Christian Democratic Workers and the Forging of German Democracy, 1920–1980

Why has democracy flourished in the Federal Republic of Germany despite that country's troubled past? Exhaustive research in German historical archives illuminates the pivotal role played by the veterans of the Christian trade unions of the Weimar Republic, the only group to participate in both of Germany's most successful political experiments after 1945, a 'Christian Democratic' party to unite Catholics and Protestants, and unified labor unions for workers of all political outlooks. They perceived that feuds between the religious confessions and competition among three rival labor federations had greatly facilitated Hitler's rise, and they resolved to bridge both chasms. Playing an influential role on the left wing of the CDU from the 1950s to the 1970s, Christian laborites alleviated class conflict through new welfare programs and laws to grant workers a powerful voice in management decisions. They took the lead in forging the distinctive 'German Model' for labor relations.

William L. Patch is the William R. Kenan Professor of History at Washington and Lee University, Virginia. He is the author of many monographs and articles, including *Heinrich Brüning and the Dissolution of the Weimar Republic* (1998).

Christian Democratic Workers and the Forging of German Democracy, 1920–1980

William L. Patch Jr.

Washington and Lee University

CAMBRIDGE
UNIVERSITY PRESS

CAMBRIDGE
UNIVERSITY PRESS

University Printing House, Cambridge CB2 8BS, United Kingdom

One Liberty Plaza, 20th Floor, New York, NY 10006, USA

477 Williamstown Road, Port Melbourne, VIC 3207, Australia

314–321, 3rd Floor, Plot 3, Splendor Forum, Jasola District Centre, New Delhi – 110025, India

79 Anson Road, #06–04/06, Singapore 079906

Cambridge University Press is part of the University of Cambridge.

It furthers the University's mission by disseminating knowledge in the pursuit of education, learning, and research at the highest international levels of excellence.

www.cambridge.org
Information on this title: www.cambridge.org/9781108424110
DOI: 10.1017/9781108539753

First published 2018

Printed in the United Kingdom by Clays, St Ives plc

A catalogue record for this publication is available from the British Library.

ISBN 978-1-108-42411-0 Hardback

Contents

Acknowledgements

I wish to extend heartfelt thanks to the National Endowment for the Humanities, which granted me a generous fellowship back in 1999 for a full year of archival research in Germany to launch this project, and to the William R. Kenan Foundation, whose endowment for my chair at Washington and Lee University has financed numerous summer research trips without which this book could not have been completed. At various stages in the research, four German experts in the field shared their insights and research findings with me generously, Tilman Mayer, Rudolf Uertz, Michael Schneider, and the late Klaus Tenfelde. Chapter 1 has benefitted greatly from advice and key documents provided by Larry Eugene Jones and Patrick Pasture. The late Frau Elisabeth Katzer (Hans Katzer's widow), Herbert Reul of the CDU of North Rhine–Westphalia and Ralf Lindemann of the CDA, and the staffs at the Archive for Christian Democratic Politics in Sankt Augustin and the Friedrich Ebert Foundation in Bonn have all gone out of their way to facilitate my access to files of documents not readily available. Thanks are also due to the staff at the Ketteler House in Cologne, who greet visiting scholars with warm hospitality. My deepest gratitude extends to my wife Ingrid for her unfailing patience and support.

Abbreviations

ACDP	Archiv für Christlich-Demokratische Politik (historical archive of the CDU, housed in the Konrad-Adenauer-Stiftung, Sankt Augustin).
BAK	Bundesarchiv Koblenz (the German National Archive, Koblenz branch).
CDA	Christlich-Demokratische Arbeitnehmerschaft (the Social Committees of Christian Democratic Workers).
CDU	Christlich Demokratische Union Deutschlands (the Christian Democratic Union).
CGB	Christlicher Gewerkschaftsbund Deutschlands (the Christian Labor Federation founded in 1959 through a merger of the CGD with the Christian unions of the Saarland).
CGD	Christliche Gewerkschaftsbewegung Deutschlands (the Christian Labor Movement that existed from 1955 to 1959).
CSU	Christlich-Soziale Union (Christian Social Union, the Bavarian ally of the CDU).
DAF	Deutsche Arbeitsfront (the German Labor Front under the Third Reich).
DAG	Deutsche Angestellten-Gewerkschaft (the white-collar German Employees' Union).
DGB	Deutscher Gewerkschaftsbund (German Labor Federation, founded in the British Occupation Zone in 1947 and the Federal Republic in October 1949).
DGB-Archiv	Historical archive of the DGB, housed in the Friedrich-Ebert-Stiftung, Bonn.
DHV	Deutschnationaler Handlungsgehilfen-Verband (German Nationalist Union of Commercial Employees, the largest white-collar union in the Weimar Republic, reconstituted in 1950 as the Deutscher Handlungsgehilfen-Verband).

DNVP	Deutschnationale Volkspartei (the conservative German Nationalist People's Party of the Weimar Republic).
DVP	Deutsche Volkspartei (the "national liberal" German People's Party of the Weimar Republic).
EDC	European Defense Community (the proposal discussed in 1950–1954 to create an integrated European army).
FDP	Freidemokratische Partei Deutschlands (the Free Democratic Party of the Federal Republic).
HAEK	Historisches Archiv des Erzbistums Köln (archive of the Cologne Archdiocese).
IG	Industriegewerkschaft (industrial union, as in IG Metall, the metalworkers' union).
KAB	Katholiche Arbeitnehmer-Bewegung (the federation of Catholic workers' clubs of western Germany).
KAB Archiv	Historical archive of the KAB, Ketteler House, Cologne.
KPD	Kommunistische Partei Deutschlands (the German Communist Party).
LANRW	Landesarchiv Nordrhein-Westfalen, Abteilungen Rheinland, Duisburg.
NATO	North Atlantic Treaty Organization.
NL	Nachlass (collection of personal papers).
NSDAP	Nationalsozialistische Deutsche Arbeiterpartei (the National Socialist German Workers' Party).
SPD	Sozialdemokratische Partei Deustchlands (the Social Democratic Party of Germany).

Introduction: Democratization and the "German Model" of Labor Relations

Democratic institutions have succeeded far better in the Federal Republic of Germany than in the Weimar Republic, and the lessons of this experience are important for anyone who hopes to encourage the spread of democracy in the world today. Most scholars focus on specialized studies of either the Weimar or the Federal Republic, however; we have very few well-researched long-term studies that seek to explain why the former collapsed and the latter flourished.[1] Many factors have been identified that help to explain the success of the Federal Republic, including Allied occupation policy after 1945, the Marshall Plan to assist economic recovery, a favorable international economic environment, a learning process among German politicians and voters, and the leveling impact on German society of the Nazi dictatorship and Second World War. Scholars cannot agree, however, on the relative importance of these factors, or what precisely Germans learned from the experience of the Third Reich.[2] The two most successful German political experiments after 1945 were undoubtedly the merger of Germany's rival labor federations for socialist, Christian social, and liberal workers into a single German Labor Federation for all workers, and the decision by most practicing Catholics and many Protestants to unite in a single political party, the Christian Democratic Union. Only one group played a leading role in

---

[1] For rare examples see Noel Cary, *The Path to Christian Democracy: German Catholics and the Party System from Windthorst to Adenauer* (Cambridge, MA, 1996), and Peter Lösche and Franz Walter, *Die SPD: Klassenpartei – Volkspartei – Quotenpartei* (Darmstadt, 1992). For thoughtful textbook accounts, see Volker Berghahn, *Modern Germany: Society, Economy and Politics in the Twentieth Century*, 2nd edn. (Cambridge, 1987); Mary Fulbrook, *A History of Germany 1918–2014: The Divided Nation*, 4th edn. (Chichester, West Sussex, 2015); and Dietrich Orlow, *A History of Modern Germany, 1871 to Present*, 7th edn. (Abingdon, 2016).

[2] See for example Ralf Dahrendorf, *Society and Democracy in Germany* (New York, 1969); A.J. Nicholls, *The Bonn Republic: West German Democracy 1945–1990* (Harlow, Essex, 1997); Lothar Kettenacker, *Germany since 1945* (Oxford, 1997); Barry Eichengreen, ed., *The Reconstruction of the International Economy, 1945–1960* (Cheltenham, 1996); Wade Jacoby, *Imitation and Politics: Redesigning Modern Germany* (Ithaca, 2000); and David Conradt and Eric Langenbacher, *The German Polity*, 10th edn. (Lanham, Maryland, 2013).

1

both these experiments, the veterans of the Christian trade unions that existed from the 1890s until 1933. This book will offer the first comprehensive history of their political role from the dissolution of the Weimar Republic until the Federal Republic of Germany achieved genuine stability and overwhelming support in the electorate.

One factor in the process of democratization has attracted special interest from social scientists, the emergence of the so-called German Model in the 1950s, a distinctive approach to social policy and labor relations characterized by high levels of public spending on social welfare programs; laws that gave workers a meaningful voice in management decisions; remarkably low strike rates (when compared to other countries); and cooperation among employers, trade unions, and elected factory councils to encourage technological innovation and improve vocational training. Many leftists deplore organized labor's willingness to cooperate with business, while many conservatives deny that the trade unions deserve any credit for economic growth. It seems undeniable, however, that this model helps to explain Germany's perennial success as an exporter of high-quality manufactured goods, its high per capita income, and its relatively low unemployment rates. The question of whether the German Model remains viable in the twenty-first century is highly controversial. The economic sociologist Wolfgang Streeck has argued forcefully that it is dead because of the weakening of organized labor and government regulatory bodies, trends that have unleashed predatory behavior by large corporations.[3] Several economists have recently presented hard evidence, however, that the German Model remains vital to explaining why the German economy has greatly outperformed most other European economies in the decade since 2006.[4] This book will shed new light on how the German Model came into being, because it was always supported most enthusiastically by the Christian trade unionists and was in some ways designed by them. Their success in this regard is still relevant to understanding the foundations of German prosperity today.

---

[3] See Tilman Mayer, Karl-Heinz Paqué, and Andreas Apelt, eds., *Modell Deutschland* (Berlin, 2013); Wolfgang Streeck, *Re-Forming Capitalism: Institutional Change in the German Political Economy* (Oxford, 2009); and Streeck's almost apocalyptic arguments in *How Will Capitalism End?* (New York, 2016).

[4] Wendy Carlin and David Soskice, "Reforms, Macroeconomic Policy and Economic Performance in Germany," in Ronald Schettkat and Jochem Langkau, eds., *Economic Policy Proposals for Germany and Europe* (Abingdon and New York, 2008), pp. 72–118; Wendy Carlin and David Soskice, "German Economic Performance: Disentangling the Role of Supply-Side Reforms, Macroeconomic Policy and Coordinated Economy Institutions," *Socio-Economic Review*, 7 (2009): 67–99; Steffen Mueller, "Works Councils and Establishment Productivity," *Industrial and Labor Relations Review*, 65 (2012): 880–898.

The early origins of the German Model seem clear. German workers organized the largest socialist labor movement in the world between 1870 and 1914 and thereby posed a great challenge to elites. The elites responded with harsh repression, but even under the Anti-Socialist Law in the 1880s, Bismarck enacted programs for public health insurance for factory workers and modest pensions for elderly or disabled workers. After the Social Democratic Party (SPD) and trade unions were decriminalized in 1890, they grew by leaps and bounds. The SPD posed a new challenge with its very popular Erfurt Program of 1891; it embraced Marx's theory that capitalism was doomed to collapse but advanced relatively moderate specific demands, such as improved safety inspection of factories, the repeal of laws forbidding unionization among certain categories of workers, and a progressive income tax. The Erfurt Program encouraged civil servants, academics, and the Protestant and Catholic clergy to offer their own plans for social reform that adopted some demands of the SPD. By 1914 social insurance and improved nutrition and urban sanitation had caused a significant increase in life expectancy for workers and alleviated anxiety. The SPD retained a Marxist definition of its ultimate goal, but reformist and Revisionist socialists exerted growing influence on its tactical decisions, and the legislative proposals of the SPD and middle-class social reformers converged.[5]

Most employers continued to combat trade unionism, however, and Germany experienced unprecedented labor strife and political violence under the Weimar Republic. It remains difficult therefore to explain how the country transitioned from the discussion of social reform before 1914 to the consensus-oriented practices of the German Model. As we shall see in Chapter 1, Germany achieved significant progress in social legislation in the Weimar Republic that was influenced directly by the Christian trade unions. However, because of competitive rivalry with the socialist Free unions, the Christian unions adopted a dubious political strategy of alliance with conservative Protestants who sometimes combated the Weimar Republic. Most Christian trade unionists favored political cooperation between Catholics and Protestants in a "Christian Democratic" party, and more and more younger colleagues demanded close cooperation with the Free trade unions to defend workers' interests. The shared experience of persecution under the Third Reich heightened their sense of workers' solidarity. The functionaries of the Christian trade unions

---

[5] Gary Steenson, *"Not One Man! Not One Penny!" German Social Democracy, 1863–1914* (Pittsburgh, 1981), esp. pp. 247–250; Gerhard A. Ritter, *Social Welfare in Germany and Britain: Origins and Development* (Leamington Spa and New York, 1983), pp. 17–130; Helga Grebing, *Geschichte der sozialen Ideen in Deutschland: Sozialismus – Katholische Soziallehre – Protestantische Sozialethik. Ein Handbuch* (Essen, 2000).

maintained an effective network under the Third Reich, and as we shall see in Chapter 2, they hurled themselves in 1945 into the effort to found today's Christian Democratic Union (CDU) and unified German Labor Federation (*der Deutsche Gewerkschaftsbund*, or DGB). They also founded the Social Committees of Christian Democratic Workers, a semi-autonomous CDU affiliate dedicated to the defense of workers' interests in the CDU and defense of the influence of Christian trade unionists in the DGB. Largely neglected by scholars, the Social Committees became a highly influential network of activists and a policy think tank; they will be the primary focus of this book.[6]

Social Democrats still comprised a majority of trade unionists after 1945, but as a result of the strategy of the Social Committees, almost two million of the six million DGB members in the 1950s and '60s voted consistently for the CDU. Blue-collar workers and their dependents comprised about one-third of CDU voters, and if one considers white-collar workers and former workers drawing pensions, a majority of CDU voters came from the working class.[7] The political scientist Wolfgang Hirsch-Weber argued already in 1959 that this overlap between the bases of support for the CDU and DGB represented the most important difference between the political systems of the Weimar and Federal Republics. In the 1920s party leaders had powerful incentives for confrontation tactics. The SPD lost support to the Communists whenever it compromised with the non-socialist parties, while each non-socialist party faced a militant competitor to its right that siphoned away middle-class supporters if it compromised with the SPD. The non-socialist parties sought blue-collar votes, but only among workers who were non-unionized or belonged to the Christian or small liberal unions; old rivalries between the labor federations therefore insulated those parties from losses among workers if they clashed with the SPD. In the 1950s, Hirsch-Weber argued, the mostly Social Democratic leaders of the DGB and mostly bourgeois leaders of the CDU both knew that their success depended largely on the support of workers whose loyalties were divided between them. Leaders on both sides therefore had a powerful incentive

---

[6] The only detailed study is the unpublished dissertation by Herlind Gundelach, "Die Sozialausschüsse zwischen CDU und DGB. Selbstverständnis und Rolle 1949–1966," phil. diss. (Bonn, 1983).

[7] An EMNID poll in November 1953 showed that 43 percent of the DGB's six million members supported the SPD, 24 percent the CDU, 6 percent the FDP, and 1 percent the KPD, while 26 percent remained undecided or backed a splinter party (DGB Archiv/NL Werner Hansen/24). In that year's Bundestag election the CDU gained 35 percent of all blue-collar votes (vs. 48 percent for the SPD) and 49 percent of the votes of white-collar workers and civil servants (vs. 27 percent for the SPD); see Frank Bösch, *Die Adenauer-CDU. Gründung, Aufstieg und Krise einer Erfolgspartei, 1945–1969* (Stuttgart, 2001), p. 157.

to seek consensus. For Hirsch-Weber this was the most important reason why confrontation tactics gave way to a conception of politics as the art of compromise.[8]

Hirsch-Weber's thesis has provoked skepticism among historians, because he relied largely on deductive reasoning. He could point to some famous bargains in the early 1950s between Chancellor Konrad Adenauer and the first DGB chair, Hans Böckler. From 1953 onward, however, Adenauer denounced the DGB as a tool of the Social Democratic opposition, and his successor Ludwig Erhard displayed an even more hostile attitude. At the summit, communication between the CDU-led government and organized labor broke down after 1953, so Hirsch-Weber's argument would only be persuasive if it could be shown that an influential corps of trade unionists in the CDU continued to explain and defend the core demands of the DGB, while a significant corps of Christian Democrats in the trade unions continued to push for compromise with the government. The initial findings by historians who have investigated that issue are bleak. The influential study of the "Adenauer CDU" by Frank Bösch concludes that, while veterans of the Christian trade unions played a major role in founding the party, it soon became dependent on financial contributions from big business. The CDU did not develop into a membership party like the SPD but relied instead on business lobbyists, scientific opinion polls, and advertising firms to conduct its election campaigns. Bösch dismisses the influence of the CDU workers' wing in the 1950s and '60s as insignificant. Maria Mitchell's recent study of the party's first years sheds additional light on the strategy of CDU leaders in overrepresenting their Protestant minority in leadership posts to seek confessional balance. The vast majority of Protestants willing to support the new party came from the middle or upper-middle class, and Mitchell supports Bösch by depicting the mostly Catholic CDU labor activists as defeated on all fronts in 1949 by the champions of free-market economics led by the Protestant neoliberal economist Ludwig Erhard. Finally, in the most thorough study available of the role of Catholic labor activists in the 1950s, Wolfgang Schroeder has shown that old personal rivalries erupted into bitter feuds in the 1950s between those who devoted themselves to political careers in the CDU, those loyal primarily to the Church, and those who served as labor organizers in the DGB. Schroeder concludes that the decision by several influential bishops to promote the revival of separate "Christian" trade unions in 1955 discredited the Catholic hierarchy among workers and

---

[8] Wolfgang Hirsch-Weber, *Gewerkschaften in der Politik. Von der Massenstreikdebatte zum Kampf um das Mitbestimmungsrecht* (Cologne, 1959).

virtually eliminated Christian Democratic influence in the DGB.[9] The arguments of Schroeder, Bösch, and Mitchell have weakened scholarly interest in the political role of Christian Democratic workers.

This book argues that these scholars have greatly underestimated the influence of trade unionists in the CDU and of Christian Democrats in the DGB. Chapters 3 and 4 will show that Christian Democratic workers did keep channels of communication open between the CDU and DGB and promoted compromise during the most polarizing debates of the 1950s. Every West German cabinet from 1949 to 1969 included at least two, and more often three, members of the Social Committees. The labor minister always came from their ranks, as did the first two ministers in charge of promoting German reunification, Jakob Kaiser and Ernst Lemmer; the first minister of defense, Theodor Blank; and housing minister Paul Lücke. Blank played a crucial role in promoting consensus over rearmament, and the former Christian trade unionist Karl Arnold exerted great influence as prime minister of Germany's most populous state, North Rhine-Westphalia. Even during their worst feuds, moreover, the leaders of the Social Committees and Catholic workers' clubs cooperated effectively in the Workers' Group of the CDU Bundestag delegation, which included thirty to sixty members throughout the 1950s and '60s and exerted great influence on social legislation.

A gifted tactician rose to lead the Social Committees in the 1960s, Hans Katzer, who ended their feud with the Catholic workers' clubs. Katzer forged a unified workers' wing of the CDU for the first time. As we shall see in Chapters 5 and 6, the Social Committees then promoted a constructive and forward-looking response by the CDU to the renunciation of Marxism by the SPD in its Godesberg Program of 1959, and the renunciation of anti-socialism by the Catholic hierarchy at the Second Vatican Council. The Social Committees became frustrated in the early 1960s, because the CDU's coalition partner, the Free Democratic Party, blocked all progress in social legislation. Therefore, they took the lead in advocating a Great Coalition between the CDU and SPD, and they sought to make the SPD respectable in the eyes of practicing Catholics. Hirsch-Weber could not know this when he wrote, but Christian Democratic labor activists achieved their greatest success at promoting the politics of compromise in the 1960s. Katzer served as labor minister in the Great Coalition cabinet of 1966–1969, and the Social Committees

---

[9] Bösch, *Adenauer-CDU*, pp. 195–235, 286–296; Maria Mitchell, *The Origins of Christian Democracy: Politics and Confession in Modern Germany* (Ann Arbor, 2012), esp. pp. 152–163; Wolfgang Schroeder, *Katholizismus und Einheitsgewerkschaft. Der Streit um den DGB und der Niedergang des Sozialkatholizismus in der Bundesrepublik bis 1960* (Bonn, 1992), pp. 403–411.

contributed to the smooth transition from Christian Democratic to Social Democratic political leadership in the 1970s. This transition demonstrated that parliamentary democracy rested on solid foundations. Even while in opposition to the SPD-led government of Helmut Schmidt, moreover, the Social Committees helped to achieve the last major legislative success for the advocates of worker participation in management, the Co-Determination Law of 1976.

This book will present substantial documentary evidence in support of Hirsch-Weber's thesis about the stabilization of democracy in the Federal Republic. Based on the personal papers of thirty Christian Democratic laborites, the archival records of the Social Committees, Catholic workers' clubs, CDU, and DGB, and the published minutes of trade union and CDU leadership conferences, it will reconstruct the activities and influence of Christian Democratic labor activists over a turbulent six decades. "To build a bridge between East and West" served as the guiding metaphor of Jakob Kaiser's speeches in 1946/ 1947, when he led the CDU in the Soviet Occupation Zone. "The bridge builders" (*Brückenbauer*) then became a term of ridicule after the Soviets suppressed civil liberties, and Kaiser appeared naive. Nevertheless, the metaphor remains apt to describe the role of Christian Democratic workers as they mediated between organized labor and the conservative politicians who dominated the federal government. After 1966 the need for bridge builders diminished as the SPD became respectable. The last veterans of the old Christian trade unions who served as DGB functionaries retired in the early 1970s, and while the Social Committees could recruit younger colleagues to become active in the CDU, few chose careers as labor organizers. Ambitious young workers now enjoyed access to higher education and many career opportunities outside the trade unions. The very successes of Christian Democratic workers undermined their influence.

Readers should be warned that a bewildering variety of church-affiliated, party-affiliated, and autonomous organizations claimed to speak on behalf of Christian workers after 1945. DGB leaders objected with good reason to the practice among Catholic priests and CDU politicians of referring to "Christian workers" as a dissident minority in the unified trade unions, because many Social Democrats were churchgoing Protestants, and at least a few, practicing Catholics. Around 1960, as we shall see, a consensus emerged that minority rights in the DGB should be defined on the basis of party affiliation, not religious outlook, and the last two chapters of this book will refer to the dissident minority as "Christian Democratic workers." In the 1950s, however, many of the dissidents backed splinter parties or no political party, so this book will refer to them in Chapters 2–4 as "Christian social workers" (with a lowercase "s" to distinguish them from members of the Bavarian Christian Social Union), meaning all workers who criticized the program and practices of the SPD and DGB on the basis of Catholic social theory or Protestant social ethics.

1   Christian Trade Unionists and the Dissolution of the Weimar Republic

Christian unions open to both Catholics and Protestants were founded in the 1890s by churchgoing workers who resented the anti-clericalism of the socialist Free unions. They spread first in Rhineland-Westphalia, because of vigorous support there from the preexisting network of church-affiliated Catholic educational and devotional clubs for workers. The Free unions accused them of dividing and weakening the labor movement, so a majority of Christian trade unionists agreed by 1901 that unified labor unions for workers of all religious and political outlooks should be their goal, unions like those of Great Britain. They promised, in other words, to merge with the Free unions if they ever renounced anti-clericalism. Some Christian trade unionists protested, however, that Christian teaching provided uniquely valuable guidance, and many denounced the internationalism of the Free unions.[1] The functionaries of the Christian unions soon developed a strong *esprit de corps* in the face of socialist attacks, and the long-term goal of unified labor unions was largely forgotten. The nationalist and anti-socialist current in the Christian unions provoked an ambivalent response to the founding of the Weimar Republic, and later to the rise of National Socialism. However, in the 1920s more and more young Christian trade unionists insisted that the interests of workers could only be served through a close alliance with the Free unions. That course prevailed during the Great Depression, when the Christian unions allied with Social Democratic workers to defend the Weimar Republic from the onslaught of the Nazi Party. They waited until after Hitler was appointed chancellor, however, to launch merger talks with the Free unions, and by then it was far too late to prevent the creation of a brutal dictatorship.

---

[1] Eric Dorn Brose, *Christian Labor and the Politics of Frustration in Imperial Germany* (Washington, DC, 1985), pp. 61–158; Michael Schneider, *Die Christlichen Gewerkschaften 1894–1933* (Bonn, 1982), pp. 51–170.

1.1   Efforts to Promote "Social Partnership" in the 1920s

In 1891 the Erfurt Program of the Social Democratic Party (SPD) called for the strict separation of church and state with the slogan "Religion is a private matter." Many Christians found that slogan offensive, because it implied that faith was irrelevant to political debates. A substantial majority of industrial workers had become estranged from the Christian churches by this time, except in a few regions (most notably the Ruhr Valley) where growing mines and factories recruited their labor force from Catholic rural areas with high rates of religious observance. Most functionaries of the SPD and socialist Free unions were also schooled in a scientific and anti-clerical worldview heavily influenced by the writings of Darwin as well as Marx.[2] Also in 1891, Pope Leo XIII encouraged the Catholic social reform movement with the encyclical *Rerum novarum*, which urged support for labor organizations to counterbalance the growing power of capital. Employers often violated workers' rights, Leo noted, so all Christians should support legislation to alleviate poverty and defend the rights of the poor. This document represented an awkward compromise, however, between Catholics who supported genuine trade unions and paternalists who supported non-striking organizations for workers in which their employers or clergy played a leading role. Leo warned emphatically that strikes are "extremely injurious to trade and to the general interests of the public," so legislation should "forestall and prevent such troubles from arising."[3]

Christian trade unions began to emerge in 1894, when several thousand coal miners in the Ruhr Valley seceded from the Free miners' union to found a Union of Christian Miners. They were soon imitated by workers in other trades, who founded a League of Christian Trade Unions in 1899; it never grew to more than one-sixth the membership of the Free unions nationwide but offered them stiff competition in Rhineland-Westphalia, Baden-Württemberg, and the Saarland. The mostly Catholic founders always sought to recruit Protestant workers, because labor organizations limited to Catholics had little chance to organize successful strikes and compete with the Free unions. They were opposed, however, by a powerful

[2] Heiner Grote, *Sozialdemokratie und Religion. Eine Dokumentation für die Jahre 1863–1875* (Tübingen, 1968); Vernon Lidtke, *The Alternative Culture: Socialist Labor in Imperial Germany* (New York, 1985); Gerhard A. Ritter and Klaus Tenfelde, *Arbeiter im Deutschen Kaiserreich 1871–1914* (Bonn, 1991), pp. 747–817.
[3] Pope Leo XIII, "Rerum novarum," May 15, 1891, published in English as "The Condition of the Working Classes," in *The Great Encyclical Letters of Pope Leo XIII* (New York, 1903), pp. 208–248 (quotation on 238–239); also available at w2.vatican.va/content/leo-xiii/. For background see Paul Misner, *Social Catholicism in Europe: From the Onset of Industrialization to the First World War* (New York, 1991).

Integralist movement in the Catholic clergy that rejected strike tactics and any mixed organizations including Protestants. The Christian unions found allies among progressive clergy in Rhineland-Westphalia and politicians of the Center Party, who founded the People's League for Catholic Germany in 1890, the largest of the many non-socialist organizations promoting social reform. The People's League supported interdenominational Christian unions that were prepared to strike if necessary, unions that were financially independent, with membership dues comparable to those of the Free unions, and with all union leaders elected by the membership. The Christian unions were led in the struggle for episcopal recognition by Adam Stegerwald, a cabinetmaker by trade and the son of Catholic peasants from Franconia, and Heinrich Brauns, the priest and economic historian who served as director of the People's League. They helped the Christian unions to gain a membership of 342,000 by 1913, versus 2.5 million for the Free unions and 107,000 for the liberal Hirsch-Duncker unions founded in the 1860s.[4]

Nationalism drove a wedge between the Free and Christian unions. Most Catholic workers developed an intensely patriotic outlook in Wilhelmian Germany that was shaped by what they learned about history at school, service in an army based on universal conscription, and the growing desire among priests and Catholic politicians after the *Kulturkampf* to prove that they were patriotic Germans. Heinrich Brauns taught Christian trade unionists in the adult education seminars of the People's League one great lesson of German history since the Wars of Liberation against Napoleon – that civic equality and increased popular participation in government were essential to mobilize the full power of the German nation against foreign enemies. Patriotism thus provided the rationale for democratization and social reform. This attitude was strongly influenced by the historian Friedrich Meinecke and by Friedrich Naumann, the former Lutheran pastor who campaigned to reconcile Protestant workers with the empire by synthesizing "national" and "social" values. Brauns and Stegerwald both doubted that Christian social theory alone could define a program clearly distinct from that of reformist socialism, so they emphasized support for the German Empire. The Christian miner Heinrich Imbusch later recalled

[4] Claudia Hiepel, *Arbeiterkatholizismus an der Ruhr. August Brust und der Gewerkverein christlicher Bergarbeiter* (Stuttgart, 1999); Brose, *Christian Labor*, pp. 181–328; membership figures in Schneider, *Die Christlichen Gewerkschaften*, pp. 111–112, 336; Bernhard Forster, *Adam Stegerwald (1874–1945). Christlich-nationaler Gewerkschafter, Zentrumspolitiker, Mitbegründer der Unionsparteien* (Düsseldorf, 2003), pp. 27–137; Horstwalter Heitzer, *Der Volksverein für das katholische Deutschland im Kaiserreich 1890–1918* (Mainz, 1979).

Brauns as both a superb teacher and a militant nationalist who could have become minister of war just as well as minister of labor.[5]

In August 1914 the SPD and Free unions embraced Germany's cause as a legitimate war of national self-defense and endorsed the call for a *Burgfrieden*, a political truce within the castle under siege. This patriotic stance greatly facilitated cooperation between the Free and Christian unions, and between the SPD and Center Party. The Christian unions supported the war effort fervently but agreed with the Social Democrats in demanding expanded powers for the government to ration food and regulate industry. In 1917 the Free and Christian unions both demanded universal and equal manhood suffrage in place of Prussia's three-class suffrage law for state elections. In January 1918 the Christian unions allied with Social Democrats and Naumannite liberal democrats in the People's League for Peace and Freedom to demand democratic reforms and the prompt negotiation of a compromise peace. The Catholic episcopate sided with conservative Protestants, however, to block all democratic reforms until the end of the war. The League for Peace and Freedom served nevertheless as a foundation for the coalition of Social, Christian, and liberal democrats that founded the Weimar Republic.[6]

Christian trade unionists had experienced great frustration in Imperial Germany, but many mourned its collapse in November 1918. Adam Stegerwald adjusted quickly to changing circumstances, however, and sought to arouse their enthusiasm for a revolution that gave workers unprecedented power. He also responded eagerly when the fear of radical revolution prompted the captains of industry to approach labor leaders with an offer to negotiate. Carl Legien of the Free unions played the leading role in these talks, but Stegerwald helped to negotiate the Stinnes-Legien Agreement of November 15, 1918, which introduced the eight-hour workday and collective bargaining throughout

---

[5] Helmut Walser Smith, *German Nationalism and Religious Conflict: Culture, Ideology, Politics, 1870–1914* (Princeton, 1995); Heitzer, *Volksverein*, pp. 24–30, 61–66, 83–129, 233–241; Friedrich Meinecke, *The Age of German Liberation*, ed. Peter Paret (Berkeley, 1977; based on lectures of 1905); Dieter Düding, *Der nationalsoziale Verein 1896–1903. Der gescheiterte Versuch einer parteipolitischen Synthese von Nationalismus, Sozialismus und Liberalismus* (Munich and Vienna, 1972); Helga Grebing, ed., *Geschichte der sozialen Ideen in Deutschland: Sozialismus, Katholische Soziallehre, Protestantische Sozialethik. Ein Handbuch* (Essen, 2000), pp. 653–712, 927–976; Heinrich Imbusch, "Heinrich Brauns," unpublished memoir in NL Platte/14/25–33.

[6] Forster, *Stegerwald*, pp. 139–199; Brose, *Christian Labor*, pp. 329–370; William L. Patch, *Christian Trade Unions in the Weimar Republic, 1918–1933: The Failure of "Corporate Pluralism"* (New Haven, 1985), pp. 24–33; Susanne Miller, *Burgfrieden und Klassenkampf. Die deutsche Sozialdemokratie im Ersten Weltkrieg* (Düsseldorf, 1974); Hans-Joachim Bieber, *Gewerkschaften in Krieg und Revolution. Arbeiterbewegung, Industrie, Staat und Militär in Deutschland 1914–1920*, 2 vols. (Hamburg, 1981).

industry. That agreement also led to the creation of the Central Association of Employers and Employees, a commission with equal numbers of industrialists and trade unionists that took charge, with the blessing of the SPD-led provisional government, of many economic regulatory functions carried out by the Imperial bureaucracy during the war. There was an overwhelming pragmatic rationale for the Central Association in view of the urgent need to demobilize millions of soldiers and convert from a war economy to a peacetime economy. However, the prewar traditions of the Free unions did not prepare them for such collaboration with business leaders, and several of the more militant Free unions refused to participate in the branch associations for each industry promised by the Central Association. The Christian unions, on the other hand, celebrated the Stinnes-Legien Agreement as an expression of their most cherished ideal of "social partnership," a bold attempt to follow the exhortation of Pope Leo in *Rerum novarum* to identify specific issues where management and labor shared vital interests. The Christian unions also participated eagerly in every branch association.[7]

For a brief time after the war, Germany seemed poised to create a system even more cooperative than the German Model of the Federal Republic. The new Weimar Republic created a powerful system of state labor arbitration, a National Economic Council that included interest group representatives to advise the Reichstag, and new oversight panels for the coal, iron, and steel industry. In early 1920 it also enacted a Factory Councils Law to require the election of a workers' council in every large plant, a council authorized to express workers' concerns to management, receive quarterly reports on the economic condition of the firm, and protect workers from arbitrary dismissal.[8] The trend toward social partnership soon encountered dramatic reversals, however, as a result of dire shortages of food and fuel, labor unrest, political violence, and galloping inflation. Employers lost their fear of socialist revolution in view of the deep divisions on the Left, and the leaders of Ruhr heavy industry took advantage of the French occupation of the Ruhr in 1923 to abolish the eight-hour workday. The Free unions withdrew from the Central Association in protest, but at year's end the German government decided

[7] Patch, *Christian Trade Unions*, pp. 34–37; Gerald Feldman and Irmgard Steinisch, *Industrie und Gewerkschaften 1918–1924. Die überforderte Zentralarbeitsgemeinschaft* (Stuttgart, 1985), pp. 11–57, 135–158; Gerald Feldman, *The Great Disorder: Politics, Economics, and Society in the German Inflation, 1914–1924* (Oxford, 1997), pp. 73–126; Heinrich August Winkler, *Von der Revolution zur Stabilisierung. Arbeiter und Arbeiterbewegung in der Weimarer Republik 1918 bis 1924*, 2nd edn. (Bonn, 1985), pp. 45–84, 267–275.

[8] Patch, *Christian Trade Unions*, pp. 54–57; Ludwig Preller, *Sozialpolitik in der Weimarer Republik*, reprint edition (Düsseldorf, 1978), pp. 226–252; Feldman, *Great Disorder*, pp. 126–254.

that work hours must be deregulated everywhere as part of a harsh austerity program designed to wring inflation out of the economy. In early 1924, state labor arbitrators established real wages at a level substantially below that of 1913, and many workers found themselves compelled to labor sixty hours a week.[9]

Nationalism and the desire to compete with the Free unions molded Adam Stegerwald's response to these developments. The Christian unions had largely exhausted their initial pool of recruitment: industrial workers in western and southwestern Germany who remained practicing Catholics. Stegerwald saw previously non-unionized Protestant workers as their only opportunity for growth. In October 1918, he therefore instructed all Christian union colleagues to seek "as many links as possible to reasonable conservative elements," especially among East Elbian landowners, to facilitate organizing drives among previously non-unionized Protestant workers, especially farmworkers. Stegerwald deputized his most talented Protestant colleague, Franz Behrens, to lead a new Christian farmworkers' union that gained a somewhat more favorable reception by big landowners than did its socialist competitor. In November 1919 Stegerwald also founded a new umbrella organization, the German Labor Federation, with the white-collar German Nationalist Union of Commercial Employees (*Deutschnationaler Handlungsgehilfen-Verband*, or DHV). Stegerwald recruited the young Catholic economist and combat veteran Heinrich Brüning to serve as that federation's secretary general. Many DHV activists were militant nationalists and racial anti-Semites, but its leaders sought to promote its development into a pragmatic and effective labor union. The DHV also had flourishing local affiliates in the mostly Protestant cities of central and northern Germany where the Christian unions had never taken root. Stegerwald's strategy therefore helped the blue-collar Christian unions to expand somewhat beyond their initial regional and confessional base; their membership peaked at over one million in 1920, a figure that later stabilized at around 600,000, and about one-third of them were Protestant. The DHV grew from 250,000 to 400,000 members in the 1920s, becoming the largest white-collar union in the Weimar Republic.[10]

Nationalism provided Stegerwald's rationale when he called for a "Christian Democratic" party to unite Catholics and Protestants in

---

[9] Patch, *Christian Trade Unions*, pp. 76–90; Feldman, *Great Disorder*, pp. 631–835; Winkler, *Revolution*, pp. 393–433, 605–734.

[10] Adam Stegerwald, "Materialien betreffend Verbesserung und Verbreitung der Organisationsbasis für die christlichen Gewerkschaften," October 1918, NL Giesberts/ 94/59–68 (quotation on 60); Patch, *Christian Trade Unions*, pp. 45–63; William L. Patch, *Heinrich Brüning and the Dissolution of the Weimar Republic* (Cambridge, 1998), pp. 24–38.

November 1920. He argued that the powerful German Empire could bear tensions between Catholics and Protestants, but that in the weak Weimar Republic, whose largely Catholic border regions were threatened by powerful enemies, "the strict political division between Catholics and Protestants creates a terrible danger." Stegerwald called for the foundation of a new party at least as large as the SPD that would be "German, Christian, Democratic, and Social." The first slogan, he explained, implied a commitment to revise the Treaty of Versailles, and "social" implied "the recognition in principle of the worker as a subject and a participant with equal rights in the process of production." Thus Stegerwald already focused in 1920 on the issue of worker participation in management decisions that became crucial for Christian laborites after 1945. His speech generated highly favorable publicity and later exerted great influence on the founders of the Christian Democratic Union. However, Stegerwald's initiative was soon thwarted by Center Party loyalists, including the leaders of the Catholic workers' clubs.[11] Thereafter Stegerwald, Brüning, and their clerical ally Heinrich Brauns promoted coalitions between the Center Party and the party most popular among Protestant workers, the monarchist German Nationalist People's Party (DNVP). Brauns enjoyed great influence over coalition policy as Reich labor minister from 1920 to 1928 in a republic where the average lifespan of a cabinet was less than one year. He and Stegerwald hoped that the DNVP would evolve along the lines of the British Conservative Party under Disraeli and come to accept parliamentary democracy and the legitimate demands of workers. Their closest ally in the DNVP was the farmworkers' leader Franz Behrens, who had already been elected to the Reichstag in 1907 for the small Christian Social Party founded by Pastor Adolf Stoecker. In December 1918, Behrens persuaded that party to merge with the DNVP and function as its pro-labor wing, but the Christian Socials included militant anti-Semites and many sentimental monarchists. Stegerwald's alliances with the DHV and Christian Socials made it very difficult for the German Labor Federation to agree on a political program.[12]

---

[11] Adam Stegerwald, "Die christlich-nationale Arbeiterschaft und die Lebensfragen des deutschen Volkes," in Gesamtverband der christlichen Gewerkschaften, *Niederschrift der Verhandlungen des 10. Kongresses der christlichen Gewerkschaften Deutschlands. Abgehalten vom 20. bis 23. November in Essen* (Cologne, 1920), pp. 183–231 (quotations on 220, 231); Patch, *Christian Trade Unions*, pp. 63–75; Noel Cary, *The Path to Christian Democracy: German Catholics and the Party System from Windthorst to Adenauer* (Cambridge, MA, 1996), pp. 73–99, 158–170; Maria Mitchell, *The Origins of Christian Democracy: Politics and Confession in Modern Germany* (Ann Arbor, 2012), pp. 39–46, 57–59.

[12] Patch, *Christian Trade Unions*, pp. 81–133; Patch, *Heinrich Brüning*, pp. 30–45; Norbert Friedrich, *"Die christlich-soziale Fahne empor!" Reinhard Mumm und die christlich-soziale Bewegung* (Stuttgart, 1997), pp. 177–260; Larry Eugene Jones, "Conservative Antisemitism in the Weimar Republic: A Case Study of the German National People's

In the realm of collective bargaining, most Christian trade unionists rejected the conciliatory stance of Stegerwald and insisted on close cooperation with the Free unions. Against Stegerwald's advice, the chair of the Christian miners' union, Heinrich Imbusch, worked closely with his Free union counterparts in May 1924 to organize a partly successful strike by Ruhr coal miners that helped to end a disastrous slump in union membership and morale. Imbusch became Stegerwald's sharpest critic within the Christian unions, largely because Imbusch was more firmly rooted in the working class as a third-generation worker in Ruhr heavy industry. Stegerwald had grown up in a peasant village, and his personal experience of labor was gained in small woodworking shops; Imbusch described him in an unpublished memoir as "by nature a petit bourgeois [*Kleinbürger*] with somewhat reactionary inclinations."[13] In Wilhelmian Germany, the Christian unions had opposed decisions to strike by the Free unions in a few important cases, most notably the Ruhr coal miners' strike of 1912. Like Imbusch, however, most younger functionaries of the Christian unions assumed in the 1920s that they must work closely with the Free unions at the collective bargaining table. In 1919/1920 the Christian unions sometimes criticized the Free for being swept along by radical members to raise unrealistic strike demands, but from 1922 onward, the Christian unions displayed almost the same propensity to strike as the Free unions. A detailed opinion survey of members of the Catholic workers' clubs of western Germany in 1925/1926 (over half of whom also belonged to the Christian unions) revealed strong feelings of hostility toward employers and government bureaucrats but very positive attitudes toward the SPD and Free trade unionists.[14]

In 1926 one Catholic labor activist, Wilhelm Elfes, called publicly for a merger of the three competing labor federations. As editor of the widely read weekly paper for the West German Catholic workers' clubs, Elfes

Party," in Larry Eugene Jones, ed., *The German Right in the Weimar Republic: Studies in the History of German Conservatism, Nationalism, and Antisemitism* (New York and Oxford, 2014), pp. 79–107.

[13] Heinrich Imbusch, "Adam Stegerwald," NL Platte/14/188–201 (quotation on 195–196); Patch, *Christian Trade Unions*, pp. 90–101; Michael Schäfer, *Heinrich Imbusch. Christlicher Gewerkschaftsführer und Widerstandskämpfer* (Munich, 1990), pp. 10–18, 130–142.

[14] "Das Problem Führer und Masse im Gewerkverein," a chapter from an unpublished history of the Christian miners' union written by Imbusch in exile, NL Platte/25/205–217; Albin Gladen, "Die Streiks der Bergarbeiter im Ruhrgebiet in den Jahren 1889, 1905 und 1912," in Jürgen Reulecke, ed., *Arbeiterbewegung an Rhein und Ruhr* (Wuppertal, 1974), pp. 111–148; Michael Schneider, *Die Christlichen Gewerkschaften*, pp. 271–322, 587–622; Heinrich August Winkler, *Der Schein der Normalität. Arbeiter und Arbeiterbewegung in der Weimarer Republik 1924 bis 1930*, 2nd edn. (Bonn, 1988), pp. 502–506; Dirk Müller, *Arbeiter, Katholizismus, Staat. Der Volksverein für das katholische Deutschland und die katholischen Arbeiterorganisationen in der Weimarer Republik* (Bonn, 1996), pp. 221–226.

prophesied that the growing power and brutality of the capitalist syndicates and trusts would compel German workers to overcome their divisions. "At present," he declared, "a great deal of time and energy is wasted
in the struggle of workers against workers. Someday the masses will
recognize – indeed, a large portion of them have already recognized – that
it is a sin against their own lives to prolong the current, self-destructive
divisions." The leaders of the Christian unions responded indignantly that
Elfes failed to understand the extent to which the three labor federations
did cooperate, and that he encouraged a dangerous pessimism that
would only benefit the Communists. Because small groups of Catholic
workers had already broken away from the Center Party to embrace
a radical socialist program, Elfes' editorial also alarmed the clerical
supervisors of the Catholic workers' clubs. They soon agreed with
Imbusch and other Christian union leaders that Elfes should become
the police chief of Krefeld and be replaced as editor by a functionary of
the Christian miners' union, Nikolaus Gross.[15] Although deprived for
some years of any opportunity to publicize his views, Elfes long remained
the most passionate advocate of working-class solidarity in the Christian
labor movement.

Stegerwald's influence over political coalitions grew in the years
1925–1927, when most laws were enacted by right-of-center parliamentary groupings led by the Center Party and DNVP. These proved the
most fruitful years of social legislation in the Weimar Republic, because
the Christian unions made it clear to business and agrarian lobbyists in
the DNVP that support for the agenda of Labor Minister Brauns was the
price of admission to cabinets and influence on tax and tariff policy.[16]
The social policy victories for Brauns included the restoration of the
eight-hour workday in steel mills, a law to provide most other workers
a 25 percent overtime bonus for work beyond eight hours, a new system
of labor courts to adjudicate violations of labor law, and most ambitious
of all, a national system of unemployment insurance. The Free and
Christian unions had long denounced the old system of municipal

---

[15] Wilhelm Elfes, "Wirtschaft, Unternehmertum und Arbeiterschaft. Die gewerkschaftliche
Zersplitterung," *Westdeutsche Arbeiterzeitung*, #9 (February 27, 1926), pp. 50–51 (source
of quotation); "Gewerkschaftliche Zersplitterung oder feste Arbeitsgemeinschaft?"
Zentralblatt der christlichen Gewerkschaften, #6 (March 22, 1926), pp. 73–76; minutes of
the "Hauptvorstand" of the Christian miners' union, March 29, 1926, p. 7, DGB-Archiv/
NL Imbusch/2; Patch, *Christian Trade Unions*, pp. 106–109; Albert Esser, *Wilhelm Elfes,
1884–1969. Arbeiterführer und Politiker* (Mainz, 1990), pp. 55–83; Vera Bücker, *Nikolaus
Gross: Politischer Journalist und Katholik im Widerstand des Kölner Kreises* (Münster, 2003),
pp. 53–56.

[16] See Michael Stürmer, *Koalition und Opposition in der Weimarer Republik 1924–1928*
(Düsseldorf, 1967).

poor relief, in which the meager benefits were linked to a strict means test, i.e. were denied to any worker who retained some assets. The Unemployment Insurance Act of July 1927 created a comprehensive national system with no means test, in which premiums and benefits were graduated according to income. This law was supported by all parties from the SPD to the DNVP. Some historians have emphasized the disagreements between Catholic and Social Democratic approaches to social policy in the 1920s, linking the former to a defense of private charitable organizations and resistance to any expansion of government power. As an opposition party the SPD naturally criticized most of Brauns's proposals as inadequate, but the thrust of social legislation in the mid-1920s was highly congenial to the socialist labor movement nevertheless. The business associations regarded Brauns as a dangerous champion of expanded government power, and the Free unions sought to retain him as labor minister under the new SPD-led cabinet formed in June 1928. It was the Center Party, not the SPD, which decided that Brauns must step down.[17]

Real wages also rose substantially from 1925 to 1929, and the business associations complained that the state labor arbitrators appointed by Brauns had imposed ruinous "political wages" dictated by the politicians' desire for popularity, not by a sober calculation of what firms could afford. Most economic historians now agree that labor arbitrators were guided primarily by the economic data, and that conditions on the labor market would have caused most of these wage increases even without state arbitration. Germany's fundamental economic problems involved high interest rates (the enduring consequence of the hyperinflation of 1923) and the suppression of competition in key industrial sectors. Nevertheless, the belief among businessmen that the "welfare state" hindered economic growth became a psychological fact that undermined investor confidence in the late 1920s.[18]

---

[17] Patch, *Christian Trade Unions*, pp. 102–117; Preller, *Sozialpolitik*, pp. 296–390; Karl Christian Führer, *Arbeitslosigkeit und die Entstehung der Arbeitslosenversicherung in Deutschland 1902–1927* (Berlin, 1990); Hubert Mockenhaupt, *Weg und Wirken des geistlichen Sozialpolitikers Heinrich Brauns* (Paderborn, 1977); Winkler, *Schein der Normalität*, pp. 293–295, 307–316, 507–509, 536–537. For accounts linking Catholicism to the defense of private charity, see David Crew, *Germans on Welfare: From Weimar to Hitler* (Oxford, 1998), pp. 16–115, and Young-Sun Hong, *Welfare, Modernity, and the Weimar State, 1919–1933* (Princeton, 1998), pp. 114–202.

[18] Knut Borchardt argues that wage increases were "excessive" in "Economic Causes of the Collapse of the Weimar Republic," in Knut Borchardt, *Perspectives on Modern German Economic History and Policy* (Cambridge, 1991), pp. 161–183. See the more persuasive analysis in Harold James, *The German Slump: Politics and Economics 1924–1936* (Oxford, 1986); Theo Balderston, *The Origins and Course of the German Economic Crisis,*

Two disastrous developments for the Weimar Republic dashed the hopes of Christian trade unionists soon after the creation of the new unemployment insurance system. The first was a lurch rightward by the DNVP. That party suffered painful losses in the Reichstag election of May 1928, and the newspaper baron and radical nationalist Alfred Hugenberg persuaded most party members to blame their Reichstag delegation's support for progressive social legislation. Hugenberg won election as DNVP chair in August 1928 and sought a united front with all radical nationalist groups to undermine the Weimar Republic, including the Nazi Party. The anti-democratic course of the DNVP meant that the Christian unions' efforts to promote the spread of "Tory democracy" had failed; the only remaining hope for a parliamentary majority was a Great Coalition involving the SPD, Center, and two liberal parties. Stegerwald drew the logical conclusion from the rise of Hugenberg and became one of the Center Party's most enthusiastic supporters of the Great Coalition cabinet led by the Social Democrat Hermann Müller.[19]

The second disastrous development for the Weimar Republic was the onset of the Great Depression. The Unemployment Insurance Act was passed during a boom year for the German economy, and it calculated premiums and benefits on the basis of highly optimistic assumptions about future unemployment rates. A painful economic slump in late 1929 caused a serious deficit in that system and in the federal budget as a whole. A collapse of government credit precluded the simple option of increasing public debt, and the Müller cabinet was compelled to debate the miserable alternatives of slashing unemployment benefits, as demanded by the liberal parties, or raising taxes to finance existing benefits, as demanded by the SPD and Free unions. Heinrich Brüning had recently won election to chair the Center Reichstag delegation, and in March 1930 he proposed a temporizing compromise, designed to allow the insurance program to scrape by for several months at least, that was endorsed by Chancellor Müller. The Social Democrats had heard credible reports, however, that President Hindenburg, the defense ministry, and many liberal politicians were conspiring to saddle them with responsibility for unpopular austerity measures and then expel them from the government anyway. The SPD Reichstag delegation therefore insisted at the end of March that unemployment insurance receive substantially increased revenue to place it on a sound basis, and Hermann Müller

---

November 1923 to May 1932 (Berlin, 1993); and Theo Balderston, *Economics and Politics in the Weimar Republic* (Cambridge, 2002).

[19] Patch, *Christian Trade Unions*, pp. 127–141; Thomas Mergel, "Das Scheitern des deutschen Tory-Konservatismus. Die Umformung der DNVP zu einer rechtsradikalen Partei 1928–1932," *Historische Zeitschrift*, 276 (2003): 323–368.

resigned after being disavowed by his own party. Brüning replaced him as chancellor with a commission from Hindenburg to form a cabinet without Social Democrats and balance the budget through any means necessary. His appointment created powerful grounds for conflict between the Free and Christian unions.[20]

1.2   The Debate between Catholic Corporatists and Socialists in the Great Depression

Many Catholic thinkers in the interwar era envisioned society as divided vertically along the lines of the *Berufsstand*, the "corporation" or "vocational association" in each branch of the economy, rather than horizontally between classes. They also developed many proposals to alleviate class conflict by granting these vocational associations a formal voice in government decisions. Christian trade unionists always rejected corporatist plans based on the example of Fascist Italy or the hierarchical doctrine of Universalism developed by Othmar Spann, a professor of social theory at the University of Vienna. Spann called for the political parties to be replaced by economic corporations uniting employers and employees in a single organization, and for parliaments to be replaced by chambers of corporations. Christian trade unionists displayed somewhat more interest in the rival school of Solidarism founded by the German Jesuit Heinrich Pesch. Solidarists endorsed autonomous trade unions and urged them to form joint committees with employers in every branch of the economy; they also exhorted the government to delegate some regulatory powers to these joint committees. Solidarists accepted the democratically elected Reichstag and political parties, but some of them argued that the upper house of parliament should represent the economic associations rather than state governments.[21] Elfriede Nebgen, who became a Christian union functionary in 1921 and worked closely thereafter with Jakob Kaiser, has testified that the Christian unions rejected even the Solidarist version of corporatism in the 1920s and only revived such proposals after

---

[20] Patch, *Bruning*, pp. 45–71; Wolfram Pyta, *Hindenburg. Herrschaft zwischen Hohenzollern und Hitler* (Munich, 2007), pp. 555–575; Ludwig Richter, *Die Deutsche Volkspartei, 1918–1933* (Düsseldorf, 2002), pp. 605–631; Winkler, *Schein der Normalität*, pp. 727–823.

[21] Paul Misner, *Catholic Labor Movements in Europe: Social Thought and Action, 1914–1965* (Washington, DC, 2015), pp. 60–83; Klein, *Der Volksverein*, pp. 285–294; Johannes Schwarte, *Gustav Gundlach S.J. (1892–1963). Massgeblicher Repräsentant der katholischen Soziallehre während der Pontifikate Pius' XI. und Pius' XII.* (Munich, 1975), pp. 18–36; William L. Patch, "Fascism, Catholic Corporatism, and the Christian Trade Unions of Germany, Austria, and France," in Lex Heerma van Voss, Patrick Pasture, and Jan De Maeyer, eds., *Between Cross and Class: Comparative Histories of Christian Labour in Europe 1840–2000* (Bern, 2005), pp. 173–201.

the Nazi seizure of power to forestall more radical projects. Some historians, however, discern an ominous line of continuity from the occasional discussion of corporatist ideas in the Christian unions after the First World War to the embrace of them in March/April 1933 and the authoritarian constitutional plans of the conservative resistance during the Second World War.[22] The available evidence suggests nevertheless that Nebgen was largely correct.

Political scientists employ the term corporatism in a value-neutral sense to describe a wide variety of political systems, ranging from formally democratic to highly authoritarian, in which key policy decisions are made through direct negotiations between the leaders of well-organized economic interest groups. In view of the polarization of party politics at the end of the First World War, Charles Maier has proposed corporatism as the explanation for the reconstruction of Western Europe in the subsequent decade.[23] This term provides a fairly accurate description of the Weimar political system in its early years, but the willingness to bargain among the interest groups faltered in 1923 and collapsed after 1927. Thereafter both the parties and interest groups proved largely incapable of forging compromises. Many Christian trade unionists perceived the revival of something like the Central Association of Employers and Employees formed in November 1918 as the best hope to overcome this stalemate; that is the only sense in which corporatism exerted a powerful influence on them.

The collapse of the willingness to compromise became apparent immediately after the Reichstag election of May 1928. The SPD scored gains in that election, but the big winner was a mélange of two dozen single-issue parties for farmers, small businessmen, inflation victims, etc., which together won a startling 14 percent of the vote. Most liberal politicians concluded that the voters had become utterly materialistic, and that the liberal parties would suffer ruinous further losses if they compromised with the SPD. The small losses by the Center Party

---

[22] Elfriede Kaiser-Nebgen to Erich Kosthorst, January 19, 1965, NL Kaiser/247, and Elfriede Nebgen, *Jakob Kaiser: Der Widerstandskämpfer*, 2nd edn. (Stuttgart, 1970), pp. 89–99. Contrast Hans Mommsen, "Gesellschaftsbild und Verfassungspläne des deutschen Widerstandes," and "Der 20. Juli und die deutsche Arbeiterbewegung," in Hans Mommsen, *Alternative zu Hitler. Studien zur Geschichte des deutschen Widerstandes* (Munich, 2000), pp. 53–158, 284–312; Michael Schneider, *Die christlichen Gewerkschaften*, pp. 697–719, 763–766; and Michael Schneider, "Zwischen Standesvertretung und Werksgemeinschaft. Zu den Gewerkschaftskonzeptionen der Widerstandsgruppen des 20. Juli 1944," in Jürgen Schmädeke and Peter Steinbach, eds., *Der Widerstand gegen den Nationalsozialismus. Die deutsche Gesellschaft und der Widerstand gegen Hitler* (Munich, 1985), pp. 520–532.

[23] Charles Maier, *Recasting Bourgeois Europe: Stabilization in France, Germany, and Italy in the Decade after World War I* (Princeton, 1975), pp. 5–15.

prompted most of its leaders to emphasize Catholic religious values as the glue holding it together, a reaction that also inspired reluctance to work with the SPD. Moreover, the Communist Party had scored a modest victory with 10.6 percent of the vote, and it denounced the Social Democrats as traitors to the working class. Vigorous competition from the Communists inspired the SPD to make aggressive campaign promises and limited its ability to compromise after the election. For all these reasons, the negotiations in June 1928 to form the Great Coalition cabinet led by the Social Democrat Hermann Müller proved extraordinarily difficult and led only to a cabinet of distinguished individuals who did not formally represent their parties. This cabinet experienced numerous crises in 1928/1929 and had a sterile legislative record; its travails inspired many thoughtful supporters of the republic to speak of a crisis of parliamentary democracy itself.[24]

Similar polarization among the economic interest groups became evident in November 1928, when the Ruhr steel industry locked out 240,000 workers rather than accept a decree by a state labor arbitrator of modest wage increases of 2 or 3 percent. The Free and Christian unions rallied support for the steelworkers in public opinion and the Reichstag, and in December the steel industrialists retreated from this challenge to the system of state arbitration. The textile industry, however, had meanwhile locked out 190,000 workers in Rhineland-Westphalia, and its sustained campaign thereafter to lower wages in all regions inflamed tempers in the Free and Christian textile workers' unions alike. Labor relations in mining and some other industries also became extremely confrontational on the eve of the Great Depression.[25]

Chancellor Brüning chose his former patron Adam Stegerwald as labor minister in April 1930, and they adopted a strategy of pragmatic corporatism inspired by the example of the Central Association of November 1918. They sought a Reichstag majority for a balanced budget by persuading the captains of industry and organized labor to agree on the following propositions:

---

[24] Larry Eugene Jones, *German Liberalism and the Dissolution of the Weimar Party System 1918–1933* (Chapel Hill, 1988), pp. 251–377; Richter, *DVP*, pp. 282–297, 490–603; Thomas Mergel, *Parlamentarische Kultur in der Weimarer Republik. Politische Kommunikation, symbolische Politik und Öffentlichkeit im Reichstag* (Düsseldorf, 2002), pp. 399–427; Patch, *Christian Trade Unions*, pp. 133–141; Winkler, *Schein der Normalität*, pp. 521–605.

[25] Discussion of labor disputes in Zentralverband christlicher Textilarbeiter, *Verhandlungen der X. Verbands-Generalversammlung, 3. Bis 7. August 1930 zu Dresden* (no place or date), pp. 128–136, 157–162; Patch, *Christian Trade Unions*, pp. 141–148; Winkler, *Schein der Normalität*, pp. 477–488, 557–572.

1. That the federal budget must be balanced quickly through an equal mixture of tax increases and spending cuts to restore public credit.
2. That wages and the cost of living should be lowered by similar proportions, to leave real wages unchanged but make German goods cheaper on the world market and thus stimulate exports. (Germany was forbidden by the reparations treaties from devaluing its currency, so Brüning hoped to accomplish the same effect through deflation.)
3. That a special tax should be imposed on the highest-paid civil servants and salaried employees to help finance unemployment insurance.

The chancellor also hoped that such an agreement would smooth the way for the government to engage in long-term borrowing for a substantial program of public works. Brüning has become infamous because of the pro-cyclical consequences of his deflationary policies, but his initial goal, as he told the cabinet on April 30, was to develop a "five-year plan ... to promote economic growth" through public works, lower transportation costs, and the stimulation of export industries. "To accelerate the return of the unemployed to the process of production," he concluded, "is one of the most important tasks of the government." The transportation, labor, and postal ministries then developed plans to raise 1.5 billion marks on foreign bond markets for infrastructure and public housing projects, a sum equivalent to 2 percent of national income.[26]

The three propositions of Brüning and Stegerwald were discussed by the Free unions and business leaders in the first two weeks of June. The labor leaders were prepared, in accord with the suggestions of Brüning, to sign a joint statement that spoke vaguely of the need "to lower the costs of production" along with consumer prices. Some conciliatory industrialists supported this line, but the Catholic steel tycoon Fritz Thyssen, an admirer of Othmar Spann's Universalism, demanded freedom for employers to undercut unilaterally the wage levels guaranteed by collective labor contracts. Most business leaders felt that Thyssen went too far, but they soon agreed that any joint statement with the trade unions must call explicitly for "the adjustment of wages to the new conditions" created by the economic slump. Labor leaders believed that any such explicit endorsement of wage reductions would discredit them among union members, so they demanded that there must be a substantial reduction in the cost of living before there could be any wage cuts. All business leaders considered that demand unreasonable, so the talks broke off on June 14. The government was therefore compelled to

---

[26] Cabinet minutes of April 30, 1930, in Tilman Koops, ed., *Akten der Reichskanzlei der Weimarer Republik. Die Kabinette Brüning I und II*, 3 vols. (Boppard am Rhein, 1982–1990), I: 65–69; Patch, *Brüning*, pp. 73–84.

defend its very unpopular budget without any support from the interest groups.[27] The collapse of these talks also inspired resistance to government borrowing for public works, because the business associations had long argued that private firms could make the best use of any credit available on foreign bond markets. In late June the autonomous governing board of the National Railway, which was dominated by industrialists, rejected the cabinet's request to increase its debt load, and the autonomous board of the *Reichsbank* vetoed most proposals for bond issues to finance highway and housing construction. The cabinet's 1.5-billion-mark program for public works was pared down to about 250 million, a sum that could not affect the unemployment rate. Resistance from the business community thus sabotaged Brüning's plan to alleviate unemployment.[28]

Relations between the Free and Christian unions deteriorated when Brüning imposed his budget through presidential emergency decree in July 1930, and then dissolved the Reichstag and called for elections when a Reichstag majority overturned that decree. The SPD targeted Catholic workers during the subsequent campaign, assuming that they were angry over Brüning's austerity measures. The Free unions also noted indignantly that the new food tariffs enacted at the insistence of President Hindenburg in April 1930 had raised the cost of living in June and July, just when government labor arbitrators began to decree wage reductions. They donated one million marks to the SPD campaign and appealed to all workers to vote for it as the only defender of the democratic republic. Their leader Theodor Leipart told a journalist in August 1930 that the government parties sought "revision of the Weimar constitution [and] greater power for the Reich President," and he discerned "strong tendencies to erect an authoritarian corporatist state," a reference to the Universalism of Othmar Spann.[29] The Christian trade unions, however, rallied to Brüning's defense. He had earned the trust of Christian labor leaders as secretary general of the German Labor Federation, and they

---

[27] See the report on these talks sent to the Free unions by Peter Grassmann on June 26, 1930, in *Gewerkschaftsquellen*, IV: 100–116 (quotations from the rival draft agreements on p. 103), and Udo Wengst, "Unternehmerverbände und Gewerkschaften in Deutschland im Jahre 1930," *Vierteljahrshefte für Zeitgeschichte*, 25 (1977): 99–119.

[28] Patch, *Brüning*, pp. 84–88.

[29] Leipart's interview on August 6, 1930, and ADGB "Wahlaufruf" of August 16, *Gewerkschaftsquellen*, IV: 119–122 (quotation on p. 119); Heinrich August Winkler, *Der Weg in die Katastrophe. Arbeiter und Arbeiterbewegung in der Weimarer Republik 1930 bis 1933* (Berlin and Bonn, 1987), pp. 125–205; Donna Harsch, *German Social Democracy and the Rise of Nazism* (Chapel Hill, 1993), pp. 79–99. With some support from the Catholic clergy, the paramilitary Austrian *Heimwehr* had recently adopted a program for an authoritarian corporatist state co-authored by Spann; see Patch, *Christian Trade Unions*, pp. 195–196.

now argued that his measures were the only rational response to the world economic crisis. They responded to attacks from the Left by reviving old accusations that the SPD and Free unions sought to undermine Christianity. Stegerwald's successor as chairman of the League of Christian Unions, Bernhard Otte, insisted during the campaign that Christians who voted for the SPD betrayed their faith. In September 1930 the Christian unions described the election outcome as a victory, because the SPD declined from 29.8 percent to 24.5 percent of the vote, while the Center Party avoided losses. The crucial result, however, was the stunning rise of the Nazi Party to 18.3 percent, following a campaign in which the best defenders of democracy had wasted much of their strength attacking each other.[30]

The rise of the Nazi Party persuaded the SPD to tolerate the Brüning cabinet, i.e. oppose any attempt to topple it on the grounds that the outcome at this juncture would be even worse, most likely a fascist government led by Hugenberg and Hitler. In private many SPD leaders expressed sympathy for Brüning's policies, but their Reichstag delegation declared on October 18, 1930, that it continued to oppose Brüning resolutely and would topple him itself when it judged the time ripe. This stance reflected an awkward compromise between the party's left and right wings.[31] The top leaders of the Free unions endorsed the policy of toleration, but it proved very difficult for them to defend because of the campaign by state labor arbitrators to lower wages. Labor Minister Stegerwald sought therefore to encourage an informal version of the Great Coalition by convening another summit conference of industrialists and trade unionists on November 12. Moderate industrialists won the upper hand over hard-liners such as Thyssen, and they soon offered an agreement attractive to Theodor Leipart. It opposed further measures of agrarian protectionism, urged a systematic campaign to lower the cost of living, and advocated agreements wherever possible to "stretch out" existing employment by introducing the forty-hour week, as demanded by the Free unions. Point 4 urged that collective labor contracts should, wherever possible, be renewed when they expired to avoid strife; if changes proved necessary, "the negotiations should be conducted with an awareness of the present economic distress and with the goal of overcoming it through voluntary agreement." Leipart defended this pact when the Free unions' national committee met on December 14, and the SPD chair Otto Wels

---

[30] Heinrich Imbusch memoir, "Heinrich Brüning," NL Platte/14/34–41; Bernhard Otte's two circulars to the Christian unions of August 20, 1930, NL Otte/2/108–13; election commentary in *Zentralblatt der christlichen Gewerkschaften*, #19 (October 1, 1930), p. 289; Patch, *Brüning*, pp. 89–103.

[31] Winkler, *Der Weg in die Katastrophe*, pp. 197–244; Patch, *Brüning*, pp. 103–108.

argued forcefully that it was needed to build a political bloc of moderates and prevent further growth by the radical Right. Most delegates insisted, however, that they could endure wage reductions imposed by state arbitrators but would suffer ruinous membership losses if they signed any agreement implying that they accepted such reductions voluntarily. Feinhals of the textile workers compared this agreement to the discredited *Burgfrieden* of August 1914, and Nikolaus Bernhard of the construction workers warned that union leaders would become "officers without soldiers" if they signed it. This debate ended the last serious attempt to revive anything resembling the Central Association of November 1918. Bernhard Otte had supported the draft agreement enthusiastically, and he warned colleagues in the Christian unions after these talks broke down that the Free unions' intransigence would only strengthen the hand of reactionary employers who rejected any dealings with organized labor.[32]

While the pragmatic version of corporatism floundered in 1930, the Christian unions became alarmed over the dissemination of authoritarian versions of Catholic corporatism. They sought to influence the Catholic discussion of social reform through the one intellectual affiliated with them who had long advocated Solidarism, Professor Theodor Brauer. The son of a cobbler, Brauer served as Stegerwald's personal secretary during the First World War and edited several union publications, while studying economics at university. In 1919 Stegerwald relied on him to draw a clear distinction between the SPD program and Christian ideas for social reform, and Brauer propagated the Solidarist vision of social harmony at several Christian union congresses. He provoked much disagreement, however, from union colleagues who experienced conflict with employers, and he soon devoted himself to an academic career. Brauer achieved success unprecedented for a Catholic worker with a doctorate in economics from the University of Bonn, a faculty appointment at Karlsruhe from 1923 to 1928, and a professorship thereafter at the University of Cologne. He published a book in 1924 that criticized both the Free and Christian unions for having ignored the laws of economics since the end of the war, for an overly ambitious legislative agenda, and for launching too many strikes. Nevertheless, Brauer always devoted himself to the adult education program for Christian union functionaries,

---

[32] Minutes of the conference with employers on November 12 and ADGB Bundesausschuss, December 14/15, 1930, *Gewerkschaftsquellen*, IV: 171–173, 187–202 (quotations on pp. 191 and 198); circulars by Otte to the Christian unions of December 10, December 15, and December 29, 1930, NL Otte/2/141–150; Wengst, "Unternehmerverbände und Gewerkschaften," pp. 111–116.

and he was regarded fondly by his students.[33] In 1930 the Christian unions provided Brauer with funding to hold regular conferences on social reform by the Königswinter Circle, which included Catholic labor leaders, economists, and the Jesuit theologians Gustav Gundlach and Oswald von Nell-Breuning. Their discussions had unanticipated consequences when Nell-Breuning received a secret commission from the general of his order to provide a draft for what became the most influential statement of Catholic social theory in the twentieth century, the encyclical *Quadragesimo Anno* issued by Pius XI in May 1931. Nell-Breuning used the Königswinter Circle as the sounding board for his ideas.[34]

Quadragesimo Anno expresses vigorous support for labor unions and welfare legislation, exhorting all Christians to display "solidarity" with the poor, but three sections proved ambiguous and problematic. The first involves the ideal of social order outlined in paragraphs 81–85, which urge "that the conflict between the hostile classes be abolished and harmonious cooperation of the Industries and Professions be encouraged and promoted." The state should encourage the formation of "guilds or associations" (*Berufsstände* in the German translation; *ordines* in the original Latin) to unite the parties divided by conflicts of interest on the labor market. "A true, genuine social order," Pius argued,

demands that the various members of a society be united together by some strong bond. This unifying force is present not only in the producing of goods or the rendering of services – in which the employers and employees of an identical Industry or Profession collaborate jointly – but also in the common good, to achieve which all Industries and Professions together ought, each to the best of its ability, to cooperate amicably.

Many Catholics interpreted this passage as a rejection of pluralist democracy, with disastrous consequences in Austria, Portugal, and Spain.[35] Nell-Breuning had sought to discourage such conclusions by including

[33] Forster, *Stegerwald*, pp. 143–146, 201–206, 272–276; Karl Dörpinghaus, "Lebenserinnerungen, I. Teil," pp. 68–69, NL Dörpinghaus/2; Johannes Albers, "Erinnerungen an meine gewerkschaftliche und politische Zusammenarbeit mit Jakob Kaiser von 1919 bis 1933," written in 1961, NL Kaiser/215/54–67 (esp. pp. 11–12); Theodor Brauer, *Krisis der Gewerkschaften*, 2nd edn. (Jena, 1924), pp. 3–11, 17–19, 36–41, 48–53.

[34] See "Der Königswinterer Kreis und sein Anteil an 'Quadragesimo anno,'" in Oswald von Nell-Breuning, *Wie sozial ist die Kirche? Leistung und Versagen der katholischen Soziallehre* (Düsseldorf, 1972), pp. 99–104, and Klein, *Der Volksverein*, pp. 285–290. The translation of *Quadragesimo anno* quoted below can be found at w2.vatican.va/content/pius-xi/it/encyclicals.index.html.

[35] Nell-Breuning, "Königswinterer Kreis," and "Octogesimo anno," in *Wie sozial ist die Kirche?*, pp. 110–112, 121–122; Gerhard Besier with Francesca Piombo, *The Holy See and Hitler's Germany*, trans. W.R. Ward (New York, 2007), pp. 87–101; Misner, *Catholic Labor Movements*, pp. 212–230.

in the encyclical a declaration that the state must respect the inalienable rights of individuals, and he proclaimed the famous principle of "subsidiarity," according to which social problems should only be addressed by local government if they cannot be solved through voluntary associations, and by the national government only if they cannot be solved by local government (paragraphs 78–80). The political implications of these passages remained unclear to many readers, however.

The second problematic passage is a commentary on the Italian Fascist labor law of 1926 (paragraphs 91–95), the only passage written by Pius XI himself:

Anyone who gives even slight attention to the matter will easily see what are the obvious advantages in the system We have thus summarily described: The various classes work together peacefully, socialist organizations and their activities are repressed, and a special magistracy exercises a governing authority. Yet ... there are not wanting some who fear that the State, instead of confining itself as it ought to the furnishing of necessary and adequate assistance, is substituting itself for free activity; that the new syndical and corporative order savors too much of an involved and political system of administration; and that ... it rather serves particular political ends than leads to the reconstruction and promotion of a better social order.

Nell-Breuning believed at the time that the praise for Fascism in the first half of this passage was a brilliant exercise in "diplomatic irony," but many Catholics deduced from the signing of the Lateran Treaties in 1929 that the pope truly sympathized with Mussolini, and they ignored the criticisms of Fascism in the second half. Heinrich Brüning felt bitter shame as a Catholic when he heard Fritz Thyssen quote Pius XI repeatedly in 1931/1932 to call for the suppression of trade unions and the right to strike.[36]

In a third problematic passage, *Quadragesimo Anno* acknowledges that democratic socialism had changed profoundly since its rupture with communism at the end of the First World War (paragraphs 111–113). "One might say," it concludes, "that, terrified by its own principles and by the conclusions drawn therefrom by Communism, Socialism inclines toward and in a certain measure approaches the truths which Christian tradition has always held sacred." The encyclical defines one irreconcilable difference nevertheless: Christians believe that man is placed on earth so that "he may fully cultivate and develop all his faculties unto the praise and glory of his Creator," but socialism "affirms that human

---

[36] Nell-Breuning, "Octogesimo anno," in *Wie sozial?*, pp. 118–120; Heinrich Brüning, *Memoiren 1918–1934* (Stuttgart, 1970), p. 136; Brüning's untitled lecture in Detroit on December 7, 1941, p. 8, Harvard University Archive/FP 93.45.

association has been instituted for the sake of material advantage alone."
Even revisionist and reformist socialists therefore embraced the process of
industrial concentration without regard for the damage inflicted on the
human psyche, because they believed that an abundance of material
possessions would endow workers' lives with meaning. Here Nell-
Breuning followed Gustav Gundlach's definition of the basic fallacy
shared by all schools of socialism, but he later acknowledged that they
had judged Social Democrats unfairly; when he first became personally
acquainted with Social Democratic labor leaders after 1945, Nell-
Breuning soon discovered that they were no more inclined than
Catholic priests to believe that the mere accumulation of material possessions could endow life with meaning.[37] Nevertheless, *Quadragesimo
Anno* inspired most parish priests to teach until the 1960s that no
socialist could be a true Christian.

These ambiguous passages sowed confusion among Catholic workers
in Germany when this encyclical was published. The Christian unions
sought to neutralize its impact by declaring that they had always followed
its principles. Bernhard Otte addressed a conference of the Königswinter
Circle in May 1932 and implored his listeners for patience, because
a corporatist order could only emerge very slowly on the basis of the
work of the trade unions. Collective bargaining agreements, he argued,
should form branch associations between management and labor in each
industry to supervise vocational training and job safety. Someday the
beneficial work of these branch associations might improve the atmosphere to the point where the Central Association of November 1918
could be revived. This very cautious speech appears to be the only
authoritative statement about Catholic corporatism by a leader of the
Christian unions before Hitler came to power.[38]

Theodor Brauer proposed two bolder reforms in line with Solidarist
theory. In a leadership conference of the German Labor Federation
on November 21, 1930, he argued that unemployment insurance should
be transferred to the control of the voluntary associations of management and labor, and that the National Economic Council should
become an upper house of parliament with jurisdiction over labor law
and social insurance. The terse press release on this meeting noted

---

[37] Nell-Breuning, "Königswinterer Kreis," in *Wie sozial?*, pp. 113–115; compare Gustav
Gundlach, "Sozialismus," in *Staatslexikon der Görres-Gesellschaft*, 5th edn. (Freiburg,
1931), vol. IV, column 1893.
[38] *Zentralblatt der christlichen Gewerkschaften*, #13 (July 1, 1931), pp. 193–194; Müller,
Arbeiter, Katholizismus, Staat, pp. 165–170; Bernhard Otte, "Wege der berufsständischen
Ordnung," in Josef van der Velden, ed., *Die berufsständische Ordnung. Idee und
praktische Möglichkeiten* (Cologne, 1932), pp. 89–102.

"skeptical remarks" by union colleagues.[39] Brauer discussed these ideas in a book published in 1931, but his co-director of the educational program for Christian union functionaries, Dr. Franz Röhr, published a critical review in the Christian union press. According to Röhr, "there can be no doubt that the social order envisioned by Brauer assumes incomparably more reason and civic virtue among individual human beings and their associations than is present among them today." It would be very dangerous, Röhr concluded, if a school of "fanatics" emerged whose response to every crisis was that "only corporatism can save us."[40]

Röhr had been a legal advisor to Walther Rathenau at the end of the First World War, and he had advocated the nationalization of the coal mines ever since 1919. Heinrich Brüning later recalled him as an admirable human being but a "radical socialist" in all questions of economic policy.[41] To understand the wave of Christian socialism that spread among Christian labor activists in 1945, it must be noted that socialism had already exerted great influence on them during the Great Depression. The bank crisis in the summer of 1931 led to shocking revelations of criminal fraud and gross blunders by business leaders, and the Christian unions demanded strong government oversight of the big banks and either the strict regulation or dissolution of the syndicates and trusts. In late October Heinrich Körner, the vice chair of the Rhineland Christian unions, called for "an orderly planned economy" so that the world would never again see mountains of wheat, cotton, and coffee burned while millions suffered privation.[42] Following brutal wage disputes with the Rhenish-Westphalian Coal Syndicate, Heinrich Imbusch appealed in January 1932 for "the transfer of mining to public ownership." His argument focused on the Syndicate's political support for the radical Right. Imbusch earned thunderous applause when he told a miners' rally on February 7 that "the heavy industrialists are a threat to the nation, they are a state within the state, they display no regard for the

---

[39] *Zentralblatt der christlichen Gewerkschaften*, #23 (December 1, 1930), pp. 358–361; *Der Deutsche*, #274 (November 22, 1930).

[40] Theodor Brauer, *Sozialpolitik und Sozialreform* (Jena, 1931); Röhr's book review in *Zentralblatt der christlichen Gewerkschaften*, #24 (December 15, 1931), pp. 375–376 (source of quotation). The leaders of the Christian miners' union noted on September 13, 1930, that Brauer requested sole control over the training of Christian union functionaries, but they voted to keep Franz Röhr as co-director with equal rights ("Gewerkverein Hauptvorstand" minutes in DGB-Archiv/NL Imbusch/2).

[41] "Franz Röhr" in *Wer ist's?*, 9th edn. (Berlin, 1928), p. 1282; Brüning, *Memoiren*, pp. 40–41, 49–50.

[42] Minutes of a Christian union leadership conference attended by Stegerwald, July 23, 1931, NL Otte/7/58–59; *Zentralblatt*, #15 (August 1, 1931), pp. 227–228, and #21 (November 1, 1931), pp. 322–323 (source of quotation); Patch, *Brüning*, pp. 172–181.

common good ... Therefore, we must remove this thorn from the flesh of the German people represented by our most ruthless businessmen." Soon thereafter Imbusch demanded the nationalization of the iron and steel industry as well as mining.[43]

Theodor Brauer opposed this assault on free enterprise. In March 1932 he declared that "the issue of nationalizing the mines must under no circumstances be linked with the issue of nationalizing the economy as a whole." Mining was a special case because of the old German legal and Catholic moral tradition that mineral wealth belonged to the community. Any attempt to nationalize all large-scale industry, however, "must result in a sort of police state, whose pressure on human beings would soon become unbearable." The Christian metalworkers' union, led by Franz Wieber, also opposed nationalization of the steel industry, and at the last congress of the Christian unions in September 1932, Brauer argued passionately against any expropriations or central state planning. The miners received vigorous support, however, from Heinrich Körner and Friedrich Baltrusch, a Protestant and the Christian unions' top expert on economic policy. The keynote address for the congress by Baltrusch called for public ownership of the largest syndicates and trusts and new government agencies to channel investment and regulate prices; his program closely resembled that of the SPD.[44]

The position of Imbusch and Körner was obviously more popular among Christian trade unionists than Brauer's. When the Christian metalworkers held their congress soon thereafter, a young delegate from Essen declared that "capitalism is to blame for our misery ... Therefore, I demand the nationalization of all large capitalist factories and their transfer to the collective ownership of the workers." Franz Wieber rebuked him, but his own son Georg noted that the "big bourgeoisie" displayed such arrogance as to make calls to nationalize heavy industry all but irresistible. Imbusch never encountered such challenges at miners' rallies, and his union only lost 7.4 percent of its members in 1932, while overall losses for the Free and Christian unions averaged 15 percent.[45]

---

[43] *Der Bergknappe*, #4 (January 23, 1932), p. 1, and #8 (February 20), p. 1 (source of quotation); Schäfer, *Heinrich Imbusch*, pp. 232–241; Patch, *Christian Trade Unions*, pp. 177–181.

[44] Theodor Brauer, "Zur Frage der Verstaatlichung des Bergbaus," *Zentralblatt*, #6 (March 15, 1932), pp. 82–85 (quotations on 82–83); "Reich und Schwerindustrie," and report on a speech by Karl Schmitz on July 10, *Zentralblatt*, #15 (August 1, 1932), pp. 194–195, 203; Gesamtverband der christlichen Gewerkschaften, *Niederschrift der Verhandlungen des 13. Kongresses der christlichen Gewerkschaften Deutschlands, 18.-20. September 1932* (Berlin, 1932), pp. 294–303, 314–317, 376–390.

[45] Christlicher Metallarbeiter-Verband, *Protokoll über die Verhandlungen der 13. General-Versammlung des Christlichen Metallarbeiter-Verbandes Deutschlands. Königswinter, 26.-28. September 1932* (no place or date), pp. 46, 74–75, 111; quarterly membership figures in

Brauer's last article for the Christian union press before Hitler's appointment as chancellor insisted that capitalism had not failed in the Great Depression; Germany simply needed a more vigorous anti-trust policy. Körner responded immediately that heavy industry must be nationalized at once. Brauer was evidently losing the debate within the Christian unions, where socialism proved a more powerful influence than Catholic corporatism during the Great Depression.[46]

1.3   The Nazi Seizure of Power

Old differences in outlook between the core membership of the blue-collar Christian unions and their Protestant allies in the white-collar DHV and Christian Social wing of the DNVP inspired conflicting responses to the rise of National Socialism. Blue-collar Christian trade unionists heeded warnings from Italian colleagues in 1922/1923 that Mussolini and his Blackshirts sought to destroy all labor unions. When the "Hitler movement" first came to national attention in 1923, the daily newspaper founded by the Christian unions reproached him for embracing Mussolini as his model; Hitler's dilettantish ideas about liberating Germany from foreign domination, it noted, had degenerated in the polarized atmosphere of Munich into vengeful schemes for the annihilation of domestic political enemies. Joseph Joos of the Catholic workers' clubs also alleged that, despite the anti-capitalist rhetoric of the National Socialist German Workers' Party (NSDAP), it depended on financing from reactionary industrialists who sought to destroy the labor unions. Any attempt by the Nazis to seize power, Joos concluded, must be crushed as ruthlessly as a Communist uprising would be.[47] A fond portrait by Heinrich Imbusch of the Jewish industrialist and statesman

Geschäftsbericht des Hauptvorstandes des Gewerkvereins christlicher Bergarbeiter Deutschlands für die Jahre 1930/32 (Essen, 1933), p. 84; Heinrich Potthoff, Freie Gewerkschaften 1918–1933. Der Allgemeine Deutsche Gewerkschaftsbund in der Weimarer Republik (Düsseldorf, 1987), pp. 348–349; Schneider, Die christlichen Gewerkschaften, pp. 452, 770–771. The Free unions lost 14.6 percent of their membership in 1932. We lack figures from 1932 for most Christian unions, but in 1931 their losses equaled those of the Free unions at 12.3 percent.

[46] Brauer, "Ende des Kapitalismus?" and rebuttal by Körner, Zentralblatt, #2 (January 15, 1933), pp. 13–19. Michael Schneider offers an exaggerated account of Brauer's influence in "Jakob Kaiser und das Ende der Christlichen Gewerkschaften 1932/33," in Tilman Mayer, ed., "Macht das Tor auf." Jakob-Kaiser-Studien (Berlin, 1996), pp. 11–42, esp. 23–27.

[47] "Die Hitlerbewegung," Der Deutsche, #23, January 28, 1923; editorial by Joos in Westdeutsche Arbeiter-Zeitung, #16 (April 21, 1923), p. 54; Patch, "Fascism, Catholic Corporatism," pp. 173–178; Jürgen Aretz, Katholische Arbeiterbewegung und Nationalsozialismus. Der Verband katholischer Arbeiter- und Knappenvereine Westdeutschlands 1923–1945 (Mainz, 1978), pp. 44–48. Contrast Michael Schneider,

Walther Rathenau illustrates the revulsion against anti-Semitism among the core membership of the blue-collar Christian unions. Rathenau was the most selfless patriot and charitable human being Imbusch had ever known. The painful memory of his assassination in 1922 prompted Imbusch to reflect that "there is no such thing as a German race," because Germany had experienced large flows of immigration from all over Europe and central Asia for twenty centuries. He concluded that anyone who had lived in the country for a time and contributed something to it was a "good German."[48]

When the white-collar DHV was founded in Hamburg in the 1890s, it had very close ties with the Pan-German League and Germany's first party of racial anti-Semites, the German Social Party. Pastor Adolf Stoecker also plunged the Christian Social Party into anti-Semitic agitation in the 1890s with arguments that differed little from those of the German Social Party, even if they were based on the theoretical premise that Jews could become decent Germans if they converted to Christianity. In the 1920s the chairman of the DHV, Hans Bechly, and its chief political strategist, Max Habermann, cultivated ties with the moderate parties, but they felt compelled to respect all points of view within their union. The DHV publishing house and adult education programs therefore disseminated strident attacks on the Weimar Republic by "conservative revolutionary" intellectuals alongside thoughtful defenses of parliamentary democracy.[49] The DHV authorized a campaign for the Reichstag in May 1924 by its functionary Franz Stöhr on the ticket of the Racial Freedom Party, which soon merged with the NSDAP. After his election Stöhr proclaimed in the DHV weekly that the antics of Marxist Jews had transformed the proceedings of the Reichstag into a nauseating farce. The Christian Social politician who edited the journal of the workers' clubs affiliated with the DNVP also published a list of twenty-eight Jewish Reichstag delegates in 1924 but warned that "these are just the ones who have emerged into the open. The others who stand behind the scenes are really pulling the strings. Is it any wonder that we find ourselves in such misery?"[50] The DHV and Christian Social movement thus left their followers susceptible to Nazi

---

"Jakob Kaiser," p. 17, which asserts that the Christian unions took no notice of National Socialism before November 1929.

[48] "Walther Rathenau," in NL Platte/14/166–169.

[49] Iris Hamel, *Völkischer Verband und nationale Gewerkschaft. Der Deutschnationale Handlungsgehilfen-Verband 1894–1933* (Frankfurt a.M., 1967); Walter Frank, *Hofprediger Adolf Stoecker und die christlichsoziale Bewegung* (Hamburg, 1935).

[50] Franz Stöhr, "Brief aus dem Reichstag," *Deutsche Handelswacht*, #20 (July 16, 1924), p. 309; editorial in Deutschnationaler Arbeiterbund, *Deutsche Arbeiterstimme*, June 1924, pp. 6–7.

propaganda in the Great Depression. The Nazis apparently won the votes of about 50 percent of DHV members in September 1930, and sixteen of the 107 Nazi Reichstag delegates belonged to that union. Habermann then sought to promote a government coalition between Brüning and Hitler. After Brüning rejected that idea, the DHV provided additional financial contributions to the NSDAP in a futile attempt to persuade it to embrace trade unionism and a progressive social policy.[51]

The blue-collar Christian unions and Catholic workers' clubs always sought to combat the NSDAP, not gain influence over it. They supported Brüning because they believed (even if some historians now disagree) that he sought to restore parliamentary democracy intact as soon as the economic crisis passed. After the election of September 1930, the League of Christian Trade Unions denounced Habermann's proposal for a coalition between Brüning and Hitler with the argument that any participation by Nazis in the government would mean "the dismantling of the democratic state." Within the cabinet, Stegerwald took the lead in persuading Brüning to oppose the Nazis and rely instead on toleration by the SPD. In January 1931, Bernhard Otte also persuaded the leaders of the Christian unions in a closed meeting that the Nazis sought to destroy all labor unions, and that it was their solemn duty "as citizens and as trade unionists ... to tolerate no National Socialist agitation in union locals and to combat National Socialist ideas with all their strength."[52]

Many Christian trade unionists did jump to the dubious conclusion that legitimate anger against the Versailles Treaty was the primary cause of Nazi electoral success. They sought therefore to establish their own patriotic credentials in the anti-Nazi struggle and applauded Chancellor Brüning's efforts to abolish war reparations. The decorated combat veteran Jakob Kaiser, who led the Rhineland provincial cartel of the Christian unions, even defended the campaign by radical nationalists in autumn 1930 to prevent screenings of the film version of *All Quiet on the Western Front*. Kaiser expressed admiration for Remarque's novel but argued that the Hollywood version made the patriotic sacrifice of German soldiers appear utterly meaningless. He concluded that "in future the fate of the nation will be determined by that segment of the working class which properly understands the newly awakened national consciousness and knows how to represent it in a dignified fashion." The Free unions, on the other hand, protested vigorously when the

[51] Patch, *Christian Trade Unions*, pp. 164–165, 196–205.
[52] Editorial in *Zentralblatt der christlichen Gewerkschaften*, #19 (October 1, 1930), p. 291; minutes of the Christian union leadership conference of January 17, 1931, NL Otte/7/ 83–84 (source of quotation); Patch, *Brüning*, pp. 130–136.

government banned this film, and they arranged private screenings at union meetings to express their opposition to militarism.[53]

This clash over *All Quiet* was virtually the last serious policy dispute between the Free and Christian unions. Otte was always inclined to defend Brüning, but in 1931 painful membership losses and pressure from the base compelled the Christian unions to join the Free in vigorous protests against new austerity measures. A joint labor deputation to Brüning on June 15, 1931, persuaded him to rescind the two most offensive provisions of his most recent emergency decree. Leipart then told Free union colleagues that their demands received much more favorable consideration from public opinion and the cabinet whenever such a united front could be presented. Leipart rewarded the Christian unions by supporting Brüning's campaign to abolish reparations in defiance of the SPD line that Germany should seek rapprochement with France. By December 1931 all three labor federations called for a synthesis of "national" and "social" values in the old spirit of Friedrich Naumann. It remains unclear whether this development reflected a patriotic consensus among union members or merely the growing influence of university-educated combat veterans on the professional staff at the national headquarters of the Free unions in Berlin.[54]

In October 1931 the mammoth Free metalworkers' union appealed for the merger of all three labor federations to present a united workers' front. In response Anton Erkelenz of the Hirsch-Duncker unions published three questions that clearly defined the preconditions for the creation of unified labor unions. Were the Free unions prepared, he asked first, to "embrace workers from all parties" and give "workers who are not socialists a home and a chance to participate?" Erkelenz considered his second question even more important, whether the unions of the future would guarantee "freedom of religious faith." Finally, he asked, were the Free unions resolved to "conduct a resolute struggle

---

[53] Kaiser's editorials in *Zentralblatt*, #19 (October 1, 1930), pp. 290–291, and #2 (January 15, 1931), pp. 17–19; Erich Kosthorst, *Jakob Kaiser: Der Arbeiterführer* (Stuttgart, 1967), pp. 53–122, 226–233; ADGB Bundesausschuss, December 14/15, 1930, *Gewerkschaftsquellen*, IV: 180; Modris Eksteins, "War, Memory, and Politics: The Fate of the Film *All Quiet on the Western Front*," *Central European History*, 13 (1980): 60–82.

[54] Patch, *Brüning*, pp. 156–164, 184, 208–214; Free union leadership conferences of June 17 and December 15, 1931, *Gewerkschaftsquellen*, IV: 327–328, 444–446; Detlev Brunner, *Bürokratie und Politik des Allgemeinen Deutschen Gewerkschaftsbundes 1918/19 bis 1933* (Cologne, 1992), pp. 223–252, 396–436. For further details see William L. Patch, "Nationalism, Socialism, and Organized Labor's Response to the Dissolution of the Weimar Republic," in Hermann Beck and Larry Eugene Jones, eds., *From Weimar to Hitler: Studies in the Dissolution of Weimar Democracy* (forthcoming from Berghahn in 2018).

against communist/Bolshevik attempts to foment revolution" and "serve the state, the nation, the Republic, and democracy?" Theodor Leipart replied with a hearty affirmative to these questions, and he argued that the three existing labor federations had for years pursued essentially the same goals with almost exactly the same methods. He asserted somewhat implausibly, however, that the Free unions already were completely independent of the SPD, and his statement on religious freedom was even more problematic. In the spirit of the SPD thesis that "religion is a private matter," Leipart reserved the right for the trade unions to attack the Christian churches if they ever meddled in politics.[55] His anti-clericalism strengthened the resolve of the leaders of the Christian unions to reject any merger talks; they alleged that the Hirsch-Duncker unions only considered the idea because they were on the brink of financial collapse.[56]

Brüning's replacement as chancellor in June 1932 by the reactionary Catholic monarchist Franz von Papen strengthened the informal cooperation between the Free and Christian unions nevertheless. Heinrich Fahrenbrach, the chair of the Christian textile workers' union, earned stormy applause at the last congress of the Christian unions in September 1932 when he called for a united front of all trade unionists. Three younger colleagues who would play leading roles in the 1950s, Jakob Kaiser, Karl Arnold, and Johannes Ernst, declared that the Weimar constitution must be defended in alliance with Social Democratic workers. Kaiser insisted that most Social Democrats were patriotic, and he concluded that "we reject the condemnation of the much maligned parliamentarism as an obsolete liberal institution ... Parliamentarism has not failed ... It only became farcical because of the behavior of the radical parties of Left and Right, foremost among them the National Socialists." The meeting hall was festooned with the Republican colors, and all speakers rejected with horror the schemes by Papen's "cabinet of barons" to restore the old "privilege state" or "caste regime" that existed before November 1918.[57]

---

[55] See the abridged version of this exchange in Ulrich Borsdorf, Hans Hemmer, and Martin Martiny, eds., *Grundlagen der Einheitsgewerkschaft. Historische Dokumente und Materialien* (Frankfurt a.M., 1977), pp. 196–209 (Erkelenz quotation on 201). These excerpts omit Leipart's remarks on religion; see the reprint of his complete article in Ulla Plener, *Theodor Leipart (1867–1947). Persönlichkeit, Handlungsmotive, Wirken, Bilanz–Ein Lebensbild in Dokumenten*, 2 vols. (Berlin, 2000–2001), II: 404–411.

[56] Leadership conference of June 18, 1931, NL Otte/7/65; Otte circular to the Christian unions, October 13, 1931, NL Otte/3/127.

[57] Gesamtverband der christlichen Gewerkschaften, *Niederschrift der Verhandlungen des 13. Kongresses der christlichen Gewerkschaften Deutschlands. Düsseldorf, 18.-20. September 1932* (Berlin, 1932), pp. 76–78, 147–174, 253–254, 296–297, 302–303, 310–323, 343–345,

Both the Free and Christian unions felt a sense of relief when General Kurt von Schleicher replaced Papen in December 1932 and rescinded his most provocative decrees. Some journalists speculated that Schleicher would form what they called a "trade union axis," i.e. a government based on the trade unions and paramilitary leagues rather than the political parties. Schleicher had no coherent plan along these lines, however, and the Christian unions remained loyal to their traditional alliance with the Center Party, as did the Free unions to the SPD. Imbusch did have some contact with Schleicher and hoped to persuade him to nationalize the coal mines, but Schleicher retained almost all of Papen's cabinet ministers, for whom such a policy was unthinkable.[58] Both the Free and Christian unions hoped in January 1933 that the Reichstag would adjourn itself voluntarily for two or three months to give Schleicher time to implement a modest program for public works to alleviate unemployment. The leaders of both labor federations were stunned when Schleicher rejected any such accommodation in late January and proposed instead to dissolve the Reichstag indefinitely, in violation of the constitution. The SPD, Center Party, and organized labor all rejected this idea emphatically.[59]

When Hindenburg dismissed Schleicher in late January, labor leaders anticipated that he would reappoint his personal favorite, Franz von Papen, and they regarded this as the worst possible outcome. They sent a joint telegram to the president on January 28, warning "that the appointment of a socially reactionary government hostile to workers would be considered a provocation by all German workers." Along with the Catholic workers' clubs, they demanded that Hindenburg uphold the Weimar constitution and repudiate all who advocated a *coup d'état*. These messages clearly rejected both Papen and Schleicher, but not necessarily a Hitler cabinet with a mandate to seek a majority in new Reichstag elections.[60] The leaders of the three labor federations met again on

352–353; Patch, *Heinrich Brüning*, pp. 272–282. Kaiser's speech is republished in Kosthorst, *Kaiser: Der Arbeiterführer*, pp. 257–270 (quotation on 264–265).

[58] Patch, *Christian Trade Unions*, pp. 212–215; Schäfer, *Heinrich Imbusch*, pp. 246–249; Heinrich Muth, "Schleicher und die Gewerkschaften 1932. Ein Quellenproblem," *Vierteljahrshefte für Zeitgeschichte*, 29 (1981): 189–215; Henry A. Turner, *Hitler's Thirty Days to Power: January 1933* (Reading, MA, 1996), pp. 19–29, 79–91; Pyta, *Hindenburg*, pp. 743–766. Axel Schildt exaggerates the significance of the "trade union axis" in *Militärdiktatur auf Massenbasis? Die Querfrontkonzeption der Reichswehrführung um General von Schleicher am Ende der Weimarer Republik* (Frankfurt a.M., 1981).

[59] Report on Schleicher's reception for Free union leaders on January 26, 1933, *Gewerkschaftsquellen*, IV: 814–817; Turner, *Thirty Days*, pp. 118–129; Winkler, *Katastrophe*, pp. 846–850; Pyta, *Hindenburg*, pp. 769–774.

[60] Telegram by the three labor federations in Anton Bolecki, ed., *Akten der Reichskanzlei der Weimarer Republik. Das Kabinett von Schleicher, 1932/3* (Boppard am Rhein, 1986), p. 314; Aretz, *KAB*, p. 68.

January 30 to discuss the possibility of a general strike. They had just agreed to declare that the appointment of Papen would be a "deliberate proclamation of hostilities against all people loyal to the constitution," when they heard with relief that Hitler had been appointed instead. All three labor federations then instructed their followers to observe developments and avoid local initiatives. Leipart told SPD leaders that the Christian unions opposed the new government and would support whatever action the Free unions proposed, a remarkable statement in view of the feud between the Free and Christian unions in the summer of 1930. Leipart argued, however, that a general strike could not succeed because of mass unemployment and the lack of any clear breach of the constitution. Karl Dörpinghaus later recalled that he had made all preparations for a strike by Christian textile workers on the lower Rhine to protest against the Nazi seizure of power, but that his union headquarters vetoed the idea.[61] Thus the leaders of the Free and Christian unions adopted the same stance.

Union leaders focused all their attention in February 1933 on the election campaigns by the SPD and Center Party. Christian trade unionists concentrated their attacks at first on the "reactionary" cabinet members Papen and Hugenberg; only gradually did they come to understand that the Nazis posed a far more dangerous threat. Heinrich Imbusch told colleagues in the Christian miners' union that "these elections will largely determine the whole future of the trade union movement and the interests of workers." They agreed to redouble their efforts to support the Center Party, while noting that "an attack on the trade union movement is possible at any time." Jakob Kaiser won the Center Party nomination for Essen and hurled himself into a successful campaign for that seat.[62] On February 11 the Catholic workers' clubs accused the government parties of seeking to create "a political order in which arbitrary power and partisanship supplant the law, and special interests supplant the common good," and "an economic order in which a just consideration of the vital interests of all groups is supplanted by one-sided favoritism for the privileged orders." Hermann Göring banned the Catholic newspapers that published this appeal and dismissed the Prussian police officials affiliated with the Christian labor

---

[61] Draft declaration by the three labor federations of January 30, final version published on January 31, and joint leadership conferences of January 30 and February 5, 1933, *Gewerkschaftsquellen*, IV: 823–829, 833–835; Winkler, *Katastrophe*, pp. 853–864; Michael Schneider, *Unterm Hakenkreuz. Arbeiter und Arbeiterbewegung 1933 bis 1939* (Bonn, 1999), pp. 34–36; Dörpinghaus, "Lebenserinnerungen, I. Teil," p. 162, NL Dörpinghaus/2.

[62] *Zentralblatt der christlichen Gewerkschaften*, #4 (February 15, 1933), pp. 37–38; Gewerkverein Hauptvorstand, February 4, 1933, NL Imbusch (Bochum)/733; Kosthorst, *Kaiser: Der Arbeiterführer*, pp. 165–169.

movement, including Wilhelm Elfes.[63] Brüning was silenced by police-
men on the campaign trail when he criticized the government for per-
secuting Social Democrats, and Adam Stegerwald was beaten senseless
by Stormtroopers when he addressed a Center Party rally in Krefeld.
Courageous activism by many thousands of trade unionists helped
nevertheless to keep the Center Party vote largely intact on March 5 in
the predominantly Catholic industrial cities of western and southern
Germany, and the SPD vote, in the Protestant cities of northern and
central Germany. The Nazis and their Nationalist partners gained
a 52 percent majority, however, and labor leaders agreed that this outcome deprived them of any rationale for a general strike.[64]

Labor leaders understood after this election that parliamentary democracy was doomed, but they clutched at the hope of preserving autonomous trade unions even if Germany became a one-party state. The Free
unions distanced themselves from the SPD soon after the election out of
fear, because Stormtroopers invaded and looted their offices in dozens of
cities. Their leaders acted under duress when they declared on March 20
that the trade unions were prepared to accept state oversight.[65] Christian
trade unionists had not yet suffered many attacks, and they acted less out
of fear than the misguided hope that Catholic corporatists enjoyed great
influence in the new government. Hitler himself had written that he
greatly admired trade unions and asked only that they purge themselves
of Marxist influence, and Vice Chancellor von Papen surrounded himself
with corporatist intellectuals. Soon after the election the Christian unions
therefore declared that workers should focus on economic reconstruction, not politics, because the time had come to create "an organic
corporatist social order." They also invited Theodor Brauer into their
inner leadership circle to draft a new program designed to preserve
autonomy for economic interest groups under the Third Reich.[66]

[63] See the press release by Bernhard Letterhaus on February 14 and Otto Müller's circular
of February 23, 1933, Kommission für Zeitgeschichte, Bonn/KAB-Archiv, and Aretz,
KAB, pp. 71–73.

[64] Patch, *Brüning*, pp. 294–295; campaign coverage in the *Kölnische Volkszeitung*, #54,
February 23, 1933, & #58, February 27, 1933; Theodor Leipart, "Die deutschen
Gewerkschaften 1933," memoir from June 1945, in Plener, *Leipart*, II: 470–477;
Winkler, *Katastrophe*, pp. 876–888; Wolfgang Jäger, *Bergarbeitermilieus und Parteien im
Ruhrgebiet. Zum Wahlverhalten des katholischen Bergarbeitermilieus bis 1933* (Munich,
1996), pp. 210–318; Dorit-Maria Krenn, *Die Christliche Arbeiterbewegung in Bayern vom
Ersten Weltkrieg bis 1933* (Mainz, 1991), pp. 293–306, 560–586.

[65] Dirk Erb, ed., *Gleichgeschaltet. Der Nazi-Terror gegen Gewerkschaften und Berufsverbände
1930 bis 1933: Eine Dokumentation* (Göttingen, 2001); Leipart to Adolf Hitler, March 21,
1933, *Gewerkschaftsquellen*, IV: 865–867; Michael Schneider, *Hakenkreuz*, pp. 57–69.

[66] Adolf Hitler, *Mein Kampf*, trans. Ralph Mannheim (Boston, 1943), pp. 40–51, 596–606;
declaration of March 8, in *Zentralblatt der christlichen Gewerkschaften*, #6 (March 15,
1933), p. 61 (source of quotation); Michael Schneider, *Hakenkreuz*, pp. 55–69;

Unveiled at a rally of the Christian unions in Essen on March 16, Brauer's program declared that the state's highest duty was to protect the "freedoms guaranteed by law." He proposed joint committees with equal representation for workers and employers in each branch of industry to supervise job training, wage levels, and working conditions; this "economic self-administration" was needed to enable the state to address its "authentically political tasks." In the discussion Bernhard Otte argued that it would be a tragic mistake "if institutions that arose from the free will and resolve of their members, and which have grown organically from the life of our people, were forcibly suppressed or compelled to develop in a direction alien to their character."[67] Brauer told the Essen rally that the existing labor unions should be the foundation for the renovation of the social order, and he later promised that they would survive as sub-groups within each *Berufsstand*, authorized to agitate for higher wages, shorter hours, and better working conditions. He said nothing about the right to strike, however. Stegerwald explained to the Essen rally that the new phraseology of corporatism meant the same thing in essence as the Christian unions' old slogans of "self-administration" and "association between employers and workers," i.e. rejection of the idolatry of the state advocated by communism, socialism, and fascism.[68] Otte sent copies of the Essen Guidelines to Hitler and Labor Minister Franz Seldte, while Brauer joined Franz von Papen's new League of the Cross and Eagle for conservative Catholics. Immediately after the Essen rally, Joseph Goebbels recorded in his diary a visit from unnamed leaders of the Christian unions who wanted to discuss their role in the Third Reich. He responded cordially but wrote privately that "they will not be able to speak of their following much longer. It's astonishing what all is offering its services to the new state."[69]

Gunther Mai, "Die Nationalsozialistische Betriebszellen-Organisation. Zum Verhältnis von Arbeiterschaft und Nationalsozialismus," *Vierteljahrshefte für Zeitgeschichte*, 31 (1983): 573–613; Larry Eugene Jones, "The Limits of Collaboration: Edgar Jung, Herbert von Bose, and the Origins of the Conservative Resistance to Hitler, 1933–34," in Larry Jones and James Retallack, eds., *Between Reform, Reaction, and Resistance: Studies in the History of German Conservatism from 1789 to 1945* (Providence and Oxford, 1993), pp. 465–501.

[67] Gesamtverband der Christlichen Gewerkschaften Deutschlands, *Die Essener Richtlinien 1933 der christlich-nationalen Gewerkschaften* (Berlin, 1933), pp. 6–35; Tim Mason, *Social Policy in the Third Reich: The Working Class and the "National Community,"* trans. John Broadwin (Oxford and Providence, 1993), pp. 73–74.

[68] *Essener Richtlinien*, pp. 46, 51–52, 61–65; Brauer, "Gewerkschaft und Berufsstand," *Zentralblatt der christlichen Gewerkschaften*, #8 (April 15, 1933), pp. 93–95.

[69] Entry of March 17, 1933, in Ralf Georg Reuth, ed., *Joseph Goebbels Tagebücher 1924–1945*, 5 vols. (Munich, 1992), II: 781; Michael Schneider, *Hakenkreuz*, pp. 68–69. Imbusch recalled in "Bernhard Otte" (NL Platte/14/164–165) that Otte became eager to establish contact with Nazi leaders immediately after the Reichstag election, so he may have participated in this delegation to Goebbels.

The doom of parliamentary government was sealed on March 23, when the Center Party joined an overwhelming Reichstag majority, opposed only by the SPD, to approve the Enabling Act to delegate law-making powers to Adolf Hitler for the next four years. Within the Center Reichstag delegation, Brüning had opposed the Enabling Act vigorously, but the party chairman, Monsignor Ludwig Kaas, urged acceptance. Stegerwald was dispatched to sound Hitler out about his intentions, and he reported that the Reichstag "will not be eliminated, as long as it does not make problems for the government. The trade unions must free themselves of Marxism, or else there will be no peace." Brüning replied that "the Enabling Act is the most monstrous thing ever demanded of a parliament," but many speakers argued that a No vote would simply provoke a bloody reign of terror by the Stormtroopers. The delegation voted by a margin of 74 to 14 to accept the law. Eight of those who voted No apparently came from the labor wing of the party, including Imbusch and Jakob Kaiser, but ten workers' delegates apparently followed Stegerwald in endorsing the law. Stegerwald told Christian union colleagues with great confidence (if Kaiser's later recollections can be trusted) that Hitler would never be able to govern without the support and advice of the Center Party. Brüning and the other naysayers then decided reluctantly to vote with the majority of their colleagues on the floor of the Reichstag. Brüning deeply regretted this decision in later years and reflected that it had been a blunder to send Stegerwald to Hitler; he had hoped that Stegerwald's forceful personality would influence Hitler, but instead Stegerwald fell under the führer's spell.[70]

Anton Erkelenz sent an urgent appeal to Stegerwald and Theodor Leipart on April 1 for a voluntary merger of the three existing labor federations as the only hope to forestall coercive action by the Nazis. Bernhard Otte opposed the idea at first, because his soundings with Franz von Papen and labor ministry officials suggested that the government would permit ongoing competition among a variety of labor organizations and might even favor the Christian unions in this competition.[71] Imbusch

[70] Rudolf Morsey, ed., *Die Protokolle der Reichstagsfraktion und des Fraktionsvorstands der Deutschen Zentrumspartei 1926–1933* (Mainz, 1969), meetings of March 20–23, 1933, pp. 622–632 (quotations on 631); Jakob Kaiser's reminiscences to Theodor Heuss on April 25, 1958, NL Kaiser/246; Brüning, *Memoiren*, pp. 652–663; Patch, *Brüning*, pp. 295–299; Forster, *Stegerwald*, pp. 592–597.

[71] Erkelenz to Stegerwald, April 1, 1933, NL Stegerwald/14/Nachtragsband/#19; Erkelenz to Leipart and Erkelenz to A. Czieslik, April 1, 1933, NL Erkelenz/136; "Vermerk" of April 1, 1933, on a visit to Papen by Otte, Bundesarchiv Berlin-Lichterfelde/R53/15/18–19 (thanks to Larry Jones for sharing this file); report by P.J.S. Serrarens of the International League of Christian Trade Unions on his conversations in Berlin on April 7/8, 1933, at the Documentation Center for Religion, Culture, and Society at the Catholic University of Leuven (=KADOC)/Archives WVA/Box 15/Doc. 40.06 (thanks to Patrick Pasture for sharing this file).

and Jakob Kaiser embraced the proposal by Erkelenz, however, and even Otte agreed to merger talks when Nazis gained control of the DHV. A power shift in that union had begun already at the DHV congress of June 1932, when Nazi delegates elected their comrade Hermann Miltzow as vice chairman. In February 1933 Max Habermann and Hans Bechly offered generous campaign contributions to the Nazis, and they expelled their most staunchly republican colleagues from the union immediately after the March election. However, Nazi DHV activists expelled Bechly and Habermann on April 10 and elected Franz Stöhr and Miltzow as co-chairs. Stöhr then advised Imbusch and Otte that a voluntary merger of all blue-collar unions offered their only hope to avoid suppression.[72]

Imbusch and Otte visited Joseph Goebbels on April 11 to ask whether the government would object if they began merger talks with the Free unions, and the propaganda minister endorsed the idea. He noted that the government could not tolerate "Marxist" unions, however, and expected all workers to participate in the "Day of National Labor" on May 1, a new official holiday to supplant the old internationalist May Day. "If the Free unions do not agree to merger by May 2 and obstruct things on May 1," Goebbels warned, "then they could hardly complain if the People takes matters into its own hands."[73] Jakob Kaiser displayed the most enthusiasm for merger of any Christian union leader. Their most urgent task, Kaiser told the Christian trade unionists of Cologne on April 12, was to persuade the new government that "the elite, the best kernel of the workers, is gathered in the trade unions," and that the workers in the Free unions had long been traveling on "the path away from the old Marxism, ... the path toward the nation." Kaiser warned, in words that may have been addressed to Otte, that the Christian unions would never earn the respect of the new government through opportunism. "It would be dishonorable to betray and vilify one's own traditions. It would be dishonorable to abandon a community that I supported yesterday, just because others now hold power. And ... it would be dishonorable to participate in the defamation of others, just because they are now weak, or because one hopes thereby to curry favor with the new powers." Many veteran Christian trade unionists, including Heinrich Imbusch, recalled old quarrels with the Free unions during

---

[72] Hamel, *Völkischer Verband*, pp. 253–262; Heinrich Imbusch, "Hans Bechli" [sic], NL Platte/14/10–12; remarks by Otte in the circular of the Christian textile workers' union, April 14, 1933, *Gewerkschaftsquellen*, IV: 892–894.

[73] Otte's report to the Christian textile workers' union, April 14, 1933, *Gewerkschaftsquellen*, IV: 894–896; Otte's report to the Christian union international, April 28, 1933, KADOC/Archives WVA/Box 15/Doc. 41.01, pp. 5–6; Goebbels, *Tagebücher*, March 24 and April 11, 1933, II: 785, 792–793.

these tense weeks, but Kaiser apparently expressed the attitude of most younger colleagues.[74]

The Free unions had meanwhile repudiated their historic alliance with the SPD in public declarations on April 5 and April 9, which called for the voluntary merger of all German labor unions "in the service of the new state." In their camp the leader of the Free unions of Hesse, Wilhelm Leuschner, displayed the most enthusiasm for merger. A decorated combat veteran like Kaiser, Leuschner had long criticized Marxist intellectuals for making the SPD radical in theory but fatalistic in practice; he sought an activist program in tune with patriotic values. He and Leipart were appalled to learn on April 13 that the Nazi Factory Cells Organization advocated what it called a "unified trade union" (*die Einheitsgewerkschaft*) in a form that did not match any reasonable definition of a trade union, an organization that would allow government officials to determine wages and working conditions, with all the organization's leaders appointed by the Nazi Party.[75] On April 19 Leuschner visited the labor ministry and found it working on a more tolerable plan influenced by Theodor Brauer for a decentralized, corporatist social order. The next day Leuschner visited Kaiser and Ernst Lemmer of the Hirsch-Duncker unions to launch merger talks by a small circle of about ten labor leaders.[76]

Leuschner entered these merger talks with a dry summary of the essential features of any genuine labor union, which must elect its leaders, be independent from the government, employers, and political parties, and enjoy the right to strike. Kaiser persuaded the Free unions, however, to accept most formulations in a rival draft by Theodor Brauer. The final text of their agreement on April 28 to form a "Leadership Ring" to prepare for merger expressed support for the "new state,"

---

[74] Speech published in Kosthorst, *Kaiser: Der Arbeiterführer*, pp. 271–280. See also Imbusch's bitter complaints about the Ruhr miners' strike of 1912 in the typescript minutes of the "Gewerkverein Generalversammlung," March 12, 1933, pp. 102–104, DGB-Archiv/NL Imbusch/1, and the ambivalent editorials about unified trade unions in *Textilarbeiter-Zeitung*, #11 (March 18, 1933), p. 2; *Die Rundschau*, #7 (April 10, 1933), pp. 27–29; and *Der Deutsche Metallarbeiter*, #15 (April 15, 1933), pp. 174–176.

[75] ADGB Bundesausschuss proceedings of April 5, 1933, letter to the government on April 9, and conference with NSBO representatives on April 13, *Gewerkschaftsquellen*, IV: 871–873, 881–882, 888–892 (quotation from Ludwig Brucker of the NSBO on 888); Joachim Leithäuser, *Wilhelm Leuschner: Ein Leben für die Republik* (Cologne, 1962), pp. 11–106; Stefan Vogt, *Nationaler Sozialismus und Soziale Demokratie. Die sozialdemokratische Junge Rechte, 1918–1945* (Bonn, 2006), pp. 118–119, 322–335.

[76] Gerhard Beier, ed., "Zur Entstehung des Führerkreises der vereinigten Gewerkschaften Ende April 1933. Dokumentation aus dem Leuschner-Nachlass," *Archiv für Sozialgeschichte*, 15 (1975): 365–392 (esp. 365–372).

which "cannot tolerate class divisions or an internationalism that turns its back on our people." It noted that labor unions must be independent of the government, employers, and political parties, but it said nothing about the right to strike. Brauer also included a declaration that the unions "recognize the significance of elemental religious forces and their constructive role in state and society." On April 24, Otte had sent an urgent request to Adolf Hitler to receive the negotiators (which went unanswered), so they obviously knew that their work meant nothing unless endorsed by the highest authority. Leipart and Leuschner apparently decided that only Brauer spoke a language that could win Hitler's approval, but they left this agreement vague enough that core elements of genuine trade unionism might be salvaged in future negotiations with the labor ministry.[77] Christian labor leaders regarded this agreement as a triumph in their long-running debate with the Free unions over basic principles, and Kaiser described it after 1945 as the founding charter for the unified labor unions of the future. No more than a half dozen Free union leaders participated in these talks, however, and they had no time to distribute the agreement for discussion; it obviously did not reflect an authentic consensus among trade unionists.[78]

While these negotiations proceeded, some opportunists in the Christian unions sought favor with the Nazis. Disputes among colleagues first arose over participation in Goebbels' Day of National Labor. On April 19, the Free unions urged all members to march on May 1, but Christian trade unionists found this idea troubling, because they had always opposed May Day demonstrations in the past. On April 21, the leaders of the Christian unions applauded the concept of the Day of National Labor, but they said nothing about marching. Kaiser, Imbusch, and Franz Wieber opposed participation, but their front weakened when Wieber died in late April. On May 1, Kaiser remained among the spectators of the parade in Berlin, but Otte and Friedrich Baltrusch accepted seats of honor in the reviewing stand. Two chairmen of small Christian unions marched (Peter Tremmel and Adolf Schaar), along with dozens of mid-ranking colleagues, some in new Stormtrooper uniforms. Many thousands of Free trade unionists marched in parades

---

[77] Beier, "Zur Entstehung des Führerkreises," pp. 374–376, 385–392 (quotations from 389–391).

[78] Gerhard Beier, "Einheitsgewerkschaft. Zur Geschichte eines organisatorischen Prinzips der deutschen Arbeiterbewegung," *Archiv für Sozialgeschichte*, 13 (1973): 207–242; Michael Schneider, *Hakenkreuz*, pp. 88–90; Jakob Kaiser, "'Einer von denen, die uns fehlen.' Zum Gedenken an Wilhelm Leuschner," eulogy from June 1947 republished in Tilman Mayer, ed., *Jakob Kaiser: Gewerkschafter und Patriot. Eine Werkauswahl* (Cologne, 1988), pp. 304–307.

all over Germany, waving the old monarchist colors as the only approved alternative to the swastika.[79]

On May 2, the Nazis dispatched armed men to occupy every Free union office in Germany. Hundreds of union functionaries were jailed, including Leipart and Leuschner; many more were beaten and publicly humiliated, and all Free union property was confiscated. Robert Ley, a high party official with no background in labor organization, announced to the world that he was the new leader of German workers. The Christian and Hirsch-Duncker unions were ignored on that day of violence, but the latter group declared its submission to Ley on May 3. That same day he summoned four leaders of the Christian unions – Otte, Kaiser, Baltrusch, and Behrens – and demanded that they too sign a "voluntary" act of submission. Three of them agreed, but Kaiser refused angrily and went into hiding when Ley had an arrest warrant issued against him. The three who signed accepted appointment to the Senate of Ley's new German Labor Front (*Deutsche Arbeitsfront*, or DAF), along with Stegerwald, Imbusch, and Brauer, and the arrest warrant against Kaiser was withdrawn. Against the objections of Imbusch and Kaiser, Otte then published a declaration to Christian trade unionists describing the DAF as the realization of their old dream of unified labor unions purged of Marxist influence. Otte also assured Christian union functionaries that Ley would hire no Free trade unionists for the DAF but would retain their services.[80] For the moment it appeared that the Christian trade unions would play a valued role in the Third Reich.

1.4   From Accommodation to Dissent

After 1945, many Christian trade unionists recalled that they had opposed the Third Reich from its inception, but even the bravest of them initially sought a *modus vivendi* with the new regime. Some actively curried favor with the Nazis to advance their own careers, most notably two Protestant union functionaries who wrote a senior DAF official in late May 1933 that Jakob Kaiser identified so closely with "the spirit of the Center Party" that he could never support the Third Reich; they

---

[79] *Zentralblatt der christlichen Gewerkschaften*, #9 (May 1, 1933), p. 105; reminiscences by Elfriede Nebgen in January 1963, NL Katzer/303; Heinrich Imbusch, "Franz Wieber," NL Platte/14/237–238; Kosthorst, *Kaiser: Der Arbeiterführer*, pp. 179–80; Schneider, *Hakenkreuz*, pp. 91–100; Winkler, *Katastrophe*, pp. 921–923, 927–928.

[80] Schneider, *Hakenkreuz*, pp. 101–102; Kosthorst, *Kaiser: Der Arbeiterführer*, pp. 180–182; undated memoir by Kaiser and Nebgen, "Die Auflösung der Gewerkschaften im Jahre 1933," NL Kaiser/362/54–56; Bernhard Otte, "Neue Wege und neue Ziele," *Zentralblatt der christlichen Gewerkschaften*, #10 (May 15, 1933), pp. 117–118; circular of the Christian textile workers' union, May 30, 1933, DGB-Archiv/NL Fahrenbrach/2.

offered to provide further names of colleagues who should be purged. The Nazis soon persecuted almost all trade unionists, however, and their brutality delivered Christian laborites from the temptation of collaborating with the regime.[81]

Heinrich Imbusch later reproached Bernhard Otte for hindering any meaningful discussion of the proper response to the formation of the German Labor Front. Otte brought Nazis to every meeting, precluding any possibility of a frank discussion, and he pinned his hopes on his private discussions with Robert Ley and other high officials. Imbusch did not await the outcome of these talks. In mid-May, Franz Stöhr warned him that he would be murdered, so Imbusch fled to the League of Nations mandate territory in the Saarland with the liquid assets of his union. Imbusch sought to persuade Fritz Husemann of the Free miners' union to do likewise, but Husemann could not believe that the Nazis would attack him, because he had never done anything wrong. Imbusch explained that the Nazis "do not want any honest representation of workers' interests ... They don't care whether we have done something wrong. For them it is enough that our existence has become inconvenient." Imbusch later read with great sadness in April 1935 that Husemann had been shot "while trying to escape" from a concentration camp. For a year after arriving in Saarbrücken, however, Imbusch refused to criticize the Third Reich in public, because he hoped to secure a guarantee from Nazi leaders that he would be left alone if he returned to his family in Essen.[82]

The Christian unions' last hope for influence involved the Nazis' desire for international respectability. In June 1933, Otte volunteered to accompany Robert Ley to Geneva to seek recognition for the DAF from the International Labor Organization, and Wilhelm Leuschner won release from prison by joining them. Leuschner maintained a stony silence in ILO meetings, however, and Otte soon abandoned this mission as hopeless. There could be no denying that the DAF was based on compulsory membership, had leaders appointed by the government, and renounced

---

[81] See the copy of a letter by Karl Dudey and Friedrich Meystre to Ludwig Brucker of the DAF, May 31, 1933, in NL Kaiser/246. For the temptation to which Austrian Christian trade unionists were exposed by the Dollfuss regime in 1934, see Anton Pelinka, *Stand oder Klasse? Die Christliche Arbeiterbewegung Österreichs 1933 bis 1938* (Vienna, 1972), pp. 35–94.

[82] Imbusch's character sketches of Otte, NL Platte/14/164–165, and Fritz Husemann, 14/94–99 (quotations on pp. 97–98); Schäfer, *Imbusch*, pp. 254–256; Detlev Peukert and Frank Bajohr, *Spuren des Widerstands. Die Bergarbeiterbewegung im Dritten Reich und im Exil* (Munich, 1987), pp. 59–72; "Fritz Husemann," in Siegfried Mielke and Günter Morsch, eds., *"Seid wachsam, dass über Deutschland nie wieder die Nacht hereinbricht." Gewerkschafter in Konzentrationslagern 1933–1945* (Berlin, 2011), pp. 96–99.

the right to strike, so the socialist and Christian trade union internationals soon agreed to deny it recognition as a labor union. Ley departed abruptly from Geneva on June 20, denounced Otte and Leuschner for sabotage, ordered Leuschner's return to prison, and expelled all Christian trade unionists from the DAF Senate. As a result of this rupture, 500 Christian union functionaries (over 90 percent of the total) were dismissed in the summer of 1933, alongside the 4,000 Free union secretaries dismissed in May. The DAF confiscated 21 million marks in Christian union assets but paid their functionaries just one month's salary in severance pay, when their contracts promised four months. The Christian trade unionist Adolf Schaar remained a DAF functionary to administer death benefits for waiters and hotel workers, but he suffered ostracism by all his former colleagues.[83]

Ley's break with the Christian unions unleashed the aggressive impulses of the Stormtroopers. In an episode that was unusually well documented but certainly not unique, three Stormtroopers burst into the Krefeld office of the Christian textile workers' union on the morning of July 14, beat Jacob Nöhsemes bloody with their truncheons, and hung a sign around his neck. He was then compelled to march around the city, halting every ten paces to repeat what stood on the sign: "I am a scoundrel [*Lump*]! I deceived the workers!" In Essen, the Nazis found a more prominent victim in September: Heinrich Hirtsiefer, the former minister of welfare in the Prussian state government. The corpulent Hirtsiefer had just protested at police headquarters that his dismissal from government service without a pension exposed him to hunger. As he left, Stormtroopers hung a sign around his neck to identify him as the "Hungering Hirtsiefer" and marched him around the city for two hours. He was then interned in the Börgermoor concentration camp and beaten repeatedly, until his wife's appeal to President Hindenburg secured his release.[84] Free trade unionists ran a greater risk of violence, to be sure, but the shared experience of Nazi brutality created a strong foundation for a unified labor movement after 1945.

[83] Jakob Kaiser, "Zur Situation in der früheren deutschen Arbeiterbewegung," November 1933, published in Siegried Mielke and Matthias Frese, eds. *Quellen zur Geschichte der deutschen Gewerkschaftsbewegung im 20. Jahrhundert. Band 5: Die Gewerkschaften im Widerstand und in der Emigration 1933–1945* (Frankfurt a.M., 1999), pp. 135–143 [hereafter cited as *Gewerkschaftsquellen*, V:]; Schaar to Kaiser, September 15, 1945, NL Kaiser/246; Patrick Pasture, *Histoire du syndicalisme chrétien international. La difficile recherche d'une troisième voie* (Paris and Montreal, 1999), pp. 164–167; Nebgen, *Kaiser: Widerstandskämpfer*, pp. 11–13; Leithäuser, *Wilhelm Leuschner*, pp. 117–128.

[84] Photostat of a criminal complaint filed by Nöhsemes on August 21, 1933, NL Dörpinghaus/1; Imbusch, "Heinrich Hirtsiefer," NL Platte/14/78–79; "Heinrich Hirtsiefer," in Mielke and Morsch, *Gewerkschafter in Konzentrationslagern*, pp. 90–95.

Their abrupt dismissal compelled the functionaries of the Christian unions to focus on material concerns. Most of them were married with children and had few resources beyond a testimonial letter from their former union supervisor, which was more likely to hinder than help them find a job. Most of them experienced at least a few months of unemployment, and some endured that fate for several years. They all assumed that the secret police and Nazi Party bosses had instructed employers to shun them. Biographical data is available for over eighty of them, and a majority established a precarious existence as small shopkeepers or traveling salesmen. Wilhelm Elfes opened a tobacco shop in Krefeld, which thrived at first because of visits from old friends and political associates; the visits soon trailed off, however, and he sank into depression. Of the Christian trade unionists who played an important role in the Federal Republic, Johannes Ernst, Anton Storch, and Johannes Platte scraped by selling life insurance, and Karl Dörpinghaus supervised the paperboys delivering a Catholic newspaper. Elisabeth Küper suffered unemployment for two years and then became the housekeeper for a well-to-do relative. Only a few colleagues prospered, such as Karl Arnold, who became co-owner of a furnace supply business in Düsseldorf, and Theodor Blank in Dortmund, who went back to school and became a technical draftsman. Only one Christian union functionary is known to have returned to factory labor, the Dortmund steelworker Paul Harmann.[85] Most ex-functionaries of the Christian unions lost ties with the world of manual labor and moved in lower-middle-class circles.

The church-affiliated Catholic workers' clubs did retain ties with factory workers after the Nazi seizure of power. In Bavaria club membership dropped from 55,000 in 1932 to 40,000 in November 1933 (a loss of 28 percent), because of the demoralizing collapse of a savings bank they had founded and a withdrawal of clerical support. However, the clubs of

---

[85] Reminiscences in Bernhard Tacke to Albert Esser, April 13, 1976, NL Tacke/13/1; Wilhelm Elfes, "Daten aus dem Leben bis 1944," NL Elfes/1/6–8; Esser, *Elfes*, pp. 112–115; Karl Dörpinghaus, "Lebenserinnerungen, I. Teil," pp. 162–169, NL Dörpinghaus/2; Hanno Ernst, biographical sketch of his father Johannes, July 1984, NL Ernst/6/4; Johannes Platte, "Anlage zum Fragebogen," December 22, 1945, NL Platte/27/23–24; Anton Storch, "Lebenserinnerungen, Erfahrungen und Erlebnisse," in Deutscher Bundestag, *Abgeordnete des Deutschen Bundestages. Aufzeichnungen und Erinnerungen*, vol. 2 (Boppard am Rhein, 1983), pp. 324–325; Detlev Hüwel, *Karl Arnold. Eine politische Biographie* (Wuppertal, 1980), pp. 51–53; Hans-Otto Kleinmann, "Theodor Blank," in Jürgen Aretz, Rudolf Morsey, and Anton Rauscher, eds., *Zeitgeschichte in Lebensbildern. Aus dem deutschen Katholizismus des 20. Jahrhunderts*, 12 vols. (Münster, 1973–2007), VI: 171–188; Brigitte Kramer, "Elisabeth Küper (1901–1991): Ein bewegtes Leben," http://heimatblaetter.heimatverein-duelmen.de /hefte/2–2003/elisabeth_kueper; Hartmann's "Lebenslauf" of July 20, 1948, NL Föcher/1.

western Germany were better managed, and despite harassment by the authorities, they lost only 8 percent of their 192,000 members during the first year of Nazi rule and 2 percent in the second. Bernhard Letterhaus organized a series of workers' pilgrimages and open-air retreats that featured veiled allusions to the persecution of Catholics by the regime; they attracted 90,000 participants in autumn 1933 and 200,000 in 1934.[86] The episcopate discouraged any oppositional movement, however, by adopting a collective policy that bishops should only protest against clear violations of the legal rights of the Catholic Church guaranteed by the Reich Concordat of October 1933, and should only convey those protests to government officials privately in written petitions or audiences. As interpreted by the German authorities, the Concordat did not even apply to "vocational associations" such as the Catholic workers' clubs, and the leaders of those clubs in the Rhineland soon became disgusted with the timidity of the bishops. Their weekly paper edited by Nikolaus Gross continued to criticize the racial worldview until it was banned in November 1938. By 1939 the Catholic workers' clubs had withered away in most regions, but with clerical support they retained 10,000 members in Cologne and Düsseldorf in 1945.[87]

A sense of grievance spread quickly among ex-functionaries of the Christian unions, but only gradually did it develop any political direction. After his expulsion from the DAF, Bernhard Otte purchased a farm in Lower Silesia to build a new existence for his large family, but after he paid the money in October 1933, the local authorities refused to allow him to take possession because he was suspected of an "attitude hostile to the state." Otte was driving in haste from Berlin to Silesia to resolve the matter when he wrapped his car around a tree; his friends suspected suicide.[88] While attending his funeral, Jakob Kaiser felt inspired to compel the DAF to honor its legal obligation as the successor of the League of Christian Trade Unions to pay another three months' salary to all discharged functionaries and refund their contributions to their pension plan. He soon obtained written declarations from 600 colleagues appointing him their legal representative, and with their financial support, he established a small office in Berlin. Robert Ley had made numerous enemies within the government, and Kaiser gained a sympathetic hearing

---

[86] Krenn, *Bayern*, pp. 354–355; Aretz, *KAB*, pp. 103–114, 140–148.

[87] Aretz, *KAB*, pp. 118–140, 150–191, 206–223, 236–237; Vera Bücker, "Bernhard Letterhaus (1894–1944)," in Karl-Joseph Hummel and Christoph Strohm, eds., *Zeugen einer besseren Welt. Christliche Märtyrer des 20. Jahrhunderts* (Leipzig, 2000), pp. 276–296; Bücker, *Nikolaus Gross*, pp. 124–157; William L. Patch, "The Catholic Church, the Third Reich, and the Origins of the Cold War," *Journal of Modern History*, 82 (2010): 396–433.

[88] Brüning, *Memoiren*, p. 676.

from several high officials. He soon created for himself the unusual position of an officially recognized litigator with the right to travel around Germany to consult with hundreds of clients about their cases. He helped to secure a new compensation law in December 1937 that established an arbitration board in the interior ministry, empowered to levy judgments against the DAF. The legal proceedings dragged on for years, but Kaiser had won almost all his claims by 1944. He later recalled his litigator's role as a cover for resistance activity from the outset, but his first petitions in autumn 1933 implored the DAF to rehire all his colleagues.[89]

In the Saarland, Heinrich Imbusch launched the first attempt to organize resistance to the Third Reich by Christian trade unionists. His colleagues there, however, were deeply divided because they had agitated for reunion with Germany ever since 1919. When Imbusch arrived in May 1933, Hitler recruited the editor of the local Christian miners' newspaper, Peter Kiefer, to serve as co-chair of the committee to promote a Yes vote for reunion in the League of Nations referendum scheduled for January 1935. Imbusch felt disgusted by Kiefer's opportunism, but only after a year of indecision did he bring his family from Essen to Saarbrücken and hurl himself into the campaign by Social Democrats and progressive Catholics for a No vote. Imbusch spoke eloquently against Nazi tyranny, but the bishops of Trier and Speyer exhorted Saar Catholics to vote Yes. Jakob Kaiser and most of his friends in Germany also opposed Imbusch, arguing that the gain to the Fatherland from a Yes vote would endure long after Nazi rule had ended. Nazi thugs beat Imbusch senseless at a rally on December 30, 1934, and the police only arrested the victim's chauffeur, after he drove the assailants away with two warning shots from his revolver. In January 1935 the pro-German side won an overwhelming 91 percent majority in the referendum, and Imbusch moved to Luxemburg and resolved to keep a very low profile.[90]

Wilhelm Leuschner visited Kaiser and Elfriede Nebgen after his release from prison in June 1934, and his revelations about the regime's brutal treatment of labor activists shocked them. They soon agreed that this regime could not last forever, and that they should organize networks of union colleagues to prepare for the creation of unified and democratic

---

[89] Nebgen, *Widerstandskämpfer*, pp. 26–33; Kaiser's correspondence with government agencies in NL Kaiser/10; Kaiser's memorandum of November 1933, "Zur Situation in der früheren deutschen Arbeiterbewegung," *Gewerkschaftsquellen*, V: 135–143; Kaiser's letters to Ludwig Grauert of November 30, 1933, December 18, 1933, and February 10, 1934, NL Kaiser/413/128–135.

[90] Schäfer, *Imbusch*, pp. 257–272; Patrik von zur Mühlen, "*Schlagt Hitler an der Saar!*" *Abstimmungskampf, Emigration und Widerstand im Saargebiet, 1933–1935* (Bonn, 1979), pp. 26–138, 217–228; Nebgen, *Kaiser: Widerstandskämpfer*, pp. 12–14, 19–22.

trade unions after it fell.[91] The extent of their support remains unclear. Leuschner headed a very large underground network of Free trade unionists in 1934/1935, but it soon withered after a wave of arrests by the Gestapo. After 1935, the surviving cells renounced any attempt to organize strikes, distribute leaflets, or prepare for an insurrection; instead they pursued the modest goals of mutual aid, intelligence gathering, and communication with colleagues abroad. Leuschner founded a business in Berlin to manufacture taps for beer kegs and therefore had reason to visit taverns all over Germany that were frequented by former colleagues. After the war broke out, he made great efforts to maintain personal contact with the surviving union cells, but he remained under police surveillance and insisted that no written record be kept of his activities. We cannot know therefore whether his wartime network numbered a few hundred members or many thousands. Even if few in number, they included colleagues very well known in their communities, such as Hans Böckler in Cologne and Willi Richter in Frankfurt am Main.[92]

Hitler's Blood Purge of June 30, 1934, helped Kaiser to organize at least small groups of Christian union colleagues as well. Most Germans took a dim view of the SA leaders who were purged, but many were troubled by the simultaneous murders of Kurt von Schleicher, Gregor Strasser, and two corporatist aides of Franz von Papen who had collaborated with Theodor Brauer in April 1933. Josef Ersing, the former head of the Christian unions in Württemberg, told Kaiser soon thereafter that he was resolved to do whatever he could to undermine this regime. Max Habermann too lost his hope that Gregor Strasser would be reconciled with Hitler and purge the Nazi Party of reactionary elements, and he sought Kaiser out in Berlin to volunteer his services. Much sympathy but no active support came from Ernst Lemmer of the Hirsch-Duncker unions, who worked as a reporter for Swiss newspapers. He was a liberal Protestant and former leader of the German Democratic Party but told Kaiser in 1936 that he would join the Center Party after Hitler's fall. Kaiser replied that "there will be no more Center Party" because his friends from the Christian trade unions all desired

---

[91] Nebgen, *Kaiser: Widerstandskämpfer*, pp. 40–41; Leithäuser, *Wilhelm Leuschner*, pp. 125–159.

[92] Gerhard Beier, *Die illegale Reichsleitung der Gewerkschaften 1933–1945* (Cologne, 1981); Beier, "Gewerkschaften zwischen Illusion und Aktion," in Schmädecke and Steinbach, *Widerstand*, pp. 99–112; Willy Buschak, *"Arbeit im kleinsten Zirkel." Gewerkschaften im Widerstand gegen den Nationalsozialismus* (Hamburg, 1993); Leithäuser, *Wilhelm Leuschner*, pp. 159–175, 199–200; Michael Schneider, *Hakenkreuz*, pp. 845–849, 970–977, 1023–1029; Michael Schneider, *In der Kriegsgesellschaft. Arbeiter und Arbeiterbewegung 1939 bis 1945* (Bonn, 2014), pp. 1159–1166.

"broader party formations."[93] At least ten provincial cells for Kaiser's network were soon organized, eight by Catholic veterans of the Christian unions in western and southwestern Germany, and two by Protestants in Breslau and Dresden.[94]

Kaiser's friends had no idea at first how the Third Reich could be toppled, but Heinrich Brüning offered strategic guidance even after his flight from Germany in May 1934. From December 1934 until 1938, Brüning conferred twice a year in Holland with his most loyal German supporters, including Joseph Joos and Bernhard Letterhaus. Brüning urged them to look for political leadership to Carl Goerdeler, the conservative mayor of Leipzig who had served in Brüning's cabinet, and to seek alliance with the army command. He warned, however, that a restoration of monarchy was the only political goal that could inspire the generals to act against Hitler.[95] In August 1935, Brüning sent a memorandum to the army command to argue for Hitler's overthrow. He sought to make this idea attractive by suggesting that only war veterans and their widows and children over age 25 should be allowed to vote in the subsequent election for a constitutional convention; it should be encouraged to restore a monarchy in principle (without naming a monarch) and to establish a lower house of parliament based on indirect elections and a corporatist upper house.[96] The problem with this strategy was that Hitler had captivated most generals through lavish funding for rearmament. They could well be motivated to rebel by the prospect of a catastrophic defeat for Germany, but Hitler enjoyed one diplomatic success after another in the 1930s. Adam Stegerwald became utterly fatalistic about the prospects for the Third Reich, so Kaiser avoided any political conversations with his mentor.

---

[93] Nebgen, *Widerstandskämpfer*, pp. 27–29, 46–47, 50–51, 65 (source of quotation); Karl Hahn, "Max Habermann und der 20. Juli," memoir in the DHV-Archiv, Hamburg.

[94] Nebgen, *Widerstandskämpfer*, pp. 33–34, 42–48; Forster, *Stegerwald*, pp. 605–618; Krenn, *Bayern*, pp. 584–585; Günter Buchstab, Brigitte Kaff, and Hans-Otto Kleinmann, *Verfolgung und Widerstand 1933–1945. Christliche Demokraten gegen Hitler* (Düsseldorf, 1986), pp. 180–190, 218–238; biographical sketches of Albers, Arnold, Ersing, Hanna Gerig, Nebgen, and Storch in Günter Buchstab, Brigitte Kaff, and Hans-Otto Kleinmann, eds., *Christliche Demokraten gegen Hitler. Aus Verfolgung und Widerstand zur Union* (Freiburg, 2004); Michael Schneider, *Kriegsgesellschaft*, pp. 1173–1176.

[95] Brüning's diary entries from December 1934–March 1935, his memorandum of May 25, 1935, and Brüning to Theodor Draper, November 1947, in Heinrich Brüning, *Briefe und Gespräche 1934–1945*, ed. Claire Nix (Stuttgart, 1974), pp. 26–27, 52, 58–66, 464–465; Brüning to Johannes Maier-Hultschin, March 13, 1946, HUG FP/93.10/Box 22/ Johannes Maier.

[96] Brüning's memorandum of August 31, 1935, given to Baroness von Willisen to convey to "Friedrich," *Briefe*, I: 466–482; see also Michael Schneider, "Zwischen Standesvertretung und Werksgemeinschaft," in Schmädecke und Steinbach, *Der Widerstand*, pp. 520–532, and Nebgen, *Widerstandskämpfer*, pp. 42–45.

Most other Christian union functionaries detested the Third Reich but saw no hope for its overthrow. Bernhard Tacke of the Christian textile workers' union, who participated in a Catholic discussion group in Mönchengladbach, later recalled that it engaged only in "spiritual resistance." His colleague Josef Schlunken concluded more pessimistically that almost every worker he knew had been won over or intimidated by the regime.[97]

There was little organized resistance to the Third Reich during the period of German military victories from 1939 to 1941, but even then some faithful Catholics argued that Germany was on the path to ruin. Wilhelm Elfes felt inspired by the outbreak of war to renounce his political apathy, and in 1940/1941 he delivered over one hundred talks to small church groups in Rhineland-Westphalia, organized by sympathetic parish priests, to remind listeners that Christ was the "prince of peace."[98] Nikolaus Gross came into contact during the war with Catholic activists from all over Germany on a new committee in Fulda to coordinate pastoral care for adult men. The priests on this committee described in general terms what they had learned from soldiers in confessional about German war crimes, and the Jesuit Alfred Delp and the leading Dominican Laurentius Siemer argued passionately that Catholics must defend universal human rights, not just the rights of the Church.[99]

Most of the civil servants and army officers in the conservative resistance movement led by Carl Goerdeler and the retired General Ludwig Beck were hostile to parliamentary democracy, but they worried about a lack of popular support and remembered that strikes had helped to topple the empire in 1918. Goerdeler insisted therefore on an alliance with credible labor leaders, and he established close contact with Kaiser and Leuschner by autumn 1941. Bernhard Letterhaus joined the nerve center of the conspiracy in the summer of 1942, when he was promoted to army captain and transferred to military counterintelligence in Berlin. The conspirators expended much energy in 1941/1942 on programmatic debates, however. The first detailed statement by Goerdeler and Beck of

[97] Peter Hoffmann, *The History of the German Resistance, 1933–1945* (Cambridge, MA, 1977), pp. 3–96; Nebgen, *Widerstandskämpfer*, pp. 54–64; Tacke to Albert Esser, April 13, 1976, NL Tacke/13/1 (source of quotation); Josef Schlunken, "Entstehung und Entwicklung der Gewerkschaften am Niederrhein," memoir from 1948, NL Dörpinghaus/1. See also the pessimistic reports about the generals' attitude in March 1938 by Letterhaus and Hermann-Josef Schmitt in Brüning, *Briefe*, I: 181–183.

[98] Esser, *Wilhelm Elfes*, pp. 112–118.

[99] Bücker, *Nikolaus Gross*, pp. 176–180; Antonia Leugers, *Gegen eine Mauer bischöflichen Schweigens. Der Ausschuss für Ordensangelegenheiten und seine Widerstandskonzeption, 1941 bis 1945* (Frankfurt a.M., 1996).

their political aims, drafted in early 1941 without input from labor leaders, closely resembled the memorandum by Brüning in 1935 for the army command. They planned to allow members of the German Labor Front to elect their leaders in future but to retain compulsory union membership, a ban on strikes, and "stewards of labor" to regulate wages and hours. They also planned to restore a hereditary monarchy, impose indirect elections for the Reichstag, and create a corporatist upper house of parliament.[100] These plans sparked lively debate in 1942 with Kaiser and Leuschner, who modified them to some extent. The final cabinet list for Goerdeler's provisional government included two Social Democrats, five veterans of the Center Party, and five conservative Protestants. The final version of its program called for the nationalization of coal mines and public utilities, but Goerdeler always advocated a monarchy, compulsory union membership, and a corporatist upper house of parliament. Elfriede Nebgen later acknowledged that Kaiser and Leuschner had reluctantly accepted a monarchy, but according to her, they rejected compulsory union membership. The Gestapo's interrogation records indicate that all the conspirators endorsed compulsory union membership, but Nebgen was doubtless correct that Leuschner and Kaiser assumed that many flaws in Goerdeler's plans could be corrected after Hitler was overthrown.[101]

In Berlin Kaiser gained support mostly from ex-functionaries of the Christian unions, but a uniquely detailed report from Duisburg suggests that many members of his provincial network had middle-class backgrounds. Karl Schmitz, the last chairman of the Christian metalworkers' union, organized a fifty-member group there in response to Kaiser's appeal to be prepared to restore democracy on "Day X," the day when the Third Reich would fall. Duisburg was a predominantly blue-collar city, but Schmitz's group included just two blue-collar workers, three white-collar workers, and three former union functionaries, alongside eight self-employed artisans, seven shopkeepers, five government employees, five teachers, four physicians, two tavern-keepers, two

---

[100] Gerhard Ritter, *Carl Goerdeler und die deutsche Widerstandsbewegung* (Stuttgart, 1954), pp. 166–196, 279–311; Hoffmann, *German Resistance*, pp. 102–202; Theodore Hamerow, *On the Road to the Wolf's Lair: German Resistance to Hitler* (Cambridge, MA, 1997), pp. 87–98, 238–316; Hans Mommsen, *Alternative zu Hitler*, pp. 53–158, 207–229, 284–312; Carl Goerdeler, "Das Ziel," in Bodo Scheurig, ed., *Deutscher Widerstand 1938–1944: Fortschritt oder Reaktion?* (Munich, 1969), pp. 53–129, esp. 83–90, 114–119, 126–129; Bücker, "Bernhard Letterhaus," pp. 287–291.

[101] Nebgen, *Kaiser: Widerstandskämpfer*, pp. 89–91, 149–150; Leithäuser, *Wilhelm Leuschner*, pp. 203–216; Ritter, *Goerdeler*, pp. 601–603; Michael Schneider, *Kriegsgesellschaft*, pp. 1204–1210; Gestapo reports of August 29 and September 13, 1944, *Gewerkschaftsquellen*, V: 291–300.

jurists, a banker, an engineer, a priest, and a housewife. It included forty-three Catholics, six free-thinkers, and one Protestant; only three were women. By war's end, fourteen had experienced Gestapo interrogation, seven were imprisoned, and one comrade had been murdered in a concentration camp. The known members of other cells in Kaiser's network included numerous lawyers, civil servants, clergymen, and businessmen.[102] Catholic religious sentiment was probably a more powerful recruiting tool for that network than working-class solidarity, but its social outlook became increasingly radical as a result of wartime privations.

Kaiser's supporters in western and southwestern Germany supported the idea of unified labor unions enthusiastically, but none of them discussed a restoration of monarchy. The most authentic record of their undocumented discussions is probably a lengthy pamphlet published by Wilhelm Elfes soon after the liberation of Mönchengladbach by the US Army, based on his wartime lectures.[103] Elfes assumed already in the summer of 1942 that his listeners desired the end of the "brown regime." He argued that the German people must not make the same blunder after the Second World War that it made after the first, when it adopted a constitution that looked democratic but left intact the power of the big industrialists, bureaucrats, and the "feudal lords" from East Elbia. Elfes championed unified labor unions, as he already had in 1926, and he also argued that democracy could not be secure without the formation of a labor party (*Partei der Arbeit*) to unite all workers. The government formed by this party should implement "the immediate transfer of large-scale capitalist industrial, transportation, and commercial enterprises to communal property in the form of producers' cooperatives [*Gemeineigentum auf genossenschaftlicher Grundlage*]," the nationalization of banks and insurance firms, the subdivision of large agricultural estates, and "the immediate restriction and to the extent possible elimination of unearned income."[104]

---

[102] Nebgen, *Kaiser: Widerstandskämpfer*, pp. 99–101; Karl Schmitz, "Die Oberbürgermeister-Dr. Gördeler-Widerstandsbewegung in Duisburg," memoir of April 1946, NL Elfes/8/24–25; Aretz, *KAB*, p. 236; Buchstab, *Verfolgung und Widerstand*, pp. 191–259; Hugo Stehkämper, "Protest, Opposition und Widerstand im Umkreis der untergegangenen Zentrumspartei," in Schmädeke and Steinbach, *Der Widerstand*, pp. 136–143, 893–910.
[103] "Ich bitte ums Wort. Zur Diskussion mit meinen Freunden. Als Manuskript abgedrückt" (no place or date), NL Elfes/2/133–157; Esser, *Elfes*, pp. 71–83, 115–123. See also Laurentius Siemer, *Aufzeichnungen und Briefe* (Frankfurt a.M., 1957), pp. 125–129, and Aretz, *KAB*, pp. 230–231.
[104] Bochum lecture, summer 1942, in "Ich bitte ums Wort," pp. 7–9.

Elfes opposed any "Christian" political party because of an anguished sense of abandonment by the episcopate in the struggle against Nazism. He wrote the following prayer in March 1944:

> See our distress, oh Lord, and hasten to help us!
> We are like sheep who have no shepherds.
> Where are the shepherds that you gave us, the messengers to
>   whom you have said, "Give them to eat!"?
> We see them not, we hear them not.
> If the fault lies in our ears and eyes, then open them! But if
>   your messengers have become tired and weak, then stir
>   them, strengthen and encourage them!

Elfes also wrote five bishops to criticize their silence in the face of Nazi crimes for encouraging "resignation" and a "paralyzing hopelessness" among Catholics. Only one replied, Bishop van der Velden of Aachen, who expressed hope that it might be possible to arrange a meeting someday.[105]

Elfes was by no means isolated in his support for a labor party. Jakob Kaiser had long opposed reviving the Center Party in its old form and favored a "Christian Democratic" party to unite Catholics and Protestants, as proposed by Adam Stegerwald in 1920. According to Nebgen, however, he decided by December 1943 that founding a labor party with Leuschner would be the natural corollary to their plan for unified trade unions, and he traveled to Cologne and won the support of the leaders of the Catholic workers' clubs for this proposal. The idea apparently gained support as well from Johannes Albers in Cologne, Karl Arnold in Düsseldorf, and other leaders of Kaiser's provincial network.[106] Kaiser's support for a labor party strongly suggests that he regarded cooperation with Goerdeler as a temporary alliance against Hitler, not an enduring foundation for postwar reconstruction.

The small group of labor leaders in the conspiracy accepted great personal risk on the eve of Colonel Stauffenberg's attempt to assassinate Hitler on July 20, 1944. Letterhaus and Leuschner accepted portfolios in Goerdeler's cabinet; Kaiser was designated the vice chair of the future unified labor federation and prepared to take charge of its operations, because the chairman Leuschner would also serve as vice chancellor.[107] Letterhaus played a leading role in the attempted coup and was arrested

---

[105] "Gebet eines Laien," NL Elfes/77/79; "Die Kirche vor einer Mission," March 1944, and reply by Joseph van der Velden on April 4, NL Elfes/77/82–87.

[106] Nebgen, *Kaiser: Widerstandskämpfer*, pp. 65, 187–188; Bücker, *Gross*, pp. 202–205.

[107] Nebgen, *Kaiser: Widerstandskämpfer*, pp. 166–171, 177–181; Hoffmann, *German Resistance*, pp. 348–369.

within a few days of its failure; the Gestapo soon imprisoned almost every plotter and most former office-holders in the SPD and Center Party. Kaiser evaded capture by hiding in the damp cellar of a house in a Berlin suburb, whose owner barely knew him but agreed to risk her life after an appeal from Elfriede Nebgen. He almost sank into despair on January 23, 1945, when the radio announced that ten of his friends had been executed on that day alone.[108] Letterhaus had been hanged already, in November 1944, but told the Gestapo nothing about the conspiracy, despite rigorous torture. He implored the German people in his final hours to remember that lies, hatred, and injustice would destroy the world. "The fatherland and the world can be saved and endure only if truth, justice, and love prevail in both private and public life." Nikolaus Gross was hanged soon thereafter.[109]

The final toll of those who died for their resistance activities also included Monsignor Otto Müller, Heinrich Körner, and Otto Gerig of the DHV. Max Habermann committed suicide as the police closed in, and the project for a labor party suffered a major blow with the execution of the only Social Democrats with whom Kaiser enjoyed close ties. Heinrich Imbusch had made his way back to Essen in January 1942 and was hidden by his family, but he died of pneumonia in January 1945. The most influential Protestant leader of the Christian unions, Franz Behrens, also died during the war.[110] In May 1945, it required a great act of will for the surviving veterans of the Christian labor movement to plan for the future amid all the blood and rubble around them. They agreed, however, that trade unionists must never again permit themselves to be divided along party lines, and that the Center Party should be discarded in favor of some more inclusive political movement. These lessons had been learned through great suffering.

---

[108] Nebgen, *Kaiser: Widerstandskämpfer*, pp. 192–215.

[109] Aretz, *KAB*, pp. 233–234; Vera Bücker, "Bernhard Letterhaus," pp. 291–295 (quotation on p. 295); Bücker, *Nikolaus Gross*, pp. 223–228.

[110] Stehkämper, "Protest, Opposition und Widerstand," in Schmädecke and Steinbach, *Der Widerstand*, pp. 903–905; Aretz, *KAB*, pp. 233–36; "Otto Gerig" and "Wilhelm Leuschner," in Mielke and Morsch, *Gewerkschafter in Konzentrationslagern*, pp. 64–69, 144–147; Leithäuser, *Wilhelm Leuschner*, pp. 239–249; articles on Julius Leber and Wilhelm Leuschner in Hans Mommsen, *Alternative zu Hitler*, pp. 313–340; Esser, *Wilhelm Elfes*, pp. 122–123; Schäfer, *Heinrich Imbusch*, pp. 294–301.

2 Christian Laborites and the Founding of the Federal Republic

Only the veterans of the Christian trade unions played a significant role in both of the most successful German political experiments after the Second World War, the creation of unified labor unions for workers of all political outlooks and a Christian Democratic party for Catholics and Protestants. They had long discussed both ideas and displayed unusual self-confidence and sense of purpose in 1945/1946, when most political groups to the right of the Social Democratic Party (SPD) were discredited and demoralized. In 1946 they also founded the Social Committees of Christian Democratic Workers, an autonomous network meant to defend the program of the old Christian unions in both the Christian Democratic Union (CDU) and the new, unified labor unions. Scholars have paid little attention to their role in founding the new unions,[1] and focused instead on the sharp debate within the early CDU over their novel program of "Christian socialism." The CDU's rejection of this program by 1949 in favor of the "social market economy" propagated by Ludwig Erhard has widely been interpreted as a crushing defeat for the workers' wing of the party.[2] In fact, the program of Christian socialism rested on three

---

[1] With the noteworthy exceptions of Helene Thiesen, "Christlich-soziale Arbeitnehmerschaft und Gewerkschaftsfrage 1945–1953," phil. diss. (Bonn, 1988), and Wolfgang Schroeder, *Katholizismus und Einheitsgewerkschaft. Der Streit um den DGB und der Niedergang des Sozialkatholizismus in der Bundesrepublik bis 1960* (Bonn, 1992).

[2] Geoffrey Pridham, *Christian Democracy in Western Germany: The CDU/CSU in Government and Opposition, 1945–1976* (London, 1977), pp. 21–55; Franz Focke, *Sozialismus aus christlicher Verantwortung. Die Idee eines christlichen Sozialismus in der katholisch-sozialen Bewegung und in der CDU* (Wuppertal, 1978), pp. 195–287; Rudolf Uertz, *Christentum und Sozialismus in der frühen CDU. Grundlagen und Wirkungen der christlich-sozialen Ideen in der Union 1945–1949* (Stuttgart, 1981); Herlind Gundelach, "Die Sozialausschüsse zwischen CDU und DGB. Selbstverständnis und Rolle 1949–1966," phil. diss. (Bonn, 1983), pp. 7–99; Horstwalter Heitzer, *Die CDU in der britischen Zone 1945–1949. Gründung, Organisation, Programm und Politik* (Düsseldorf, 1988); A.J. Nicholls, *Freedom with Responsibility: The Social Market Economy in Germany, 1918–1963* (Oxford, 1994), pp. 90–247; Frank Bösch, *Die Adenauer-CDU. Gründung, Aufstieg und Krise einer Erfolgspartei 1945–1969* (Stuttgart and Munich, 2001), pp. 21–83; Maria Mitchell, *The Origins of Christian Democracy: Politics and Confession in Modern Germany* (Ann Arbor, 2012), pp. 39–63, 119–163.

assumptions that most Christian laborites perceived to be unrealistic by 1949 – that the German people were doomed to suffer decades of poverty, that big business and big landowners had installed Hitler in power, and that socialist economic reforms would persuade the Soviet Union to accept German national reunification. By promptly adjusting their program to changing circumstances, the veterans of the Christian trade unions preserved considerable influence in both the trade unions and CDU.

2.1   The Formation of Unified Labor Unions and the CDU

The occupation powers banned all political meetings and strikes in Germany at the end of the war. Most Germans displayed little inclination for political activism, because they were absorbed in the struggle for survival. Their cities were full of rubble, and millions of refugees from Eastern Europe aggravated a dire housing shortage. Food and fuel remained desperately scarce, and many goods could only be obtained on the black market.[3] In the bombed-out cities along the Rhine and Ruhr in particular, most veterans of the Christian trade unions agreed with the gloomy reflections of Wilhelm Elfes, who published his wartime lectures to small groups of dissident Catholics soon after the US Army appointed him mayor of Mönchengladbach in April 1945, at a time when Allied military censorship silenced almost all German writers. Elfes proclaimed that Germans no longer formed a "bourgeois nation" (*Bürgervolk*) but rather a "nation of workers."

The hour demands that the broad masses of working people must provide the foundation, content, and leadership for Germany's political and social order. The logic of facts and all political considerations demand it, for only working people can muster the tremendous energies needed to rebuild order at home, and only they are capable of building bridges to the surrounding world, of carrying out the work of understanding and reconciliation with other peoples.[4]

Thousands of copies of this privately printed manifesto were distributed in the spring and summer of 1945, and Elfes won many admirers for the energy and skill with which he led the task of rebuilding a city almost

---

[3] Theodor Eschenburg, *Jahre der Besatzung 1945–1949. Geschichte der Bundesrepublik Deutschland: Band I* (Stuttgart, 1983), pp. 9–77; Christoph Klessmann and Peter Friedemann, *Streiks und Hungermärsche im Ruhrgebiet 1946–1948* (Frankfurt a.M., 1977); Jeffry Diefendorf, *In the Wake of War: The Reconstruction of German Cities after World War II* (Oxford, 1993).

[4] "Der Christ in der Politik. Überlegungen in einem verschwiegenen Versteck vor der Gestapo (Herbst und Winter, 1944/45)," in Wilhelm Elfes, "Ich bitte ums Wort. Zur Diskussion mit meinen Freunden. Als Manuskript gedruckt" (fifty-page booklet, no place or date), NL Elfes/2/132–57 (quotation on pp. 37–38). Elfes had begun to develop this idea in a letter to Msgr. Otto Müller on June 21, 1943, NL Elfes/77/73–74.

completely destroyed by bombing. Elfes argued that it would require several decades to regain the living standard of 1938; if the new German democracy could not offer prosperity, he reasoned, then it must achieve an equitable distribution of wealth by nationalizing large-scale industry and subdividing large agricultural estates. His pessimism about Germany's economic prospects was shared by all advocates of Christian socialism in 1945/1946. Elfes isolated himself politically, however, because for some months he declined all invitations to join a Christian Democratic party, pursuing instead his wartime idea of a labor party to unite all workers.[5]

Most veterans of the Christian trade unions soon abandoned the idea of a labor party because of the swift revival of the SPD. They expected Social Democrats to acknowledge that their failure to renounce Marxism had been a major cause of the dissolution of the Weimar Republic, but most Social Democrats took great pride in their party's historic role as a champion of democracy and international reconciliation. The SPD soon gained recognition by the occupation authorities, and it found a vigorous leader in Kurt Schumacher, a resolute foe of both Nazism and Communism who had suffered grievously in Hitler's concentration camps. Many Social Democrats were more inclined at the war's end to seek alliance with Communists than with Catholic workers.[6] Jakob Kaiser soon encountered disappointment when he explored the prospects for a labor party in Berlin. He had only discussed the idea with two Social Democrats, Wilhelm Leuschner and Julius Leber, who were both executed for resistance activities. One of Kaiser's first contacts when he emerged in May 1945 from the cellar where he hid from the Gestapo was Theodor Leipart, the former leader of the socialist Free unions, who helped Kaiser to arrange union merger talks with three Free trade unionists and Ernst Lemmer of the liberal Hirsch-Duncker unions. The Free

---

[5] Johannes Albers to Elfes, November 2, 1945, NL Elfes/79/45; Elfes to Dr. Wilhelm Kaiser, November 21, 1945, and to Görlinger, November 21, 1945, NL Elfes/34/81–84; Wilhelm Elfes, "Christ und Sozialist," *Frankfurter Rundschau*, October 29, 1946, republished in Elfes' pamphlet "Christen und Sozialisten" (Mönchengladbach, 1947; NL Elfes/2/158–65); Albert Esser, *Wilhelm Elfes, 1884–1969. Arbeiterführer und Politiker* (Mainz, 1990), pp. 115–136. Elfes rejected the label of "Christian socialism," calling himself instead both a Christian and a socialist.

[6] Albrecht Kaden, *Einheit oder Freiheit. Die Wiedergründung der SPD 1945–46*, 3rd edn. (Hannover, 1990); Frank Moraw, *Die Parole der "Einheit" und die Sozialdemokratie. Zur parteiorganisatorischen und gesellschaftspolitischen Orientierung der SPD in der Periode der Illegalität und in der ersten Phase der Nachkriegszeit, 1933–1948* (Bonn, 1973); Kurt Klotzbach, *Der Weg zur Staatspartei. Programmatik, praktische Politik und Organisation der deutschen Sozialdemokratie 1945 bis 1965* (Bonn, 1982), pp. 39–97; Stefan Berger, *Social Democracy and the Working Class in Nineteenth and Twentieth Century Germany* (Harlow, England, 2000), pp. 94–162, 180–185.

trade unionists insisted that Communists join these talks, however, and by the time the Soviet military government authorized their Free German Labor Federation on June 14, Kaiser had been demoted from second to fourth place in the leadership team. The Berlin SPD reconstituted itself the next day with an aggressive program demanding the nationalization of all big banks, insurance firms, mines, and electrical plants. Distressed by what he perceived as a revival of Marxism, Kaiser soon joined the talks organized by his former Center Party colleagues Andreas Hermes and Heinrich Krone to found a new Christian Democratic party.[7]

Kaiser did not seek at first to commit Christian Democrats to a socialist program, accepting the argument by Hermes (a former agrarian lobbyist) that they must appeal primarily to middle-class voters. Kaiser also embraced Hermes' proposed name, the Christian Democratic Union of Germany, where "Union" signified alliance between Catholics and Protestants from all social classes, and "Germany," a claim to found a party representing the entire nation in the national capital. Kaiser played a major role in drafting the first CDU platform, published on June 26; six of the thirty-five members of the drafting committee belonged to his wartime circle of trade unionists, and Kaiser and Lemmer were elected to the #3 and #4 posts in the party leadership. Their platform called for the immediate restoration of civil liberties and property rights, measures to support small business and family farmers, and the subjugation of "mining and other key monopolistic enterprises" to "state power," which could be interpreted either as a call for nationalization or trust-busting.[8] Some friends urged Kaiser to return to Rhineland-Westphalia, where most of his supporters lived, but he resolved to persevere in Berlin, because it was the only city where meaningful dialogue could take place with the four occupation powers. Germany's fate, he declared, would be decided in Berlin.[9]

---

[7] "Aufruf des Berliner Zentralausschusses der SPD," June 15, 1945, in Klaus-Jörg Ruhl, ed., *Neubeginn und Restauration. Dokumente zur Vorgeschichte der Bundesrepublik Deutschland 1945–1949*, 3rd edn. (Munich, 1989), pp. 185–188; Elfriede Nebgen, *Jakob Kaiser: Der Widerstandskämpfer*, 2nd edn. (Stuttgart, 1970), pp. 225–232; Werner Conze, *Jakob Kaiser: Politiker zwischen Ost und West, 1945–1949* (Stuttgart, 1969), pp. 11–19; Mitchell, *Origins of Christian Democracy*, pp. 60–62.

[8] "Aufruf der Christlich-Demokratischen Union," June 26, 1945, in Ruhl, *Neubeginn*, pp. 188–192 (quotation on 190); Heinrich Krone, *Tagebücher 1945–1966*, ed. Hans-Otto Kleinmann, 2 vols. (Düsseldorf, 1995–2003), June 16–22, 1945, I: 15–18; Conze, *Kaiser: Politiker*, pp. 19–25; Ralf Thomas Baus, *Die Christlich-Demokratische Union Deutschlands in der sowjetisch besetzten Zone 1945 bis 1948* (Düsseldorf, 2001), pp. 69–97.

[9] Kaiser's circular of December 8, 1945, "Gleichlautend an meine engeren Freunde aus den früheren Christlichen Gewerkschaften," NL Kaiser/92/147–152, published in Tilman Mayer, ed., *Jakob Kaiser: Gewerkschafter und Patriot. Eine Werkauswahl* (Cologne, 1988), pp. 192–196; Kaiser to Albers, January 18, 1946, NL Kaiser/164a/75–76.

Many of Kaiser's admirers in western Germany dedicated themselves to founding new trade unions. In most West German cities, the first organizing committee for new unions was elected at an assembly of Social Democrats and Communists in spring 1945, convened either by ex-functionaries of the Free unions or younger leaders of spontaneously elected factory councils. In almost every city of Rhineland-Westphalia, however, veterans of the Christian trade unions soon joined these committees and co-signed the first petitions for recognition by the occupation authorities. In Duisburg for example, an organizing committee emerged on May 14 with four Communists and four Social Democrats, but Matthias Föcher of the Christian metalworkers' union persuaded a workers' assembly two weeks later to elect a new committee with three Communists, three Social Democrats, and three Christian trade unionists. That ratio corresponded roughly to the relative strength of the three currents in Duisburg in 1932.[10] The unionizing drive received a boost in early June when the Catholic bishops of Rhineland-Westphalia exhorted Catholic workers to participate in unified labor unions, as long as they observed neutrality regarding partisan politics and religion. Pope Pius XII had already offered similar advice to Italian workers, and he confirmed in a circular to all German bishops on November 1, 1945, that Catholic workers should be allowed to join unified labor unions, "as long as the extraordinary conditions of this age endure."[11]

Veterans of the Christian miners' and textile workers' unions proved especially active. Johannes Ernst was sent to a concentration camp in August 1944 but became the district leader of the unified miners' union of Aachen soon after the war. In Bochum, Johannes Platte, the

[10] Siegfried Mielke, ed., *Quellen zur Geschichte der deutschen Gewerkschaftsbewegung im 20. Jahrhundert. Band VI: Organisatorischer Aufbau der Gewerkschaften 1945–1949* (Cologne, 1987; hereafter *Gewerkschaftsquellen*, VI:), 32–38, 219–221, 227–233; Ulrich Borsdorf, "Der Weg zur Einheitsgewerkschaft," in Jürgen Reulecke, ed., *Arbeiterbewegung an Rhein und Ruhr. Beiträge zur Geschichte der Arbeiterbewegung in Rheinland-Westfalen* (Wuppertal, 1974), pp. 385–413; Ulrich Borsdorf, "'Ein grosser Tag für die deutschen Arbeiter': Die Gründung des 'Freien Deutschen Gewerkschaftsbundes Aachen' am 18. März 1945," *Gewerkschaftliche Monatshefte*, 36 (1985): 234–248; Eberhard Schmidt, *Die verhinderte Neuordnung 1945–1952. Zur Auseinandersetzung um die Demokratisierung der Wirtschaft in den westlichen Besatzungszonen und in der Bundesrepublik Deutschland*, 7th edn. (Frankfurt a.M., 1977), pp. 21–35; Hans-Otto Hemmer and Kurt Thomas Schmitz, eds., *Geschichte der Gewerkschaften in der Bundesrepublik Deutschland. Von den Anfängen bis heute* (Cologne, 1990), pp. 19–83.

[11] Minutes of the "Konveniat der Bischöfe der Kölner und der Paderborner Kirchenprovinz," June 4–6, 1945, in Ludwig Volk, ed., *Akten deutscher Bischöfe über die Lage der Kirche, 1933–1945*, 6 vols. (Mainz, 1985), VI: 513–514; papal address to the Catholic workers' clubs of Italy, March 1945, and circular to the German bishops, in Katholische Arbeitnehmer-Bewegung Deutschlands, *Texte zur katholischen Soziallehre. Die sozialen Rundschreiben der Päpste und andere kirchliche Dokumente*, 6th edn., 3 vols. (Kevelaer, 1985), I: 183–194 (quotation on 192).

son and grandson of coal miners, rose to become chief editor of the miners' weekly paper by 1947. A great admirer of Heinrich Imbusch, Platte lectured both trade union and CDU audiences on the historic achievements of the old Christian unions.[12] Theodor Blank co-founded the new unions and CDU of Dortmund and became vice chair of the miners' union in the British Zone in 1946. Karl Dörpinghaus and Bernhard Tacke of the Christian textile workers' union played leading roles as labor organizers along the lower Rhine, as did Albert Hillenkötter in northern Westphalia. Anton Storch, an ex-functionary of the Christian woodworkers' union, co-founded the new labor federation and CDU in Hanover. Storch and Tacke found that almost all veterans of the Free unions were good colleagues who supported the idea of a nonpartisan labor federation and respected the sensibilities of churchgoers.[13]

In southern Germany, Christian trade unionists played a much smaller role in the new unions. Adolf Leweke and Josef Arndgen, the last chairman of the Christian leather workers' union, joined the fifteen-member organizing committee for the Free German Labor Federation of Hesse, but Arndgen soon chose a political career in the CDU.[14] In Munich and Stuttgart as well, about half of the Christian trade unionists who co-founded unified labor unions soon opted for political or civil service careers. The US military government concluded in 1947 that most trade unionists in its occupation zone supported the SPD; the Communist minority of 10–15 percent was slightly larger and far more active than the "Christian" minority.[15]

---

[12] Capsule biography of his father by Hanno Ernst, July 1984, NL Ernst/6/4; Johannes Ernst to August Schmidt, August 30, 1947, NL Ernst/4; Platte's "Lebenslauf" from 1950, NL Platte/15/33–34, and his lectures from 1946 in NL Platte/3/140–163.

[13] Hans-Otto Kleinmann, "Theodor Blank," in Jürgen Aretz, ed., *Zeitgeschichte in Lebensbildern. Band VI* (Mainz, 1984), pp. 178–188; Blank's circular of January 24, 1946, NL Kaiser/164a/123; memoir by Josef Schlunken (1948), "Entstehung und Entwicklung der Gewerkschaften am Niederrhein," NL Dörpinghaus/1; Karl Dörpinghaus, "Lebenserinnerungen, I. Teil," pp. 192–194, NL Dörpinghaus/2; Bernhard Tacke to Albert Esser, April 13, 1976, NL Tacke/13/1; Tacke to Detlev Hüwel, February 2, 1977, NL Tacke/10/5; Tacke to Robert Marzell, January 11, 1978, NL Tacke/11/5; August Heeke to Jakob Kaiser, February 12, 1946, NL Kaiser/164b/58; Anton Storch, "Lebenserinnerungen, Erfahrungen und Erlebnisse," in Deutscher Bundestag, *Abgeordnete des Deutschen Bundestages. Aufzeichnungen und Erinnerungen*, vol. 2 (Boppard am Rhein, 1983), pp. 326–328.

[14] Leweke's memorandum of May 16, 1945, NL Kaiser/80/68–69; Gerhard Beier, *Willi Richter. Ein Leben für die soziale Neuordnung* (Cologne, 1978), pp. 156–157, 215–216; Hans-Otto Kleinmann, *Geschichte der CDU* (Stuttgart, 1993), pp. 39–40; Anne Weiss-Hartmann, *Der Freie Gewerkschaftsbund Hessen 1945–1949* (Marburg, 1977), pp. 40–48.

[15] *Gewerkschaftsquellen*, VI: 501–503, 522–525, 363–365, 371–372, 563–568, 632–634; Josef Ersing to Kaiser, January 8, 1946, NL Kaiser/164a/186–187; Michael Fichter, *Besatzungsmacht und Gewerkschaften. Zur Entwicklung und Anwendung der*

The most influential Christian trade unionists in the new unions were Karl Arnold and Michael Rott. Arnold won election as the first chair of the new labor federation of Düsseldorf and retained close ties to union colleagues after the British military governor appointed him mayor in January 1946.[16] In Bonn, Kaiser's friend Rott became vice chair of a union organizing committee in late April 1945 and forged a partnership with Hans Böckler in Cologne, the former leader of the Free unions in the Rhineland. Rott joined Böckler's five-man coordinating committee for the Rhineland in early June and persuaded it to add Karl Arnold and Bernhard Deutz to become a Committee of Seven, with three Christian trade unionists, three Social Democratic Free trade unionists, and one Communist. It embraced the principle that leadership posts should be distributed according to the relative strength in each region of the different labor currents before 1933, which implied that Christian trade unionists deserved about one-third of the posts in Rhineland-Westphalia but only one-tenth in many other regions.[17]

The Christian trade unionists supported Hans Böckler's radical vision of the *Einheitsgewerkschaft*, a labor federation united in three senses:

1. Fusion of the three federations that existed until 1933 for workers of different political outlooks;

US-Gewerkschaftspolitik in Deutschland, 1944–1948 (Opladen, 1982), pp. 112–115; "U.S. Zone Trade Unions," report of July 21, 1947, in Siegfried Mielke and Peter Rütters, eds., *Gewerkschaften in Politik, Wirtschaft und Gesellschaft 1945–1949. Quellen zur Geschichte der deutschen Gewerkschaftsbewegung im 20. Jahrhundert: Band VII* (Cologne, 1991; hereafter *Gewerkschaftsquellen*, VII:), pp. 425–438.

[16] Detlev Hüwel, *Karl Arnold. Eine politische Biographie* (Wuppertal, 1980), pp. 83–90.

[17] See the petitions by Oswald Seifert and Rott of May 14/15, 1945, *Gewerkschaftsquellen*, VI: 221–223. The "Siebener Ausschuss" did not keep records, and some socialists later challenged the assertions by Christian laborites that it was based on parity between the Free and Christian unions. Eberhard Schmidt asserts in *Die verhinderte Neuordnung*, pp. 37–41, that it included four Free trade unionists, two Christian trade unionists, and one Communist, but he apparently confuses the Rhineland committee with a committee founded just for Cologne in March 1945. The petition seeking government recognition by the new, five-man "Landesausschuss der Rheinischen Gewerkschaften" to Oberpräsident Dr. Fuchs in Bonn on June 3, 1945 (NL Rott/2/9) lists three Social Democrats and two Christian trade unionists as members. The most knowledgeable witnesses agree that the expanded Committee of Seven formed in September or October included Böckler and two other Social Democrats, the Communist Konrad Skrentny, and the Christian trade unionists Rott, Bernhard Deutz, and Karl Arnold. See the memorandum for Werner Hansen by DGB archivists on November 18, 1955, NL Hansen/4; Bernhard Deutz to Hans Katzer, March 15, 1956, NL Katzer/592; Bernhard Tacke to Detlev Hüwel, February 2, 1977, NL Tacke/10/5; Borsdorf, "Weg zur Einheitsgewerkschaft," pp. 403–405; Thiesen, "Christlich-soziale Arbeitnehmerschaft," pp. 51–53; and Karl Lauschke, *Hans Böckler. Band 2: Gewerkschaftlicher Neubeginn 1945 bis 1951* (Frankfurt a.M., 2005), pp. 17–29.

2. Unified industrial unions for blue- and white-collar workers (plus civil servants in the public sector); and
3. A centralized labor federation that controlled the finances and strike decisions of its member unions.[18]

Most German trade unionists embraced the first principle in 1945, but the second caused debate, and the third proved highly controversial; the British authorities in particular feared that centralization would stifle internal democracy. Karl Arnold sought to overcome their resistance with the following petition:

> The transition from the old partisan labor federations to the new unified German trade union makes strong, centralized leadership indispensable. German workers lacked any leadership for 12 years and were therefore exposed to many dangerous influences. Today's mental confusion and radicalizing tendencies can only be combated successfully by functioning trade unions with authority and a unified will. The selection of union leaders ... cannot be left up to the labor forces in the various factories, because then accidental, radical majorities would often prevail instead of objective considerations.[19]

Arnold obviously anticipated a fierce struggle against the Communists by veterans of the Free and Christian unions. Johannes Ernst believed that the sense of solidarity uniting workers in the same vocation provided the strongest foundation for union work, but he supported Böckler's approach for the moment because of the shortage of trained labor organizers. Karl Schmitz, the last chair of the Christian metalworkers' union, supported Böckler more vigorously and testified that his plan corresponded to the wartime plans of the Resistance. Michael Rott displayed the most enthusiasm for Böckler's plan and hurled himself into the campaign for British approval.[20]

Böckler's position weakened after the Social Democrats who led the Hessian trade unions in the US occupation zone called for a decentralized federation of autonomous industrial unions. The British endorsed that model and pressured Böckler in September 1945 by halting all new permits to organize labor unions in their zone. In December Böckler and his colleagues capitulated, and largely autonomous industrial unions

---

[18] See Böckler's memoranda from June 3, 1945, and August/September 1945 in *Gewerkschaftsquellen*, VI: 107–110, 235–242.

[19] Karl Arnold, "An die Alliierte Militärregierung der Nord-Rheinprovinz," July 31, 1945, NL Rott/2/9.

[20] Johannes Ernst, "Gründung, Entwicklung und Aufgaben des Industrieverbandes," lecture of September 1946, NL Ernst/6/5; memorandum on the plans of the "Gördeler-Widerstandsgruppe," sent to Böckler by Schmitz on January 1, 1946, NL Katzer/594; Michael Rott, "Zur gewerkschaftlichen Lage," October 10, 1945, NL Rott/2/9; Rott, "Bericht zur gewerkschaftlichen Lage in der Nord-Rheinprovinz," August 8, 1946, NL Rott/2/10.

began to grow rapidly in the British Zone. In April 1947 they founded an umbrella organization with narrowly restricted powers, the German Labor Federation of the British Zone (*Deutscher Gewerkschaftsbund,* or DGB), with 1.8 million members, loosely allied with another 900,000 in the American Zone.[21] Böckler thus came close to achieving unity in his first two definitions of the term but not the third.

Christian trade unionists supported Böckler more vigorously in the debate over the proper form of union organization than did many of his Social Democratic party colleagues. Michael Rott became perhaps the most persuasive advocate of Böckler's principle that the national railway, postal system, and all government administrative offices and enterprises should have unified "industrial unions" including blue-collar workers, white-collar workers, and civil servants. He became vice chair of the new Public Service and Transport Workers' Union (*Gewerkschaft ÖTV*), and he championed its demands for unlimited freedom to unionize in the public sector and the right to strike for civil servants and government employees. Böckler and Rott celebrated the united front of workers and civil servants who had launched a general strike in 1920 to defeat the monarchist Kapp Putsch, and they argued that the breakdown of this alliance in later years had greatly facilitated the Nazi seizure of power. Civil servants were far less likely to support the SPD than blue-collar workers, so the prospects for organized labor in the growing public sector depended in large measure on the engagement of Christian Democrats such as Rott.[22]

Only in the Saarland and among white-collar workers did the foundation of unified labor unions provoke serious debate among veterans of the Christian labor movement. The Catholic steelworkers and coal miners of the Saarland were cut off from other German regions under French occupation. In the summer of 1945 three supporters of Jakob Kaiser joined a committee in Saarbrücken to organize unified labor unions, and the French military governor vetoed an application by other veterans of the Christian miners' union to revive separate Christian unions. The most

[21] Minutes of a trade union conference of December 7, 1945, declaration of December 19, and membership tables in *Gewerkschaftsquellen*, VI: 255–268, 288–290, 431–432; Rolf Steininger, "England und die Gewerkschaftsbewegung 1945/46," *Archiv für Sozialgeschichte*, 18 (1978): 41–116; Wade Jacoby, *Imitation and Politics: Redesigning Modern Germany* (Ithaca, 2000), pp. 55–69; Fichter, *Besatzungsmacht*, pp. 196–197.

[22] Rott's memorandum from May 1945 and speech of February 27, 1946, *Gewerkschaftsquellen*, VI: 103–105, 275–276; "Bericht über die am 10. Januar 1946 … stattgefundene Eisenbahner-Konferenz aller führenden Kollegen im R.B.D.-Bezirk Köln," with speeches by Böckler and Rott, NL Rott/2/13; Michael Rott, "Bericht zur gewerkschaftlichen Lage in der Nord-Rheinprovinz," August 8, 1946, NL Rott/2/10; Franz Josef Furtwängler, *ÖTV. Die Geschichte einer Gewerkschaft* (Stuttgart, 1955), pp. 295–314, 599–616.

influential Catholic politicians in the Saarland argued, however, that unified labor unions promoted the spread of Communism, and they mobilized allies in the French Christian trade unions. In May 1947 a Christian democratic French foreign minister therefore approved the founding of Saar Christian trade unions, which gained 80,000 members by 1950.[23] Among veterans of the old white-collar DHV (*Deutschnationaler Handlungsgehilfen-Verband*), Jakob Kaiser's friend from his resistance days, Karl Hahn, sought in 1945/1946 to rally support for the new, unified industrial unions. A majority advocated separate unions for white-collar workers, however, and many DHV veterans cooperated with Social Democrats in founding the new German Employees' Union (*Deutsche Angestellten-Gewerkschaft*, or DAG), which broke away from the DGB in 1948 with about 150,000 members. The DAG played the leading role among white-collar workers in the commercial sector, while the DGB's member unions remained dominant among white-collar workers in industry. Karl Hahn then agreed in 1950 to chair a revived DHV (where the "D" now stood simply for *deutsch* rather than *deutschnational*); it attracted the most right-wing veterans of the old DHV, many of them former Nazis, and initially gained only about 10,000 members.[24] The overwhelming majority of blue-collar Christian trade unionists outside the Saarland supported unified labor unions nevertheless.

Veterans of the Christian trade unions had meanwhile played a major role in founding the Christian Democratic Union in Rhineland-Westphalia. The secondary school teacher Leo Schwering took the first step when he assembled eighteen former members of the Cologne Center Party at Walberberg Abbey on June 17, 1945, to found a Christian Democratic Party in the spirit of Adam Stegerwald's Essen Program of 1920. This meeting was hosted by the Dominican resistance activists Laurentius Siemer and Eberhard Welty, and it included one figure from the Christian labor movement, the former Reichstag delegate Peter Schlack. That trio drafted a radical platform in the spirit of Wilhelm Elfes, calling for "a true Christian socialism" based on the principle that "the scope of communal property should be expanded to whatever extent is required by the public welfare. The postal system and railroads, coal mining, and energy production are to be considered public services.

---

[23] Reports by Alois Lenhart to Jakob Kaiser on January 3 and March 13, 1946, NL Kaiser/ 164b/108–110; Patrick Pasture, *Histoire du syndicalisme chrétien international. La difficile recherche d'une troisième voie* (Paris and Montreal, 1999), pp. 239–242.

[24] Reports to Kaiser by Hahn on April 27, 1946, and by Bernhard Deutz on May 4, 1946, NL Kaiser/92/119 and 164a/160–161; Hemmer and Schmitz, *Geschichte der Gewerkschaften*, pp. 41–46; "Bericht über die Konferenz der christlichen Fachinternationalen" in Utrecht on May 31, 1951, and Karl Hahn to August Vanistendael, July 19, 1951, in NL Katzer/ 618/Christliche Gewerkschaften.

Banking and insurance are to be subject to state control." Papal encyclicals had condemned socialism repeatedly in the name of the "natural right" to private property, but the theologian Welty argued that the highest moral value in the social theory of Thomas Aquinas, the common good, demanded a dramatic expansion of public ownership of the means of production at this historical juncture. After 100,000 copies of this manifesto were distributed throughout Rhineland-Westphalia, Center Party veterans recruited a number of Protestants untainted by collaboration with the Third Reich to formulate a more authoritative party program, proclaimed on September 2 at simultaneous rallies in Cologne, Düsseldorf, and Bochum. Many veterans of the Christian unions participated in these discussions, and Karl Arnold sat on the seven-man committee that finalized the text. This program retained in Points 16–21 the core economic demands of Welty's manifesto but omitted any reference to "Christian socialism."[25]

Christian trade unionists in the Rhineland found a vigorous leader when Johannes Albers, who had been liberated from a Berlin prison by the Red Army, made his way back to Cologne in June 1945. Albers greatly admired Jakob Kaiser but also enjoyed good ties with Mayor Konrad Adenauer, having served on the Cologne city council from 1924 to 1933. He reported to Kaiser in October 1945 that Michael Rott had entered into "a sort of marriage with Hans Böckler in which we have nothing to say." Albers demanded influence and respect for Christian trade unionists within both the labor unions and the Christian Democratic Party. With the help of Bernhard Deutz, he compiled a list of names and addresses of former comrades in Rhineland-Westphalia that included 1,000 entries by October. Albers went beyond the narrow circle of ex-functionaries of the Christian unions to revive contact with factory workers and miners who had held unpaid office in factory councils or union locals before 1933.[26]

Albers endorsed Wilhelm Elfes' gloomy assessment of economic prospects, and he also agreed with Elfes that German workers and small

---

[25] Programs of June and September 1945 in Helmuth Pütz, ed., *Konrad Adenauer und die CDU der britischen Besatzungszone, 1946–1949. Dokumente zur Gründungsgeschichte der CDU Deutschlands* (Bonn, 1975), pp. 105–113 (quotations on 106–108; hereafter cited as *CDU Protokolle: Britische Zone*); "Bericht über die Gründungsversammlung der Christlich Demokratischen Partei des Rheinlands," September 2, 1945, NL Rott/1/2; Leo Schwering, *Frühgeschichte der Christlich-Demokratischen Union* (Recklinghausen, 1963), pp. 34–40, 52–60, 82–91, 122–123; Uertz, *Christentum und Sozialismus*, pp. 23–59; Heitzer, *CDU*, pp. 35–70; Mitchell, *Origins*, pp. 42–53.

[26] Albers to Kaiser, October 6, 1945, and January 7, 1946, NL Kaiser/164a/55–56, 61–65; Deutz to Kaiser, January 13, 1946, NL Kaiser/164a/159–160; Thiesen, "Christlich-soziale Arbeitnehmerschaft," pp. 60–64; biographical sketch of Albers in Günter Buchstab, Brigitte Kaff, and Hans-Otto Kleinmann, eds., *Christliche Demokraten gegen Hitler. Aus Verfolgung und Widerstand zur Union* (Freiburg, 2004), pp. 72–80.

farmers were the victims of the Third Reich, because Hitler had been hoisted into the saddle by the heavy industrialists and big landowners. Albers presented this argument most forcefully at a somber retreat in Walberberg in July 1945, where eighty-seven veterans of the Christian unions assembled to honor the martyrs of the Resistance. Albers noted that Christian trade unionists had always experienced some friction with their Social Democratic "class comrades" (*Klassengenossen*), a striking departure from the vocabulary of Catholic social theory, but he insisted that these disagreements were relatively unimportant.

> Far more difficult was the struggle that we had to wage against the hard-liners from the business camp. We have not forgotten Kirdorf, Thyssen, ... and the others ... For the sake of human dignity and the dignity of labor, and to bring order to the state and society, the workers demanded the right to co-determination [*Mitbestimmung*] and a role in shaping the business enterprise and the economy as a whole. That was demanding too much. In its hatred of democracy and the labor movement, big business took the money that it refused to give for a decent wage to the workers and gave it with an open hand to the partner in its newly formed marriage since 1930, the criminal Hitler. And so the struggle was decided in 1933 against the workers, and elitism, political and social reaction, and megalomania could triumph.

The trade unions must be united, Albers concluded, and the balance of power tilted away from big business to guarantee that nothing like the Nazi seizure of power ever happened again. Historical research suggests that Albers exaggerated the support for the Nazis from big business, but his view closely resembled that of most Social Democrats, and this interpretation of history became a founding premise of Christian socialism.[27]

Although he hesitated to commit himself so far in public, Albers wrote privately to his mentor Adam Stegerwald in mid-August that the steel industry must be "nationalized" (*verstaatlicht*) along with the coal mines, and that systematic planning and "producers' cooperatives" should be introduced throughout the economy. He described the arguments by Eberhard Welty for Christian socialism as the product of many months of wartime discussions with himself and their martyred laborite comrades Nikolaus Gross, Bernhard Letterhaus, and Heinrich Körner. Körner (as we saw in Chapter 1) had already advocated an essentially socialist response to the Great Depression in 1931/1932.[28] Stegerwald had lapsed

---

[27] See the two drafts of this speech in NL Albers/2/1, "Einkehrtag, July 14/15, 1945" (quotation from the final draft). Compare Henry A. Turner, *German Big Business and the Rise of Hitler* (Oxford, 1985), and Jonathan Wiesen, *West German Industry and the Challenge of the Nazi Past, 1945–1955* (Chapel Hill, 2001).

[28] Albers to Stegerwald, August 15, 1945, NL Stegerwald/12/1/#1247. See also Eberhard Welty, *Die Entscheidung in die Zukunft. Grundsätze und Hinweise zur Neuordnung im deutschen Lebensraum* (Heidelberg, 1946), and Laurentius Siemer, *Aufzeichnungen*

into a collaborationist attitude under Hitler's rule, but he was plunged into depression in 1943 by the death of one son and severe wounding of two others on the Russian Front. Imprisonment from August to October 1944 as a former Center Party leader helped to open his eyes to the true nature of the regime, and Stegerwald remembered the democratic ideals that guided most of his career when the US Army appointed him prefect of Franconia in May 1945. Albers' report from Cologne influenced his first postwar speech, delivered in Würzburg on August 21, which embraced the call for unified industrial unions.[29] At a second rally on October 13, Stegerwald offered a fourteen-point platform for the new Christian Social Union of Bavaria that borrowed heavily from Welty's program of June 1945, including the call for "a true Christian socialism." Stegerwald planned to merge this party with the Christian Democratic parties emerging elsewhere but preferred "social" to "democratic" in the name as a pledge to serve the interests of workers and peasants. Stegerwald also reiterated Albers' argument that industrialists and East Elbian landowners had installed Hitler in power.[30]

Albers arranged for the seventy-one-year-old Stegerwald to visit Cologne on October 20, 1945, to meet with former colleagues. Stegerwald lectured them for eight hours during a twenty-four-hour visit, tapping a rich vein of personal experience that included discussions with every German chancellor since Bethmann Hollweg. Stegerwald also argued a clear thesis, that the Catholic episcopate had often intervened disastrously in German politics, and that its agents in the Catholic workers' clubs had sabotaged every constructive initiative by the Christian trade unions. Stegerwald described in detail the campaign by clerical hard-liners to prohibit any collaboration with Protestants before 1914, obstruct democratic reforms during the First World War, thwart the attempt in 1920 to found a Christian Democratic Party, and elect Monsignor Ludwig Kaas as chair of the Center Party in 1928 instead of Stegerwald. For the past century, Stegerwald alleged, the Catholic clergy had responded to the growing independence of educated middle-class Catholics by tightening the reins that bound Catholic workers and women. "It can be predicted," Stegerwald concluded, "that political reaction will emerge again in the foreseeable future. In that situation, Catholic workers must learn from the past

und Briefe (Frankfurt a.M., 1957), pp. 157–159. For Körner's background, see above, pp. 30–32.

[29] See Stegerwald's memorandum of August 18, 1945, NL Stegerwald/12/1/#1246; Stegerwald to Albers, August 20, 1945, with enclosed speech to be delivered the next day, "Wo stehen wir?", NL Stegerwald/12/1/#1248; and Bernhard Forster, *Adam Stegerwald (1874–1945)* (Düsseldorf, 2003), pp. 612–661.

[30] Stegerwald, "Wohin des Wegs?", pp. 15–19, 29–32, NL Stegerwald/12/1.

and never again allow themselves to be misused for reactionary aims in the political, economic, and religious spheres." He presented strong historical evidence for this thesis.[31]

Stegerwald's audience included one influential priest, Hermann-Josef Schmitt, the son of a metalworker and the former secretary general of the national federation of Catholic workers' clubs in the Weimar Republic. After liberation from Dachau, Schmitt had walked home to Cologne to secure a pledge of support by Archbishop Josef Frings (who was elevated to the rank of cardinal soon thereafter) for the revival of church-affiliated workers' clubs. Schmitt now assured Stegerwald that Frings, who had been active in the Catholic workers' clubs as a young priest, truly sympathized with workers and sought to achieve social justice. Stegerwald replied bluntly that Frings could die tomorrow, that his successor would not be chosen by workers, and that if Schmitt ever disagreed with his bishop, he would be posted to a remote peasant village. The Catholic workers' clubs had treated their members like children before 1933, Stegerwald insisted; if they were revived at all, they should sever ties with the Church. Schmitt was appalled by the suggestion.[32] This clash exposed lingering tensions between veterans of the Christian unions and the Catholic workers' clubs.

Soon after this conference, a former Catholic who had joined the German Communist Party denounced Stegerwald publicly as a Nazi sympathizer. There was no foundation for his most serious charge, that Stegerwald had betrayed comrades to the Gestapo, but he hit the mark when he alleged that Stegerwald had written several bishops in 1941/1942 to urge support for the German war effort. Stegerwald died in December before he could respond to this attack.[33] After pained reflection, Albers, Kaiser, and other senior veterans of the Christian unions agreed that they must defend Stegerwald's reputation. His anti-clerical interpretation of German history struck a responsive chord; Stegerwald's admirers agreed that these issues were not fit for public discussion, but that his insights

---

[31] See Stegerwald's summary of his remarks, "Aus meinen Erlebnissen im Kampf gegen den Integralismus und die politische Reaktion in katholisch-kirchlichen Kreisen," sent to Albers in late October 1945, NL Katzer/565; Albers to Kaiser, January 7, 1946, NL Kaiser/164a/61–65; and William L. Patch, *Christian Trade Unions in the Weimar Republic, 1918–1933: The Failure of "Corporate Pluralism"* (New Haven, 1985), pp. 20–32, 63–71, 133–141.

[32] Stegerwald to Albers, November 9, 1945, NL Kaiser/164a/38–40; Hermann-Josef Schmitt to Wilhelm Elfes, November 27, 1945, KAB Archiv/5/2; William L. Patch, "The Legend of Compulsory Unification: The Catholic Clergy and the Revival of Trade Unionism in West Germany after the Second World War," *Journal of Modern History*, 79 (2007): 848–880 (esp. 849–853).

[33] Wilhelm Gerst, "Fragen an Herrn Adam Stegerwald," *Frankfurter Rundschau*, November 20, 1945 (NL Kaiser/164a/33–35); Forster, *Stegerwald*, pp. 672–674.

must be incorporated into their training seminars for future leaders of the trade unions and CDU.[34]

Veterans of the Christian trade unions secured an influential position in the Christian Democratic Party of Rhineland-Westphalia in autumn 1945. They comprised eleven of forty-one members of its central committee for the Rhineland, and Karl Arnold chaired the party in Düsseldorf, as did Albers in Cologne. Albers' first speech as Cologne party chair advocated a "socialist order ..., a socialism out of Christian duty" (*Sozialismus aus christlicher Verantwortung*).[35] In Westphalia, Christian laborites comprised eight of twenty-two members of the first CDU executive committee, and the first party chair was Johannes Gronowski, a veteran of the Christian metalworkers' union and Catholic workers' clubs and the last provincial prefect of Westphalia in the Weimar Republic. Another ex-functionary of the Christian metalworkers' union, Joseph Schrage, was appointed mayor of Olpe by the US Army in May 1945 and represented it in the state parliament until his death in 1953.[36] The early CDU included many farmers, businessmen, artisans, and free professionals, to be sure, but in heavily blue-collar cities it granted a major leadership role to workers. In the mining town of Bockum-Hövel near Hamm, for example, the party's founder and chair was a functionary of the Catholic workers' clubs, Wilhelm Deist, who led his party to an absolute majority in the first municipal election with a promise to transfer ownership of the local coal mine to the miners. The six candidates on his winning ticket included two miners and a mine foreman.[37]

Albers' program also gained support at the first national conference of Christian Democrats, when 250 delegates from every German region except Bavaria assembled in Bad Godesberg on December 14. They agreed to adopt the Berlin party name, "Christian Democratic Union," and they embraced Albers' slogan, "Socialism out of Christian Duty." Leo Schwering later recalled that the Christian trade unionists were the

---

[34] Jakob Kaiser to Frau Zenta Stegerwald, December 8, 1945, Albers to Kaiser, January 7, 1946, Josef Ersing to Thomas Esser, January 7, 1946, and Kaiser to Ersing, January 27, 1946, NL Kaiser/164a/30, 36, 61–65, 188–189; Ersing to Kaiser, February 28, 1946, NL Kaiser/15/246.

[35] "Mitgliederliste des Landesvorstandes," October 15, 1945, "Bericht über die Sitzung der Personalkommission," October 20, and "Bericht über die Sitzung des Landesvorstandes der CDU Rheinland," November 19, 1945, NL Rott/1/2; "Vortrag des Parteivorsitzenden Joh. Albers auf der Kundgebung am 2. Dez. 1945 in der Universität Köln," NL Albers/2/1.

[36] Heitzer, *CDU*, pp. 88–89; Karl Teppe, "Johannes Gronowski," *Zeitgeschichte in Lebensbildern*, VIII: 77–94; Erhard Lange, "Landrat Josef Schrage (1881–1953). 'Dem heimatgebundenen Wirken am nächsten ...'," *Olpe in Geschichte und Gegenwart*, 10 (2002): 105–142.

[37] See the two campaign posters from September 1946 sent by Deist to Westphalian party headquarters, NL Gronowski/12/57–63.

best organized faction by far at this conference. Most middle-class delegates also agreed with them that a wave of socialism was sweeping Europe, and that the German people faced many years of dire hardship. Albers and Deutz reported the happy outcome of this conference in the first of many newsletters that they distributed to their growing list of Christian laborite colleagues.[38]

Christian trade unionists also gained respect from middle-class party colleagues through their vigorous support for cooperation with Protestants. When veterans of the old Center Party reconstituted it in Westphalia in October 1945, they attacked the CDU as "socially reactionary," because most Protestants who joined it were middle-class and anti-socialist. Albers, Heinrich Strunk, and other veterans of the Christian trade unions replied emphatically, however, that no matter how much influence Catholic workers achieved in a revived Center Party, this party as a whole would be doomed to a marginal role. They defended the ideal of cooperation between Catholics and Protestants embraced at the Essen Congress of the Christian unions in 1920, and they spread the word that the last Center Party chairman, the exiled Heinrich Brüning, sternly condemned any attempt to revive it. Support for the CDU by all former leaders of the Christian unions severely restricted the growth of the new Center Party.[39]

In Berlin Christian laborites gained new influence when the Soviet military government deposed Andreas Hermes as chair of the eastern CDU in December 1945, after he condemned its policy of confiscating large agricultural estates without compensation. Kaiser and Ernst Lemmer agreed to become the new CDU chair and vice chair, reasoning that trade unionists had a better chance to influence the Soviets than did the farm lobbyist Hermes. Kaiser's rise to high office thrilled his admirers in Rhineland-Westphalia.[40] Kaiser now took a strong interest in Christian socialism, embracing most arguments by his friends Albers and Elfes. He declared at a mass rally on February 13, 1946, that big business

---

[38] Albers and Deutz to "Lieber Freund," December 14, 1945, NL Rott/2/16; Albers and Deutz to "Lieber Freund," January 12, 1946, NL Kaiser/164a/59–61; Schwering, *Frühgeschichte*, pp. 150–165; Uertz, *Christentum und Sozialismus*, pp. 59–65; Heitzer, *CDU*, pp. 174–182.

[39] Karl Zimmermann circular of November 15, 1945, and Albers circular on the conference of Christian union veterans on February 16, 1946, NL Katzer/566; Heinrich Strunk to Wilhelm Hamacher, November 21, 1945, NL Kaiser/96/93–100; Ute Schmidt, *Zentrum oder CDU. Politischer Katholizismus zwischen Tradition und Anpassung* (Opladen, 1987); Noel Cary, *The Path to Christian Democracy: German Catholics and the Party System from Windhorst to Adenauer* (Cambridge, MA, 1996), pp. 210–251.

[40] Circular to CDU colleagues by Andreas Hermes, December 20, 1945, NL Andre/4/1; CDUD circular of January 5, 1946, NL Rott/1/1; Conze, *Kaiser: Politiker*, pp. 42–52; Baus, *CDU*, pp. 203–252.

had installed Hitler in power. Kaiser argued that "just as the French Revolution inaugurated the era of the bourgeoisie, we ... live in the era of the breakthrough of the masses of laboring people as the decisive factor in the life of the nation." The recent elections in Great Britain, France, and Italy revealed that all peoples yearned for a new social order. Kaiser now developed the bridging metaphor that dominated his speeches for the next two years: "To me it seems that Germany has been given the great task of finding the synthesis between eastern and western ideas ... We are to be a bridge between East and West." Christian socialism would always respect parliamentary democracy and individual liberties, Kaiser declared, but it rejected those forms of private property that conveyed "power over human beings." The CDU therefore demanded "communal ownership of mineral wealth, sharp restrictions on land ownership, and the sharpest control of all large-scale property in private hands."[41]

For Kaiser, Christian socialism represented above all a guarantee to the Soviets that imperialism would not revive in Germany, and relations between the CDU and Soviet military government did improve after he took office. We now know that this détente only resulted from a Soviet decision to concentrate for the moment on suppressing the SPD, but Kaiser's strategy appeared successful for a time, and his speeches enjoyed great resonance in Rhineland-Westphalia.[42] Albers assembled 200 veterans of the Christian trade unions on February 16, 1946, to express support for Kaiser and discuss their experiences in the CDU and trade unions. Karl Arnold declared that "the Christian Democratic Union is the torch-bearer of a newly awakened Christian Socialism ... and will pursue this goal with the utmost resolution." The delegates then resolved to support the CDU, because "it is determined to create socialism out of Christian duty." They also agreed to found a network of local clubs of veterans of the Christian trade unions, which in most cities were named the "Social Committees" (Sozialausschüsse). Albers established a central office for these clubs in Cologne and hoped that they would become powerful defenders of the program of the old Christian unions within both the CDU and German Labor Federation. He wrote Kaiser, however, that for the moment they could rely on just a few active colleagues. "Our comrades are more or less already too old and have become tired. Those who remain have mostly fled into government jobs, and it seems

---

[41] "Christlicher Sozialismus und Einheit," in Mayer, *Jakob Kaiser*, pp. 212–230 (quotations on 217–218, 222).
[42] Baus, *CDU*, pp. 255–278; Albers and Deutz to Kaiser, February 25, 1946, NL Kaiser/164a/83–85; Wilhelm Elfes to Kaiser, June 24, 1946, NL Elfes/9/12.

impossible to pry them out again." The Social Committees could only play a significant role if they inspired younger colleagues to join the struggle.[43]

2.2 Jakob Kaiser and the Debate over Christian Socialism

Veterans of the Christian trade unions suffered their first attacks after the war from Communists in the trade unions who denounced their program of Christian socialism as a sham. In a Ruhr Valley plagued by shortages, the KPD founded 285 factory cells by March 1946 with 13,000 members. In the first postwar factory council elections in the Ruhr coal mines, Communist candidates out-polled the Social Democrats, while Christian social candidates ran a distant third with 14 percent of the vote. The Communists avoided attacks on veterans of the Free unions but sought to eliminate the influence of Catholic laborites.[44] In Duisburg, for example, Matthias Föcher delivered a speech to celebrate labor unity at the founding congress of the local metalworkers' union on March 17, 1946, where the organizing committee had nominated eleven veterans of the Free unions for the leadership and ten from the Christian and Hirsch-Duncker unions. The organizing committee had also resolved to act with their colleagues from nearby Hamborn, however, and Communists dominated the large group of Hamborners who arrived during Föcher's speech. Föcher reported to Hans Böckler that "I have never experienced such confusion, disorder, unreasonableness, and tactlessness, or such disregard of all democratic rules." The meeting eventually elected a whole new leadership team with a Communist majority. Föcher accepted a post with the Public Service Workers' Union and began to look for a government job.[45]

An alliance between veterans of the Free and Christian unions soon defeated this Communist offensive. Christian Democrats helped to elect

[43] See Albers' account of the proceedings on February 16, sent on March 10, 1946, NL Katzer/566; Albers to Kaiser, January 23, 1946, NL Kaiser/164a/77; and Thiesen, "Christlich-soziale Arbeitnehmerschaft," pp. 60–67.

[44] Christoph Klessmann, "Betriebsgruppen und Einheitsgewerkschaft. Zur betrieblichen Arbeit der politischen Parteien in der Frühphase der westdeutschen Arbeiterbewegung 1945–1952," *Vierteljahrshefte für Zeitgeschichte*, 31 (1983): 272–307 (esp. pp. 274–276); Klessmann and Friedemann, *Streiks und Hungermärsche*, pp. 68–70; W. Weibels of Essen to Kaiser, January 30, 1946, NL Kaiser/164b/185–186; report by Heinrich Strunk to CDU leaders in *CDU Protokolle: Britische Zone*, March 18, 1947, p. 298.

[45] Föcher's speech of March 17, 1946, and Föcher to Willi Stock, April 1, 1946, NL Braukmann/4/Gewerkschaftsgeschichte; Föcher to Böckler, March 19, 1946, NL Braukmann/2/Gewerkschaftsgeschichte; Föcher to Gocklen, Arnold, Albers, and Schrage, April 21, 1947, NL Gockeln/18; Thiesen, "Christlich-soziale Arbeitnehmerschaft," pp. 71–73.

the moderate Social Democrat August Schmidt as the first chair of the unified miners' union of the Ruhr in March 1946, with an executive committee granting equal representation to Communists, Social Democrats, and Christian Democrats. Schmidt's policy that miners should work overtime in exchange for improved rations proved unpopular, but in December 1946 Christian Democrats helped him again to win a narrow victory over the Communist candidate to chair the miners' union of the whole British Zone. In return Schmidt helped to defeat a Communist initiative to remove Johannes Ernst as the district leader for Aachen.[46] Hans Böckler nurtured the anti-communist alliance at the first congress of the trade unions of the British Zone in August 1946. Because the unions had a strong tradition of simple majority voting rather than proportional representation, only thirty-five of the 400 elected delegates represented the Christian social current, but Böckler helped them to gain six of twenty-two seats on the zonal oversight committee. Johannes Ernst held the keynote address on the plight of miners, and his resolution, approved unanimously, advocated "the transfer of mining to public ownership." The Christian trade unionist Anton Storch was also delegated to take charge of the unions' efforts, in cooperation with the military government, to rebuild the social insurance funds for health insurance and old age and disability pensions. Böckler was a lifelong Social Democrat, but he always insisted on the unions' complete independence from the SPD, and he resolved to combat any Communist agitation within the unions; he regarded the veterans of the Christian unions as valuable allies in both causes.[47]

The Soviets strengthened this anti-communist alliance in West Germany when they suppressed the SPD in their occupation zone in 1946 and sent thousands of Social Democrats to labor camps. When the German Labor Federation (DGB) of the British Zone was constituted in April 1947, Böckler secured the election of Matthias Föcher as vice chair after his preferred candidate, Michael Rott, died in an automobile accident. A second Catholic laborite was elected to the executive committee to

---

[46] Ulrich Borsdorf, "Speck oder Sozialisierung? Produktionssteigerungskampagnen im Ruhrbergbau 1945–1947," in Hans Mommsen and Ulrich Borsdorf, eds., *Glück auf, Kameraden! Die Bergarbeiter und ihre Organisationen in Deutschland* (Cologne, 1979), pp. 345–366; Willi Agatz to I.V. Bergbau, Bezirksleitung Aachen, August 27, 1947, and Ernst to August Schmidt, August 30, 1947, NL Ernst/4; Albers to Johannes Platte, September 19, 1947, NL Platte/26/180.

[47] Gewerkschaftliches Zonensekretariat, *Protokoll: Gewerkschafts-Konferenz der britischen Zone vom 21. bis 23. August 1946 in Bielefeld* (Bielefeld, no date), pp. 16–17, 24–25 (source of quotation), 32, 40–48; Bernhard Deutz to Kaiser, August 24, 1946, NL Kaiser/164a/165–166; Thiesen, "Christlich-soziale Arbeitnehmerschaft," p. 71; Lauschke, *Hans Böckler*, pp. 197–207.

coordinate efforts to organize women workers, Thea Harmuth, a former manager of Christian consumers' cooperatives and a co-founder of the Bavarian CSU.[48] Böckler also appointed Werner Hansen to chair the DGB state federation of North Rhine-Westphalia, a moderate Social Democrat who had returned to Cologne from British exile. During the Second World War, a majority of the Free trade unionist émigrés in Britain had supported a radical socialist program for Germany's future unions that was designed to promote a united front between Social Democrats and Communists. Hansen had rejected that program, however, arguing that unity among German workers could only be achieved if they dropped any demand for a "socialist economy" and proclaimed instead "the religious and partisan political neutrality" of the future united labor federation. In April 1947 Hansen wrote a fellow Social Democrat that the DGB would never allow a Communist to join its executive committee, because "we do not want the discussions of this body to become an open book for the Communist Party and thus for Moscow." Like Böckler, Hansen regarded the veterans of the Christian trade unions as valued allies not only against the Communists but also against the politicians at SPD headquarters; he feared that the SPD would interfere aggressively in union affairs if the Christian social minority ever withdrew from the DGB.[49] There was some grumbling at the early meetings of the Social Committees that the DGB did not grant them enough posts, but Albers took pride in the fact that at least 200 salaried DGB functionaries in the British Zone belonged to the Social Committees.[50]

In West Germany the Communist wave crested soon after the war, but the Social Committees faced more widespread and sustained attacks within the CDU. In October 1945 Konrad Adenauer gained time for party work when the British authorities deposed him as mayor of Cologne, and he argued forcefully that Christian Democrats must appeal primarily to non-socialist voters. The most influential veterans of the Christian unions agreed nevertheless that Adenauer was the politician best qualified to unify their new party and win elections. Even the radical Wilhelm Elfes believed at this time that Adenauer supported the

---

[48] Thiesen, "Christlich-soziale Arbeitnehmerschaft," pp. 71–73; Klessmann, "Betriebs-gruppen und Einheitsgewerkschaft," pp. 278–281.

[49] Hans Gottfurcht, "Entwurf einer programmatischen Erklärung der Landesgruppe deutscher Gewerkschafter in Gross-Britannien," January 1943, and the critique written by Werner Hansen under the pseudonym Heidorn on April 4, 1943, "Zum Entwurf einer Prinzipien-Erklärung der Landesgruppe" (source of first quotation), NL Hansen/20; Hansen to Josef Kappius, April 21, 1947, Gewerkschaftsquellen, VII: 384.

[50] "Tagung in Hilden am 11. August 1947," NL Platte/3/133–134.

substance of workers' demands despite his aversion to the socialist label. A firm alliance was forged at Adenauer's 70th birthday party on January 6, 1946, where most guests came from the left wing of the CDU. They all agreed that Adenauer should chair the Rhineland CDU and be its candidate to lead the whole British Zone, and within a month he won election to both positions. Michael Rott explained to Kaiser that Karl Arnold possessed the intellect and character needed to lead the party, but that the large Cologne contingent would never accept a leader who did not come from their city; aside from Arnold, only Adenauer was qualified. The founders of the Social Committees thus displayed more concern for the success of the CDU as a whole than for the influence of their faction within it.[51]

The influence of their faction soon declined as Adenauer strengthened the powers of a new coordinating committee for the state parties in the British Zone, in which workers' representatives held only about one-tenth of the seats.[52] Adenauer wrote a new party program that was adopted by this committee in Neheim-Hüsten on March 1, 1946. Avoiding any mention of Christian socialism, it demanded the "strengthening of the economic position and freedom of the individual, and prevention of any concentration of economic power that could jeopardize economic or political freedom, whether in the hands of individual persons, corporations, or private or public organizations." This "principle of dividing power" (*das machtverteilende Prinzip*) was more in tune with the famous papal encyclical *Quadragesimo Anno* than were the manifestos of Christian socialism. Adenauer did make one concession to laborites by calling for the "socialization" (*Vergesellschaftung*) of the coal mines, but he rejected "nationalization" (*Verstaatlichung*), because he sought to distribute ownership shares broadly among small private investors and municipal governments.[53]

Adenauer also challenged Albers' interpretation of the Nazi seizure of power in his first major address as party leader, delivered in Cologne on March 24, 1946.

---

[51] Adenauer to Albers, Arnold, Strunk, Rott, Christine Teusch, Fräulein Franken, and Gumppenberg, January 6, 1946 (summarizing their agreement that day), NL Rott/1/2; Albers to Kaiser, January 7, 1946, NL Kaiser/164a/61–65; Wilhelm Elfes, "Vor zwanzig Jahren," LANRW/RWN/72/1/29; Rott to Dr. Wolf in Aachen, December 23, 1945, NL Rott/1/2; Rott to Jakob Kaiser, February 14, 1946, NL Rott/3/22; Hans-Peter Schwarz, *Adenauer*, 2 vols. (Stuttgart, 1986–1991), I: 482–508; Hüwel, *Karl Arnold*, pp. 67–72.

[52] See the minutes of the first two meetings of the "Zonenausschuss" in *CDU Protokolle: Britische Zone*, pp. 113–122.

[53] Neheim-Hüsten Program, *CDU Protokolle: Britische Zone*, pp. 132–133; Schwarz, *Adenauer*, I: 494–496, 508–510.

It is not right to say that the big bosses, the senior military leaders and big industrialists bear all the guilt. True, they bear a considerable burden of guilt ... But the broad masses of the people, farmers, small business people, workers, intellectuals, did not have the proper mentality, or else the chain of victories for National Socialism in the year 1933 and thereafter would not have been possible. The German people ... has suffered for many decades from a false view of the state, of power, and of the position of the individual. It made the state into an idol and placed it on an altar. It sacrificed the dignity and value of the individual person to this idol.

Adenauer concluded that the baneful influence of "Prussia" and "materialism" on the whole German people was the most important cause of the Nazi seizure of power. Scholars continue to debate whether Adenauer or Albers offered the more authentic historical insight, but Adenauer's view soon dominated the CDU. His arguments persuaded Albers himself to emphasize thereafter the dangerous role played in German history by "idolatry of the state" among all social classes.[54] For politicians Adenauer became most persuasive when he rejected Christian socialism as a losing campaign strategy. He told CDU leaders in June 1946 that "in both scholarship and everyday speech, the term socialism already has a definite meaning. With the slogan of socialism, we will win over five people, but twenty will run away."[55]

After the adoption of the Neheim-Hüsten Program by a committee on which he did not sit, Albers sought to rally support for the rival program adopted by the national CDU conference in Bad Godesberg in December 1945 under the motto, "Socialism out of Christian Duty." He invited Jakob Kaiser for a speaking tour of the Ruhr Valley in late March 1946 that attracted large and enthusiastic crowds. Albers also distributed to all Social Committees the speeches of Arnold, Elfes, and Kaiser. They all agreed, he concluded, that the CDU must create

a new socialist right of property ... that transfers to public ownership with government supervision all enterprises that are ripe for this, such as mines, power plants, chemical plants, large steel plants, banks, insurance, and shipping firms ... Toil and poverty are the inescapable lot of the German people. After the lost war, to make life bearable and worth living for the working population, for the workers of the head and the hand, a planned economy to satisfy human needs [Plan- und Bedarfsdeckungswirtschaft] is essential.

---

[54] Konrad Adenauer, Reden 1917–1967. Eine Auswahl, ed. Hans-Peter Schwarz (Stuttgart, 1975), pp. 82–84; Albers' speech of September 1946, "Die christlichen Arbeiter und die CDU," pp. 1–3, NL Albers/2/1; Schwarz, Adenauer, I: 508–516; Maria Mitchell, "Materialism and Secularism: CDU Politicians and National Socialism, 1945–1949," Journal of Modern History, 67 (1995): 278–308.

[55] Zonenausschuss, June 26–28, 1946, CDU Protokolle: Britische Zone, pp. 149–150.

Albers, Arnold, and Heinrich Strunk also wrote Adenauer privately that his proposals for economic reform did not go nearly far enough to satisfy the trade unions, and that his attacks on the SPD were too harsh.[56]

Unfortunately for Albers, his slogans provoked controversy even among veterans of the Christian unions. Anton Storch wrote him in July 1946 that all their friends in Hanover "rejected the term 'Christian Socialism' and the phrase 'socialism out of Christian duty,'" because they were so unclear. They preferred the plan for "economic democracy" advanced by the Free unions in 1928, which in Storch's experience was perfectly acceptable to middle-class party colleagues, including Adenauer. The veterans of the Christian unions in the Bavarian CSU adopted a similar position.[57] Albers held a meeting of sixty Christian trade unionists in Krefeld on August 8 to rally support for Christian socialism, but it sent mixed signals. Albers relied on a functionary of the Rhenish CDU to organize this conference, Karl Zimmermann, who supported Adenauer's line. Zimmermann emphasized that papal encyclicals condemned every form of socialism, and his speech gained much wider distribution than did that of Albers.[58]

The idea of "Christian socialism" also provoked attack by influential clerics. After Eberhard Welty published his arguments in book form in 1946, Germany's most prominent Jesuit social theorists, Gustav Gundlach and Oswald von Nell-Breuning, protested that their Dominican colleague misunderstood papal teaching. Welty soon reported to Wilhelm Elfes that a major offensive against Christian socialism had begun among the bishops, and that "somebody has already mentioned my name in Rome in this connection and sought to discredit me."[59] Welty avoided political

---

[56] Speech by Kaiser in Essen, March 31, 1946, in Mayer, *Jakob Kaiser*, pp. 231–242; Johannes Albers, "Grundgedanken zum Thema Christlicher Sozialismus. Diskussionsmaterial," May 1, 1946, NL Katzer/566 (quotations from pp. 11–12); Strunk to Adenauer, March 11, 1946, and Albers to Adenauer, July 15 and August 14, 1946, NL Albers/3/2; Albers to Kaiser, July 16 and August 15, 1946, NL Kaiser/164a/86–88.

[57] Storch to Albers, July 24, 1946, quoted in Heitzer, *CDU*, pp. 495–496; declaration by Josef Donsberger at the CSU Landesausschuss, September 6, 1946, in Barbara Fait and Alf Mintzel, eds., *Die CSU 1945–1948. Protokolle und Materialien zur Frühgeschichte der Christlich-Sozialen Union*, 3 vols. (Munich, 1993), I: 545. For background see Rudolf Kuda, "Das Konzept der Wirtschaftsdemokratie," in Heinz Vetter, ed., *Vom Sozialistengesetz zur Mitbestimmung* (Cologne, 1975), pp. 253–274.

[58] There is a twenty-six-page typescript in NL Albers/2/2 of his speech of August 8, but he could only distribute a two-page summary in printed form (NL Kaiser/122/59). Contrast the published sixteen-page pamphlet by Zimmermann, "Das politisch-soziale Weltbild des christlichen Arbeiters," pp. 6–9 (NL Katzer/566). For Zimmermann's background see Buchstab, *Christliche Demokraten gegen Hitler*, pp. 36, 455–456.

[59] Hejo Schmitt to Nell-Breuning, November 25, 1946, and reply of November 29, KAB Archiv/5/45; Welty to Elfes, April 16, 1947, NL Elfes/79/199; Uertz, *Christentum und Sozialismus*, pp. 122–164; Johannes Schwarte, *Gustav Gundlach S.J. (1892–1963)* (Munich, 1975), pp. 347–349, 466–489.

activism for several years thereafter. In Krefeld a Catholic discussion group heard lectures by a factory owner and a priest in autumn 1946 and concluded that "there is no 'Christian Socialism,' because there is no support or confirmation of this doctrine by the Catholic Church."[60] In the CDU of Recklinghausen a feud erupted between Mayor Wilhelm Bitter (a magazine publisher) and the local leader of the miners' union, Heinrich Gutermuth, over the union's proposal to socialize the mines. Gutermuth had belonged to the Christian miners' union from 1920 to 1933, but Bitter denounced him to Westphalian CDU leaders for behaving "almost like a Communist." The local Catholic workers' clubs sided with Bitter, arguing that Gutermuth ignored papal teaching. Gutermuth left the CDU and joined the SPD in May 1947, and he later rose to chair the miners' union.[61] The attacks of Bitter thus deprived the Social Committees of one of their most effective supporters in the trade unions. In Mönchengladbach, Elfes himself provoked attack by many party colleagues for his socialism and efforts to cooperate with the SPD. By March 1948 the trade unionist Bernhard Tacke was the only CDU city council member to support Elfes, so he resigned as mayor.[62]

In the face of such attacks, Albers and Karl Arnold backed away from the slogan of Christian socialism by the end of the year 1946. Albers soon agreed that socialization should take place only in a decentralized form, because of the German people's dangerous tendency to idolize the state. Sharp attacks by the SPD on the CDU during the municipal election campaign in North Rhine-Westphalia in September reinforced Albers' party loyalty, and the CDU's impressive victory over the SPD by a margin of 49 percent to 30 percent inspired confidence in Adenauer's leadership.[63] Albers avoided any reference to Christian socialism when he convened 400 delegates of the Rhenish-Westphalian Social Committees to discuss the creation of a "New Order" on November 8, 1946. Their resolution condemned both capitalism and collectivism, calling for the transfer of mining and large-scale industry to "communal ownership" (*Gemeinbesitz*) to implement "the principle of democracy in the whole economy." One delegate still called for "socialism out of Christian

---

[60] Franz Müller to Johannes Albers, November 25, 1946, NL Rott/2/16.

[61] CDU Landesverband Westfalen leadership conference of May 2, 1947, NL Gronowski/ 1/8–15; circular by Bernhard Winkelheide to the Catholic workers' clubs, June 2, 1947, NL Platte/26/141–143.

[62] See Esser, *Wilhelm Elfes*, pp. 159–162, and Tacke, "Erinnerungen an die Gründungszeit der CDU in Mönchengladbach," March 16, 1976, NL Tacke/13/1.

[63] See Heitzer, *CDU*, pp. 616–620, and Albers' two speeches from September 1946, "Die christlichen Arbeiter und die CDU," pp. 1–4, and "Grundfragen der Sozialisierung," NL Albers/2/1.

duty," but the published account of the proceedings interjected criticism of this speech.[64]

Many ideas of Christian socialism can still be found in the CDU Ahlen Program of February 1947, but not the phrase itself. The first state election in North Rhine-Westphalia was scheduled for April, and Albers secured a key role in writing the campaign platform. Albers and Adenauer developed rival drafts but agreed in late January on a compromise text that was adopted in Ahlen on February 3. Adenauer granted Albers significant concessions, because the idea of socialization enjoyed great popularity during this cold and hungry winter, as food rations in Ruhr cities sank to their lowest levels ever.[65] The Ahlen Program endorses "the principle of dividing power" and ignores the phrase "Christian socialism," but it goes well beyond the Neheim-Hüsten Program by calling for the socialization of the steel industry as well as mines, and it declares that "the government control of banks and insurance companies that began already before 1933 should be further developed" (Points II/4 and II/6). It echoes trade union demands that workers be given "the representation they deserve" on corporate boards of supervisors (Part III), and Part IV declares that "economic planning and direction will be necessary to a large extent for a long time." Adenauer later spoke as if the Ahlen Program rejected Christian socialism decisively, but it incorporated most of the demands by Albers and Kaiser and closely resembled the plan for "economic democracy" published by the DGB in January 1947.[66]

The final discussion of the Ahlen Program overlapped with a debate over socialization in the appointed state parliament of North Rhine-Westphalia. In late January the SPD introduced a bill to socialize the coal and steel industry that gained a favorable response in public opinion, and Albers and Karl Arnold persuaded Adenauer that the CDU must offer an alternative. On March 4 Adenauer and Arnold co-sponsored a bill to establish a "communal economy" in coal and steel, where ownership would be divided among small private investors and municipalities, with a rule that government bodies must own a majority of all

[64] Karl Zimmermann, ed., "Neues Wollen, neue Ordnung. Bericht über die Tagung der Sozialausschüsse der CDU Nordrhein-Westfalen," Herne, November 8/9, 1946 (no place or date), pp. 11–13, 15–18 (NL Katzer/566); Hüwel, Karl Arnold, pp. 76–78.

[65] CDU Protokolle: Britische Zone, October 21–24 and December 17/18, 1946, pp. 206–207, 224–225, 254–256; Albers to Adenauer, November 26, 1946, NL Albers/3/2; Hüwel, Karl Arnold, pp. 94–109; Schwarz, Adenauer, I: 539–541; Focke, Sozialismus, pp. 251–260; Uertz, Christentum und Sozialismus, pp. 166–185; Heitzer, CDU, pp. 496–505; Klessmann and Friedemann, Streiks und Hungermärsche, pp. 35–49.

[66] "Das Ahlener Programm," CDU Protokolle: Britische Zone, pp. 280–286; Adenauer to Albers, November 2, 1947, NL Albers/1/1947. Compare "Wirtschaftsdemokratie" (pamphlet from January 1947) and "Leitsätze der Gewerkschaften zur Sozialisierung," January 27, 1947, Gewerkschaftsquellen, VII: 729–739.

shares.[67] Adenauer gave Albers free rein to interpret the Ahlen Program during the state election campaign, and Kaiser arrived from Berlin to launch it at a mass rally organized by the Social Committees. The CDU won 37.5 percent of the vote in North Rhine-Westphalia in April, vs. 32 percent for the SPD, 14 percent for the KPD, 10 percent for the Center Party, and 6 percent for the liberal Free Democratic Party (FDP). The CDU share had declined since the municipal elections of 1946, but in view of the deteriorating economic situation, the losses would doubtless have been much greater without the Ahlen Program. Adenauer and Albers agreed that it enjoyed great popular resonance and confounded the CDU's enemies on the Left.[68]

When the new state parliament convened, Adenauer supported Josef Gockeln of the Catholic workers' clubs as prime minister, but the great majority of CDU delegates backed Karl Arnold. He offered the state ministry of economics and other key posts to the SPD and small cabinet roles to the KPD and Center Party, and he won unanimous election in June 1947. Arnold declared that he had a duty as a trade unionist to support a "Great Coalition" with the SPD.[69] Adenauer favored confrontation with the SPD, arguing that democracy could not flourish without vigorous debate between the two largest parties. At this time, however, many CDU leaders in other states shared Arnold's preference for broad coalitions to confront material hardship. In late 1946 an all-party government emerged in Württemberg-Baden, a Great Coalition led by the CSU in Bavaria, and a Great Coalition led by the SPD in Hesse. The Hessian CDU even agreed to a provision in the state constitution mandating public ownership of the coal, iron, and steel industries, although the US Military Government vetoed any attempt to implement that proposal.[70]

The rivalry between Arnold and Gockeln reflected the most serious problem for the Social Committees within the CDU, opposition by the revived network of Catholic workers' clubs. Many parish priests believed after the war that there had been far too many Catholic vocational associations in the Weimar Republic. Hermann-Josef Schmitt

---

[67] Albers to Kaiser, January 26, 1947, NL Kaiser/164a/94–95; Hüwel, *Karl Arnold*, pp. 129–131.

[68] Karl Zimmermann, ed., "Erbe und Aufgabe. Bericht über die Tagung der Sozialausschüsse der CDU der britischen Zone," February 21/22, 1947 (Recklinghausen, no date; NL Elfes/ 34/127–152); *CDU Protokolle: Britische Zone*, remarks by Albers and Adenauer on March 18, 1947, pp. 289, 297–298; Hüwel, *Karl Arnold*, pp. 110–111; Heitzer, *CDU*, pp. 325–327.

[69] Hüwel, *Karl Arnold*, pp. 111–117; Arnold to Fritz Henssler, May 27, 1947, ACDP/ Splitternachlass Arnold/1.

[70] Kleinmann, *Geschichte der CDU*, pp. 74–75; Carolyn Eisenberg, *Drawing the Line: The American Decision to Divide Germany, 1944-1949* (Cambridge, 1996), pp. 261–274.

could only find three German prelates eager to revive the Catholic workers' clubs, his patron Cardinal Frings in Cologne, Archbishop Lorenz Jaeger in Paderborn, and Bishop Michael Keller in Münster. They agreed to exhort all parish priests to found workers' clubs after Schmitt accepted a form of episcopal oversight more stringent than that which existed before 1933. The clubs of Rhineland-Westphalia soon reconstituted the Catholic Workers' Movement (*Katholische Arbeiterbewegung*, or KAB) with a network of thirty full-time lay functionaries who provided legal aid and other services for members, led by Gockeln in Düsseldorf, Johannes Even in Cologne, and Bernhard Winkelheide in Recklinghausen. They served as the movement's public spokesmen, but the KAB's course was set by Schmitt and his clerical colleagues who supervised the clubs in each diocese. One year after the war ended, the KAB only counted 42,000 members, however, compared with 147,000 in 1930; Schmitt felt compelled therefore to demonstrate loyalty to the bishops as he sought more active support from them.[71]

In January 1946 Albers provoked conflict with the KAB when he sought CDU approval of statutes for the Social Committees of Christian Democratic Workers. They featured a plan to conduct seminars for young workers, but Gockeln insisted that only the KAB should conduct adult education for Catholic workers. Hermann-Joseph Schmitt reproached Albers by invoking the memory of their martyred comrades: "I must say that I never expected to see you of all people, Mr. Albers, so jeopardize the work of Nikolaus Gross and Bernhard Letterhaus in its delicate opening phase. I deplore your stance very much, but if you want a fight, you can have one."[72] When Albers published an ambitious organizational plan in June, Schmitt protested to Adenauer that the Social Committees sought to create an autonomous mass organization with its own dues and publications that would choke the KAB to death. Adenauer too condemned Albers' plan, because it called for the Social Committees to formulate positions on social and economic policy but restricted membership to workers; the CDU, Adenauer declared, could never permit one social class to define its positions.[73] Albers briefly considered secession

---

[71] Patch, "Legend of Compulsory Unification," pp. 851–853.

[72] "Bericht über die Sitzung des Landesvorstandes [der CDU]," January 8, 1946, NL Rott/1/2; circular by Albers and Bernhard Deutz to "Lieber Freund," January 12, 1946, NL Kaiser/164a/59–61; Schmitt to Albers, January 25, 1946, KAB Archiv/5/21.

[73] Johannes Albers, "Was ist und was soll der Sozialausschuss?" (June 1946), NL Katzer/566; Schmitt to Albers, June 14, and Schmitt to Adenauer, July 1, 1946, KAB Archiv/5/21; Adenauer to Albers, June 19, 1946, reply of July 5, and Adenauer to Albers, July 6 and July 14, 1946, NL Albers/3/2; *CDU Protokolle: Britische Zone*, pp. 148–150, 159; Heitzer, *CDU*, pp. 372–375; Thiesen, "Christlich-soziale Arbeitnehmerschaft," pp. 105–107.

from the CDU but soon gained Adenauer's sympathy with a more modest proposal in September 1946, which defined the Social Committees as an "organ of the CDU" that would serve as "the interpreter of workers' wishes ... The party leadership must understand these wishes if it hopes to take account of them when making decisions."[74] The KAB remained hostile, however, and boycotted the first national congress of the Social Committees in November 1947. When Adenauer heard of this boycott, he withdrew his agreement to speak, writing Albers that "I have learned to my great sorrow that open conflict has broken out between the KAB and Social Committees." Albers scribbled in the margin that Adenauer really meant "to my great joy." The party leader obviously exploited this quarrel to strengthen his own authority.[75]

The Adenauer loyalist Karl Zimmermann also sabotaged an initiative to strengthen the alliance with the DGB at the First National Congress of the All-German Social Committees of the CDU/CSU on November 28–30, 1947. Here Karl Arnold and Jakob Kaiser called for a "new social order" in which workers gained respect and material well-being; Kaiser explained that "I am thinking of a truly social, or I could also say, a socialist order."[76] The DGB vice chair Matthias Föcher then presented a strong case that the trade unions could best promote membership growth among white-collar workers and civil servants by hiring more Christian Democratic functionaries, because the SPD was not popular among these social groups needed to expand the base of organized labor. Hans Böckler attended the rally and agreed that veterans of the Christian trade unions deserved a larger share of DGB offices. The leaders of the DGB and Social Committees intended to launch a major union recruitment drive among Christian Democratic workers. Karl Zimmermann summarized Föcher's speech in the published record, however, as "a massive attack on the policy of the unified unions that was echoed by all discussants." Zimmermann also declared that Böckler might have good intentions but was very weak. Föcher and other Catholic DGB functionaries complained bitterly that Zimmermann's distorted report had antagonized DGB leaders and stifled interest

---

[74] Albers to Karl Arnold, July 16, 1946, NL Albers/3/2; Adenauer to Albers, August 23, 1946, and Albers to Adenauer, September 10, 1946, NL Albers/3/2.

[75] Gockeln to Adenauer, November 7, 1946, NL Gronowski/12/1–5; Gockeln to Albers, November 24, 1947, and Adenauer to Albers, November 29, 1947, NL Albers/1/1947; Heitzer, CDU, pp. 377–380.

[76] Karl Zimmermann, ed., "Erste Reichstagung der gesamtdeutschen Sozialausschüsse der CDU/CSU in Herne in Westfalen am 28., 29. und 30. November 1947" (Heidelberg, 1948), p. 19.

among Christian Democrats in joining a union. The Social Committees severed ties with Zimmermann soon thereafter.[77]

In January 1948 Adenauer and Albers finally agreed on statutes for the Social Committees that incorporated Albers' definition of goals but Adenauer's view of proper procedure. The Social Committees were denied the right to levy membership dues, and they were obliged to secure approval by party organs of all leadership elections and press releases. The latter rule conflicted with Albers' vision of the Social Committees as an autonomous workers' movement, and it was often ignored. The Social Committees were left with only one independent source of income, however, appeals to those who had gained political or union office with their help to donate a portion of their salaries.[78]

The programmatic debate among Christian Democrats was complicated by the efforts of the Berlin CDU to play a national leadership role. In 1946 Jakob Kaiser urged every CDU state party to send delegates to his party congresses in Berlin, and the Berlin CDU sought to correspond regularly with all provincial offices. Adenauer insisted, however, that contacts with Berlin should occur only at the infrequent meetings of the CDU/CSU inter-zonal coordinating committee.[79] Kaiser sought recognition as the CDU's chief spokesman to the Allied occupation authorities, and he proposed that all German parties should form a "national representation" to express the wishes of the German people to the world until nationwide elections could be arranged. Adenauer believed that Kaiser was naive about Soviet intentions and failed to comprehend the growing rift between the Soviets and the Western powers. Open conflict erupted on February 5, 1947, when Kaiser urged the inter-zonal coordinating committee to create a foreign policy bureau in Berlin, headed by himself. Adenauer insisted that the bureau should be led by a professional diplomat and located in a region free of Soviet influence; in the heat of argument he even insinuated that the Berlin CDU was led by fanatical nationalists plotting Germany's clandestine rearmament. After an exhausting debate, the conference decided not to create any foreign policy

---

[77] Ibid., pp. 4–9, 29–30; Föcher to Albers, March 23, 1948, NL Katzer/593; Föcher to Mina Amann, March 23, 1948, NL Föcher/2; correspondence by Karl Dörpinghaus in January 1948 with Alex Maier and Johannes Platte, NL Dörpinghaus/3.

[78] Heitzer, CDU, pp. 383–386; Albers' circular of December 1947, NL Dörpinghaus/3.

[79] "Erste Sitzung des Zwischenzonenverbindungsausschusses," February 14, 1946, in Brigitte Kaff, ed., Die Unionsparteien 1946–1950. Protokolle der Arbeitsgemeinschaft der CDU/CSU Deutschlands und der Konferenzen der Landesvorsitzenden (Düsseldorf, 1991), p. 6 (hereafter Arbeitsgemeinschaft CDU/CSU); Conze, Kaiser: Politiker, pp. 69–78; Heitzer, CDU, pp. 244–272.

bureau.[80] Adenauer's judgment of the international situation proved sound when the US government proclaimed the Truman Doctrine and proposed the Marshall Plan for European economic recovery soon thereafter. Kaiser visited Kurt Schumacher in late May to seek support for a "national representation," but the SPD chairman took the same anti-Soviet line as Adenauer; indeed, Schumacher denounced Kaiser for collaborating with the military authorities who had sent thousands of Social Democrats to labor camps. This quarrel left Kaiser without any viable alternative to Adenauer's policy of close alliance with the West.[81]

Kaiser moved toward Adenauer's position when he protested against the curtailment of civil liberties in the Soviet Zone at a Berlin rally in July 1947:

Measures regarding compulsory labor and repeated waves of expropriation have caused much unrest. Unrest is also spread throughout the population by the fact that internment camps still exist in which Germans are being held who cannot be regarded as Nazi activists or war criminals ... We understand that the occupation powers were not always able to observe all the rules and forms of the law in the immediate postwar period with all its confusion. But now, two years after the end of the war, there is no longer any reason to ignore normal legal procedures.

Kaiser also proclaimed a clear mission for the eastern CDU at its party congress in September: "We must be and will be the sea wall [*Wellenbrecher*] against dogmatic Marxism and its totalitarian tendencies." Kaiser then won reelection as party chair with all votes but one.[82]

Kaiser angered the Soviets in November 1947 when he rejected demands to participate in a German People's Congress, summoned to denounce the Marshall Plan in the name of all "anti-fascist" parties and social organizations. The Berlin CDU leadership endorsed Kaiser's stand but promised to respect party colleagues who decided to attend, and over 200 Christian Democrats participated in the congress on December 6. A Red Army officer then urged Kaiser to resign, because he had lost the confidence of his party, but Kaiser replied that only a CDU party congress could remove him. At a tense meeting of eastern CDU leaders on

---

[80] *Arbeitsgemeinschaft CDU/CSU*, February 5/6, 1947, pp. 46–57. See also "Dreimal CDU," memorandum from January 1947 by Alfred Gerigk, NL Kaiser/58/2–6; Elfriede Nebgen, "Notiz betr. 1. Tagung der CDU/CSU in Königstein/Taunus im Februar 1947," March 22, 1954, NL Kaiser/58/56; Conze, *Kaiser: Politiker*, pp. 69–133; and Schwarz, *Adenauer*, I: 518–529.

[81] See Kaiser's report to party colleagues on June 2, 1947, *Arbeitsgemeinschaft CDU/CSU*, pp. 110–114; Conze, *Kaiser: Politiker*, pp. 135–149; and Eisenberg, *Drawing the Line*, Chapters 5–8.

[82] Kaiser's speeches of July 12 and September 6, 1947, in Mayer, *Jakob Kaiser*, pp. 308–324, 334–352 (quotations on 315 and 350); Conze, *Kaiser: Politiker*, pp. 165–174; Baus, *CDU*, pp. 353–386.

December 11, Kaiser reproached the congress participants for cowardice, but a majority agreed that Soviet pressure had become irresistible. On December 20 a Red Army colonel persuaded CDU regional leaders to sever ties with Kaiser, and he announced publicly that he could no longer function as party chair, because "there no longer appears to be any practical opportunity in the Eastern Zone to continue the democratic and honest course of the Union."[83] Karl Arnold and many other West German CDU leaders flew to Berlin to express solidarity with Kaiser on December 28, but Adenauer sent his regrets. Kaiser still hoped that the Soviets could be persuaded to "reach an understanding with the German people," rather than "attempt to transform us into unfree and dependent persons." The Russians should understand that "upright men are more valuable than dishrags who say Yes to everything." His party colleagues then declared unanimously that they still had confidence in Kaiser and Lemmer, who remained the leaders of the CDU in the Soviet Zone until a party congress decided otherwise. This resolution had no practical effect, however, because the Soviets banned Kaiser from travel in their zone.[84]

Ernst Lemmer continued for a few months to serve as the second vice chair of the Free German Labor Federation, but in June 1948 its theoretical journal denounced the program of Christian socialism as hopelessly confused, declaring that only "scientific socialism" could achieve progress. A few days later, the Soviets imposed a blockade on West Berlin, and all West German labor leaders condemned the Free German Labor Federation as a tool of government repression.[85] Lemmer then joined Kaiser in West Berlin to help organize a new CDU affiliate and democratic labor unions. Kaiser's premise that Christian socialism could help to bridge the chasm between West and East had obviously been discredited. The East German press now denounced Kaiser's "bridge" as a "bridgehead" for US imperialism, and Kaiser acknowledged ruefully that so many "Trojan horses" had crossed his bridge that it must be demolished. He maintained nevertheless that the attempt to build it had been necessary,

[83] See the conflicting accounts by Kaiser and Otto Nuschke in *Arbeitsgemeinschaft CDU/CSU*, December 28/29, 1947, pp. 153–174; Kaiser's declaration published on December 21, 1947, in Mayer, *Jakob Kaiser*, pp. 390-392 (source of quotation); Conze, *Kaiser: Politiker*, pp. 185–207; and Baus, *CDU*, pp. 386–408.

[84] *Arbeitsgemeinschaft CDU/CSU*, pp. 145–52, 174–197; Wilhelm Dietsch, "Notizen über die Berliner Verhandlungen am 28. und 29.12.47," NL Lemmer/43/6 (quotations from pp. 2–4).

[85] Minutes of February 3–5 and August 17–19, 1948, in Werner Müller, ed., *Quellen zur Geschichte der deutschen Gewerkschaftsbewegung im 20. Jahrhundert. Band XIV: Die Interzonenkonferenzen der deutschen Gewerkschaften 1946–1948* (Bonn, 2007), pp. 404–412, 468–487; Heinz Sanke, "Sozialismus und Christentum," *Die Arbeit*, II/#6 (June 1948), pp. 164–167.

and that it must be rebuilt when circumstances became favorable. As Werner Conze has observed, Kaiser's actions in the Soviet Zone and his ultimate failure did more than all the wise speeches of Adenauer to open the eyes of the German people to the true nature of Soviet Communism.[86]

2.3   The Founding of the Social Market Economy in 1948

By autumn 1946, long before the neo-liberal economist Ludwig Erhard exerted any influence on the CDU, most leaders of its labor wing judged that the slogan of Christian socialism was counterproductive, but they continued to support its core ideas. After Kaiser's removal as chair of the eastern CDU in December 1947, they understood that it would require a great deal more than a mildly socialist economic program to persuade the Soviets to allow German national reunification. Most of them remained highly pessimistic about economic trends, however, and the most important premise of Christian socialism had always been that a democracy which could not offer prosperity must achieve an equitable distribution of wealth. Only the decisions about economic policy by the Frankfurt Economic Council in 1948, made largely under American influence, revived hopes for prosperity. Veterans of the Christian trade unions played a pivotal role in its decision that the West German economy would be based primarily on free markets and private enterprise.

West German political life began at the federal level in June 1947, when the US and British military governors authorized the convening of a proto-parliament in Frankfurt am Main for their combined occupation zones, the Economic Council (*Wirtschaftsrat*), with a cabinet of five German directors of administrative agencies. Elected by the state parliaments, the fifty-two members of the original Economic Council included twenty Social Democrats, twenty Christian Democrats, three Communists, and nine delegates from the small non-socialist parties. Four Christian Democrats were veterans of the Christian trade unions, Anton Storch, Theodor Blank, Peter Schlack, and the Bavarian Hugo Karpf; they could therefore achieve a laborite majority if they voted with the SPD and KPD. At first Blank displayed a militant attitude, moreover, when he reported to Westphalian party colleagues that their delegation included far too many businessmen.[87] The CDU/CSU caucus soon developed an *esprit de corps* nevertheless as the representatives of

---

[86] Conze, *Kaiser: Politiker*, pp. 207–215, 224–241, 256; Baus, *CDU*, pp. 413–414, 449–451.

[87] Thilo Vogelsang, *Das geteilte Deutschland*, 9th edn. (Munich, 1978), pp. 71–76; introduction to Rainer Salzmann, ed., *Die CDU/CSU im Parlamentarischen Rat. Sitzungsprotokolle der Unionsfraktion* (Stuttgart, 1981), pp. 9–19 (hereafter *CDU Protokolle: Wirtschaftsrat*);

different interest groups defended each other against attacks from the Left. Most delegates agreed that the CDU should name three of the agency directors, and the SPD two. The SPD demanded control of the economics ministry, but Adenauer, Blank, and Storch persuaded their delegation to reject this demand, because the SPD already controlled most state economics ministries. The SPD declared therefore on July 24 that it would not accept any directorships but rather go into "constructive opposition." This decision made the CDU the governing party at the federal level and the SPD, the opposition, a division of roles that endured until 1966.[88]

For six months the Economic Council encountered nothing but frustration as it sought to revive production. When it was doubled in size in January 1948, another three Christian laborites arrived, Heinrich Strunk from Essen, Bernhard Winkelheide of the KAB, and Hans Schütz of the CSU. Blank persuaded all the Christian laborites to listen carefully to Ludwig Erhard, a nonpartisan economist who led the council's office for monetary policy. Erhard argued forcefully that the creation of free markets in which prices were determined solely by fair competition offered the only hope for a rapid transition from a simple economy designed for war to the far more complex economy required to satisfy the manifold needs of consumers. Policy-makers had become obsessed with the equitable distribution of the small stock of existing goods, he concluded, when they needed to revive free markets to expand that stock.[89] When the post of Bizonia Economics Director became vacant in February 1948, Theodor Blank was one of the first two CDU delegates to nominate Erhard. Some scholars attribute all opposition to Erhard within the CDU to the Social Committees, but many businessmen, economists, and government officials argued at the time that wage and price controls must be retained until the production of coal and steel could be expanded. The CDU delegation was deeply divided over the merits of Erhard's policy; the Free Democratic Party supported him enthusiastically, however, so the Christian Democrats also voted for him on March 2 to "promote fruitful cooperation in future with the

remarks by Blank, Westphalian CDU leadership conference of July 26, 1947, NL Gronowski/1/53–55.

[88] *CDU Protokolle: Wirtschaftsrat*, July 21–22, 1947, pp. 43–46; Wolfgang Benz, *Von der Besatzungsherrschaft zur Bundesrepublik. Stationen einer Staatsgründung 1946–1949* (Frankfurt a.M., 1984), pp. 65–68.

[89] Ludwig Erhard, "Freie Wirtschaft und Planwirtschaft," editorial of October 14, 1946, republished in Peter Gillies, Daniel Koerfer, and Udo Wengst, *Ludwig Erhard* (Berlin, 2010), pp. 160–163; Nicholls, *Freedom with Responsibility*, pp. 151–205; Alfred Mierzejewski, *Ludwig Erhard: A Biography* (Chapel Hill, 2004), pp. 27–57; Volker Hentschel, *Ludwig Erhard. Ein Politikerleben* (Bremen, 1998), pp. 42–61.

FDP."[90] When the US authorities announced that they would introduce a new currency for Bizonia on June 20, Erhard proposed that the Economic Council grant him broad decree powers to decide which commodities should be freed from price controls. He secured the CDU's support with a solemn promise that, although prices might rise briefly, the power of competition would soon bring them down again. Blank embraced this argument and served as his party's chief spokesman in the crucial Economic Council debate on June 18 over Erhard's "enabling act," which passed over the fierce opposition of the SPD and KPD. Erhard made vigorous use of these powers in July to deregulate the prices of most consumer goods.[91]

The extent to which Blank consulted his colleagues in the Social Committees about this crucial decision remains unclear. Storch later recalled that they had always intended to dismantle price controls, but Hugo Karpf recollected more plausibly that the Christian laborites in Frankfurt had agonized over this decision, because it contradicted their program. Erhard scheduled two private meetings with them in early June, Karpf recalled, and gained their confidence with his persuasive arguments. Blank later asserted that Jakob Kaiser had traveled from Berlin to Frankfurt to implore him to oppose Erhard, and that Albers had even threatened to expel him from the Social Committees. He probably exaggerated, however, because Albers told CDU activists in Cologne on the day after the crucial vote that this was a "painful but necessary measure," which offered the best hope for economic revival. Blank probably saw an opportunity for personal advancement by depicting himself as the only trade unionist capable of understanding Erhard's logic.[92] Kaiser delivered several public speeches in May/June 1948 about the threat posed by Soviet Communism. Regarding economic policy, he simply

---

[90] *CDU Protokolle: Wirtschaftsrat*, February 23 and March 1–2, 1948, pp. 138–144, 154–157 (quotation on 157); Nicholls, *Freedom with Responsibility*, pp. 159–205; Mierzejewski, *Ludwig Erhard*, pp. 60–64. For one-sided accounts of the opposition to Erhard, see Hentschel, *Ludwig Erhard*, pp. 61–64, and Mitchell, *CDU*, pp. 152–161.

[91] *CDU Protokolle: Wirtschaftsrat*, May 24, June 4, and June 16, 1948, pp. 199–200, 211–217, 225–230; Benz, *Besatzungsherrschaft*, pp. 127–150; Vogelsang, *Das geteilte Deutschland*, pp. 77–81.

[92] Storch, "Lebenserinnerungen," pp. 328–329; report by Rainer Salzmann on an interview with Karpf on June 15, 1983, *CDU Protokolle: Wirtschaftsrat*, pp. 25–26; report on an interview with Blank on January 13, 1971, in Erich Kosthorst, *Jakob Kaiser: Bundesminister für gesamtdeutsche Fragen, 1949–1957* (Stuttgart, 1972), pp. 26–27; speech by Albers, "Bezirksvorsteherkonferenz, Samstag, 19.6.1948," pp. 1–2, NL Albers/3/4; Gundelach, "Sozialausschüsse," pp. 92–93. Heinrich Tilly of the Westphalian Social Committees expressed suspicion of Blank's personal ambition in a letter to Albers on December 8, 1947, NL Albers/1/1947.

observed that the CDU rejected all dogmas, including both Marxism and the "dogma of neo-liberalism."[93]

Erhard deregulated prices while a wage freeze remained in effect, because many economists feared that a wage-price spiral would undermine the new currency. Bizonia experienced a 10 percent increase in the cost of living from July to October 1948 and no change in nominal wages, and the SPD and KPD denounced Erhard and the CDU as agents of big business.[94] Adenauer sought to rally support for Erhard at a CDU party congress in late August, where Erhard proclaimed the ideal of a "socially committed market economy," which combined free competition with government policies to promote full employment and social welfare, echoing the concept of a "social market economy" recently developed by the Münster economics professor Alfred Müller-Armack.[95] The response by the leaders of the Social Committees was fairly positive. Anton Storch had recently been elected labor director for Bizonia, becoming Erhard's cabinet colleague; he praised Erhard for seeking to shield the poor from hardship but warned that workers could no longer accept wage controls. Albers noted that "the thunderous applause for Professor Erhard should not deceive this party congress about the critical mood among most workers and consumers ... The belief must spread that everyone is getting ahead, not just a few." He praised the accomplishments of the Economic Council nevertheless and denounced threats by some trade unionists of a general strike if Erhard was not dismissed. Jakob Kaiser declared that the CDU must find a "middle course" that "allows measures of a liberal and – let us speak the word calmly – of a socialist character, as long as they serve the people." This congress united the CDU in a campaign for municipal elections in North Rhine-Westphalia, and Storch gave that campaign a boost in September when he persuaded the Economic Council to dismantle wage controls. The CDU achieved modest electoral gains on October 15, while the SPD gained more ground, and the Center Party and KPD suffered heavy losses.[96] Both of Germany's largest parties benefitted from the polarizing debates in Frankfurt at the expense of the splinter parties.

---

[93] See Jakob Kaiser, "Überwindet den Dogmatismus," May 1, 1948, in Mayer, *Jakob Kaiser*, pp. 424–428, and Conze, *Kaiser: Politiker*, pp. 231–241.

[94] Benz, *Besatzungsherrschaft*, pp. 134–150; DGB leadership conference of July 20/21, 1948, and "Entschliessung zur Lohn- und Preispolitik," *Gewerkschaftsquellen*, VII: 581, 1130–1132.

[95] *CDU Protokolle: Britische Zone*, pp. 657–678 (Erhard quotation on 658); Nicholls, *Freedom with Responsibility*, pp. 11–14, 136–146, 234–236.

[96] *CDU Protokolle: Britische Zone*, pp. 692–698, 700–703 (Albers quotation on 700), 708–709 (Kaiser quotation); Heitzer, *CDU*, p. 634.

DGB leaders actually saw no alternative to Erhard's policy and worked with the Social Committees to combat radical currents among workers. Hans Böckler convened an extraordinary congress of the DGB of the British Zone a few days before the currency reform to rally support for the Marshall Plan. In an impassioned debate with the Communist Willi Agatz, Böckler declared that Germany must accept US leadership to promote economic revival. He acknowledged that this policy would delay efforts to socialize industry but promised to resume that struggle when Germany regained sovereignty. The Social Democratic chair of the miners' union, August Schmidt, accused Agatz of seeking "uproar, chaos, and the perpetuation of misery for partisan political reasons." He assured miners that "life goes on, despite everything, and it is even getting better, although slowly."[97] After the currency reform, the SPD and Center Party passed a law for state ownership of the coal mines of North Rhine-Westphalia, but as Böckler feared, the British military governor vetoed it under American pressure.[98] Thereafter the state DGB chair Werner Hansen sent Johannes Albers a list of modest proposals to cope with the rising cost of living, and he assured Albers that union leaders sought to prevent radical attacks on Erhard.[99] Albers renewed his anti-communist alliance with DGB leaders at a cordial meeting on September 27, and they agreed to form a joint committee to arbitrate disputes about violations of partisan neutrality in the unions. Hansen then invited nominations by Albers to fill vacant union posts in five different cities, and Albers forwarded to Ludwig Erhard with a hearty endorsement the DGB's suggestions for measures to slow the rise in the cost of living. Albers warned Erhard that workers were losing confidence in his policy.[100] In October Theodor Blank wrote Albers to demand an end to all criticism of the Economic Council within the Social Committees, but Albers replied that it was healthy to allow constituents to voice complaints about an Economics Director who did not even belong to the CDU. "We have no reason," Albers concluded,

---

[97] DGB Bundesvorstand, *Protokoll. Ausserordentlicher Bundeskongress des Deutschen Gewerkschaftsbundes für die britische Zone vom 16.-18. Juni 1948 in Recklinghausen* (Cologne, no date), pp. 35–64; pamphlets by August Schmidt from June and August 1948, *Gewerkschaftsquellen*, VII: 392–399 (quotations on 394 and 396).

[98] Hüwel, *Karl Arnold*, pp. 134–137; John Gimbel, *The American Occupation of Germany: Politics and the Military, 1945–1949* (Stanford, 1968), pp. 233–236.

[99] Hansen to Albers, September 10, 1948, reply of September 16, and Hansen to Albers, September 18, 1948, NL Katzer/576.

[100] DGB Vorstand, September 27, 1948, *Gewerkschaftsquellen*, VII: 400–403; Hansen to Albers, September 28 and October 1, 1948, NL Katzer/576; Albers to Erhard, October 15, 1948, NL Katzer/570.

to sail in the wake of Professor Erhard, who posed as such a liberal two months ago. It must be our task to defend our own position against these liberals and the liberal people in our delegation ... The orderly market economy [*die Marktwirtschaft in Ordnung*], that must come, but not in the form conceived by Professor Erhard.[101]

The cost of living rose quickly in September and October 1948, and DGB leaders became alarmed by plummeting morale among union members. They also became angry when Ludwig Erhard denounced protests against his measures as "the hysterical squawking of collectivists of every kind," who feared that the German people might liberate itself from the "tyranny of a power-hungry and soulless bureaucracy and boss-ocracy [*Bonzokratie*]." Erhard thus revived the favorite Nazi slogans to vilify the trade unions, and the DGB of the British Zone resolved on October 26 to undertake "energetic measures to alter the currently insupportable conditions."[102] It agreed with union colleagues from the American zone in early November to undertake a twenty-four-hour general strike to demand the "restoration of systematic food rationing," swift and drastic punishment for price gougers and tax cheats, "economic planning in the industrial sector," "the transfer of basic industries and big banks to communal ownership," "democratization of the economy," and the ratification by the military governors of all state laws already passed to achieve economic reform.[103] This decision violated an old principle of the Christian unions that strikes should not be launched to compel government bodies to accept policy demands.

Debate erupted between trade unionists and CDU party loyalists when Albers assembled the leaders of the Social Committees to discuss this confrontation on November 6. Anton Storch predicted that a general strike would aggravate the coal shortage, encourage Communist agitation, and spread panic. Peter Schlack denounced the DGB's call for the draconian punishment of "price-gouging" retailers and concluded that "this path leads to Communism!" Their Dutch colleague Joseph Serrarens promised financial support from the International League of Christian Trade Unions if Christian unions were revived in Germany, but none of the other speakers pursued that idea. Matthias Föcher emphasized that workers had suffered a painful decline in real wages, and Johannes Platte and Karl Arnold agreed with the DGB on the need for

---

[101] Blank to Albers, October 14, 1948, and reply of October 16, NL Katzer/593.

[102] Gerhard Beier, *Der Demonstrations- und Generalstreik vom 12. November 1948* (Frankfurt a.M., 1975), pp. 34–38 (Erhard quotation on 37); Hans Thoma to Hans Böckler, October 18, 1948, NL Hansen/22; DGB leadership conference of October 26, 1948, and Böckler to V. Tewson, October 27, 1948, *Gewerkschaftsquellen*, VII: 997–1000.

[103] Union leadership conferences of November 4–6, 1948, *Gewerkschaftsquellen*, VII: 1001–1013.

stronger laws against excessive retail mark-ups. Albert Hillenkötter conceded that the Christian unions had always condemned "political strikes," but he suggested that the Allied military governors were the DGB's real target, and that strikes "for reasons of foreign policy" were legitimate. Albers eventually secured agreement to send a delegation to Böckler promising to support most of his policy demands if the DGB abandoned the strike. He also issued a balanced press release to support the DGB's goals while criticizing the tactic of a general strike as counterproductive. Distorted press reports (probably inspired by Adenauer) created the false impression, however, that the Social Committees had resolved to found Christian trade unions if the general strike took place, and Albers encountered an icy reception by DGB leaders on November 8. Albers emphasized that the Social Committees made no threats and wanted to help organized labor to achieve its goals, but as soon as he left, the DGB leaders voted unanimously to proceed with their twenty-four-hour protest strike on November 12.[104]

After the SPD called for his resignation, Ludwig Erhard won a vote of confidence in the Economic Council on November 10 by a margin of fifty-two to forty-three. His majority included all seven workers' representatives in the CDU/CSU delegation, who tipped the scales in his favor. Albers had traveled to Frankfurt to confer with them, and they persuaded him that any step back toward the system of price controls would be disastrous. After the vote, Albers told reporters that "Christian Democratic trade unionists emphatically reject the attempt to exert political pressure via the trade unions." The Social Committees thus joined the ranks of Erhard's defenders, and in old age Theodor Blank looked back on 1948 as the year when they exerted their greatest historical impact by making possible the adoption of the social market economy.[105]

Most veterans of the Christian unions within the DGB supported the protest strike nevertheless. Almost every economic enterprise in Bizonia was shut down on November 12. At the decisive meeting of the Bizonia

[104] "Notizen der Tagung am 6/7. Nov. 1948 im Adam Stegerwaldhaus," NL Katzer/257; conflicting press releases by the Social Committees and CDU on November 7, 1948, NL Katzer/570; DGB Bundesvorstand meeting of November 8, 1948, *Gewerkschaftsquellen*, VII: 1013–1014, 1026–1030. Adenauer briefly attended the conference in the Stegerwald House and later reported misleadingly in private correspondence that Kaiser and Albers had promised to organize a secession from the DGB if it carried out a general strike; see for example Adenauer to Johannes Even, November 22, 1948, KAB Archiv/5/21. The minutes of the conference show that it rejected any such ultimatum.

[105] Albers' circular to the Social Committees, November 10, 1948, and DUD press release of November 11, 1948, NL Katzer/570; *CDU Protokolle: Wirtschaftsrat*, November 8, 1948, p. 290; Theodor Blank, "Die Christlich Demokratische Arbeitnehmerschaft in der CDU," speech of October 12, 1968, NL Blank/13.

Trade Union Council on November 10, the Social Democratic union leaders from Bavaria opposed the strike, but Matthias Föcher insisted that it must proceed. Föcher also delivered a radio address that evening to defend the strike as "a necessary consequence of the fact that all legitimate claims and demands of the workers have been ignored."[106] The unions made careful preparations to keep water and electricity flowing, safeguard perishable food items, and prevent coal mines from flooding. At the request of the Allied military governors, they avoided public demonstrations, but 9.25 million workers remained at home out of a total labor force of 11.7 million in an impressive display of labor unity. Almost as many work days were lost due to a strike on November 12 as in all West German strikes for the next twenty years combined.[107]

Albers received dozens of letters about this strike from activists in the Social Committees, whose conflicting opinions provide some evidence for the gloomy conclusion by Grete Juchem of Cologne that "Christian workers are, to put it in quite modern terms, atomized." A majority clearly opposed the strike, however, and the Social Committees of Essen, Wuppertal, and Leverkusen condemned it publicly.[108] Many colleagues reproached Föcher, because he had agreed to oppose the general strike in the Königswinter conference but then championed it after prodding by Hans Böckler. August Heeke expressed the prevalent view among veterans of the Christian unions in the DGB: "Now the first general strike lies behind us. Let's hope that it is the last one."[109]

The general strike revived old fears of organized labor among middle-class Christian Democrats. Adenauer wrote Albers angrily "that people were compelled to stay away from work and to close shops with outright terrorist and Nazi methods." Adenauer vowed to place "Christian trade unions" on the agenda for the next CDU leadership conference, but Albers evidently persuaded him to drop the idea.[110] Albers sought patiently to achieve a course correction by the Economic Council while persuading union leaders that another political strike would shatter

[106] Union leadership conferences of November 10/11, 1948, *Gewerkschaftsquellen*, VII: 1032–1042; Föcher's radio broadcast of November 10, 1948, NL Katzer/570.
[107] Beier, *Generalstreik*, pp. 40–45; conference to prepare for the strike on November 7, 1948, *Gewerkschaftsquellen*, VII: 1014–1023.
[108] Grete Juchem to "Herr Kollege," November 10, 1948, and related correspondence in NL Katzer/570.
[109] Josef Berntzen (Hamm Social Committee) to Albers, November 8, 1948, NL Katzer/ 570; Leweke to Albers, December 7, 1948, NL Katzer/592; Krehle to Albers, November 16, 1948, and Heeke to Albers, November 16, 1948, NL Katzer/570.
[110] Adenauer to Albers, November 16, 1948, NL Albers/3/2; Adenauer to Johannes Even, November 22, 1948, KAB Archiv/5/21. No discussion of "Christian trade unions" is recorded in the minutes of the next CDU leadership conference on February 24/25, 1949, *CDU Protokolle: Britische Zone*, pp. 775–866.

labor unity. The Social Democrat Werner Hansen also told DGB colleagues that the most important lesson from this strike was the need "to maintain contact with the socially progressive colleagues of the CDU and with the CDU Social Committees, which represent their socially active and enlightened elements."[111] Many veterans of the Free and Christian unions thus sought to preserve their alliance against the radical Left. Fortunately for them, the debate over economic policy subsided at year's end, when the rise in the cost of living slowed to a virtual standstill, as Erhard had predicted. Bizonia achieved impressive economic growth in the year 1949, and real wages rose by 15 percent.[112] These developments undermined the economic pessimism that played such a large role in the formation of Christian socialism, and the public began to pay attention to the deliberations of a constitutional convention whose initial debates had been largely ignored.

2.4   The Basic Law and First Bundestag Election

The prospects for West German democracy depended on the spread of the belief that politics is the art of compromise. Influential elements in both the CDU and SPD favored confrontation tactics, however, when the military governors of the Western powers first called for a constitutional convention. The Social Committees exerted their greatest influence on the drafting of that constitution at the outset of the process, in July 1948, when Karl Arnold was elected by the state prime ministers to head the team that negotiated with the military governors about procedure. During the recent debates in the Economic Council, Kurt Schumacher had denounced the CDU for betraying German national interests, and Arnold and Jakob Kaiser agreed that the SPD must not be given any reason to adopt the same attitude toward the constitutional convention. Arnold therefore told the military governors that West Germans would do nothing to imply acceptance of the permanent division of Germany. Instead of a "National Assembly" elected by the people, they would only accept a "Parliamentary Council" elected by the state parliaments; instead of a "constitution" ratified by popular referendum, they would only adopt a provisional "Basic Law," ratified by the states. This limited charter facilitated the search for consensus with the SPD.[113]

---

[111] Speech by Albers on December 12, 1948, and "Tagung der Sonderausschüsse der Arbeitsgemeinschaft," December 18/19, 1948, NL Katzer/315; DGB Bundesvorstand, December 16/17, 1948, *Gewerkschaftsquellen*, VII: 1048.

[112] Nicholls, *Freedom with Responsibility*, pp. 228–233.

[113] Hüwel, *Karl Arnold*, pp. 191–200; Peter Merkl, *The Origin of the West German Republic* (Westport, CT, 1982), pp. 50–62; Benz, *Besatzungsherrschaft*, pp. 156–175, 191–194.

When the sixty-five voting delegates of the Parliamentary Council convened in Bonn on September 1, 1948, the CDU and SPD each commanded twenty-seven votes, but Adenauer won election as chairman with the support of the small non-socialist parties. Kaiser served as one of the five delegates from West Berlin, but to his dismay the Allied military governors decreed that they would participate only as non-voting observers. Kaiser retained influence nevertheless by persuading CDU leaders that he should continue to represent the CDU of the Soviet Zone in their inter-zonal conferences.[114] Kaiser sought above all to persuade his party colleagues in Bonn to create a powerful federal government. When Adenauer exhorted them on September 28 to secure independent sources of tax revenue for the states, Kaiser replied emphatically: "We must not only consider the question of viable states but of a viable Germany ... The most important thing is a strong Germany. The legacy of this war cannot be overcome by the parts, but only by the whole."[115] Kaiser soon agreed with Adenauer to support a bicameral legislature with a popularly elected, American-style Senate as the upper house. They experienced a painful defeat in November, however, when the CSU agreed with the SPD to create a weak Bundesrat (federal council) that represented the state governments and could only vote on issues directly affecting them. Kaiser and Adenauer developed a spirit of partnership in these debates, after Kaiser made it clear that he accepted a subordinate role.[116]

All parties sent their best experts on constitutional law to the Parliamentary Council, and the only voting delegate from a trade union background was the Christian Democrat from Olpe in Westphalia, Josef Schrage. He gained a seat on the Committee for Basic Principles and emerged as the Parliamentary Council's most vigorous defender of trade unionism. The DGB had resolved to confine its demands for the Basic Law to the "classic fundamental rights" of workers, and Hans Böckler wrote Adenauer in October 1948 to request the following article:

The right to form associations for the protection and promotion of labor and economic conditions is guaranteed for everyone and for every occupation. All measures and agreements that seek to restrict or prohibit this freedom are illegal.

---

[114] Merkl, *Origin*, pp. 58–60; *Arbeitsgemeinschaft CDU/CSU*, August 20 and September 21, 1948, pp. 237–238, 246–247; Kaiser's speech of September 19, 1948, in Mayer, *Jakob Kaiser*, pp. 457–459, 463–464; Conze, *Kaiser: Politiker*, pp. 245–246.

[115] See the two records of the meeting in Rainer Salzmann, ed., *Die CDU/CSU im Parlamentarischen Rat. Sitzungsprotokolle der Unionsfraktion* (Stuttgart, 1981), pp. 33–34, 597 (hereafter *CDU Protokolle: Parlamentarischer Rat*).

[116] *CDU Protokolle: Parlamentarischer Rat*, September 23, 1948, pp. 27–30, 592; Merkl, *Origin*, pp. 66–71; Conze, *Kaiser*, p. 254; Kaiser to Wilhelm Elfes, December 28, 1948, NL Elfes/34/224.

The trade unions' right to strike is guaranteed. Whoever participates in a union-authorized strike that does not violate a collective labor contract does not break the law.

Labor leaders considered this request noncontroversial, but their general strike on November 12 created an angry backlash in the Parliamentary Council.[117]

When the Committee for Basic Principles discussed freedom of association on November 24, Theodor Heuss of the FDP and Hermann von Mangoldt of the CDU demanded that the Basic Law also endorse the right *not* to join a union; if the DGB opposed such a clause, they argued, then it was demanding the right to "compel" workers to join. The SPD delegates noted that DGB leaders would feel offended by this provision, but Josef Schrage responded more forcefully. "I know from experience," he declared, "that joining a trade union is completely voluntary and that every proper trade unionist rejects coercive measures. This principle has to my knowledge never been abandoned by the trade unions ... I therefore see no reason to state this explicitly." Germany had nothing like the "closed shop" permitted in the US, Schrage explained, but all gains achieved by the unions benefited every worker. The survival of German trade unions depended therefore on moral pressure against the "parasites" who profited from their endeavors without paying dues, but the clause demanded by Heuss would encourage parasitical behavior. Heuss then demanded that the Basic Law recognize the right to strike only "for the regulation of wages and working conditions," but Schrage protested that there were other legitimate grounds to strike, for example if an employer violated the rights of factory councils. When other delegates sought a prohibition of strikes by civil servants, Schrage proposed that the Basic Law make no mention of strikes at all, following the example of the Weimar constitution.[118] Schrage soon persuaded DGB leaders to support this minimalist approach and rally support from the SPD. The original Basic Law therefore said nothing about the right to strike and simply guaranteed in Article 9 "the right to form associations in order to safeguard and improve working and economic conditions." Schrage thus rescued the DGB from a danger that it had not foreseen.[119]

[117] Union leadership conference of September 30–October 1, 1948, and Böckler to Adenauer, late October 1948, *Gewerkschaftsquellen*, VII: 862–871 (quotation on 867); Beier, *Generalstreik*, pp. 25–33.

[118] Eberhard Pikart and Wolfram Werner, eds., *Der Parlamentarische Rat 1948–1949: Akten und Protokolle. Band 5: Ausschuss für Grundsatzfragen*, 2 vols. (Boppard am Rhein, 1993), II: 685–692, 696–701.

[119] Michael Feldkamp, ed., *Der Parlamentarische Rat 1948–1949: Akten und Protokolle. Band 14: Hauptausschuss*, 2 vols. (Munich, 2009), I: 521–533; *CDU Fraktionsprotokolle: Parlamentarischer Rat*, December 3, 1948, pp. 254–257; Fritz Tarnow to the DGB

Adenauer agreed with Kaiser that it would be desirable to achieve a broad consensus in favor of the Basic Law, but he feared that Kurt Schumacher cared only about partisan advantage and would denounce it as a foreign imposition. Adenauer therefore warned CDU leaders to prepare for the possibility that a narrow majority based on the CDU and FDP might offer the only hope for passage, but Kaiser assured them that most SPD leaders were more reasonable than Schumacher.[120] Adenauer's greatest fear was that if the SPD rejected the Basic Law, the Social Committees would side with it, and the CDU might disintegrate along class lines. It soon became clear, however, that regionalism posed the true threat to party unity, after south German colleagues observed an upsurge in support for regional parties. At a CDU/CSU leadership conference on January 8, 1949, Bavarian Prime Minister Hans Ehard led an assault on numerous articles of the draft Basic Law. The debate became highly emotional when Ehard accused Jakob Kaiser of describing Bavaria as "one of the countries south of Germany," and Kaiser retorted that whoever had told Ehard this was a fool or a liar. Adenauer jumped to Kaiser's defense, because the Social Committees actually supported his position on all controversial issues in the Parliamentary Council.[121]

Kaiser stood at Adenauer's side during the final negotiations with the party leaders and military governors that achieved agreement on a draft constitution on April 25, 1949. Both men became indignant the next day when Hans Ehard informed CDU leaders that the CSU would reject the Basic Law, because it ignored Bavaria's demands for fiscal autonomy and failed to protect the rights of the Catholic Church. This stand was surprising, because Pope Pius XII himself had signaled acceptance of the Basic Law. Kaiser exclaimed that what Adenauer had achieved in the past week was "almost like a miracle ... We can only succeed together. This is not about Berlin and not about Bavaria and not about South Württemberg, this is about Germany. If we do not solve the German question, then no state can be helped!"[122] The Basic Law won approval

leaders of Württemberg-Baden, December 28, 1948, *Gewerkschaftsquellen*, VII: 878–879; Beier, *Generalstreik*, pp. 51–57.
[120] *CDU Protokolle: Parlamentarischer Rat*, November 9, 1948, and January 4, 1949, pp. 139–140, 301–313; *CDU Protokolle: Britische Zone*, February 25, 1949, pp. 820–821; Merkl, *Origin*, pp. 97–98.
[121] *Arbeitsgemeinschaft CDU/CSU*, January 8/9, 1949, pp. 260–262, 284–296, 300–309, 318–319.
[122] *CDU/CSU Arbeitsgemeinschaft*, April 26, 1949, pp. 520–528, 550–551 (source of quotation); Merkl, *Origin*, pp. 99–102, 115–124, 137–142. For Adenauer's discussions with Church leaders about the Basic Law, see also Norbert Trippen, *Josef Kardinal Frings (1887–1978)*, 2 vols. (Paderborn, 2003–2005), I: 363–384.

by a two-thirds majority of the Parliamentary Council on May 8 and was soon ratified by every state except Bavaria. When the Bavarians renewed their complaints at the next CDU/CSU leadership conference, Adenauer quickly turned the podium over to Kaiser for another speech on the need for national unity.[123]

As the deliberations of the Parliamentary Council drew to a close, so did the Soviet blockade of Berlin, and Kaiser focused his energies on Rhineland-Westphalia and the Social Committees. He and Albers established a proper headquarters in the former conference center of the Christian unions in Königswinter, across the Rhine from Bonn, which they reopened as the Adam Stegerwald House in November 1948. The KAB asserted a claim to this valuable property as a minority shareholder in the charitable foundation that financed its construction in the early 1920s, but the old Christian trade unions were the majority shareholder, and the new DGB could have taken possession, because the British authorities recognized it as the legal heir of the Christian unions. Hans Böckler won Kaiser's gratitude by renouncing all claims in favor of the Social Committees.[124] Albers and Kaiser also found a loyal and energetic aide in Hans Katzer, born in 1919, whose father had been prominent in the Kolping Clubs for Catholic journeymen artisans and the Cologne city council. After training as a commercial employee, Katzer fought on the Eastern Front and rose to become a company commander. He attended the first postwar congress of the Berlin CDU and found inspiration in Kaiser's speeches. Albers then secured a job for Katzer in the Cologne Employment Office, where he met Kaiser's daughter. By 1949 Katzer had become chair of the Cologne Social Committee and Kaiser's son-in-law, and he was appointed full-time manager of the Social Committees in 1950. He later confessed that young combat veterans like himself understood nothing about politics, but he brought orderly record-keeping to what had been a chaotic operation under Albers.[125]

---

[123] Merkl, *Origin*, pp 125–126, 153–159; Benz, *Besatzungsherrschaft*, pp. 220–228; Schwarz, *Adenauer*, I: 597–600; *Arbeitsgemeinschaft CDU/CSU*, pp. 593–595.

[124] Jakob Kaiser to Hans Böckler, September 29, 1947, NL Katzer/575; Albers to "Verbandspräses Dr. Schmidt" (i.e. Hermann-Josef Schmitt), October 14, 1947, KAB Archiv/5/21; Schmitt to Nell-Breuning, July 6, 1948, KAB Archiv/5/45; memoir by Elfriede Kaiser-Nebgen, "Unser Haus in Königswinter," October 1, 1977, and commentary by Bernhard Tacke, sent to Katzer on March 3, 1978, NL Tacke/11/5; recollections of Heiner Budde in Wolfgang Schroeder, ed., *Gewerkschaftspolitik zwischen DGB, Katholizismus und CDU 1945 bis 1960. Katholische Arbeiterführer als Zeitzeugen in Interviews* (Cologne, 1990), pp. 218–219.

[125] Katzer's reminiscences in Schroeder, *Zeitzeugen in Interviews*, pp. 162–177; radio interview with Katzer on February 14, 1978, ACDP/01–684/23/1; Tilman Mayer, "'Gerechtigkeit schafft Frieden.' Die Gesellschaftspolitik Hans Katzers," in Ulf Fink, ed., *Hans Katzer. Partnerschaft statt Klassenkampf* (Cologne, 1989), pp. 11–37.

Disagreements between Adenauer and the Social Committees revived during the first Bundestag election campaign. Adenauer saw the election as a referendum on the concept of a "social market economy" that should lead to a coalition government by the CDU and FDP. Karl Arnold and most CDU leaders in Hesse, Württemberg, and Rheinland-Pfalz preferred a Great Coalition, however, and Kaiser championed that strategy when the CDU/CSU campaign committee met in March 1949. Kaiser opposed sharp attacks on the SPD, arguing that the best election outcome would be for the CDU and it to emerge equally strong and form a progressive coalition. Adenauer replied emphatically that "Social Democracy will employ all means at its disposal, including the worst slanders and most malicious lies, to achieve a plurality" and then create an anti-Christian government with the KPD.[126]

Adenauer sought consensus in support of the social market economy by inviting Ludwig Erhard to address the CDU leaders of the British Zone in late February 1949. After Erhard explained his program, Adenauer proposed a committee to work with him to draft a campaign platform, and he invited Albers to participate. Albers protested that "the presentation by Professor Erhard suspends central provisions of the Ahlen Program." Adenauer replied that every program must deal with questions acute at the moment. "In the coming election campaign, this question is acute: planned economy or market economy." Kaiser sought to mediate by declaring that, despite Erhard's reputation for being a doctrinaire liberal,

I like very much the ideas that he presented. They are irreplaceable principles that must be preserved. It is just the same with conservative ideas, which malicious people call reactionary. They too must not be lost, and it is the task of our party to bring these irreplaceable ideas ... into harmony with the new ideas that must also come into being.

Erhard must have resented this attempt to reduce him to a sort of museum exhibit, but he assured Albers and Kaiser that "I embrace your ethical theses" regarding social policy. "I cannot imagine," Erhard concluded, "that you would ever raise social policy demands that I would not be willing to accept, as long as they are based on realities and not mere fantasies." The conference then agreed that a committee including Albers and several supporters of Erhard would draft a campaign platform on economic policy. Soon thereafter the Stegerwald House announced a formal decision to the Social Committees that the "term socialism ... is not appropriate at this time in the current conflict

---

[126] *Arbeitsgemeinschaft CDU/CSU*, March 5, 1949, pp. 394–398; Schwarz, *Adenauer*, I: 607–609.

of political forces in the world" to describe their goals, although the goals remained unchanged.[127]

This decision by the CDU in February resulted in the Düsseldorf Guidelines, adopted by the CDU of the British Zone on July 15, 1949, and soon endorsed by its sister parties. They offer the following definition of the CDU's economic model:

The "social market economy" is the socially bound version of the commercial economy, in which the achievements of free and capable human beings are brought into an order that guarantees the highest level of economic profit and social justice for all. This order is created through freedom and controls, which . . . take place through genuine competition and independent control of monopolies. Genuine competition exists when a competitive order is assured that gives everyone equal chances and fair competitive conditions and then rewards the best achievement in free competition. Coordination among all participants is guided through fair market prices. Fair market prices are the engine and the steering mechanism of the market economy.

This language was obviously inspired by Erhard. The preamble endorses "the principles of the Ahlen Program," but the Düsseldorf Guidelines contradict them when they reject "the system of the planned economy, regardless of whether its planning agencies are centralized or decentralized, state-directed or organized according to economic self-administration." The Ahlen Program had endorsed planning in a decentralized form based on "economic self-administration."[128]

After he saw the final draft of the Düsseldorf Guidelines, Albers offered a last flicker of defiance when he told a rally of Ruhr workers on May 8 that "as far as I am concerned, you can call what we want *socialism*." He later described their goal, however, as the achievement of a healthy "social order," and this phrase became the enduring slogan of the Social Committees. Albers' manuscript declared that the CDU would impose "communal ownership" on mining, the steel industry, and the large-scale chemical industry, and that workers were becoming "the dominant element" in the economy. At the last minute, however, he penciled in "communal ownership *if necessary*" and changed "dominant" to "equal."[129] Albers' enthusiasm for the campaign revived when he and Josef Gockeln were appointed to head a committee to

---

[127] *CDU Protokolle: Britische Zone*, pp. 854–859, 863–864; Josef Bock, "Informationsdienst Nr. 4," March 10, 1949, NL Katzer/255. Mitchell, *CDU*, pp. 160–161, ends her account of this CDU conference with Kaiser's statement that Erhard was a "doctrinaire liberal," giving the impression of a stark clash of views.

[128] "Düsseldorfer Leitsätze der CDU," July 15, 1949, *CDU Protokolle: Britische Zone*, pp. 866–880 (quotations on 866–868); Heitzer, *CDU*, pp. 515–520.

[129] Albers, "Rede in Wetter/Ruhr, 8.5.1949," pp. 5–9, NL Katzer/315.

draft Social Policy Guidelines to complement the Economic Policy Guidelines. They spoke the traditional language of Catholic social theory and called for "implementation of the right of workers to consultation and co-determination" in management decisions, while declaring that "every human being has a natural right to work."[130]

At the urging of Albers, Jakob Kaiser was elected to replace him as chair of the Social Committees on May 15, and Kaiser took charge of efforts to secure healthy Bundestag representation for the workers' wing of the CDU. The nominations process for the Bundestag election was highly decentralized, however. Candidates for each district were chosen by the CDU county committees, while the state parties controlled the state lists of candidates who achieved proportional representation by receiving the pooled votes of the unsuccessful candidates in districts. Both Kaiser and Adenauer feared that small cliques of local notables would choose candidates with little talent or popular appeal. Kaiser implored Adenauer to influence the process in favor of workers, women, refugees from the East, and youth, and Adenauer agreed. Kaiser himself was soon nominated in a secure district in Essen (which he had represented briefly in 1933), and Albers in Cologne, but most other CDU county committees proved hostile to laborites.[131] In May the Social Committees agreed with the church-affiliated workers' clubs on a joint list of workers' nominees, but when Albers forwarded their "unified slate" to Adenauer, he listed the candidates of the Social Committees in slots 1–15, those of the KAB as 16–22, and those of the Protestant workers' clubs as 23–24. KAB leaders concluded angrily that the Social Committees did not respect them.[132] Only four of the fifteen candidates proposed by the Social Committees won Bundestag seats (Albers, Blank, Kaiser, and Aloys Lenz), plus another four listed by the KAB (Even, Gockeln, Martin Heix, and Winkelheide). Most of the DGB functionaries endorsed by the Social Committees failed to win nomination, because of a backlash against organized labor after the general strike of November 1948. Seven leaders of the Social Committees won election outside North Rhine-Westphalia nevertheless, and Kaiser

[130] CDU pamphlet from July 1949, "Düsseldorfer Leitsätze über Wirtschaftspolitik, Landwirtschaftspolitik, Sozialpolitik, Wohnungsbau" (Frankfurt a.M., no date), pp. 24–26; Heitzer, *CDU*, pp. 515–516.

[131] "Sammlung der christlich-demokratischen Arbeiterschaft," report by Josef Bock on a conference of the Social Committees on May 15/16, "Informationsdienst Nr. 5," May 22, 1949, NL Katzer/257; remarks by Kaiser and Adenauer, *Arbeitsgemeinschaft CDU/CSU*, May 19, 1949, pp. 562–622; Conze, *Kaiser: Politiker*, pp. 70–71, 135–146, 254–255; Heitzer, *CDU*, pp. 635–637.

[132] Albers to Adenauer, June 21, 1949, NL Katzer/313; circular to the Westphalian Social Committees by Bernhard Winkelheide and Wilhelm Alef, May 23, 1949, NL Katzer/257; Willi Heitkamp to Even, June 17, and reply of June 21, 1949, KAB Archiv/3/35.

reckoned that 30 of the 139 CDU/CSU delegates in the first Bundestag were blue- or white-collar workers who supported the program of the Social Committees. He invited them to a special caucus at the Stegerwald House just before the Bundestag convened and thus founded an enduring institution, the "Workers' Group" in the CDU Bundestag delegation.[133]

West Germany's first Bundestag campaign became famous for its angry exchanges between Adenauer and Kurt Schumacher of the SPD. Jakob Kaiser also became involved in furious polemics after Schumacher argued that the CDU had been the first party to capitulate to the Communists in the Soviet Zone, in December 1945, when Kaiser volunteered to replace Andreas Hermes as party chair. Kaiser responded on May 15, 1949, that Christian Democratic workers must "become an ever stronger source of security against all totalitarian and collectivist forces. This defense is not limited to the Communists but must also extend to Social Democracy, which contrary to the strivings of its champions in the Resistance has not yet achieved moderation and tolerance." Kaiser portrayed the fusion of the SPD and KPD in the Soviet Zone in 1946 as an enthusiastic merger, when it was in fact a hostile takeover.[134] Schumacher responded aggressively, and at campaign rallies in late July, Kaiser denounced him for "totalitarian gestures, neurotic exaggeration, lapses into crass intolerance, ... and outmoded, reactionary Marxist doctrines." He repeated the accusation that many Social Democrats had eagerly joined the Socialist Unity Party in 1946, adding that Social Democrats had played the same role all over Eastern Europe. "Here too the same disastrous capitulation and delivery of the state to Communism. The will to resist during this tragic process remained alive only in Christian circles."[135] This rhetoric was not healthy for democracy, and Karl Arnold and Anton Storch avoided such attacks. Albers also distanced himself from Kaiser when he told DGB leaders on July 3 that not only Christian Democracy but also "democratic socialism rejects every totalitarian theory; now everything depends on securing respect in the trade unions for both these poles, which are of such historic value for Europe, on making sure that they can coexist and cooperate." Albers

---

[133] Schlack to Karl Arnold, May 24, 1949, NL Katzer/313; Martin Heix to Johannes Even, July 8, 1949, KAB Archiv/3/35; Kaiser to Josef Gockeln, August 16, 1949, NL Kaiser/248/12.

[134] "Sammlung der christlich-demokratischen Arbeiterschaft," report by Josef Bock on a conference of the Social Committees on May 15/16, "Informationsdienst Nr. 5," May 22, 1949, NL Katzer/257.

[135] Kaiser's speech of July 23, 1949, NL Kaiser/74/182–244, esp. 200–201, 205–225, 230–233; Kaiser's speech of July 31, 1949, NL Kaiser/74/83–135, quotations on 111–117.

knew that the influence of Christian Democrats in the trade unions depended on their anti-communist alliance with Social Democrats.[136]

The CDU/CSU won a narrow election victory on August 14 with 31 percent of the national vote, versus 29 percent for the SPD, 12 percent for the Free Democratic Party, and 5.7 percent for the KPD. The Parliamentary Council had agreed that proportional representation should be restricted through a 5 percent hurdle to discourage splinter parties, but the first suffrage law only applied this rule at the state level, so three regional parties gained representation with less than 5 percent of the national vote, the Bavaria Party, German Party (based in Lower Saxony), and Center Party. Adenauer declared to the press on the morning after the election that "the overwhelming majority of the German people do not want to have anything to do with socialism in any form." Karl Arnold and Josef Gockeln told reporters, however, that a Great Coalition between the CDU and SPD would be the most logical conclusion from these results. That line probably reflected the wishes of most workers who voted for the CDU.[137]

Adenauer outmaneuvered Arnold by arranging for twenty-six distinguished party colleagues to meet at his home in Rhöndorf on August 21. Arnold did not receive an invitation, but Kaiser and Theodor Blank participated. Kaiser had promised Arnold and Gockeln to advocate a Great Coalition at this conference, but the minutes record no attempt by him to do so. Adenauer argued for a narrow coalition with the FDP and German Party, and a majority agreed with him, while six colleagues from Hesse and southwestern Germany called for a Great Coalition. Even they agreed, however, that Ludwig Erhard must become the minister of economics, and Erhard declared that he could never serve in a cabinet with Social Democrats. Theodor Blank argued passionately that only Erhard's policy could reduce unemployment, and he predicted that economic growth and progressive social legislation would doom the SPD to decline. Kaiser then supported the majority view, observing that "Schumacher is Germany's misfortune."[138]

Karl Arnold gained support from the KAB for a Great Coalition but no further allies. His young aide Rainer Barzel wrote Hermann-Josef Schmitt that "we need a free economy. What Erhard offers us, however,

---

[136] Storch, "Lebenserinnerungen," pp. 331–332; Hüwel, *Karl Arnold*, pp. 205–206; Albers, "Zusammenkunft mit den Gewerkschaften in Düsseldorf," July 3, 1949, NL Katzer/315.

[137] Udo Wengst, ed., *Auftakt zur Ära Adenauer. Koalitionsverhandlungen und Regierungsbildung 1949* (Düsseldorf, 1985), pp. xxxviii–xxxix, 9–10 (hereafter *Quellen: Koalitionsverhandlungen 1949*); Hüwel, *Karl Arnold*, pp. 206–207; Benz, *Besatzungsherrschaft*, pp. 249–270.

[138] Minutes of August 21, 1949, *Quellen: Koalitionsverhandlungen 1949*, pp. 33–41 (quotation on 40); Schwarz, *Adenauer*, I: 619–626; Kosthorst, *Kaiser: Minister*, pp. 67–70.

is a monopoly economy without competition. That explains the prices and the real incomes that are too low ... Please think of the consequences that will result from the identification of the Church with social reactionaries." Schmitt then wrote Adenauer that a coalition with the pro-business FDP would upset the delicate balance of social forces within the CDU that made it "a beginning of that vision of social order that the Church has discerned since *Quadragesimo Anno*." Schmitt concluded that participation by the SPD in a coalition government might cause a schism in that party, benefitting the CDU, while its relegation to the opposition could only foster radicalism.[139] Arnold sought further support by organizing a conference of eighty former Christian trade unionists on August 29, but it refused to adopt a position on coalition policy after Albers defended Kaiser vigorously. Johannes Platte of the miners' union supported Arnold at this meeting but found that Albers intimidated many colleagues by questioning the integrity of those who stood on the DGB payroll.[140]

Kaiser prepared for a leadership conference of the Social Committees on August 31 by distributing in advance detailed position papers to the participants, including twenty-seven Bundestag delegates. They challenged the priorities of Ludwig Erhard by demanding government action to promote full employment, subsidize housing construction, and strengthen worker participation in management decisions. The paper on economic policy argued that many of the SPD's ideas to promote full employment and the socialization of heavy industry should be supported. Kaiser warned that Kurt Schumacher's attitude made the "small coalition" preferred by Adenauer all but inevitable; it if emerged, he concluded, the Social Committees must act as "the social conscience and the social engine of this cabinet." Kaiser won the meeting's support after promising that the Social Committees would enjoy two cabinet posts, with himself in charge of a ministry to promote national reunification and Anton Storch as labor minister.[141]

---

[139] Barzel to Hejo Schmitt, August 25, 1949, and reply of August 26, KAB Archiv/5/21; Schmitt to Adenauer, August 29, 1949, and reply of August 31, *Quellen: Koalitionsverhandlungen 1949*, pp. 80–82, 134–136. See also the undated and unsigned "Betrachtungen zum Wahlausgang," which appears to reflect the shared thoughts of Arnold and Gockeln, NL Katzer/313.

[140] Report by Albers to the CDU Bundestag delegation on September 1, 1949, *Quellen: Koalitionsverhandlungen 1949*, pp. 152–153; "Erklärung der Konferenz der ehemaligen christlichen Gewerkschaftler vom 29.8.49 in Düsseldorf," NL Braukmann/12; Platte, "Aktennotiz" of August 30, 1949, NL Platte/28/88–89; Kosthorst, *Kaiser: Minister*, pp. 74–75.

[141] Bock's invitation of August 26 and policy papers of August 30, 1949, NL Kaiser/248/17–29; Jakob Kaiser, "Die Stellung der christlich-demokratischen Arbeiterschaft zur Koalitionsbildung," and "Sozialpolitische Aufgaben der Bundesregierung," August 29,

Adenauer's coalition policy triumphed at a CDU/CSU leadership conference later on August 31 and the first meeting of their Bundestag delegation the next day. On August 31 Adenauer still faced resistance. The leader of the Hessian Social Committees, Josef Arndgen, recalled the dramatic congress of the Christian trade unions in September 1932 where Kaiser had appealed for alliance with the Social Democrats in the struggle against Nazism. "If we had succeeded then at forming a close coalition government with Social Democracy," Arndgen declared, "I do not think this disaster would have occurred whose consequences now confound us." The position of Adenauer's critics weakened during this debate, however, when Kurt Schumacher told a press conference that the SPD would never accept the economic policy of Ludwig Erhard. By the next day, the opposition to Adenauer had collapsed. Kaiser moved that the Bundestag delegation elect Adenauer as its chancellor candidate, and the vote was unanimous. All the delegates but one voted to endorse Adenauer's coalition policy, and Kaiser won election to the negotiating team to conduct talks with the FDP and German Party. Even before those talks concluded, Adenauer won by just one vote the absolute Bundestag majority required for election as chancellor on September 15. Karl Arnold had sought at least to secure the election of a candidate supported by the SPD to the largely ceremonial office of federal president, but Adenauer insisted on the liberal democrat Theodor Heuss to cement his coalition with the FDP. Arnold did win election himself with the support of state governments led by the SPD as president of the Bundesrat, thwarting Adenauer's plan to grant this office to the Bavarian Hans Ehard. Adenauer and some other CDU leaders reproached Arnold bitterly for placing his own ambition above the welfare of their party.[142]

All the most famous veterans of the Christian trade unions had by now chosen political careers, but less prominent colleagues did secure influence at the top level of union leadership as Hans Böckler organized the national founding congress of the German Labor Federation in October 1949. Böckler designated Matthias Föcher as one of the two vice chairs in the national federation and placed him in charge of the DGB press and educational programs. When SPD leaders protested against that decision, Böckler told them to mind their own

1949, NL Kaiser/414/11–21 (quotation on 14); "Sozialer Kurs," *Ruhr-Nachrichten*, September 1, 1949 (NL Braukmann/12).
[142] *Quellen: Koalitionsverhandlungen 1949*, pp. 89–134 (Arndgen quotation on 112), 140–202, 281–297, 312–314; Schwarz, *Adenauer*, I: 626–630; Hüwel, *Karl Arnold*, pp. 205–221.

business.[143] Böckler also nominated Thea Harmuth as a second Christian social representative on the eleven-member executive committee, to take charge of recruitment drives among women. Several women delegates at the congress supported a Social Democratic candidate instead, but Böckler cut off their protests with the declaration that "I pursue the goal, as I have emphasized often in the past, ... of giving the Christian current a somewhat stronger position in the future executive committee than it has had in the past."[144] About one-fourth of DGB members were practicing Catholics, and Böckler sought to integrate them into union life. He encouraged Föcher to incorporate the study of Catholic social theory and the history of the Christian labor movement into all programs to train union functionaries, and to respond vigorously if any functionary lapsed into anti-clericalism. Föcher also hired an expert on Catholic social theory, Dr. Franz Deus, to direct the DGB academy at Hattingen on the Ruhr.[145]

Storch, Föcher, and Kaiser played key roles in the future confrontations between the Adenauer government and organized labor, but the task of promoting compromise obviously exceeded their powers. Success depended on whether a significant constituency could be mobilized within the CDU to explain and defend the core demands of organized labor, and within the DGB to explain and defend CDU policy. The Social Committees now defined as their foremost goals "co-determination" (*Mitbestimmung*), i.e. a strong voice for workers in corporate management decisions; "co-ownership" of the means of production (*Miteigentum*) to redistribute wealth; and an economic policy dedicated to full employment. These goals were far more modest than those envisioned in 1945 by the champions of Christian socialism but reflected more penetrating analysis of social and economic trends.

---

[143] Siggi Neumann to Hans Böckler, September 19, 1949, and reply of September 27, *Gewerkschaftsquellen*, VII: 467–468.

[144] Deutscher Gewerkschaftsbund, *Protokoll: Gründungskongress des Deutschen Gewerkschaftsbundes, München, 12.-14. Oktober 1949* (Cologne, 1950), pp. 237–242 (quotation on 238); capsule biography of Harmuth at www.fes.de/archiv/adsd_neu/inh alt/nachlass/nachlass_h/harmuth-th.htm.

[145] Schroeder, *Katholizismus und Einheitsgewerkschaft*, pp. 365–367; Lauschke, *Hans Böckler*, pp. 344–352; capsule biography of Deus from 1966, ACDP/04–013/59.

3   The Debate over Co-Determination (*Mitbestimmung*), 1949–1953

By supporting the formation of a government in 1949 that excluded the SPD, the Social Committees assumed responsibility to defend the interests of West German workers. The veterans of the Christian trade unions took that duty seriously and championed in particular the controversial demand by organized labor for co-determination (*Mitbestimmung*), i.e. a powerful voice for workers in corporate management decisions. Those veterans also held enough key positions in the cabinet, CDU, and German Labor Federation (DGB) to promote compromise during some of the most explosive political debates in the early history of the Federal Republic. They received vigorous support from Chancellor Konrad Adenauer at first, because he sought the backing of organized labor for his pro-Western foreign policy, which was opposed by the SPD. After the DGB endorsed Adenauer's controversial first steps toward economic and political integration with the West, Adenauer hurled himself into the effort to enact the parity Co-Determination Law of 1951 for the coal, iron, and steel industries, the greatest legislative victory for organized labor in the history of the Federal Republic. However, the powerful business lobby rejected any application of this model to other branches of industry, and the Catholic clergy and Catholic workers' clubs, although sympathetic to co-determination in principle, soon expressed alarm over the growing power of the trade unions. In 1952/1953, Adenauer and several influential spokesmen for the Catholic Church began to attack the DGB as a tool of the SPD. Because of old personal rivalries and new Cold War tensions, bitter feuds soon erupted between Christian labor activists loyal primarily to the CDU, those loyal to the Catholic Church, and those loyal to the new, unified trade unions.[1]

---

[1] This development has been analyzed in detail by Wolfgang Schroeder in *Katholizismus und Einheitsgewerkschaft. Der Streit um den DGB und der Niedergang des Sozialkatholizismus in der Bundesrepublik bis 1960* (Bonn, 1992). Schroeder offers an exaggerated conclusion, however, that this feud marked the virtual demise of the Catholic social movement in Germany.

3.1   Konrad Adenauer's "Option for the West"

Adenauer's primary objective as chancellor was to promote economic, political, and military integration with Western democracies to prevent the spread of Communism. His approval ratings plummeted in 1950, however, when he embraced two specific initiatives toward that end: the proposal by French Foreign Minister Robert Schuman to create the European Coal and Steel Community (the kernel of today's European Union) and requests by the US government to contribute to the military defense of Western Europe. SPD leaders argued passionately that Adenauer's policy subordinated the Federal Republic of Germany to the Western powers, antagonized the USSR, and hindered negotiations for national reunification. Adenauer replied that the only hope for reunification was to strengthen the Western alliance and achieve a level of prosperity that would exert a magnetic attraction on impoverished East Germans. The Social Committees' chairman Jakob Kaiser implored Adenauer to seek consensus with the SPD during these debates, and he became the most persistent critic of Adenauer's line within the cabinet and CDU leadership.[2]

Kaiser's skirmishes with the chancellor began with the definition of the responsibilities of his new ministry. During the election campaign Adenauer offered to put Kaiser in charge of a "new Eastern Ministry" whose tasks would include programs to integrate the millions of ethnic German refugees from the East into West German society. In September 1949 he decided to create a separate Ministry of Refugees, however, and announced that Kaiser's ministry would simply educate the West German people about the importance of national reunification and seek to influence public opinion abroad. Kaiser was happy to conduct propaganda for national reunification but hoped to accomplish more. He also rejected the designation "Eastern Ministry" because he regarded the French-occupied Saarland as an important theater in the struggle for national reunification. He persuaded Adenauer to accept the name "Ministry for All-German Affairs" (*Bundesministerium für gesamtdeutsche Fragen*), but its responsibilities were undefined when the cabinet took office. Kaiser's staff developed ambitious plans to influence public opinion at home and abroad, cultivate German patriotism in the Saarland,

---

[2] See Hans-Peter Schwarz, *Adenauer*, 2 vols. (Stuttgart, 1986–1991), I: 617–956, II: 7–105; Rainer Zitelmann, *Adenauers Gegner. Streiter für die Einheit* (Erlangen, 1991); Gordon D. Drummond, *The Social Democrats in Opposition, 1949–1960: The Case Against Rearmament* (Norman, Okla., 1982); Ronald Granieri, *The Ambivalent Alliance: Konrad Adenauer, the CDU/CSU, and the West, 1949–1966* (New York and Oxford, 2003); and Steven Brady, *Eisenhower and Adenauer: Alliance Maintenance under Pressure, 1953–1960* (Lanham, 2010).

send agents into East Germany to collect intelligence, and prevent infiltration by Communist agents. Adenauer avoided any debate over this mission statement but encouraged his finance minister to grant such modest funding that few of these goals could be pursued.[3]

Kaiser consolidated his primary base of support within the CDU when a national organization was founded for the Social Committees of Christian Democratic Workers at a congress in Oberhausen in February 1950. Their statutes invited membership by civil servants as well as blue- and white-collar workers. Their stated goals were to "gather and activate all Christian democratic workers to exert influence on political life according to the principles of the Christian Democratic Union," educate workers about those principles, and "represent workers within the CDU." The leaders of the Social Committees wanted to collect dues from all members, but the Catholic workers' clubs renewed their strenuous objections to that idea and mobilized support among trade union activists who feared that a financially powerful mass organization might serve as the basis to revive separate Christian trade unions. The statutes therefore stated that anyone could become a member by signing a declaration of support and participating in meetings; dues would be collected only from members who gained office in politics, government administration, or the trade unions. Only dues-paying members of the CDU could be elected to office in the Social Committees.[4]

The size of the Social Committees remains very difficult to judge. The Social Committees of the Rhineland, where the movement was strongest, simply counted as members all CDU members who identified themselves as blue- or white-collar workers, a group numbering 29,160 in 1950. The Westphalian Social Committees reported vaguely in late 1949 that the CDU there had about 120,000 members, of whom about 50 percent were workers. In Hesse 5,000 of the 20,000 CDU members were workers, but only about 2,500 participated in meetings of the Social Committees. The CDU of the Rhineland had agreed in 1947 to hire a small network of full-time "social secretaries" to help the Social

---

[3] Erich Kosthorst, *Jakob Kaiser. Bundesminister für gesamtdeutsche Fragen, 1949–1957* (Stuttgart, 1972), pp. 11–12, 81–100; Stefan Creuzberger, *Kampf für die Einheit. Das gesamtdeutsche Ministerium und die politische Kultur des Kalten Krieges 1949–1969* (Düsseldorf, 2008), pp. 41–72.

[4] Johannes Even to Johannes Albers, November 3, 1949 (NL Katzer/617) and November 24, 1949 (NL Even/1); KAB, "Sitzung des geschäftsführenden Verbandsvorstandes," November 21, 1949, KAB Archiv/1/1; Johannes Platte to Heinrich Strunk, November 29, 1949, NL Strunk/2/42; CDA "Satzungsentwurf" adopted on December 20, 1949, NL Katzer/256; printed "Satzung der Sozialausschüsse der CDU," February 1950, NL Dörpinghaus/3 (source of quotations); Schroeder, *Katholizismus und Einheitsgewerkschaft*, pp. 288–291.

Committees organize factory cells, and a few other state parties followed that example, but the network never grew to the point that it could develop reliable membership rolls.[5] The Social Committees soon founded a monthly magazine, *Social Order*, which sold 11,000 copies by 1954, about 5,000 of them to individual subscribers. Of that group, 51 percent lived in North Rhine-Westphalia, 13 percent in Baden-Württemberg, and about 8 percent each in Hesse and the Rhenish Palatinate. This regional pattern resembled that of the old Christian trade unions before 1933. Somewhere around 40,000 workers participated more or less regularly in the meetings of the Social Committees, and their network of factory cells grew to a membership of about 110,000 by 1958.[6]

Kaiser gained a second base of support with the foundation in June 1950 of the "CDU in Exile," an association of Christian Democrats who had fled the Soviet Occupation Zone and resided in West Germany. It attracted a small but distinguished membership of about 300, including Ernst Lemmer and Heinrich Krone. The CDU state chairs all agreed to recognize the CDU in Exile as a state party organization representing Germans under Soviet occupation, and they awarded it a very generous 100 voting delegates at the CDU's first national party congress in October 1950. Adenauer won election there as party chair with 302 votes of 335 cast, but Kaiser won 304 votes as vice chair. The CDU in Exile held periodic conferences thereafter to support Kaiser's line that calculations of expediency must never eclipse the moral imperative to seek national reunification.[7]

The CDU in Exile also included many veterans of the anti-Hitler resistance, who backed Kaiser's line that no former Nazis should play a prominent leadership role in the CDU. Support from it enabled Kaiser to obstruct Adenauer's proposal at the first CDU congress to elect Kurt Georg Kiesinger as the party's executive secretary. Kiesinger had belonged to the NSDAP from 1933 to 1945 and worked during the war

---

[5] "Bericht über die Tagung der Landessozialsekretäre," November 6, 1949, NL Katzer/246; Josef Mick to Dr. Bock, July 24, 1950, NL Katzer/390.

[6] Hans Katzer circular to the Social Committees, April 12, 1954, with attached "Bezieherzahl der *Sozialen Ordnung*," ACDP/04–013/159; Katzer's "Geschäftsbericht" for the "8. Bundestagung der Sozialausschüsse der CDA" in May 1958, *Soziale Ordnung*, XII/#5 (May 1958), p. 75.

[7] Brigitte Kaff, ed., *Die Unionsparteien 1946–1950. Protokolle der Arbeitsgemeinschaft der CDU/CSU Deutschlands und der Konferenzen der Landesvorsitzenden* (Düsseldorf, 1991), meetings of July 31 and September 11, 1950, pp. 716–717, 727; Kosthorst, *Kaiser: Minister*, pp. 162–166; CDU, *Erster Parteitag der Christlich-Demokratischen Union Deutschlands. Goslar, 20.–22 Oktober 1950* (Bonn, no date), pp. 23–25, 110–111; "Beschluss-Protokoll über die Sitzung des legalen Hauptvorstandes der Exil-CDU," December 7, 1950, NL Kaiser/110b/141–45.

in the foreign ministry to conduct propaganda abroad. Kaiser insisted that this record disqualified him. Kiesinger enjoyed vigorous support from the Württemberg CDU and Adenauer, but he weakened his position by supporting a youth league, the First Legion, that Kaiser denounced as "neo-fascist" in a meeting of CDU leaders in December 1950. Evidence soon emerged to support that allegation, and Adenauer distanced himself from Kiesinger in 1951. Kiesinger gained an influential position nevertheless as the CDU Bundestag delegation's chief foreign policy spokesperson and later rose to become chancellor and party chairman despite his past.[8] As we shall see in Chapter 6, Chancellor Kiesinger displayed a marked aversion to his labor minister, Kaiser's son-in-law Hans Katzer.

Adenauer had meanwhile achieved a first success for his pro-Western foreign policy with the Petersberg Accord of November 22, 1949, in which France, Great Britain, and the US recognized the conditional sovereignty of the Federal Republic of Germany. They agreed to make West Germany a full-fledged member of the international control commission to supervise Ruhr heavy industry, but they only promised to curtail, not terminate, their program to demolish German factories that had produced munitions during the war. Kurt Schumacher of the SPD therefore denounced Adenauer in a passionate Bundestag debate on November 24 for sacrificing German interests to those of international capitalism. Adenauer had secured the support of organized labor, however, by promising Hans Böckler that he would appoint a DGB representative as vice chair of the German delegation to the Ruhr Authority. As the Bundestag debate began, the DGB published a declaration supporting the Ruhr Authority, and the SPD's opposition soon collapsed.[9] Böckler

---

[8] Hauptvorstand der Exil-CDU to Adenauer, October 25, 1950, NL Kaiser/110b/160–61; "Aktennotiz" of November 11, 1950, on a discussion of the "Erste Legion" by the Rhenish CDU, NL Kaiser/108/124–25; CDU Bundestag delegation, November 29, 1950, in Helge Heidemeyer, ed., *Die CDU/CSU-Fraktion im Deutschen Bundestag. Sitzungsprotokolle 1949–1953* (Düsseldorf, 1998; hereafter *Fraktionsprotokolle 1949–53*), p. 319; Günter Buchstab, ed., *Adenauer: "Es musste alles neu gemacht werden." Die Protokolle des CDU-Bundesvorstandes 1950–1953*, 2nd edn. (Stuttgart, 1986), meetings of December 5, 1950, and September 6 and October 29, 1951, pp. 11–12, 65–66, 89–92 (hereafter *Vorstandsprotokolle 1950–53*); Kaiser's circular to the Social Committees, December 21, 1950, NL Katzer/238; Die Erste Legion, "Politischer Brief Nr. 4," June 28, 1951, NL Kaiser/114/70–72; Kaiser's speech to the CDU Bundesausschuss, September 22, 1951, NL Kaiser/237/386–91; Kosthorst, *Kaiser: Minister*, pp. 165–167; Schwarz, *Adenauer*, I: 649–651; Günter Buchstab et al., eds., *Kurt Georg Kiesinger 1904–1988. Von Ebingen ins Kanzleramt* (Freiburg, 2005), pp. 201–227, 269–302.

[9] Herbert Blankenhorn, *Verständnis und Verständigung. Blätter eines politischen Tagebuchs 1949 bis 1979* (Frankfurt a.M., 1980), November 21, 1949, pp. 80–81; Böckler to Adenauer, November 21, 1949, in Siegfried Mielke and Peter Rütters, eds., *Gewerkschaften in Politik, Wirtschaft und Gesellschaft, 1945–1949. Quellen zur Geschichte*

faced criticism from SPD headquarters but won the support of union leaders by arguing that "we must always remain on the ground of *Realpolitik*," and "must keep free of any influence from the outside, whether it be from political parties or other organizations." He reminded colleagues that the Free unions had often defended themselves against SPD interference before 1933, and that today's unified labor unions obviously had a greater obligation to do so.[10] In May 1950 Robert Schuman proposed to replace the Ruhr Authority with a "common market" for the French and German coal, iron, and steel industries: the European Coal and Steel Community. Adenauer promptly embraced the Schuman Plan, and the Social Committees agreed that it would yield major economic benefits. Their leaders helped to persuade the DGB to endorse the Schuman Plan in March 1951, despite opposition by the SPD, and the Bundestag ratified this treaty in January 1952.[11]

Adenauer tackled the issue of rearmament after North Korea invaded South Korea in June 1950. He had long believed that West Germany must gain the capacity to defend itself against attack from the East, but public opinion at home and abroad remained hostile to the idea. The Korean War inspired the US government to champion West German rearmament, however, and Jakob Kaiser supported the idea. He was conferring with advisors in Königswinter when the news from Korea arrived; one of them joked nervously that nothing stood between them and the East German border except the Helmstedt volunteer fire brigade. Adenauer sent the Americans a confidential proposal on August 29 to create a heavily armed federal border police as an interim solution, which provoked the resignation of Interior Minister Gustav Heinemann. Kaiser regarded this progressive Protestant as a valuable political ally and sought to mediate between him and Adenauer, but he shared Adenauer's bewilderment when Heinemann argued that the

der deutschen Gewerkschaftsbewegung im 20. Jahrhundert: Band 7, pp. 993–994; CDU Bundestag delegation, November 23, 1949, *Fraktionsprotokolle 1949–53*, pp. 94–95; Granieri, *Ambivalent Alliance*, pp. 31–35; Schwarz, *Adenauer*, I: 671–687.

[10] DGB leadership conferences of December 19, 1949, and January 6 and 24/25, 1950, in Josef Kaiser, ed., *Der Deutsche Gewerkschaftsbund 1949 bis 1956. Quellen zur Geschichte der deutschen Gewerkschaftsbewegung im 20. Jahrhundert: Band XI* (Cologne, 1996; hereafter *Gewerkschaftsquellen*, XI:), pp. 19–22, 29–40 (quotations on 32 and 40).

[11] Blankenhorn, *Tagebuch*, May 8, 1950, pp. 100–101; DGB leadership conferences of March 11/12 and May 7, 1951, *Gewerkschaftsquellen*, XI: 149–153, 177–182; Otto Lenz, *Im Zentrum der Macht. Das Tagebuch von Staatssekretär Lenz 1951–1953*, ed. Klaus Gotto et al. (Düsseldorf, 1988), March 8 and May 30, 1951, pp. 55, 88; Schwarz, *Adenauer*, I: 699–727; Kosthorst, *Kaiser: Minister*, pp. 128–139; Detlev Hüwel, *Karl Arnold. Eine politische Biographie* (Wuppertal, 1980), pp. 268–271; Kurt Kotzbach, *Der Weg zur Staatspartei. Programmatik, praktische Politik und Organisation der deutschen Sozialdemokratie 1945 bis 1965* (Berlin and Bonn, 1982), pp. 194–210.

events of 1918 and 1945 must be understood as God's judgment that the German people should never bear arms again.[12] In September 1950 Kaiser's friend Wilhelm Elfes, the former mayor of Mönchengladbach, also denounced the idea of rearmament. Embittered over his marginalization within the CDU because of his socialist views, Elfes argued that the US was no less imperialistic than the USSR, and that Adenauer only sought to acquire tanks so that he could crush demonstrations by German workers. Kaiser, Johannes Albers, and Karl Arnold rejected these arguments emphatically.[13]

The Social Committees were plunged into the middle of the foreign policy debate in October 1950 when Adenauer appointed Theodor Blank to coordinate preparations to rearm. Blank had fought in the Second World War, attaining the rank of first lieutenant, but he was no expert on military affairs. Adenauer decided nevertheless that this plainspoken vice chair of the miners' union would be the ideal candidate to assure foreign governments and the German people that the new German army would renounce the old spirit of Prussian militarism. Blank gained the peculiar title of "Deputy to the Chancellor for Questions Relating to the Augmentation of Allied Troops," and he secured a large budget for a new "Blank Office." He instructed the civil servants and former officers gathered there to draft plans for an army of "citizens in uniform" that would accept parliamentary oversight and respect the civil rights of soldiers.[14]

In 1951 Adenauer agreed with the US government that the most politically acceptable form of rearmament would be to support a French proposal to create a "European Defense Community" (EDC) to develop an integrated European army. Blank led the German delegation in talks

---

[12] CDU Bundestag delegation, September 6, 1950, *Fraktionsprotokolle 1949–53*, p. 301; Kosthorst, *Kaiser: Minister*, pp. 142–143; Granieri, *Ambivalent Alliance*, pp. 48–53; David Clay Large, *Germans to the Front: West German Rearmament in the Adenauer Era* (Chapel Hill, 1996), pp. 35–55, 64–70; Norbert Wiggershaus, "Die Entscheidung für einen westdeutschen Verteidigungsbeitrag 1950," in *Anfänge westdeutscher Sicherheitspolitik 1945–1956*, ed. Militärgeschichtliches Forschungsamt, 4 vols. (Munich, 1982–1997), I: 325–402.

[13] Wilhelm Elfes, "Totengedenkfeier," speech of September 10, 1950, NL Elfes/81/72–79; Elfes' letters from September-October 1950 to Karl Arnold, Carl Severing, and others in NL Elfes/4/13–32; Kosthorst, *Kaiser: Minister*, pp. 142–155; Albert Esser, *Wilhelm Elfes, 1884–1969. Arbeiterführer und Politiker* (Mainz, 1990), pp. 189–202; Herlind Gundelach, "Die Sozialausschüsse zwischen CDU und DGB. Selbstverständnis und Rolle 1949–1966," phil. diss. (Bonn, 1983), pp. 141–142; Karl Arnold, "Arbeiterschaft und europäische Neuordnung," in *Essener Kongress 1950 der christlich-demokratischen Arbeitnehmerschaft: Christlich, Deutsch, Demokratisch, Sozial, Europäisch* (Bonn, no date; found in NL Katzer/631), pp. 65–73.

[14] Large, *Germans*, pp. 111–113; Hans-Jürgen Rautenberg, "Zur Standortbestimmung für künftige deutsche Streitkräfte," in *Anfänge westdeutscher Sicherheitspolitik*, I: 777–788; Dieter Krüger, *Das Amt Blank. Die schwierige Gründung des Bundesministeriums für Verteidigung* (Freiburg, 1993), pp. 29–36, 51–57.

that yielded an EDC treaty in May 1952, but the French government hesitated to seek parliamentary ratification in the face of sharp attacks from both French rightists and Communists (opposition which proved so tenacious that the whole project collapsed in 1954).[15] Kaiser appealed to Adenauer to involve SPD leaders in the EDC negotiations, but Adenauer replied that they were completely unreasonable. Blank followed Kaiser's advice, however, by conferring repeatedly with Social Democrats to seek forms of parliamentary oversight and screening procedures for officer candidates acceptable to them. Blank told reporters that the debate with the SPD over *whether* to rearm must not be aggravated by a debate over *how* to rearm.[16] A passionate debate over rearmament continued for several years, but Blank's approach helped to achieve acceptance of the new *Bundeswehr* by the SPD in the late 1950s.

The Basic Law made no provision for plebiscites, but the Christian pacifists Gustav Heinemann, Wilhelm Elfes, and Martin Niemöller soon allied with the German Communist Party to demand a popular referendum on rearmament, because Adenauer had not raised this issue during the Bundestag election campaign. In April 1951 Elfes addressed a peace rally organized by Communists, and in July he argued in an open letter to Adenauer that "the result of armament will be war." His CDU party local in Mönchengladbach promptly expelled him, and he was shunned by the KAB and other Catholic organizations. Protestant pacifists enjoyed some support even at the highest ranks in the Evangelical Church, but Pius XII and the Catholic bishops championed rearmament to prevent the spread of communism.[17]

Anger over French policy in the Saarland created powerful allies for Kaiser in his debates with Adenauer. Adenauer sought to persuade his cabinet and CDU leaders that Saarlanders did not care about national reunification, because their connection with France improved their standard of living. He also insisted that disputes over the Saarland must not delay the great work of European integration. Kaiser maintained that most Saarlanders yearned for

---

[15] Large, *Germans*, pp. 118–135; Krüger, *Amt Blank*, pp. 36–48.

[16] Otto Lenz, *Tagebuch*, January–February 1952, pp. 208, 224–229, 259, 266; Heinrich Krone, *Tagebücher*, ed. Hans-Otto Kleinmann, 2 vols. (Düsseldorf, 1995–2003), January 27, 1952, I: 97; "Theo Blank: Der härteste Schädel in Bonn," *Der Spiegel*, VI/#50 (December 10, 1952), pp. 6–13; Rautenberg, "Standortsbestimmung," in *Anfänge westdeutscher Sicherheitspolitik*, I: 788–863.

[17] Elfes to Adenauer, July 8, 1951, NL Elfes/39/11–16; Elfes to Joseph Joos, October 5, 1951, and reply of October 12, NL Elfes/39/102–03; Elfes to Hejo Schmitt, November 5, 1951, NL Elfes/2/98; Esser, *Wilhelm Elfes*, pp. 200–205; Alice Holmes Cooper, "The West German Peace Movement and the Christian Churches: An Institutional Approach," *Review of Politics*, 50 (1988): 171–185; Peter Kent, *The Lonely Cold War of Pope Pius XII: The Roman Catholic Church and the Division of Europe, 1943–1950* (Montreal, 2002).

reunion with Germany, and many party and cabinet colleagues shared his indignation over the strict ban by the French authorities of any newspaper or party that favored reunion. In March 1952 Adenauer acknowledged to the cabinet that the French had brutally expelled several thousand German patriots from the Saarland; many leaders of the CDU and FDP agreed with Kaiser that such actions revealed a refusal by France to accept Germany as an equal partner.[18] That summer, Kaiser persuaded Adenauer to confer with leaders of the pro-German parties in the Saarland, sister parties of the CDU and SPD that were not legally recognized. Kaiser also persuaded the chancellor to authorize a Bundestag debate over civil liberties in the Saarland, and to confer with Social Democrats to find a common approach. Adenauer assured CDU leaders on November 20 that his goal in future talks with France would be "to achieve the ability of the Saar populace to express their will freely." Kaiser expressed relief that he had been mistaken to think that "the chancellor wanted to sacrifice the Saarland on the altar of Europe." Adenauer shot back that if it ever did become necessary to choose between "creating Europe or allowing Europe to fail for the sake of the Saarland, then his choice could not be in doubt." Kaiser had nevertheless achieved a significant course correction in Adenauer's foreign policy.[19]

The rearmament treaties cleared a first parliamentary hurdle on December 5, 1952, after a raucous debate in the Bundestag. When Robert Tillmanns of the Berlin CDU defended them, the Social Democrats yelled, "He's one of the bridge builders!" They thus recalled Kaiser's idealistic slogans from 1946, when he sought an understanding with the Soviet Union. Tillmanns replied that at least he had never merged with the Communist Party, like so many Social Democrats in the Soviet Zone. Watching in the gallery, Adenauer's chief of staff Otto Lenz feared that the Social Democrats would assault Tillmanns physically. "But then the full moon of Kaiser [his shaved skull] hurled itself into the stormy sea and parted the combatants with soothing gestures, ... and calm gradually returned. The chancellor found this episode richly amusing." Kaiser warned Adenauer after this debate that "we have a fragmented people and a fragmented parliament." Adenauer agreed to receive Erich

---

[18] Adenauer's remarks to the cabinet on March 25, 1952, Point F, and cabinet minutes of March 28, Point C, and April 1, Points B.a. and B.e., Bundesarchiv, *Kabinettsprotokolle Online 1952*; Kosthorst, *Kaiser: Minister*, pp. 117–123.

[19] Bundesarchiv, *Kabinettsprotokolle Online 1952*, meetings of September 3, 1952, Points 1.b and 1.c, September 26, Point C, October 10, Point C, October 21, Point A, and November 5, 1952, Point A; Otto Lenz, *Tagebuch*, September 3, November 20, and December 2, 1952, pp. 425, 473 (source of quotations), 485; Schwarz, *Adenauer*, II: 21–36; Drummond, *Social Democracy*, pp. 83–99.

Ollenhauer, the new SPD chair who had succeeded the recently deceased Schumacher, for a private meeting to improve the atmosphere.[20]

Otto Lenz was a former friend of Kaiser from the Berlin CDU but felt that he had become completely unrealistic. He asked Adenauer several times in 1952 whether Kaiser should not be dismissed from the cabinet for insubordination, and in moments of exasperation, the chancellor sometimes agreed. Lenz noted at year's end, however, that Adenauer had "sentimental inhibitions" regarding Kaiser.[21] Adenauer doubtless sensed that Kaiser's arguments enjoyed great resonance; indeed, Kaiser's criticisms helped Adenauer to shape and explain his foreign policy in a way that could rally popular support. The foreign policy debate diverted the attention of the leaders of the Social Committees, however, from the issues of social and economic policy that were of primary concern to Christian Democratic workers. Because of a distracted leadership, the Social Committees were slow to develop sound procedures to achieve their core mission, to ascertain and explain to CDU leaders the wishes of their blue-collar constituents.

3.2   Christianity and the Search for Consensus over Co-Determination

Christian Democratic workers and their clerical allies felt obliged in light of Catholic social theory and Protestant social ethics to promote worker participation in management decisions, a concept Germans call *Mitbestimmung*, or "co-determination." The Weimar Republic had introduced co-determination in a weak form with the Factory Councils Law of 1920, which required management to consult with elected factory councils and authorized those councils to name two members of the supervisory board of large joint-stock corporations, the *Aufsichtsrat*, which had only represented shareholders and creditors in the past. The socialist Free unions campaigned in the 1920s to strengthen the factory councils with the slogan of "economic democracy," and the Christian unions, with the slogan of "social partnership." They both argued that German workers took a lively interest in the success of their firms, and that productivity rose when workers learned more about the firm's problems and shared their practical experience with management.[22] These arguments laid

---

[20] Otto Lenz, *Tagebuch*, December 5 and 10, 1952, pp. 490–491, 496.

[21] Otto Lenz, *Tagebuch*, June 23, July 14, August 18, and December 3, 1952, pp. 372, 392, 412, 485.

[22] See William L. Patch, *Christian Trade Unions in the Weimar Republic, 1918–1933* (New Haven, 1985), pp. 54–57, 126, 146–148; Nathan Reich, *The Organization of Industrial Relations in the Weimar Republic* (New York, 1938); and Hans-Otto Hemmer,

the foundation for the German model of labor relations that emerged in the 1950s.

Elected factory councils emerged spontaneously in most German cities in spring 1945 and sometimes exerted great influence. In April 1946 all four occupation powers agreed, however, to promulgate a Factory Councils Law that reduced them to a purely advisory role. Only in the Ruhr steel industry was a strong form of co-determination implemented, after the British military authorities sequestered the ownership shares of the industrialists, who were then viewed as Hitler's accomplices. When the British Labour Government decreed in November 1946 that the United Steelworks trust must be dissolved, it consulted the German metalworkers' union about the organization of the successor firms but not the former shareholders. The new steel corporations therefore adopted the unions' ideal of parity co-determination, with supervisory boards comprised of five representatives elected by the workers and five by the shareholders (whose votes were cast for now by British-appointed stewards), plus a "neutral" eleventh member named by the British. The metalworkers' union could name two of the five workers' representatives, and the factory council the other three. The top echelon of corporate management also included a labor director who was hired by the workers' representatives to be in charge of personnel matters. The DGB celebrated these steel firms as Germany's first true example of "economic democracy" and hoped to apply this model to all large corporations.[23]

The German business associations rejected parity co-determination with the following arguments:
1) That the survival of free enterprise required the election of the entire supervisory board by the annual shareholders' meeting;
2) That whatever voice workers gained in management decisions should only involve social issues regarding the dining hall and other amenities, not personnel issues that involved hiring and firing, and certainly not the core economic decisions by management; and

---

"Betriebsrätegesetz und Betriebsrätepraxis in der Weimarer Republik," in Ulrich Borsdorf et al., eds., *Gewerkschaftliche Politik: Reform aus Solidarität* (Cologne, 1977), pp. 241–269.

[23] Gabrielle Müller-List, ed., *Montanmitbestimmung. Das Gesetz über die Mitbestimmung der Arbeitnehmer in den Aufsichtsräten und Vorständen der Unternehmen des Bergbaus und der Eisen und Stahl erzeugenden Industrie vom 21. Mai 1951* (Düsseldorf, 1984; hereafter *Quellen: Montanmitbestimmung*), pp. XXX–XLIII; Horst Thum, *Mitbestimmung in der Montanindustrie. Der Mythos vom Sieg der Gewerkschaften* (Stuttgart, 1982), pp. 18–36; Isabel Warner, *Steel and Sovereignty: The Deconcentration of the West German Steel Industry, 1949–54* (Mainz, 1996), pp. 5–9; Karl Lauschke, *Die halbe Macht. Mitbestimmung in der Eisen- und Stahlindustrie 1945 bis 1989* (Essen, 2007), pp. 17–36.

3) That whatever voice workers gained must be exercised only by employees of the firm, and never by "outsiders" appointed by the trade unions.

In September 1949 the leaders of the FDP and German Party advanced all these arguments in their coalition talks with Adenauer, but he replied cautiously that the CDU was bound only by the Ahlen Program of February 1947, which promised workers "the representation they deserve" on corporate supervisory boards.[24]

Within the CDU influential businessmen supported the FDP's position, including Adenauer's close friend, the Cologne banker Robert Pferdmenges, and the steel industrialist Günter Henle. They had played a key role as fundraisers in the first Bundestag election campaign, and they and Economics Minister Ludwig Erhard rejected parity co-determination as incompatible with free markets.[25] Nevertheless, Jakob Kaiser endorsed the DGB's call to "democratize the economy" at a rally of the Social Committees on October 9, 1949, and the meeting resolved that "in corporate supervisory boards, parity representation of labor and capital must be secured in an appropriate form, because they are equally important factors in economic life." Johannes Albers then introduced a Bundestag resolution calling on the government to introduce a co-determination bill promptly, which passed with the support of the CDU and SPD on November 4.[26]

The idea of co-determination enjoyed great sympathy from both the Catholic and Protestant clergy. The Evangelical pastors with the strongest interest in social issues, such as Eberhard Müller and Johannes Lilje, believed that hostility to organized labor had been a great failing of the Evangelical churches in the past, and many of them sought détente with the SPD after 1945. They modestly denied possessing any Christian "social theory" such as that outlined in papal encyclicals, but they sought

---

[24] Jonathan Wiesen, *West German Industry and the Challenge of the Nazi Past, 1945–1955* (Chapel Hill, 2001), pp. 156–159, 180–188; Heinrich Hellwege to Adenauer, September 14, 1949, reply of the same day, and Gustav Heinemann's account of his discussion with Adenauer on September 15, in Udo Wengst, ed., *Auftakt zur Ära Adenauer. Koalitionsverhandlungen und Regierungsbildung 1949* (Düsseldorf, 1985), pp. 407–410, 420.

[25] Frank Bösch, *Die Adenauer-CDU. Gründung, Aufstieg und Krise einer Erfolgspartei 1945–1969* (Stuttgart, 2001), pp. 195–235; A.J. Nicholls, *Freedom with Responsibility: The Social Market Economy in Germany, 1918–1963* (Oxford, 1994), pp. 144, 338–340.

[26] Jakob Kaiser, "Unterlagen für die Rede am 9. Oktober 1949," NL Kaiser/248/93–107; "Bericht über die Tagung der Sozialausschüsse," October 9/10, 1949, NL Katzer/257; resolution quoted from the CDA "Informationsdienst," Nr. 5, October 17, 1949, LANRW/CDA Rheinland/911; Albers' speech of October 23, 1949, NL Katzer/315; CDU Bundestag delegation, October 19, 1949, *Fraktionsprotokolle 1949–53*, p. 37; excerpts from the Bundestag debate of November 4, *Quellen: Montanmitbestimmung*, pp. 3–5.

to promote respect for "social ethics," i.e. to guarantee that human beings would be treated as ends in themselves in economic life, never as a means to an end. Müller pursued this goal by founding the Evangelical Academy at Bad Boll in Württemberg in 1945, and Lilje founded a similar academy at Hermannsburg after he won election as the Evangelical bishop of Hanover. There he assembled eighty influential industrialists and DGB leaders to discuss co-determination on October 21–23, 1949. Pastor Johannes Doehring opened the conference by declaring that "the roots of human respect and responsibility must not lie in the garden cultivated on the weekend; instead, they must be planted at the workplace. Factory management and the factory council must see to it that human dignity is secured inside the factory, not just outside it." No breakthroughs were achieved in the subsequent debate, but each side acknowledged that the other had offered valuable suggestions.[27]

Soon after he was elevated to the rank of cardinal in February 1946, Archbishop Josef Frings of Cologne launched a more sustained effort to promote consensus among Catholics: the Social Discussion Circle was chaired by Hermann-Josef Schmitt of the KAB and brought leaders of the Catholic workers' clubs together with Catholic businessmen and scholars. The Jesuit social theorist Oswald von Nell-Breuning addressed the Circle's first meeting. He and Schmitt sought to persuade the group that papal encyclicals endorsed a powerful voice for workers in management, and that satisfying the trade unions' demand for co-determination would encourage them to drop harmful demands to nationalize industry. The Circle soon agreed that workers must be "a responsible element" in management and should elect some members of all corporate supervisory boards. When it met again in March 1948, Schmitt argued that workers deserved a voice not only in social and personnel issues but also "economic" decisions, including the hiring of senior managers. He agreed with employers, however, that all workers' representatives should be employees of the firm.[28]

Hoping to achieve something dramatic for workers, the KAB secured great influence over planning for the most important event in Catholic life controlled by the laity, the annual Congress of German Catholics that

[27] See "Hermannsburger Gespräche," minutes of the conference in NL Katzer/223, quotation on p. 4, and Martin Möller, *Evangelische Kirche und Sozialdemokratische Partei in den Jahren 1945–1950. Grundlagen der Verständigung und Beginn des Dialoges* (Göttingen, 1984), pp. 172–187.

[28] Summary of the discussion of June 20, 1946, and Schmitt's memorandum of April 8, 1948, "Zur Frage des Mitbestimmungsrechtes," HAEK/NL Hermann-Josef Schmitt/118; Norbert Trippen, *Josef Kardinal Frings (1887–1978)*, 2 vols. (Paderborn, 2003–2005), I: 397–400.

convened in Bochum on August 31, 1949, under the motto "Justice Creates Peace." The congress attracted around half a million participants, and the uniformed ranks of the Catholic workers' clubs dominated the opening and closing ceremonies.[29] The KAB arranged for DGB Vice Chair Matthias Föcher to address the congress, which culminated with a debate over co-determination between him and the industrialist Franz Greiss. Greiss argued that only shareholders and senior managers were qualified to decide personnel and economic questions. Föcher replied that political democracy could not endure without economic democracy, which must apply to basic economic decisions by management. To the surprise of most journalists, the congress sided with Föcher unambiguously in the following resolution:

The human being stands in the middle of every macro- and micro-economic discussion. The right of co-determination in social, personnel, and economic questions for all employees is recognized. The right of co-determination is a natural right in the order willed by God and is to be affirmed like the right to property.[30]

The DGB distributed this Bochum Resolution to all union locals, and Hans Böckler quoted extensively from papal encyclicals at the founding congress of the national DGB soon thereafter. Hermann-Josef Schmitt found Böckler's speech thrilling and termed his endorsement of the Bochum Resolution "a success for which we never dared to hope."[31]

The Bochum Resolution provoked an outcry in the business press, however, and several Catholic bishops distanced themselves from it. Nell-Breuning explained to Schmitt that it had been a blunder to describe co-determination as a universal "natural right," because conditions in Latin America and elsewhere differed greatly from those in Germany. The strongest claim that the Vatican might accept was that German workers had achieved such a level of education and self-restraint that co-determination would promote the "common good" at this stage in German historical development. The bishops of western Germany criticized the Bochum Resolution sternly when they met

[29] KAB, "Protokoll über die Sitzung des gführ. Verbandsvorstandes," June 29, 1949, KAB Archiv/1/1; Zentralkomitee der Deutschen Katholikentage, *Gerechtigkeit schafft Frieden. Der 73. Deutsche Katholikentag vom 31. August bis 4. September 1949 in Bochum* (Paderborn, 1949), pp. 11–14, 58–68, 90–97.

[30] *Katholikentag 1949*, pp. 193–205, 213; Thomas Grossmann, *Zwischen Kirche und Gesellschaft. Das Zentralkomitee der deutschen Katholiken 1945–1970* (Mainz, 1991), pp. 238–250.

[31] DGB circular of September 16, 1949, NL Kaiser/9/27; DGB, *Protokoll: Gründungskongress des Deutschen Gewerkschaftsbundes. München, 12.-14. Oktober 1949* (Cologne, 1950), pp. 198–203; "DGB greift Bochumer Beschlüsse auf," *Ketteler-Wacht*, October 15, 1949; Schmitt to Bernhard Michalke, October 11, 1949 (source of quotation), KAB Archiv/5/2.

in November, and thereafter the KAB denounced any role for the trade unions in co-determination, seeking to differentiate its position from that of the SPD.[32]

Most Catholic workers regarded co-determination as their "right" nevertheless, and Schmitt drafted a program endorsing this right for adoption at a KAB congress in July 1950. He and Even traveled to Rome in late May to seek Vatican approval. There the senior Vatican advisor Gustav Gundlach raised several objections to their program, but they were received cordially by Pius XII and left Rome content. They were sickened to learn upon arriving home that Pius XII had just delivered an address condemning the demand for co-determination in "economic" questions as a violation of the natural right to property. Press reports that the KAB had been disavowed impelled Cardinal Frings and Adenauer to cancel their promised speeches at the KAB Congress, and Jakob Kaiser rejected an appeal to step in as the government representative. The KAB suffered humiliation when no bishop, cabinet minister, or CDU leader attended its congress.[33]

Labor Minister Storch had meanwhile persuaded the cabinet not to draft a co-determination bill until the DGB and business leaders could seek agreement. He favored, in other words, a pragmatic corporatist approach like that sought by Chancellor Brüning in the year 1930. Walter Raymond, the president of the National League of Employers' Associations, had visited Hans Böckler on November 15, 1949, and they agreed to seek consensus before this complex issue became subject to unpredictable parliamentary debates. Böckler assured Raymond that "the highest goal in all our joint efforts is to increase production. The right of co-determination can therefore never be implemented in a form that reduces production."[34] Serious negotiations began on March 30, 1950, when the DGB demanded equal representation for workers and shareholders in all corporate supervisory boards, with the workers' representatives to be chosen jointly by the factory council and trade unions.

---

[32] Nell-Breuning to Schmitt, November 2, 1949, KAB Archiv/5/8; William L. Patch, "The Legend of Compulsory Unification: The Catholic Clergy and the Revival of Trade Unionism in West Germany after the Second World War," *Journal of Modern History*, 79 (2007): 848–880 (esp. 856–859).

[33] Reports to Nell-Breuning by Schmitt on May 25, 1950, KAB Archiv/5/45, and Johannes Even on July 11, KAB Archiv/3/20; Patch, "Compulsory Unification," pp. 859–861; Pius XII, "Address to the Catholic International Congress for Social Study," June 3, 1950, *Catholic Mind*, August 1950, pp. 507–510.

[34] Storch to Föcher, November 9, 1949, and Raymond's memorandum on his conversation with Böckler, *Quellen: Montanmitbestimmung*, pp. 6–7; cabinet minutes of November 29, 1949, Point 1, Bundesarchiv, *Kabinettsprotokolle Online 1949*. For the negotiations between management and labor in 1930, see pp. 22–26 of this volume.

Business leaders replied that they could never grant more than one-third of the seats to workers, who must be chosen solely by the factory council. Raymond wrote Adenauer after this meeting that the DGB's demand to control delegations in every corporate board would create "an instrument with whose help the whole economy can be influenced from a central agency. In no democratic system has there ever been such a concentration of power as the trade unions here demand with their slogan of 'economic democracy.'"[35]

When the leaders of management and labor met again on May 24, Adenauer opened the proceedings with a lecture on the deterioration of East–West relations. "It is necessary in view of this situation," the chancellor concluded, "that social peace be maintained in Germany." He then left Storch to conduct the negotiations, and the DGB offered a concession by agreeing that at least one-half of the workers' representatives on corporate boards must be employees of the firm. Employers offered no concession in return, however, and in mid-June an exasperated Böckler told DGB leaders that they must prepare for protest strikes to achieve parity.[36] Storch pursued agreement in three more rounds of talks, and on July 5 the DGB restricted its demand for parity to firms with more than 1,000 employees. The employers' representatives rejected parity for firms of any size, however, arguing that this was the only logical conclusion from Chancellor Adenauer's appeals "to build an ideological dike for the protection of the Western cultural world against the East." DGB leaders then informed Storch that further negotiations were pointless.[37] On July 15 Böckler told DGB leaders that "the trade unions can no longer abandon the demand for parity . . . because it has been presented to all our congresses, conferences, and rallies as the unconditional demand of the trade unions." When the larger DGB national committee assembled three days later, an overwhelming majority resolved that "only a genuine renovation of the economy through responsible co-determination" could preserve social peace, and that the DGB must "employ trade union methods of struggle."[38] This resolution created the potential for a dramatic confrontation with the government.

As this confrontation loomed, tensions mounted between the leaders of the Social Committees and their allies in the DGB and Catholic

---

[35] See the employers' memorandum of March 30, the two sets of minutes, and Raymond to Adenauer, April 4, 1950, *Quellen: Montanmitbestimmung*, pp. 33–52.

[36] Minutes of May 24 and June 2, 1950, *Quellen: Montanmitbestimmung*, pp. 63–75, 78–89; DGB Bundesvorstand, June 13, 1950, *Gewerkschaftsquellen*, XI: 62–64.

[37] *Quellen: Montanmitbestimmung*, pp. 112–129 (quotation on 126).

[38] DGB leadership conferences of July 15, 1950, *Quellen: Montanmitbestimmung*, pp. 134–135, and July 18/19, *Gewerkschaftsquellen*, XI: 74–75.

workers' clubs. Theodor Blank denounced DGB leaders to their faces in September 1950 for propagating the "dogma" of the planned economy, but several veterans of the Christian trade unions repudiated Blank's remarks.[39] Matthias Föcher concluded from Blank's outburst that influential elements in the CDU planned to revive separate Christian trade unions, and he wrote all DGB-affiliated unions to request the names and addresses of all veterans of the old Christian unions now employed by them. He and Böckler had decided, Föcher explained, to organize counterdemonstrations whenever the Social Committees criticized the DGB.[40] Föcher employed this tactic to steal the thunder of a congress of the Social Committees held in Essen on November 18; four days earlier he had assembled 250 veterans of the Christian trade unions to denounce anyone who attempted to split the DGB. Journalists found this proliferation of Christian social conferences bewildering, and the congress of the Social Committees attracted little publicity.[41] The KAB had meanwhile come to oppose efforts by the Social Committees, Karl Arnold, and his cabinet colleague Johannes Ernst to revive a Great Coalition government with the SPD in North Rhine-Westphalia. The trade unionist Ernst in particular sought to promote cooperation with the SPD as the new state labor minister, and Arnold formed a provisional coalition with the small Center Party to pursue that goal. Because the SPD opposed confessional schools, however, the KAB agreed with Adenauer that Arnold should form an anti-socialist coalition with the Free Democrats instead. In October 1950 Johannes Even publicly denounced Arnold's tactics, declaring that the prime minister was now opposed by large segments of the CDU. Arnold's friends concluded that the KAB sought to replace him with one of its leaders.[42] By autumn 1950 a great many veterans of the old Christian labor movement felt compelled to decide whether their primary loyalty was to the CDU, the DGB, or the Catholic Church, and to attack former comrades who made a different choice.

---

[39] DGB Bundesausschuss, September 26/27, 1950, *Gewerkschaftsquellen*, XI: 112–114.

[40] See Föcher's circulars of September 30 and October 17, 1950, NL Braukmann/9.

[41] Föcher's speech of November 14, 1950, NL Föcher/2; "Konferenz der ehemaligen christlichen Gewerkschaftler innerhalb des Deutschen Gewerkschaftsbundes" on November 14, 1950, NL Katzer/806; Josef Arndgen to Matthias Föscher (sic!), November 16, 1950, NL Katzer/806; Storch to Kaiser, December 20, 1950, NL Kaiser/41/360.

[42] Circular by Albers, Hillenkötter, and Mick to the Social Committees, July 10, 1950, NL Katzer/245; Johannes Even, "Eine misslungene Regierungsbildung," *Ketteler-Wacht*, #20, October 15, 1950, p. 2; Johannes Platte to Even, October 25 and November 4, 1950, and replies of November 3 and 23, KAB Archiv/3/20; Hüwel, *Karl Arnold*, pp. 159–165, 224–235.

3.3 Adenauer, the DGB, and the Co-Determination Laws of 1951 and 1952

After months of uncertainty about co-determination, Ludwig Erhard provoked a decisive confrontation on November 20, 1950, when he suggested in a public speech that the government might abolish the existing system of parity in the Ruhr steel industry. Outraged DGB leaders met the next day and authorized the metalworkers' union to strike, but they also agreed not to oppose rearmament. The metalworkers soon voted to strike if the government did not promise before February 1, 1951, to anchor in German law the steelworkers' existing rights under Allied occupation statutes, and the miners' union soon resolved to strike if coal miners did not receive the same rights. Adenauer still needed the DGB's support for rearmament, so he promptly intervened. Businessmen expected him to refuse to negotiate under threat, but he arranged a cordial private meeting with Hans Böckler on January 11, 1951, and agreed to preside over negotiations between management and labor to secure parity co-determination in coal and steel.[43]

Adenauer ignored this issue for the moment, but Christian social activists sought anxiously to persuade labor leaders that "political strikes" were immoral and dangerous. Shortly before meeting Adenauer, Böckler received a delegation of Catholic and Protestant church representatives led by Johannes Even, Nell-Breuning, and Pastor Eberhard Müller. Müller explained that "strikes to manipulate parliamentary resolutions" offended the Christian conscience because of "the upheavals associated with them and the challenge to the fundamental political order." Böckler replied that only progress toward social justice could prevent the spread of communism, but the government had remained passive for a year.

We want at long last [Böckler declared] to have equal political and economic rights and cannot simply defer to accidental parliamentary majorities. How did this majority come into being? Does it promote the common good, or does it also represent people who avoided losses through hoarding and black marketeering and even today issue false manifestoes for whole shiploads of goods? ... Bolshevism can only be opposed constructively, not with police methods. We do not want class rule, neither by the employers nor by the trade unions. We want shared rule, in which capital will always retain the leading role because of its traditions and intellect.

This largely unknown speech offered a powerful summation of Böckler's vision of social reform near the end of his life. Josef Gockeln of the KAB

---

[43] *Quellen: Montanmitbestimmung*, pp. LI–LVII, 161–162, 169–170, 176, 185–186, 188, 193, 197, 218–228; DGB Bundesvorstand, November 21, 1950, *Gewerkschaftsquellen*, XI: 121–129.

replied that "the strike slogan conflicts with the prerogatives and dignity of parliament" and "would offend the conscience of Christians of both denominations." Böckler then agreed that it would be best if Adenauer's mediation could prevent a strike.[44]

Böckler pondered this discussion carefully and reported to DGB colleagues on the clergy's concern "that state authority must not be endangered" if protest strikes took place.[45] Nell-Breuning also pondered this discussion and wrote Böckler six days later that workers had every right "to defend with tooth and claw" the rights they had won in the new steel corporations. Nell-Breuning hoped nevertheless that Böckler did not intend to argue as a general rule that the trade unions "hold it to be compatible with the democratic order to employ forcible means ... to exert pressure on the legislative body formed through democratic elections or the government elected by that body, so that it will bow to the will of one group." Christians believed, Nell-Breuning concluded, that an injustice should be suffered, if resistance would disrupt public order. Nell-Breuning later heard that Böckler found this letter valuable and discussed it with DGB colleagues. When the letter was shown to Cardinal Frings, however, he reproached Nell-Breuning for offering "too many concessions" to the DGB. Böckler died soon thereafter, and Nell-Breuning wrote Hermann-Josef Schmitt that the Social Democratic labor leader had understood his moral reasoning better than the cardinal.[46]

The leaders of the Social Committees were outraged by the DGB's threat of "political strikes." Jakob Kaiser and the workers' representatives in the CDU Bundestag delegation reproached IG Metall on January 6 for "bringing our young democracy into the most extreme danger ... To pressure the legislature with the threat to strike is a breach of the constitution. Such a strike must be considered a revolutionary act." This rhetoric was overblown, because neither the Basic Law nor any statute restricted the right to strike.[47] On January 8 the DGB accused the Social Committees of plotting to split the unions, and

---

[44] Minutes of the meeting on January 6, 1951, in the confidential newsletter, "Information der Wirtschaftsgilde: Sozialer Sachbericht Nr. 21," January 10, 1951, KAB Archiv/5/7.

[45] DGB executive committee, January 8, 1951, *Quellen: Montanmitbestimmung*, pp. 199–200.

[46] Nell-Breuning to Böckler, January 12, 1951, and Nell-Breuning to Hejo Schmitt, January 31 and April 25, 1951, KAB Archiv/5/45.

[47] CDA circular by Josef Bock, January 8, 1951, NL Katzer/238; DGB press release of November 30, 1950, NL Hansen/23. For the debate among the legal experts, see *Quellen: Montanmitbestimmung*, LVI–LVII, and the vague legal opinion by Professor Rolf Dietz for the employers' associations of January 10, 1951, which termed the DGB's action illegal because it was "a flagrant violation of good morals" (KAB Archiv/5/45).

Föcher arranged for a declaration by forty-five veterans of the Christian unions that the Social Committees had no right to speak for Christian social members of the DGB. Karl Arnold also distanced himself from Kaiser by telling DGB leaders "that I will do everything to influence the negotiations in a manner favorable to you."[48] The leaders of the Social Committees met soon thereafter, and Arnold reported accurately that trade unionists simply feared the loss of existing rights. Kaiser and Albers insisted, however, that DGB leaders were causing trouble on orders from the SPD. Kaiser then reported to Otto Lenz that most leaders of the Social Committees favored a rupture with the DGB, and that "he is very much against the DGB and wants to revive the old Christian trade unions." Lenz felt that Kaiser was distraught, however, and did not truly mean what he said.[49] For the moment Kaiser had lost touch with his blue-collar constituents.

Veterans of the Christian trade unions in the DGB could not understand why the Social Committees opposed the campaign for parity co-determination. They complained that the politicians in the Social Committees had frozen union colleagues out of their leadership conferences and defended capitalist interests, because they relied on the CDU for funding. Johannes Platte and Josef Berntzen resigned in protest from the Social Committees, although not from the CDU. Bernhard Tacke, the vice chair of the textile workers' union, complained to Kaiser's aide Josef Bock that "the greatest worry" at all recent conferences of the Social Committees "was always that the trade unions might gain too much power ... You are well on your way to destroying all the painstaking work of our colleagues in the unions." The Oberhausen Bundestag delegate and KAB functionary Martin Heix reproached the leaders of both the Social Committees and KAB.

We have been defeated by our own leaders. They have inflicted the most severe damage on us through their selfishness and lack of leadership qualities. Their obsession with office and desire for personal gain have made them incapable of seeing beyond themselves .... The whole great tradition of the Christian labor movement, which has achieved glorious things for decades, has been squandered

---

[48] DGB leadership conference, January 8, 1951, *Quellen: Montanmitbestimmung*, p. 200; Föcher to Albers, January 9, 1951, and "'Befremdend.' Gewerkschaftler gegen die Sozialausschüsse," *Frankfurter Allgemeine Zeitung*, January 10, 1951 (NL Katzer/580); DGB Bundesausschuss, January 12, 1951, *Gewerkschaftsquellen*, XI: 136 (source of quotation).

[49] "Kurzer Bericht über die Sitzung des Hauptvorstandes," January 13, 1951, NL Katzer/255; Josef Bock circular of January 16, 1951, and press release of January 13, 1951, NL Katzer/238; Otto Lenz, *Tagebuch*, January 15–18, 1951, pp. 1, 8.

by a few people in a few weeks. What a tragedy! We are now combating ourselves and whipping up our friends in the countryside and the factories against each other.[50]

Heix exaggerated, but he identified a real danger that high government officials might forget the concerns of their constituents. Kaiser placed the question, "What are Christian workers thinking?" on the agenda for the Social Committees' leadership conference of June 1, 1951, and his young colleague Josef Mick, who led the team of CDU "social secretaries" for the Rhineland, conducted actual research to prepare for the discussion. Mick kept silent, however, when it became clear that his senior colleagues only wanted to discuss the question, "What should Christian workers be thinking?"[51]

Adenauer maneuvered with great energy and skill in late January 1951 to hammer out an accord between the leaders of management and labor in coal and steel. They agreed to give each side five seats on corporate supervisory boards, with a representative of capital as chair, and to give the workers' representatives control over the appointment of a labor director at the top echelon of corporate management. After much debate, Adenauer secured agreement to add a "neutral" eleventh board member to break possible ties who was acceptable to a majority on both sides of the board. The workers' representatives would be elected by the factory council in consultation with the trade unions; the unions could nominate three members, while the other two must be employees of the firm. Adenauer thus secured a bargain almost identical to that imposed by the British in 1947 and highly favorable to organized labor, despite the fact that the balance of social forces in West Germany had shifted toward big business since then.[52]

Adenauer could not enact this bargain into law unilaterally, however, and powerful opposition soon emerged. In late January the FDP cabinet ministers and business lobbyists in the CDU Bundestag delegation denounced any negotiation under what they called the "illegal pressure" of the DGB's "unconstitutional" threat to strike. They rejected Anton Storch's accurate observation that productivity had risen in the steel

---

[50] Tacke to Dr. Bock, January 17, 1951, and Heix to Dr. Bock, February 6, 1951, NL Katzer/265. See also the protest letters from seven other Christian social DGB functionaries in NL Katzer/265 and two more in NL Katzer/580.

[51] Mick to Kaiser, June 12, 1951, NL Albers/1/1950–55.

[52] Documentation in *Quellen: Montanmitbestimmung*, pp. 231–271; Otto Lenz, *Tagebuch*, January 17/18, 1951, pp. 5–8; Schwarz, *Adenauer*, I: 783–790; Gabriele Müller-List, "Adenauer, Unternehmer und Gewerkschaften. Zur Einigung über die Montanmitbestimmung 1950/51," *Vierteljahrshefte für Zeitgeschichte*, 33 (1985): 288–309; Thum, *Mitbestimmung*, pp. 71–93, 146–149.

industry since the introduction of parity co-determination, and Ludwig Erhard declared without evidence that productivity would plummet in the mines if it was extended to the coal industry. The DGB functionary Aloys Lenz warned CDU colleagues that the unions' strike threat was serious, and that a strike would topple the government. The majority agreed, however, that "if we seek to avoid this strike at any cost, then we will create a disastrous precedent for future political development."[53] The cabinet soon withdrew some of Adenauer's concessions to labor from the government bill, and this process accelerated in February during Bundestag committee hearings. Anton Sabel of the Social Committees championed Adenauer's bill as chair of the Bundestag labor committee, but the corporate lawyer Gerhard Schröder mobilized opposition by telling CDU colleagues that it "achieved a hyper-centralism of the trade unions that does not exist anywhere else in the world."[54]

The Social Committees now forged an alliance with the DGB that secured passage of Adenauer's bill. When DGB leaders celebrated their bargain with Adenauer as a great victory, their Christian social colleague Thea Harmuth warned immediately that they must secure the active support of the CDU workers' delegates before the Bundestag debate began. After Albers complained that Christian Democrats were grossly underrepresented in the existing organs of co-determination, the Social Democratic DGB leader Willi Richter implored all union colleagues to promise every CDU Bundestag delegate they knew "that the trade unions do not intend to ignore their group" in future nominations for these posts.[55] Such assurances helped to grease the wheels of legislation, but the Social Committees were influenced more by the popularity of the DGB's demands. In late February they finally launched a systematic effort to collect reports from every local Social Committee about the views of the membership. Those reports confirmed the judgment of the CDU social secretaries, who organized

---

[53] CDU Bundestag delegation, January 23, 1951, *Fraktionsprotokolle 1949–53*, pp. 340–342; Brentano to Adenauer, January 23, 1951, *Quellen: Montanmitbestimmung*, pp. 249–250; Bundesarchiv, *Kabinettsprotokolle-Online*, January 23, 1951, item B, and January 24, Point #1; Otto Lenz, *Tagebuch*, January 23, 1951, pp. 16–17.

[54] Lenz, *Tagebuch*, January 30, 1951, p. 25; *Kabinettsprotokolle Online*, cabinet minutes of January 30, 1951, Point #1; Sabel to CDU parliamentary leaders, February 15, 1951, NL Sabel/1/1; CDU Bundestag delegation, February 13, 1951, *Fraktionsprotokolle 1949–53*, pp. 353–354 (source of quotation).

[55] DGB Bundesausschuss, January 29, 1951, *Quellen: Montanmitbestimmung*, pp. 279–281; Thea Harmuth to Matthias Föcher, February 7, 1951, NL Katzer/265; "Protokoll der erweiterten Vorstandssitzung der rheinischen Sozialausschüsse," February 10, 1951, NL Katzer/255; DGB Bundesvorstand, March 11/12, 1951, *Gewerkschaftsquellen*, XI: 147–148.

factory cells, that most Christian Democratic workers agreed with the DGB about co-determination.[56]

To promote his bill, Adenauer arranged a meeting between DGB leaders and the CDU parliamentary leadership on March 19, and Karl Arnold warned party colleagues that he would secure a veto in the Bundesrat if the Bundestag passed a bill unacceptable to organized labor.[57] When the CDU Bundestag delegation met on April 3, Johannes Even of the KAB joined the representatives of the Social Committees in a fight to restore the provisions of Adenauer's original bill. On April 9 Adenauer secured the delegation's approval of a bill very close to his original plan, which passed the Bundestag the next day with the votes of the CDU/CSU and SPD, against the opposition of the FDP and German Party. DGB leaders celebrated this law as "a great success, one of the greatest in the history of the trade unions." The Social Committees also celebrated this result and claimed much of the credit.[58]

Hans Böckler had died in February 1951, and many Christian Democrats feared a lurch to the left by his successors. In May the DGB broke openly with the SPD to support the Schuman Plan, however, and in June the Christian social minority helped to elect as DGB chair the moderate Social Democrat Christian Fette. Fette advocated patient negotiations with employers over the gradual extension of parity co-determination to other branches of industry, and he endorsed Adenauer's thesis that West Germans must "make our contribution to defense for the preservation of our freedom." Kaiser and Otto Lenz both found his inaugural speech most impressive and concluded that the achievement of parity co-determination in coal and steel had strengthened the pragmatists in the DGB.[59]

[56] Bock circular of February 23, 1951, NL Katzer/238; "Sitzung der Sozialsekretäre," March 3, 1951, NL Katzer/257.

[57] CDU Bundestag delegation, March 8 and 16, 1951, *Fraktionsprotokolle 1949–53*, pp. 372, 378–379; Otto Lenz, *Tagebuch*, March 13–16, 1951, pp. 58–59; DGB circular of March 20, 1951, and von Brentano to Schröder and Sabel, March 28, 1951, *Quellen: Montanmitbestimmung*, pp. 457–458, 466–468; DGB Bundesausschuss, April 2/3, 1951, *Gewerkschaftsquellen*, XI: 166–168.

[58] CDU Bundestag delegation, April 3 and 9, 1951, *Fraktionsprotokolle 1949–53*, pp. 383–387; "Sitzung des erweiterten Vorstandes der Sozialausschüsse von Nordrhein," March 17, 1951, NL Katzer/246; Aloys Lenz to Kaiser, August 28, 1951, NL Katzer/392; Thum, *Mitbestimmung*, pp. 95–97; final terms of the law in *Quellen: Montanmitbestimmung*, pp. 526–529; DGB Bundesausschuss, April 16, 1951, *Gewerkschaftsquellen*, XI: 172–173 (source of quotation); CDA circulars by Josef Bock of April 5, 1951, LANRW/CDA Rheinland/913, and April 12, NL Katzer/238.

[59] DGB leadership conferences of March 11/12 and May 7, 1951, *Gewerkschaftsquellen*, XI: 149–151, 177–182; "Bericht über die Hauptvorstandssitzung" of the Social Committees, June 1, 1951, NL Katzer/238; DGB, *Protokoll. Ausserordentlicher Bundeskongress des Deutschen Gewerkschaftsbundes, Essen, 22. und 23. Juni 1951* (Cologne, 1951), pp. 38,

Adenauer had declared repeatedly that coal and steel formed a special case, and DGB leaders agreed initially that they must demonstrate the success of parity co-determination in this sector before seeking to apply it elsewhere. Labor leaders became upset, however, when the Allied High Commissioners announced in July 1951 that they would restore unfettered private ownership in the coal-iron-steel sector. Acting on the basis of a confidential agreement with Adenauer, the Allies then distributed to the former shareholders in the component firms of the old United Steelworks and Rhenish-Westphalian Coal Syndicate shares of equal value in the new, decartelized coal and steel firms. The Social Committees and DGB had both demanded that the government acquire a one-third ownership stake, but Adenauer insisted that they must choose either parity co-determination or a government stake.[60] After this disappointment Christian Fette experienced mounting pressure from union colleagues to demonstrate that his support for Adenauer's foreign policy yielded tangible benefits.

Adenauer proclaimed himself "a friend of the trade unions" in a closed meeting of CDU leaders on September 6. "It is impossible to govern against the unions," he emphasized.

For the CDU it would be catastrophic if we drove the DGB into the arms of the SPD and impelled them to conduct the next election campaign together. It is better if at least the top leadership of the unions respects partisan political neutrality. We must cooperate with the unions in a way that is successful, but without sacrificing any of our fundamental principles.

Adenauer promised in particular to reject any demand for the socialization of industry or parity co-determination outside of coal and steel.[61] Fette clung to the most optimistic interpretation of his subsequent discussions with the genial Adenauer, but more and more colleagues pointed out that the chancellor made no concessions. In November Fette himself concluded that Adenauer was not negotiating in good faith regarding co-determination for sectors

---

143–151 (Fette quotation on 148); Otto Lenz, *Tagebuch*, May 30 and June 26, 1951, pp. 88, 103–104; Jakob Kaiser to Heinrich Strunk, June 27, 1951, NL Strunk/1/166; Thum, *Mitbestimmung*, pp. 98–108.

[60] DGB Bundesvorstand, July 24, 1951, and report by Hans vom Hoff on his talks with Adenauer, September 4, *Gewerkschaftsquellen*, XI: 198–203, 218–219; Otto Lenz, *Tagebuch*, August 10, 1951, pp. 126–127; "Protokoll der Tagung" of the Workers' Group in the CDU Bundestag delegation, September 9, 1951, pp. 31–44, NL Katzer/392; CDU Bundestag delegation, September 7 and 10, 1951, *Fraktionsprotokolle 1949–53*, pp. 432–435; Thum, *Mitbestimmung*, pp. 116–130; Warner, *Steel and Sovereignty*, pp. 11–90.

[61] *Vorstandsprotokolle 1950–53*, pp. 56–57.

outside coal and steel, and DGB leaders voted on December 3 to suspend all contacts with the government.[62]

KAB leaders became overtly hostile to the DGB in the winter of 1951/52, because demonstrations by Catholic workers in support of organized labor's co-determination demands inspired fears of socialist infiltration. Hermann-Josef Schmitt discerned "the Marxist cloven hoof" and "cultural totalitarianism" when Christian Fette delivered a speech on January 31, 1952, calling for the unions to play a more active role in cultural life. Nell-Breuning sought in vain to persuade his old friend that German trade union leaders had renounced Marxism ever since the 1890s.[63] The Catholic bishops of western Germany followed Schmitt's advice at their closed meeting in March 1952 by registering "grave concern over the development of the unified trade unions, which are placing an ever greater burden on the conscience of their Catholic members. The possibility of founding a Christian or perhaps a Catholic trade union must be considered carefully. The task of training capable Catholic labor leaders is therefore a vitally important mission of the Church."[64] This resolution implied an expanded mission for the KAB – to form a cadre for Christian trade unions.

Soon thereafter Johannes Even launched a strident public attack on anti-clericalism in the DGB. He castigated the unions for allowing Social Democrats and even Communists to control their personnel decisions and educational programs, but his case was not well grounded. Even asserted for example that only one-eighth of the functionaries of the miners' union came from "the Christian camp," when over one-fourth were veterans of the Christian miners' union. The worst case of anti-clericalism he cited was an advent celebration by one DGB county organization that included satirical poems about Christmas by Erich Kästner and Kurt Tucholsky in addition to traditional Christmas carols. The KAB had only learned of this incident, however, through a letter from Matthias Föcher to describe his prompt intervention to discipline

---

[62] DGB leadership conferences, *Gewerkschaftsquellen*, XI: 229–237, 242–257; Thum, *Mitbestimmung*, pp. 129–134.

[63] "Der Sozialausschuss Hagen zum Betriebsverfassungsgesetz," resolution of May 29, 1952, enclosed in Otto Brötling to KAB headquarters, May 31, KAB Archiv/5/45; DGB Kreisausschuss Kempen to the KAB, June 6, 1952, KAB Archiv/5/22; resolution supporting the DGB by 24 Catholic workers in Düsseldorf, June 1952, enclosed in Schmitt to Karl Braukmann, August 13, 1952, KAB Archiv/5/22; Schmitt to Cardinal Frings, February 1, 1952, KAB Archiv/5/4; KAB, "Protokoll über die Sitzung des gführ. [KAB] Verbandsvorstandes," February 26, 1952, KAB Archiv/1/1; KAB, "Stellungnahme zu der Rede des Vorsitzenden des DGB Christian Fette über Soziale Kulturpolitik," KAB Archiv/3/32; Nell-Breuning to Schmitt, February 6 and March 1, 1952, and replies of February 7 (source of quotation) and March 3, KAB Archiv/5/45.

[64] "Konveniat der westdeutschen Bischöfe," March 3–5, 1952, HAEK/CR II/2.19, 11.

the union functionary involved. Even concluded that the DGB had reverted to the militant anti-clericalism of the Free unions in the 1890s, and he compared the current situation to the year 1933, when Catholic workers had followed their conscience and refused to participate in the German Labor Front. His evidence did not support these conclusions.[65]

Johannes Even's greatest fear, he confided to a friend, was that Catholic workers would develop a "split personality [*gespaltenes Bewusstsein*] and only listen to us about religious matters, while in politics, economic policy, and even cultural policy the program of the DGB will be the alpha and omega for them. This disintegration is proceeding unstoppably." KAB leaders thus blamed the DGB for the long-term process of secularization in German society. Their confrontation course was controversial even among Catholic bishops, however; the Jesuit Johannes Hirschmann soon conveyed word to DGB headquarters that the KAB enjoyed active support from only a few of them, and that the Vatican still endorsed participation by Catholics in the DGB. Oswald von Nell-Breuning compared the thinking of KAB leaders to what he termed the "very dangerous" movement of Integralism in the Catholic Church before 1914. He observed with regret to DGB leaders that more and more prominent Catholics acted as if only one political program could be deduced from Catholic teaching, when in fact a variety of programs were compatible with any set of religious norms.[66]

The government parties agreed in January 1952 on a factory council bill for sectors outside coal-iron-steel that offered workers "at most one-third" of the seats on corporate supervisory boards. The Social Committees had demanded "at least one-third," hoping for voluntary agreements on parity in some sectors, but they were overruled. The government bill also weakened union influence on the choice of workers' representatives, included no provision for a labor director, and excluded the public sector altogether. Both the DGB and Social Committees held that public-sector employees deserved the same rights as those in the private sector, but the cabinet proposed a separate bill for them on February 22 that did not offer

[65] Johannes Even, "Gewerkschaften im Zwielicht," 28-page pamphlet (Cologne, no date, NL Katzer/804), pp. 11–15, 20, 27–28; Föcher to Hejo Schmitt, November 18, 1950, and reply of November 25, KAB Archiv/5/5; Matthias Föcher, "Gewerkschaften im Zwielicht?" (Düsseldorf, no date; NL Katzer/804); "Vertreter der IG Bergbau stellen 'Weissbuch' der KAB richtig," DGB press release of April 17, 1952, KAB Archiv3/32.

[66] Even to Dr. Rössler, June 6, 1952, KAB Archiv/3/31; Karl Braukmann, "Niederschrift über ein Gespräch mit Pater Hirschmann" on June 9, 1952, NL Braukmann/7; remarks by Nell-Breuning in "Niederschrift über ein Gespräch zwischen Vertretern des Deutschen Gewerkschaftsbundes mit Vertretern katholischer und evangelischer Verbände und Institutionen," March 9, 1954, DGB-Archiv/5/DGAI001854.

any equivalent for representation on corporate supervisory boards. After attempts to amend these bills failed, DGB leaders resolved on May 9, 1952, to "appeal to our members to undertake trade union methods of struggle."[67]

The DGB opened its campaign with protest demonstrations and one-hour shutdowns of public transportation in key cities on May 15; it built up to a dramatic two-day strike by typesetters at the end of May that interrupted production of almost every newspaper. Union members supported these actions, but they outraged public opinion. They also coincided with the final round of negotiations over the European Defense Community treaty, and Adenauer concluded erroneously that the DGB had resolved to prevent rearmament. The chancellor therefore refused to negotiate until the unions terminated all strikes and demonstrations.[68] Adenauer instructed the interior ministry to prepare for government operation of public utilities, food distribution, and hospitals during a general strike, ignoring assurances by DGB leaders that German trade unions never had and never would allow such vital services to be interrupted. Adenauer also instructed Otto Lenz to prepare a contingency plan to revive separate Christian trade unions. Lenz employed as his agent Karl Hahn, chair of the conservative white-collar DHV, who soon reported generous offers of financial support from foreign Christian trade unions, German businessmen, and the US High Commissioner John McCloy. Jakob Kaiser and Theodor Blank also supported the project, Hahn asserted, if funding could be obtained from non-business sources.[69] Adenauer thus prepared for all-out war against the DGB.

Hahn's report about Kaiser's attitude appears unreliable, because the Social Committees now defended the position of the DGB. Many of their regional conferences expressed support for labor's demands, most

---

[67] Anton Sabel to Heinrich Krone, January 10, 1952, NL Sabel/1/1; CDU Bundestag delegation, January 22, 1952, *Fraktionsprotokolle 1949–53*, pp. 497–498; DGB leadership conferences of April 10 and May 9, 1952, *Gewerkschaftsquellen*, XI: 287–290, 311–316; Thum, *Mitbestimmung*, pp. 134–135.

[68] Theo Pirker, *Die blinde Macht. Die Gewerkschaftsbewegung in der Bundesrepublik*, 2 vols. (Berlin, 1979), I: 254–270; Hans-Otto Hemmer and Kurt Thomas Schmitz, eds., *Geschichte der Gewerkschaften in der Bundesrepublik Deutschland. Von den Anfängen bis heute* (Cologne, 1990), pp. 113–127; Otto Lenz, *Tagebuch*, May 12–29, 1952, pp. 325, 344, 347, 351; CDU Bundestag delegation, May 13–27, 1952, *Fraktionsprotokolle 1949–53*, pp. 551, 556, 561–563.

[69] Otto Lenz, *Tagebuch*, entries of May 1952 and February 26, 1953, pp. 329, 334, 341, 348–349, 567; "Bericht über die Konferenz der christlichen Fachinternationalen" in Utrecht, May 31, 1952, NL Katzer/618/Christliche Gewerkschaften; Ludwig Rosenberg's reports to DGB leaders of June 26 and July 8, 1952, on his negotiations with the interior ministry, NL Hansen/16.

notably the state convention of the Westphalian Social Committees in January 1952. Here 80 percent of the delegates belonged to a DGB-affiliated union; they reelected as chair the militant leader of the textile workers' union in the Münsterland, Albert Hillenkötter, and resolved to fight to improve co-determination rights.[70] Kaiser and Albers met with DGB leaders on May 19 and then sent mediation proposals to all CDU Bundestag delegates. They called for a workers' share on corporate boards of "at least one-third," freedom for workers to elect union experts as their representatives, expanded powers for factory councils, and a single law for the public and private sectors. After the cabinet rejected these proposals, Albers warned Adenauer that in all rallies he had addressed recently, "the main topic of the passionately conducted debate was co-determination. Those attending supported your foreign policy without reservation. But with regard to the demands of the trade unions, the overwhelming majority of those who spoke, at least 90 percent, took the side of the unions." Albers thus supported the substance of the DGB's demands while opposing the tactic of political strikes as counterproductive. He concluded that significant concessions must be made to avoid driving the DGB into the arms of the SPD.[71]

Arnold, Kaiser, and Albers brought DGB leaders together with Adenauer on June 13. In exchange for a promise to suspend all strikes during the negotiations, Adenauer agreed to form a mediation commission, to be hosted by Arnold, with four Bundestag delegates from the government parties and four representatives of the DGB. The DGB then assured union members that its proposals would "not only be considered but also in large measure implemented."[72] The government parties had become quite hostile to the DGB, however, and confident that public opinion supported them. The two negotiators chosen by the CDU Bundestag delegation, Gerhard Schröder and Anton Sabel, promised

[70] "Niederschrift der Landesdelegiertenkonferenz des Sozialausschusses der CDU-Wesftfalen," January 12/13, 1952, ACDP/03–002/125/1; "Unsere Stellung zum Betriebsverfassungs-Gesetz," *Soziale Ordnung*, Sonderdruck, March 1952; "Betriebsverfassungsgesetz und Personalvertretungsgesetz," speech by Hans Katzer on May 18, 1952, ACDP/04–013/166/3.

[71] *Kabinettsprotokolle Online*, May 20, 1952, Topic A, report by Kaiser on his talks with the DGB; Otto Lenz, *Tagebuch*, May 20, 1952, p. 336; DGB Bundesvorstand, June 4, 1952, *Gewerkschaftsquellen*, XI: 318–319; "Vermittlungsvorschläge zum Betriebsverfassungsgesetz," CDA circular of May 28, 1952, ACDP/04–013/164; Albers to Adenauer (unsigned carbon copy), May 25, 1952, NL Katzer/808; Albers' speech of May 30, 1952, NL Katzer/317; Albers' essay, "'Politische Streiks': Gewerkschaftsschädigend und unerlaubt," sent to Johannes Platte on June 6, 1952, NL Platte/28.

[72] DGB leadership conferences of June 4 and June 14, 1952, *Gewerkschaftsquellen*, XI: 319–327; Otto Lenz, *Tagebuch*, June 9–13, 1952, pp. 358–363; press releases by Otto Lenz, June 10, and Karl Arnold, June 11, 1952, NL Katzer/224; Thum, *Mitbestimmung*, pp. 137–138.

party colleagues that these talks would lead to no substantive alterations in the government bill. Albers replied that labor leaders were in full retreat, and that the CDU must "build a bridge" for them, but a large majority rejected any concessions.[73] Schroeder and Sabel then excluded Arnold from any active role in the talks of their mediation commission that began on June 30. By July 14, Fette only requested that the Bundestag debate be postponed until after the summer holidays, but he could not secure even that concession. He reported to DGB leaders the next day that the atmosphere at this meeting had been "the most unfriendly imaginable." Fette proposed a four-hour "warning strike" by all workers but acknowledged that prospects for success were dim. The DGB leadership decided to abandon this hopeless struggle.[74]

Within the CDU Bundestag delegation, representatives of farmers and small business now demanded complete exemption from the Factory Councils Law, and tempers flared on July 15. Josef Arndgen threatened to vote for all amendments proposed by the SPD, and Aloys Lenz denounced the "reactionary" farmers for toppling Heinrich Brüning in 1932. As the Bundestag vote began on July 19, CDU leaders feared massive defections, but only Oskar Rümmele of the Railroad Workers' Union voted No, while Albers, Kaiser, three other workers' delegates, and two small businessmen abstained.[75] The KAB celebrated the Factory Councils Law of 1952 (*Betriebsverfassungsgesetz*) as a great victory for Christian social doctrine over the trade union bureaucracy. Hans Katzer drew the more sobering lesson for the Social Committees that attacks on the DGB really sought to harm the fundamental interests of all workers. "Even if Christian trade unions had existed," he argued, "they would have been compelled to pursue the same goals in shaping the Factory Councils Law as the DGB." He thus acknowledged that the great majority of Christian Democratic workers agreed with the DGB about co-determination; this was not just a demand of the SPD or trade union bureaucracy. Bernhard Tacke considered resigning from the CDU in protest, but Kaiser retained his support with the promise of a leading role in the Social Committees. Kaiser, Albers, and Katzer all concluded from this confrontation that the Social Committees must cooperate more

---

[73] CDU Bundestag delegation, June 17, 1952, *Fraktionsprotokolle 1949–53*, pp. 570–572.

[74] Karl Arnold to Albers and Kaiser, June 16, 1952, NL Katzer/224; DGB Bundesausschuss, July 12 and July 15, 1952, *Gewerkschaftsquellen*, XI: 335–337, 348–357; Hans Katzer, CDA *Rundbrief* Nr. 4, July 10, 1952, NL Katzer/239; CDU Bundestag delegation, July 8 and 14/15, 1952, *Fraktionsprotokolle 1949–53*, pp. 580–585; Thum, *Mitbestimmung*, pp. 140–142.

[75] CDU Bundestag delegation, July 15 and 18, 1952, *Fraktionsprotokolle 1949–53*, pp. 585–589.

closely with the DGB, and Tacke became their most influential ally within the unions when he succeeded Föcher as DGB vice chair in 1956.[76] Organized labor had suffered a humiliating defeat, and debate erupted over Christian Fette's leadership at the DGB national congress of October 1952. Siggi Neumann of the SPD had lobbied tirelessly to purge the defenders of Adenauer's foreign policy from the DGB leadership and rally support for Walter Freitag of the metalworkers' union to replace Fette. Some labor activists also called for the expulsion of any union member who had voted for the Factory Councils Law, a course likely to provoke a mass exodus of Christian Democrats. Fette still enjoyed support from several smaller trade unions, however, and August Schmidt of the miners' union and the Christian social minority campaigned for his reelection to maintain partisan political neutrality. Freitag's supporters sought to reduce opposition by reporting accurately that he enjoyed very good relations with the veterans of the Christian trade unions in IG Metall.[77] All but three of the thirty delegates who spoke on the first day of the congress reproached Fette for gullibility in his dealings with Adenauer, and many also attacked his support for the Schuman Plan and rearmament. Schmidt, Föcher, and Tacke proposed that Fette and Freitag be elected as equal co-chairs, but that motion failed by a few votes to win the two-thirds majority needed to alter union statutes. Freitag then defeated Fette by a vote of 184 to 154 in one of the most tightly contested elections in the history of German trade unionism.[78]

Hans Böckler had exhorted union leaders to decline political mandates, but now the DGB was led by a Social Democratic Bundestag delegate.

---

[76] Johannes Even, "Das Betriebsverfassungsgesetz auf der Waage," 40-page pamphlet (no place or date; NL Katzer/567); "Niederschrift über die Vorstandssitzung" of the Westphalian Social Committees, August 16, 1952, ACDP/03–002/127/1; Tacke to Hans Katzer, January 20, 1953, and Kaiser to Tacke, January 23, 1953, NL Kaiser/40/1–2.

[77] DGB leadership conferences of July 30 and October 4, 1952, Hans Brümmer to Viktor Agartz, July 31, and Neumann's report to the SPD of October 22, 1952, *Gewerkschaftsquellen*, XI: 357–360, 364–372, 378–382; Brümmer to the DGB Bundesvorstand, August 25, 1952, in Walter Dörrich and Klaus Schönhoven, eds., *Die Industriegewerkschaft Metall in der frühen Bundesrepublik. Quellen zur Geschichte der deutschen Gewerkschaftsbewegung im 20. Jahrhundert: Band X* (Cologne, 1991; hereafter *Gewerkschaftsquellen*, X:), pp. 236–239; Fritz Biggeleben to Jakob Kaiser, July 18, 1952, NL Kaiser/160/264; Föcher to Kaiser, August 5, 1952, NL Katzer/614; biographical sketch of Freitag for the press, "DGB: Wer ist der neue Mann?", October 8, 1952, NL Hansen/1a; Thum, *Mitbestimmung*, pp. 142–145. Bruno Trawinski had praised Freitag for fair treatment of the Christian social minority in his union in a letter to Kaiser of November 30, 1950, NL Katzer/265.

[78] Deutscher Gewerkschaftsbund, *Protokoll: 2. Ordentlicher Bundeskongress, Berlin, 13. bis 17. Oktober 1952* (Düsseldorf, no date), pp. 117–189, 390–406; Hemmer and Schmitz, *Geschichte der Gewerkschaften*, pp. 127–133.

Adenauer remained calm, however, noting accurately that Freitag was no more radical than Fette. Siggi Neumann reported to SPD headquarters nevertheless that the decisions of the DGB Congress "demonstrate the moral authority of the Party within the trade unions" and "signify the victory of Social Democratic consciousness over organizational egotism."[79] Three economic experts at DGB headquarters who had supported the Schuman Plan were soon dismissed after evidence surfaced that they had expressed deplorable opinions under the Third Reich. Freitag was not responsible for this purge, but he proved less energetic than Böckler or Fette when it came to resisting SPD interference in union affairs. Matthias Föcher soon complained to his new boss about a proliferation of SPD cells at union headquarters.[80]

Soon after Freitag's election, Cardinal Frings issued his first public criticism of the DGB. KAB leaders had pressed him to call for the revival of Christian trade unions; he supported the idea but encountered opposition by other bishops and Vatican officials who saw no reason to attack the firmly anti-communist DGB. Frings therefore offered indirect support when he told a KAB rally on November 30, 1952, that the German bishops had sought to revive Christian trade unions in 1945 but encountered fierce opposition by the Allied military governments. He read out an affidavit by Archbishop Jaeger of Paderborn, conveying his recollection of a dramatic confrontation at British military headquarters in August 1945 with a British general who declared that the Allies would only permit unified labor unions. Many newspapers reported the next day that the DGB existed only because of interference in German affairs by the occupation powers. Prominent veterans of the Christian trade unions responded at once that their comrades had consulted neither German bishops nor British generals when deciding to join unified labor unions in 1945, and they pointed out gross discrepancies between Jaeger's recollections and the historical record. The western German bishops had publicly endorsed unified labor unions in June 1945, and two contemporary records of the meeting at British military headquarters in August (one by Jaeger's own secretary) indicate that the two bishops present had reiterated that position, while the British declared that Catholics were free to found Christian trade unions

---

[79] Otto Lenz, *Tagebuch*, October 17 and 29, 1952, pp. 436, 451; CDU Bundesvorstand, October 17, 1952, *Vorstandsprotokolle 1950–53*, p. 161; Siggi Neumann memorandum of October 22, 1952, *Gewerkschaftsquellen*, XI: 376.

[80] Pirker, *Blinde Macht*, II: 33–38; Föcher to Freitag, February 6, 1952, DGB-Archiv/5/DGAI000003; Bernhard Tacke, "Anmerkungen zu 'Willi Richter. Ein Leben für die soziale Neuordnung' von Gerhard Beier," October 2, 1978, NL Tacke/11/5.

in future, if they wished.[81] Jaeger and Frings avoided publicity after some of these discrepancies came to light, but Frings told the CDU parliamentary leader Heinrich Krone in January 1953 that Christian trade unions must be founded soon. This development provided some confirmation for Adam Stegerwald's prophecy to the founders of the Social Committees in October 1945 that the Catholic clergy would prove their most dangerous opponent.[82]

3.4   "To Elect a Better Bundestag!": The DGB and the Election Campaign of 1953

During the emotional debate over the Factory Councils Law of 1952, Adenauer told DGB leaders repeatedly that they must secure a parliamentary majority if they wanted a law favorable to organized labor. He thus left them little alternative but to intensify support for the SPD in the next Bundestag election campaign, but any step in that direction provoked outrage among Christian Democrats over breaches of partisan political neutrality in the unified labor unions. Adenauer evidently anticipated a confrontation with organized labor, because he exhorted CDU leaders for a year in advance of the Bundestag election of September 1953 to campaign vigorously against the SPD in alliance with the FDP. Jakob Kaiser and Karl Arnold replied again and again that the CDU should hold open the door for a Great Coalition, because workers might become radicalized if the SPD remained in opposition for another four years.[83]

Concern about partisan tendencies in the trade unions mounted after a purge of Christian Democrats at the DGB state congress for North Rhine-Westphalia in February 1953. Werner Hansen proposed the reelection of his Christian social colleagues to the state committee, but most delegates were angry about the Factory Councils Law; the minority lost three of its five seats, including the vice-chairmanship. This result angered all Christian social union functionaries, and Jakob Kaiser declared at a national congress of the Social Committees that it violated

---

[81] Patch, "Legend of Compulsory Unification," pp. 864–871; Helene Thiesen, "Christlich-soziale Arbeitnehmerschaft und Gewerkschaftsfrage 1945–1953," phil. diss. (Bonn, 1988), pp. 166–168.

[82] Krone, *Tagebücher*, January 30, 1953, I: 111. For Stegerwald's reunion with old comrades in Cologne in October 1945, see pp. 70–71 above.

[83] "Tagung der Arbeitnehmerabgeordneten des Deutschen Bundestags," September 7, 1952, NL Katzer/310; CDU Bundesvorstand meetings from December 1952 to July 1953, *Vorstandsprotokolle 1950–53*, pp. 242–247, 261–263, 269–278, 318–320, 395–399, 542–561, 598–606; Otto Lenz, *Tagebuch*, December 3–15, 1952, pp. 485, 501–503.

a solemn agreement among trade unionists in the anti-Hitler Resistance that a colleague from the Christian unions should always lead their state organization in Rhineland-Westphalia.[84] On March 1 the KAB sent DGB leaders eight peremptory demands to avoid schism, including a quota of leadership posts in every union proportional to the number of "Christian" members. Kaiser expressed a fervent desire to preserve labor unity, but Johannes Even argued that competition between rival labor federations would strengthen organized labor. The cautious Adenauer told CDU leaders that they should follow Kaiser's lead.[85]

Walter Freitag sought to appease the Social Committees by instructing Hansen to conduct a new election for his state leadership team. Freitag told the DGB National Committee on April 29 that Hans Böckler had indeed promised Kaiser, Albers, and Karl Arnold in Freitag's presence that a representative of their group would always have one of the top two leadership posts in North Rhine-Westphalia. Freitag felt bound by this agreement and did "not want to do anything that would lead to the foundation of Christian trade unions."[86] In June Freitag identified a candidate for state vice chair acceptable to both the majority and minority, Peter Claassen, the Wuppertal district leader of the Public Service Workers' Union and a veteran of the Christian unions. Freitag also arranged a meeting with the leaders of the Social Committees and three meetings with Catholic and Protestant church representatives. The representatives of the Social Committees and Evangelical Church raised suggestions in these meetings designed to preserve labor unity, but KAB leaders displayed open hostility. Freitag promised them all that the DGB would not subsidize the SPD election campaign or tell union members which party to support.[87]

---

[84] Dörpinghaus to the DGB Bundesvorstand, February 14, 1953, NL Dörpinghaus/1; Hermann Meinzer to Albers, February 17, 1953, NL Katzer/544; protest letter to Walter Freitag of February 26, 1953, signed by nine DGB leaders, *Gewerkschaftsquellen*, XI: 400–402; Föcher to Kaiser, April 8, 1953, NL Kaiser/9/ 35–36; speech by Kaiser in *Bundestagung der Sozialausschüsse der christlich-demokratischen Arbeitnehmerschaft. Köln, 28. Februar und 1. März 1953* (Königswinter, no date; found in NL Katzer/631), pp. 72–74.

[85] Johannes Even, "Um die Einheit der Gewerkschaften," *Ketteler-Wacht*, #5, March 1, 1953; CDU Bundesvorstand, March 11 and April 21, 1953, *Vorstandsprotokolle 1950–53*, pp. 435–437, 457–468, 482–483, 512–513.

[86] Wilhelm Backes to Albin Karl, March 17, Werner Hansen to the DGB Bundesausschuss, April 1, and Hansen to Freitag, April 21, 1953, DGB-Archiv/5/DGAI000003; DGB Bundesausschuss, April 29, 1953, *Gewerkschaftsquellen*, XI: 408–410.

[87] Strategy memorandum for Freitag, "Für Stockholm," May/June 1953, DGB-Archiv/5/ DGAI000003; Eberhard Müller's report to Professor Höffner on a meeting with Freitag, written on April 20, 1953, NL Katzer/586; DGB Bundesausschuss, April 29, 1953, *Gewerkschaftsquellen*, XI: 403–405; Kaiser's report to CDU leaders on his meeting with

In March 1953 Kaiser sought to persuade CDU leaders that the best way to neutralize partisan tendencies in the trade unions would be to add several influential DGB leaders to the CDU Bundestag delegation, and Adenauer agreed. Kaiser had received a confidential list from DGB headquarters of eleven favored candidates, starting with Matthias Föcher, but only one gained a CDU nomination, Franz Varelmann of Hanover.[88] Trade unionists had become unpopular among middle-class Christian Democrats because of a modest revival of strike activity in 1951/52; the chair of the CDU in Bocholt, for example, denounced Albert Hillenkötter to Westphalian CDU headquarters for ignoring pleas by party colleagues to end a local strike by textile workers. The KAB therefore found willing listeners when it exhorted CDU county committees to scrutinize candidates who were union functionaries with great care, because they had probably become "infected with socialist ideas."[89] Kaiser and Adenauer did help to secure the nomination of Heinrich Scheppmann of the miners' union, but the successful nominees from North Rhine-Westphalia included just three DGB functionaries, versus six KAB functionaries. Albers complained that the CDU displayed far less interest than the old Center Party in nominating vigorous advocates of workers' interests.[90] Strike rates remained extremely low in comparison with the period before 1933, but CDU county committees displayed an allergic reaction to any labor strife.

The CDU nominations policy left the DGB no choice but to strengthen the SPD if it hoped to influence legislation. On July 18 the DGB leadership resolved therefore to appropriate two million marks for a "nonpartisan" campaign "to elect a better Bundestag," to be supervised by three

Freitag on May 9, 1953, *Vorstandsprotokolle 1950–53*, pp. 571–572; Albers' report to CDU parliamentary leaders on May 11, 1953, *Fraktionsprotokolle 1949–53*, p. 708; Franz Deus's summary of the DGB receptions for Protestants and Catholics on May 22 and June 2, 1953, and detailed transcript of the latter meeting, DGB-Archiv/5/ DGAI001854.

[88] *Vorstandsprotokolle 1950–53*, pp. 467–468; Hans Katzer's note on a telephone call from Karl Pottmann at DGB headquarters on December 11, 1952, NL Kaiser/172/4–5.

[89] Josef Sonnenschein (from Bocholt) to Josef Blank, May 5, 1952, ACDP/03–002/130; Hillenkötter to Johannes Even, August 5, 1952, NL Even/1; Kaiser to Hillenkötter, August 29, 1952, NL Katzer/618; "Die grossen Gefahren," *Ketteler-Wacht*, July 1, 1953, and complaints about this article by Josef Berntzen and Matthias Föcher, NL Katzer/312.

[90] Kaiser to Adenauer, February 9, 1953, NL Kaiser/172/4–5; CDU Bundesvorstand, May 22 and July 20, 1953, *Vorstandsprotokolle 1950–53*, pp. 571–574, 623–625, 640; "Niederschrift über die am 18.4.53 in Hamm stattgefundenen Vorstandssitzung" of the Westphalian Social Committees, NL Katzer/247; "Niederschrift der Vorstandssitzung des Sozialausschusses [Westfalens]," May 23, 1953, ACDP/03–002/127/1; Hans Katzer "Vermerk" of July 22, 1953, NL Katzer/552; Albers to Landrat Johnen, July 20, 1953, LANRW/CDA Rheinland/912.

Social Democrats and Matthias Föcher. Föcher told colleagues in the Social Committees that he opposed this decision and feared the growing influence of left-wing socialists at DGB headquarters. His warnings gained confirmation when the DGB published an aggressive election manifesto on July 30. All union members must vote, the DGB declared, because business interests had often triumphed under Adenauer.

Reactionaries have gained an ever stronger influence on key positions in our civil and foreign service in the last four years . . . . Vote only for those men and women who are either union members or have demonstrated through their conduct in the past that they will fulfill the legitimate wishes and demands of the unions in the new Bundestag.

Whoever desires peace and progress, freedom and unity, and whoever does not want to see again the reign of violence and war, terror and nights of bombing, they all must help with their votes to elect a better Bundestag to exclude those forces that want to plunge the German people into disaster for a second time.

Many DGB county organizations also distributed pamphlets that called explicitly for union members to vote SPD, or helped to distribute SPD campaign materials.[91]

Walter Freitag insisted that this DGB manifesto avoided any breach of partisan political neutrality, but all CDU leaders were outraged. Kaiser declared on July 31 that the DGB proclamation was

partisan in its one-sided positions, partisan in its formulations, partisan in its signatures . . . It is intolerable that the leadership of the DGB and its member unions lies almost exclusively in the hands of Social Democrats . . . That must be changed, if we are to be able to remain in the DGB.

Adenauer accused the DGB of "totalitarian tendencies" and told CDU leaders that "no state can tolerate that such an organization . . . proceeds in such fashion against the government and undermines the state."[92] Kaiser rejected the KAB's call to secede from the DGB, however, because that would give radical socialists complete control of the unions. On August 7 the Social Committees resolved instead to found "Christian social caucuses" within the unions. Kaiser based this plan on

---

[91] DGB Bundesausschuss, July 18, 1953, and election manifesto of July 30, *Gewerkschaftsquellen*, XI: 418–420, 431–433; Hans Katzer, "Vermerk" on a meeting on July 20 of Föcher with Christian social delegates to the congress of the miners' union, NL Katzer/552; report by Hans Düngelhoff of Bottrop to CDA headquarters, September 16, 1953, NL Katzer/619; CDU Landessozialausschuss Rheinland-Pfalz to CDA headquarters, September 6, 1953, NL Katzer/806; Anton Sabel to Walter Freitag, September 8, 1953, NL Sabel/1/3.

[92] Kaiser's speech in a CDA circular of August 1, 1953, LANRW/CDA Rheinland/913; Otto Lenz, *Tagebuch*, July 31, 1953, p. 674 (source of Adenauer quotation); Thiesen, "Christlich-demokratische Arbeitnehmerschaft," pp. 191–193.

the example of Austria, where Christian trade unionists had joined unified trade unions in 1945 but won recognition in 1951 of their right to form a caucus within each union for supporters of the Austrian People's Party. They held annual congresses and received a quota of union leadership posts.[93]

By August 20 the Social Committees had distributed one million leaflets advocating Christian social caucuses, with attached "declarations of solidarity" for workers who wanted to join them. Few German workers followed Austrian developments, however, and they did not know what to make of this appeal. Of the several dozen letters of response preserved, almost half supported the plan as a step toward founding Christian trade unions, and almost half opposed it; only a handful agreed that caucuses were desirable in themselves.[94] KAB leaders rejected caucuses as meaningless and vowed to secede if the DGB did not accept their eight demands for radical reform of March 1. "Only a clearly defined Christian labor movement can help us," Johannes Even declared at a KAB rally on August 23, "that will oppose the socialist program with its own vision of social order. Do not say 'a minority movement.' A resolute minority with a clear program is more valuable than a confused mass movement in which everything is submerged in the collective." Some speakers in the following discussion urged consultation with the Social Committees, but they were shouted down by those who reproached Kaiser and Albers for cowardice.[95]

The initial response to the DGB election manifesto by Christian Democrats reflected anxiety that it might prove effective, but on September 6 the CDU scored a dramatic victory with 45 percent of the popular vote, versus just 29 percent for the SPD, and an absolute majority of Bundestag seats. The CDU won 35 percent of all blue-collar

---

[93] "Vorstandssitzung am 7.8.1953 in Essen: Gewerkschaftliche Situation," summary of Kaiser's speech in NL Katzer/399; "Antwort auf den Wahlaufruf des Deutschen Gewerkschaftsbundes: 'Fraktioneller Zusammenschluss,'" CDA press release of August 7, 1953, and "'Das Mass ist voll.' Aufruf der CDU-Sozialausschüsse," *Der Tag*, August 4, 1953, NL Kaiser/102/57–58; "Richtlinien zum Aufbau der Fraktion 'Christlicher Gewerkschafter,'" NL Katzer/641; Ludwig Reichhold, *Geschichte der christlichen Gewerkschaften Österreichs* (Vienna, 1987), pp. 567–629.

[94] See the correspondence from August/September 1953 in NL Katzer/619, and Katzer's circular to the Social Committees, August 20, 1953, LANRW/CDA Rheinland/608. Karl Arnold wrote Kaiser on September 23 (NL Katzer/292) that most letters to him opposed any action that might split the DGB.

[95] See Johannes Even, "'Vor der Entscheidung.' Rede anlässlich der Sondertagung der KAB am 23. August 1953 in Recklinghausen" (Cologne, no date), pp. 10–11, 14–15, and the two anonymous reports to Katzer about this conference and related press clippings in NL Katzer/617.

votes, versus 48 percent for the SPD, and among white-collar workers and civil servants, it defeated the SPD, 49 percent to 27 percent. Thrilled by this victory, Johannes Even told reporters three days later that only the resignation of the entire DGB executive committee would satisfy him; otherwise Christian trade unions would be founded immediately.[96] Adenauer agreed with Kaiser and Arnold, however, in opposing that idea. Adenauer warned CDU leaders that any effort to found new unions would cost millions of marks, and Arnold predicted that hardly anyone would join them. They agreed to avoid any initiative until the Social Committees and KAB agreed on a plan.[97]

The top leaders of the Social Committees conferred with the KAB in Cologne on the morning of September 12 and then assembled all forty-seven members of their National Committee in Düsseldorf that afternoon. At the first meeting Kaiser and Arnold opposed the foundation of Christian trade unions, because they could never become a significant force, and the influence of workers in the CDU depended on cooperation with the powerful DGB. The KAB leaders agreed reluctantly to support one more attempt at negotiation with the DGB, and Kaiser and Arnold were assigned to draft a letter presenting their joint demands. The larger Düsseldorf conference then endorsed the idea of a joint letter, but several DGB functionaries implored Kaiser and Arnold not to raise demands that contradicted union statutes, or utter threats that would poison the atmosphere. Kaiser assured them that he still sought to preserve labor unity.[98] To retain the support of the KAB, Kaiser and Arnold were compelled nevertheless to include eight aggressive demands in their letter to the DGB on September 16, including the immediate co-opting of three additional "Christian workers" into the DGB Central Committee and enough into each member union's leadership to assure Christian workers "the influence they deserve." A parity committee with equal representation for the majority and minority should plan all educational programs, and a parity tribunal

[96] Election results in Bösch, *Adenauer-CDU*, pp. 156–157; "Christliche Arbeitnehmer: DGB muss sich ändern," *Westfalen Blatt*, September 10, 1953 (NL Katzer/617); "CDU stellt den DGB vor die Entscheidung," *Die Welt*, September 10, 1953 (NL Katzer/622); Josef Thur to Katzer, reporting on Even's press conference of September 9, NL Katzer/292.

[97] Lenz, *Tagebuch*, September 8 and 10, 1953, pp. 693–697; CDU Bundesvorstand, September 10, 1953, *Vorstandsprotokolle 1953–57*, pp. 6–13, 38–58.

[98] "Notiz über die Besprechung im Kettelerhaus," September 12, 1953, NL Katzer/618/ Besprechungen mit KAB; "Protokoll der Sitzung des Hauptvorstandes der Sozialausschüsse in Düsseldorf," September 12, 1953, NL Katzer/386; "Warnung in letzter Stunde," *Rheinische Post*, September 14, 1953 (NL Katzer/622).

should judge alleged violations of partisan neutrality and religious tolerance.[99]

These demands outraged DGB leaders. IG Metall had already resolved on September 11 to reject any outside interference, and its press chief accused the Social Committees of serving big business with their attempt to split the unions. When the DGB Central Committee met on September 18, everyone rejected Kaiser's demands, and several speakers compared the CDU's attitude to that of the Nazis after their election victory in March 1933. Föcher sought to calm them by reporting that KAB leaders wanted to found Christian trade unions, but that "Karl Arnold seeks to rein in the KAB." There was no need to accede to any of these demands, Föcher declared, but they should confer with Kaiser and Arnold.[100] On September 30 the DGB National Committee formally rejected the eight demands, but Freitag sent a personal letter offering to receive Kaiser and Arnold. KAB leaders insisted that the DGB had brusquely rejected an "ultimatum," but Kaiser and Arnold welcomed the opening of a "dialogue."[101]

Hard-liners on both sides pressed for a rupture. Cardinal Frings told a KAB rally on September 19 that "I personally no longer believe in the dogma that only unified trade unions can effectively defend workers' interests." August Vanistendael of the International League of Christian Trade Unions then promised generous financial support for new Christian trade unions in Germany, and Bernhard Winkelheide insisted that no good Catholic could defend the DGB.[102] At the opposite

[99] See the draft for this letter sent by Arnold to Kaiser on September 14 and the undated draft by Katzer in NL Katzer/292; "Niederschrift über die Besprechung mit der KAB am 16.9.53 im Kettelerhaus," with five drafts of the letter, NL Katzer/618/Besprechungen mit KAB; and the final draft in *Gewerkschaftsquellen*, XI: 438–441.

[100] IG Metall leadership conference, September 11/12, 1953, *Gewerkschaftsquellen*, X: 290–299, 306–307; DGB Bundesvorstand, September 18, 1953, *Gewerkschaftsquellen*, XI: 441–453; report to Kaiser on the latter meeting by Arnold's aide Alfermann, September 18, 1953, NL Katzer/622; "Gleichschaltung oder Spaltung," SPD press release of September 10, 1953, NL Katzer/292; Werner Hansen, "Rundschreiben Nr. 217" to the DGB of Nordrhein-Westfalen, September 26, 1953, NL Katzer/621.

[101] Telegram from Katzer to Kaiser, September 27, 1953, on a telephone call from Arnold, NL Katzer/88; DGB leadership conferences of September 30 and October 5, 1953, and Freitag to Arnold and Kaiser, October 1, *Gewerkschaftsquellen*, XI: 454–470; "Vorletzte Mittel," *Rheinischer Merkur*, September 25, 1953, and "KAB beansprucht Eigenrecht," *Aachener Volkszeitung*, September 30, 1953 (NL Katzer/617); dpa press release of September 29, "Arnold fordert zu nüchterner Betrachtung des Gewerkschaftsproblems auf" (NL Hansen/20); Arnold to Freitag, September 29, 1953, DGB-Archiv/5/DGAI000003; "DGB lehnt ab. Gespräch geht weiter," *Rheinische Post*, October 1, 1953 (NL Katzer/622); "Dokumente zur Gewerkschaftsfrage," *Soziale Ordnung*, VII/#10 (October 1953), pp. 3–4.

[102] "Der KAB-Ruf von Mönchen-Gladbach," *Aachener Volkszeitung*, #219, September 21, 1953, and two clippings from the *Ruhr-Nachrichten* of September 21, NL Katzer/617;

extreme, the leaders of the metalworkers', chemical workers', and public service workers' unions denounced Freitag for agreeing to receive Kaiser and Arnold. At a DGB state leadership conference on October 2, Werner Hansen compared Adenauer's recent speeches to those of Hitler in March 1933, and Peter Claassen denounced his fellow Catholic workers in the CDU for losing control of their party to reactionaries and capitalists. Freitag could not keep his first appointment with Kaiser and Arnold because of these attacks.[103]

They never acknowledged this, but the attitude toward the DGB among leaders of the Social Committees was transformed by the dismal failure of their campaign to collect declarations of solidarity with Christian social caucuses. Some regional leaders of the Social Committees refused to distribute the leaflets at all, because they sympathized either with the KAB or the DGB. Even where, as instructed, the leaflets were all handed out to workers leaving their factories, they were often discarded immediately, like every other leaflet distributed during the frantic last days of the Bundestag election campaign.[104] Hans Katzer eventually acknowledged to the leaders of the Social Committees that this effort had not been "an impressive success," but he asserted that 40,000 declarations had been returned. Buried in his files was the sobering truth that he had received fewer than 5,000. Only fifty-one returned from Essen, Kaiser's own Bundestag district, where 30,000 Christian trade unionists lived in 1929.[105] Kaiser and Albers had always assumed that they enjoyed a following at least as large as the

confidential report by Alfermann for Kaiser, September 21, 1953, NL Katzer/622, and for Arnold that same day, NL Katzer/292.

[103] IG Metall leadership conference, October 6, 1953, and letters to the DGB Bundesvorstand by Otto Brenner and Hans Brümmer, *Gewerkschaftsquellen*, X: 317–324; Walter Freitag to DGB Bundesvorstand, October 9, 1953, DGB-Archiv/5/DGAI001710; Hubert Jipp to Arnold and Kaiser, October 4, 1953, NL Katzer/630; memorandum on the leadership conference of IG Chemie on October 23–25, 1953, NL Kaiser/362/32; Paul Nowak, "Bericht über die Tagung der Angestellten im DGB," with speeches by Hansen and Claassen on October 2, 1953, NL Kaiser/621; Hans Zankl to Jakob Kaiser, October 5, 1953, NL Katzer/621; overview of contacts between the leaders of the Social Committees and DGB in NL Kaiser/362/52–53.

[104] Martin Heix to Katzer, August 27, 1953, NL Katzer/619; "Niederschrift der Vorstandssitzung des Sozialausschusses der CDU [Westfalens]," October 3 and October 24, 1953, ACDP/03–002/127/1; Albert Hillenkötter to Helmut Schönfeld, October 20, 1953, ACDP/03–002/130; CDU Kreisverband Siegen to Katzer, November 4, and CDU Kreispartei Lemgo to Katzer, November 20, 1953, NL Katzer/298.

[105] Tables on the results of the campaign in NL Katzer/641, including a break-down by city on November 1, 1953, a breakdown by trade, and a final total of 5,000 on January 1, 1954; transcript of Katzer's oral report to the Social Committees' "Vorstandssitzung" on April 10, 1954, with the number 40,000 penciled in at the last moment, NL Katzer/387.

membership of the old Christian trade unions, but this data confirmed the warnings by Karl Arnold that most churchgoing workers today would ignore any appeal to join Christian trade unions, because the DGB defended their interests more effectively. Thereafter, leaders of the Social Committees never gave serious consideration to proposals for secession from the DGB.

When Kaiser finally gained an audience with the DGB National Committee on December 11, he embraced labor unity but warned that others might weaken the movement by founding Christian trade unions. He recounted in detail the convergence in theory and practice between the Free and Christian trade unions in the 1920s and the agreement among Resistance leaders to establish unified labor unions after Hitler's fall, but he reported malaise among Christian workers today. "Christian workers do not feel at home in the trade unions," Kaiser warned. "We cannot simply have the old Social Democratic terminology and the old Social Democratic objectives. The trade unions were more advanced before 1933 than today." The DGB doomed itself to membership stagnation, he concluded, by offending workers who were not committed Social Democrats. The leaders of the metalworkers' and public service workers' unions replied, however, that every political party contained many Christians; when Kaiser complained of discrimination against Christians, he really spoke on behalf of a political party that often opposed workers' interests. The DGB did suffer painful membership losses in the fall and winter of 1953/1954, however, for which Kaiser offered a plausible explanation.[106]

KAB leaders also received clear indications that Christian trade unions would enjoy very little support among workers, but they chose to ignore them. On October 22, 1953, they sought agreement on an action plan with clerical colleagues from southern Germany, four conservative representatives of Protestant workers' clubs, several leaders of Catholic factory cells, and representatives of the International League of Christian Trade Unions. All the factory cell leaders reported that hardly any workers would join a Christian trade union, and their clerical

---

[106] Compare the draft, "Jakob Kaiser vor dem Ausschuss des DGB am 11. Dezember 1953," NL Katzer/540, with the slightly different transcript of the remarks delivered, in Josef Kaiser, ed., "'Wir können da keine Heimat finden, wo wir mit unseren Auffassungen immer wieder erdrückt werden.' Jakob Kaiser vor dem Bundesausschuss des Deutschen Gewerkschaftsbundes am 11. Dezember 1953," *Internationale wissenschaftliche Korrespondenz zur Geschichte der Arbeiterbewegung*, 34 (1998): 37–81 (esp. 54–56, 59–65, 75–78). See also Werner Hansen's summary of the meeting in NL Hansen/20; Thea Harmuth to Kaiser, December 14, 1953, NL Katzer/619; and the DGB Bundesvorstand minutes of February 23, 1954, and Hans Brümmer to Kaiser, March 20, 1954, *Gewerkschaftsquellen*, XI: 496–515.

colleague from Stuttgart estimated that fewer than 10 percent of the members of the Catholic workers' clubs in Baden-Württemberg would do so. Gockeln, Schmitt, and Even insisted that Christian unions must be founded soon, but the leaders of the Christian International declared that they would offer funding only if agreement could be reached with Jakob Kaiser, because the project was doomed without his support.[107] KAB leaders took heart nevertheless when the Catholic bishops of western Germany resolved in a closed meeting on November 3–5 that "we understand very well why Christian workers have decided that it is their ethical duty to go their own way and found Christian trade unions. They can rest assured that the German episcopate sympathizes with their efforts and respects this decision of conscience." The bishops refused to publish this resolution, but Schmitt assured the next KAB leadership conference that "the attitude toward the KAB among the bishops is good." In his mind this news evidently outweighed all negative reports about the attitude among workers.[108]

Johannes Even acknowledged in an editorial on December 1 that the attempt to found Christian trade unions must be postponed. He noted that social theorists from the Jesuit and Dominican Orders had "confused" Catholics by defending the DGB, and he attacked Kaiser and Arnold for seeking more negotiations with it. "Let us all acknowledge that they acted with good intentions," Even concluded, "but they have inflicted grave harm on Christian workers and the Christian social idea." Adenauer too earned a reprimand for praising those who negotiated with the DGB.[109] Soon thereafter the most widely circulated magazine for Catholics attacked Kaiser's motives as well as his judgment. "Kaiser may belong to those Christian politicians," its editor suggested, "who want to retain the goodwill of the Left at any cost, so that they can remain in the great game after the demise of the chancellor ... The transparent Kaiser strategy of speaking with a forked tongue has now led to a grave conflict of conscience among Christian workers." These personal attacks infuriated Kaiser and his colleagues.[110]

---

[107] See the confidential report on this meeting to Kaiser and Arnold by C.G. Schweitzer on October 23, 1953, NL Kaiser/362/40–43.

[108] "Protokoll der Beratungen auf dem Konveniat der westdeutschen Bischöfe," November 3–5, 1953, HAEK/CR II/2.19, 13; KAB, "Protokoll über die Sitzung des gführ. Verbandsvorstandes," November 19, 1953, KAB Archiv/1/1.

[109] Johannes Even, "Ende des Ersten Aktes," *Ketteler-Wacht*, December 1, 1953.

[110] Hermann Rössler, "In der Krise," *Mann in der Zeit*, January 1954 (NL Kaiser/327/34); Kaiser's letter to the editor, December 31, 1953, with copies to the papal nuncio and German bishops, NL Kaiser/427/8–15; "Polemik an der Jahreswende," *Soziale Ordnung*, VIII/#1 (January 1954), pp. 1–2.

By now many younger Catholics in the trade unions had become equally disillusioned with the KAB, senior union functionaries, and the career politicians who led the Social Committees. They wanted the trade unions to become less hierarchical and shift some authority from salaried functionaries to unpaid volunteers in union work, but they also distrusted the clumsy interventions in union affairs by the KAB and Social Committees. Groups of young Catholic trade unionists in Rhineland-Westphalia began to hold weekend retreats in 1952, many organized by Maria Weber, a functionary at DGB headquarters. They formed an alliance with Father Herbert Reichel, a young Jesuit who had just published a history of the DGB, and they discussed plans to reform the DGB in the light of Catholic social theory. Reichel became both the spiritual advisor and political strategist for this network, which soon called itself the Christian Social Collegium (*Christlich-soziale Kollegenschaft*).[111]

The Collegium burst into public view when Matthias Föcher lost control of a conference for 600 Christian social trade unionists that he convened in Essen on October 31, 1953. Föcher planned a rally to defend the DGB, but to achieve an impressive turnout he invited many younger colleagues who were not salaried union functionaries. Collegium activists resolved in advance that a genuine debate must take place, and they formulated proposals to invigorate grass-roots democracy in the unions.[112] On October 31 Labor Minister Storch offered a vigorous rebuttal of Föcher's opening address to defend the DGB, and he encouraged younger colleagues to raise their demands. After a stormy debate, the majority endorsed an eight-point reform program resembling that sent to the DGB by Kaiser and Arnold on September 16. They also demanded, however, that DGB leaders discuss these issues with the Christian Social Collegium, not the KAB or Social Committees.[113] The emergence of the Collegium made it very difficult for journalists

---

[111] Schroeder, *Katholizismus und Einheitsgewerkschaft*, pp. 318–320, 390–394; Thiesen, "Christlich-demokratische Arbeitnehmerschaft," pp. 169–172; Nell-Breuning to Hermann-Josef Schmitt, July 22, 1951, and Schmitt to Nell-Breuning, April 19, 1952, KAB Archiv/5/45; Werner Holzgreve to Hans Brosch, August 27, 1952, enclosed in a report to Joseph Blank on September 17, ACDP/03–002/133/1.

[112] Helmut Schorr, circular of October 10, 1953, and circular by Aloys Lenz with attached "Stellungnahme zur Lage der christlich-sozialen Kollegenschaft innerhalb des Deutschen Gewerkschaftsbundes," October 26, 1953, NL Katzer/584.

[113] Report on the conference by Aloys Lenz to Kaiser, November 1, 1953, NL Kaiser/362/22–25; C.G. Schweitzer to Kaiser and Arnold, November 2, 1953, NL Katzer/630; Leo Maur to Hermann-Josef Schmitt, November 2, 1953, KAB Archiv/5/8; eight-point resolution of November 1, 1953, NL Katzer/544; Thiesen, "Christlich-soziale Arbeitnehmerschaft," pp. 208–210.

to distinguish among the many rival Christian social organizations that sought to negotiate with the DGB.

The estrangement of some colleagues from the KAB and DGB left many local Social Committees with stagnating membership and declining morale. The Social Committees had developed a more vigorous internal democracy since 1949 nevertheless. Local meetings now discussed important policy issues thoroughly, and the results of those discussions shaped the articles in *Social Order* and thoughtful position papers by standing committees on social insurance, family policy, co-determination, home ownership, and other issues. The Social Committees had developed sound procedures to achieve the most basic objective defined by Johannes Albers in September 1946, to serve as the "interpreter of workers' wishes" for the CDU leadership.[114] Their careful study of social policy enabled them to set the course for the workers' wing of the CDU. Despite all their feuding, the leaders of the Social Committees, KAB, and Christian social trade unionists responded to the same constituents with the same interests. There was no fundamental conflict between the members of the KAB and Social Committees; their disputes resulted almost entirely from clerical influence in the KAB.[115] As we shall see in the next chapter, they almost always collaborated effectively in parliamentary debates over social policy.

---

[114] See Albers to Konrad Adenauer, September 10, 1946, NL Albers/3/2, and the reports from the "Arbeitskreise" in the published *Bundestagung der Sozialausschüsse* of February 28/March 1, 1953.

[115] When KAB leaders finally authorized the first scientific poll of their members' views, conducted in spring 1969, it found that 84 percent supported the DGB's position in the ongoing debate over parity co-determination; very few echoed the militant anti-socialist line established by Hermann-Josef Schmitt. See Institut für Demoskopie Allensbach, "Die Katholische Arbeitnehmer-Bewegung. Bericht über eine repräsentative Mitglieder-Befragung," completed on May 6, 1969, esp. Tables 39 and T25-T27, KAB Archiv/33/80.

4 The Influence of Christian Democratic Workers on Welfare Legislation, 1953–1957

Labor Minister Anton Storch aroused much anticipation when he agreed to address the national congress of the Social Committees in February 1953 on the topic, "From Social Policy to Social Reform." He noted that many Social Democrats admired the Beveridge Plan of 1942 to abolish poverty, ignorance, disease, and unemployment in postwar Britain, which called for numerous entitlements for all citizens, to be financed through taxation. Storch opposed that approach for Germany, because it could build on six decades of experience as the world leader in public health insurance, old age and disability pensions, and unemployment insurance. Unlike the Beveridge Plan, German social insurance retained a link between the level of dues paid by individuals and their benefits, and it was supervised by elected representatives of those who paid the premiums, not a centralized bureaucracy. This approach, Storch argued, provided "social security" while fostering a sense of responsibility for one's own fate; it thus nurtured the capacity for personal initiative upon which economic growth depended. Regardless of what today's observer might think about the relative merits of German social insurance and British entitlements, Storch's argument was very well suited to defend social spending in a party committed to free-market economics. However, Storch acknowledged painful gaps in the German system and promised a new approach by a second Adenauer cabinet. "In the final analysis," he concluded, "to achieve social reform through social policy means that we must create a modern legal status and material security for all who work ... We must ... draw together all these different social issues into a comprehensive social plan." The speech earned hearty applause, but some listeners deplored its lack of detail.[1]

[1] Anton Storch, "Von der Sozialpolitik zur Sozialreform," in CDA, *Bundestagung der Sozialausschüsse der christlich-demokratischen Arbeitnehmerschaft. Köln, 28. Februar und 1. März 1953* (Königswinter, n.d.; NL Katzer/631), pp. 10–18; Arthur Rohbeck to Hans Katzer, March 4, 1953, NL Katzer/240. For background see Hans Günter Hockerts, *Sozialpolitische Entscheidungen im Nachkriegsdeutschland. Alliierte und deutsche*

The Federal Republic of Germany did lead the world in spending on social security. As measured by the International Labor Organization, total West German expenditure on social programs rose dramatically from 10.3 billion marks in 1949 to 19.3 billion in 1953, amounting to 20 percent of national income, the highest proportion for any industrialized country. This increase resulted from a scramble to deal with the consequences of the Second World War, however, not from any government plan. All experts agreed that Germany had developed a confusing patchwork quilt of social programs, and that benefits often did not go to the needy. People of independent means sometimes received multiple benefits, for example if they had lost property in East Germany, while senior citizens and war invalids who depended entirely on their pensions often lived below the poverty level. Storch had promised the Bundestag repeatedly to undertake a comprehensive reform of social policy, but the labor ministry was severely understaffed; only in March 1953 could two officials be spared to begin the review. The Social Committees, Catholic workers' clubs, and social policy experts in the CDU Bundestag delegation all prodded the labor ministry forward during Adenauer's second term, and the Social Committees hired an insurance expert, Arthur Rohbeck, to work full time at the Stegerwald House. As Katzer told a rally of the Social Committees in May 1954, their election victory obliged Christian Democrats to translate their ideals into specific legislative proposals.[2]

4.1   Rearmament and the Growing Divisions among Christian Democratic Workers

The demands of the Social Committees always faced powerful opposition from business lobbyists in the CDU, who took the lead in funding that party's election campaigns. Progress toward social reform depended on the ability of the Social Committees to persuade CDU leaders that their election prospects depended on implementing measures strongly desired by the blue- and white-collar workers and their dependents who made up well over 70 percent of the electorate and a narrow majority of CDU voters. Experience suggested that this effort required cooperation between the Social Committees and the powerful DGB, whose strikes

Sozialversicherungspolitik 1945 bis 1957 (Stuttgart, 1980), pp. 220–230, and Hans Günter Hockerts, *Der deutsche Sozialstaat. Entfaltung und Gefährdung seit 1945* (Göttingen, 2011), pp. 43–62.

[2] Hockerts, *Sozialpolitische Entscheidungen*, pp. 115–118, 195–220; Hans Katzer, "Die Sozialausschüsse im Ringen um eine neue Gesellschaftsordnung," speech of May 9, 1954, ACDP/03–002/125/1.

and demonstrations offered the strongest evidence regarding workers' demands. Many middle-class Christian Democrats were outraged by any evidence of collusion between the Social Committees and organized labor, however, so great discretion was required. DGB leaders also sought to collaborate with the Social Committees, because they were eager to influence the federal government. For them too discretion was required, because many union members regarded the Adenauer government as militaristic and reactionary. The alliance between the Social Committees and organized labor was often disrupted by the ongoing debate over rearmament and the hostility to labor unions among middle-class Christian Democrats and Catholic clerics.

Chancellor Adenauer's preoccupation with rearmament posed an obstacle to social reform. The SPD challenged the constitutionality of rearmament, so the chancellor formed a broad coalition after his election victory in September 1953 that commanded a two-thirds majority in the Bundestag capable of amending the Basic Law. His coalition with the FDP, German Party, and the league representing ethnic Germans expelled from Eastern Europe added several foes of organized labor to his second cabinet, including two former Nazis. To serve as his chief of staff, Adenauer also replaced the resistance veteran Otto Lenz with Hans Globke, a former interior ministry bureaucrat under the Third Reich who had written the official commentary on the anti-Semitic Nuremberg Laws of 1935. Globke had never joined the Nazi Party, however, and Jakob Kaiser testified repeatedly that he had supported the resistance during the war. Adenauer considered removing the undisciplined Kaiser from the cabinet, along with Labor Minister Storch, whom he considered barely competent, but he decided that they were too popular.[3] Until West Germany finally achieved NATO membership in May 1955, Chancellor Adenauer was often completely absorbed in complex diplomatic negotiations.[4]

The debate over rearmament also weakened the advocates of social reform by compelling Karl Arnold to renounce cooperation with Social Democrats as prime minister of North Rhine-Westphalia. In that state's election of June 1954, the CDU increased its share of the vote, but losses by the Center Party left what Arnold called his "Christian coalition" with only 99 of 200 seats. The Social Committees advocated a Great Coalition with the SPD, but Arnold insisted that their cabinet must support

---

[3] Press clippings about Kaiser's testimonials for Globke in NL Kaiser/115; Hans-Peter Schwarz, *Adenauer*, 2 vols. (Stuttgart, 1986–1991), II: 111–120; Erich Kosthorst, *Jakob Kaiser. Minister für gesamtdeutsche Fragen 1949–1957* (Stuttgart, 1972), pp. 280–282.

[4] See Schwarz, *Adenauer*, II: 120–168, and David Clay Large, *Germans to the Front: West German Rearmament in the Adenauer Era* (Chapel Hill, 1996), pp. 176–223.

Adenauer's foreign policy in the Bundesrat. When the SPD rejected that demand, Arnold formed a coalition with the Free Democrats instead. This decision antagonized Arnold's supporters on the left wing of the CDU, and he sought to mollify them by appointing Johannes Platte of the miners' union as state labor minister. It now became impossible, however, for Arnold to revive the threat with which he had exerted great influence on the parity Co-Determination Law of 1951 for coal, iron, and steel – that he would veto legislation unfavorable to organized labor by casting his state's votes with the SPD bloc in the upper house of parliament.[5]

Soon thereafter a passionate debate over rearmament broke out within the DGB, which disrupted the efforts by the Social Committees to ally with it. The militant leader of the metalworkers' union, Otto Brenner, had agreed with the moderate DGB chair Walter Freitag and Christian social trade unionists that the DGB should develop an Action Program to reduce the length of the work week to forty hours, while achieving wage increases sufficient to prevent any loss of weekly earnings. They also agreed that rearmament should be excluded from the agenda of the next DGB congress in October 1954, and that the DGB expert Viktor Agartz would deliver a keynote address to provide an economic rationale for the Action Program. The Marxist theoretician Agartz had been the SPD's most influential champion of a centrally planned economy in 1947/1948, and he remained the figure at DGB headquarters whose views diverged most sharply from those of the Christian social minority. In recent years, however, Agartz had sought to prove his usefulness to the DGB by compiling new statistics to advance an old thesis supported by all trade unionists: that wage increases promoted economic growth by stimulating aggregate consumer demand. He agreed with DGB leaders that this would be the topic of his congress speech.[6]

---

[5] Detlev Hüwel, *Karl Arnold. Eine politische Biographie* (Wuppertal, 1980), pp. 262–267; Ludger Gruber, *Die CDU-Landtagsfraktion in Nordrhein-Westfalen 1946–1980. Eine parlamentshistorische Untersuchung* (Düsseldorf, 1998), pp. 319–322; letters to Arnold by Peter Claassen on July 10, 1954, and Johannes Platte and Karl Braukmann on July 13, NL Braukmann/6/Briefwechsel Arnold.

[6] Discussion between Agartz and IG Metall leaders on November 5, 1953, in Walter Dörrich and Klaus Schönhoven, eds., *Quellen zur Geschichte der deutschen Gewerkschaftsbewegung im 20. Jahrhundert. Band X: Die Industriegewerkschaft Metall in der frühen Bundesrepublik* (Cologne, 1991), pp. 325–355 (hereafter *Gewerkschaftsquellen*, X:); Andrei Markovits, *The Politics of the West German Trade Unions: Strategies of Class and Interest Representation in Growth and Crisis* (Cambridge, 1986), pp. 83–87, 188–190; Theo Pirker, *Die blinde Macht. Die Gewerkschaftsbewegung in der Bundesrepublik*, 2 vols. (Berlin, 1979), II: 90–104, 107–128; Wolfgang Schroeder, "Christliche Sozialpolitik oder Sozialismus. Oswald von Nell-Breuning, Viktor Agartz und der Frankfurter DGB-Kongress 1954," *Vierteljahrshefte für Zeitgeschichte*, 39 (1991): 179–220.

Nobody anticipated that the DGB Frankfurt Congress would occur just before the decisive international negotiations over West German NATO membership. DGB youth groups held pacifist rallies on the eve of the congress, and six delegates mounted the rostrum on the opening day to denounce rearmament. Following listless discussions of labor law and social policy, Viktor Agartz then diverged from his assigned topic in a three-hour diatribe that electrified the delegates. Agartz denounced the US Military Government for having crippled the labor movement in 1947/1948 when it vetoed state laws to socialize heavy industry. "By disregarding these democratic votes," Agartz declared,

the decisive foundation was laid for the renewed strength of reaction in West Germany. One should not always point to the East with the assertion that the government of the German Democratic Republic was supported by Russian tanks. The structure and order of the West German economy have undoubtedly been shaped in the same way by the bayonets of the Western occupation powers.

West Germany did not have a democracy, Agartz declared, because the political parties "with few exceptions" had been bought by the special interests. Agartz concluded that workers would be compelled to pay the enormous cost of rearmament, and that "the presence of an army has always posed a dangerous threat to the domestic security of the people." This speech earned thunderous applause from the delegates but dismayed union leaders. The Christian Democratic vice chair of the textile workers' union, Bernhard Tacke, denounced Agartz's thesis "that democracy cannot be defended, indeed, that there is no democracy to defend." Such radicalism, Tacke observed, only encouraged fatalism in practice. Even Otto Brenner, who was denounced as a Marxist himself by conservative Christian Democrats, expressed disappointment to union colleagues, because Agartz had failed to provide a coherent rationale for the DGB Action Program.[7]

Shortly before Agartz's speech, one congress delegate began to circulate a hastily drafted motion rejecting "any contribution to defense until all opportunities to negotiate with the goal of understanding between the peoples have been exhausted and the unity of Germany is restored." It soon collected signatures from a majority of delegates, many of whom

---

[7] Deutscher Gewerkschaftsbund, *Protokoll: 3. ordentlicher Bundeskongress, Frankfurt a.M., 4. bis 9. Oktober* 1954 (Frankfurt a.M., no date), pp. 107–108, 113–115, 144–145, 190–194, 202–203, 215–216, and Agartz speech on 423–468 (quotations on 429, 436–439, 466); remarks by Tacke to the DGB Bundesausschuss, November 15, 1954, in Josef Kaiser, ed., *Quellen zur Geschichte der deutschen Gewerkschaftsbewegung im 20. Jahrhundert. Band XI: Der Deutsche Gewerkschaftsbund, 1949 bis 1956* (Cologne, 1996; hereafter *Gewerkschaftsquellen*, XI:), p. 628; remarks by Brenner to leaders of his union, December 14/15, 1954, *Gewerkschaftsquellen*, X: 547–551.

apparently failed to notice that the last phrase committed them to a position far more radical than that of the SPD, which only demanded that all opportunities to negotiate be exhausted. The congress debates revealed so much pacifist sentiment, however, that DGB leaders felt compelled to endorse this motion, which passed against only four Nay votes.[8] The KAB appealed to Catholic workers to leave the DGB in protest, but Adenauer and Jakob Kaiser opposed that demand. Adenauer noted that Freitag was doing his best to neutralize a sudden revival of Communist agitation in the unions, and he agreed to meet with the DGB chair to discuss ways to prevent any revival of militarism during the process of rearmament. Kaiser told CDU leaders that there had been positive developments at the Frankfurt Congress, beginning with the decision to depict Adam Stegerwald as one of the four great pioneers of trade unionism in the convention hall. The Christian Democratic delegates had supported the reelection of Freitag as DGB chair, he concluded; accepting the motion against rearmament had been necessary to retain him.[9]

The Social Committees had recently persuaded the CDU to hire a well-connected DGB functionary, Hans Zankl, to head a new office for trade union affairs at CDU headquarters and represent the party at labor conferences.[10] Zankl assured the CDU that labor leaders had no intention of actively supporting the SPD-led campaign against rearmament. Even Otto Brenner had said nothing against rearmament at the Frankfurt Congress; he only demanded that if it did take place, then the arms contracts should go to German rather than US firms. All DGB leaders devoted themselves to defining attainable short- and medium-term objectives in their Action Program, which was published in March 1955. It showcased the demand for a forty-hour work week with wage increases sufficient to prevent any loss of weekly income, and it gained enthusiastic

---

[8] DGB, *3. Kongress 1954*, pp. 374–375, 578–585, 806–807, 811; Pirker, *Blinde Macht*, II: 133–138.

[9] Johannes Even, "Bedrohliche Entwicklung der Einheitsgewerkschaft," *Ketteler-Wacht*, November 1, 1954 (NL Katzer/617); CDU Bundestag delegation, October 12, 1954, in Helge-Heidemeyer, ed., *Die CDU/CSU-Fraktion im Deutschen Bundestag. Sitzungsprotokolle 1953–1957*, 2 vols. (Düsseldorf, 2003), I: 298–299 (hereafter *Fraktionsprotokolle 1953–57*); Günter Buchstab, ed., *Adenauer: "Wir haben wirklich etwas geschaffen." Die Protokolle des CDU-Bundesvorstands 1953–1957* (Düsseldorf, 1990; hereafter *Vorstandsprotokolle 1953–57*), October 11, 1954, pp. 261–276, 316–317; "Adenauer trifft mit Walter Freitag zusammen," *Die Welt*, #233, October 13, 1954 (NL Katzer/623); Schwarz, *Adenauer*, II: 157–163.

[10] Katzer to Bruno Heck, July 23, 1954, reply of August 4, and Katzer's handwritten "Vermerk" of September 7, NL Katzer/87; Zankl's undated "Lebenslauf," NL Katzer/593; Hans Zankl, "Meine Tätigkeit an der Bundesgeschäftsstelle," memorandum of February 7, 1955, NL Katzer/87.

support from the Social Committees. Pragmatic reformism was the dominant tendency in organized labor, and union leaders did what they could to revive cooperation with the Social Committees.[11]

The diplomatic talks over rearmament led to a new debate over the Saarland in February 1955, when Adenauer endorsed a French proposal to hold a referendum on independence in that region. The French government had abandoned the project for a European Defense Community in 1954, and the US and Great Britain had then proposed that West Germany be accepted as an equal partner in NATO. Adenauer offered to accept independence for the Saarland to secure French approval of West German NATO membership. Jakob Kaiser detested this bargain but abstained in the Bundestag vote approving the referendum, after Adenauer warned him bluntly that a Nay vote would lead to his dismissal from the cabinet. Adenauer's gambit succeeded when West Germany became a NATO member in May 1955, with the only restriction on its freedom to rearm being a West German pledge not to develop weapons of mass destruction.[12] In exchange for legal recognition by France of the pro-German Saar parties during the referendum campaign, Adenauer then issued a declaration urging Saarlanders to vote for independence. The pro-independence parties featured Adenauer's image on their posters, but Kaiser's agents in the Ministry for All-German Affairs helped to secure a decisive rejection of independence by 68 percent of Saar voters in October 1955. Adenauer then negotiated a treaty with France that cleared the way for the accession of the Saarland to the Federal Republic of Germany on January 1, 1957. Kaiser rejoiced over this development and concluded that German national sentiment remained far more powerful than Adenauer believed; Adenauer retorted that only his skillful diplomacy had enabled the Saarlanders to decide their own fate.[13]

[11] Hans Zankl, "Aktennotiz für Herrn Dr. Heck," February 5, 1955, NL Zankl/1/1; remarks by Brenner, DGB, 3. Bundeskongress 1954, p. 104; "Aktionsprogramm des DGB," March 30, 1955, Gewerkschaftsquellen, XI: 682–688; remarks by Katzer to DGB leaders in "Niederschrift über die erste Besprechung des Siebener-Ausschusses," December 16, 1955, NL Katzer/592; Gordon Drummond, The German Social Democrats in Opposition, 1949–1960: The Case against Rearmament (Norman, 1982), pp. 133–149; Hans-Otto Hemmer and Kurt Thomas Schmitz, eds., Geschichte der Gewerkschaften in der Bundesrepublik Deutschland. Von den Anfängen bis heute (Cologne, 1990), pp. 185–247.

[12] Adenauer to Kaiser, February 18, 1955, reply of February 20, and Adenauer to Kaiser, February 23, 1955, in Mayer, Jakob Kaiser, pp. 614–618; Kosthorst, Kaiser: Minister, pp. 340–349; Bruno Thoss, "Der Beitritt der Bundesrepublik Deutschland zur WEU und NATO im Spannungsfeld von Blockbildung und Entspannung (1954–1956)," in Anfänge westdeutscher Sicherheitspolitik 1945–1956, ed. Militärgeschichtliches Forschungsamt, 4 vols. (Munich, 1982–1997), III: 1–234

[13] CDU Bundesvorstand, September 20, 1956, Vorstandsprotokolle 1953–1957, pp. 1016–1017; Kosthorst, Kaiser: Minister, pp. 349–354; Schwarz, Adenauer, II:

The former Christian trade unionist Theodor Blank had meanwhile gained appointment as West Germany's first defense minister in June 1955, and he sought to engage the leaders of the DGB and SPD in efforts to guarantee parliamentary control of the military, screen applicants for the officer corps, and assure the humane treatment of recruits. He made promises about the pace of rearmament that could not be kept, however, and in 1956 he felt obliged to advocate military conscription with an eighteen-month term of service as the necessary corollary to NATO membership. That demand proved highly unpopular, and in September 1956 the Bavarian CSU disavowed Blank by demanding a twelve-month term. The Social Committees discerned anti-worker prejudice in the attacks on Blank, and the security expert Herbert Blankenhorn judged that he had done an excellent job as defense minister but faced obstacles that would overwhelm any man.[14] The CSU leader Franz Josef Strauss condemned Blank before their Bundestag delegation on September 26 for relying on the advice of generals in politically delicate matters, and for purchasing too many weapons from the US instead of German firms. Blank replied angrily that "it is more than martyrdom to be required to conduct defense policy when the defense minister only learns from the newspaper what the defense policy is." Most CDU leaders concluded from this outburst that Blank suffered from nervous exhaustion, and Adenauer requested his resignation on October 16 to make way for Strauss. Blank accepted this decision stoically but complained to leaders of the Social Committees in private that Strauss was the tool of German industrialists seeking arms contracts.[15] Strauss soon notified the NATO allies that German rearmament would be a much slower process than they had expected, and partly because of his gradualist approach, the prophecy by Agartz that rearmament would impose a crushing financial burden on

---

225–234; Stefan Creuzberger, *Kampf für die Einheit. Das gesamtdeutsche Ministerium und die politische Kultur des Kalten Krieges 1949–1969* (Düsseldorf, 2008), pp. 110–112.

[14] "Niederschrift über die Vorstandssitzung" of the Westphalian Social Committees, January 28, 1956, NL Katzer/251; Heinrich Krone, *Tagebücher*, ed. Hans-Otto Kleinmann, 2 vols. (Düsseldorf, 1995–2003), entries of April-July 1956, I: 210–211, 217, 223; CDU Bundesvorstand, September 20, 1956, *Vorstandsprotokolle 1953–57*, pp. 1028–1031, 1061–1067, 1074–1077; Herbert Blankenhorn, *Verständnis und Verständigung. Blätter eines politischen Tagebuchs 1949 bis 1979* (Frankfurt a.M., 1980), October 5, 1956, pp. 253–254; Large, *Germans to the Front*, pp. 234–261; Hans Ehlert, "Innenpolitische Auseinandersetzungen um die Pariser Verträge und die Wehrverfassung 1954 bis 1956," in *Anfänge westdeutscher Sicherheitspolitik*, III: 430–552.

[15] CDU Bundestag delegation, September 26 and October 16–22, 1956, *Fraktionsprotokolle 1953–57*, II: 1213–1223 (quotation on 1218), 1267–1274; Krone, *Tagebücher*, October 6, 1956, I: 231; "Niederschrift über die Hauptvorstandssitzung der Christlich-Demokratischen Arbeitnehmerschaft," November 12, 1956, remarks by Blank on p. 7, ACDP/04–013/1/2; Schwarz, *Adenauer*, II: 270–280.

workers did not come true. Because of rapid economic growth and a reduction in the occupation costs levied by the Allies, West German military spending actually declined from a painful 14 percent of national income in the years 1952–1955 to a more tolerable 8–9 percent in 1956–1959.[16] Rearmament created less of an economic barrier to social reform than a political hindrance, because it disrupted the alliance between the Social Committees and organized labor.

Growing hostility toward the DGB in the Catholic clergy created another obstacle to social reform. The leaders of the Catholics workers' clubs resolved in January 1954 to found a new Christian labor federation with financial support from the International League of Christian Trade Unions. After the DGB Frankfurt Congress, Bishop Keller of Münster declared in a closed meeting of western German bishops in early November that "there can be no avoiding the foundation of a separate union." Soon thereafter Bernhard Winkelheide and Johannes Even of the KAB agreed with two conservative leaders of the small Protestant workers' clubs of Rhineland-Westphalia to establish an office to draft a program for Christian trade unions, after August Vanistendael of the Christian International agreed to pay the expenses.[17]

In response to these maneuvers by the KAB, Jakob Kaiser persuaded the leaders of the Social Committees in January 1955 that it would be almost impossible to found new unions, because Christian workers did not perceive anything in recent actions by the DGB that raised profound "questions of conscience." The CDU held so much political power, however, that Christian Democrats could certainly increase their influence in the unified labor unions significantly, if only all Christian social factions would cooperate.[18] Kaiser then met with KAB leaders on January 27 to argue that they had already made good progress, because their colleagues now included about 700 of the 5,000 functionaries in the

[16] Large, *Germans to the Front*, pp. 261–264; Werner Abelshauser, "Wirtschaft und Rüstung in den fünfziger Jahren," in *Anfänge westdeutscher Sicherheitspolitik*, IV: 88–185 (statistics on 89).

[17] KAB, "Protokoll über die Sitzung des gführ. Verbandsvorstandes," January 18 and October 26, 1954, KAB Archiv/1/1; "Protokoll des Westdeutschen Bischofskonveniats," November 3–5, 1954, HAEK/CR II/2.19, 14; anonymous report to Katzer on Even's secret meeting with Vanistendael on November 8, 1954, NL Katzer/617; Wolfgang Schroeder, *Katholizismus und Einheitsgewerkschaft. Der Streit um den DGB und der Niedergang des Sozialkatholizismus in der Bundesrepublik bis 1960* (Bonn, 1992), pp. 170–171.

[18] Hans Katzer, "Niederschrift über die am 8. Januar 1955 in Essen stattgefundene Besprechung mit etwa 60 hauptamtliche Gewerkschaftssekretäre," NL Katzer/292; "Rededisposition" for Kaiser's remarks and "Niederschrift über die Besprechung mit den hauptamtlichen Gewerkschaftern" in Königswinter on January 22, 1955, NL Katzer/540.

DGB, a ratio similar to that of 1929 between the functionaries of the Christian and Free unions. Johannes Even retorted that today's Christian social DGB functionaries were compelled to obey radical socialist superiors or face dismissal. He acknowledged that new Christian unions might not attract more than 8,000 members initially but suggested that another 10,000 would join if Kaiser endorsed the enterprise. Whatever their size, Even concluded, unions must be founded that were based on a program truly compatible with Christianity. Hermann-Josef Schmitt, the priest who was the true leader of the KAB, added that "our people in the trade unions are losing more and more of their principles. There is a loss of [moral] substance that is absolutely frightful." Hans Katzer replied bluntly that it was the KAB's mission to educate Catholic workers about morality; if moral substance was being lost, Schmitt should not blame the trade unions. Kaiser wrote Even a few days later that if radical forces ever did gain control of the DGB, new unions could be founded in alliance with moderate Social Democrats. The true fault line in organized labor, he concluded, did not divide Christians from socialists but rather moderates from radicals.[19]

Chancellor Adenauer was profoundly skeptical of the prospects for new Christian unions, but he also feared that the DGB sought to prevent rearmament. His initial response to the Frankfurt Congress had been mild, but he became fearful by May 1955 and told CDU leaders that the DGB was becoming ever more radical. "The trade unions are at present the true holders of power in the Federal Republic," Adenauer declared, and would remain so until an army had been created. "The whole situation will change ... the moment the Federal Republic has an army again. A state without an army is powerless ... If people act against democracy, and it has nothing to defend it but its principles, then it is lost." When a new army had been created, "then no transport strike will be possible, because the army can then arrange buses and God knows what." Jakob Kaiser then exclaimed, "God forbid that a day comes when German soldiers ... intervene against rebellious trade unionists or other demonstrators." Kaiser insisted that "the German Labor Federation is not so bad."[20] Adenauer's rhetoric encouraged many middle-class CDU leaders to hope for a schism of the DGB nevertheless.

The radical speech by Viktor Agartz to the Frankfurt DGB Congress had meanwhile become a lightning rod for criticism among Catholics, so the Jesuit social theorist Oswald von Nell-Breuning resolved to defend

---

[19] Hans Katzer, "Niederschrift über die Aussprache mit der KAB am 27. Januar 1955," and Kaiser to Even, January 30, 1955, NL Katzer/618/Aktionsausschuss.
[20] CDU Bundesvorstand, May 2, 1955, *Vorstandsprotokolle 1953–57*, pp. 428, 469–472.

labor unity by driving this Marxist out of the DGB. In Munich he asked a large audience on January 11, 1955, "Where is Dr. Viktor Agartz leading the DGB?" Nell-Breuning offered the following provocative answers: "1) into a maze of delusions regarding the state and social and economic policy; 2) he leads toward political and class struggle radicalism; 3) ... he leads toward irresponsibility; 4) he leads toward the schism of the DGB."[21] Agartz avoided any direct response but commissioned a junior colleague at the DGB Economic Research Institute, Walter Horn, to publish a vitriolic rebuttal in May. Horn compiled a long list of apparent contradictions in Nell-Breuning's published utterances since the late 1920s. He concluded that Nell-Breuning's numerous "errors ... are doubtless the historically necessary consequence of Catholic social doctrine itself," because its rigid, centuries-old norms could not take account of changing social and economic realities. Horn also launched an ad hominem attack, alleging that Nell-Breuning "seeks to interpret recent history falsely or even to falsify the data deliberately."[22]

On May 25 Nell-Breuning informed Georg Reuter, the DGB official in charge of publications, that Horn's pamphlet amounted to criminal libel and made it impossible for him to defend labor unity in future. All Catholic DGB functionaries were outraged by Horn's pamphlet, and the DGB vice chair Matthias Föcher commissioned an analysis by Dr. Franz Deus, the Catholic director of the DGB academy in Hattingen. Deus concluded that Horn's pamphlet rejected Catholic doctrine itself, not just particular assertions by Nell-Breuning, and grossly distorted Catholic teaching. He also noted that for years Agartz had marginalized his most distinguished colleagues at the Economic Research Institute and favored his Marxist friend Horn and the radical pacifist Theo Pirker.[23] Walter Freitag launched inquiries which suggested that Horn might have ties with the East German government. Agartz denied any foreknowledge of Horn's pamphlet, but he had instructed DGB staff to assist Horn, and Georg Reuter had approved the pamphlet in advance and instructed all DGB organs to distribute it.

---

[21] "Oswald von Nell-Breuning contra Viktor Agartz," *Gesellschaftspolitische Kommentare*, February 1, 1955 (DGB-Archiv/5/DGAI001191); Schroeder, "Christliche Sozialpolitik oder Sozialismus," pp. 194–199.

[22] Walter Horn, "Oswald von Nell-Breuning S.J. kontra Oswald von Nell-Breuning S.J." (Cologne: Bund-Verlag, 1955), pp. 1, 26–27 (DGB-Archiv/5/DGAI001777).

[23] Nell-Breuning to Georg Reuter, May 15, 1955, DGB-Archiv/5/DGAI001777; Reichel to Föcher, May 29, 1955, Hans Deckers to Föcher, June 7, and Franz Deus to Karl Braukmann, June 26, 1955, in NL Braukmann/6/Nell contra Nell; Karl Braukmann's "Aktennotiz" on a discussion with Karl Arnold, Tacke, Platte, and Sabel on June 11, 1955, DGB-Archiv/5/DGAI001777.

Freitag soon persuaded the DGB Central Committee to express regret over the personal attacks in the pamphlet, and he halted its distribution.[24] Werner Hansen, the Social Democratic state chair of the DGB of North Rhine-Westphalia, expressed sympathy for Nell-Breuning and revealed to Katzer that Reuter was maneuvering to succeed Freitag. Hansen vowed to resign from the DGB if Reuter succeeded, and he backed up his professions of good will by securing the election of a fourth Christian social representative to his state leadership team.[25]

DGB leaders had already stopped inviting Agartz to their meetings in early 1955, because the SPD's economic experts agreed with Nell-Breuning that his economic methodology was obsolete. In late June Horn published a diatribe against this new alliance between clericalism and "neo-socialists" in a leftist Hamburg weekly. "National Socialism was also a kind of neo-socialism," Horn declared, and "there are reputable scholars in the world who consider the imposition of clerico-fascism possible in Germany." Thereafter SPD leaders agreed with Freitag that Agartz and Horn behaved outrageously.[26] Agartz provoked a final rupture in July when he gave Freitag two letters suggesting that a colleague at the Economic Research Institute with whom he disagreed was an East German agent. After thorough investigation, DGB leaders judged that these letters had been forged, and that Agartz had made a practice for years of seeking and perhaps fabricating documents to eliminate rivals at DGB headquarters. On October 8 the DGB announced that Agartz had been suspended from his duties, and it dismissed Horn and Pirker a few days later. On October 13 the CDU commended the DGB for taking steps well suited "to improve the climate within the trade unions," and Heinrich Krone appealed confidentially to Winkelheide and Even to desist from any attempt to found Christian trade unions, because he and

---

[24] Else Viehöver to Freitag, May 22, 1955, and reply of June 6, and two unsigned, undated reports for Freitag, "Betr.: Dr. Walter Horn," DGB-Archiv/5/DGAI001777; Föcher to Nell-Breuning, June 14, 1955, NL Braukmann/6/Nell contra Nell; Albin Karl to Freitag, June 23, and Nell-Breuning to Freitag, June 24 and June 30, 1955, *Gewerkschaftsquellen*, XI: 689–696; Freitag to Wilhelm Biedorf of the Bund-Verlag, June 30, 1955, and Biedorf to Freitag, December 19, 1955, enclosed in Freitag's circular of December 20 to DGB leaders, DGB-Archiv/5/DGAI001777.

[25] Hans Katzer, "Niederschrift über die am 14. Juni 1955 stattgefundene Besprechung mit dem Vorstand des [DGB] Landesbezirks NRW," NL Kaiser/12/20–22; "Niederschrift über die Sitzung des [DGB] Landesbeamtenausschusses" in late May 1955, NL Hansen/22.

[26] Walter Horn to Georg Reuter, June 11, 1955, published in *Die Andere Zeitung*, #8, June 30, 1955 (DGB-Archiv/5/DGAI001777); Nell-Breuning to Thea Harmuth and Matthias Föcher, August 15, 1955, and Professor Weisser to Föcher and Harmuth, August 17, 1955, DGB-Archiv/5/DGAI001777; DGB Bundesvorstand, August 9, 1955, *Gewerkschaftsquellen*, XI: 729–730.

Adenauer had concluded that it would fail.[27] Nell-Breuning had thus accomplished a great deal with his attack on Agartz.

On October 14 Johannes Even of the KAB announced nevertheless to the leaders of other Christian social organizations that impetuous young colleagues would assemble in Essen the next day to found a Christian labor federation. One leader of the Kolping Clubs responded immediately that the DGB's purge of radicals eliminated any rationale for such an initiative. KAB leaders felt constrained to act, however, by a deadline on the offer of subsidies from the International League of Christian Trade Unions and demands for clarity about their futures by the handful of disgruntled young DGB functionaries who had been recruited to staff the new organization. On October 15 about 180 workers invited by the KAB therefore assembled in Essen to announce their secession from the DGB, and on October 30 they founded the Christian Labor Movement of Germany (*Christliche Gewerkschaftsbewegung Deutschlands*, or CGD), with Johannes Even as president.[28]

Seldom has any initiative been repudiated so quickly by supposed allies. The Social Committees declared that the small group in Essen did not represent anyone, and Heinrich Krone told CDU parliamentary leaders that Adenauer regarded this initiative as "inopportune."[29] Some DGB leaders suspected the Social Committees of complicity, but Freitag, Föcher, and Bernhard Tacke assured them that the KAB had acted alone. "There is no doubt," Tacke explained, "that Even and Winkelheide desire schism; personal factors play a role here, ambition and wounded vanity." On November 4 Freitag invited Jakob Kaiser to name seven representatives to meet regularly with DGB leaders to discuss the "protection of minorities." Karl Arnold condemned the attempt to split the unions in a radio address that evening, and similar declarations came from the Social Committees, Christian Social

---

[27] Krone, *Tagebücher*, I: 191; "Personalveränderungen im DGB," DUD press release of October 13, 1955 (source of quotation), and DGB press releases of October 13 and October 17, 1955, NL Katzer/624; DGB Bundesvorstand, November 22 and December 6, 1955, *Gewerkschaftsquellen*, XI: 795–799, 813–815; Schroeder, "Christliche Sozialpolitik oder Sozialismus," pp. 217–218; Pirker, *Blinde Macht*, II: 151–154.

[28] Hans Katzer, "Niederschrift über die Sitzung des Aktionsausschusses vom 14. Oktober 1955," NL Katzer/618/Aktionsausschuss; ultimatum to the DGB of October 22, 1955, *Gewerkschaftsquellen*, XI: 756–758; "Winkelheide: In letzter Minute," *Rheinische Post*, October 26, 1955 (NL Katzer/592); Schroeder, *Katholizismus und Einheitsgewerkschaft*, p. 180.

[29] "Richtigstellung," CDA press release of October 18, 1955, ACDP/04–013/160/1; "Die Sozialausschüsse ... distanzieren sich," CDA Westfalen press release of October 20, 1955, NL Katzer/250; CDU Fraktionsvorstand, October 17, 1955, *Fraktionsprotokolle 1953–57*, I: 837.

Collegium, and the most prominent social activists in the Evangelical Church.[30]

The Christian Labor Movement enjoyed powerful clerical support nevertheless. Cardinal Frings secured the following resolution by the western German bishops on November 5: "Now that Christian workers have resolved to found new Christian trade unions, as a result of genuine inner conflict and after lengthy deliberation in complete freedom, we respect this well-founded decision and expect sympathy for it, especially in clerical circles." They also issued pastoral guidelines instructing priests to help parishioners make "a correct decision of conscience" by explaining why the bishops considered DGB membership a grave threat to faith.[31] The bishops' declarations secured a respectful hearing for the CGD among CDU leaders. Jakob Kaiser told them on November 10 that this initiative would harm their party, but a majority agreed that the CDU must adopt a position of benevolent neutrality, because many party members admired the CGD. A few conservatives sought to revive the legend that the occupation powers had imposed unified trade unions in 1945 over the emphatic protests of the bishops, and such prominent figures as Franz Josef Strauss published explanations of their "neutrality" that consisted entirely of attacks on the DGB.[32]

The Christian Labor Movement was not a federation of unions but rather a single organization with regional offices for workers of all trades, financed with 500,000 marks in interest-free loans from the International League of Christian Trade Unions and smaller loans from the KAB. For many months it published no membership figures, and estimates by knowledgeable observers ranged from 5,000 to 20,000.[33] Even and Winkelheide had no trade union experience and refused to lay down

[30] "Düsseldorf, 31. Oktober 1955," minutes of a meeting of Freitag, Arnold, Kaiser, Katzer, and Föcher, and Freitag to Kaiser, November 4, 1955, NL Kaiser/102/83–84; DGB Bundesvorstand, November 1, 1955, and January 3, 1956, *Gewerkschaftsquellen*, XI: 766–784 (Tacke quotation on 772), 821–830; Arnold's radio speech and other declarations in *Gesellschaftspolitische Kommentare*, #22, November 15, 1955 (NL Kaiser/334/8–15); petition to Adenauer by the "Arbeitsgemeinschaft evangelischer Sozial- und Arbeiterpfarrer," October 6, 1955, NL Kaiser/276/33–34.

[31] "Protokoll der Beratungen auf dem Konveniat der westdeutschen Bischöfe" on November 3–5, 1955, and Anhang I, "Haltung der Geistlichen in der Gewerkschaftsfrage," issued on November 6, HAEK/CR II/2.19, 16.

[32] *Vorstandsprotokolle 1953–57*, November 10, 1955, pp. 698–708; CDU Bundestag delegation, November 8, 1955, *Fraktionsprotokolle 1953–57*, I: 861; "In Gewerkschaftsfragen neutral!" *Kölnische Rundschau*, November 12, 1955 (NL Kaiser/280/3); Adolf Süsterhenn, "Was dem einen Recht ist," *Rheinischer Merkur*, November 18, 1955 (NL Katzer/814); F.J. Strauss to the *Frankfurter Neue Presse*, November 25, 1955 (NL Platte/6/7).

[33] Press clippings about the CGD in NL Kaiser/285/89–91; Schroeder, *Katholizismus und Einheitsgewerkschaft*, pp. 188–192.

any of their other offices for union work. To run the CGD, they relied on a handful of ex-functionaries of the DGB, who sometimes proved unreliable. One of the most prominent was Werner Holzgreve, a co-founder of the Christian Social Collegium who had lost patience with its strategy to reform the DGB. Holzgreve resigned from the CGD in May 1956, however, and described it to reporters as utterly chaotic and ineffective.[34] Even and Winkelheide showed signs of desperation when they convened a second "Founding Congress" of the CGD in June 1956. When pressed by the delegates to provide membership figures, Winkelheide shouted that "the actual number MUST remain secret, or else we will no longer be interesting!" By February 1957 the CGD claimed 22,000 members, but its senior functionary Hubert Sturm then resigned and announced to the press that the actual number was 12,000 at most. The organization incurred a massive deficit each month, Sturm reported, and should be liquidated at once.[35]

The mere existence of the CGD nevertheless encouraged middle-class Christian Democrats to attack the Social Committees for defending the DGB. The Westphalian CDU headquarters, which was run by Theodor Blank's brother, Josef, authorized Winkelheide to present "informational talks" about the CGD to party meetings, and it hired several CGD activists to represent the CDU and Social Committees as the "social secretaries" who organized factory cells. The outraged protests by Albert Hillenkötter and other Christian Democratic DGB functionaries against this favoritism were ignored.[36] The influence of the Social Committees suffered further in February 1956 when the FDP toppled Karl Arnold as prime minister of North Rhine-Westphalia and formed a coalition with the SPD, because Adenauer had quarreled with the FDP in Bonn. Three CDU delegates opposed Arnold in the very close vote of confidence, and his friends suspected the KAB of taking revenge on the CDU's foremost defender of labor unity.[37] KAB leaders

---

[34] See Holzgreve's letter of resignation, March 20, 1956, and his declaration of May 7, attached to the Cologne DGB circular of May 29, 1956, NL Katzer/815.

[35] "Bericht über den Verlauf des CGD-Bundeskongresses" of June 15–17, 1956, NL Katzer/815; "Christliche Gewerkschaft gescheitert," *Frankfurter Allgemeine Zeitung*, #45, February 22, 1957 (with related press clippings in NL Katzer/815).

[36] CDA Westfalen, "Niederschrift über die Vorstandssitzung der Sozialausschüsse," January 28, 1956, and "Protokoll der Landesvorstandssitzung der Sozialausschüsse," April 1956, ACDP/03–002/454/1; dossiers on this dispute sent by Hillenkötter to the CDU Landesvorstand Westfalen on April 13, 1956, NL Katzer/592, and to Kaiser on May 5, NL Katzer/815; Hillenkötter's circular to party colleagues, June 7, 1956, NL Katzer/251.

[37] Hüwel, *Karl Arnold*, pp. 288–299; Gruber, *CDU Landtagsfraktion*, pp. 322–324; Mick to Albers, February 27, 1956, NL Albers/1/1956–1959; Karl Braukmann to Johannes Even, February 29, 1956, and reply of March 13, KAB Archiv/3/32.

and the Catholic clergy endorsed the "social reform" advocated by Labor Minister Storch and the Social Committees, but their decision to revive Christian trade unions inflicted grave damage on the political alliances necessary to make it happen.

In October 1956 the SPD strengthened its position further in the municipal elections in North Rhine-Westphalia. With the splinter parties in decline, the vote for the CDU rose from 35.6 percent in 1952 to 38.2 percent, but that for the SPD surged from 36.1 to 44.2 percent. The CDU fared worst in large cities and lost control of the mayor's office in Essen, Cologne, and Düsseldorf. This result marked the beginning of the transformation of the Ruhr Valley into the "Red Ruhr," a bastion of SPD power from the late 1950s to the 1980s. Jakob Kaiser argued that the SPD had profited from disenchantment with the CDU among blue-collar voters. Some CDU leaders challenged this assessment, but Adenauer secured agreement that they must achieve impressive gains in social policy to have any hope of winning the next Bundestag election; the voters must see genuine progress toward the "social reform" long promised by Labor Minister Storch.[38]

4.2   Social Policy Debates in the Bundestag

Despite their feuds, the Bundestag delegates from the KAB and Social Committees represented constituents with the same interests, and they cooperated in social policy debates. The details of legislative deliberations remain difficult to reconstruct, however, because the most important decisions were made not in the well-documented meetings of the entire CDU/CSU Bundestag delegation but by fewer than thirty colleagues in its executive committee (*Fraktionsvorstand*), who often kept no record of their discussions. The executive committee only presented a controversial issue for debate by the whole delegation after agreement on basic principles had been achieved in small working groups (*Arbeitskreise*) that included the most influential representatives of the interest groups affected. This rule avoided heated debates in the delegation as a whole, but only at the expense of many delays. In Adenauer's second term the delegation included eight working groups that corresponded to the eight committees in the Bundestag. This organization crudely reflected the

---

[38] *Vorstandsprotokolle 1953–57*, November 23, 1956, pp. 1135–1147; Kaiser to Hans Toussaint, November 2, 1956, NL Kaiser/114/296; Hüwel, *Karl Arnold*, pp. 301–308; municipal election results at www.wahlergebnisse.nrw.de/kommunalwahlen. See also Karl Rohe, "Political Alignments and Re-alignments in the Ruhr, 1867–1987," in Karl Rohe, *Elections, Parties, and Political Traditions: Social Foundations of German Parties and Party Systems, 1867–1987* (New York, 1990), pp. 107–144.

vision of social order in the papal encyclical *Quadragesimo Anno*. According to Heinrich Krone, the CDU Bundestag delegation rejected the rigid discipline of the SPD, because it respected freedom of conscience; instead of imposing a closed caucus [*Fraktionszwang*] in important Bundestag votes, it sought consensus through persuasion and artful compromise. Krone boasted to party colleagues in 1956 that the spirit of "Christian solidarity" made their delegation the most unified in the Bundestag, even though it contained the most socially diverse membership.[39]

The delegation's Working Group IV on social policy was chaired by Peter Horn, a health insurance expert from Hesse and cautious member of the Social Committees. Workers' delegates comprised the strongest element in it, but important social policy bills were discussed jointly with Working Group II on economic policy, where business lobbyists predominated. Only when Groups II and IV agreed on basic principles could the whole delegation discuss a bill. Heinrich von Brentano chaired the delegation from 1949 to 1955 but focused his attention on foreign policy; his deputy Krone became the parliamentary leader for domestic policy even before he succeeded Brentano as chair in June 1955. Krone had become a career Center Party politician already in 1922; he came from a humble family of peasants and artisans, had old ties to the Catholic social movement, and was a personal friend of Jakob Kaiser. The Workers' Group therefore backed him enthusiastically against Kurt Georg Kiesinger in the election to chair their delegation in 1955.[40] Of the twenty-eight members of the delegation's executive committee in February 1955, seven represented workers (Albers, Arndgen, Even, Lücke, Pelster, Rümmele, and Schütz), five of whom had begun their careers in the old Christian trade unions.[41]

Despite Krone's assertions about Christian solidarity, the CDU/CSU Bundestag delegation had a remarkable history of split voting. Of the 167 roll-call votes in the Bundestag's second term, it voted unanimously in only 44, mostly involving foreign policy. In some votes the party took no

[39] Heinrich Krone, "Die Arbeit der CDU/CSU-Bundestagsfraktion," in CDU, *6. Bundesparteitag der CDU, 26.–29. April 1956 in Stuttgart* (Hamburg, no date), pp. 80–82; Hans-Peter Schwarz, "'Für mich ist das Fegefeuer, wenn ich in die Fraktion muss.' Die CDU/CSU-Fraktion in der Ära Adenauer, 1949–1963," in Hans-Peter Schwarz, ed., *Die Fraktion als Machtfaktor. CDU/CSU im Deutschen Bundestag, 1949 bis heute* (Munich, 2009), pp. 9–37; Geoffrey Pridham, *Christian Democracy in Western Germany, 1945–1976: The CDU/CSU in Government and Opposition* (New York, 1977), pp. 69–81.

[40] Introduction by Helge Heidemeyer to *Fraktionsprotokolle 1953–57*, and meetings of June 6 and June 15, 1955, I: 650–651, 669; Krone, *Tagebücher*, biographical introduction and entries of June 1955, I: 180–181.

[41] *Fraktionsprotokolle 1953–57*, January 25 and February 16, 1955, I: 540, 553.

stand, but in 101 votes the CDU did take a stand, and one or more delegates rejected it. Religious denomination and other factors had little influence on a delegate's tendency to deviate; occupation was the key variable, and workers defied their party most often.

Deviations from the Party Line by CDU/CSU Bundestag Delegates, 1953–1957

Number of deviations	Career Politicians (15)	Large and Small Business (58)	Free Professions (45)	Miscellaneous (15)	Farmers (34)	Civil Servants (39)	Labor (30)
0	73%	47%	40%	33%	32%	23%	17%
1–3	27%	45%	44%	40%	47%	59%	30%
4 or more	0%	8%	16%	27%	21%	18%	53%
	100%	100%	100%	100%	100%	100%	100%

The compilers of this table only counted thirty workers' representatives, based on their published résumés, but sixty-one delegates joined the Workers' Group by 1956, including many civil servants who belonged to public-sector labor unions. Many delegates listed as "miscellaneous" or "civil servants" in this table could be counted as "labor," but the authors have clearly shown that the workers' delegates displayed more dissatisfaction with the party line and more willingness to provoke confrontation than did members of any other vocational group.[42] To investigate whether these confrontation tactics proved successful, this section will discuss the three bills most important to the Social Committees in the mid-1950s: the law to regulate co-determination in the public sector, the Supplemental Co-Determination Law of August 1956, and the "dynamic" pension reform of 1957.

4.2.1   The Government Personnel Representation Law of June 1955

The DGB and Social Committees both sought to extend co-determination rights to government employees after Adenauer insisted in 1952 that they be excluded from the Factory Councils Law. Members of the Social Committees had played a leading role in efforts to unionize the public sector, and the Social Committees promised the DGB in 1952 to secure

---

[42] George Rueckert and Wilder Crane, "CDU Deviancy in the German Bundestag," *Journal of Politics*, 24 (1962): 477–488 (table on 486); list of sixty-one "Arbeitnehmervertreter der CDU/CSU im Bundestag" on November 1, 1956, NL Katzer/255. See also the attendance records in "Zusammenstellung der Tagungen der Arbeitnehmerabgeordneten," 1952–1956, ACDP/04–013/131/1.

rights "of equal value" in the public and private sectors. The Social Committees and DGB agreed that public-sector employees deserved a strong voice in all decisions made by their job supervisors, but not in policy decisions by parliamentary bodies. In September 1952 the Social Committees opposed the first cabinet bill for a Personnel Representation Law because it violated this principle, and in April 1953 they persuaded the CDU Hamburg Party Congress to demand a "personnel representation law ... that takes account of the special nature of public service without in any way discriminating against the civil servants, employees, and blue-collar workers in public service." Opposition by the Social Committees helped to prevent the government bill from advancing in the first legislative term.[43]

The government introduced a modified bill in March 1954, but the Social Committees still found it objectionable. As chair of the Bundestag labor committee, Anton Sabel headed a joint Bundestag subcommittee, which included representatives of the civil service committee, to review the bill. In the summer of 1954 Sabel worked with the Social Democratic DGB leader Willi Richter to secure majorities on this subcommittee for amendments that gave elected personnel committees a voice in the hiring and promotion of colleagues, allowed the participation of union functionaries in their deliberations, and referred disputes with a supervisor to the ordinary labor courts, where the unions enjoyed strong influence, not administrative panels of senior civil servants. However, in October the interior and justice ministers persuaded the cabinet to reject all these amendments.[44]

Tough bargaining took place within the CDU Bundestag delegation in March 1955 to reconcile the committee and cabinet versions of the bill. Sabel's principal opponent was the CSU delegate, Josef Ferdinand Kleindinst, chair of the Bundestag civil service committee, who enjoyed support from business lobbyists and others fearful of union influence in the public sector. The law would apply to 1.2 million untenured blue- and white-collar workers as well as 800,000 tenured civil servants, but many CDU Bundestag delegates spoke only about the latter group. Adenauer himself sympathized with Kleindinst and apparently told Sabel privately that his version of the bill would never become law as long as Adenauer

---

[43] Herlind Gundelach, "Die Sozialausschüsse zwischen CDU und DGB. Selbstverständnis und Rolle 1949–1966," phil. diss. (Bonn, 1983), pp. 116–122; CDU, *4. Bundesparteitag, 18.–22. April 1953, Hamburg* (Hamburg and Bonn, no date), p. 75.

[44] Katzer circular to the Social Committees, June 30, 1954, ACDP/04–013/159; Adolf Leweke, "Personalvertretungsgesetz in Sicht," *Soziale Ordnung*, VIII/#6 (June 1954), p. 7; Bundesarchiv, *Kabinettsprotokolle Online*, meeting of October 22, 1954, Point 4; Sabel to Storch and Kaiser, October 28, 1954, NL Sabel/2/3; Gundelach, "Sozialausschüsse," pp. 123–125.

remained chancellor.[45] On March 16 Sabel presented his amendments to his Bundestag delegation nevertheless and received vigorous support from the Workers' Group. Heinrich von Brentano insisted that the delegation take no stand, however, and wrote Sabel angrily that such debates over fundamental principles should never occur in the delegation until the Working Groups had reached agreement. Civil servants denounced Sabel to reporters for seeking the "complete Bolshevization of the administration," and most of the provisions demanded by Kleindinst gained majorities on March 17 in the Bundestag's penultimate vote on the bill. Sabel led a group of forty CDU delegates who voted with the SPD, but the civil service lobby gained victory with the votes of 200 Christian Democrats plus the small coalition parties.[46]

This Bundestag vote provoked a storm of protest by the Social Committees, and Katzer branded it a flagrant breach of the promises made by the CDU Hamburg Party Congress. "If changes are not made in the final vote in line with the committee bill by Anton Sabel," Katzer concluded, "then rights will be lost which factory councils in the public sector have enjoyed for the past ten years" on the basis of state laws and collective bargaining agreements.[47] Sabel and seven Bundestag colleagues wrote Brentano on March 28 that Kleindinst had inserted amendments at the last minute which made the bill even more unfavorable to workers than the original cabinet bill, and they demanded a restoration of Sabel's provisions in the final vote. Sabel predicted correctly that the DGB and especially its Public Service and Transport Workers' Union would regard this version of the bill as a massive assault on organized labor. Georg Schneider of the white-collar German Employees' Union, which sometimes criticized the militant tactics of the DGB, editorialized that the recent parliamentary vote had revealed "anti-union complexes" in the CDU; this bill would inflict grave harm on two million public-sector employees.[48]

---

[45] CDU Bundestag delegation, March 7 and 14, 1955, *Fraktionsprotokolle 1953–57*, I: 571, 577; Josef Mick to Albers, March 11, 1955, reporting what Katzer had heard from Sabel about his conversation with Adenauer, NL Albers/1/1950–1955.

[46] *Fraktionsprotokolle 1953–57*, March 16, 1955, I: 578–582, 587–588; Brentano to Sabel, March 17, 1955, NL Sabel/1/2; "Personalräte: Rechte Hand und linke Hand," *Der Spiegel*, IX/#16 (April 13, 1955), pp. 9–10 (source of quotation).

[47] CDA Kreissozialausschuss Essen to all CDU/CSU Bundestag delegates, March 18, 1955, LANRW/CDA Rheinland/695; CDA Kreissozialausschuss Düsseldorf, circular of March 19, 1955, NL Katzer/249; Katzer to Heinrich von Brentano, March 19, 1955, with enclosed press release, "Bedrohliche Entwicklung," ACDP/04–013/167/2 (source of quotation); Anton Becker, "Rundschreiben Nr. 5" to the Westphalian Social Committees, March 21, 1955, NL Katzer/249.

[48] Anton Sabel and friends to Brentano, March 28, 1955, NL Sabel/1/2; editorials by Sabel and Georg Schneider, *Soziale Ordnung*, IX/#4 (April 1955), pp. 4–5; DGB

On March 21 Heinrich Krone appointed a seven-man commission to seek consensus within the delegation that included three workers' delegates, three civil servants, and an Evangelical theologian as chair. After two months of negotiations, a majority agreed to follow Kleindinst by rejecting jurisdiction for the labor courts and a right for union representatives to participate in meetings of personnel committees. Sabel prevailed, however, in defining broad powers for the personnel councils of blue- and white-collar workers to "co-determine" work hours, holiday schedules, pay scales, and promotion decisions. The most controversial issue involved the powers of the councils for tenured civil servants, but Sabel secured a 4:3 vote that they too should have the right to "co-determine" hiring and promotion decisions. Katzer reported to the Social Committees that Sabel had won a great victory.[49]

Following a tense debate on June 7, the CDU Bundestag delegation as a whole voted to reverse that last victory by Sabel and strip personnel councils for civil servants of any voice in promotion decisions. Artur Jahn of the railroad workers' union then wrote all CDU/CSU workers' delegates that they must attend the Bundestag vote the next day, because "there is danger that crucial provisions will be included in the Personnel Representation Law against our wishes." If they did not approve of the bill's final version, he concluded, they should adjourn the debate and huddle to decide on a course of action. Sabel informed the CDU parliamentary leadership that his friends could not accept the decision on promotions, and it amended the CDU bill at the last minute to allow "co-determination" in the promotion of civil servants up to the pay grade of A1a, excluding those who worked in academia or the arts. This compromise secured a unified CDU vote in favor of the bill on June 8, and it passed despite opposition by the SPD and FDP. Krone took pride in the spirit of unity among his colleagues, which transcended conflicts of material interest. Katzer declared in the name of the Social Committees that the CDU's promises to public sector employees had been kept. The final law still provoked criticism by the DGB, but its leaders thanked the union-affiliated Bundestag delegates from all parties who had defeated the most intolerable demands of the civil service lobby. The confrontation tactics by forty CDU workers' delegates thus achieved a noteworthy success, a law that

Bundesausschuss, March 30, 1955, *Gewerkschaftsquellen*, XI: 674–676; Hans Zankl, "Bericht vom 2. Gewerkschaftstag der Gewerkschaft ÖTV," May 3–7, 1955, pp. 7–9, NL Katzer/552.

[49] *Fraktionsprotokolle 1953–57*, March 21–28 and May 23, 1955, I: 591, 594, 600, 641; Katzer, "Rundschreiben Nr. 4/55," May 25, 1955, pp. 1–5, ACDP/04–013/160/1.

created a more collegial work environment for two million public sector employees.[50]

4.2.2   The Supplemental Co-Determination Law of August 1956

Debate erupted between business lobbyists and laborites in the CDU because of a loophole in the parity Co-Determination Law of 1951 for coal, iron, and steel. After 1945 the Allied military governments pursued an aggressive decartelization policy by dissolving both horizontally integrated trusts such as the United Steelworks and vertically integrated industrial combines. Many German business leaders believed that they had been left with too many small firms that could not compete with European and American giants. In 1952 the Allied High Commissioners terminated their decartelization program, and some German businesses resumed the quest for horizontal and vertical integration through the formation of holding companies, i.e. combines with several component firms. In December 1953 the revived Mannesmann holding company secured a verdict from the Düsseldorf district court that parity co-determination did not apply to it, only the Factory Councils Law of 1952, which granted workers only one-third of the seats on the corporate supervisory board and did not require the appointment of a "labor director" at the top echelon of management. The metalworkers' and miners' unions discerned a plot to sabotage parity co-determination by transferring key decisions to the holding companies, and they demanded a law to close this loophole.[51]

Labor Minister Storch agreed that organized labor had a grievance, and he presented a bill to the cabinet on January 8, 1954, to require that parity co-determination apply to any holding company whose "predominant function" was to produce coal, iron, and/or steel. Adenauer termed this bill highly controversial, however, and demanded consultation with the coalition parties.[52] The Workers' Group in the CDU Bundestag delegation agreed to support the DGB's demands on January 10, and Anton Sabel again secured a pivotal role as chair of a joint subcommittee

[50] *Fraktionsprotokolle 1953–57*, June 7/8, 1955, I: 654, 662; Artur Jahn circular to "Werter Kollege," June 7, 1955, ACDP/04–013/131/1; Krone, *Tagebücher*, June 8, 1955, I: 179; Krone to Sabel, June 10, 1955, NL Sabel/1/2; Hans Katzer, "Soziale Mehrheit für das Personalvertretungsgesetz," *Soziale Ordnung*, IX/#6 (Beilage for June 1955), p. 1; Gundelach, "Sozialausschüsse," pp. 125–26; Pirker, *Blinde Macht*, II: 165–167.

[51] Erich Potthoff, *Der Kampf um die Montanmitbestimmung* (Cologne, 1957), pp. 55–65, 81–112; Potthoff's report to the leadership of IG Metall, January 14/15, 1954, *Gewerkschaftsquellen*, X: 407–418; Isabel Warner, *Steel and Sovereignty: The Deconcentration of the West German Steel Industry, 1949–54* (Mainz, 1996), pp. 95–230.

[52] Bundesarchiv, *Kabinettsprotokolle Online*, meeting of January 29, 1954, Point 3.

of the Bundestag committees for labor and social policy that included Johannes Even, Heinrich Scheppmann, and the Mannesmann executive Wolfgang Pohle. Sabel assured Adenauer that he did not seek to extend co-determination rights, only to preserve them where they existed, and on February 1 he persuaded a majority on the subcommittee to demand prompt legislation.[53] The Social Committees hoped that if they fulfilled the unions' legislative wishes, then the unions would acknowledge "the obligation to pay the proper attention to Christian workers when filling the positions in question." They resolved on February 22 that holding companies must have a board of supervisors based on parity and a labor director chosen by the workers' representatives. Most CDU business lobbyists accepted the former demand but rejected the latter.[54]

After the DGB placed the issue of holding companies on the agenda for its Frankfurt Congress of October 1954, the cabinet and CDU addressed it again in September. Sabel and other workers' delegates pressed for a bill to introduce parity co-determination and a labor director in every holding company for which 75 percent or more of turnover came from coal, iron, and steel. Johannes Albers noted that this sector had not lost one day to strikes since the introduction of parity co-determination in 1951, and he warned that failure to pass this bill would provoke unrest. "One cannot expect the trade unions to renounce co-determination rights already achieved," he concluded. Wolfgang Pohle now opposed any bill, however, and chairman Brentano concluded that the CDU should not take a position but simply acknowledge the right of Sabel to introduce his bill, which he did on September 24.[55] Storch had gained cabinet approval for his bill the day before, but only after bowing to pressure from Ludwig Erhard and the FDP to drop any provision for labor directors. At the DGB Frankfurt Congress, the CDU Bundestag delegate and functionary of the miners' union, Heinrich Scheppmann, promised to fight for Sabel's

---

[53] Anton Sabel, "An die Mitglieder des Arbeitskreises für Arbeit und Soziales in der CDU/CSU-Fraktion," January 11, 1954, with enclosed "Entwurf eines Gesetzes zur Ergänzung des Gesetzes über die Mitbestimmung der Arbeitnehmer," ACDP/08–005/67/2; "Aktennotiz über die 1. Sitzung des Unterausschusses 'Mitbestimmung in den Holding-Gesellschaften der Montanindustrie,'" January 18, 1954, and "2. Sitzung," February 1, 1954, NL Sabel/2/3; Sabel to Adenauer, January 18, 1954, NL Sabel/1/2.

[54] "Zusammengefasste Niederschrift über die Sitzung des Wirtschaftspolitischen Ausschusses der Sozialausschüsse," January 22, 1954, ACDP/04–013/159 (source of quotation); "Niederschrift über die Tagung der Arbeitnehmerabgeordneten" of the CDU, February 22, 1954, NL Katzer/310; "Niederschrift über die Sitzung des Arbeitskreises für Sozialpolitik der Sozialausschüsse," February 22, 1954, NL Sabel/1/4; "4. Sitzung des Unterausschusses 'Mitbestimmung-Holding,'" February 23, 1954, NL Sabel/2/3; Wolfgang Pohle to Sabel, July 7, and Robert Pferdmenges to Adenauer, July 8, 1954, NL Sabel/2/3.

[55] *Fraktionsprotokolle 1953–57*, September 22, 1954, I: 349–357.

bill against the cabinet's inferior version but warned that big business would mobilize powerful opposition. Thereafter the legislative process stalled because of sharp disagreement between the social policy and economic policy working groups in the CDU Bundestag delegation.[56]

Some observers argued that workers had lost interest in the issue, but they soon learned otherwise. The steel industrialist Hermann Reusch provoked outrage among his workers when he told a shareholders' meeting on January 11, 1955, that parity co-determination had only resulted from "brutal extortion" by the trade unions and should be replaced everywhere by the milder provisions of the Factory Councils Law of 1952. Over 13,000 steelworkers in Oberhausen spontaneously went on strike for twenty-four hours, against the advice of local union functionaries. The unions then organized a second twenty-four-hour protest strike on January 22 that involved a stunning 820,000 miners and metalworkers.[57] Prime Minister Karl Arnold condemned Reusch's speech and told reporters that "the state will know how to defend the right of co-determination, which has worked well in practice, against everyone." Some business lobbyists in the CDU defended Reusch, however, and Adenauer equivocated; he criticized Reusch's speech before CDU leaders but also expressed outrage that a handful of union bosses could "compel" hundreds of thousands of workers to strike against their wishes.[58]

CDU parliamentary leaders refused to consider the issue again until Sabel reported in April 1956 that the Bundestag labor committee had adopted a compromise bill endorsed by Wolfgang Pohle. This bill required labor directors, but in holding companies they would be elected by a simple majority of the supervisory board, not the workers' representatives alone. Sabel had also agreed that the workers' representatives would be elected by assemblies of all employees, not the factory council,

---

[56] Bundesarchiv, *Kabinettsprotokolle Online*, Kabinettsausschuss für Wirtschaft, September 20, 1954, Point 1, and cabinet meeting of September 23, Point 1; "Aktive Sozialpolitik," *Soziale Ordnung*, VIII/#10 (October 1954), p. 6; DGB, *3. Bundeskongress 1954*, pp. 82–83, 504–505, 512; CDU Bundestag delegation, November 15, 1954, *Fraktionsprotokolle 1953–57*, I: 469–470.

[57] Report from the Düsseldorf office of IG Metall, January 13, 1955, *Gewerkschaftsquellen*, X: 565–566; DGB Bundesvorstand, January 16 and February 1, 1955, *Gewerkschaftsquellen*, XI: 634–635, 649–650; note by Katzer on January 18, 1955, on a confidential report by "Herr Sch[eppmann]," NL Katzer/625; Potthoff, *Montanmitbestimmung*, pp. 112–117; Karl Lauschke, *Die halbe Macht. Mitbestimmung in der Eisen- und Stahlindustrie 1945 bis 1989* (Essen, 2007), pp. 115–119.

[58] "Arnold zur Erklärung von Dr. Reusch," press release of January 14, 1955, NL Hansen/24; CDU Bundestag delegation, January 18, 1955, *Fraktionsprotokolle 1953–57*, I: 532–535; CDU Bundesvorstand, February 5, 1955, *Vorstandsprotokolle 1953–57*, pp. 340–341.

a procedure that weakened trade union influence. Pohle spread the word, however, that he still rejected any labor director and had only voted for Sabel's bill to prevent the labor committee from endorsing an even worse SPD bill. Pohle informed Sabel that he reserved the right to introduce amendments on the floor of the Bundestag, but Sabel replied sharply that his friends were also prepared to introduce amendments in cooperation with the SPD. "It is seldom possible in political life," Sabel declared, "to implement one's views completely. Compromises demand concessions from all sides."[59] Pohle refrained from introducing amendments during the decisive Bundestag debate on June 7 and abstained in the final vote, and the Supplemental Co-Determination Law passed with an overwhelming majority, opposed only by the FDP. It applied to all eight holding companies then in existence and thereby promoted labor peace in the Ruhr, but others formed thereafter with holdings so diverse that the law did not apply.[60] Debate over this issue revived therefore under Adenauer's successors.

4.2.3   The "Dynamic" Pension Reform of January 1957

The most important act of social legislation in Adenauer's second term came after a four-year debate over pension reform. Germany's system of publicly administered old-age pensions for blue- and white-collar workers had relied on the formation of large capital reserves that were destroyed by the Second World War and currency reform. By 1953 the labor ministry had succeeded at providing pensions calculated as if the retiree's contributions had been paid in today's D-marks, but the results were not very impressive. As Anton Storch explained to the cabinet in November 1953, so many workers had earned such low wages and paid dues at such low rates for most of their careers that pensions usually amounted to only 30–40 percent of one's income before retirement. He called for a bold revaluation of pensions, based on the premise that the retiree had always paid dues according to today's wage levels and rates, so that retirement would not cause an abrupt decline in the standard of living. Finance Minister Fritz Schäffer of the CSU demanded, however, that any increase of pensions be linked to a means test, that planning for "social reform" be removed from the labor ministry and entrusted to an independent

---

[59] Report by Sabel to the CDU Fraktionsvorstand, April 16, 1956, *Fraktionsprotokolle 1953–57*, II: 1047; Sabel to Krone, May 2, Pohle to Sabel, May 28, and Sabel to Pohle, June 1, 1956, NL Sabel/1/2; Potthoff, *Montanmitbestimmung*, pp. 124–132.

[60] *Fraktionsprotokolle 1953–57*, June 5–6, 1956, II: 1102–1105; Pirker, *Blinde Macht*, II: 167–172; Lauschke, *Die halbe Macht*, pp. 119–131.

commission of experts, and that the finance ministry be allowed to borrow money against the surplus funds accumulating in the unemployment insurance system. Storch replied firmly that means tests were demeaning, that pensions must be regarded as entitlements, and that pension reform should begin at once, not wait for a new commission to study social reform. He also laid claim to the surplus funds in the unemployment insurance chest to launch pension reform. The cabinet agreed that the labor ministry should continue planning for pension reform, but say nothing about it in public.[61]

Schäffer's idea of an independent commission gained support in the following weeks from other ministries and the press, so Storch gave a radio interview on January 13, 1954, to describe his disagreement over means testing with unnamed opponents in the government who ignored the distinction between poor relief and social insurance. The labor minister proclaimed his resolve to achieve pensions "that can be described as socially just."[62] On February 19 Storch obtained permission from the cabinet to discuss pension reform at an upcoming conference of experts, where he promised a general increase of all pensions, without means testing. Storch secured the support of the Workers' Group in the CDU Bundestag delegation on February 22, and on April 6 he persuaded the cabinet to postpone indefinitely any discussion of an independent commission. At the CDU party congress in May, speakers earned the loudest applause when they addressed pension reform, and Storch promised to present a bill in June. *Social Order* then polemicized against the outmoded view (articulated by Schäffer in cabinet meetings)

that it was never the purpose of our pension system to grant pensions that would be the sole source of income, but that self-help and family obligations should continue to provide support. For the little man there is not much chance of self-help after nights of bombing and the currency reform ... We must acknowledge that the pension must now provide the sole source of support for pensioners in most cases.[63]

---

[61] Cabinet meeting of November 5, 1953, Point 1, Bundesarchiv, *Kabinettsprotokolle Online*; Hockerts, *Sozialpolitische Entscheidungen*, pp. 237–249.

[62] Anton Storch, interview with the Hessischen Rundfunk, January 13, 1954, published in the *Bulletin des Presse- und Informationsamtes der Bundesregierung*, January 16, 1954, pp. 75–76.

[63] Cabinet meetings of February 19, 1954, Point 4, and April 6, 1954, Point 9, Bundesarchiv, *Kabinettsprotokolle Online*; "Niederschrift über die Tagung der Arbeitnehmerabgeordneten," February 22, 1954, NL Katzer/310; remarks by Brentano and Storch, CDU, *5. Bundesparteitag der CDU. Köln, 28.-30. Mai 1954* (Bonn, no date), pp. 41, 128–132; Adolf Leweke, "Die alten Leute," *Soziale Ordnung*, VIII/#7–8 (July–August 1954), pp. 12–13; Hockerts, *Sozialpolitische Entscheidungen*, pp. 251–260.

Storch had revealed enough about internal government debates to mobilize public opinion without committing a flagrant breach of cabinet discipline.

Adenauer blocked further progress, however, when he told cabinet ministers on June 1, 1954, that "comprehensive social reform" must be their top priority. The cabinet then created an inter-ministerial planning committee, where the labor ministry representative was usually outvoted by his colleagues from the finance and interior ministries. Storch notified CDU parliamentary leaders that Fritz Schäffer obstructed pension reform, and they demanded "the fastest possible increase in old-age pensions." Adenauer ignored this plea, however, and told the cabinet on July 13 that an independent commission must be appointed, and that the government must avoid "partial solutions" while it deliberated.[64] This stance doomed the cabinet to paralysis until the SPD caused a political stampede on September 1 by introducing a very popular bill to grant every pensioner a thirteenth month's payment for Christmas. Storch then presented a slightly more generous government bill that passed the Bundestag unanimously on October 14. The cabinet also agreed to drop the idea of an independent commission and reaffirm the labor ministry's jurisdiction over planning. The Social Committees in particular rejected an independent commission, because it would only help the finance ministry to subordinate social to fiscal considerations.[65]

The cabinet remained deeply divided over pension reform in the year 1955. Storch revealed to the CDU workers' delegates on January 10 that the labor ministry sought pensions for everyone equal to 70–75 percent of the retiree's former income, the basic rule for civil service pensions, and they expressed enthusiastic support. Adenauer challenged that approach, however, when he wrote all cabinet ministers on January 16 to express grave concern about the emergence of a "caretaker state" (*Versorgungsstaat*), in which the citizens demanded the elimination of all risk from their lives. He thus encouraged Fritz Schäffer, Ludwig Erhard, and Franz Josef Strauss to argue that spending on social programs must

---

[64] Cabinet meetings of June 1, 1954, Point 2, and July 13, Point 3, Bundesarchiv, *Kabinettsprotokolle Online*; CDU Bundestag delegation, June 21, 1954, *Fraktionsprotokolle 1953–1957*, I: 167.

[65] Cabinet meetings of September 14, 1954, Topic B, September 22, Topic A, and September 29, Point 1, Bundesarchiv, *Kabinettsprotokolle Online*; CDU Bundestag delegation, September 14/15, 1954, *Fraktionsprotokolle 1953–57*, I: 295–300, 325–326; Jakob Kaiser's "Vermerk" of September 27, 1954, NL Kaiser/441/35–36; "Sozialreform eine fiskalische Angelegenheit?" *Soziale Ordnung*, VIII/#9 (September 1954), p. 3; Hockerts, *Sozialpolitische Entscheidungen*, pp. 265–271.

be reduced.[66] Schäffer also obstructed progress by refusing to approve funding for the additional labor ministry officials which the cabinet agreed were needed to draft legislation. Adenauer expressed impatience with Storch by inviting four professors of social policy to draft their own proposals for social reform, completed in late May, which called for a radical reorganization of all social benefits to avoid duplication of effort. Storch attacked their plan as utterly impractical, however, and the Social Committees agreed. Adenauer deplored Storch's mental rigidity in the cabinet meeting of July 13 and then left on vacation.[67] Storch sought publicity thereafter and gained enthusiastic support at the national congress of the Social Committees in September 1955, which resolved that pensions must correspond to 75 percent of the retiree's previous income, and that "pensions already granted are to be adjusted to the prevailing wage niveau." This demand reflected one of the first public discussions of the idea of "dynamic" pensions, adjusted not merely to the cost of living but to match improvements in the living standard of employed workers, a demand not raised by the DGB until January 1956.[68] Within the CDU, many criticized this resolution as overly ambitious, and Adenauer offered no guidance because of preoccupation with foreign policy. For the second year in a row, the SPD therefore caught the CDU off guard when it introduced a bill in late September to grant pensioners an extra half month's payment every four months. The CDU again felt compelled to offer a slightly more generous interim bill of its own, which gained unanimous Bundestag approval on November 17.[69]

The logjam in the cabinet finally broke up when Adenauer forged an alliance with the labor ministry at year's end. After reading with approval an article by a young economist employed by the League of Catholic Businessmen, Wilfrid Schreiber, Adenauer invited him

---

[66] "Bericht über die Tagung der Arbeitnehmerabgeordneten" on January 9/10, 1955, NL Katzer/310; Adenauer's circular to the cabinet, "Betr.: Entwicklung zum Versorgungsstaat," January 16, 1955, and replies in NL Kaiser/435.

[67] Hockerts, *Sozialpolitische Entscheidungen*, pp. 288–299; "Niederschrift über die Vorstandssitzung der Sozialausschüsse," July 2, 1955, ACDP/03–002/454/1; cabinet meeting of July 13, 1955, Point 1, Bundesarchiv, *Kabinettsprotokolle Online*.

[68] Anton Storch, "Zur Reform der sozialen Leistungen," *Soziale Ordnung*, IX/#10 (October 1955), pp. 6–7, plus Beilage with "Entschliessungen der VII. Bundestagung: Arbeitskreis IV;" Hans Stützle, "Begleiterscheinungen der Rentenreform," *Soziale Ordnung*, X/#10 (October 1956), p. 162.

[69] CDU Bundestag delegation, September 21, 1955, *Fraktionsprotokolle 1953–57*, I: 791–801; Hockerts, *Sozialpolitische Entscheidungen*, pp. 307–308. Hans-Peter Schwarz ignores Adenauer's distinctly unhelpful role before December 1955 when he declares that pension reform could not have taken place "without constant pressure on the part of the chancellor" (*Adenauer*, II: 280).

on December 13 to explain to several cabinet ministers his proposal for "dynamic" pensions whose value would be adjusted periodically to match wage increases. Schreiber rejected the old idea that workers should accumulate a capital reserve sufficient to support them in retirement, arguing that it was a morally praiseworthy gesture of "solidarity between the generations" for retirees to be supported by those currently employed. He emphasized that pension increases financed in this way could not cause inflation, because they simply transferred consumption power from younger to older citizens. Labor ministry officials then gave Adenauer a thick stack of briefing papers to work through over the Christmas holiday, and on January 18, 1956, he persuaded the cabinet committee on social reform to endorse their plan, including a complex formula to calculate the initial value of pensions based on employment history and the annual adjustment of pensions to match increases in current wages and salaries. Ludwig Erhard and Fritz Schäffer rejected the latter proposal emphatically, however. Despite Schreiber's cogent arguments to the contrary, Erhard insisted that the labor ministry plan would cause inflation. The economics minister noted that employers had often succeeded in opposing demands for wage increases with the argument that an increase in the cost of living would harm retirees; dynamic pensions would leave Germany with "no adequate brake to bring movements to raise wages to a halt and would therefore not sufficiently oppose inflationary tendencies."[70]

Storch argued persuasively to cabinet colleagues that Erhard exaggerated the risk of inflation; indeed, his plan would reduce aggregate consumer demand slightly through a modest hike in pension insurance premiums. The labor minister sought consensus nevertheless by agreeing that pensions should not be adjusted automatically to match wage increases; "instead other factors such as the overall development of the standard of living and productivity will be considered." The cabinet then notified the press that its proposal should be called "productivity pensions" rather than "dynamic pensions." Support from Adenauer enabled the labor ministry to complete its bill for cabinet consideration by May 1956, which provided pensions for all blue- and white-collar workers who turned sixty-five that were equal to 60 percent of former income for those who had contributed dues

[70] Ministerausschuss für Sozialreform, meetings of December 13, 1955, and January 18, 1956, Point 1a, Bundesarchiv, *Kabinettsprotokolle Online*; Hockerts, *Sozialpolitische Entscheidungen*, pp. 309–330; Hockerts, *Der deutsche Sozialstaat*, pp. 72–76; Schwarz, *Adenauer*, II: 283–284.

for forty years, rising to 75 percent for those who had contributed for fifty years.[71]

Every major business association denounced Storch's plan in the following months. Private insurance firms feared that it would put them out of business by requiring even the best paid employees to enroll in the public system. Bankers and the employers' associations argued that it would destroy the stability of the German mark, deprive business of investment capital, and require a crushing burden of contributions from those still working. When Storch explained his plan to the CDU Bundestag delegation on March 20, the observer from the government press office noted that "the delegation divided between a social and a 'capitalist' wing. Remarks by representatives of one side or the other provoked hostile personal comments from the opposite side."[72] When Storch visited the Stegerwald House on March 18, his hosts declared with satisfaction that "the demands of the Social Committees ... have been met." Storch replied, "Yes, the SPD has also acknowledged that without reservation." This exchange suggests that Storch was prepared to collude with the SPD to advance his bill, and he may have encouraged that party to publish an even more generous proposal on April 18.[73] Thereafter Storch's supporters in the CDU warned repeatedly that the SPD bill would pass if his was rejected.

In late April 1956 a CDU party congress endorsed Storch's bill unanimously, after several speakers agreed with him that it would not cause inflation. Jakob Kaiser had been assigned to speak on communist oppression in East Germany, but he landed a shrewd blow for pension reform by quoting the following declaration in the second East German Five-Year Plan: "Social insurance must actively promote the raising of labor productivity and the intensification of socialist labor discipline." In cabinet meetings Kaiser had heard much the same argument by Ludwig Erhard about the benefits to the economy of meager pensions, but he now pronounced this argument a prime example of "communist tyranny." Communism could only be defeated, he declared, if West

---

[71] Ministerausschuss für Sozialreform, February 17, 1956, and cabinet meetings of May 15, Point 2, and May 23, Point 2, Bundesarchiv, *Kabinettsprotokolle Online*; Arthur Rohbeck, "Um die neue Rentenformel," *Soziale Ordnung*, X/#3 (March 1956), pp. 37–39; Anton Storch, "Die Alters- und Invaliditätssicherung," *Soziale Ordnung*, X/#4 (April 1956), pp. 51–52; Hockerts, *Sozialpolitische Entscheidungen*, pp. 336–352.

[72] Hockerts, *Sozialpolitische Entscheidungen*, pp. 378–393; CDU Bundestag delegation, March 20, 1956, *Fraktionsprotokolle 1953–57*, II: 1024–1028 (quotation from footnote 14).

[73] Hans Katzer's report to the Social Committees on their leadership conference of March 17/18, 1956, NL Katzer/389; Hockerts, *Sozialpolitische Entscheidungen*, pp. 342–348.

Germany anchored "the fundamental principles of freedom and human dignity" in its social system and created a "comprehensive order based on social justice."[74] The KAB held a major congress soon thereafter, where the leadership ignored current policy debates, but the delegates displayed great interest in pension reform. Their guest speaker Anton Böhm earned thunderous applause when he declared that the opponents of dynamic pensions advanced "all sorts of ostensibly expert arguments that are revealed upon closer examination to be for the most part merely the defense of special interests." The congress embraced a resolution from the floor demanding that pensioners be assured a humane existence.[75] Storch's bill thus proved extraordinarily popular.

As the summer holidays ended, business representatives in the CDU mounted a furious assault on Storch's bill nevertheless. On September 20 the Hamburg banker Hugo Scharnberg lectured the CDU Central Committee in the spirit of Ludwig Erhard that the trade unions would lose all restraint in their wage demands if they no longer feared that pensioners on fixed incomes would suffer from inflation. Adenauer replied angrily that all of Scharnberg's "chatter about jeopardizing the currency" meant nothing to a pensioner who had to survive on 75 marks a month. "That is not fit for a human being! I want to give working people the best guarantee that we can in law that when they become elderly, they can live a decent life and don't need to run around like beggars." When his turn to speak came, Johannes Albers confessed that Adenauer had taken the words out of his mouth. The CDU business lobbyists remained adamant, however, and Krone reported to Adenauer that the divisions in their delegation appeared insurmountable. Krone then appointed a nine-member commission to seek consensus that tilted toward labor by including three businessmen, a budget expert, and five members of the Social Committees, with Peter Horn as chair.[76]

Jakob Kaiser strengthened Adenauer's support for pension reform when he persuaded the chancellor to address a DGB national congress for the first time in October 1956. Adenauer earned applause with a firm promise that "pension reform will come within the next few months,

---

[74] CDU, 6. Bundesparteitag der CDU, 26–29 April 1956 in Stuttgart (Hamburg, no date), pp. 59–60 (source of quotations), 98–99, 102–103, 135–136, 143–147, 152–153; see also Jakob Kaiser, "Zehn Jahre Christlich-Demokratische Union Essen," speech of January 22, 1956, NL Kaiser/315/27–31.

[75] KAB, Bericht über den 20. Verbandstag der KAB Westdeutschlands in Marl i. W. vom 10.–13. Mai 1956 (Cologne, no date), pp. 19–20, 52–72 (quotation on 63), 131–132.

[76] CDU Bundesvorstand, September 20, 1956, Vorstandsprotokolle 1953-57, pp. 1025-1026, 1056-1060 (quotation on 1058-1059); CDU Bundestag delegation, September 26 and October 1, 1956, Fraktionsprotokolle 1953–57, II: 1224–1232, 1242–1247; Krone, Tagebücher, September 26, 1956, I: 229–230.

including the productivity pension." The DGB emphasized its interest in the issue by electing as chairman Willi Richter, its top expert on social insurance. The atmosphere at the congress remained tense, however, because of the recent imposition of military conscription, and Adenauer heard repeated cries from the floor: "First pensions, then rearmament!" Adenauer concluded that this was an eminently reasonable demand, because the quest for social security must advance along with the quest for national security. The chancellor therefore secured cabinet resolutions on October 17 and 24 supporting Storch's bill.[77]

Fritz Schäffer and Ludwig Erhard continued nevertheless to attack core principles of Storch's bill in newspaper interviews and public speeches. Storch reported to the Social Committees on November 12 that they sought to sabotage pension reform in alliance with business lobbyists from all parties. Schäffer "no longer feels bound to cabinet resolutions," Storch explained, because he had obtained a study projecting that the bill would require contributions of 30 percent of a worker's earnings within ten years. "Whatever happens," Storch concluded, "the law must be passed in the next three weeks, if necessary with the well-intentioned elements in the SPD." Anton Sabel "warned above all against resorting to the idea of passing the law with the opposition. Then we would forfeit a valuable propaganda theme for our future election campaign." This meeting welcomed Theodor Blank back to the leadership of the Social Committees after his recent fall as defense minister, and he agreed with Sabel that the bill must be passed by the government parties. Blank proposed that the Social Committees convene an "extraordinary congress" to give Storch a platform, and they did so on November 28.[78] Storch and Kaiser cared less about which party took credit for pension reform than they did about its substance, but most colleagues in the Social Committees retained a lively interest in winning elections; they agreed with Adenauer that it would be political suicide if one faction of the CDU allied with the SPD to enact pension reform against the other faction. After Kaiser abstained in a Bundestag procedural vote to warn his party not to water down Storch's bill further, Sabel wrote him "that a few CDU people strain so hard to look toward the SPD in preparation for the

[77] DGB, *4. ordentlicher Bundeskongress, Hamburg, 1. bis 6. Oktober 1956* (Cologne, no date), p. 18 (source of quotation); "Zusammengefasste Niederschrift der CDA Hauptvorstandssitzung," September 8, 1956, pp. 6–8, NL Katzer/389; cabinet meetings of October 17, 1956, Point 4, and October 24, Point 7, Bundesarchiv, *Kabinettsprotokolle Online*; Hockerts, *Sozialpolitische Entscheidungen*, pp. 365–377, 400–408.

[78] "Niederschrift über die Hauptvorstandssitzung," November 12, 1956, NL Katzer/255; *Soziale Ordnung*, X/#11 (November 1956), pp. 179–180, and X/#12 (December 1956), pp. 183–186, 195–196.

coming Bundestag election that their eyeballs might pop out of their heads." Kaiser replied stiffly that "I have never counted among those colleagues who oppose the SPD as a matter of principle, especially when it comes to social policy decisions."[79]

The threat to CDU unity receded in the third week of November, when Peter Horn's mediation commission achieved consensus in the Bundestag delegation. The final round of negotiations began with a heartfelt speech by Josef Schüttler, a functionary of the metalworkers' union from Baden-Württemberg, who asked his colleagues to ponder why, of all their voters in 1953, 31 percent were blue-collar workers, 18 percent white-collar workers, and 13 percent working-class pensioners.

They were attracted by the program the CDU proclaimed for a new order and believed that this order would also be achieved ... True, much has been achieved for economic growth and foreign policy, which should not be minimized. But has a real effort at reform been made at home? Has it been shown that forces are at work who approach these questions from a truly Christian perspective on life? Here the voter has been disappointed, a voter who cannot be held simply with Christian principles but who must also see realities ... If economic interests continue to be revered as they have been until now, no success will be possible.

Adenauer responded that "Schüttler is largely correct ... The CDU must avoid appearing, like the old Center Party, to be a heap of special interests [*Haufen von Interessenten*], and we will acquire that reputation if we do not always observe, emphasize, and proclaim at every opportunity the principle of Christian balance [*Ausgleich*]."[80]

Horn's commission met daily for the next week, and Horn persuaded the workers' delegates to make a few concessions. No wage data from the year before retirement would apply when calculating the initial value of the pension, which slightly lowered the value, and the government would not be obliged to adjust the value of existing pensions, only to present a formal economic report each year to assist the Bundestag in considering whether the value should be adjusted. Business lobbyists hoped to persuade the Bundestag not to act on these reports, but as the supporters of pension reform anticipated, it resolved with little debate each year for the next twenty years to increase existing pensions to match increases in wages and salaries. Thus "dynamic" pensions were achieved

---

[79] CDU Bundesvorstand, November 23, 1956, *Vorstandsprotokolle 1953–57*, pp. 1105, 1135–1146; Sabel, Arndgen, and Horn to Heinrich Krone, December 14, 1956, Kaiser to Sabel, December 14, Sabel to Kaiser, December 17, and Kaiser to Sabel, December 26, 1956, NL Kaiser/41/5–8; Hockerts, *Sozialpolitische Entscheidungen*, pp. 394–395.

[80] CDU Bundestag delegation, November 13, 1956, *Fraktionsprotokolle 1953–57*, II: 1318–1320.

in practice.[81] Adenauer praised Horn to CDU leaders on November 23 for achieving consensus but implied unfairly that Storch's "lack of energy" had caused the long delay in pension reform. That delay had been caused by Ludwig Erhard, Fritz Schäffer, and the CDU business lobbyists, and Storch had struggled against these powerful foes with great skill. He became a scapegoat in his hour of triumph, however, and Adenauer resolved to dismiss him at the first opportunity.[82]

Krone still displayed anxiety when his delegation met on the eve of the final parliamentary debate over pensions in January 1957, but the leaders of every interest group promised not to introduce amendments. When it became clear that the bill would pass, Willi Richter persuaded the SPD to support it, so on January 22 it received 398 Aye votes from the 440 Bundestag delegates. This reform increased pensions from 30–40 percent of previous earnings to an average of 60 percent, and for the next twenty years it proved feasible, as the labor ministry had forecast, to make these pensions "dynamic" while financing them with contributions that did not exceed 14 percent of earnings (paid half by employers and half by employees). No other law in German history has proved as popular or done so much to strengthen the confidence of citizens in their government. The Social Committees took great pride in this legislation, which also enhanced their prestige within the DGB.[83]

4.3   The Crisis of the Social Committees in 1957

The preceding case studies indicate that the workers' wing of the CDU exerted great influence on social policy, but they also reveal a certain isolation within the party. The Social Committees had hoped to forge enduring alliances with youth groups, refugees from the East, artisans, and small farmers to guarantee that the CDU would be a populist rather than a "bourgeois" party. Most of these groups adopted a hostile attitude toward organized labor, however, and the legislative agenda of the

---

[81] Hockerts, *Sozialpolitische Entscheidungen*, pp. 395–397, 408–412; Arthur Rohbeck, "Das Versprechen wurde eingelöst," *Soziale Ordnung*, XI/#1 (January 1957), pp. 3–5.

[82] *Vorstandsprotokolle 1953–57*, pp. 1105–1106; see also Adenauer's remarks to President Heuss on October 9, 1956, in Hans Peter Mensing, ed., *Adenauer – Heuss. Unter vier Augen: Gespräche aus den Gründerjahren 1949–1959*, 2nd edn. (Berlin, 1999), p. 210.

[83] CDU Bundestag delegation, January 14/15, 1957, *Fraktionsprotokolle 1953–57*, II: 1377–1391; Hockerts, *Sozialpolitische Entscheidungen*, pp. 376–377, 418–425; Hockerts, *Der deutsche Sozialstaat*, pp. 81–85; DGB Bundesvorstand, January 8/9, 1957, in Jens Hildebrandt, ed., *Quellen zur Geschichte der deutschen Gewerkschaftsbewegung im 20. Jahrhundert. Band XII: Der Deutsche Gewerkschaftsbund 1956–1963* (Bonn, 2005; hereafter *Gewerkschaftsquellen*, XII:), p. 94; "Die soziale Tat," *Soziale Ordnung*, XI/#1 (January 1957), pp. 1–2; Artur Saternus, "Die Erhöhung der Renten ist gesichert," *Welt der Arbeit*, #4, January 28, 1957, p. 1.

Social Committees advanced only when they persuaded the professional politicians who led the CDU that it would derive a great electoral benefit.

The isolation of the Social Committees within the CDU became apparent during debates over the treatment of sick workers. White-collar workers who became ill enjoyed a legal guarantee that their employer would continue to pay their salary for up to six weeks before they would need to apply for disability benefits. Sick blue-collar workers, on the other hand, were required to apply to their health insurance fund for "sick pay" that was lower than their previous earnings and linked to strict medical testing. The DGB demanded in 1954 that sick blue-collar workers be treated in exactly the same way as white-collar workers, calling for the "continued payment of wages" by employers (*Lohnfortzahlung*), and the Social Committees embraced this demand in September 1955. When the SPD presented a bill to accomplish this soon thereafter, the Social Committees sought to persuade the CDU Bundestag delegation to support it. The bill would cost employers money, however, because workers' contributions financed 50 percent of the current sick pay from health insurance, and it upset small employers in particular, who wanted health insurance to administer the program. One CDU farmers' representative exclaimed that if this bill became law, "then we should not even show our faces any more in the countryside."[84] After pension reform had been achieved, Willi Richter notified Jakob Kaiser confidentially in May 1957 that "continued payment of wages" was now the DGB's top legislative priority. Heinrich Krone then concluded that the issue might provide the SPD with a valuable slogan in the next election campaign, so he insisted that his Bundestag delegation seek compromise with that party. The CDU and SPD passed a new law at the end of May that allowed blue-collar workers to claim supplemental benefits from employers that would raise sick pay to 90 percent of previous earnings. The DGB protested, however, that health insurance would continue to bear most of the financial burden, while blue-collar workers still faced a requirement for medical testing from which white-collar workers were absolved.[85] Only under

---

[84] Willi Richter's speech in DGB, *3. Bundeskongress 1954*, p. 286; "Entschliessungen der VII. Bundestagung der Sozialausschüsse," Arbeitskreis IV, Point 3, *Soziale Ordnung*, IX/#10 (Beilage for October 1955); CDU Bundestag delegation, October 25, 1955, *Fraktionsprotokolle 1953–57*, I: 846–849.

[85] Richter to Kaiser, May 15, 1957, NL Kaiser/102/110; CDU Bundestag delegation, May 21 and 27, 1957, *Fraktionsprotokolle 1953–57*, II: 1485, 1488; Krone, *Tagebücher*, May 31, 1957, I: 255–256; Arthur Rohbeck, "Gesetz zur Verbesserung der wirtschaftlichen Sicherung der Arbeiter im Krankheitsfalle," *Soziale Ordnung*, XI/#8 (August 1957), pp. 120–121.

the Great Coalition of 1966–1969 was this issue resolved to the satisfaction of organized labor, at the behest of Hans Katzer as labor minister.

The Social Committees encountered even greater disappointment regarding their proposal to supplement "co-determination" in industry with "co-ownership" of the means of production (*Miteigentum*). Karl Arnold had presented a simple plan for co-ownership to the second CDU party congress in 1951, and countless meetings of the Social Committees thereafter discussed some variant of his proposal for an "invested wage," i.e. the diversion of a portion of any wage increase into small ownership shares that a worker would be forbidden to sell for a certain number of years. The Social Committees hoped that such programs would transform the mentality of workers, and that workers would someday control such a large ownership stake in large corporations that there would be little disagreement between the representatives of capital and labor on corporate supervisory boards. Hans Katzer distributed a draft bill in November 1952, and the leaders of the KAB and League of Catholic Businessmen jointly published similar proposals in December.[86] For years the CDU Bundestag delegation did not consider the idea, however, because of disagreements between its working groups for economic and social policy. Bernhard Tacke of the DGB criticized the idea on the grounds that "the worker must retain the personal right to dispose of all wages earned." He also feared that an invested wage would expose workers to the risk of capital losses and tie them to one firm, restricting mobility. Far more influential within the CDU was the critique of the leading business lobbyist Fritz Hellwig, who declared in March 1956 that if the Social Committees intended to compel any employer to offer such a plan, then the Economic Policy Working Group must oppose them. The Social Committees were compelled to report to the CDU parliamentary leadership in April 1957 that they did not have a bill that could be presented to the Bundestag this term.[87]

[86] CDU, *Zweiter Parteitag der Christlich-Demokratischen Union Deutschlands. Karlsruhe, 18. bis 21. Oktober 1951* (Bonn, no date), pp. 30–31, 168, 170; "Vorstandssitzung der gesamtdeutschen Sozialausschüsse," March 15, 1952, NL Katzer/317; Hans Katzer circular, "Gedanken zum Miteigentum. Arbeitsergebnis einer Vorbesprechung," November 6, 1952, NL Katzer/239; Johannes Even to Hans Berger and Heinrich Dinkelbach, November 8, 1952, NL Even/1; Yorck Dietrich, *Eigentum für jeden. Die vermögenspolitischen Initiativen der CDU und die Gesetzgebung 1950–1961* (Düsseldorf, 1996), pp. 49–76, 122–162.

[87] Tacke to Katzer, January 9, 1953 (source of quotation), and February 13, 1957, NL Katzer/7; Katzer circular of March 28, 1956, with enclosed letter by Hellwig to Arndgen of March 16, and "Protokoll der Sitzung des Sonderausschusses 'Wirtschaftliches Miteigentum,'" March 12, 1956, ACDP/04–013/160/2; "Entwurf eines Gesetzes über das Miteigentum von Arbeitnehmern," April 17, 1956, NL Katzer/7; CDU

The Social Committees enjoyed somewhat more success with regard to housing policy thanks to Paul Lücke. Most of their activists distrusted the tendency to describe home ownership as a panacea for social problems, focusing instead on co-ownership of the means of production. Johannes Albers had noted in the last months of the Weimar Republic, however, that the KPD of Cologne won its votes in the neighborhoods where the housing shortage was most acute, and he concluded that "settlement on the edge of the city to create family homes is a task that must be solved, despite all hardship." After 1945 Albers chaired the Cologne Housing Cooperative, which was allied with Catholic charities, and he became the first chair of the Bundestag Committee for Reconstruction and Housing. Adenauer granted control of the housing ministry to the FDP, however, and Albers became involved in bitter disputes with the liberal minister. He therefore turned over the committee chairmanship to his younger and more patient colleague Lücke in 1950.[88]

Born in 1914, Paul Lücke did not have a trade union background but did come from a poor blue-collar family in the upper Bergland, northeast of Cologne. He worked in a stone quarry for several years, earned a degree in mechanical engineering in 1938, and lost a leg in combat in 1944. Lücke became active in the Rhenish Social Committees after the war and joined the Workers' Group in the CDU Bundestag delegation in 1949. As a Bundestag candidate he termed the housing shortage "the number 1 problem left behind by the war," the problem that must be solved as the precondition for solving all other social problems. Inspired by the success of a project to build forty single-family houses in Engelskirchen with small plots of land, financed in part by donated labor, Lücke became the most persuasive champion of the idea popular with the Catholic clergy that home ownership could "de-proletarianize" German workers and promote the formation of stable families. The FDP agreed with the SPD, however, that the government should encourage the rapid construction of numerous rental units. Lücke sided with the SPD by advocating government support for affordable, low-cost housing, but he differed with it by arguing that within this "social housing" sector, a large quota of units should be row houses or single-family dwellings offered for purchase. During Adenauer's second term he worked tirelessly to build consensus

---

Fraktionsvorstand, April 19, 1957, *Fraktionsprotokolle 1953–57*, II: 1466; Dietrich, *Eigentum für jeden*, pp. 193–269.

[88] Johannes Albers, "Die politische Entwicklung und die Kölner christliche Arbeiterschaft," speech of December 26, 1932, pp. 3–5, 9, NL Albers/2/1; Albers' remarks to the CDU Bundestag delegation, November 22, 1949, *Fraktionsprotokolle 1949–53*, pp. 85, 88; Günter Schulz, *Wiederaufbau in Deutschland. Die Wohnungsbaupolitik in den Westzonen und der Bundesrepublik von 1945 bis 1957* (Düsseldorf, 1994), pp. 84–92, 175–195.

with the representatives of builders, renters, charitable associations, mortgage lenders, trade unions, and state governments. Lücke's Second Housing Construction Law passed the Bundestag with the support of the CDU and FDP in May 1956, and after the Bundesrat amended it, the SPD also voted Aye in an almost unanimous final Bundestag vote in June. It announced the bold objective of building 1.8 million housing units with government subsidies in the next six years. Lücke renounced his original demand for a fixed quota of single-family dwellings, but the law instructed state and local governments to prioritize the sale of "family homes" with a yard. Reports by the state governments on their progress toward this goal would guide the future allocation of subsidies by the federal government. Lücke earned the applause of the Social Committees, Cardinal Frings, and CDU leaders, and he became the consensus choice as housing minister when the CDU won the next election. Many municipal governments argued, however, that Lücke's policy discriminated against big cities, where high land prices and problems with traffic and infrastructure made it almost impossible to attain his ideal.[89]

Christian Democratic workers did make some progress toward stronger influence in the DGB in 1956/1957. The Social Committees engaged in more careful planning to influence the Hamburg DGB Congress of October 1956 than they had in 1954. Jakob Kaiser persuaded most DGB leaders that Anton Sabel should succeed Matthias Föcher as DGB vice chair, because the trade unions would benefit if the leading representative of their Christian social minority actually enjoyed the confidence of the CDU. Sabel decided that he would prefer the secure position of president of the Federal Employment Agency, however, which he led from 1957 until 1968.[90] The DGB functionaries belonging to the Social Committees then agreed that Bernhard Tacke, the vice chair of the textile workers' union, was their most effective

[89] Paul Lücke, "Gedanken anlässlich meiner Vorstellung als Kandidat für den Bundestag im Rhein.-Berg. Kreis," 1949, p. 5, NL Lücke/151; CDU Bundestag delegation, May-June 1954 and May 2, 1956, *Fraktionsprotokolle 1953–57*, I: 129–131, 148–149, and II: 1071–1072; Heinrich Krone, *Tagebücher*, May 3, 1956, I: 211–212; Cardinal Frings, "Predigt am Vorabend des 1. Mai 1957," pp. 4–6, KAB Archiv/5/4; "Wohnungsbau: Bürger im Grünen," *Der Spiegel*, XII/#29 (July 16, 1958), pp. 25–34; Günter Schulz, *Wiederaufbau*, pp. 257–314.

[90] Kaiser to Sabel, January 25, 1954, NL Kaiser/41/3; Jakob Kaiser, "Notizen im Anschluss an meine Besprechung mit Walter Freitag" on March 9, 1954, NL Kaiser/102/70–72; Hans Katzer, "Niederschrift über die am 14. Juni 1955 stattgefundene Besprechung mit dem Vorstand des [DGB] Landesbezirks NRW," NL Kaiser/12/20–22; DGB Bundesvorstand, May 7 and June 18, 1957, *Gewerkschaftsquellen*, XII: 145–146, 155; Hans Zankl, "Informationen," circular to the "Sekretärsvereinigung" of July 25, 1957, NL Katzer/544.

colleague, and he was endorsed by Kaiser. Tacke received the votes of fifty-five of the sixty-eight Christian Democratic DGB functionaries who met to discuss the succession at the Stegerwald House in August 1956, and he gained the endorsement of all sixteen DGB union chairs soon thereafter. The Social Committees had exerted no comparable influence on the original choice of Föcher as DGB vice chair. The Social Committees also nominated the young Maria Weber, a former leader of the Christian Working Youth of Essen now active in the Christian Social Collegium, to succeed the deceased Thea Harmuth as their second representative on the DGB executive committee.[91]

In March 1956 the Social Committees sought to enhance their influence over the choice of a successor to Walter Freitag as DGB chair by forming special working groups for members who belonged to each DGB-affiliated union, so that they could discuss union business at meetings attended only by union colleagues. Kaiser then wrote a personal letter to each union chair on May 11 to argue that the membership and influence of the unions would grow if they helped to secure healthy representation for the Christian Democratic minority at the next DGB congress. He helped to secure the election of thirty CDU members as voting delegates to the Hamburg Congress (up from seventeen in 1954), who were joined by twenty-eight invited CDU guests, including Kaiser, Storch, Karl Arnold, Herbert Reichel, and Chancellor Adenauer.[92] Willi Richter won election as Freitag's successor without opposition, after the chair of the nominating committee reported that this proposal had been approved during discussions "with colleagues who occupy important government offices today and were active before among the Christian workers." Richter enjoyed the confidence of the SPD but also had friendly ties with Arndgen, Sabel, and Storch, and he could be expected to focus attention on pragmatic efforts to achieve incremental improvements in

---

[91] "Notizen über die Tagung am 4.8.56 im Adam Stegerwald-Haus," NL Zankl/4/1; "Der neue Bundesvorstand des DGB," *Soziale Ordnung*, X/#10 (October 1956), pp. 155–156; Stefan Remeke, *Anders links sein. Auf den Spuren von Maria Weber und Gerd Muhr* (Essen, 2012), pp. 71–76, 92–98.

[92] "Niederschrift über die zweite Besprechung des Siebener-Ausschusses," March 13, 1956, and "3. Besprechung," March 28, 1956, NL Katzer/592; "Zusammengefasste Niederschrift über die Hauptvorstandssitzung der Sozialausschüsse," March 17/18, 1956, NL Katzer/390; Katzer's circular to the Social Committees, March 28, 1956, NL Katzer/389; "Niederschrift über die Besprechung des gewerkschaftlichen Arbeitskreises," April 18/19, 1956, ACDP/04–013/160/2; Jakob Kaiser to Otto Brenner, May 11, 1956, *Gewerkschaftsquellen*, XI: 845–847 (with identical letters to other union leaders in NL Katzer/555); folder on "Delegierte/Gastdelegierte," NL Katzer/811, with résumés of CDU congress delegates; table on party affiliations of the delegates to the DGB congress in 1954, NL Katzer/555. Wolfgang Schroeder misleadingly credits Herbert Reichel for this result in *Katholizismus und Einheitsgewerkschaft*, pp. 210–212.

social policy.[93] Richter consulted regularly with Christian social colleagues and secured the approval of Hans Katzer before publishing the DGB manifesto for the Bundestag election of 1957, which avoided criticism of the current government and focused instead on the unions' legislative demands for the future. *Social Order* published this manifesto with an approving commentary, and Richter intervened energetically when Katzer brought to his attention violations of partisan neutrality during the campaign by local union officials. No DGB chair since Böckler had worked so hard to demonstrate that the DGB was independent of the SPD.[94]

Despite Richter's collegiality, the Catholic bishops exerted mounting pressure on their flock to support the Christian Labor Movement. It gained new strength in January 1957 when 40,000 Christian trade unionists from the Saarland, the only German region where vigorous Christian unions had revived after the war, became citizens of the Federal Fepublic. In anticipation of this development, Bishop Keller of Münster persuaded the bishops of western Germany on March 22, 1956, to notify all Catholic organizations that they were *not* neutral regarding union affiliation:

> It is false to draw the conclusion that individual Catholics may choose their own standpoint based on personal taste or their purely individual views. Still less can anyone feel justified to deny the right of the Christian trade unions to exist or to combat them in public or covertly ... The reasons that led to the foundation of Christian unions are well known: frequent violation of neutrality in questions of fundamental religious, social, and cultural significance. We remind everyone ... above all of the need for a union organization that dedicates itself actively to the realization of Christian social doctrine.

At first this declaration was not published, only sent to the leaders of Catholic organizations, but the bishops responded to press leaks by publishing it on May 3.[95]

---

[93] Gerhard Beier, *Willi Richter. Ein Leben für die soziale Neuordnung* (Cologne, 1978), pp. 241–244; DGB, *4. Bundeskongress 1956*, pp. 625–627.

[94] DGB Bundesvorstand, August 13, 1957, and "Erklärung des DGB-Bundesvorstandes zur Bundestagswahl 1957," *Gewerkschaftsquellen*, XII: 172, 177–178; "Vermerk. Betr.: Christliche Kollegenschaft," reception by Richter on August 16, 1957, for Katzer, Heckhausen, and Weber-Walsum, DGB-Archiv/5/DGAI001191; "Der Wahlaufruf des DGB," *Soziale Ordnung*, XI/#8 (August 1957), pp. 113–114; Hans Katzer circular to the Social Committees, August 1957, ACDP/04–013/160/2; Katzer to the CDA Betriebsgruppe Opel in Rüsselsheim, August 21, 1957, NL Katzer/624; circular by Willi Richter to the DGB Bundesvorstand, September 23, 1957, DGB-Archiv/5/DGAI001854.

[95] "Protokoll der Beratungen auf dem Konveniat der westdeutschen Bischöfe," March 21–23, 1956, HAEK/CR II/2.19, 15; "Erneute Stellungnahme der Westdeutschen Bischöfe zur

Publication of the bishops' declaration caused a storm of protest. Chancellor Adenauer bellowed to CDU leaders that it had ruined their efforts to influence Catholic workers. "It demands that only the Christian trade unions be supported. It has smashed your Social Committees and the Christian Collegium of Father Reichel ... This cries out to heaven." Bernhard Tacke posed the following anguished questions in an open letter to Frings on May 16, co-signed by 107 Catholic functionaries in the DGB:

Is a Catholic forbidden to belong to a union affiliated with the DGB?
Is a Catholic forbidden to be a functionary of the DGB or one of the unions that forms it?
Is a Catholic forbidden to attend class at a school of the DGB, or one of the unions in it ... ?
Is a Catholic worker obliged ... to join one of the unions affiliated with the International League of Christian Trade Unions, even if he is persuaded that only the unified unions are strong enough to represent his legitimate interests effectively?[96]

After six weeks Frings replied tersely that there was "no objective justification" for these questions, and Tacke resented this dismissive note for the rest of his life. When German journalists posed Tacke's questions in Rome, however, Vatican spokesmen declared without hesitation that "no Catholic is obliged to leave the DGB, and no Catholic is obliged to join a Christian trade union." Heinrich Krone learned when he visited the Eternal City in November that senior Vatican officials regarded the DGB as a reality that should be accepted.[97]

The old feud between the KAB and Social Committees had thus flared up again as the CDU considered nominations for the Bundestag election of 1957, and the Social Committees also experienced a leadership crisis. Jakob Kaiser suffered a minor stroke in January 1957; he soon returned to work against his doctor's advice and suffered a massive second stroke in

Frage der Christlichen Gewerkschaften," March 16, 1957, KAB Archiv/5/4; CGD press release of May 6, 1957, NL Katzer/809.

[96] Complaint by the Catholic DGB secretaries of Paderborn to Archbishop Jaeger, May 8, 1957, NL Zankl/8/4; remarks by Adenauer in CDU Bundesvorstand, May 11, 1957, *Vorstandsprotokolle 1953–57*, pp. 1249–1250; Tacke to Jakob Kaiser, May 7, 1957, NL Katzer/809; "Kardinal Frings soll Stellung nehmen zu DGB-Mitgliedschaft," *Westdeutsche Allgemeine Zeitung*, June 4, 1957 (source of quotation, NL Katzer/809).

[97] "Antwort von Kardinal Frings enttäuscht CDU-Gewerkschaftler," *Westdeutsche Allgemeine Zeitung*, #170, July 25, 1957, and "Kein objektiver Anlass," CGD press release of July 26, 1957 (NL Katzer/809); Tacke to Franz Kusch, July 21, 1980, with enclosed copy of the letter to him by Cardinal Frings of July 3, 1957, NL Tacke/13/6; "Der Vatikan und der deutsche Wahlkampf," *Frankfurter Allgemeine Zeitung*, #143, June 25, 1957; Krone, *Tagebücher*, I: 273.

mid-April. He then withdrew as a Bundestag candidate and lay bedridden in his Berlin apartment for the remaining four years of his life. Krone noted sadly in his diary that Kaiser would never return to politics. "Jakob Kaiser is an honest man, . . . and a loyal comrade. His strength was and is the struggle for justice and the struggle against all injustice . . . Jakob Kaiser is a patriot in the true sense of the world. Although a Frank from Bavaria, he reveres Prussia and everything that made this country great through order and discipline."[98] In North Rhine-Westphalia, state labor minister Johannes Platte promoted cooperation between the DGB and CDU, but he suffered personal disaster after Karl Arnold was toppled as prime minister in 1956. The CDU did not offer him any position, and the miners' union refused to rehire him, so Platte was compelled to retire on a meager disability pension for miners no longer capable of working. Ernst Leuninger, the vice chair of the Hessian state DGB and a founding member of the Hessian CDU, defected to the SPD in June 1957, and Anton Sabel withdrew from politics as president of the Federal Employment Agency.[99] Thus several of the Social Committees' most powerful pieces were removed from the chessboard.

Johannes Albers had meanwhile become profoundly discouraged. He wrote Kaiser in July 1956 that "I view future developments with anxiety and fear when I now see how the bourgeois element becomes ever stronger in the party, and the workers ever weaker." In 1957 Albers became involved in numerous disputes over Bundestag nominations and complained bitterly to Adenauer that the CDU of Essen, the historic capital of the Christian labor movement, had awarded Kaiser's seat to a businessman.[100] Albers decided to withdraw from the Bundestag to assure seats for both Hans Katzer in Albers' district in Cologne and Josef Mick on the state nominations list. The only gain for worker representation in the Rhineland came when Karl Arnold won a landslide victory in Geilenkirchen. Arnold then succeeded Kaiser as chair of the Social Committees, but he died of a massive heart attack in 1958.[101] The chair of the Westphalian Social Committees, Anton Becker, noted in July 1957 that his colleagues had exerted little influence over nominations. KAB leaders expressed even more frustration; they were not allowed any role in the deliberations over the state nominations list,

[98] Kosthorst, *Kaiser: Minister*, p. 354; Krone *Tagebücher*, June 13, 1957, I: 257.

[99] See Platte's letter to Anton Sabel from late 1957, NL Platte/18/55, and Hans Zankl, "Informationen," circular to the "Sekretärsvereinigung," July 25, 1957, NL Katzer/544.

[100] Albers to Kaiser, July 16, 1956, NL Kaiser/100/52; Albers to Adenauer, July 17, 1957, NL Kaiser/172/161–163.

[101] Mick to Albers, May 2, 1956, NL Albers/1/1956–1959; Zankl to Albers, May 20, and Zankl to Karl Arnold, May 20, 1957, NL Mick/1/2; Hüwel, *Karl Arnold*, pp. 320–326.

and when they sought a personal audience with Adenauer, he could not be reached. This was doubtless their punishment for the bishops' recent declaration in favor of Christian trade unions.[102] The Social Committees retained three Bundestag seats from Lower Saxony but lost a seat in Hesse after Sabel's retirement. In all, forty-nine CDU/CSU workers' delegates won election in September 1957 (twenty-five from North Rhine-Westphalia), the same number as in 1953, while their Bundestag delegation grew from 244 to 270 members.[103]

For the first (and perhaps last) time in the history of free elections in Germany, a single party list won an absolute majority of the popular vote in 1957. Favorable winds filled the CDU sails during the campaign after four years of rapid economic growth, and the critics of rearmament appeared foolish after the Soviets' brutal suppression of the Hungarian uprising of November 1956. This election victory resulted in large measure, however, from the impressive record of social legislation achieved by Anton Storch and the Workers' Group in the CDU Bundestag delegation. The new pension system, co-determination in the public sector, and defense of parity co-determination in holding companies persuaded a great many voters that they had a truly "social" as well as a "market" economy. The pollsters all agreed that the CDU fared especially well among Catholic blue-collar workers and senior citizens, the two groups most affected by these laws.[104]

The strangest election result was the overrepresentation of the minuscule Christian Labor Movement. Even Josef Arndgen, one of the most energetic advocates of workers' interests, resigned from the DGB-affiliated leatherworkers' union during the campaign to join the CGD, and several colleagues imitated him. They did not intend to alter their pro-worker policies but reasoned that they could achieve more progress if they severed ties with a labor federation that, in the view of most CDU members, sought to create a socialist economy and served the partisan interests of the SPD. Their actions strengthened the negative stereotype of the DGB in the minds of Christian Democrats, however, and nurtured unrealistic expectations about how labor unions should be expected to behave. In the newly elected Bundestag the CGD and

---

[102] "Niederschrift über die Vorstandssitzung der Sozialausschüsse Westfalens," February 23, 1957, ACDP/03–002/454/1; "Niederschrift über die Sitzung des Landesvorstandes der Sozialausschüsse Westfalens," July 27, 1957, ACDP/03–002/127/1; KAB, "Protokoll über die Sitzung des gführ. Verbandsvorstandes," July 18, 1957, KAB Archiv/1/1.

[103] Hans Wellmann to Hermann-Josef Russe, April 23, 1957, ACDP/04–013/167/2; Anton Sabel to Adolf Cillien, February 27, 1957, NL Sabel/1/2; "Unsere Abgeordneten im 3. Deutschen Bundestag," *Soziale Ordnung*, XI/#10 (October 1957), p. 154.

[104] U. W. Kitzinger, *German Electoral Politics: A Study of the 1957 Campaign* (Oxford, 1960).

DGB-affiliated unions each received dues from about eighteen CDU delegates. The party thus granted 60,000 Christian trade unionists as much representation as two million CDU voters in the DGB.[105] To restore a healthy relationship with Germany's only effective labor unions became the primary goal of the Social Committees thereafter.

[105] Arndgen to Adolf Lewecke, August 13, 1957, NL Arndgen/3/2; Hans Zankl, "Vorstandssitzung, Landessozialausschuss Rheinland," September 1957, NL Zankl/2/1; "Nüchternes Rechenexempel für die CDU," *Gesellschaftspolitische Kommentare*, #4, February 15, 1959, p. 39.

5   Seeking a New Path in the Twilight of the Adenauer Era

The Social Committees devoted a special issue of their magazine to publicize a discussion at the Catholic Academy of Bavaria in January 1958 between Catholic theologians and prominent Social Democrats. The SPD delegation, led by Carlo Schmid, proclaimed its desire for "peaceful coexistence" with the Catholic Church, and the Jesuit theologian Gustav Grundlach acknowledged that the SPD had taken great pains to distance itself from its Marxist heritage. Disagreements emerged over school policy, but the discussion remained quite cordial. Gundlach's attitude was remarkable, because he had inspired the papal declaration in *Quadragesimo Anno* that every form of socialism, even revisionist or reformist socialism, was a "materialistic" creed incompatible with Christianity. *Social Order* observed with satisfaction that, whereas German politics had for decades resembled "a thinly veiled civil war," political debate was now evolving into a civilized "competition ... over the best rationale for and application of fundamental values professed in common."[1] This prediction received powerful confirmation in 1959, when the SPD adopted its new Godesberg Program, and Pope John XXIII invited all bishops around the world to prepare for a great ecumen-ical council to reform the Church. Many Christian Democrats were bewildered by these developments, but the Social Committees eagerly embraced the new era of "civilized competition" with the SPD.

The trend toward consensus politics was obscured when Chancellor Adenauer secured a Bundestag resolution in March 1958 authorizing the German military to acquire nuclear weapons if invited to do so by NATO. Adenauer probably took this step more for reasons of domestic politics

---

[1] "Christentum und Sozialismus," *Soziale Ordnung*, supplement to XII/#3 (March 1958), pp. 37–44 (quotations on 39, 42–43). See also the detailed record of the conference in Munich on January 11/12, 1958, in Adolf Arndt and Gustav Gundlach, eds., *Christentum und demokratischer Sozialismus* (Munich, 1958), and Thomas Grossmann, *Zwischen Kirche und Gesellschaft. Das Zentralkomitee der deutschen Katholiken 1945–1970* (Mainz, 1991), pp. 301–305. For the anti-socialism of *Quadragesimo Anno*, see above, pp. 28–29.

than national security; NATO never issued such an invitation, but the CDU had benefited at the polls from every polarizing debate over foreign policy in the past. This Bundestag resolution caused great indignation on the Left, especially among scientists and intellectuals, and the SPD launched an emotional appeal for a "Struggle against Atomic Death."[2] The Christian social labor leaders Bernhard Tacke and Maria Weber shared the indignation of their Social Democratic colleagues in the DGB leadership, which resolved unanimously on March 28 to join and subsidize this anti-nuclear campaign. Tacke appealed to the current leaders of the Social Committees to display the same independence of judgment regarding Adenauer's foreign policy that Jakob Kaiser had displayed in the past, but they protested that DGB leaders had no mandate from union members to issue pronouncements about foreign policy. The DGB chair Willi Richter was shouted down when he attempted to defend his position before the Eighth National Congress of the Social Committees. Many CDU leaders accused the DGB falsely of planning a general strike, and in May the Gladbeck CDU pressured its Bundestag delegate to switch his union affiliation to the Christian trade unions.[3] As with the debate over NATO membership a few years earlier, the anti-nuclear movement disrupted the alliance with organized labor sought by the Social Committees. The SPD disengaged from this campaign, however, after another defeat in July 1958, when the CDU won an absolute majority in the state election in North Rhine-Westphalia. Despite attracting large crowds to rallies, the Struggle against Atomic Death had no impact on voting trends.[4]

The defeat in North Rhine-Westphalia encouraged "modernizers" in the SPD, led by the former Communist Herbert Wehner and his younger

---

[2] Hans-Peter Schwarz, *Adenauer*, 2 vols. (1986–1991), II: 385–415; Ronald Granieri, *The Ambivalent Alliance: Konrad Adenauer, the CDU/CSU, and the West, 1949–1966* (New York and Oxford, 2003), pp. 98–113; Steven Brady, *Eisenhower and Adenauer: Alliance Maintenance under Pressure, 1953–1960* (Lanham, Maryland, 2010), pp. 216–223; Kurt Klotzbach, *Der Weg zur Staatspartei. Programmatik, praktische Politik und Organisation der deutschen Sozialdemokratie 1945 bis 1965* (Berlin and Bonn, 1982), pp. 393–396, 467–472; Gordon Drummond, *The German Social Democrats in Opposition, 1949–1960: The Case Against Rearmament* (Norman, 1982), pp. 217–226.

[3] "Niederschrift über die Sitzung des Hauptvorstandes der Sozialausschüsse," March 22/23, 1958, ACDP/04–013/1/2; DGB Bundesvorstand meetings of March-May 1958 in Jens Hildebrandt, ed., *Quellen zur Geschichte der deutschen Gewerkschaftsbewegung im 20. Jahrhundert. Band XII: Der Deutsche Gewerkschaftsbund 1956–1963* (Bonn, 2005; hereafter *Gewerkschaftsquellen*, XII:), pp. 266–276, 280–285, 301–303, 307–309; Tacke to Albers, April 14, 1958, and Tacke to Jakob Kaiser, April 15, NL Katzer/311; "8. Bundestagung der Sozialausschüsse," *Soziale Ordnung*, XII/#5 (May 1958), pp. 75–76; "Aktennotiz über die Besprechung am Freitag, den 23. Mai 1958," minutes of a summit conference between the DGB and Social Committees, NL Albers/1/1956–1959; CDU Stadtgruppe Gladbeck to all CDU Bundestag delegates, May 8, 1958, NL Zankl/1/3.

[4] Klotzbach, *Staatspartei*, pp. 472–475; Drummond, *Social Democrats*, pp. 234–241.

colleagues Willy Brandt and Helmut Schmidt, to insist that their party move toward the middle of the political spectrum. They secured passage of a new program at the Godesberg Party Congress in November 1959 under the motto, "Move with the times!" All previous SPD programs had opened with a detailed statement of principles, but this one simply observed that democratic socialism was "rooted in Christian ethics, humanism, and classical philosophy." The SPD declared itself "in favor of national defense" and dropped any demand to nationalize industry, calling instead for a modern, countercyclical fiscal and monetary policy to promote full employment. The following conclusion from the section on "The Economy" was quoted often in the press:

Free choice of consumer goods and free choice of working place are essential foundations, and free competition and free entrepreneurship are important elements of Social Democratic economic policy ... The totalitarian command economy destroys freedom. The Social Democratic Party therefore favors the free market wherever free competition exists. Where markets are dominated by individuals or groups, a variety of measures must be taken to preserve economic freedom. As much competition as possible, as much planning as necessary!

The section on "Trade Unions in the Economy" praised the system of parity co-determination in coal and steel as "the beginning of a new economic order," but otherwise this program was largely compatible with the principles of Ludwig Erhard.[5]

Konrad Adenauer insisted that the Godesberg Program signified no change in the policies of SPD leaders, who remained determined to impose centralized state economic planning, withdraw from NATO, and slash military spending.[6] *Social Order* commented more thoughtfully that the SPD had carried out a skillful "adaptation to the political, social, and economic development since 1945" and drawn closer to the principles of the CDU. The SPD deserved respect for acknowledging that it had pursued "a false political path" since 1945; now the CDU must ponder carefully how to distinguish itself from the SPD in future. In December, Oswald von Nell-Breuning reported to a closed meeting of Catholic social activists in Dortmund that every statement about social and economic

[5] SPD, "Basic Programme of the Social Democratic Party of Germany" (Bonn, 1959), available at http://germanhistorydocs.ghi-dc.org/pdf/eng/Parties%20WZ%203%20ENG%20FI NAL.pdf; Klotzbach, *Staatspartei*, pp. 388–454; Harold Schellenger, *The SPD in the Bonn Republic: A Socialist Party Modernizes* (The Hague, 1968); Julia Angster, *Konsenskapitalismus und Sozialdemokratie. Die Westernisierung von SPD und DGB* (Munich, 2003).

[6] CDU Bundesvorstand, January 29, 1960, in Günter Buchstab, ed., *Adenauer: ". . . um den Frieden zu gewinnen." Die Protokolle des CDU Bundesvorstands 1957–1961* (Düsseldorf, 1994; hereafter *Vorstandsprotokolle 1957–61*), pp. 587–589; see also Adenauer's remarks on September 16, 1959, and July 6 and August 23, 1960, pp. 393–395, 703–711, 788.

policy in the Godesberg Program was compatible with papal encyclicals. Most participants agreed that it would be impossible in future for any bishop to issue a statement implying that no Catholic was permitted to vote for the SPD, as several had done in the last Bundestag election campaign. Judgments of the SPD in the Catholic press remained mostly hostile, but many CDU politicians and senior clerics now agreed with the Social Committees that Adenauer's purely negative response to the Godesberg Program was unfair and short-sighted.[7] The CDU could not rely in future on clerical influence to prevent workers from voting for the SPD.

5.1   Hans Katzer and the Unification of Christian Democratic Workers

After Jakob Kaiser suffered a massive stroke in April 1957, his son-in-law Hans Katzer became the chief strategist for the Social Committees. He lacked Kaiser's moral passion and gripping life story but displayed far more tactical skill. His thinking was not shaped by the former status of the independent and well-financed Christian trade unions of the Weimar Republic; Katzer dealt with current political realities. His long-term goal was to persuade the Catholic bishops to withdraw support from the non-viable Christian trade unions founded in 1955, so that the Social Committees could revive their alliance with the powerful DGB. His most urgent task, however, was to achieve a positive relationship with the Catholic workers' clubs. Katzer set out to create for the first time a unified workers' wing of the CDU.[8]

Their exhilarating election victory in September 1957 encouraged many Christian Democrats to believe that what they called the "social question" had been resolved and that workers no longer had genuine grievances. Noting impressive gains among blue-collar voters, Adenauer told CDU leaders on September 19 that socialism was dead as an ideology; he hoped that young workers could be drawn "away from thinking in terms of class." The Protestant theologian Eugen Gerstenmaier argued

---

[7] "Geh mit der Zeit," *Soziale Ordnung*, XIII/#12 (December 1959), pp. 177–178; "Das Grundsatzprogramm der SPD," minutes by Franz Deus of the "Tagung des Wirtschafts- und Sozialrates der Kommende" in Dortmund on December 3/4, 1959, pp. 3–6, 9–13, NL Deus/1/1; Grossmann, *Zentralkomitee*, pp 306–320; Heinrich Krone, *Tagebücher, 1945–1969*, ed. Hans-Otto Kleinmann, 2 vols. (Düsseldorf, 1995–2003), November 18, 1959, I: 387; CDU Bundesvorstand, January 29, 1960, *Vorstandsprotokolle 1957–61*, pp. 601–602.

[8] See the overview of Katzer's career in Tilman Mayer, "Gerechtigkeit schafft Frieden. Die Gesellschaftspolitik Hans Katzers," in Ulf Fink, ed., *Hans Katzer. Partnerschaft statt Klassenkampf* (Cologne, 1989), pp. 11–37.

that most workers had already renounced class conflict. He proclaimed at the CDU party congresses before and after the election that the government could not do any more for its citizens without stifling their sense of individual responsibility, and that the economy could not afford any further increase in spending on welfare programs. Economics Minister Ludwig Erhard agreed. "I am convinced," Erhard told the party congress of 1958, "that the German worker is happy, and that this accursed era of class conflict, which divided human beings into hostile camps and did not allow our nation [*Volk*] to become aware of itself, has been overcome."[9] The leaders of the Social Committees replied forcefully that workers still had many grievances, and that the CDU must continue to redress them through progressive social legislation if it hoped to win future elections. They were doubtless correct that the reports of the death of social class as an objective reality and of class consciousness as an attitude were premature to say the least.[10]

When Adenauer assembled a new cabinet in October 1957, he insisted that Anton Storch be replaced as labor minister by Theodor Blank, his favorite Christian trade unionist ever since Blank had forged an alliance with Ludwig Erhard in the Frankfurt Economic Council in 1948. The leaders of the Social Committees felt that Storch did not deserve dismissal after accomplishing his great pension reform, and they complained when Blank failed to attend their next meeting. Johannes Albers conveyed to Blank the "heartfelt request that you will not allow your connection with the workers to be dissolved," reminding him that the Social Committees had salvaged his career after his fall as defense minister.[11] Two other longtime members of the Social Committees also belonged to the cabinet, Housing Minister Paul Lücke and Ernst Lemmer as Minister for All-German Affairs. Jakob Kaiser's old friend Lemmer had risen to chair the CDU of West Berlin and shared most of Kaiser's positions, but not his willingness to provoke controversy; Kaiser chided him for avoiding CDU leadership conferences when he anticipated conflict. Lemmer kept a low profile in Bonn after the chancellor's aide Hans Globke conveyed a stern

[9] CDU Bundesvorstand, September 19, 1957, *Vorstandsprotokolle 1956–61*, pp. 4–6, 9, 21–22, 33–36; CDU, *7. Bundesparteitag der CDU. Hamburg, 11.-15. Mai 1957* (Hamburg, no date), pp. 17–22; CDU, *8. Bundesparteitag der CDU. Kiel, 18.-21. September 1958* (Hamburg, no date), pp. 92–101, 203 (source of Erhard quotation).

[10] Speech by Albers on February 22, 1958, *Soziale Ordnung*, XII/#3 (March 1958), p. 50; Elfriede Nebgen, "Um die geistigen Grundlagen," *Soziale Ordnung*, XII/#10 (October 1958), pp. 157–159; Johannes Albers, "Wir stehen im Wort," *Soziale Ordnung*, XII/#12 (December 1958), pp. 189–191. See also Ralf Dahrendorf, *Society and Democracy in Germany* (New York, 1967), Chapters 6–7.

[11] Albers to Storch, October 28, 1957, and Albers to Blank, October 28, 1957, ACDP/ 04–013/1/2.

warning to avoid pronouncements about foreign policy.[12] Lücke had no trade union experience but came from a blue-collar family, and he regarded participation in the conferences of the Social Committees as vital to rally popular support for his housing policy. Despite some disagreements, Katzer preferred him to Blank as a trustworthy defender of workers' interests.[13]

Karl Arnold was the consensus choice to replace the incapacitated Kaiser as chairman of the Social Committees, but he died of a massive heart attack in July 1958 while leading the CDU state election campaign in North Rhine-Westphalia. Albers then wrote Kaiser to ask whether he should step in again to chair the organization or leave that task to the younger Blank, who was "very eager" to play this role. Kaiser replied promptly that "you must not decline this responsibility," and he and Katzer arranged for the election of Albers on July 11. Several pro-CDU newspapers described Albers as an "interim chairman," and reported that Blank would soon replace him and suppress the "trade union radicalism" spreading in the Social Committees. Most activists in the Social Committees resented such meddling, however, and rallied behind Albers.[14]

Arnold's death revealed that the influence of the Social Committees had declined in their regional bastion of North Rhine-Westphalia. Already during the nominations process for the state election campaign, Albers had noted that several workers who retired from politics were replaced by middle-class nominees. He reminded the Rhineland CDU chair that blue- and white-collar workers had comprised 40 percent of their first state parliamentary delegation in 1946, and he asked, "How are we going to conduct the campaign against the socialists when our election districts do not put forward any prominent representatives of workers and instead fill the delegation with teachers, school inspectors, and similar personages?"[15] After the election, the KAB nominated its chair Josef Gockeln as prime minister, but three-fourths of the CDU parliamentary delegates supported Franz Meyers instead, a corporate

---

[12] Kaiser to Lemmer, February 4, 1955, and reply of February 7, NL Kaiser/3/51–53; Stefan Creuzberger, *Kampf für die Einheit. Das gesamtdeutsche Ministerium und die politische Kultur des Kalten Krieges 1949–1969* (Düsseldorf, 2008), pp. 78–87.

[13] See Katzer to Lücke, June 16, 1959, and Lücke's reply of June 19, NL Lücke/79/1.

[14] Albers to Kaiser, July 4, 1958, and reply of July 7, NL Katzer/311; Hans Katzer, "Wir stehen im Wort," *Soziale Ordnung*, XII/#7 (July 1958), p. 108; "Niederschrift über die Sitzung des Landesvorstandes der Sozialausschüsse Westfalens," September 15, 1958, ACDP/03–002/127/1; A.B., "Zwiedenken," *Rheinischer Merkur*, August 1, 1958 (NL Katzer/616); Dietrich Schwarzkopf, "Ein Trostpflaster für den linken CDU-Flügel," *Der Tagesspiegel*, September 6, 1958 (NL Kaiser/269/25).

[15] Albers to Wilhelm Johnen, March 19, 1958, NL Albers/1/1956–1959.

lawyer from Mönchengladbach. Meyers promised to appoint two workers' representatives to his cabinet, but no candidate from the Social Committees could gain support, so Meyers brought the ailing, seventy-year-old Johannes Ernst out of retirement as labor minister and then described the director of the Mönchengladbach Chamber of Commerce as his cabinet's second "workers' representative," a man who belonged to the KAB but had functioned as a business lobbyist since 1945. Albers and Josef Mick published an indignant protest against this distortion of the concept of a workers' representative.[16] The Westphalian CDU also provoked skepticism by asserting that twenty-one of its state parliamentary delegates, 55 percent of the total, were "workers" (*Arbeitnehmer*), a tally that included high-ranking civil servants, corporate managers, and a university professor. The Social Committees reckoned that twelve of fifty-one CDU delegates elected in the Rhineland were blue- or white-collar workers, and nine of thirty-eight in Westphalia, yielding an overall proportion of 24 percent of the CDU delegation, far lower than that of 1946 but still higher than that of most other CDU state delegations in 1958. Johannes Ernst was soon replaced as labor minister by the much younger Konrad Grundmann, a white-collar worker in the dairy industry, member of a DGB-affiliated union, and activist in the Rhineland Social Committees. Grundmann helped to check the regional decline of worker influence and rose to chair the Rhineland CDU from 1963 to 1969.[17]

Hans Katzer knew that any genuine revival of worker influence in the CDU depended on cooperation between the Social Committees and KAB, so he revived the idea proposed by Jakob Kaiser in 1955 for a great Christian Social Workers' Congress. The KAB's decision to revive Christian trade unions had thwarted Kaiser's project, but anger over the DGB's role in the "Struggle against Atomic Death" revived this idea. The leaders of the Social Committees declared in July 1958 "that despite

---

[16] "Der fixe Franz," *Der Spiegel*, XII/#31 (July 30, 1958), pp. 17–25; Karl Braukmann to Albers, July 14 and July 29, 1958, NL Braukmann/5/4; Albers and Mick to Franz Meyers, July 26, 1958, LANRW/CDA Rheinland/909; "Rechtsanwälte regieren an Rhein und Ruhr," *Die Welt*, #175, July 31, 1958 (clipping in NL Katzer/254).

[17] Paul Wiechert to Katzer on the election results in Westphalia, August 1, 1958, NL Katzer/253; "Arbeitnehmervertreter," undated summary from 1959 of their position in the Rhineland CDU, LANRW/CDA Rheinland/909; capsule biography of Grundmann at www.landtag.nrw.de. Compare Ludger Gruber, *Die CDU-Landtagsfraktion in Nordrhein-Westfalen 1946–1980* (Düsseldorf, 1998), pp. 66–70. Gruber finds that the proportion of white-collar workers declined hardly at all from 1947 to 1958, from 41 to 39 percent, while blue-collar workers declined from 3 to 2 percent. He uses a broad definition of white-collar, however, and excludes functionaries of the unions, KAB, or Social Committees from the blue-collar category, so the count by the Social Committees gives a better sense of who represented workers.

constantly reiterated warnings by Christian social workers, the evolution of the DGB and its member unions into one-sided, partisan political unions has made ever accelerating progress." They called for a "comprehensive Christian workers' congress ... to examine the situation in the trade unions." Several newspapers reported that many participants at this meeting had called for a mass exodus from the DGB, but Katzer denied this report and sought cooperation with both KAB and DGB colleagues.[18]

The initial responses to Katzer's appeal were discouraging. KAB leaders refused to commit themselves, and the DGB denounced the idea of any congress devoted to criticism of the unions. Most Christian social DGB functionaries agreed that they could only participate in a congress with non-members of their unions if it was devoted to criticism of the CDU for neglecting workers' interests.[19] The recently elected leader of the Christian Labor Movement, Bernhard Winkelheide of the KAB, had grown discouraged about its prospects, however, and he sought cooperation with the Social Committees. Katzer elicited a very positive response when he published a documentary history in August 1958 to demonstrate that both sides in the debate about reviving Christian trade unions had honorable motives and serious arguments. On September 13 Winkelheide praised the Social Committees at a rally of the Christian Labor Movement and endorsed a Christian Social Workers' Congress. He appealed for a "truce of the castle" (*Burgfrieden*) among all Christian social organizations, and the KAB then sent its most influential leaders to negotiate with the Social Committees.[20]

When these negotiations proved difficult, Bishop Franz Hengsbach stepped forward as a mediator. Recently chosen to head the newly created, heavily blue-collar diocese of Essen, Hengsbach met separately with the KAB, Social Committees, and Christian Social Collegium and then

---

[18] Karl Braukmann, "Aktennotiz" for Bernhard Tacke, June 25, 1958, and "Niederschrift über die Hauptvorstandssitzung der Sozialausschüsse," July 11/12, 1958, NL Braukmann/5/4; "Dem DGB droht die Spaltung," *Kölner Stadt-Anzeiger*, #159, July 14, 1958 (ACDP/ 04–013/1/2); Hans Katzer, "Aktennotiz" of July 18, 1958, NL Katzer/616; Hans Katzer, "Wir stehen im Wort," *Soziale Ordnung*, XII/#7 (July 1958), pp. 108–109 (source of quotation).

[19] Katzer to Schmitt, Johannes Even, and Gockeln, July 14, 1958, reply by Schmitt of August 8, and reply by Gockeln of August 12, ACDP/04–013/42/1; Karl Braukmann to Albers, July 14 and September 2, 1958, NL Braukmann/5/4; Tacke to Albers, July 14, 1958, NL Katzer/ 544; "Die Arbeitnehmer wollen Einheitsgewerkschaften," DGB press release of July 24, 1958, ACDP/04–013/001/2; Hans Zankl's correspondence with three dozen Christian Democrats in the DGB from July 1958 in ACDP/04–013/1/2.

[20] "Dokumentation zur Gewerkschaftsfrage," *Soziale Ordnung*, XII/#8 (August 1958), pp. 121–141; speech by Winkelheide on September 13, 1958, NL Katzer/816; KAB Westdeutschlands, "Sitzung des Verbandsvorstandes," September 22, 1958, KAB Archiv/1/1.

distributed rules of etiquette for the "cooperation of Christian forces belonging to trade unions." Christians who belonged to rival unions should never attack each other, the bishop declared; instead they should cooperate in factory council elections and develop a common social program.[21] Katzer also received support from CDU headquarters in Bonn, which commissioned him in December 1958 to monitor attempts by other political parties to violate the terms of the Factory Councils Law by "politicizing" German factories. Katzer, Albers, and Winkelheide soon launched a joint "Christian Social Factory Campaign," an effort by the Social Committees and six church-affiliated organizations to influence the next factory council elections by securing fair representation on DGB nominations lists; only in factories where local union officials denied all reasonable requests did they seek to nominate separate lists of "Christian social" candidates. Albers also announced that the seven organizations had agreed to convene a great Christian Social Workers' Congress to demand "a genuine social reform that will give the 75 percent of our population who are wage- and salary-earners the feeling that social justice is the foundation of all decisions in our social and political life." Katzer sent copies of their manifesto to numerous CDU leaders and church dignitaries, earning their praise.[22]

Katzer and Albers sought to involve the Christian Social Collegium in their Factory Campaign, but they discovered that its leaders had developed radical ambitions. The Collegium had begun to publish harsh criticism of the DGB and sought to organize unauthorized caucuses within each member union. Its chief strategist, Father Herbert

[21] "Niederschrift über die Besprechung der Vertreter der Katholischen Arbeiter-Bewegung Westdeutschlands und der Sozialausschüsse der CDA," October 22, 1958, ACDP/ 04–013/42/1; Ernst Schmitz, "Bericht über eine Aussprache auf Einladung des H.H. Bischofs von Essen," October 4, 1958, involving Herbert Reichel and several leaders of the Collegium, ACDP/04–013/98/2; "Zusammenarbeit der christlichen Kräfte im gewerkschaftlichen Raum. Einige Grundsätze und Spielregeln," draft sent by Hengsbach to Albers for comment on October 13, 1958 (source of quotation), and Albers to Hengsbach, November 13, 1958, NL Albers/1/1956–1959; Albers to Hengsbach, October 23, 1958, LANRW/CDA Rheinland/912. For background see Christian Plostica, "Katholische Arbeitervereine und katholisches Milieu in Essen nach dem Zweiten Weltkrieg, 1945–1958," M.A. diss. (Bochum, 1998).
[22] Hans Katzer, "Im Geiste des Betriebsverfassungsgesetzes," DUD press release #233 of December 4, 1958, ACDP/04–013/33/3; "Protokoll über die Sitzung der christlich-sozialen Betriebsaktion 1959 für Westfalen und das Ruhrgebiet," Essen, January 2, 1959, ACDP/04–013/33/3; Hans Katzer, "Ansprache auf der konstituierenden Sitzung des christ-lich-sozialen Arbeiterkongresses," Cologne, January 6, 1959, ACDP/04–013/129/2; Johannes Albers, "Proklamation der Chr.-Soz. Betriebsaktion," Cologne, January 6, 1959, NL Katzer/579 (source of quotation); "Hartes Ringen um Betriebsräte," Rheinische Post, January 7, 1959 (ACDP/04–013/33–3); "Einheit in Vielfalt," Soziale Ordnung, XIII/#2 (February 1959), pp. 17–19; Bishop Michael Keller to the Social Committees, January 7, 1959, and related correspondence in ACDP/04–013/37/2.

Reichel, also wrote CDU headquarters to denounce both the Social Committees and KAB for interfering with his efforts to reform the DGB. Reichel insisted that leadership by the clergy offered the only hope: "Only the Church has the authority and despite the developments of recent years the trust needed to gather Catholics together in service of the Church."[23] Heinrich Krone invited Katzer and Reichel to CDU headquarters to seek a common line, but his two guests reproached each other for personal ambition and bad judgment. At a closed meeting of Collegium leaders three weeks later, their national spokesperson August Weimer predicted a decisive confrontation at the next DGB national congress in September 1959. He concluded that "if, despite all our efforts, no genuinely unified trade unions are possible, then we need a genuine alternative on Day X." Reichel agreed that "if we are outlawed [by the DGB], then genuinely unified trade unions will be founded."[24] They evidently hoped to found a third labor federation alongside the DGB and Christian Labor Movement. Willi Richter decided not to take any disciplinary action against the Collegium, however, after seeking the advice of Oswald von Nell-Breuning, and the DGB Congress in September proved quite harmonious. The moderate Social Democrat Ludwig Rosenberg delivered an address on economic policy that resembled the Godesberg Program, and he quoted the encyclical *Quadragesimo Anno* at length. Richter was then reelected as DGB chair without opposition, with Bernhard Tacke and Rosenberg as vice chairs.[25] Reichel hoped that the DGB would create martyrs for his movement, but it refused to oblige.

The Social Committees had meanwhile avoided conflict with the DGB during their Christian Social Factory Campaign while improving cooperation with the Catholic workers' clubs. Their veteran representative in Aachen reported to the Stegerwald House, for example, that his opposite number in the Aachen KAB had agreed for the first time to regular meetings to coordinate their activities. In Westphalia, Hesse, and

---

[23] Ernst Schmitz, "Niederschrift über die Verhandlung" with Collegium leaders at the Cologne CDU office on November 14, 1958, NL Zankl/2/1; Herbert Reichel, "Gewerkschaftlicher Lagebericht" for CDU leaders, December 28, 1958, NL Zankl/3/1.

[24] "Akten-Notiz über das Gespräch bei Dr. Krone zwischen Dr. Reichel und Leo Schütze einerseits und Hans Katzer und Josef Arndgen andererseits unter Teilnahme von Dr. Barzel," January 5, 1959, and Hans Zankl's "Bericht über die Tagung in Walberberg" on January 27, 1959, in NL Zankl/1/3.

[25] "Niederschrift über eine Aussprache mit Vertretern konfessioneller Gruppen" at DGB headquarters, April 2, 1959, minutes of a similar meeting on July 10, and Ludwig Rosenberg to Willi Richter, July 30, 1959, DGB-Archiv/5/DGAI001191; Rosenberg's speech in DGB, *Protokoll: 5. ordentlicher Bundeskongress Stuttgart, 7. bis 12. September 1959* (Cologne, no date), pp. 390–438; Hans Katzer, "Kongress der vertagten Entscheidungen," *Soziale Ordnung*, XIII/#10 (October 1959), pp. 145–148.

Baden-Württemberg as well, the Social Committees reported good cooperation with the Catholic workers' clubs and an increased willingness by trade union functionaries to negotiate with them when they presented a united front. Summing up the campaign in a report to Adenauer, Katzer declared that "cooperation with the leaders of the Catholic and Protestant workers' clubs was outstanding, with extraordinarily positive results in the factories."[26] In 1959 Winkelheide turned over the chairmanship of the reorganized Christian trade unions to Peter Gier from the Saarland. Winkelheide championed cooperation between the KAB and Social Committees thereafter and won election to chair the Workers' Group in the CDU Bundestag delegation in 1962.[27]

In June 1959 the KAB finally agreed to discuss plans for a Christian Social Workers' Congress. The Kolping Clubs then resolved the old debate about the agenda by proposing a congress devoted to clarifying the fundamental differences between the "Christian Social Idea" and liberalism, socialism, and totalitarianism.[28] His friends in the DGB still wanted nothing to do with the Christian trade unions, so Katzer decided that no organizations would sign the invitations to the congress, only distinguished individuals such as Albers, Johannes Even of the KAB, August Weimer of the Collegium, and Peter Gier. Bernhard Tacke agreed to exhort his DGB colleagues to participate after Katzer promised to add him to the executive council of the Social Committees.[29] Katzer and Even

---

[26] Sozialsekretär Wilhelm Prümm (Aachen), "Erfahrungsbericht über die Betriebsratswahlen 1959," June 3, 1959, ACDP/04–013/33/2; summary of regional reports at the Factory Action conference on March 6, 1959, enclosed in Lutz Esser to Henrich, April 2, 1959, ACDP/04–013/37/2; Manfred Jordan, "Abschliessender Bericht über die Betriebsratswahl 1959 –Bezirk Industriegebiet Ost," July 1959, ACDP/04–013/33/2; Willi Krampe, "Betriebsrätewahlen im Erzbistum Paderborn," ACDP/04–013/139/1; "Geschäftsbericht der Sozialausschüsse ... der CDU Westfalen/Lippe für die Jahre 1957, 1958 u. 1959," October 24, 1959, ACDP/03–002/125/1; Joseph Riedel, "Bericht von der Tagung der Betriebsvertrauensleute" of the Hessian Social Committees, September 16, 1958, ACDP/04–013/51/2; Riedel to Katzer, February 3 and May 14, 1959, ACDP/04–013/33/2; German Stehle (Stuttgart) to CDA headquarters, June 3, 1959, ACDP/04–013/33/2; Katzer to Adenauer, July 6, 1959, NL Katzer/89.

[27] See "Christlich-soziale Gewerkschaftseinheit," *Rheinischer Merkur*, July 3, 1959, p. 1 (NL Katzer/816), and the praise for Winkelheide in Franz Deus to Bishop Hengsbach, January 16, 1963, NL Deus/1/1.

[28] Hans Katzer, "Kurzprotokoll über eine Besprechung der Christlich-Sozialen Verbände," June 22, 1959, and attached "Grundlage zur Vorbereitung des Arbeiterkongresses, wie sie vor zwei Jahren erarbeitet wurde," ACDP/04–013/42/1; Erwin Häussler to CDA headquarters, July 20, 1959, ACDP/04–013/42/1; Norbert Henrich for the Kolping Clubs to Katzer, July 30, 1959, ACDP/04–013/41/1; "Kurzprotokoll über eine Besprechung der Christlich-Sozialen Verbände," September 29, 1959, ACDP/04–013/42/1.

[29] Johannes Even and Hans Katzer to August Weimer, October 7, 1959, and reply of October 19, ACDP/04–013/42/1; Karl Braukmann, "Aktennotiz: Sitzung des Bundesvorstandes der Sozialausschüsse" on November 4/5, 1959, NL Braukmann/5/4;

agreed that "the impression cannot be allowed to emerge that this is essentially a Catholic congress," but among Protestant groups they could only secure the participation of the small network of Evangelical workers' clubs of North Rhine-Westphalia. The more influential Evangelical Action League for Workers' Questions included supporters of the SPD, and it declined the invitation. Confessional balance remained the most intractable problem for the organizers of the event.[30]

The long awaited Christian Social Workers' Congress finally met in Cologne on March 26, 1960, with an impressive array of guests including Federal President Heinrich Lübke, three federal cabinet ministers, Willi Richter, and two state prime ministers. The speeches were not scintillating, but the congress proved a major success, because it took place in a harmonious atmosphere and passed joint resolutions in the name of a combined membership of 1.5 million that gained massive publicity. Newspaper reporters expressed astonishment at the sight of DGB functionaries sitting beside representatives of the Christian trade unions in discussion groups that developed joint position papers. Many speakers demanded legislation to promote a more equitable distribution of wealth and "continued payment of wages" for sick blue-collar workers by their employers, so that they would be treated like white-collar workers. Katzer also denounced attempts by big business to undermine parity co-determination in coal and steel through corporate mergers. One Social Democratic reporter predicted that the resurrection of "the left wing of the CDU" would create many headaches for the leaders of that party, but the pro-CDU press also praised the congress enthusiastically.[31] The congress elected a standing committee that met regularly thereafter to forge common positions among the member organizations regarding social policy. Katzer and two colleagues from that committee were

---

"Beschlussprotokoll der Hauptvorstandssitzung" of the Social Committees, December 4/5, 1959, ACDP/04–013/8/1; "Beschluss-Protokoll über die Sitzung des Vorbereitungskomitees Christlich-Sozialer Arbeitnehmer-Kongress," December 16, 1959, ACDP/04–013/42/1; Katzer's correspondence with Tacke from December 1959 and January 1960, ACDP/04–013/134/2.

[30] "Besprechung des Organisationskomitees für die Vorbereitung des Arbeitnehmerkongresses," January 5, 1960, NL Mick/7/3 (source of quotation); Katzer to Arnold Poepke, February 23, 1960, Poepke to Eberhard Müller, February 24 and April 7, 1960, Müller to Katzer, March 5, 1960, and Katzer's "Vermerk über die Besprechung mit Herrn Pfarrer Dr. Eberhard Müller" on March 10, 1960, in ACDP/04–013/40/1.

[31] See Hans Katzer, "Christlich-sozial in unserer Zeit," and the other congress speeches in NL Mick/7/3, with numerous press clippings, including Kurt Gehrmann, "Gibt es wieder einen linken CDU-Flügel?" *Neue Rhein Zeitung*, March 29, 1960, and Josef Mick, "Christlich-Sozialer-Arbeitnehmerkongress 1960," *Betriebsräte-Briefe der CDA des Rheinlandes*, Nr. 91, April 1960. See also "Lübke beim christlich-sozialen Arbeitnehmerkongress," *Frankfurter Allgemeine Zeitung*, March 28, 1960 (NL Dörpinghaus/1).

elected to the CDU Central Committee soon thereafter, and Adenauer expressed "very great joy" over the success of the congress, because "for years he had regretted the fact of tension and conflict among all these organizations."[32]

The Christian Social Collegium disintegrated six months after this congress, after Herbert Reichel secured a resolution by its leaders on October 8, 1960, that it "no longer considers itself a group within the unions," because of the "unrestrained social democratization" of the DGB. A few of Reichel's followers then joined the Christian trade unions, but most remained DGB members and severed ties with the Collegium. Reichel's decision reflected frustration over Katzer's success at persuading most Catholics in the DGB that "minority rights" should be defined in terms of party affiliation, not religion. Heinrich Wittkamp led the opposition to Reichel within the Collegium and deplored his stubborn refusal to cooperate with the Social Committees.[33]

Subcommittees for DGB members within the Social Committees grew rapidly after the Collegium broke with the DGB. They had been founded in March 1956 to give the members of DGB-affiliated unions the opportunity to discuss "internal union problems only within the circle of fellow members of the union in question," but they had stagnated in the face of opposition by the DGB vice chair, Matthias Föcher.[34] Bernhard Tacke breathed new life into the enterprise at a conference in the Stegerwald House in February 1960, where Katzer promised his DGB colleagues autonomy to develop positions for communication to the leaders of the DGB, Social Committees, and CDU; Katzer asked only that they issue no press releases unless cleared with him. The Social Committees would pay the cost of their meetings, while Tacke's office at DGB headquarters provided logistical support. Katzer hoped that this initiative would

---

[32] CDA "Hauptvorstandssitzung," April 14, 1960, ACDP/04–013/8/1; "Zusammengefasste Niederschrift über das Gespräch des Ständigen Ausschusses . . . mit . . . Konrad Adenauer" on March 2, 1961, ACDP/04–013/40/1, quotation on p. 2. See also the minutes of the "Ständiger Ausschuss Christlich-Sozialer Arbeitnehmerkongresse" of June 13 and October 24, 1960, ACDP/04–013/40/1, and the "Entwurf einer Geschäftsordnung des Ständigen Ausschusses," NL Winkelheide/2/2.

[33] "Einheitsgewerkschaft gescheitert!" Collegium resolution and related press clippings in DGB-Archiv/5/DGAI001197; Wittkamp's remarks in "Bericht über eine Tagung christlich-sozialer GdED Kollegen" on April 2/3, 1960, ACDP/04–013/136/2; Wittkamp's reminiscences in "Aufgaben und Zielsetzung der Arbeitsgemeinschaft christlich-demokratischer DGB-Gewerkschafter," speech of January 27, 1962, p. 4, ACDP/04–013/139/2; Wolfgang Schroeder, *Katholizismus und Einheitsgewerkschaft. Der Streit um den DGB und der Niedergang des Sozialkatholizismus in der Bundesrepublik bis 1960* (Bonn, 1992), pp. 261–264, 332–334.

[34] Circular by Katzer to the Social Committees, March 28, 1956 (source of quotation), NL Katzer/389; "Niederschrift über die Besprechung des gewerkschaftlichen Arbeitskreises" on April 18/19, 1956, ACDP/04–013/160/2.

strengthen Tacke's position in the DGB by showing its leaders that he enjoyed the confidence of their Christian Democratic minority. Tacke emphasized that there were now so many practicing Christians in the SPD that one could no longer distinguish between "Christian" and "socialist" camps. All DGB leaders desired political influence, however, and would respect efforts to defend "minority rights" based on affiliation with the majority party in the Bundestag. Several veteran colleagues applauded this initiative as the most promising they had ever seen in all the attempts to enhance their influence on both the CDU and DGB.[35] When Tacke's colleagues assembled again in September, he dismissed Reichel's attacks on the DGB by noting that "even among our people, the view is spreading that Social Democrats too can get into heaven." At their next meeting in November, the senior DGB functionaries Maria Weber, Adolf Müller, Heinrich Wittkamp, and August Weimer all renounced their earlier support for the Collegium and exhorted their friends to join the Social Committees. Albers noted with satisfaction that "today we are more unified than in the last years." Katzer warned, however, that the Social Committees must maintain a pose of strict neutrality regarding which trade unions their members should join; they still faced intense suspicion in the CDU, where Christian trade unionists now outnumbered the members of DGB-affiliated unions in the Bundestag delegation by a tally of seventeen to thirteen.[36]

In late November 1960, Tacke's network adopted its formal name, Association of Christian Democratic DGB Trade Unionists (*Arbeitsgemeinschaft christlich-demokratischer DGB-Gewerkschafter*), with Tacke as chair and Wittkamp as the full-time manager. Katzer promised to publish any articles they submitted to *Social Order*, and they promised to expand its circulation.[37] The network grew slowly but steadily for the next two years. Some tensions remained between Tacke, who thought

---

[35] Hans Zankl, "Protokoll der konstituierenden Sitzung des 'Arbeitskreises der christlich-demokratischen Mitglieder des DGB' in den 'Sozialausschüssen der Christlich-demokratischen Arbeitnehmerschaft,'" February 27, 1960, NL Zankl/2/1.

[36] Hans Zankl, "Notizen aus der Sitzung des DGB-Arbeitskreises," September 24, 1960, NL Zankl/1/3, Tacke quotation on p. 2; Wittkamp to Katzer, October 27, 1960, reporting on his discussions with Tacke and Maria Weber, ACDP/04–013/146/3; Zankl, "Protokollnotizen aus der Sitzung des 'DGB-Arbeitskreises der Sozialausschüsse der Christlich-Demokratischen Arbeitnehmerschaft,'" November 11, 1960, ACDP/04–013/146/3, Albers quotation on p. 9.

[37] "Gewerkschaftsausschuss der Sozialausschüsse von Nordrhein und Westfalen: Beschlussprotokoll über die Sitzung," November 23, 1960, ACDP/04–013/140; "Gewerkschaftlicher Arbeitskreis des DGB: Niederschrift über die Sitzung des Vorbereitungsausschusses," November 26, 1960, ACDP/04–013/140; "Protokoll über die Besprechung zwischen den Kollegen Bernhard Tacke, Hans Katzer und Heinrich Wittkamp," January 28, 1961, ACDP/04–013/146/3.

its purpose was to reform the CDU, and Collegium veterans who sought to reform the DGB. Wittkamp reckoned that there were now about 280 Christian Democratic colleagues among the 5,000 functionaries of the DGB, a significant decline since 1953 that reflected the furor over the revival of Christian trade unions. He exhorted the DGB to broaden its appeal among workers by hiring more Christian Democratic functionaries; Wittkamp noted that the miners' union, which treated its minority best, enrolled 70 percent of all miners, while the organization rate for industry as a whole was only 30 percent.[38]

Katzer's success at unifying the workers' wing of the CDU encouraged Adenauer to display new interest in supporting party colleagues in the DGB. In September 1960 the senior Christian Democrat in IG Metall, Fritz Biggeleben, visited the chancellor to complain that his union had hired a Social Democrat the last two times a Christian Democratic district leader retired.[39] Adenauer promptly commissioned Johannes Albers to negotiate with the union chairman Otto Brenner in the chancellor's name, to demand that the next congress of IG Metall adopt resolutions "that will assure adequate representation in its leadership organs of the members of this union who belong to us." Brenner readily agreed to receive Albers, and Biggeleben assured the chancellor that his intervention had made a great impression. The promotions policy of IG Metall became slightly more even-handed thereafter, and Brenner persuaded his union congress in September 1962 to expand their central committee to add two Christian Democratic colleagues.[40]

Another sign of growing influence for the Social Committees came at a CDU leadership conference on November 18, 1960. Earlier that day Adenauer had ridiculed the Godesberg Program in a public rally, because it described the trade unions as agents of democratization. The trade unions, Adenauer exclaimed, were "the most undemocratic thing there is." In the subsequent closed meeting of the CDU Central Committee, Katzer's friend Rainer Barzel reminded everyone that at least one-third of

---

[38] Wittkamp to Katzer, November 17, 1961, ACDP/04–013/146/3; Wittkamp to Lutz Esser, April 13, 1962, ACDP/04–013/141/1; Wittkamp, "Aufgaben und Zielsetzung der Arbeitsgemeinschaft christlich-demokratischer DGB-Gewerkschafter," speech of January 27, 1962, pp. 2–3, ACDP/04–013/139/2. Compare Tacke's critique of the CDU in "Probleme unserer gesellschaftlichen Entwicklung," speech of March 24, 1963, LANRW/CDA Rheinland/832.

[39] See the correspondence with Biggeleben in NL Zankl/8/4, and Zankl's newsletter, "Notizen, Berichte, Informationen aus dem Gewerschaftsleben," February 24, 1960, NL Katzer/616.

[40] Adenauer to Albers, September 26, Albers to Brenner, September 29, and Biggeleben to Adenauer, October 7, 1960, NL Zankl/8/4; report by Otto Brenner to the DGB Bundesvorstand, September 25, 1962, *Gewerkschaftsquellen*, XII: 862.

CDU voters were blue-collar workers, and that a large proportion of them belonged to the DGB. "If placed before the question: CDU or DGB," Barzel warned, "even many of our friends will prefer the DGB." He exhorted Adenauer to avoid personal attacks on union leaders and phraseology that could be exploited by the SPD at election time; the CDU should simply argue "that the trade unions are undemocratic in the sense that they have no respect for the minority. That would also make the work of our colleague Katzer easier." Adenauer replied that the DGB was undemocratic because it "compelled" workers to join, a charge without foundation. Katzer then reminded everyone that the DGB deserved much credit for Germany's economic miracle, opposed Communism steadfastly, and launched very few strikes. The DGB deserved criticism when it violated the rights of its Christian Democratic minority, Katzer concluded, but most other attacks on it by CDU politicians alienated blue-collar voters. Katzer received unexpected support from the Protestant theologian Eugen Gerstenmaier, who bluntly told a colleague who disagreed with Katzer, "Excuse me, but nothing that dumb has ever been said by any of us in public." The victory of Barzel and Katzer in this debate provides evidence for the thesis of Wolfgang Hirsch-Weber that the overlap in the bases of support for the CDU and DGB gave leaders on both sides a powerful incentive for compromise.[41]

Katzer had assembled a young leadership team at the Stegerwald House that shared his determination to forge a discreet alliance with the DGB, led by Karl-Heinz Hoffmann and Hermann Josef Russe. Russe was born into a blue-collar family in Bochum but earned a prep school degree in 1941. He worked as a coal miner after the war but devoted himself to university study in 1948 and earned a degree in economics. Russe took charge of the Social Committees' adult education programs in 1952. Born in 1928, Karl-Heinz Hoffmann had worked in a chemical factory after the war, joined the chemical workers' union and CDU, and served as a CDU social secretary in the Rhineland; Katzer hired him in 1960 to take charge of relations with factory cells and trade unions in the Stegerwald House. He, Katzer, and Russe all sought to develop strong personal relationships with DGB leaders, working closely with Adolf Müller, the son of a functionary in the old Christian metalworkers' union in Remscheid who became vice chair of the DGB state organization of North Rhine-Westphalia in 1958 and won election to the Bundestag in 1961.[42]

---

[41] CDU Bundesvorstand, November 18, 1960, *Vorstandsprotokolle 1957–61*, pp. 875–884 (Barzel on 875–876, Gerstenmaier on 882); for the Hirsch-Weber thesis, see pp. 4–5 in the present volume.

[42] See the biographical sketches of Müller, Hoffmann, and Russe on de.wikipedia.org; Hoffmann's c.v. from 1954 in NL Katzer/259; and the interview with Adolf Müller in

Katzer's team achieved some financial independence from the CDU by establishing the Jakob Kaiser Foundation in December 1961, a charitable organization dedicated to adult education for which contributions were tax deductible. In the 1960s the DGB donated 25,000–30,000 marks per year to the Kaiser Foundation alongside the 100,000 it gave to the SPD-affiliated Friedrich Ebert Foundation. IG Metall apparently matched the DGB contribution from 1963 onward, and smaller sums flowed in from other unions and paid advertisements in *Social Order*.[43] The leaders of the Social Committees denied press reports that they were subsidized by organized labor, but trade union contributions to their national headquarters approached in size the monthly subsidy of 8,000–9,000 marks from the CDU.[44] The overall CDU contribution remained much larger, because state and county party offices paid for the network of social secretaries who organized factory cells, and the CDU provided generous funding for factory council election campaigns. Katzer had tapped into a significant new revenue stream nevertheless, because unity on the workers' wing of the CDU gave the Social Committees new importance in the eyes of DGB leaders.

5.2 The Stagnation of Social Policy

Despite the trend toward unity on the workers' wing of the CDU, the social policy record of the third Adenauer cabinet proved much weaker than that of the second. Many Christian Democrats opposed any expansion of welfare programs. Ludwig Erhard also enjoyed growing influence as the man widely credited for West Germany's "economic miracle" and Adenauer's likely successor. Erhard had become preoccupied with the fear of inflation and did everything he could to prevent budget deficits or "excessive" wage increases, which according to him must never exceed

Wolfgang Schroeder, ed., *Gewerkschaftspolitik zwischen DGB, Katholizismus und CDU, 1945 bis 1960. Katholische Arbeiterführer als Zeitzeugen in Interviews* (Cologne, 1990), pp. 61–76.

[43] Hans Katzer, "Jakob-Kaiser-Stiftung," *Soziale Ordnung*, XVI/#1 (January 1962), pp 1–3. The minutes of the DGB Bundesvorstand record a contribution of 25,000 marks to the Kaiser Foundation in 1966, and 30,000 for the years 1967–1968 (*Gewerkschaftsquellen*, XIII: 326, 474, 630); on November 27, 1973, K. Probst of the Kaiser Foundation wrote Heinz Oskar Vetter with thanks for raising the annual subsidy to 35,000 (DGB-Archiv/5/DGCS000105). Karl-Heinz Hoffmann recorded in a "Vermerk" for Katzer on January 17, 1963 (ACDP/04–013/141/1), that according to Fritz Biggeleben, IG Metall wanted to contribute and inquired how much the DGB was giving, so that this sum could be matched.

[44] See the carefully worded denial in the circular by Russe to the Social Committees in June 1967, ACDP/04–013/12/1, and Konrad Kraske to Katzer, January 14, 1963, NL Katzer/89, announcing that the CDU's monthly subsidy would be increased to DM 9,000.

measurable gains in productivity per work hour. As labor minister, Theodor Blank proved far less skillful than Anton Storch at rallying political support; he made no effort to coordinate his initiatives with the Social Committees or DGB, and his appeals to public opinion were sometimes clumsy. Blank suffered growing isolation as he grappled with a crisis in the coal industry and the complex issue of health insurance reform.

5.2.1   The Coal Crisis

Many Social Democrats blamed Ludwig Erhard for the coal crisis that began in 1958, because he had persuaded the cabinet in March 1956 to deregulate the price of coal, one of the few commodities to which the great experiment with price deregulation in 1948 did not apply. In 1956 there was an acute coal shortage, however, and the miners' union agreed with management that the price of coal must be allowed to rise to encourage increased production.[45] Unfortunately for German miners, the world market price of petroleum declined steadily thereafter, and it came to be used more and more to heat German homes and generate electricity. The Ruhr mines experienced the sudden growth of stockpiles of unsold coal in the winter and spring of 1958, and the mine operators began to reduce production by ordering unpaid holidays for miners. Ludwig Erhard downplayed the significance of this development in a report to the cabinet on April 30 and even expressed satisfaction that "the marketing difficulties in coal have served to brake wage demands by the trade unions in all sectors of industry." Adenauer implored his cabinet colleagues not to express such views in public, and he warned against "underestimating the political aspect of these marketing difficulties. If unemployment spreads, the Ruhr can develop into a witches' cauldron. Communist agitation will not neglect this opportunity." The former vice chairman of the miners' union, Labor Minister Blank, noted that there would soon be a state election in North Rhine-Westphalia and implored the cabinet on May 7 to announce that it would not permit the mining industry to go under. On June 3 the cabinet finally granted the wishes of Adenauer and Blank with a declaration to the press "that domestic coal production is and will remain the essential foundation of German energy policy. The Federal Government will therefore strive to remain as close as possible to the current level of employment in coal mining."[46]

[45] See Heinrich Gutermuth's speech to a miners' congress on May 18, 1956, pp. 15–17, 26–27, NL Katzer/553, and Christoph Nonn, *Die Ruhrbergbaukrise. Entindustrialisierung und Politik 1958–1969* (Göttingen, 2001), pp. 32–42, 69–70.
[46] Cabinet meetings of April 30, 1958, point E, May 7, point C, and June 3, Point G, Bundesarchiv, *Kabinettsprotokolle Online*; Nonn, *Ruhrbergbaukrise*, pp. 71–82.

The CDU election victory in North Rhine-Westphalia in July 1958 relieved the immediate pressure on the cabinet, but the demand for coal declined further. The mines set a new record for unpaid holidays in October, and in a sector long plagued by labor shortage, there were now 3,000 unemployed miners. The coal industry demanded steep tariffs on all energy imports, and the leader of the miners' union, Heinrich Gutermuth, planned a wave of protest demonstrations for early November to support this demand.[47] On October 29 the Rhenish Social Committees appealed to Adenauer for the protection of German coal. "Through neglect of domestic coal mining we will become ever more dependent on foreign countries for our energy supplies," they declared, and the recent Suez Crisis showed how quickly imports could be disrupted; "radicalism and nihilism" had been banished with great difficulty from the mines after 1945 but would revive if the marketing crisis continued. The leaders of the Westphalian Social Committees heard an alarming report on November 22 that 100,000 miners could be laid off soon, and they too exhorted the government to enact protective tariffs at once.[48]

Adenauer echoed the arguments of the Social Committees in a CDU leadership conference in late November. "You know that the industrial region [on the Ruhr] is a hotbed of Communist agents," the chancellor declared, "and that political unrest in the industrial region can have an extraordinarily harmful effect throughout the country." Erhard replied that there was no crisis, because the average miner had lost only four days' wages that year, and he rejected any tariffs or subsidies for coal, because they would then be demanded by many other branches of industry. West Germany now enjoyed an annual trade surplus of six billion marks, the economics minister concluded, and profited like no other country from free trade. Adenauer replied that "it does not help me if a few branches of the German economy achieve a great export surplus, and other branches ... go to the dogs. I don't think that's right, to say nothing of the political consequences." Blank supported Adenauer, noting that the mountains of coal in the Ruhr today looked just like those Blank had seen as a youth in the Great Depression. "I maintain from personal experience ... that one of the reasons why the Nazis came to power was

---

[47] Bundesarchiv, *Kabinettsprotokolle Online*, cabinet meeting of September 3, 1958, Point C, and "Kabinettsausschuss für Wirtschaft," October 23, 1958, Point 1.a; Nonn, *Ruhrbergbaukrise*, pp. 99–102.

[48] Albers, Johannes Ernst, and Hermann Weber to Chancellor Adenauer, October 29, 1958, NL Katzer/254, published in *Soziale Ordnung*, XII/#11 (November 1958), pp. 184–185 (source of quotation); "Niederschrift über die erweiterte Landesvorstandssitzung" of the Westphalian CDA, November 22, 1958, ACDP/03–002/127/1; Nonn, *Ruhrbergbaukrise*, p. 103.

this great dying out that began on the Ruhr at the end of the 1920s. The more mines that died, the larger the SA columns on the street." Adenauer, Blank, and Albers agreed that Heinrich Gutermuth, a veteran of the old Christian miners' union despite being a Social Democrat, was the most reasonable of labor leaders, and that the government must work with him to combat radicalism. Adenauer implored Erhard's admirers to ponder what would happen to their precious free market principles if the SPD won the next election and nationalized the mines.[49]

Erhard could not defeat Adenauer in open debate but proved skillful at obstructing policies that he considered irrational. Gutermuth pressured the cabinet by organizing a rally for 80,000 miners in Bochum on January 25, 1959, the largest demonstration in the Ruhr since 1949. He denounced the economics ministry for an "economic Stalingrad on the Ruhr," alleging that the miners' "standard of living has been sacrificed on the altar of liberal free market principles. The accusation is sweeping through the coal pits that we confront high treason against the national economic interests of mining and its employees." On the eve of this rally, Erhard agreed to support a tariff on imported coal high enough to elim-inate competition from American mines, but he rejected any attempt to restrict oil imports.[50] Erhard responded to Gutermuth's attacks at a closed retreat for DGB activists in the Christian Social Collegium. In the modern economy, he insisted, "there is no organized security. Genuine security comes from within. It is the feeling that arises when you know that justice prevails . Where free competition reigns ... there is no unearned income. Higher nominal and real incomes thereby become possible." "Security" both national and social had been the central theme of Adenauer's winning election campaigns in 1953 and 1957, but Erhard argued that only flexibility and mobility could solve the coal crisis.[51]

Neither Erhard nor Adenauer anticipated the magnitude of the lay-offs that would result from oil imports and the introduction of labor-saving machinery in the mines. The number of West German coal miners declined from a peak of 604,000 in 1957 to 388,000 in 1965 and just 230,000 in 1972. The decline of coal output was far more gradual, from

---

[49] CDU Bundesvorstand, November 27, 1958, *Vorstandsprotokolle 1957–61*, pp. 263–311 (quotations on 263–264, 299–305); see also "Weisse Halden," *Der Spiegel*, XII/#45 (November 5, 1958), pp. 22–26.

[50] Heinrich Gutermuth, "Wirtschaftliches Stalingrad an der Ruhr," speech of January 25, 1959, NL Katzer/554; CDU Bundestag delegation, January 27, January 29, and February 3, 1959, in Reinhard Schiffers, ed., *Die CDU/CSU-Fraktion im Deutschen Bundestag. Sitzungsprotokolle 1957–1961*, 2 vols. (Düsseldorf, 2004; hereafter *Fraktionsprotokolle 1957–61*), I: 311–318; Nonn, *Ruhrbergbaukrise*, pp. 109–118.

[51] Hans Zankl, "Bericht über die Tagung in Walberberg," January 27, 1959, NL Zankl/1/3, quotation on p. 5.

149 to 103 million tons per year, as production became mechanized.[52] The Ruhr suffered its first large mine closing with mass layoffs in June 1959, and the miners' union organized a new wave of demonstrations in August to demand a steep tax on imported oil. The Social Committees embraced this demand, and in mid-September the cabinet proposed a steep tax of 30 marks per ton. Serious opposition emerged, however, from other branches of industry, the SPD, and CDU Bundestag delegates from northern and southern Germany, who all defended the rights of consumers and argued that economic growth depended on cheap energy prices. The tax only passed the Bundestag after the CDU lowered the rates to a level that did not alter market trends significantly.[53]

The policy debate between Adenauer and Erhard soon erupted into struggle for control of the CDU. Erhard was the most popular West German politician by far, but Adenauer believed that he lacked the political skills and knowledge of foreign policy needed to be a good chancellor. In February 1959 Adenauer therefore sought to draft his economics minister for the ceremonial office of federal president, but the CDU Bundestag delegation rejected the idea. Adenauer then announced on April 9 that he would accept nomination as president himself, and the response was enthusiastic. Johannes Albers concluded that Erhard would inevitably become the next chancellor, but he appealed confidentially to Heinrich Krone to seek election as CDU party chair, because Krone could best retain the confidence of Catholic workers and "preserve the old spirit of the Center Party" when the neo-liberal Protestant Erhard led the government.[54] Adenauer remained determined to prevent the election of Erhard to succeed him as chancellor, and he became angry when most party colleagues ignored his advice. On June 5 Adenauer therefore stunned the press and CDU by announcing that he must remain chancellor in view of the revival of East-West tensions, because Erhard did not enjoy the trust of NATO allies. The leaders of the Social Committees feared that Adenauer's erratic behavior could lead "to a crisis of the party, even of democracy itself," but Krone persuaded them to issue a restrained press release that they disagreed with Adenauer's decision but continued to support his policies. Erhard was mortally offended by Adenauer's attacks

---

[52] Nonn, *Ruhrbergbaukrise*, p. 385.
[53] Landessozialausschuss Rheinland, resolution of August 29, 1959, NL Ernst/4; "Niederschrift über die Sitzung der [CDU] Arbeitnehmerabgeordneten," September 14, 1959, NL Katzer/424; CDU Bundestag delegation, September 14, 1959, *Fraktionsprotokolle 1957–61*, II: 461–462; CDU Bundesvorstand, September 16, 1959, *Vorstandsprotokolle 1957–61*, pp. 395–396; Nonn, *Ruhrbergbaukrise*, pp. 120–139.
[54] Johannes Albers, "Aktennotiz über die Besprechung mit Herrn Dr. Krone" on April 11, 1959, and Albers to Adenauer, April 14, 1959, LANRW/CDA Rheinland/912; Schwarz, *Adenauer*, II: 502–516.

but agreed to remain in the cabinet, and CDU leaders became polarized between Adenauer loyalists and supporters of the heir apparent. Hans Katzer enjoyed the respect of both camps, because he sometimes criticized Erhard's policies but insisted that Adenauer had treated him unfairly.[55]

Adenauer shored up his support from the Social Committees when he joined Albers that autumn in a plea to CDU leaders to nominate more working-class candidates. Albers reproached the members of the CDU Central Committee, because only six out of sixty were blue- or white-collar workers. "Do not get red in the face," Albers concluded, "if a trade union secretary from the DGB declares his support for the CDU and wants to work in it! I must note that still today there are many trade union secretaries who support the CDU and would like to work in it, but they are not respected and are not accepted by many groups among us." These remarks provoked contradiction, but Adenauer declared that Albers was correct and must be heeded, if the CDU wanted to win elections. Katzer and Albers agreed thereafter that Adenauer displayed far more sympathy for their concerns than did most other CDU leaders.[56]

5.2.2   The Campaign for Health Insurance Reform

Theodor Blank sought when he took office as labor minister to address the growing skepticism in the CDU about the moral and economic impact of the "welfare state." He therefore advocated cost-neutral reforms of social insurance programs to reduce waste, direct benefits to the most needy, and encourage a sense of responsibility for their own fate among the insured.[57] Blank soon learned that officials in the labor ministry worried most about the rising cost of health care, and he advised Chancellor Adenauer to declare that the top social policy priority for his third term would be health insurance reform. Adenauer and Blank agreed that they should introduce both popular improvements in coverage and a painful system of co-payments by the insured for each medical service, to contain costs. Blank then called publicly on February 13, 1958, for "some contribution to

---

[55] CDU Bundestag delegation, June 5, 1959, *Fraktionsprotokolle 1957–61*, I: 391–406; "Zusammengefasste Niederschrift über die Hauptvorstandssitzung der Sozialausschüsse," June 5/6, 1959 (source of quotation), ACDP/04–013/8/1; reminiscences about Katzer by the Erhard loyalist Erik Blumenfeld in Fink, *Hans Katzer*, pp. 42–43; Schwarz, *Adenauer*, II: 516–526; Volker Hentschel, *Ludwig Erhard. Ein Politikerleben* (Berlin, 1998), pp. 443–470.

[56] CDU Bundesvorstand, November 9, 1959, *Vorstandsprotokolle 1957–61*, pp. 450–459 (quotation on 456); Albers to Jakob Kaiser, November 14, 1959, LANRW/CDA Rheinland/912.

[57] See Blank's reminiscences in "Die Christlich Demokratische Arbeitnehmerschaft in der CDU," speech of October 12, 1968, NL Blank/13, and the compilation of key passages from his speeches of 1958/59 in "Auf dem Wege zu einer Sozialpolitik neuen Stils," *Soziale Ordnung*, XIII/#9 ("Beilage" of September 1959).

the cost of treatment by the insured." The old system of free visits to the doctor and free prescription drugs was very popular, however, and many physicians believed that it conferred important health benefits by neutralizing reluctance to visit the doctor among the poor.[58]

While labor ministry officials drafted a complex bill, their chief of staff, State Secretary Wilhelm Claussen, told reporters that co-payments were needed to discourage those "who run to the doctor for every trivial case and involve the health insurance apparatus to obtain a bottle of cough syrup." Those who formulated social policy, he declared, "must finally have the courage to be unpopular ... [and] can no longer behave as if health insurance were a cow that is milked on earth and fed in heaven." Such declarations prompted some of Blank's friends to warn him that, following his controversial role as the architect of rearmament, another bold attempt to prove that he had "the courage to be unpopular" might end his political career.[59] Blank nevertheless reiterated his call for co-payments in a newspaper interview on July 19, and he foolishly revived the implausible threat to organize a mass secession from the DGB if it did not terminate all support for the SPD. The DGB responded with a blistering attack on co-payments, because they would place the burden of paying for reform on the poorest workers and increase "the danger of delay and a worsening of diseases not detected quickly."[60]

In autumn 1958 Blank secured cabinet approval for nine principles to govern health insurance reform that reflected a lofty sense of ethics but a lack of political realism. Blank rejected as too expensive for employers the most popular reform idea, championed by the DGB and Social Committees, the "continued payment of wages" for sick blue-collar workers by employers. He insisted that the insured must contribute something to the cost of every doctor's visit, medication, and day in hospital, and he called for doctors to be paid a fee for each service rendered, not (as at present) a lump sum per month. The cabinet approved these principles without debate on November 5 but did not discuss health insurance again for another year.[61] That hesitation

---

[58] See "Das sozialpolitische Programm," *Soziale Ordnung*, XII/#4 (April 1958), pp. 58–59, and Ursula Reucher, *Reformen und Reformversuche in der gesetzlichen Krankenversicherung (1956–1965). Ein Beitrag zur Geschichte bundesdeutscher Sozialpolitik* (Düsseldorf, 1999), pp. 19–63.

[59] See "Krankenkassen: Geld, Geld," *Der Spiegel*, XII/#48 (November 26, 1958), pp. 34–50 (quotation on 34).

[60] DGB Bundesvorstand, August 5, 1958, *Gewerkschaftsquellen*, XII: 337–341 (quotation on 340).

[61] See Bundesarchiv, *Kabinettsprotokolle Online*, Ministerausschuss für Sozialreform 1955–1960, October 24, 1958, Point 1, and cabinet minutes for November 5, 1958, Point 5.

doubtless resulted from the harsh public criticism of Blank's plans, and Christian Democratic workers were especially critical. The surviving records of discussions in Christian social factory cells and local meetings of the Social Committees all reflect fierce opposition to co-payments and resentment of the labor ministry bureaucrats who blamed the system's problems on malingering workers.[62]

In the summer of 1959 Heinrich Krone advised Blank to drop the issue of health insurance until the next legislative term, but the labor minister insisted on proceeding. Blank reported to the cabinet that the SPD might introduce a bill that contained only the most attractive features of his plan, without any measures to contain costs, so it approved his bill in November 1959 and introduced it to the Bundestag in January 1960.[63] The bill provoked outrage among trade unionists, and the DGB appropriated 600,000 marks for agitation against it, more than it had contributed to the entire "Struggle against Atomic Death." Representatives of the hospitals and physicians also attacked the bill, as did regional conferences of the Social Committees in Rhineland-Westphalia and Baden-Württemberg. A despondent Heinrich Krone confided to his diary in March 1960 that "it does not appear that we will pass health insurance reform in this Bundestag. We will lose the election."[64]

Adenauer reproached the Social Committees at the CDU party congress of April 1960 for criticizing the labor minister in public. He suggested jovially that if they had a "family quarrel" with Blank, they should "approach an older relative and ask him if he would not be willing to take part in such a discussion." Heinrich Scheppmann, the former coal miner who chaired the Bundestag labor committee, replied sharply that this advice assumed that the other family member did not decide without consulting you to "disseminate proposals to the public that cause outrage, and which we are then supposed to defend.[65] Scheppmann introduced a resolution adopted unanimously at a prior caucus of the congress

---

[62] "Selbstbeteiligung?" *Soziale Ordnung*, XIII/#1 (January 1959), pp. 8–11; report by Erwin Brenner to Lutz Esser on January 14, 1959, on discussions in the MAN-Werk in Nuremberg, ACDP/04–013/40/2; "Protokoll über die erweiterte Landesvorstandssitzung" of the Social Committees of Westphalia, March 7, 1959, NL Katzer/254; Sozialauschuss Duisburg, "Protokoll der erweiterten Vorstandssitzung," February 1, 1960, LANRW/CDA Rheinland/696.

[63] Bundesarchiv, *Kabinettsprotokolle Online*, cabinet meetings of October 28, 1959, Point 3, and November 20, Point 2; Krone, *Tagebücher*, I: 374, 378–379, 398; Reucher, *Reformen*, pp. 139–148.

[64] DGB Bundesvorstand, February 2–4, 1960, *Gewerkschaftsquellen*, XII: 532–536; CDU Bundestag delegation, February 16, 1960, *Fraktionsprotokolle 1957–61*, II: 560–561; Krone, *Tagebücher*, March 15, 1960, I: 411; Reucher, *Reformen*, pp. 148–162.

[65] CDU, *9. Bundesparteitag der CDU. Karlsruhe, 26.-29. April 1960* (Hamburg, no date), pp. 29, 137–140, 173–176 (quotations on 140, 173).

delegates belonging to the Social Committees, which demanded the "continued payment of wages" by employers for sick blue-collar workers, and replaced the idea of co-payments with a small, one-time fee for commencing treatment at the onset of illness. After tense discussions among party leaders behind closed doors, Scheppmann withdrew this motion in favor of a simple endorsement of "continued payment of wages," which passed by an overwhelming majority. No congress resolution mentioned co-payments.[66]

Blank continued to fight for his plan within the CDU Bundestag delegation in May, arguing that "one should not shrink back with fright from public opinion. When the Social Market Economy was introduced in the [Frankfurt] Economic Council, people thought at first that we could not take this step against public opinion, but then it proved to be correct." Scheppmann retorted that the CDU would lose the next election if it passed a bill that was opposed by "all the insured and all interest groups except for the employers' associations."[67] Soon thereafter Krone persuaded Blank over a bottle of wine to replace co-payments with the small one-time fee proposed by Scheppmann, but they could not rally their party behind this idea. Physicians complained bitterly to Adenauer, because Blank's plan remained so vague that they had no idea how their incomes would be affected, and business lobbyists insisted on co-payments for each service. Krone confided to his diary on July 12 that his delegation was hopelessly divided.[68]

After politicians returned from their summer vacations, the DGB functionary and CDU Bundestag delegate August Weimer published a simple plan to improve compensation from health insurance so that sick blue-collar workers would be paid 100 percent of previous earnings for each day of illness. Business lobbyists denounced the Weimer Plan, but it proved so popular that Adenauer and Krone agreed in January 1961 to abandon comprehensive reform and concentrate on passing it. Krone secured his delegation's support on February 7, and the Bundestag passed the bill on May 31. It still disappointed the DGB, because workers

---

[66] Ibid., pp. 173–174, 181–182, 185–186, 227–228, 242–243; confidential report for DGB leaders on the CDU Party Congress, May 4, 1960, DGB-Archiv/5/DGAI001793; Gundelach, "Sozialausschüsse," pp. 205–207.

[67] CDU Bundestag delegation, May 10, 1960, *Fraktionsprotokolle 1957–61*, II: 612–618 (quotations on 616–617).

[68] CDU Bundestag delegation, May 20 and May 25, 1960, *Fraktionsprotokolle 1957–61*, II: 626–633; Krone, *Tagebücher*, May–July 1960, I: 420–421, 432–435; "Sitzung des eng-er-en Parteivorstands," July 6, 1960, *Vorstandsprotokolle 1957–61*, pp. 705–727; "Kurz-Protokoll der Sitzung des Hauptvorstands" of the Social Committees, July 9, 1960, ACDP/04–013/8/1; Arthur Rohbeck, "Krankenversicherungsreform am Scheideweg," *Soziale Ordnung*, XIV/#7 (July 1960), pp. 122–123.

contributed much of the funding through their health insurance premiums and remained subject, unlike white-collar workers, to mandatory medical testing. Katzer rejoiced nevertheless, because the Social Committees had gained something and given up nothing in exchange.[69] Theodor Blank was virtually ignored during these discussions.

5.2.3   *"Property for Everyone!"*

The Social Committees had long argued that Christian principles demanded a more equitable distribution of wealth and therefore sought to promote "co-ownership" of the means of production (*Miteigentum*) through an "invested wage," i.e. agreements to grant a portion of any wage increase in the form of small ownership shares that workers would be forbidden to sell for some years. In May 1957 the CDU launched its Bundestag election campaign with speeches by Ludwig Erhard on "Prosperity for All!" and Karl Arnold on "Property for Everyone!" Erhard acknowledged that the methods employed to promote economic growth over the last decade had resulted in greater inequality in the distribution of wealth, and he declared that "the CDU has adopted the policy goal of achieving an ever broader diffusion of ownership of the means of production ... No other weapon could strike such a deadly blow to collectivist and totalitarian ideologies as this policy, which seeks social justice and balance." He was vague about details but did make one specific promise, a law to privatize the Volkswagen firm, with a discount on ownership shares for Volkswagen employees.[70] In January 1958 Karl Arnold introduced a Volkswagen privatization bill to the Bundestag, declaring that "property is a natural right granted to human beings by the Creator" and "the foundation of freedom." Big business, the SPD, and the DGB all opposed the bill, however, and debate in the Bundestag was delayed for two years by a legal dispute over the control of Volkswagen between the federal government and the SPD-led state government of Lower Saxony.[71]

---

[69] August Weimer, "Ein weiterer Schritt zur Gleichstellung der Arbeiter," *Soziale Ordnung*, XIV/#10 (October 1960), p. 176; Krone, *Tagebücher*, January 27-February 1, 1961, I: 468; CDU Bundestag delegation, September 27, 1960, February 6/7, 1961, and May 30, 1961, *Fraktionsprotokolle 1957–61*, II: 676–677, 680–681, 759–767, 831; Katzer, "Die christlich-soziale Idee setzt sich durch," *Soziale Ordnung*, XV/#6 (June 1961), p. 89; Reucher, *Reformen*, pp. 182–185.

[70] CDU, *7. Bundesparteitag 1957*, pp. 146–164 (quotation on 148).

[71] "Eigentum für jeden," *Soziale Ordnung*, XII/#2 (February 1958), pp. 20–21 (source of quotation); Gundelach, "Sozialausschüsse," pp. 190–193; Yorck Dietrich, *Eigentum für jeden. Die vermögenspolitischen Initiativen der CDU und die Gesetzgebung 1950–1961* (Düsseldorf, 1996), pp. 321–331.

The Social Committees soon gained new support for their ideas in both the labor unions and the CDU. The DGB had long opposed the "invested wage," but Willi Richter and Ludwig Rosenberg concluded in April 1958 that the Social Committees had generated so much interest in the idea among workers that they must develop a plan of their own. They proposed "social investment funds" managed by the trade unions, not individually owned shares, but the Social Committees applauded this shift in course. In May 1958 a national congress of the Social Committees resolved that each worker should be able to acquire 10,000 marks' worth of shares by retirement. Nobody would be compelled to participate, but everyone should be encouraged through discounts on stock purchase by employees and tax breaks.[72] Katzer advocated this plan in July during a weekend retreat for the CDU Bundestag delegation's property subcommittee. "In 1945 we all agreed," he declared, "that we should achieve a new social order. Today in 1958 that thesis cannot be propounded in many party organs without being challenged, but it remains correct." The existing co-determination laws had taken a step toward drawing workers "away from the path of class struggle and toward recognition of the idea of partnership." Now the time had come to promote a more equitable distribution of ownership of the means of production, not through confiscation of existing wealth but through shaping the ways in which new wealth formed. Katzer persuaded the subcommittee to endorse a bill for tax breaks to encourage firms to offer plans for an "invested wage."[73]

Small business lobbyists opposed Katzer's plan, and deliberations in the CDU Bundestag delegation stalled because of discord between its working groups for economic and social policy.[74] In January 1961 the CDU leadership concluded that the legislative term might end without any accomplishments for workers, so it finally introduced Katzer's bill "For the Formation of Wealth by Workers," a modest proposal to exempt up to 312 marks per year of a worker's savings from all taxes and contributions to social insurance. Workers could devote these sums to the purchase of ownership shares in any corporation, shares in their own firm, or savings accounts, but the bill promised employers tax breaks if they

---

[72] DGB Bundesvorstand, April 15, 1958, *Gewerkschaftsquellen*, XII: 296–298; "Breite Streuung des Eigentums," and "Der DGB jetzt auch für Eigentumsstreuung," *Soziale Ordnung*, XII/#6 (June 1958), pp. 91–95; Erwin Häussler, "Zu neuen Ufern," *Soziale Ordnung*, XII/#9 (September 1958), pp. 150–152.

[73] "Niederschrift über die Verhandlungen des Unterausschusses Eigentum der CDU/CSU-Fraktion," July 8/9, 1958, NL Katzer/7 (quotations on pp. 8–9).

[74] Resolution by the CDA Hauptvorstand, June 8, 1959, NL Katzer/255; CDU Bundestag delegation, June 23 and October 2, 1959, *Fraktionsprotokolle 1957–61*, I: 444–445, and II: 463–464; CDU Bundesvorstand, November 9, 1959, *Vorstandsprotokolle 1957–61*, p. 500; Krone, *Tagebücher*, November 14–19, 1959, I: 386–387.

offered employees small ownership shares in the firm at a discount.[75] Business lobbyists withdrew their objections after the Social Committees agreed to exclude the trade unions from any role. The so-called 312 Marks Law only applied to agreements between an employer and individual workers, or between an employer and the factory council; trade unions could not incorporate its provisions into collective bargaining agreements. It passed the Bundestag on May 30, 1961, but very few firms made use of its provisions.[76]

The bill to privatize Volkswagen finally became law in April 1961, and an impressive 1.5 million citizens purchased Volkswagen shares that year. Only 7.5 percent of them were blue-collar workers, however, so this program did not really address the concerns of the Social Committees. During the Bundestag election campaign of 1961, the Social Committees could only claim two accomplishments since their great election victory in 1957, a modest improvement of sick pay for blue-collar workers and the ineffective 312 Marks Law. The participants in their Ninth National Congress in March 1961 could find almost nothing to say about Adenauer's third term in office and devoted all their attention to proposals for the fourth.[77] The Bundestag with the largest proportion of CDU delegates had proved a great disappointment to advocates of social reform.

5.3   The Slow Rise and Rapid Fall of Ludwig Erhard

The CDU/CSU suffered a painful reverse in the Bundestag election of September 18, 1961, when its share of the vote declined from 50.2 to 45.3 percent, while the SPD rose from 31.8 to 36.2 percent, and the FDP, to an unprecedented 12.8 percent. Christian Democrats could not agree on whether this set-back resulted primarily from their poor record in social policy (as argued by the Social Committees and KAB), disaffection with Adenauer, or the attractiveness of the SPD's Godesberg Program, but most sensed the need for new leadership. Adenauer had certainly

---

[75] Hans Katzer, "Die Idee der Partnerschaft in der sozialen Marktwirtschaft," and "Regierungsentwurf eines Gesetzes zur Förderung der Vermögensbildung der Arbeitnehmer," *Soziale Ordnung*, Beilage to XV/#1 (January 1961), pp. 17–20.

[76] "Ein weiterer Schritt zum 'Eigentum für alle'," *Soziale Ordnung*, XV/#2 (February 1961), pp. 28–30; Hans Katzer, "Die christlich-soziale Idee setzt sich durch," *Soziale Ordnung*, XV/#6 (June 1961), pp. 89–90; "Gesetz zur Förderung der Vermögensbildung," with commentaries by Blank and Katzer, *Soziale Ordnung*, Beilage to XV/#7 (July 1961), pp. 111–115; Gundelach, "Sozialausschüsse," pp. 198–200; Dietrich, *Eigentum*, pp. 365–408.

[77] Dietrich, *Eigentum*, pp. 332–351; "VW-Aktien für VW-Angehörige," *Soziale Ordnung*, XV/#2 (February 1961), p. 31; "9. Bundestagung der Sozialausschüsse," *Soziale Ordnung*, XV/#3 (March 1961), pp. 37–52; "Die Arbeit der Arbeitnehmer-Abgeordneten," *Soziale Ordnung*, XV/#8 (August 1961), p. 138.

committed a political blunder when he virtually ignored the alarming construction of the Berlin Wall during the campaign and allowed the telegenic mayor of West Berlin, Willy Brandt, to seize the spotlight.[78] The influence of Adenauer's heir apparent, Ludwig Erhard, increased after this election, and he finally became chancellor in 1963. To the dismay of the Social Committees, Erhard had developed a visceral loathing for organized labor and refused to consider any proposals by the DGB. His disdain for both the SPD and trade unions reduced his effectiveness as chancellor and harmed the CDU.

The workers' wing of the CDU maintained its number of Bundestag seats despite the shrinking size of the delegation, because of effective cooperation during the nominations process among all the groups in the Christian Social Workers' Congress. Activists in the Westphalian Social Committees complained, however, that the nominees included few "genuine workers," and nationwide only four successful candidates were DGB functionaries.[79] Of the 251 new CDU/CSU delegates, forty-one classified themselves as blue- or white-collar workers, alongside forty-nine members of the free professions, forty-nine civil servants and teachers, forty-five farmers, thirty-three business lobbyists, and twenty-three representatives of small business; eleven belonged to miscellaneous occupations or did not list any. The Workers' Group actually grew to fifty-eight members (23 percent of the total), because of participation by civil servants. Fifty-three were Catholic and five Protestant, and only four were women. Among those who revealed a trade union affiliation, there were nineteen members of the minuscule Christian Labor Federation, sixteen from DGB-affiliated unions, and five from the white-collar German Employees' Union.[80]

---

[78] CDU Bundesvorstand, August 25, 1961, *Vorstandsprotokolle 1957–61*, pp. 1005–1060; CDU Fraktionsvorstand, September 21, 1961, in Corinna Franz, ed., *Die CDU/CSU-Fraktion im Deutschen Bundestag. Sitzungsprotokolle 1961–1966*, 3 vols. (Düsseldorf, 2004; hereafter *Fraktionsprotokolle 1961–66*), I: 4; Johannes Even's KAB circular of September 23, 1961, and his memorandum, "Zur Beurteilung der Bundestagswahlen 1961," NL Mick/1/3; Geoffrey Pridham, *Christian Democracy in Western Germany: The CDU/CSU in Government and Opposition, 1945–1976* (London, 1977), pp. 123–134; Schwarz, *Adenauer*, II: 640–672, 713–719.

[79] Documentation on nominations in NL Mick/1/3; "Bezirksvorstandssitzung des Sozialausschusses der CDU Ost-Westfalen-Lippe," July 22, 1961, ACDP/03–002/133/1; Albert Hillenkötter to Hans Zankl, August 25, 1961, NL Zankl/9/1; "Landesvorstandssitzung der Sozialausschüsse der Christlich-Demokratischen Arbeitnehmerschaft [Westfalens]," October 21, 1961, ACDP/03–002/127/1.

[80] "Zusammensetzung der CDU/CSU-Fraktion im 4. Deutschen Bundestag," compiled by CDU headquarters on October 11, 1961, NL Lücke/147; "Die Arbeitnehmergruppe der CDU/CSU," *Soziale Ordnung*, XV/#12 (December 1961), p. 204; Deutsches Industrieinstitut, "Der 'linke Flügel' der CDU/CSU," Sondermaterial Nr. 1/1962 (NL

The Free Democratic Party had become essential for a parliamentary majority, and it declared on the day after the election that it would only form a coalition with the CDU if Ludwig Erhard became chancellor. Some CDU leaders supported this idea, but Adenauer still believed that Erhard would be a disaster, and he gained support from the workers' wing of his party. Alarmed by FDP demands for a roll-back of welfare programs, the Standing Committee of the Christian Social Workers' Congress resolved on September 18 that Adenauer must remain chancellor, and Johannes Albers demanded his reelection when CDU leaders gathered the next day. Adenauer achieved consensus with a confidential promise to step down as chancellor in two years to clear the path for Erhard.[81]

The Social Committees sought to offer Adenauer options by exploring the possibility of a Great Coalition with the SPD. Hans Katzer reported to Adenauer on September 20 that he had conferred twice with Georg Leber, the leader of the construction workers' union and one of the few practicing Catholics in the SPD Bundestag delegation, who reported strong interest in a coalition among SPD leaders and a willingness to retain Adenauer as chancellor. The KAB supported this idea, and even Cardinal Frings told Adenauer and Krone that he preferred the SPD to the FDP. Adenauer told CDU parliamentary leaders on September 21 that many Social Democrats were now prepared to share responsibility for the most difficult decisions facing government. "We must not treat the SPD," he concluded, "in such a way that it pulls back from everything. In future he will not say, 'not with the SPD' . . . One must leave the FDP in some uncertainty." *Social Order* then editorialized that a "strong government" must be formed to deal with the crisis created by the Berlin Wall. The FDP, however, had become a mere "collection of political eccentrics with emphatically nationalistic undertones," whose "lack of programmatic or personal cohesion adds up to a weakness that stands in stark contradiction to the necessity of forming the most stable government possible at this moment."[82] National security offered a powerful rationale for a Great Coalition.

Tacke/12/3); "Arbeitnehmergruppe der CDU/CSU-Fraktion," list with union affiliations compiled by CDA headquarters in 1962/63, NL Deus/1/1.

[81] Minutes of September 19, 1961, in Günter Buchstab, ed., *Adenauer: "Stetigkeit in der Politik." Die Protokolle des CDU-Bundesvorstands 1961–1965* (Düsseldorf, 1998; hereafter *Vorstandsprotokolle 1961–65*), pp. 7, 18–19, 34–36, 44–47; Schwarz, *Adenauer*, II: 672–675.

[82] "CDU: Katzer von links," *Der Spiegel*, XV/#42 (October 11, 1961), pp. 27–28; Johannes Even, "Vertraulich," KAB circular of September 23, 1961, NL Mick/1/3; CDU Fraktionsvorstand, September 21, 1961, *Fraktionsprotokolle 1961–66*, I: 7 (source of Adenauer quotation); Krone, *Tagebücher*, September 25-October 4, 1961, I: 532–537; "Ernüchtert in die Zukunft," *Soziale Ordnung*, XV/#10 (October 1961), pp. 157–159; Daniel Koerfer, *Kampf ums Kanzleramt. Erhard und Adenauer* (Darmstadt, 1987), p. 567.

Many CDU leaders and almost everyone in the Bavarian CSU opposed a Great Coalition, however, so Heinrich Krone felt compelled to make concessions in his coalition talks with the FDP. On October 20 he signed an agreement that the next government would not extend co-determination rights for workers, launch new social programs, or raise taxes. Katzer detested this agreement and argued for a Great Coalition to his Bundestag delegation on October 27. Theodor Blank retorted that "a coalition with the SPD would be comfortable, because the SPD would behave in a genteel fashion toward the CDU/CSU to come to power in 1965. But for that very reason, such a coalition would be wrong." Krone soon gained approval of his agreement, and Katzer warned the Social Committees that they bore a great responsibility to serve as the "social conscience" of the new government.[83]

Ludwig Erhard gained new self-confidence when the coalition with the FDP formed, and in early 1962 he denounced organized labor for "excessive" wage demands that created inflationary pressure. These attacks were popular among middle-class voters, but DGB leaders and Christian Democratic workers were appalled.[84] Katzer persuaded Erhard to meet with the Social Committees' economics experts on March 1, 1962, when Erhard lectured them that free competition inevitably lowered profit rates and promoted a more equitable distribution of wealth. Soon thereafter he delivered a radio address to ridicule vague demands for "justice" in the distribution of wealth; those who advocated further "progress" in social policy, Erhard concluded, "perhaps want to do good, but will certainly accomplish evil." Katzer felt wounded and complained to Erhard that he only criticized wage increases and said nothing about the many other causes of inflation. Erhard replied that he was not attacking anyone in the CDU, only those outside the party who "lead us ever further away from the responsibility of the individual and into collectivism."[85]

---

[83] CDU Bundestag delegation, October 24 and 27 and November 3/4, 1961, *Fraktionsprotokolle 1961–66*, I: 60–73, 94–99, 104–110 (quotation on 71–72); Johannes Even, "Die Koalitionsverhandlungen," KAB circular of late October 1961, NL Mick/1/3; Hans Katzer, "Bürgerblock gegen Arbeiterblock?", *Soziale Ordnung*, XV/#11 (November 1961), pp. 173–174.

[84] CDU Bundesvorstand, February 7, 1962, *Vorstandsprotokolle 1961–65*, pp. 106–111, 139; CDU Bundestag delegation, March 13 and April 4, 1962, *Fraktionsprotokolle 1961–66*, I: 206–210, 230–235; Bernhard Tacke to Kurt Schmücker, March 12, 1962, ACDP/07–004/522/1; DGB Bundesvorstand, February 6 and April 3/4, 1962, *Gewerkschaftsquellen*, XII: 740–741, 789–790; Josef Mick's speech to the Rhenish Social Committees on February 10, 1962, pp. 4–5, LANRW/CDA Rheinland/915; Hentschel, *Ludwig Erhard*, pp. 535–536.

[85] "Protokoll über die Besprechungen zwischen Bundeswirtschaftminister Prof. Dr. Ludwig Erhard und dem wirtschaftspolitischen Ausschuss der Sozialausschüsse," March 1 and March 23, 1962 (source of second Erhard quotation), NL Katzer/64; "Masshalten!" radio address by Erhard on March 21, 1962, published in

Even his old ally Theodor Blank clashed with Erhard soon thereafter. By May 1962 the coal mines had laid off 150,000 workers. With another state election approaching, the CDU of North Rhine-Westphalia and Chancellor Adenauer called for new measures to protect German coal from imported oil, but Erhard rejected the idea.[86] As its labor contract neared expiration, the miners' union demanded a wage increase of 10.6 percent to keep pace with increases in other trades, but the employers replied that they could afford no increase at all. Blank offered his mediation in June and proposed an 8 percent wage increase, to be subsidized through government payment of a portion of the dues owed to the miners' health insurance and pension funds. To secure agreement, Blank promised the employers with Adenauer's approval that the government would do everything it could to guarantee steady demand for coal. Erhard wrote Blank privately that he was "absolutely not in agreement" with these promises, but Blank scribbled in the margin that Erhard "*was* in agreement." Erhard concluded in his letter that "what saddens me most about this matter is that you in particular, with whom I have always enjoyed such a good and harmonious cooperative relationship, would take such a step without my knowledge. That places a great strain on our relationship ... I hope you will understand my need to express my disappointment frankly." Blank wrote in the margin, "I too am disappointed."[87] Erhard had apparently agreed to this initiative in private but now sought to establish his credentials as a champion of free enterprise.

As Blank feared, the CDU suffered losses in North Rhine-Westphalia on July 8, declining from 50.5 to 46.4 percent of the state vote, while the SPD rose from 39.2 to 43.2 percent. CDU losses were heaviest in the Ruhr, and the Duisburg Social Committee reported that "for the first time the SPD appears to have succeeded at making a breakthrough among churchgoing workers." The SPD campaign was launched with an outreach to the Catholic clergy in May, when the party held its national congress in Cologne and organized an exhibit on the history

---

Helmut Engel, ed., *Ludwig Erhard* (Berlin, 2010), pp. 242–250 (first Erhard quotation on 246); Katzer's remarks in the handwritten minutes, "Hauptvorstand Sozialausschüsse 5. u. 6. Mai 1962 Berlin," NL Franz Deus/2/3.

[86] Circular by the CDU Rheinland Wirtschaftsausschuss, April 13, 1962, NL Lücke/147; CDU Bundestag delegation, May 15, 1962, *Fraktionsprotokolle 1961–66*, I: 270–272; cabinet minutes of May 14, 1962, Point 2, Bundesarchiv, *Kabinettsprotokolle Online*.

[87] DGB Bundesvorstand, June 5, 1962, *Gewerkschaftsquellen*, XII: 810–813; Krone, *Tagebücher*, June 20, 1962, II: 72; CDU Bundestag delegation, June 26, 1962, *Fraktionsprotokolle 1961–66*, I: 313; "Die CDU verhindert Streik in Nordrhein-Westfalen," campaign leaflet from June/July 1962, NL Lücke/147; Erhard to Theodor Blank, July 26, 1962, NL Blank/22/Privatkorrespondenz als Minister.

of the Catholic social movement in consultation with the archdiocese. The SPD had sought détente with the Catholic Church for several years, but this election apparently offered the first hard evidence that this strategy could yield electoral benefits.[88] The CDU campaign was also undermined by feuds in Westphalia between Christian trade unionists and DGB activists. Four of the five social secretaries hired by the Westphalian CDU came from the Christian trade unions, and they undermined the position of DGB functionaries in the Social Committees such as Albert Hillenkötter. They caused so much strife that there were no functioning Social Committees at all in five of the eleven counties of eastern Westphalia by 1963.[89]

Wiser from experience, Labor Minister Blank had meanwhile decided to bundle the unpopular reforms of health insurance that he considered necessary with two very popular ideas into a "Social Package." Early in the new legislative term he instructed the labor ministry to prepare the following three bills:

1. To achieve the "continued payment of wages" by employers for sick blue-collar workers, as demanded by the DGB and Social Committees;
2. To improve support payments for parents with two or more children; and
3. To introduce co-payments by the insured for all medical services.

This plan required an iron resolve that all three bills must be passed together. Blank secured approval of this strategy by a CDU party congress in early June 1962 and outlined it to the Bundestag on June 15. Predictably, the Social Committees and KAB embraced the first two proposals but requested more details about the third. For months, none could be provided, however, because Blank remained deadlocked in negotiations with the FDP.[90]

---

[88] "An der Wendemarke," *Soziale Ordnung*, XVI/#8 (August 1962), pp. 131–133; Kreissozialausschuss Duisburg to CDU Kreisverbandesvorstand, September 13, 1962, LANRW/CDA Rheinland/696; CDU Bundesvorstand, February 7 and June 2, 1962, *Vorstandsprotokolle 1961–65*, pp. 114, 141–142, 273–275; Thomas Gauly, *Katholiken. Machtanspruch und Machtverlust* (Bonn, 1992), pp. 153–166.

[89] "Niederschrift über die Sitzung des Vorstandes der Sozialausschüsse der CDA Westfalen/Lippe," May 26, 1962, ACDP/03–002/127/1 (typescript first draft); Albert Hillenkötter to Hans Zankl, June 1962, NL Zankl/9/1; "Besprechung mit dem geschäftsführenden Bundesvorsitzenden der CDU," December 21, 1962 (a meeting of J.H. Dufhues with Albers, Mick, Russe, and Katzer), NL Katzer/88; report by Rudi Priebe to the Westphalian Social Committees, August 15, 1963, ACDP/03–002/133/1.

[90] CDU, *11. Bundesparteitag der CDU. Dortmund, 2.-5. Juni 1962* (Hamburg, no date), pp. 48–60; CDU, *Fraktionsprotokolle 1961–66*, I: 292–296, 356–357; Theodor Blank, "Die Ziele unserer Sozialpolitik heute und morgen," and report on his Bundestag speech of June 15, *Soziale Ordnung*, XVI/#6 (June 1962), pp. 94–95, and #7 (July 1962), p. 124; "Niederschrift über die Sitzung des Landesvorstandes der Sozialausschüsse Westfalen/ Lippe," September 29, 1962 (three-page typescript draft plus two-page mimeo),

As the DGB prepared for a national congress in October 1962, many analysts anticipated an all-out struggle between "traditionalists" who demanded the nationalization of large-scale industry, led by the metal-workers' and chemical workers' unions, and "reformers" who supported the SPD Godesberg Program, led by Ludwig Rosenberg at DGB head-quarters and Georg Leber of the construction workers' union. The Social Committees felt ambivalent about this struggle, because the reformers closest to them in program enjoyed close ties to SPD headquarters. Karl-Heinz Hoffmann sensed a great opportunity nevertheless, because the two factions were so evenly matched that each needed the support of Christian Democratic trade unionists.[91] The leadership struggle failed to materialize, however, because Otto Brenner had actually committed IG Metall to support the Godesberg Program. The metalworkers simply pursued incremental gains within the existing economic order, and the moderate Rosenberg won election as DGB chair without opposition, while Bernhard Tacke and Maria Weber won more votes for the executive committee than they had in 1959.[92] Only the issue of government "emer-gency powers" provoked controversy. An SPD party congress had recently endorsed in principle the popular idea that the Basic Law should be amended to authorize the cabinet to issue decrees and deploy troops in a state of emergency. Emergency powers raised the specter of strike-breaking, however, and Brenner persuaded a two-thirds majority at the DGB congress to resolve that "we reject any additional regulation of a state of emergency or emergency services, because both plans tend to restrict fundamental rights ... and to weaken democratic forces in the Federal Republic." This was the one issue where all "traditionalists" in the labor unions rejected the new flexibility of the SPD.[93]

ACDP/03–002/127/1; Gundelach, "Sozialausschüsse," pp. 241–244; Reucher, *Reformen*, pp. 189–207.

[91] Deutsches Industrieinstitut, "Berichte zu Gewerkschaftsfragen," Nr. 1/1962 (May 1962), ACDP/04–013/134/2; Hans Zankl, "Aktennotiz. Betr.: Personalveränderungen beim Deutschen Gewerkschaftsbund," May 16, 1962, ACDP/07–004/522/1; unsigned memo-randum by Hoffmann from late 1962, "Politische Auswirkungen auf das Verhältnis DGB-CDU," ACDP/04–013/141/1.

[92] Fritz Biggeleben, "Rückblick auf Essen. Ein Nachwort zum 7. Gewerkschaftstag der IG Metall," *Allgemeine Sonntags-Zeitung* (Würzburg), Nr. 39, 1962 (NL Zankl/8/3); Lutz Esser, "Der Realismus der IG Metall," *Soziale Ordnung*, XVI/#10 (October 1962), p. 183; DGB, *Protokoll: 6. ordentlicher Bundeskongress. Hannover, 22. bis 27. Oktober 1962* (Cologne, no date), pp. 15–21, 450–451, 456–461; Andrei Markovits, *The Politics of the West German Trade Unions: Strategies of Class and Interest Representation in Growth and Crisis* (Cambridge, 1986), pp. 183–197; Angster, *Konsenskapitalismus und Sozialdemokratie*, pp. 415–461.

[93] DGB, *6. Bundeskongress 1962*, pp. 204–256, 960–964 (quotation on 960); Michael Schneider, *Demokratie in Gefahr? Der Konflikt um die Notstandsgesetze: Sozialdemokratie, Gewerkschaften und intellektueller Protest (1958–1968)* (Bonn, 1986), pp. 27–92.

Soon after this DGB congress, the CDU made its first serious attempt to form a national coalition with the SPD in response to the *Spiegel* Affair, an uproar over the arrest for treason of prominent journalists who had revealed deficiencies in West German military preparedness. The FDP ministers resigned from Adenauer's cabinet on November 19, 1962, when they learned that Defense Minister Franz Josef Strauss of the Bavarian CSU had lied to the Bundestag when he denied involvement in these arrests. The FDP merely sought the resignation of Strauss, but several CDU leaders seized this opportunity to pursue a Great Coalition instead. Paul Lücke had established close contact with Georg Leber by March 1962 and believed that he truly supported the core values of Catholic social theory. Lücke had long argued that proportional representation should be replaced with the British form of majority suffrage to promote the emergence of a two-party system; this proposal would require a two-thirds Bundestag majority to amend the constitution, which could only be achieved through a Great Coalition. The parliamentary leaders Heinrich Krone and Heinrich von Brentano also favored a Great Coalition, because the FDP had become impossible to work with, while the Social Committees yearned for it to overcome the stagnation of social policy. They found an unexpected ally in the aristocratic CSU maverick, Baron Karl von Guttenberg, who had become alarmed by the erratic foreign policy line of the FDP. That summer von Guttenberg had discreetly approached the most influential SPD leader, Herbert Wehner, and established that Wehner despised the FDP, supported majority suffrage, and endorsed continuity in foreign policy. The baron formed an alliance with Lücke when they heard of the resignation of the FDP ministers.[94]

Lücke advised Adenauer on November 26 to form a Great Coalition on the conditions that he remain chancellor, and that the SPD support "majority suffrage, emergency powers legislation, and finance reform." Adenauer asked him to conduct exploratory talks, and Lücke met with Wehner that evening; he found the discussion "very positive in both human and political terms." Wehner assured Lücke that he knew all about the horrors of Communism from personal experience and would do anything necessary to preserve democracy.[95] The next day Brentano

[94] Paul Lücke, *Ist Bonn doch Weimar? Der Kampf um das Mehrheitswahlrecht* (Frankfurt a.M., 1968), esp. pp. 34–36; Lücke to Paul Adenauer, March 30 and April 12, 1962, and Lücke to Franz Meyers, July 11, 1962, NL Lücke/22/1; Krone, *Tagebücher*, June 13, 1962, II: 69–70; Schwarz, *Adenauer*, II: 769–793; Ulrich Wirz, *Karl Theodor von und zu Guttenberg und das Zustandekommen der Grossen Koalition* (Grub am Forst, 1997), pp. 146–152, 176–180, 196–198.

[95] Entry for November 26, 1962, in Lücke's diary fragment from November/December (source of first quotation), and "Telegr. an Min. Schröder in Asien," sent

persuaded the CDU Bundestag delegation to give Adenauer a free hand to negotiate with both the SPD and FDP. Most delegates expected a mere gesture toward the SPD as a bargaining tactic, but Lücke and von Guttenberg plunged into serious talks with Wehner to develop an ambitious program for constitutional amendments to stabilize democracy. The most influential DGB leaders, including Otto Brenner, also supported this initiative.[96]

At a tense meeting of the CDU Central Committee on December 3, Lücke and von Guttenberg read aloud a detailed government platform endorsed by Wehner, the SPD chairman Ollenhauer, and Adenauer. Theodor Blank opposed any Great Coalition, however, and argued that majority suffrage would only benefit the SPD. Blank reminded CDU leaders that Wehner had always been one of their most aggressive foes, concluding that "I must emphatically reject any attempt to spread the legend this morning that Mr. Wehner has transformed himself." Albers and Katzer championed a Great Coalition nevertheless, and Adenauer secured approval for serious negotiations with the SPD.[97] Ludwig Erhard entered the fray when the CDU Bundestag delegation met that evening. He noted that the CDU had succeeded for thirteen years by denouncing the SPD as utterly unreliable. "If one now says that the SPD has become trustworthy, then one cannot say to the voters that they should trust the SPD less than the CDU. Then there will be nothing to distinguish us from them." Adenauer replied that if the CDU enacted more and better laws in 1963–1965 with the SPD than it had in 1961–1963 with the FDP, it would gain credit in the eyes of the voters. His position mirrored that of the Social Committees and was forward-looking. Krone noted sadly in his diary, however, that for Blank and Erhard, "there is only the old Social Democracy. Many in the delegation cannot find their way."[98]

---

on November 26, NL Lücke/106/5; Lücke's report to the CDU Bundesvorstand on December 3, 1962, *Vorstandsprotokolle 1961–65*, pp. 366–368 (source of second quotation). Lücke sought to protect Adenauer by telling CDU leaders that he had opened talks with Wehner on his own initiative, but his diary entry and telegram from November 26 reveal that he had prior authorization.

[96] CDU Bundestag delegation, November 27, 1962, *Fraktionsprotokolle 1961–65*, I: 424–427; Lücke's diary entries of November 27–29, 1962, and drafts for a government program negotiated with Wehner in NL Lücke/106/5; Krone, *Tagebücher*, November 28, 1962, II: 123; Karl-Heinz Hoffmann, "Stellungnahme verschiedener Gewerkschaften und Funktionäre zur Regierungsbildung und zur grossen Koalition," December 5, 1962, ACDP/04–013/141/1.

[97] See Lücke's typescript speech with handwritten corrections, "Zur Lage," December 3, 1962, NL Lücke/106/5; CDU Bundesvorstand, December 3, 1962, *Vorstandsprotokolle 1961–65*, pp. 358–401 (quotation on 377); and Schwarz, *Adenauer*, II: 796–803.

[98] CDU Fraktionsvorstand and Bundestag delegation, December 3, 1962, *Fraktionsprotokolle 1961–66*, I: 446–465 (Erhard quotation on 457–458); Krone, *Tagebücher*, II: 125.

These coalition talks soon broke down, because CDU leaders could only rally support in their party with the promise of suffrage reform, while SPD experts calculated that 30 percent of their delegates would fail to win reelection under majority suffrage. On December 6 Erich Ollenhauer informed the chancellor that the SPD could not consider suffrage reform until after the next Bundestag election, and Adenauer concluded that he must promise to resign soon, to revive the coalition with the FDP. Krone reflected that the film of the Erhard chancellorship must be screened, but he hoped that it would be short, and that the hour of the Great Coalition would arrive soon. The CDU Bundestag delegation formally elected Erhard as the next chancellor in April 1963 with the understanding that he would take office at the end of the summer.[99]

Many Christian Democrats were bewildered by these developments, but the delegates of the Social Committees displayed great optimism and self-confidence when they assembled for their Tenth National Congress in Oberhausen in July 1963. They mourned the loss of their founder, Johannes Albers, who had died in March and was remembered as "the advocate of the little man." Katzer was the consensus choice to succeed him as chairman, opposed only by the delegates from Baden-Württemberg, where the Christian trade unions enjoyed great influence. The theme of the congress was that the CDU must now display the same energy and skill in shaping the social order as it had displayed in the 1950s in shaping the international order. Katzer organized discussion groups on every aspect of domestic policy, led by knowledgeable guests.[100] Newspaper reporters were struck in particular by the high niveau of the discussion on tax policy, which yielded seventy-seven proposals to make the tax code more progressive without raising the overall burden. Some pro-business journals denounced the Social Committees as Marxist, but CDU parliamentary leaders agreed that their tax plan deserved careful consideration, and Adenauer praised Katzer again for achieving unity on the workers' wing of the party.[101] Unfortunately for Katzer, the favorable publicity for this congress made business lobbyists perceive the Social

---

[99] Krone, *Tagebücher*, December 4–29, 1962, II: 125–128, 131, 137; Globke to Lücke, December 5, 1962, notes for Adenauer by Lücke of December 5 and 7, and Adenauer to Ollenhauer, December 5, 1962, NL Lücke/106/5; Klotzbach, *Staatspartei*, pp. 520–529; Wirz, *Guttenberg*, pp. 231–236; Schwarz, *Adenauer*, II: 826–839.

[100] "10. Bundestagung der Sozialausschüsse. Oberhausen, 6–7. Juli 1963," *Soziale Ordnung*, XVII/#8–9 (August–September 1963), pp. 143–194 (Albers eulogy on 144).

[101] CDU Bundesvorstand, July 9, 1963, *Vorstandsprotokolle 1961–65*, pp. 485–486, 515–518; CDU Fraktionsvorstand, July 9, 1963, *Fraktionsprotokolle 1961–66*, I: 718–719; "Linksdruck in der CDU," *Die Zeit*, July 12, 1963, www.zeit.de/1963/28/linksdruck-in-der-cdu; "Wichtiges Glied der CDU. Sozialausschüsse der Christlich-Demokratischen Arbeitnehmerschaft tagten in Oberhausen," *Union in Deutschland Informationsdienst*, XVII/#28 (July 11, 1963), pp. 1–2.

Committees as a serious threat, perhaps for the first time since 1948, and conflict between the representatives of capital and labor in the CDU intensified thereafter.

Ludwig Erhard finally achieved his dream when he became chancellor in October 1963, but he soon committed serious political blunders. Erhard proposed to divide the offices of chancellor and CDU chair to promote collegiality, but he failed to advance any candidate for the latter post, leaving it to the hostile Adenauer. Erhard also failed to remove the Adenauer loyalist Blank from the cabinet. He offered the labor ministry to Katzer and then to Housing Minister Lücke, but both men declined, so Erhard retained Lücke and Blank in their old posts. Katzer later recalled that he saw no opportunity to accomplish anything in the cabinet with only two years remaining in the legislative term. Erhard also vowed to prevent the FDP from strengthening its cabinet position, but he eventually dismissed Ernst Lemmer and surrendered the Ministry of All-German Affairs to it. The Social Committees and KAB praised Erhard in public, but their leaders concluded privately that anti-worker tendencies would grow stronger in the new cabinet.[102]

Erhard's top priority in domestic policy was to enact Theodor Blank's Social Package. The Free Democrats disagreed with many of the labor minister's proposals, however, and they pushed the coalition to the brink of crisis in January 1964 by joining with the SPD to obstruct consideration of the Social Package in the Bundestag committees. Katzer told CDU leaders that the FDP had obviously resolved to block any concessions to workers, because it wanted to pose in the next election campaign as the only champion of business interests; he called for a new strategy that did not depend on its support. Blank sought agreement with the FDP, however, by proposing a new plan to drop co-payments for medical treatment in favor of a business-friendly calculation of health insurance premiums, to be paid 60 percent by workers in future instead of 50 percent, so that workers would have an incentive to contain costs. Blank had discussed this plan with the chair of the Bundestag labor committee, Heinrich Scheppmann, but he had not consulted the Social Committees. Katzer and Winkelheide protested that they had made some progress toward explaining the need for co-payments to constituents, but had no idea how to defend a drastic increase in workers' premiums. The Social

---

[102] Krone, *Tagebücher*, August 10 and September 30-October 16, 1963, II: 207, 226–234; Tilman Mayer, "Gerechtigkeit schafft Frieden," p. 18; Alfons Müller, "Niederschrift über die Sitzung des Ständigen Ausschusses Christlich-Sozialer Arbeitnehmerkongresse," October 19, 1963, NL Winkelheide/2/2; Lutz Esser, "Zweite Halbzeit – Hoffnung auf Erhard," *Soziale Ordnung*, XVII/#10 (October 1963), p. 195; Gundelach, "Sozialausschüsse," pp. 265–267; Hentschel, *Ludwig Erhard*, pp. 597–598.

Committees were spared that burden, because the FDP itself rejected Blank's plan after it was condemned by most business leaders alongside organized labor. Despite the almost universal condemnation of his proposal, Blank denounced Katzer to CDU leaders for sabotaging it because of personal ambition.[103]

Tensions were mounting in the CDU because of the foundation in December 1963 of a new Business Council (*Wirtschaftsrat*) of the CDU, which bore the party name but was autonomous according to its statutes and welcomed all businesspersons as members regardless of their party affiliation. The Business Council won endorsement of those statutes by top CDU leaders after promising to submit all nominations for leadership posts to them for approval. The Social Committees protested that the Business Council claimed the right to speak for the CDU about economic policy without submitting to party discipline, and Katzer believed that it had been founded to neutralize the growing influence of the Social Committees.[104] In February 1964 the chair of the Business Council and CDU state chair for North Württemberg, Klaus Scheufelen, explained to CDU leaders that its statutes proclaimed autonomy merely for tax purposes (i.e. to evade the law that contributions to political parties were not tax deductible), but that the CDU retained control. Adenauer's deputy as managing chairman of the CDU, J.H. Dufhues, supported Scheufelen with the argument that this club would extend CDU influence among businessmen. Katzer retorted that "in practice the effect is the opposite, namely the influence of business in the Union!" The Business Council soon became a fund-raising machine potent enough, however, that most CDU leaders refused to offend it.[105]

The Social Committees believed that the channels of communication in their party had broken down, because their chief representative in the cabinet ignored them, while their parliamentary representative Scheppmann had become overtly hostile. Scheppmann even insinuated to party colleagues that Jakob Kaiser, Karl Arnold, and Johannes Albers

---

[103] CDU Bundesvorstand, November 12, 1963, and February 25, 1964, *Vorstandsprotokolle 1961–65*, pp. 531–533, 648–662; CDU Bundestag delegation, February 3–4, 1964, *Fraktionsprotokolle 1961–66*, II: 972–996; Hans Katzer, "Sozialprogramm statt Sozialpaket," *Soziale Ordnung*, XVIII/ #3 (March 1964), pp. 45, 52–53, 56–57; Reucher, *Reformen*, pp. 222–231.

[104] See Economics Minister Kurt Schmücker to J.-H. Dufhues, December 5, 1963, and the letters of complaint by the Social Committees in NL Katzer/60, and Gundelach, "Sozialausschüsse," p. 283.

[105] CDU Bundesvorstand, February 25, 1964, *Vorstandsprotokolle 1961–65*, pp. 672–676 (quotation on 675); Hans-Otto Kleinmann, *Geschichte der CDU 1945–1982* (Stuttgart, 1993), pp. 146–148, 478–480; Frank Bösch, *Die Adenauer-CDU. Gründung, Aufstieg und Krise einer Erfolgspartei 1945–1969* (Stuttgart, 2001), pp. 386–387.

had only defended the DGB because it enriched them with consulting contracts.[106] The leaders of the Social Committees resolved unanimously on March 7, 1964, that "a reform of health insurance dues according to the ideas of Scheppmann and Blank cannot be accepted under any circumstances," and that Katzer should replace Blank as CDU vice chair at their upcoming party congress. Most CDU leaders agreed, however, that their party must still enact Blank's Social Package and could not reject him for party office without disavowing its own program. On the last day of the CDU congress, Blank therefore defeated Katzer by a vote of 266 to 124, with 55 abstentions, in the only contested election. Russe later told colleagues in the Westphalian Social Committees that Adenauer had been persuaded at the last minute to advise Blank to withdraw from consideration, but that Blank refused.[107] Representatives of the Business Council introduced a sharp tone to the congress debates and secured large majorities against all motions by the Social Committees. Katzer's supporters agreed that he had accomplished something valuable nevertheless by winning enough votes to demonstrate that Blank did not represent the workers' wing of the party. Russe calculated that blue- and white-collar workers comprised 40 percent of CDU members but only 18 percent of congress delegates, and that almost all of them had voted for Katzer.[108]

CDU leaders began to pay more attention to workers' demands after their party sank from 45 percent to 43 percent of the vote in the September municipal elections in North Rhine-Westphalia, while the SPD rose from 40.7 to 46.6 percent. In Cologne the two parties were almost tied in 1961, but the SPD now won by twenty points. Katzer concluded from this landslide in his hometown that "if the CDU continues to nurture the impression that it has abandoned the course of a people's party and become

---

[106] See Katzer to Scheppmann, April 28, 1964, Scheppmann to Dufhues, May 8, Otto Laipold to Scheppmann, May 12, and Scheppmann to Elfriede Kaiser-Nebgen, June 24, 1964, NL Katzer/60.

[107] Russe's "Vermerk zur Hauptvorstandssitzung am 7. März 1964," "Beschlussprotokoll, Hauptvorstandssitzung 7.3.64" (two-page typescript, source of quotation), and "Beschlussprotokoll, Hauptvorstandssitzung 7.3.64" (five-page handwritten first draft), ACDP/04–013/8/2; CDU Bundesvorstand, March 14, 1964, *Vorstandsprotokolle 1961–65*, pp. 684–700; CDU, *12. Bundesparteitag der CDU. 14.-17. März 1964, Hannover* (Hamburg, no date), pp. 495–500; "Entwurf: Protokoll über die am 4. April 1964 ... stattgefundene Vorstandssitzung des Landessozialausschusses Westfalen," ACDP/03–002/127/2, pp. 1–2.

[108] CDU, *12. Bundesparteitag 1964*, pp. 272–292, 325–328; Franz Deus, "Bericht über die Hauptvorstandssitzung der Sozialausschüsse" on May 9, 1964, NL Deus/2/3. See also the report on the undemocratic procedures for choosing congress delegates in "Analyse der Delegation zum 12. Bundesparteitag der CDU," November 2, 1964, NL Katzer/396.

a business party, there can be no helping it."[109] Winkelheide and Katzer discussed social policy at length with Chancellor Erhard on September 24 and persuaded him that they should involve the trade unions in efforts to promote share ownership by workers through amendment of the 312 Marks Law. They assured Erhard that Georg Leber was eager to incorporate its provisions into collective labor agreements for construction workers, and that his example would become so popular that it would be followed by other unions. Erhard promised business leaders, however, to reject any other proposal that imposed new costs on them. The amended 312 Marks Law (passed with SPD support in May 1965 against the FDP) therefore remained the only legislative victory for the Social Committees under Erhard.[110]

The Social Committees enjoyed more success in 1965 at influencing Bundestag nominations than they did at shaping the legislative agenda. Katzer sought to strengthen the hard core of the Workers' Group that supported cooperation with the DGB, and in January 1965 he secured the nomination in Westphalia of his aide Russe to replace the retiring Scheppmann.[111] Joseph Mick secured renomination on the Rhineland state list for Katzer, himself, and their DGB ally Adolf Müller, and a new seat for their KAB ally Heinz Budde. Three supporters of Katzer's line joined the Bundestag delegation from Hesse, Josef Riedel, August Weimer, and Otto Zink, and another from Hamburg, Gerhard Orgass, a functionary of the construction workers' union. After the election the Workers' Group included fifty-four members, and it was younger on average than the previous group and more sympathetic to the DGB.[112]

---

[109] "Niederschrift über die Klausurtagung der Arbeitnehmergruppe der CDU/CSU-Fraktion," September 29/30, 1964, NL Lücke/160 (quotation on p. 2); "Landesvorstand der Sozialausschüsse" of Westphalia, October 24, 1964, ACDP/03–002/127/2; "Letzter Denkzettel," *Soziale Ordnung*, XVIII/#10 (October 1964), pp. 209–211; Winfried Herbers, *Der Verlust der Hegemonie. Die Kölner CDU 1945/46–1964* (Düsseldorf, 2003), pp. 332–342.

[110] Report by Winkelheide and Katzer, "Niederschrift über die Klausurtagung der Arbeitnehmergruppe der CDU/CSU-Fraktion," September 29/30, 1964, pp. 2–5, NL Lücke/160; "Stellungnahme des DGB zur Vermögensbildung," *Gewerkschaftsquellen*, XIII: 125–127; "Eigentum steht im Brennpunkt," *Soziale Ordnung*, XVIII/#10 (October 1964), pp. 218–221; Hans Katzer, "Soziales Sofortprogramm," *Soziale Ordnung*, XVIII/#12 (December 1964), pp. 249–250; "Bilanz des 4. Bundestages," *Soziale Ordnung*, XIX/#8 (August 1965), pp. 119–121; Gundelach, "Sozialausschüsse," pp. 276–277.

[111] "Niederschrift über die Sitzung des Landesvorstandes der Sozialausschüsse der CDU Westfalen-Lippe," January 16, 1965, and Rudolf Nickels to J.H. Dufhues, January 19, 1965, ACDP/03–002/127/2.

[112] Documentation in NL Mick/2/1, including the "Niederschrift über die erste Sitzung der 'Siebener-Kommission,'" February 19, 1965, and that commission's evolving list of Rhineland nominees developed at subsequent meetings; "Die Arbeitnehmergruppe der

Despite frequent appeals for fiscal discipline, Erhard could not prevent the government parties from enacting generous new programs during the election campaign to benefit farmers, war veterans, and other groups, which caused a rapidly mounting budget deficit. On the campaign trail, the chancellor nevertheless blamed Germany's mild inflation entirely on "excessive" wage demands by the trade unions. After an especially sharp attack in Bremen, delivered while IG Metall held a congress there, Fritz Biggeleben published an open letter to Erhard on behalf of Christian Democrats in that union to "reject emphatically the unfounded attacks on the trade unions that you made in Bremen." Most Christian Democratic DGB functionaries agreed that Biggeleben had gone too far, but Bernhard Tacke noted sadly that "Chancellor Erhard has shown in this campaign that he has no understanding for the unions."[113] When Erhard held a speech in Krefeld soon thereafter, the DGB county committee welcomed him with a leaflet alleging that he had insulted German workers as "layabouts, incompetents, and malingerers." Adolf Müller rushed to Krefeld to defend the chancellor, but Erhard later told Katzer that party colleagues such as Biggeleben and and Tacke played a destructive role as "token Christian Democrats" (*Konzessionsschulzen*), who lacked the will and capacity to restrain the militant socialists who controlled the DGB.[114]

Erhard rejoiced when the CDU and CSU won 47.6 percent of the national vote on September 19, 1965, their second best result to date. Although the SPD also increased its share from 36.2 to 39.3 percent, most polls had predicted that the CDU would only defeat it by two or three points, so this was an impressive victory. The SPD scored significant gains among Catholics, however, and an unprecedented number of

CDU/CSU Bundestagsfraktion," *Soziale Ordnung*, "Sonderbeilage Nr. 2" of October 1965.

[113] Hentschel, *Ludwig Erhard*, pp. 786–799; letter to Erhard of September 11, 1965, by "Die Delegierten und Gastdelegierten des 8. Ordentlichen Gewerkschaftstages der IG Metall, die der CDU angehören," NL Zankl/1/3 (source of Biggeleben quotation); "Niederschrift über die Sitzung des gewerkschaftlichen Arbeitskreises," October 23, 1965 (Tacke quotation on p. 2), and Biggeleben to Tacke, November 12, 1965, ACDP/ 04–013/138; "Stellungnahme der Arbeitsgemeinschaft Christlich-Demokratischer DGB-Gewerkschafter zu den Vorgängen auf dem IG-Metall Kongress," October 23, 1965, and Tacke to Katzer, December 8, 1965, ACDP/04–013/27/2.

[114] Christel Krienen to Karl-Heinz Hoffmann, October 5, 1965, with enclosed leaflet published on September 12 by the DGB Kreisausschuss Krefeld, "Die Erhard Saga" (source of first quotation), ACDP/04–013/169/1; speech by Adolf Müller to a rally of the Social Committees in Krefeld, September 16, 1965, LANRW/CDA Rheinland/647; Hans Katzer, "Vermerk über das zweite Gespräch der Verhandlungskommission der CDU/CSU bei Bundeskanzler Erhard" on October 5, 1965, NL Katzer/378 (Erhard's critique of the trade unions on pp. 7–9).

voters had switched parties. The clearly defined social milieus that molded voting behavior in the 1950s were eroding.[115]

The Social Committees secured the inclusion of Katzer in the commission to negotiate the next coalition. They reluctantly endorsed a revived government with the FDP, but in accord with the priorities of the DGB, they demanded that the new cabinet study how parity co-determination could be expanded from coal-iron-steel to other branches of industry. Erhard firmly rejected that demand, so Katzer was surprised when the chancellor invited him again in early October to become labor minister. With the prospect of a full legislative term to accomplish something, Katzer agreed.[116] Katzer was dismayed, however, when Erhard delivered a stern speech to his Bundestag delegation on October 20 about the need for fiscal austerity. Regarding social policy, the chancellor declared that "we have undoubtedly done too much of a good thing, or done it too rapidly." Erhard demanded a freeze on all social policy initiatives and expressed concern that the "dynamic" pensions introduced in 1957 had created inflationary pressure.[117] When Katzer reported that the CDU Workers' Group found this speech deeply disturbing, Erhard made some concessions to secure his service as labor minister and free himself of the Adenauer loyalist Blank. Erhard elevated Paul Lücke to the influential post of interior minister and promised to defend dynamic pensions. He revealed to Katzer that Blank had "caused him many problems when told that he was no longer wanted in the cabinet. The behavior of Blank had confirmed that his dismissal was urgently necessary."[118] Blank was in fact stunned by his dismissal, because he believed that Erhard stood

---

[115] Erwin Scheuch, "Wachsender Wohlstand hilft der SPD," *Der Spiegel*, XIX/#42 (October 13, 1965), pp. 47–49; Konrad Kraske's analysis in CDU Bundesvorstand, September 20, 1965, in Günter Buchstab, ed., *Kiesinger: "Wir leben in einer veränderten Welt:" Die Protokolle des CDU-Bundesvorstands 1965–1969* (Düsseldorf, 2005; hereafter *Vorstandsprotokolle 1965–69*), pp. 3–6; Werner Kaltefleiter, "Kanzler-Wähler und Partei-Wähler," *Soziale Ordnung*, XIX/#10 (October 1965), pp. 143–146.

[116] CDA Bundesvorstand, "Zusammengefasste Niederschrift über die Sitzung" of September 20, 1965, ACDP/04–013/27/1; CDA Bundesvorstand meeting of September 25, and "Vorstellungen der Christlich-Demokratischen Arbeitnehmerschaft zum Regierungsprogramm der 5. Legislaturperiode des Deutschen Bundestages," ACDP/ 04–013/27/2; Hans Katzer, "Vertraulicher Vermerk. Regierungsbildung 1965: Erstes Gespräch der Verhandlungskommission," September 24, 1965, and "Vermerk über das zweite Gespräch" on October 5, NL Katzer/378; "Katzer-Jammer rechts," *Der Spiegel*, XIX/#41 (October 6, 1965), p. 46.

[117] CDU Bundestag delegation, October 20, 1965, *Fraktikonsprotokolle 1961–66*, III: 1589–1590.

[118] Hans Katzer, "Gespräch bei Bundeskanzler Erhard," October 25, 1965, three-page typescript, NL Katzer/379 (source of quotation); Krone, *Tagebücher*, II: 421–423; Klaus Hildebrand, *Von Erhard zur Grossen Koalition, 1963–1969* (Stuttgart, 1984), pp. 152–160.

heavily in his debt, but he was partially consoled by election as vice chair of the CDU Bundestag delegation. Blank told the Westphalian Social Committees that Erhard had become the tool of business leaders who demanded Blank's head because of the strengthening of the 312 Marks Law.[119]

The new labor minister confronted a grim situation when Erhard submitted to the cabinet a plan to balance the budget in late November that called for budget cuts of three billion marks, almost half of them from social programs enacted just before the election. Erhard responded logically to new evidence that the budget deficit was causing inflation, but this bill created the impression that the CDU had deceived the voters; as Adenauer pointed out, no governing party had ever moved so abruptly after an election to dismantle programs it enacted just before. The Workers' Group in the CDU Bundestag delegation helped Katzer to make this plan more palatable with small tax increases on the well-to-do, and to delay rather than cancel most of the promised increases in social benefits.[120]

Erhard appeared to reach the pinnacle of power when elected CDU chair as well as chancellor in March 1966. His decline began almost immediately, however, because an inflation rate near 4 percent impelled the *Bundesbank* to raise interest rates, slowing economic activity. Most economists now agreed that profligate spending by federal, state, and local government was the primary cause of inflation, so Erhard proposed a "reform of the financial constitution." The chancellor and economics ministry drafted three complex Stabilization Laws that summer to restrict the fiscal autonomy of state and local government and make possible an effective countercyclical policy involving all public-sector investments. The Social Committees supported this plan enthusiastically as an expression of the most "modern" economic thought (meaning Keynesian) that would benefit workers by assuring full employment. Erhard described the goal of his Stabilization Laws to CDU leaders as the preservation of "the magic triangle" of full employment, economic growth, and a stable currency, but he insisted that the last goal was most important. His thinking was molded by years of worry that a rapidly growing economy

---

[119] CDU Bundestag delegation, October 26, 1965, *Fraktionsprotokolle 1961–66*, III: 1599; "Regierungsbildung: Vors Brett," and "Ex-Minister," *Der Spiegel*, XIX/#45 (November 3, 1965), pp. 30–34; "Niederschrift über die Vorstandssitzung der Sozialausschüsse der CDA Westfalen-Lippe," October 30, 1965, and "Notiz für Herrn Laipold" by Joseph Grosskortenhaus, November 2, 1965, ACDP/03–002/127/2.

[120] CDU Bundestag delegation, October 20, November 9, and November 23, 1965, *Fraktionsprotokolle 1961–66*, III: 1594–1596, 1605–1611, 1632–1633.

might overheat; for Erhard, "countercyclical" implied reductions in government spending.[121] The Stabilization Laws would require a two-thirds Bundestag majority to amend the Basic Law, but Erhard offered the SPD no political incentive to support them. The chancellor dismissed suggestions by Lücke and Heinrich Krone that this reform could only be achieved by a Great Coalition. Erhard also ignored requests by DGB leaders for a meeting to discuss his plans, because he regarded organized labor as his enemy.[122] The DGB supported the Stabilization Laws in principle, but its economics expert Wilhelm Haferkamp warned labor leaders in September that the cabinet "lacks any coherent economic policy." The chancellor had launched this project only because he feared inflation, and he stubbornly ignored new data suggesting that Germany was on the brink of recession.[123] A similar critique was sent confidentially to CDU leaders by Erhard's former collaborator, the distinguished economist Alfred Müller-Armack, after Erhard dismissed his concerns in a personal meeting. Müller-Armack criticized Erhard's stubborn optimism and argued that, while the consumer goods sector still flourished for now, a dangerous recession had already begun in the capital goods sector. Erhard only sought to reduce government spending, Müller-Armack concluded, when Germany urgently needed more public-sector investment and lower interest rates. Erhard's reputation for economic expertise had been severely undermined.[124]

Erhard's economic policy cost his party dearly in the state election in North Rhine-Westphalia in July 1966. The coal mine operators had announced a new round of pit closings in February, but Erhard rejected

[121] Speeches by Erhard to the CDU Bundesvorstand, May 6, 1966, *Vorstandsprotokolle 1965–69*, p. 176, the Bundestag delegation on June 14, *Fraktionsprotokolle 1961–66*, III: 1829–1830, and the CDU Präsidium on June 16, NL Lücke/140/2; "Stellungnahme des wirtschaftspolitischen Arbeitskreises der Sozialausschüsse der CDA zum Entwurf eines Gesetzes zur Förderung der wirtschaftlichen Stabilität," July 20, 1966, NL Lücke/150/1; Pridham, *Christian Democracy*, pp. 159–161; Schwarz, *Adenauer*, II: 902–22; Hentschel, *Ludwig Erhard*, pp. 819–832, 850–855, 862–865.
[122] Krone, *Tagebücher*, II: 503, August 5, 1966; exchange between Erhard and Lücke in the CDU Präsidium, August 27, 1966, NL Lücke/140/2. On April 22 Erhard had persuaded the Präsidium to ignore questions from the DGB about its policies, and on April 26, to ignore a request by DGB leaders for a meeting (minutes in NL Lücke/140/2).
[123] See Haferkamp's reports to the DGB Bundesvorstand on September 6 and November 15, 1966, *Gewerkschaftsquellen*, XIII: 319, 328–329 (source of quotation), 344–346, and Hans Zankl's memorandum for CDU leaders, "Stellungnahme des DGB zum Stabilisierungsgesetz," October 18, 1966, ACDP/07–004/518/2.
[124] Alfred Müller-Armack, "Die konjunkturelle Lage, das Stabilisierungsgesetz und die nächsten wirtschaftspolitischen Aufgaben," twenty-eight-page memorandum of September 7, 1966, sent to Lücke with a cover letter of September 14, NL Lücke/24; Hentschel, *Ludwig Erhard*, pp. 865–869.

any measures to sustain demand for coal.[125] The chancellor also appeared indifferent when the steel industry demanded government subsidies to offset German tax and trade policies that placed it at a disadvantage versus French and Italian competitors. The state labor minister Konrad Grundmann of the Social Committees championed that request, but Erhard rejected it in May, and the Krupp Works announced lay-offs soon thereafter. When the miners' union threatened a strike in June to secure a wage increase of 8.5 percent, Grundmann appealed to the chancellor to mediate, but Erhard refused again. The chancellor assured party colleagues that the SPD could not exploit this issue, because "we have done too much for coal . . . I have said again and again, where in the world has there ever been an economic branch confronted with the necessity of restructuring that has received such massive assistance?"[126] Erhard was stunned when the CDU share declined in the state election on July 10 from 46.4 to 42.8 percent, while the SPD surged from 43.3 to 49.5 percent. The SPD won 60 percent of the vote in the Ruhr industrial district. Der Spiegel pronounced this result "the beginning of the political end for Chancellor Erhard," and for once it did not exaggerate.[127] By September 1966 all leaders of the CDU and CSU agreed that they faced electoral catastrophe if Erhard remained chancellor, and a majority, as we shall see in the next chapter, soon agreed with the Social Committees that they must seek a Great Coalition with the SPD.[128]

5.4   Vatican II and the Origins of the Great Coalition

The erosion of support for Ludwig Erhard was accelerated by a complex reform process within the Catholic Church that baffled many German politicians. A fresh wind had begun to blow in 1959, when Pope John XXIII invited all bishops to a great ecumenical council; he announced no agenda but simply invited them to write him with their concerns. During the three years of preparations for this Second Vatican Council, CDU

---

[125] CDU Bundestag delegation, March 1, 1966, *Fraktionsprotokolle 1961–66*, III: 1719–1720; CDU Bundesvorstand, May 6, 1966, *Vorstandsprotokolle 1965–69*, pp. 178–183; Nonn, *Die Ruhrbergbaukrise*, pp. 270–284.

[126] "Stahl, Stahl: Überlegungen zur Lage eines Wirtschaftszweiges," *Soziale Ordnung*, XX/#6 (June 1966), p. 12; CDU Präsidium, May 19, 1966, p. 2, NL Lücke/140/2; Grundmann to Erhard, June 8, 1966, NL Blank/15; CDU Bundestag delegation, June 14, 1966, *Fraktionsprotokolle 1961–66*, III: 1828 (source of quotation); "Ruhr Bergbau: Klar zum Gefecht," *Der Spiegel*, XX/#26 (June 20, 1966), pp. 22–33.

[127] CDU Bundesvorstand, July 11, 1966, *Vorstandsprotokolle 1965–69*, pp. 196–235; "NRW-Wahlen: Lack ab," *Der Spiegel*, XX/#30 (July 18, 1966), pp. 15–25 (quotation on 15).

[128] See Hentschel, *Ludwig Erhard*, pp. 865–877, and Wirz, *Karl von Guttenberg*, pp. 431–437.

leaders feared that it might proclaim some new dogma that would antag-
onize Protestants. They were greatly relieved therefore when Pope John
created a new Vatican department to seek better relations with other
Christian churches. Cardinal Josef Frings of Cologne soon emerged as a
champion of progressive reforms and secured an invitation for the
Evangelical Church of Germany to send an official observer. Shortly before
the first council session, Heinrich Krone attended the annual Congress of
German Catholics in August 1962 and observed that those who spoke of
the need for cooperation among all Christians earned the loudest applause;
he noted with satisfaction that "the age of struggle with each other is over in
the thinking of German Catholics."[129] Konrad Adenauer felt alarmed,
however, by the prospect that Catholics might lose all taste for struggle.
After visiting Rome in January 1960, he told Krone that Pope John was "a
good and dear man," but that "the Vatican lacks insight and toughness in
the struggle against the danger of world Communism."[130]

Conservative Catholics were disoriented by Pope John's encyclical,
Mater et Magistra, issued in May 1961.[131] It endorsed core arguments
of the Social Committees that workers should "gradually come to share in
the ownership of their company," have a larger voice in management, and
influence all economic policy decisions by government (paragraphs 77,
91–97). Pope John praised the Christian trade unions around the world,
but he also praised "those dear sons of Ours who in a true Christian spirit
collaborate with other professional groups and workers' associations
which respect natural law and the freedom of conscience of their members," a label that could well apply to the German Labor Federation
(par. 102). The encyclical also emphasized the importance of the "lay
apostolate." "Differences of opinion in the application of principles can
sometimes arise even among sincere Catholics," it noted, and Catholics
must respect those who disagreed with them. They should plunge into the
world, associate with non-Catholics, and "show themselves animated by
a spirit of understanding and unselfishness, ready to cooperate loyally in
achieving objects which are good in themselves, or can be turned to good"
(par. 238–239, 254–255).

No major issues were resolved at the first session of Vatican II in autumn
1962, but *Social Order* noted that Vatican conservatives had suffered major

---

[129] John W. O'Malley, *What Happened at Vatican II* (Cambridge, MA, 2008), pp. 15–25,
33–43; Norbert Trippen, *Josef Kardinal Frings (1887–1978)*, 2 vols. (Paderborn, 2003–
2005), II: 210–313; Krone, *Tagebücher*, I: 386, 395; and II: 14, 57–61, 86 (source of
quotation), 98; remarks by Adenauer and Gerstenmaier to CDU leaders on July 6,
1960, *Vorstandsprotokolle 1957–1961*, pp. 712–713.
[130] Krone, *Tagebücher*, January 26, 1960, I: 400–401; see also Schwarz, *Adenauer*, II: 603–606.
[131] See Grossmann, *Zentralkomitee*, pp. 163–164, and the German and English translations
of the encyclical at w2.vatican.va/content/john-xxiii/.

defeats regarding the agenda. Its reporter marveled at the "democratic spirit" displayed by the council, which had developed into "a parliament in the best sense of the word. Caucuses emerged that struggled against each other with skill and passion. Back-benchers from the provinces and overseas missions stood up and courageously registered their complaints. Influential cardinals of the curia, who ... hoped to seize control of the council, were voted down or trapped by strict procedural rules." Theology did not depend on majority resolutions, *Social Order* acknowledged, but this council dealt with issues of enormous political as well as theological importance, so Catholic workers took great comfort from the evidence that "resolutions will be adopted, of which it can be said with confidence that they are representative of the entire Catholic Church."[132]

In April 1963 Pope John published his last encyclical, *Pacem in Terris*, addressed to "all men of good will."[133] It argued that "Everyone must sincerely cooperate in the effort to banish fear and the anxious expectation of war from men's minds," because "lasting peace among nations cannot consist in the possession of an equal supply of armaments but only in mutual trust" (par. 113). Pope John exhorted Catholics to cooperate with non-Catholics and unbelievers in all projects that might benefit the world, because the "false philosophy" in which many movements for social reform had originated did not prevent them from playing a beneficial role today (par. 158–160). Adenauer complained in a closed meeting of CDU leaders that this document undermined any rationale for episcopal condemnation of the SPD, and Heinrich Krone traveled to Rome to complain that the Vatican ignored the grave threat still posed by Communism. *Social Order* praised the encyclical nevertheless. Pius XII, it argued, had become the "ally of the West," as "uncompromising as the crusading popes of the Middle Ages," but John preached "reconciliation between the confessions, between the poor and rich, between blacks and whites and even Reds, between the nations." This editorial provoked complaints, so Hans Katzer apologized to the journal's readers for its disrespectful tone and commissioned an article by the Dominican theologian Eberhard Welty to explain the similarities between the thinking of Pius XII and John XXIII.[134] John passed away soon thereafter, but the

---

[132] N.O., "Der Fall Ottaviani," *Soziale Ordnung*, XVI/#12 (December 1962), inside front cover; compare O'Malley, *Vatican II*, pp. 94–159, and Trippen, *Kardinal Frings*, II: 313–348.

[133] Go to w2.vatican.va/content/john-xxiii/.

[134] Krone, *Tagebücher*, March 9 and April 13, 1963, II: 167, 181–183; CDU Bundesvorstand, March 14 and April 26, 1963, *Vorstandsprotokolle 1961–65*, pp. 410, 446, 473–478; N.O., "Frieden auf Erden," *Soziale Ordnung*, XVII/#5 (May 1963), inside front cover; *Soziale Ordnung*, XVII/#6 (June 1963), initial editorial note by

reform process at Vatican II had taken on a life of its own and yielded bold council decrees under Paul VI.

For some years it remained unclear how or even whether these encyclicals and council decrees would transform the practices of German Catholicism. In the 1950s conformity was not simply imposed on Catholics by their bishops; the lay vocational and devotional associations represented in the Central Committee of German Catholics also displayed a powerful desire for unity and aligned themselves closely with the CDU. Catholics were never truly united, but they maintained the appearance through ostracism of those who criticized the Church hierarchy or CDU. The numerous victims of ostracism included the novelist Heinrich Böll, the blue-collar pacifist Wilhelm Elfes, and the veteran of the Christian miners' union, Heinrich Gutermuth, after he switched party affiliation in 1947 from CDU to SPD. Gutermuth remained a practicing Catholic as he rose to chair the powerful miners' union, but he confessed to DGB colleagues in 1961 that he could not obtain an appointment with any bishop.[135] The bishops and KAB leaders who supported Christian trade unions sought to ostracize all Catholic DGB functionaries, even if they remained practicing Catholics and CDU members, by denouncing them as careerists who had already succumbed to the plague of materialism that would spread if Catholic workers remained in contact with Social Democrats in unified labor unions. Father Herbert Reichel had ridiculed that hostile stereotype in the 1950s as leader of the Christian Social Collegium, but after 1960 he propagated it aggressively to support his new thesis that no Catholic could in good conscience belong to a DGB-affiliated union. The old Christian Labor Movement had been thoroughly reorganized in 1959 as the Christian Labor Federation (*Christlicher Gewerkschaftsbund*, or CGB), which claimed a fairly impressive membership of 200,000, mostly from the Saarland Christian unions and white-collar DHV. Some bishops therefore intensified their support, and in 1960 the leadership conferences of the KAB and Central Committee of German Catholics heard their most emphatic pleas ever for "unity and resolve" (*Einheit und Geschlossenheit*), code words for the ostracism of DGB Catholics.[136]

Katzer and letters to the editor on p. 116; Eberhard Welty, "Pacem in Terris," *Soziale Ordnung*, XVII/#7 (July 1963), pp. 127–130.

[135] DGB Bundesvorstand, August 1, 1961, *Gewerkschaftsquellen*, XII: 693–95; Grossmann, *Zentralkomitee*, pp. 138–161, 299–317; Trippen, *Kardinal Frings*, I: 504–537; Gauly, *Katholiken*, pp. 41–152.

[136] Deutsches Industrieinstitut, "Berichte zu Gewerkschaftsfragen: Zur Gründung des Christlichen Gewerkschaftsbundes Deutschlands," July 1, 1959, NL Zankl/8/1; DGB memorandum of December 11, 1961, "Betrifft: Christlicher Gewerkschaftsbund (CGB) und 'Christlich-soziale Kollegenschaft,'" DGB-Archiv/5/DGAI001197; remarks by

Among the first German commentators on *Mater et Magistra*, Herbert Reichel argued that Pope John wanted all Catholic workers to join Christian trade unions, but the Social Committees argued more plausibly that he supported the "lay apostolate" of Catholics in the DGB.[137] The DGB soon commissioned its Catholic employee Franz Deus, director of the DGB academy at Hattingen on the Ruhr, to hold public lectures on the encyclical, where he distributed free copies to thousands of union colleagues. Reichel derided these efforts by the DGB to mask its socialism, but Deus secured approval of his lectures from his own bishop, Hengsbach of Essen. In May 1961 Hengsbach also pioneered a new style of pastoral outreach by hosting 109 Catholic factory council members in the Ruhr coal mines from both the Christian trade unions and DGB. The meeting was acrimonious, but Hengsbach signaled clearly that DGB Catholics belonged to his flock and would be heard.[138]

The rationale for ostracizing DGB Catholics was very weak, because the Vatican had declared repeatedly that Catholic workers were free to join the DGB. Hans Katzer and Bernhard Tacke agreed therefore that it should be possible to isolate the clerical supporters of the Christian unions. When Tacke assembled his leading DGB colleagues in January 1961 to found their Association of Christian Democratic DGB Trade Unionists, most of the discussion revolved around the attitude of the Catholic bishops. The most alarming report came from Bavaria, where the CSU and senior clergy exerted great pressure on all DGB Catholics to join the CGB.[139] In June 1962 Franz Deus and Maria Weber complained to Bishop Hengsbach that the Central Committee of German Catholics had avoided any contact with DGB Catholics for the last two years, despite the bishops' stated policy that Catholics in all unions deserved equal treatment. They learned that the clerical champions of the Christian unions had exerted great pressure on the episcopate, but Hengsbach promised to

---

Hermann-Josef Schmitt in KAB, "Sitzung des Verbandsvorstandes," September 19, 1960, KAB Archiv/1/1; Schroeder, *Katholizismus und Einheitsgewerkschaft*, pp. 261–265, 330–334, 390–401; Grossmann, *Zentralkomitee*, pp. 154–160, 447–449. See also the polemical account by the CGB leader Bernhard Koch, *100 Jahre Christliche Gewerkschaften* (Würzburg, 1999), pp. 284–306.

[137] Hans Zankl, "Bericht über eine Rede des Hochw. Herrn Pater Dr. Reichel SJ," November 17, 1961, ACDP/07–004/522/1; Norbert Iserlohe, "Nach 70 Jahren: 'Mater et magistra,'" *Soziale Ordnung*, XV/#8 (August 1961), pp. 130–132; speech by Josef Mick to the "Hauptversammlung der Rheinischen Sozialausschüsse," February 10, 1962, p. 12, LANRW/CDA Rheinland/915.

[138] See the documentation on Deus's lectures in NL Deus/1/2, and "Notizen zum ersten Treffen katholischer Betriebsräte aus dem Bergbau mit dem H.H. Bischof," May 26, 1961, NL Deus/1/1.

[139] "Arbeitskreis christlich-demokratischer Mitglieder des DGB," January 5, 1961, ACDP/04–013/146/3; see also the interview with Franz Prinz in Schroeder, *Zeitzeugen in Interviews*, pp. 312–324.

resist it.[140] In December 1962 the mildly progressive secretary general of the Central Committee, Heinrich Köppler, announced that Cardinal Frings was prepared to receive Bernhard Tacke and Maria Weber. Wilhelm Wöste, the conservative priest who had succeeded Hermann-Josef Schmitt as clerical supervisor of the KAB in Cologne, responded with a classic plea for ostracism. He complained to Frings that Christian trade unionists were persecuted by DGB colleagues in every factory. "In my opinion," Wöste concluded,

a reception for Mr. Tacke and his colleagues would have a very unfavorable impact. The new activation of the Association of Christian Democratic DGB Trade Unionists has provoked concern and alarm . . . among many in the Catholic vocational organizations and the CDU . . . A reception of this group by Your Eminence would grant it too much importance and cause great disappointment among many truly faithful Catholic workers.

Frings decided not to receive the DGB Catholics.[141]

Konrad Adenauer soon helped Fritz Biggeleben of IG Metall to breach the wall around Cologne's cardinal. Biggeleben reported confidentially to Bernhard Tacke that he had visited the outgoing chancellor in April 1963 to complain about the sharp personal attacks on DGB Catholics by Herbert Reichel, and Adenauer exclaimed, "You must tell this to Cardinal Frings!" Biggeleben replied that Frings would not receive him, but Adenauer promised to smooth the way; Biggeleben should simply telephone the cardinal's office for an appointment. This DGB Catholic was then received for one hour by Frings on April 20; the atmosphere was cool at first, because Frings had been "informed in a one-sided fashion about developments in the trade unions," but soon became friendlier. Frings deplored Reichel's behavior but explained that he could only intervene if Reichel caused scandal within the Cologne archdiocese.[142]

The DGB Catholics finally entered into meaningful dialogue with Catholic leaders when Bishop Hengsbach arranged for Tacke and his associates to be received by Heinrich Köppler on September 12, 1963. Tacke expressed concern for the future of Catholicism because of the contrast between the "almost unconditional support for DGB trade unionists" by leaders of the Evangelical Church and the silence of most Catholic bishops. Köppler replied that most bishops now acknowledged

---

[140] See the two notes about the meeting with Hengsbach on June 29, 1962, in NL Deus/1/1.

[141] "Niederschrift über die Sitzung des geschäftsführenden Ausschusses der Arbeitsgemeinschaft christlich-demokratischer DGB-Gewerkschafter," January 3, 1963, ACDP/04–013/140; Tacke to Cardinal Frings, March 19, 1963, ACDP/04–013/141/1; Wöste to Frings, March 29, 1963, KAB Archiv/5/4.

[142] Biggeleben to Tacke, April 23, 1963, NL Zankl/8/4.

"that the foundation of Christian trade unions has remained unsuccessful." He noted sadly that the attitude of the KAB made it all but inevitable that active supporters of Catholic social theory would soon die out in the DGB, and he promised to nourish an atmosphere in Catholic organizations that would make a career as labor organizer appear attractive again to young Catholic workers.[143] Cardinal Frings himself received Tacke at long last on June 27, 1964, along with Hans Katzer, Maria Weber, Adolf Müller, and Franz Deus. Tacke found the discussion most gratifying, because Frings acknowledged that their work in the DGB was an important form of the "lay apostolate." When the leading Christian Democrats in the DGB met again in October, most expressed enthusiasm about their current relationship with their local bishop, although the delegate from Bavaria noted that conditions remained almost unbearable there.[144] In May 1966 the DGB and IG Metall both sent large delegations to Rome to celebrate the seventy-fifth anniversary of *Rerum novarum*, a signal that relations between the labor movement and Catholic Church had entered a new phase. Bishop Kempf of Limburg told an IG Metall congress a few days later that the Catholic Church in the US had always enjoyed very good relations with the American trade unions, which had "helped both of them to serve people better." He hoped that the ties recently established between these two forces in Germany would grow stronger.[145]

The course of the CDU under Chancellor Erhard encouraged new sympathy for the DGB among leading Catholics. In 1964 the social policy experts on the Central Committee noted with dismay the growing influence of the Business Council in the CDU and warned that its rejection of all proposals based on Christian social theory might drive idealistic Christians into the SPD. They also applauded the proposals by the Catholic but Social Democratic chair of the construction workers' union, Georg Leber, to encourage property formation by workers.[146] Heinrich Köppler told an assembly of Christian Democratic DGB trade unionists in January 1965 that SPD leaders had worked skillfully to

---

[143] "Aktennotiz über eine Besprechung beim Zentralkomitee der deutschen Katholiken," September 12, 1963, three-page typescript in NL Tacke/11/4.

[144] Tacke to Cardinal Frings, June 29, 1964, and "Niederschrift über die Sitzung der Arbeitsgemeinschaft christlich-demokratischer DGB Gewerkschafter," October 24, 1964, ACDP/04–013/140.

[145] Katholische Nachrichten-Agentur press release #130 of June 6, 1966 (source of quotation), ACDP/04-013/163; Fritz Biggeleben, "Die gewerkschaftspolitische Situation," speech of June 18, 1966, NL Zankl/8/3.

[146] Grossmann, *Zentralkomitee*, pp. 402–405; Georg Leber to Paul Lücke, September 14, 1964, with enclosed "Programm zur Vermögensbildung der Arbeitnehmer im Baugewerbe," NL Lücke/23; Bishop Höffner to Georg Leber, October 13, 1964, NL Deus/1/1.

reduce areas of disagreement with the Church. He estimated that 17 percent of practicing Catholics and 40–50 percent of all baptized Catholics were now "open to voting SPD," and he concluded that the CDU could not rely on Catholic organizations to combat that party in future. "For the CDU as a party this trend may not be welcome," he concluded, "but it is very significant for the development of our state."[147]

An open challenge to the old policy of ostracism soon emerged within the KAB, led by its director of adult education, Heinz Budde, and the editor of the KAB magazine, Wolfgang Vogt. They led a faction of young progressives who argued already in 1957 for cooperation with the Social Committees and the withdrawal of support from the Christian trade unions. Vogt was a great admirer of Jakob Kaiser, having been inspired by him to join the CDU in the Soviet Zone. The decrees of Vatican II inspired Vogt and Budde to argue that the KAB must welcome as members not only DGB Catholics but even Social Democrats. After Johannes Even died in November 1964, Budde challenged the more senior Winkelheide for election as the lay chairman of the KAB, but Winkelheide won, after Wilhelm Wöste prohibited any debate between the candidates.[148] In January 1966 Budde drew Wöste into the first open debate before KAB leaders about their relationship with the SPD. Wöste argued that the KAB had benefitted greatly from exerting all its influence on one political party. "The CDU needs the unified influence of the KAB to be protected from further liberalization," he concluded, "and the SPD needs a clear front of Christian social forces against it, so that it will change even more." Budde replied forcefully that the KAB must become the common home of all Catholic workers, "without discrimination, favoritism, or preferential treatment of any kind ... It cannot permit itself to ignore the new boundaries and possibilities indicated by the spirit of the [Second Vatican] Council. It must not ignore the exhortation of John XXIII and Paul VI, who have called for cooperation with 'all persons of good will.'" Wöste then retained a narrow majority for the old position that avowed members of the SPD should not be accepted as club members.[149] In September 1967 Budde and Vogt finally persuaded the KAB central committee that the KAB

---

[147] "Katholische Kirche und SPD," speech of January 9, 1965, ACDP/04–013/138.
[148] KAB, "Niederschrift über die Sitzung des Verbandsvorstandes," March 31, 1965, and "Protokollnotiz über die Wahl des 1. und 2. Vorsitzenden auf dem 23. Verbandstag der KAB in Dortmund," May 29, 1965, KAB Archiv/1/4; recollections of Budde in Schroeder, *Zeitzeugen in Interviews*, pp. 212–227; Wolfgang Vogt, "So lernte ich 'uns' kennen," in Uwe Schummer, ed., *CDA 1945 bis 1995* (Bergisch Gladbach, 1995), pp. 41–43.
[149] KAB, "Niederschrift über die Verbandsvorstandssitzung," November 24, 1965, and the minutes of January 3, 1966, with attached memoranda by Wöste and Budde, "KAB und

should simply encourage all members to join a trade union, without expressing any preference. In May 1968 a KAB congress resolved that Social Democrats were welcome to join the Catholic workers' clubs.[150] The KAB thus adopted the position encouraged by John XXIII five years after his death.

The Social Committees also worked to end the trade union controversy among Catholics by facilitating union mergers. In December 1962 Katzer and Johannes Albers reported to the CDU "managing chairman" J.H. Dufhues on the harmful impact of the many local feuds between DGB Catholics and Christian trade unionists, and they secured his agreement "that the long-term goal should be to lead the Christian unions back into the unified trade unions under honorable conditions."[151] In December 1963 the two founders of the Christian Labor Federation, Johannes Even and Bernhard Winkelheide, confessed to Katzer and Tacke that it was not viable and should merge with the DGB. Social Democrats at DGB headquarters hindered Tacke's efforts, however, to bring them together with the DGB chair Ludwig Rosenberg.[152] The Social Committees encouraged discussion of reunification in their seminars for young workers, and they finally achieved a breakthrough in December 1965, when Karl-Heinz Hoffmann received an appeal for assistance by the leaders of the Christian miners' and metalworkers' unions in the Saarland. He helped them to negotiate merger agreements that were ratified by 83 percent of Christian miners and 56 percent of metalworkers in March-April 1966. The former agreement took effect and led to significant growth for the unified miners' union, but the latter vote did not yield a qualified majority. Otto Brenner promised generous treatment nevertheless for any member or functionary of the Christian metalworkers' union who joined IG Metall, and Hoffmann reckoned that about 2,300 did so, while 2,000 remained in the Christian union, and 3,000 dropped out of union life. Some CGB leaders denounced the Social Committees for treachery, but most Catholic journalists

---

SPD," and "Einige Anmerkungen zur Diskussion über das Verhältnis KAB-SPD," KAB Archiv/1/4.

[150] KAB, "Niederschrift über die Sitzung des Verbandsvorstandes," January 10, 1967, attached "Thesen zur Diskussion über die Gewerkschaftsfrage" by Budde and Vogt, and the minutes of September 8, 1967, KAB Archiv/1/7; "Niederschrift über die Sitzung des Verbandsvorstandes," June 20, 1968, KAB Archiv/1/2.

[151] "Besprechung mit dem geschäftsführenden Bundesvorsitzenden der CDU," December 21, 1962, NL Katzer/88, quotation on p. 2.

[152] See Tacke's report in "Niederschrift über die Sitzung der Arbeitsgemeinschaft christlich-demokratischer DGB Gewerkschafter," October 24, 1964, pp. 1–2, and Adolf Müller's remarks in "Niederschrift über die 2. Sitzung der Verhandlungskommission 'Katholische Kirche'," March 31, 1964, p. 6, ACDP/04–013/140.

applauded the Social Committees for securing highly favorable merger terms. By December 1966 the CGB claimed fewer than 100,000 members, down from 200,000 in 1960.[153]

Disillusionment with the policies of the CDU had spread broadly among the Catholic clergy of North Rhine-Westphalia by the time of its state election campaign in 1966. A new round of mine closings in 1965 inspired some Catholic priests in the Ruhr to join anti-government protest marches for the first time, and such protests became widespread by June 1966. CDU politicians were stunned when the Catholic bishops of North Rhine-Westphalia decided not to recommend any party in this campaign. Instead they declared in the spirit of Vatican II that "there can be legitimate disagreements among Christians about the ordering of earthly things. In such cases, nobody has the right to claim the authority of the Church exclusively for himself and his opinion." Post-election interviews with hundreds of activists in the Catholic lay associations revealed a paralyzing loss of confidence in Chancellor Erhard as a result of price increases, the first signs of rising unemployment, and the breach of promises made during the 1965 Bundestag campaign. The CDU had relied heavily on volunteers from these organizations in all previous campaigns, but many of them remained idle in 1966.[154] After the SPD defeated the CDU, Theodor Blank warned party colleagues dramatically that "if the mass of Catholic workers have once voted for the SPD, and if they no longer feel as they once did that this would jeopardize their eternal salvation, then I tell you that the chances for a CDU majority are gone forever." Katzer rejected Blank's premise, arguing instead that the CDU had benefited from the widespread belief that only it could assure national security during the Cold War; he agreed, however, that neither

---

[153] Report by Karl-Heinz Hoffmann, "Niederschrift über die Sitzung des Geschäftsführenden Bundesvorstandes der Sozialausschüsse," June 13, 1966, ACDP/04–013/17/1; "Niederschrift über die Sitzung des Bundesvorstandes der Sozialausschüsse," June 25, 1966, pp. 12–14, ACDP/04–013/25/2; "Sitzung der Arbeitsgemeinschaft Christlich-Demokratischer DGB-Gewerkschafter in den Sozialausschüssen," July 9, 1966, ACDP/04–013/138. See also the press clippings in ACDP/04–013/163, including "Kursverfall bei CGB-Aktien," *Süddeutsche Zeitung,* March 17, 1966, p. 4; Alfred Horné, "Wohin soll ich mich wenden? Die Christen und die Einheitsgewerkschaft," Bayerischer Rundfunk broadcast of May 9, 1966; and Paul Seiler, "Jahreswende – Zeitenwende?" *CGB Korrespondenz,* December 1966 (source of membership figures).

[154] CDU Präsidium, June 3, 1966, p. 3, NL Lücke/140/2; "Ruhr Bergbau: Klar zum Gefecht," and "NRW-Wahlen: Lack ab," *Der Spiegel,* XX/#26 (June 20, 1966), pp. 22–33, and #30 (July 18, 1966), pp. 15–25 (bishops' quotation on 15); Günter Giesen, "Ergebnis der Befragung," summary of several hundred interviews of Catholic activists sent to Bruno Heck and Paul Lücke on August 25, 1966, NL Lücke/150/1; Grossmann, *Zentralkomitee,* p. 324.

the hope for salvation nor fear of Communism could save their party in future.[155]

The Great Coalition of 1966–1969 resulted to a large extent from revulsion among Catholics against the liberal policies of Ludwig Erhard, a revulsion that the Social Committees nurtured systematically. The most dramatic breach in the old Catholic practice of ostracism came after the Great Coalition formed, when the Central Committee of German Catholics elected the Social Democrat Georg Leber as a new member in 1967. The new members also included eight CDU politicians, but the addition of even one Social Democrat was a stunning development. Maria Weber and Adolf Müller of the DGB were elected soon thereafter, and the growing influence of DGB functionaries in Catholic life promoted acceptance of the SPD as well. In 1966 Müller had been the only DGB Catholic permitted to speak at the Bamberg Catholic Congress (Karl-Heinz Hoffmann called him "a voice crying in the wilderness"), but three DGB Catholics helped to shape the agenda of the Essen Catholic Congress of 1968. This was the most important way in which the Social Committees played a bridging role in German society. Catholic bishops attacked the SPD again in the 1970s because of fierce debates over abortion and pornography, but the old identification of Catholic lay organizations with the CDU, efforts to foment schism within the labor unions, and practices of ostracism did not revive.[156]

---

[155] CDU Bundesvorstand, July 11, 1966, *Vorstandsprotokolle 1965–69*, pp. 196–235 (remarks by Katzer on 224–226, Blank quotation on 230).
[156] Grossmann, *Zentralkomitee*, pp. 186–215; Karl-Heinz Hoffmann, "Rechenschaftsbericht der Arbeitsgemeinschaft Christlich-Demokratischer DGB-Kollegen," speech of June 15, 1968, ACDP/04–013/148/2 (quotation on pp. 3–4); Gauly, *Katholiken*, pp. 255–293.

6 The Political Success and Organizational Decline of Christian Democratic Workers, 1966–1980

The Social Committees and their Christian Democratic colleagues in the trade unions rejoiced when Kurt Georg Kiesinger formed the first Great Coalition cabinet at the federal level in November 1966. Hans Katzer and Paul Lücke joined that cabinet and played important roles in its successful efforts to overcome West Germany's first economic recession and reform the political system. They helped to nurture a consensus among elites and voters alike that Social Democrats could be entrusted with power, a consensus which grew so strong that the Free Democrats resolved in 1969 to form a coalition with the SPD.[1] The influence of the Social Committees then declined abruptly, because many labor leaders felt free to ignore the CDU as an opposition party, and "bridge builders" had become largely unnecessary. The Social Committees sought to regain influence by launching a bold campaign to commit the CDU to support parity co-determination, and thus demonstrate to trade unionists that the SPD had abandoned their most important concerns to preserve its coalition with the FDP. That campaign was doomed because of the power of business lobbyists in the CDU, but the Social Committees pushed their party far enough to the left to achieve a co-determination law in 1976 more favorable to organized labor than the FDP would have permitted otherwise. The Social Committees thus helped to consolidate an approach toward labor relations in the Federal Republic far more consensual than that of most other industrialized countries.

6.1 Crisis Management under the Great Coalition, 1966–1969

The immediate cause of Ludwig Erhard's fall was a dispute over how to balance the budget. The cabinet achieved a budget compromise

---

[1] See Peter März, "Zweimal Kanzlersturz: Adenauer 1963, Erhard 1966," in Hans-Peter Schwarz, ed., *Die Fraktion als Machtfaktor. CDU/CSU im Deutschen Bundestag 1949 bis heute* (Munich, 2009), pp. 39–65.

in September 1966, but because of a sudden decline in tax receipts, its Free Democratic finance minister demanded in early October that another 3.5 billion marks be cut from next year's spending. The FDP rejected any tax increases, so he sought to eliminate a planned payment of 500 million marks to the pension system and repeal the 312 Marks Law to encourage property formation by workers, a program cherished by the Social Committees. Labor Minister Katzer fought for the principle established by his predecessors that the government must pay a subsidy each year to safeguard "dynamic" pensions as the population aged, and he threatened to resign if these FDP demands were accepted. Katzer received vigorous support from the CDU Bundestag delegation, but the FDP remained adamant, and its ministers resigned from the cabinet on October 27.[2]

The Social Committees had long championed a Great Coalition with the SPD, and most Christian Democrats now agreed that the FDP was incapable of constructive compromise. Paul Lücke and Karl von Guttenberg quickly reactivated their contacts with SPD leaders and spread the word that they distrusted all CDU chancellor candidates except Kurt Georg Kiesinger, who had long sought consensus with Social Democrats over foreign policy and cultivated good relations with them as prime minister of Baden-Württemberg. This news tipped the choice toward Kiesinger when the CDU Bundestag delegation elected its chancellor candidate on November 10, and he launched coalition talks with the SPD.[3] The Social Committees sent Kiesinger an ambitious social policy program on November 12 that climaxed with a call for "economic co-determination by workers," and the German Labor Federation transmitted an emphatic appeal for the extension of parity co-determination to all large corporations.[4] SPD leaders told

---

[2] Hans Katzer, "Stabilität und Fortschritt," *Soziale Ordnung*, XX/#10 (October 1966), pp. 2–9; "Niederschrift über die Sitzung des Geschäftsführenden Bundesvorstandes der Sozialausschüsse," October 10, 1966, ACDP/04–013/17/1; Bundesarchiv, *Kabinettsprotokolle Online*, cabinet meeting of October 26, 1966, Point A; Klaus Hildebrand, *Von Erhard zur Grossen Koalition 1963–1969* (Stuttgart, 1984), pp. 217–225.

[3] Heinrich Krone, *Tagebücher, 1945–1969*, ed. Hans-Otto Kleinmann, 2 vols. (Düsseldorf, 1995–2003), October 30–November 10, 1966, II: 518–521; "Kurzprotokoll der Sitzung des Bundesvorstandes der Sozialausschüsse," November 12, 1966, ACDP/04–013/25/2; Ulrich Wirz, *Karl Theodor von und zu Guttenberg und das Zustandekommen der Grossen Koalition* (Grub am Forst, 1997), pp. 444–453; Rudolf Morsey, "Die Grosse Koalition – Vorgeschichte und Nachwirkungen," in Günter Buchstab et al., eds., *Kurt Georg Kiesinger 1904–1988. Von Ebingen ins Kanzleramt* (Freiburg, 2005), pp. 393–419.

[4] "20 Thesen zur Sozial- und Gesellschaftspolitik," *Soziale Ordnung*, XX/#12 (December 1966), pp. 4–6, quotation from Thesis #20; "Erklärung des DGB an die neue Bundesregierung," December 3, 1966, and DGB Bundesvorstand, December 6, in Wolther von Kieseritzky, ed., *Quellen zur Geschichte der deutschen Gewerkschaftsbewegung*

Kiesinger, however, that they would not demand any strengthening of co-determination rights this term; they sought respectability above all and agreed that their government declaration should simply promise to appoint a panel of experts to study the issue. Paul Lücke and Herbert Wehner persuaded Kiesinger that the Great Coalition should promise to implement the constitutional amendments which they had discussed in 1962, involving emergency powers, "reform of the financial constitution," and majority suffrage to replace proportional representation. Kiesinger told party colleagues that majority suffrage would be desirable, but Lücke argued passionately that the survival of democracy depended on it, because proportional representation fragmented the party system and encouraged irresponsible behavior by the splinter parties. By focusing attention on that issue, Lücke gained support for a Great Coalition among CDU conservatives who sought to strengthen government authority. Wehner rallied support in the SPD with the argument that the FDP contained too many reactionaries to be a viable partner.[5] Thus the political alignment championed by Karl Arnold in 1949 finally emerged.

Kiesinger assembled a talented cabinet with eleven Christian and nine Social Democrats, including Willy Brandt as foreign minister, Wehner as Minister for All-German Affairs, and the Social Democratic Keynesian economist Karl Schiller as minister of economics. The CSU leader Franz Josef Strauss accepted the difficult post of finance minister, and Lücke and Katzer retained their posts at interior and labor. Helmut Schmidt soon became leader of the SPD Bundestag delegation, while Rainer Barzel returned as his opposite number for the CDU. Barzel later recalled that Willy Brandt opened their first discussion of cabinet personnel by claiming the labor ministry for the SPD. Kiesinger appeared to accept that demand, so Barzel pulled him aside to insist that the CDU could never win an absolute majority again without the votes of nearly half of all workers; Katzer was their best resource in that struggle and must not be sacrificed. Lücke and Katzer soon lost their special role as trusted intermediaries between the SPD and CDU, however, because Kiesinger

im 20. Jahrhundert. Band XIII: Der Deutsche Gewerkschaftsbund 1964–1969 (Bonn, 2006; hereafter *Gewerkschaftsquellen*, XIII:), pp. 368–369, 374.
[5] CDU Präsidium, November 22 and November 28, 1966, NL Lücke/140/2; Krone, *Tagebücher*, II: 521–524, 1966; CDU Bundesvorstand, November 13–26, 1966; CDU Bundesvorstand, November 8 and November 29, 1966, in Günter Buchstab, ed., *Kiesinger: "Wir leben in einer veränderten Welt." Die Protokolle des CDU-Bundesvorstands 1965–1969* (Düsseldorf, 2005; hereafter *Vorstandsprotokolle 1965–69*), pp. 360–361, 375–419; Paul Lücke, *Ist Bonn doch Weimar? Der Kampf um das Mehrheitswahlrecht* (Frankfurt a.M., 1968); Wirz, *Karl von Guttenberg*, pp. 459–466; Wayne Thompson, *The Political Odyssey of Herbert Wehner* (Boulder, 1993), pp. 245–252.

developed a good working relationship with Wehner in the cabinet, Strauss with Schiller, and Barzel with Helmut Schmidt. When differences arose between these coalition partners, the top party leaders conferred directly with each other.[6]

As the unemployment rate crept upward, an atmosphere of crisis gripped the country in December 1966, and Katzer found himself plunged into renewed debate within the cabinet over unpleasant fiscal alternatives. Without naming names, Kiesinger reminded his first cabinet meeting that Katzer had threatened dramatically to resign if austerity measures were imposed during the last months of the Erhard cabinet. "Tough measures are sometimes the most popular measures," Kiesinger declared, and "he would never be deterred by threats of resignation from implementing that which he considered necessary." Katzer replied that "he regards it as essential to express in the government declaration that nothing will change in the principles of our pension system. This was the precondition for his agreement to take office [under Erhard] and remains his precondition." Katzer noted that he had already consented to reductions in social expenditure amounting to 3.5 billion marks but could never abandon the principle of "dynamic" pensions whose value rose in step with wages. Katzer leaked the details of this exchange to the press and notified the Social Committees "that the preservation of the social budget will require assistance from parliament, because new difficulties will doubtless emerge in the cabinet."[7] Soon thereafter Katzer told reporters that the unemployed deserved a 20 percent increase in jobless benefits. The cabinet had agreed on 10 percent, and Kiesinger reprimanded Katzer sternly. Josef Mick appealed to Barzel, however, to resist calls to balance the budget at the expense of social programs, and *Social Order* editorialized that increased jobless benefits would promote economic recovery by stimulating consumer demand. After the SPD proposed an even larger increase, Barzel and Kiesinger agreed with Helmut Schmidt to raise jobless benefits by 15 percent.[8] Thus a social policy alliance emerged between the Social Committees and the SPD Bundestag delegation.

[6] See Stefan Marx, "In der ersten Grossen Koalition, 1966–1969," in Schwarz, *Die Fraktion als Machtfaktor*, pp. 87–112, and Rainer Barzel, *Ein gewagtes Leben. Erinnerungen* (Stuttgart, 2001), pp. 236–238.

[7] Bundesarchiv, *Kabinettsprotokolle Online*, cabinet meeting of December 7, 1966, Point 1; "Bonn: Kabinett. Eine Lage Bier," *Der Spiegel*, XX/#51 (December 12, 1966), pp. 29–30 (which reproduces almost verbatim the exchange between Erhard and Katzer from the confidential cabinet minutes); "Niederschrift über die Sitzung des Geschäftsführenden Bundesvorstandes [der Sozialausschüsse]," December 12, 1966, three-page typescript, ACDP/04–013/17/1 (source of last quotation).

[8] Cabinet minutes of January 11, 1967, Point A, *Bundesarchiv Kabinettsprotokolle Online*; Mick to Barzel, January 16, 1967, NL Mick/20/2; CDU Bundestag delegation, February 14, 1967, in Stefan Marx, ed., *Die CDU/CSU-Fraktion im Deutschen*

Katzer won another victory when the cabinet decided in January to close the budget deficit for 1967 without major cuts to social programs; instead, some tax breaks would be eliminated, and spending reduced for agricultural subsidies, defense, and foreign aid. Karl Schiller also won approval for 2.5 billion marks in long-term borrowing for investments in the national railway, telecommunications, and highway system, a program inspired by memories of the disastrous consequences of a one-sided policy of fiscal austerity under the Brüning Cabinet in 1930/1931. This development is often explained as the result of a new embrace of Keynesian economics by the cabinet, but Brüning had actually sought to adopt the same mix of policies in May/June 1930. His plan for long-term borrowing for infrastructure investments was actually three times larger than Schiller's as a proportion of national income, but it provoked insurmountable opposition by the autonomous boards of the *Reichsbank* and National Railway. In 1967 German bankers and industrialists proved far more willing to cooperate with the government to prevent mass unemployment.[9] By June the government had also enacted a modified version of Ludwig Erhard's proposed Stability Laws to facilitate countercyclical planning of all public investments, and a three-year budget plan that foresaw modest reductions in social spending. Katzer achieved a difficult balancing act during these negotiations. Kiesinger told CDU leaders that the labor minister had proved truly helpful in securing the most stringent austerity measures that could be achieved under this coalition, while the DGB chair Ludwig Rosenberg issued the following testimonial in a conversation with Willy Brandt: "Recent experience has shown that he [Rosenberg] can rely on Hoffmann, Katzer, and the Social Committees in critical political questions." Katzer later recalled that he developed a genuine friendship with the sagacious Rosenberg (who was Jewish as well as Social Democratic) and came to rely on his advice.[10]

Bundestag. Sitzungsprotokolle 1966–1969, 2 vols. (Düsseldorf, 2011; hereafter *Fraktionsprotokolle 1966–69*), I: 77–79, 87–89; "Ein Konzept für morgen," and "Die süsse Arbeitslosigkeit," *Soziale Ordnung*, XXI/#2 (February 15, 1967), pp. 9–10.

[9] Cabinet meetings of January 11, 1967, Point F, January 18, Point C, and January 19, #2, Bundesarchiv, *Kabinettsprotokolle Online*; "Haushalt 67: In den Klingelbeutel," *Der Spiegel*, XXI/#5 (January 23, 1967), pp. 15–16; Hildebrand, *Von Erhard zur Grossen Koalition*, pp. 283–287; Gabriele Metzler, "Die Reformprojekte der Grossen Koalition im Kontext ihrer Zeit," in Buchstab, *Kurt Georg Kiesinger*, pp. 421–452. For Brüning's failure, see pp. 22–24 above.

[10] DGB Bundesvorstand, meetings of May–July 1967, and Willy Brandt's notes, "Gespräch mit Ludwig Rosenberg am 19. September 1967," *Gewerkschaftsquellen*, XIII: 457–460, 473–479, 489–491, 524–525 (quotation on 525); CDU Bundestag delegation, May 9, June 13, and June 20, 1967, *Fraktionsprotokolle 1966–69*, I: 248–258, 338–350, 359–371; Kiesinger's report to the CDU Bundesvorstand, July 17, 1967, *Vorstandsprotokolle 1965–69*, pp. 618–622, 634–635; Hans Katzer, "Ein Augenzeuge berichtet," in

Another sign of progress since 1930 toward consensus politics came with the success of the so-called Concerted Action, a series of three-way conferences of government, labor, and business leaders convened by Karl Schiller. In December 1966 the economics minister told DGB leaders that he embraced their demand for lower interest rates to stimulate recovery, but that, in exchange, the *Bundesbank* demanded "concerted action" (*konzertierte Aktion*) between the government and social partners to reduce the danger of inflation. Its first goal would be to issue non-binding "orientation data" regarding what range of future wage increases would be compatible with economic growth, a term chosen by Schiller because organized labor detested the idea of "wage guidelines." Thereafter, Schiller promised, the social partners could raise any other issue for discussion that concerned them. The DGB promptly endorsed Concerted Action, and soon thereafter the *Bundesbank* lowered the discount rate from 5 percent to 4.5 percent.[11] After studying the economics ministry's statistical reports, the most influential leaders of business and organized labor conferred with Schiller again on March 1-2, 1967, and declared jointly that the economy would probably grow at a nominal rate of about 4 percent in 1967, and the cost of living rise by 2 percent, so that it would be reasonable to expect nominal wages and salaries to rise by 3–4 percent. For six months thereafter, almost every new collective labor contract adhered to these parameters. Bernhard Tacke played a key role in Concerted Action as the DGB coordinator for collective bargaining strategy, but he agreed with the militant Otto Brenner of IG Metall that Schiller underestimated the inflation rate, and that real wages were actually falling. Both men feared that Concerted Action would undermine union autonomy, but it proved so popular that all labor leaders felt compelled to participate. The influence of Catholic corporatism had obviously declined since 1930, because Tacke and Katzer always remained skeptical critics of this experiment in "social partnership" launched by an agnostic Keynesian Social Democrat.[12]

Uwe Schummer, ed., *CDA 1945 bis 1995* (Bergisch-Gladbach, 1995), p. 34; Hildebrand, *Von Erhard zur Grossen Koalition*, pp. 289–294.
[11] Reports by Tacke and Haferkamp to the DGB Bundesvorstand, December 14, 1966, and minutes of January 10, 1967, *Gewerkschaftsquellen*, XIII: 378–383, 389–391 (quotations on 389–390); Schiller's report to the cabinet on January 11, 1967, Point F, *Kabinettsprotokolle-Online*; Bernhard Tacke, "Zusammengefasste Ergebnisse in den bisher stattgefundenen vierzehn Gesprächen im Rahmen der 'Konzertierten Aktion,'" March 1969, pp. 1–2, NL Tacke/2/1. For the failure of similar talks in 1930, see pp. 22–26 above.
[12] DGB Bundesvorstand, March 1–7, 1967, and January 16, 1968, *Gewerkschaftsquellen*, XIII: 415–417, 429–431, 605–610; "Massiver Angriff auf den Lebensstandard?" (interview with Otto Brenner), *Der Spiegel*, XXI/#14 (March 27, 1967), pp. 39–45; Bernhard Tacke, "Konzertierte Aktion und autonome Tarifpolitik," speech of May 31, 1967, NL

The Social Committees' collaboration with the SPD caused a backlash in the CDU. The Bielefeld CDU party manager, for example, reported to his superiors in February 1967 that "influential personages whose goodwill and support we need have declared their intention to resign from the CDU, if the party does not at last clearly condemn the arrogance of the Social Committees." Rudi Nickels of the Westphalian Social Committees sought to persuade CDU functionaries that they enjoyed a great opportunity, because blue-collar workers now regarded Hans Katzer as their only champion in the cabinet. Nickels asked bluntly, "What is better, to win future elections or finance your party organization with money from the industrialists?" Many of them complained nevertheless that Katzer infuriated donors with his attempts to outflank the SPD to the left.[13] At the CDU party congress in May 1967, an overwhelming majority elected Kiesinger as party chair, rejecting arguments by the Social Committees that this office should be separate from the chancellorship. The delegates also rejected the party leadership's recommendation to elect Katzer and Konrad Grundmann to the CDU Central Committee, leaving the CDU vice chair Paul Lücke as the only representative of the Social Committees in the party leadership. This rebuff did not weaken Katzer's position as labor minister, but Grundmann suffered a major embarrassment as chair of the large CDU state organization of the Rhineland, which expected a seat on the Central Committee.[14]

The Social Committees responded aggressively to this disappointment at their Offenburg National Congress in July 1967. The delegates overwhelmingly reelected Hans Katzer as their leader and purged three of his Christian trade unionist critics from their central committee. They also gave thunderous applause to a plea for parity co-determination in all

Tacke/2/1; Tacke to Katzer, July 9, 1968, and reply of August 2, ACDP/04–013/23; Hans-Otto Hemmer and Kurt Thomas Schmitz, eds., *Geschichte der Gewerkschaften in der Bundesrepublik Deutschland. Von den Anfängen bis heute* (Cologne, 1990), pp. 249–279.

[13] Erich Bischoff (Bielefeld) to Otto Laipold, February 3, 1967 (source of first quotation), and "Niederschrift über die Sitzung des Bezirksvorstandes der Sozialausschüsse der CDU Ostwestfalen-Lippe," February 11, 1967, ACDP/03–002/133/2; Rudi Nickels, "Besprechungspunkte für Kreisgeschäftsführertagung," May 3, 1967, ACDP/ 03–002/130 (second quotation on p. 2); "Vermerk über das von Herrn Minister Kurt Schmücker inszenierte Gespräch zwecks Koordinierung der Wirtschafts- und Sozialpolitik," May 2, 1967, ACDP/04–013/30.

[14] CDA, "Aktennotiz Betr.: Parteivorsitz der CDU," January 16, 1967, ACDP/ 04–013/25/2; "Vermerk" by K.H. Hoffmann for Katzer, January 18, 1967, ACDP/ 04–013/17/1; CDU Bundesvorstand, May 2 and May 21, 1967, *Vorstandsprotokolle 1965–69*, pp. 504–506, 530–536 578–607; "Beschlüsse des geschäftsführenden Bundesvorstandes [der Sozialausschüsse]," April 28, 1967, ACDP/04–013/30; CDU, *15. Bundesparteitag der CDU. Braunschweig, 22./23. Mai 1967* (Oberhausen and Düsseldorf, 1967), pp. 178–194; report by Grundman to the Rhenish CDU, May 26, 1967, NL Mick/10/2.

branches of industry by the Jesuit theologian Hermann Josef Wallraff, who proposed that corporate supervisory boards should include representatives of workers, shareholders, and government in the ratio of 40:40:20. Out of respect for CDU leaders, Katzer hindered any vote to endorse this plan, but in their Offenburg Declaration, the Social Committees demanded "stronger co-determination rights for the factory council and a position of equality for labor in the supervisory boards of large enterprise." This phrase was not in the declaration's first draft but was added at the last minute in response to pleas by DGB supporters in the Westphalian Social Committees.[15] Some pro-business journals denounced this resolution, but sympathetic press coverage was organized by the brash young Norbert Blüm, recently employed to edit *Social Order*. A former altar boy, Blüm had worked for a decade on the Opel assembly line in Rüsselsheim and then earned a doctorate in sociology from the University of Bonn; his unusual life story and lively sense of humor made him a magnet for journalists. Blüm persuaded the CDU secretary general Bruno Heck that a vigorous discussion of co-determination helped to integrate workers into their party, and Heck promised to improve relations between the Social Committees and CDU county offices. The top CDU leaders agreed, however, following two tense discussions of the Offenburg Declaration that no majority would ever emerge in their party for any extension of parity co-determination beyond coal and steel, and that they must discourage such hopes.[16]

Economic activity revived in the summer of 1967, and the cabinet's attention shifted toward reforms of the political system. SPD leaders agreed with a majority of the voters that the Basic Law should be amended to give the federal government meaningful emergency powers, but Otto Brenner had secured another resolution by a DGB national congress in May 1966 to reject the idea categorically. Bernhard Tacke condemned Brenner's stance for depriving organized labor of any influence. He agreed with the government that some legislation must be enacted to transfer to German authorities in a regulated form powers currently enjoyed in an

---

[15] "Wallraff," memorandum of May 8, 1967, ACDP/04-013/32/2; "Niederschrift über die Landesvorstandssitzung der Sozialausschüsse Westfalen-Lippe," June 16, 1967, ACDP/03-002/128/1; "12. Bundestagung der Sozialausschüsse," *Soziale Ordnung*, XXI/#7 (July 1967), pp. 2–24; "Offenburger Erklärung: Ein Beitrag der Sozialausschüsse der CDA zur Diskussion des Parteiprogramms der CDU," July 9, 1967, pp. 5, 14–15 (pamphlet in NL Mick/8/3).

[16] "12. Bundestagung der Sozialausschüsse .... Pressestimmen," NL Mick/8/3; Norbert Blüm, "Aktenvermerk: Redaktionssitzung," June 29, 1967, and "Aktenvermerk: Sitzung der CDU-Redakteure," July 10, 1967 (conferences chaired by Bruno Heck), ACDP/04-013/86; CDU Präsidium, June 30 and July 17, 1967, NL Lücke/150/2; Blüm's capsule biography and reminiscences in Schummer, *CDA 1945 bis 1995*, pp. 133–145.

unregulated form by the commanders of Allied troops based in Germany, and he endorsed Interior Minister Lücke's appeal to labor leaders to help draft improved legislation. Tacke gained new influence when he was elected to chair the DGB commission to study the issue of emergency powers in December 1966.[17] Lücke secured cabinet approval in March 1967 for bills to authorize the government to issue decrees and deploy troops in case of foreign invasion, domestic upheaval, or natural disaster. His bills displayed more solicitude for civil liberties than had earlier drafts, but they still authorized labor conscription in a state of emergency, and they aroused passionate opposition among the intellectuals and student radicals in the loosely organized movement calling itself the "Extra-Parliamentary Opposition." Lücke assured party colleagues in June 1967 that support for his plan was spreading among trade unionists and the public at large, but student demonstrations against emergency powers grew larger and more militant in the following months nevertheless.[18] In March 1968 student radicals sought to disrupt the SPD Party Congress in Nuremberg, and Willy Brandt himself was assaulted as he entered the congress hall. The SPD resolved, however, to forge ahead with emergency powers legislation, which gained final passage with a two-thirds Bundestag majority on May 30, 1968. Tacke deplored the premise of these laws that labor unrest would probably emerge in any "state of emergency," arguing that the trade unions were the most reliable defenders of democracy. He secured a resolution by the DGB Central Committee nevertheless that the will of the Bundestag must be respected.[19]

Lücke had removed himself from this debate in March 1968 by resigning from the cabinet to protest its failure to advance suffrage reform. The panel of experts he appointed had endorsed majority suffrage in November 1967, and Lücke pressed for action to prevent the right-wing extremist National Democratic Party from entering the next Bundestag under proportional representation. The debate over emergency

---

[17] Interior ministry report on "Gewerkschaftliche Äusserungen" regarding emergency powers, January 28, 1966, NL Lücke/107/1; reports by Tacke to the "Arbeitsgemeinschaft Christlich-Demokratischer DGB-Gewerkschafter," March 5 and July 9, 1966, ACDP/ 04-013/138; DGB Bundesvorstand, December 6, 1966, Gewerkschaftsquellen, XIII: 375; Hans Zankl memorandum of November 22, 1966, ACDP/07-004/522/1; Michael Schneider, Demokratie in Gefahr? Der Konflikt um die Notstandsgesetze (Bonn, 1986), pp. 81–174.

[18] CDU Bundestag delegation, June 27, 1967, Fraktionsprotokolle 1966-69, I: 394–396; Michael Schneider, Demokratie in Gefahr?, pp. 174–228.

[19] "SPD-Parteitag: Komplott bei Adelheid," Der Spiegel, XXII/#13 (March 25, 1968), pp. 27–31; DGB leadership conferences of March 29–June 19, 1968, and resolution of May 19, Gewerkschaftsquellen, XIII: 648–659, 678–680, 688–699, 703–706; Tacke's speech to a DGB rally on May 11, 1968, DGB-Archiv/5/DGCY000007.

powers made it extremely difficult, however, for SPD leaders to ask their party to consider another momentous constitutional amendment.[20] Lücke expected vigorous support from the chancellor, but Kiesinger waited until January 1968 to confer with SPD leaders about the issue, and they reached no agreement. The SPD party congress in March then resolved that suffrage reform must be studied thoroughly and discussed again at the next congress; Wehner informed Lücke confidentially that a majority of delegates had opposed suffrage reform, so this was the best result that could be achieved.[21] Lücke then submitted his resignation, hoping to stimulate action by all party leaders who had signed the coalition agreement promising suffrage reform. Kiesinger's only response, however, was to tell party colleagues that he was not obliged to resign himself, because he had never argued like Lücke that the survival of democracy depended on suffrage reform. Lücke confided to a friend several years later that Kiesinger had promised him when the cabinet formed "to dissolve the government if necessary and call for new elections before he allowed the quest for suffrage reform to fail. Mr. Kiesinger did not keep his word." CDU colleagues admired Lücke's dedication to principle, but he never served in the cabinet again.[22]

Throughout Kiesinger's time in office, militants in the Social Committees and trade unions encouraged each other to challenge the decision by CDU and SPD party leaders that co-determination did not belong on the legislative agenda. Their first battle involved the preservation of parity co-determination where it existed. In February 1967 the factory councils of the Rhenish Steel Works holding company complained to the cabinet that it had recently carried out an acquisition which left coal and steel no more than 45 percent of total sales. This merger had required approval by the workers' representatives on the supervisory board, which was granted in exchange for a pledge that nothing would change in the organs of parity co-determination, but

---

[20] CDU Bundestag delegation, February–December 1967, *Fraktionsprotokolle 1966–69*, I: 80, 257–258, 326, 555, 586, 591; report to Lücke on divisions in the SPD, November 7, 1967, NL Lücke/110/4; CDU Bundesvorstand, December 4, 1967, *Vorstandprotokolle 1965–69*, pp. 723–730, 737–747; Lücke, "Klare Mehrheiten!" *Soziale Ordnung*, XXI/ #12 (December 1967), p. 3.

[21] Interior ministry "Protokoll über die Sitzung des persönlichen Mitarbeiterstabes," December 6, 1967, NL Lücke/110/5; Stefan Marx, ed., *Der Kressbronner Kreis. Die Protokolle des Koalitionsausschusses der ersten Grossen Koalition aus CDU, CSU und SPD* (Düsseldorf, 2013), meeting of January 11, 1968, pp. 13–18; Wehner to Lücke, March 24, 1968, NL Lücke/133.

[22] CDU Bundestag delegation, March 26, 1968, *Fraktionsprotokolle 1966–69*, I: 801–832; letters of support for Lücke after his resignation in NL Lücke/110/1; Lücke to Johannes Schauff, December 18, 1974, quoted in Morsey, "Die Grosse Koalition," in Buchstab, *Kiesinger*, pp. 410–411 (source of quotation).

now management planned to elect a supervisory board with only one-third of the seats reserved for workers at the next shareholders' meeting. Katzer therefore proposed an amendment to the Supplemental Co-Determination Law of 1956, requiring that the proportion of coal and steel in total sales must fall below 50 percent for five years in a row before parity co-determination ceased to apply.[23] The leaders of big business denounced this bill for interfering with the "natural course" of mergers, but after some agonizing, the CDU parliamentary leader Rainer Barzel recommended its passage. He explained to his delegation that "if we do not come in the Ruhr with its structural problems of coal and steel to the creation of new and larger concerns with the agreement of the trade unions, ... then the Ruhr will continue to decline." If the CDU did not recover its popularity in North Rhine-Westphalia by the time of the next Bundestag election, Barzel concluded, "then we can achieve the most lovely results in Baden-Württemberg and Bavaria and Lower Saxony, and we will still be in opposition." Katzer's bill passed the Bundestag on April 27, maintaining parity co-determination at Rhenish Steel and two other holding companies for several years.[24]

Regarding the far more controversial issue of whether parity co-determination should be extended beyond coal and steel, Katzer assured DGB leaders in May 1967 that he exercised jurisdiction over the appointment of the commission of experts promised in Kiesinger's government declaration and would press for it to work swiftly. Only in November, however, could he secure cabinet agreement about its composition. Katzer recruited the young Professor Kurt Biedenkopf as chair, an expert on business law who had recently become rector of the new Ruhr University in Bochum. Three more law professors and five economists rounded out the team of "independent experts."[25] Kiesinger told CDU leaders firmly at year's end that the deliberations of this

[23] "Protokoll der Sitzung des Arbeitskreises Mitbestimmung [der Sozialausschüsse]," July 21, 1966, and memorandum of September 1966, ACDP/04–013/32/2; Adolf Müller to Kiesinger, February 10, 1967, petition to Kiesinger of February 16 by the Betriebsräte Rheinische Stahlwerke, and Stingl to Barzel, February 21, 1967, ACDP/08–005/67/2; CDU Bundestag delegation, February 21, 1967, *Fraktionsprotokolle 1966–69*, I: 115–130.

[24] "Auszüge zum Thema 'Aushöhlung' aus dem Referat von Dr. Hanns-Martin Schleyer ... auf dem Wirtschaftstag der CDU/CSU," January 26, 1967, ACDP/08–005/67/2; "Aktennotiz: Vertrauliche Mitteilung!", minutes of a conference on February 17, 1967, between the CDU Präsidium and Schleyer and other business leaders, NL Mick/20/2; CDU Bundestag delegation, March 7 and March 14, 1967, *Fraktionsprotokolle 1966–69*, I: 142–149, 212–216 (Barzel quotation on 215–216).

[25] DGB leadership conferences of May 2 and November 2/3, 1967, and press release of September 5, *Gewerkschaftsquellen*, XIII: 457–458, 523, 547, 559; Kurt Biedenkopf to Franz Deus, June 21, 1966, NL Deus/2/1; cabinet minutes of November 8, 1967, point B, *Bundesarchiv Kabinettsprotokolle Online*; "Sozialpolitische Informationen," December 4, 1967, pp. 1–2, ACDP/08–005/66/2.

commission would be "all that will happen in this legislative term" regarding co-determination. Shortly before the Biedenkopf Commission convened, Kiesinger also informed his labor minister curtly that he had received numerous requests "to reassure the public about the neutrality of the commission of experts" and would therefore place it under the direct supervision of the chancellor's office.[26]

The Offenburg Declaration nurtured hopes in the DGB and fears in the CDU that the Social Committees would introduce their own co-determination bill. Karl-Heinz Hoffmann did favor such action, and at a rally of the Social Committees in October 1967 he proposed the formation of an "Association to Promote Co-Determination" to unite the Social Committees, DGB, and Catholic and Protestant workers' clubs. Union leaders responded enthusiastically, beginning with Wilhelm Gefeller of the chemical workers' union, but Katzer and Bernhard Winkelheide rejected the idea. Hoffmann felt a sense of urgency, because he believed that parity co-determination could only be enacted under a Great Coalition, but his senior colleagues sought to maintain good relations with CDU leaders.[27] Hoffmann's agitation generated pressure on the SPD nevertheless to demonstrate that it had not turned its back on the trade unions. The DGB and IG Metall organized mass rallies for co-determination in March 1968, and Ludwig Rosenberg complained to friends in the SPD that the Social Committees made greater efforts than their party to rally public support for the core demands of organized labor. The SPD party congress of March 1968 therefore instructed its Bundestag delegation to introduce a bill as soon as possible to extend parity co-determination. This resolution inspired the Westphalian Social Committees to petition CDU headquarters to add a similar plank to the next CDU platform, and Hoffmann distributed a draft bill for discussion by the Social Committees.[28]

[26] CDU Bundesvorstand, December 4, 1967, *Vorstandsprotokolle 1965–69*, p. 716; Kiesinger to Katzer, January 22, 1968, NL Katzer/379.

[27] Hoffmann to "Lieber Willi" (Gefeller), October 16, 1967, and reply of October 24, ACDP/04–013/132/1; DGB Bundesvorstand, November 2, 1967, and March 29, 1968, *Gewerkschaftsquellen*, XIII: 548, 653; "Zusammengefasste Niederschrift über die konstituierende Sitzung des Arbeitskreises 'Mitbestimmung' der Sozialausschüsse," November 3, 1967, ACDP/04–013/32/2; "Protokoll über die Sitzung des Arbeitskreises der Parlamentarier der Sozialausschüsse," November 15, 1967, NL Lücke/160; circular by Hoffmann on December 6, 1967, with attached "Entwurf einer Arbeitsvorlage zur wirtschaftlichen Mitbestimmung," NL Mick/3/3; "Niederschrift über die Sitzung des Geschäftsführenden Bundesvorstandes [der Sozialausschüsse]," February 9, 1968, ACDP/04–013/30; "Rechenschaftsbericht der Arbeitsgemeinschaft Christlich-Demokratischer DGB-Kollegen," June 15, 1968, pp. 14–19, ACDP/04–013/148/2.

[28] Brenner to the DGB Bundesvorstand, February 6, 1968, and Rosenberg to Oberbürgermeister Ludwig, June 4, 1968, *Gewerkschaftsquellen*, XIII: 625–627; "Der Mensch ist wichtiger als die Sache. Landestagung 1968 der Sozialausschüsse

Co-determination proved the most divisive issue by far as the CDU drafted its Action Program for the next Bundestag election. J.H. Dufhues told CDU leaders in June 1968 that they must not adopt a program intolerable for the Social Committees, but he also revealed that several prominent businessmen would resign from the party if it endorsed any extension of parity co-determination. Kiesinger belittled the issue by reporting that "a leading Social Democrat" had confided to him that only union functionaries cared about co-determination, while "it is much more important to the worker that he receive a four-week vacation." KAB leaders soon ascertained, however, that 84 percent of their members supported the DGB's demands to extend co-determination rights, and the Social Committees agreed that the great majority of Christian Democratic workers in large factories demanded parity. When Karl-Heinz Hoffmann gained an important post as vice chair of the Public Service and Transport Workers' Union, the Social Committees chose another champion of parity co-determination to replace him as their general manager: Norbert Blüm.[29] Konrad Grundmann secured agreement by the CDU of the Rhineland on the following compromise formula for the Action Program: "Whether a more extensive form of co-determination in large enterprises is possible and desirable must be studied carefully. In any alteration of corporate structure, there must be no monopoly of influence for one interest group outside the firm, and the ability of the firm to succeed in international competition must not be undermined." Katzer persuaded the leaders of the Social Committees that this was the best outcome that could be expected, and the CDU party congress adopted it in November. Katzer warned the delegates, however, that the debate over co-determination could not be suppressed, because industrial concentration and the rising educational niveau of German workers caused growing interest in the issue.[30] The SPD nurtured that

Westfalen-Lippe" on March 29/30, 1968, with attached motion to amend the CDU Action Program, ACDP/03–002/126/1; Hoffman's circular to the Social Committees in May/June 1968, "Zur Diskussion gestellt!" NL Mick/10/1.

[29] CDU Bundesvorstand, June 21, 1968, *Vorstandsprotokolle 1965–69*, pp. 950–965 (quotation on 960); Institut für Demoskopie Allensbach, "Die Katholische Arbeitnehmer-Bewegung. Bericht über eine repräsentative Mitglieder-Befragung," completed on May 6, 1969, Tables 39 and T25-T27, KAB Archiv/33/80; "Informationen der Sozialausschüsse der CDA," September 19, 1968, LANRW/CDA Rheinland/609; "Protokoll über die Vorstandssitzung der Sozialausschüsse der CDA des Rheinlandes," October 1, 1968, NL Mick/10/1; Norbert Blüm, "Mitbestimmung," speech of September 14, 1968, published in "GK-Informationen," Nr. 57, October 10, 1968, ACDP/08–005/67/2.

[30] "Aktennotiz über das Gespräch zwischen den Vorständen der Wirtschaftsvereinigung und der Sozialausschüsse der CDA des Rheinlandes," August 28, 1968, and CDA Rheinland, "Informationen," Nr. 64, August 29, 1968 (source of quotation), NL Mick/10/1; CDU Bundesvorstand, September 20, 1968, *Vorstandsprotokolle 1965–69*, pp. 1204–1222; speeches by Mick, Blank, and Katzer on October 12, 1968,

interest in December by introducing a bill to extend to all large corporations the system of parity co-determination in coal and steel, as demanded by the DGB. The CDU reproached it for posturing, because it had waited so long to present this bill that the Bundestag obviously could not enact it this term. The bill revived enthusiasm for the SPD among trade unionists nevertheless.[31]

Katzer displayed an iron resolve to achieve this term at least one old demand of the Social Committees and DGB, the "continued payment of wages" by employers for sick blue-collar workers, so that they would receive the same treatment as white-collar workers. This proposal shifted to employers a burden that had been financed through health insurance, and the CDU endorsed it only if linked to painful co-payments by the insured for all medical services. Katzer told a reporter in June 1968, however, that it might be necessary to enact continued payment of wages first to nurture a willingness among workers to accept co-payments. Economics Minister Schiller and the DGB applauded this initiative, arguing that continued payment of wages would stimulate consumer demand and accelerate economic recovery by lowering health insurance premiums. In September Katzer told his Bundestag delegation that, while comprehensive health insurance reform was impossible this term, they could link continued payment of wages to "the beginning of a reform." Barzel supported Katzer with a warning that the SPD could seize on this issue during the next election campaign.[32]

In January 1969 Katzer and the social policy experts of the CDU proposed to link continued payment of wages with a plan to lower health insurance premiums from 11 percent to 9 percent of wages, raise the income ceiling for mandatory coverage to DM 990 per month to add more affluent contributors (plus matching payments by their employers), and impose a co-payment of three marks per day for hospital stays.

LANRW/CDA Rheinland/896; CDU, *16. Bundesparteitag der Christlich Demokratischen Union Deutschlands. Berlin, 4. bis 7. November 1968*, (Monschau, Eifel, 1968), pp. 250–255.

[31] CDU Bundesvorstand, January 16, 1969, *Vorstandsprotokolle 1965–69*, pp. 1307–1308; CDU Bundestag delegation, meetings of January 14 and January 21, 1969, *Fraktionsprotokolle 1966–69*, CD-Supplement, p. 980, and II: 1292–1398; CDU memorandum, "Betrifft: Mitbestimmungsgesetze der SPD," January 14, 1969, ACDP/ 08–005/67/2.

[32] Bernhard Tacke, "Zusammengefasste Ergebnisse in den bisher stattgefundenen vierzehn Gesprächen im Rahmen der 'Konzertierten Aktion,'" March 1969, pp. 7–8, NL Tacke/2/ 1; Tacke to Katzer, July 9, 1968, and reply of August 2, ACDP/04–013/23; Katzer's report in the "Niederschrift über die Klausurtagung der Arbeitnehmergruppe der CDU/ CSU-Fraktion," September 17, 1968, NL Lücke/160; CDU Bundestag delegation, September 24–30, 1968, *Fraktionsprotokolle 1966–69*, CD Supplement, pp. 823–824, 835–854 (Katzer quotation on 838), 864–869, 909. For background see pp. 187–88, 218–221, in the present volume.

The SPD rejected any co-payments, however, and demanded a 1,200-mark income ceiling, which would cost business an additional 1.2 billion marks per year. Katzer implored his delegation to make some concession for a swift agreement, because the price of a bargain would only rise as the date of the election neared.[33] Business lobbyists in the CDU rejected any concessions, however, so the SPD forged ahead with a bill to reject co-payments in any form, lower premiums even further, and raise the income ceiling to DM 2,000 by 1972. That bill proved so popular that the CDU capitulated in June to the demand for continued payment of wages without co-payments and a 1,200-mark ceiling. When party colleagues complained, Katzer observed tartly that he could have obtained a better bargain if they had followed his lead nine months ago.[34]

Katzer thus achieved a demand raised by every congress of the Social Committees since 1955. He could also take credit for an innovative law to link unemployment insurance with educational programs for the unemployed and improved job placement services (the Jobs Promotion Act of June 1967) and other measures to improve vocational training. Trade union leaders regarded him as a highly effective labor minister. As Blüm observed, each legislative battle fought by the Social Committees had also advanced a noble principle: "partnership" with the co-determination laws of 1951/1952, "security" with the pension reform of 1957 and 312 Marks Law, "equality" with the continued payment of wages, and "the right to work" with the Jobs Promotion Act. Katzer had also been compelled to preside over several rounds of painful austerity measures, however, that reduced social spending by nine billion marks. His time in office did not greatly enhance his popularity.[35]

---

[33] CDA "Informationen," Nr. 8, January 16, 1969 (NL Lücke/166/1) and Nr. 10, February 24, 1969 (LANRW/CDA Rheinland/610); CDU Bundestag delegation Arbeitskreis IV, minutes of February 4 and February 25, 1969, ACDP/08–005/11/1; CDU Bundestag delegation, January–February 1969, *Fraktionsprotokolle 1966–69*, CD Supplement, pp. 989, 1001, 1074–1078, and II: 1302–1305, 1367–1368; "Koalitionsgespräch" of February 11, 1969, *Kressbronner Kreis*, pp. 225–226; "Protokoll über die Bundesvorstandssitzung der Sozialausschüsse der CDA," February 8, 1969, ACDP/04–013/15/2.

[34] "Koalitionsgespräch" of February 21 and June 10, 1969, *Kressbronner Kreis*, pp. 229–230, 260–261; CDU Bundesvorstand, March 6, 1969, *Vorstandsprotokolle 1965–69*, pp. 1388–1401; CDU Bundestag delegation, March 18 to June 11, 1969, *Fraktionsprotokolle 1966–69*, II: 1384–1385, 1401–1410, 1438, 1502–1503, 1534–1535, 1553–1566, and CD Supplement, pp. 1157–1158, 1194, 1221–1234; CDA "Informationen," Nr. 11, March 19, 1969, pp. 1–2, and Nr. 14, May 22, 1969, NL Lücke/161/1.

[35] Blüm's remarks in "Protokoll der Sozialsekretärskonferenz," February 4, 1970, ACDP/04–013/15/2; Tilman Mayer, "Gerechtigkeit schafft Frieden. Die Gesellschaftspolitik Hans Katzers," in Ulf Fink, ed., *Partnerschaft statt Klassenkampf* (Cologne, 1989), pp. 11–37 (esp. 20–28); Hemmer and Schmitz, *Geschichte der Gewerkschaften*, pp. 271–272.

Kiesinger hoped to revive the Great Coalition after the Bundestag election, but that outcome became unlikely when the SPD and FDP joined forces to elect the Social Democratic pacifist Gustav Heinemann as president of the Federal Republic in March 1969. The young Helmut Kohl, doubtless the most astute political analyst among CDU leaders, deduced at once from this decision that the leaders of the SPD and FDP had decided to form a coalition, that co-determination was the only issue dividing their parties, and that the SPD could obtain a coalition if it promised the FDP not to introduce a co-determination bill for another four years.[36] SPD leaders worried about the reaction by organized labor to such a bargain, but the DGB became less likely to oppose it when Ludwig Rosenberg retired in May 1969. The most capable candidate to succeed him advanced a controversial plan to centralize authority within the DGB, so the union chairs agreed to elect the more cautious vice chair of the miners' union, Heinz Oskar Vetter. The new chairman took office in a weak position and apparently felt compelled to seek the favor of SPD headquarters. Kiesinger also offended DGB leaders by withdrawing at the last minute his agreement to address the DGB congress that elected Vetter.[37] By failing to court organized labor, Kiesinger lost his best chance to rally support for the Great Coalition.

In 1969 many CDU county committees made opposition to any extension of parity co-determination a litmus test for nominating Bundestag candidates. The Westphalian Social Committees complained that their wishes were ignored, and Konrad Grundmann found that the struggle over nominations in the Rhineland caused "difficulties of a magnitude that we have never before experienced."[38] The Social Committees did secure one new seat for Ferdinand Breidbach, a skilled metalworker and former chair of the Young Christian Democratic Workers of the Rhineland who worked in the publicity office at DGB headquarters. He won nomination in a heavily blue-collar district in Duisburg that the

---

[36] CDU Bundesvorstand, March 6, 1969, *Vorstandsprotokolle 1965–69*, pp. 1344–1350, 1395–1396; Hildebrand, *Von Erhard zur Grossen Koalition*, pp. 389–401.

[37] DGB leadership conferences of March 3–April 1, 1969, *Gewerkschaftsquellen*, XIII: 813–816, 825–827, 832–841; "Protokoll über die Sitzung des geschäftsführenden Ausschusses der DGB-Arbeitsgemeinschaft," January 25 and May 2, 1969, ACDP/ 04–013/94/2; Heinz Bus, "Organisatorischer Geschäftsbericht" for the DGB-Arbeitsgemeinschaft for 1969–1970, pp. 2–3, ACDP/04–013/126; "Informationen der Sozialausschüsse der CDA," Nr. 14, May 22, 1969, LANRW/CDA Rheinland/610; Andrei S. Markovits, *The Politics of the West German Trade Unions: Strategies of Class and Interest Representation in Growth and Crisis* (Cambridge, 1986), pp. 112–114.

[38] "Informationen der Sozialausschüsse der CDU," Nr. 14, May 22, 1969, LANRW/CDA Rheinland/610; "Niederschrift über die Landesvorstandssitzung der Sozialausschüsse [Westfalens]," May 7, 1969, ACDP/03–002/128/1; Grundmann to Mick, May 16, 1969, NL Mick/6/1 (source of quotation).

CDU had no chance of winning, plus a secure nomination on the state list.[39] The CDU candidates disagreed sharply with each other about co-determination during the campaign, and Kiesinger appealed for patience with the effort to achieve consensus within their party when he addressed a national congress of the Social Committees on July 5. Norbert Blüm replied firmly that nobody could persuade the Social Committees to abandon their support for parity co-determination, which was based on lived experience.[40]

On September 28, 1969, the CDU and CSU won 46.1 percent of the national vote, a slight decline since 1965, while the SPD share rose to 42.7 percent; the FDP suffered heavy losses but still entered the Bundestag with 5.8 percent. The SPD and FDP commanded a small parliamentary majority, and Willy Brandt and the Free Democrat Walter Scheel quickly seized the initiative to form a coalition. The SPD had scored gains among white-collar workers, women, and young voters. In regional terms the most striking result was that the CDU lost to it by three points in North Rhine-Westphalia, which the CDU had carried by five points in 1965. As Barzel had warned his Bundestag delegation in March 1967, despite achieving "the most lovely results" in southern Germany and Lower Saxony, the CDU found itself in opposition, because it had failed to revive its popularity in Germany's most populous state.[41]

6.2   Adjusting to the Role of Opposition, 1969–1972

When Willy Brandt became the first Social Democratic chancellor since 1930, he told reporters that his would be a "government of domestic reforms," but the SPD and FDP agreed on little other than foreign policy. The leaders of the Social Committees guessed correctly that Brandt had

---

[39] "Niederschrift über die Vorstandssitzung der CDA Duisburg," October 4, 1968, "Niederschrift über die Sitzung des CDA-Hauptausschusses Duisburg," November 16, and Hans Görtz to the CDU Kreisparteivorstand, November 18, 1968, LANRW/CDA Rheinland/697.

[40] "Aktenvermerk für Herrn Bundesminister Hans Katzer," June 11, 1969, ACDP/04–013/86; CDU Bundesvorstand, June 20, 1969, *Vorstandsprotokolle 1965–69*, pp. 1478–1481; "Katzer warnt die Gegner der Mitbestimmung in der CDU," *Die Welt*, July 7, 1969, in "CDA Informationen: Pressestimmen zur 13. Bundestagung," LANRW/CDA Rheinland/621.

[41] "Niederschrift über die Sitzung des Landesvorstandes" of the Rhineland CDU, October 10, 1969, with attached "Analyse" by Wolfgang Vogt, NL Mick/6/1; Bruno Heck, "Zusammenfassender Bericht über die Nachuntersuchung zur Bundestagswahl 1969," CDU circular of February 23, 1970, NL Lücke/143/3; "Wahlen: Analyse," *Der Spiegel*, XXIII/#41 (October 6, 1969), pp. 36–44; Hildebrand, *Von Erhard zur Grossen Koalition*, pp. 400–404. For Barzel's warning, see above, p. 263.

promised the FDP not to extend parity co-determination, and they hoped to embarrass him by exposing the contradictions between the DGB program and the new cabinet's policies. Several members of the Rhineland Social Committees who belonged to IG Metall wrote its chair Otto Brenner already on October 4, 1969, to demand that he fight for parity co-determination even against party colleagues in the government, and he promised to do so. Brandt's government declaration to the Bundestag promised to "dare more democracy" but was vague about domestic policy and said nothing about co-determination in large corporations. The DGB noted this silence regarding its foremost policy demand but concluded charitably "that in contrast to all government declarations since 1949, this is the first time that the wishes of workers and their trade unions have been incorporated to a large extent." The Social Committees were doubtless correct that old bonds with the SPD created a euphoria among union functionaries unrelated to the details of cabinet personnel and policies.[42]

The leaders of the CDU closed ranks at their Mainz Party Congress in November 1969. Hans Katzer was dismayed by the abrupt end of his tenure as labor minister but resolved to consolidate his influence in the CDU. The Social Committees nominated him again as CDU vice chair and presented him as part of a "reform trio" including Helmut Kohl and Gerhard Stoltenberg, the youthful prime ministers of the Rhenish Palatinate and Schleswig-Holstein. All three men won election to the presidium by comfortable margins. The Social Committees' candidates Konrad Grundmann and Hermann Josef Russe failed to win election to the larger Central Committee, and this new rebuff for Grundmann led to his demotion from chair to vice chair of the Rhineland CDU, which demanded a leader with influence in the national party. Norbert Blüm did win a seat on the Central Committee, however, with Kohl's support;

---

[42] Undated "Fortsetzung des Protokolls der Bundesvorstandssitzung [der Sozialausschüsse]" from early October 1969, ACDP/04–013/25/2; Wilhelm Riether and friends to Otto Brenner, October 4, 1969, and reply of October 16, LANRW/CDA Rheinland/848; transcript of Brandt's Bundestag speech of October 28, 1969, http://dipbt.bundestag.de/doc/btp/06/06005.pdf, pp. 20–34, quotation on 20; DGB Bundesvorstand, October 7/8, 1969, and press release of October 28 in Klaus Mertsching, ed., *Quellen zur Geschichte der deutschen Gewerkschaftsbewegung im 20. Jahrhundert. Band XVI: Der Deutsche Gewerkschaftsbund 1969–1975* (Bonn, 2013; hereafter *Gewerkschaftsquellen*, XVI:), pp. 113–121 (DGB quotation on 121); "Mitbestimmung: Miese Dialektik," *Der Spiegel*, XXIII/#42 (October 13, 1969), pp. 44–47; CDA "Informationen," Nr. 19, November 5, 1969, NL Lücke/161/1; Karl Dietrich Bracher, Wolfgang Jäger, and Werner Link, *Republik im Wandel, 1969–1974: Geschichte der Bundesrepublik Deutschland: Band 5/1*, (Stuttgart, 1986), pp. 15–26; Arnulf Baring, *Machtwechsel. Die Ära Brandt-Scheel*, 3rd edn. (Stuttgart, 1982), pp. 148–199, 244–245; Hemmer and Schmitz, *Geschichte der Gewerkschaften*, pp. 273–279; Klaus Kempter, *Eugen Loderer und die IG Metall. Biografie eines Gewerkschafters* (Filderstadt, 2003), pp. 230–246.

Blüm then felt compelled to deny rumors that he had undermined Russe and functioned as Kohl's agent.[43] The Biedenkopf Commission presented its long-awaited report on co-determination to Chancellor Brandt on January 21, 1970, and its findings refuted many arguments by business lobbyists. In the unanimous judgment of the experts, based on testimony by hundreds of witnesses with practical experience, under the system of parity co-determination in coal and steel the workers' representatives on corporate supervisory boards sought above all to enhance the firm's efficiency, for the sake of higher wages and job security. All workers' representatives understood and accepted the rules of the market-oriented economy. They were more reluctant than other board members to endorse lay-offs, but senior managers agreed that their ability to gain approval of the strategy they considered necessary did not depend on whether workers' representatives occupied one-half or one-third of the board seats. Co-determination had preserved social peace without undermining the economic rationality of management decisions. The report concluded nevertheless that conditions in coal and steel were unique, and that parity co-determination would probably not succeed elsewhere. For other industries it proposed a twelve-member supervisory board in every corporation employing at least one thousand workers, with six members elected by the shareholders and four by workers; senior management would then nominate the last two, who must be approved by a majority on both sides. This approach had been suggested by the Evangelical Church in December 1968 as a method to encourage the search for consensus but assure shareholders a majority of seven to five in practice, because the last two seats could only be filled through a quid pro quo between capital and labor.[44]

---

[43] Elfriede Kaiser-Nebgen to Erich Kosthorst, November 6, 1969 (describing a conversation with Katzer), NL Katzer/305; report on preparations for the party congress by the Rhenish Social Committees in CDA "Informationen," Nr. 19, November 5, 1969, pp. 4-5, NL Lücke/161/1; "Ergebnis-Protokoll der Sitzung, Geschäftsführender Bundesvorstand [der Sozialausschüsse]," November 6, 1969, ACDP/04–013/15/2; CDU, *17. Bundesparteitag der CDU. Mainz, 17./18. November 1969* (Bonn, 1969), pp. 152–154, 165–166, 187; report on Grundmann's difficulties in the "C-inform" newsletter of November 27, 1969, p. 3, and "Ein Arbeiter war ihnen zu 'farblos'," *Welt der Arbeit*, November 28, 1969 (clippings in NL Mick/6/1); report by Blüm in the "Ergebnisprotokoll der Landessozialsekretärskonferenz," December 1/2, 1969, ACDP/04–013/119.

[44] "Mitbestimmung im Unternehmen. Bericht der Sachverständigenkommission zur Auswertung der bisherigen Erfahrungen bei der Mitbestimmung" (Bochum, January 1970), Bundestag *Drucksache* VI/334, esp. pp. 41–47 (available online at www.bundestag.de). See also "Sozialethische Erwägungen zur Mitbestimmung der Wirtschaft in der Bundesrepublik Deutschland. Eine Studie der Kammer für soziale Ordnung" (Hamburg, 1968), sent to all Bundestag delegates by the Evangelical Bishop Hermann Kunst on December 10, 1968, ACDP/08–005/67/2.

Hans Katzer sought to rally support for this recommendation. Biedenkopf had sent him the report five days before it was delivered to the chancellor, and Katzer told CDU leaders on January 23 that, while nobody was completely satisfied with its conclusions, nobody was truly dissatisfied either. It called for "more co-determination, both with respect to quality and the number of firms covered," and it advocated a model "essentially similar to that proposed by the Evangelical Church," which should reduce opposition. Heinz Vetter also offered a positive initial commentary to labor leaders, describing the Biedenkopf Model as a meaningful step toward parity. The central committees of the CDU and DGB both hesitated to endorse it, however, and powerful opposition soon mobilized. The leaders of big business declared that all members of corporate boards must be elected directly, with the shareholders guaranteed a majority. IG Metall and Norbert Blüm demanded genuine parity, however, and the DGB formally rejected the Biedenkopf Model on March 4. Adolf Müller later judged that it would have been enacted by an overwhelming Bundestag majority if the CDU had endorsed it promptly.[45]

CDU leaders soon became preoccupied with Willy Brandt's quest for détente with Communist regimes and found little time to discuss domestic policy. Kiesinger reported with alarm to party colleagues in April 1970 that Brandt might extend diplomatic recognition to the German Democratic Republic. As chancellor, Kiesinger had worked closely with Brandt to improve relations with East Germany, but he now displayed a passionate opposition to Brandt's *Ostpolitik* that gained support from the CSU and the leagues of ethnic Germans expelled from Eastern Europe. Norbert Blüm warned CDU leaders, however, that most younger Germans applauded *Ostpolitik*, and that the CDU would

---

[45] Biedenkopf to Katzer, January 16, 1970, ACDP/01–684/1/2; CDU Bundesvorstand, January 23, 1970, in Günter Buchstab and Denise Lindsay, eds., *Barzel: "Unsere Alternativen für die Zeit der Opposition." Die Protokolle des CDU-Bundesvorstands 1969–1973* (Düsseldorf, 2010; hereafter *Vorstandsprotokolle 1969–73*), pp. 157–161 (Katzer quotation on 158–159); DGB Bundesvorstand, February 3, 1970, *Gewerkschaftsquellen*, XVI: 198–200; Blüm's remarks in "Protokoll der Sozialsekretärskonferenz," February 2–4, 1970, ACDP/04–013/15/2; "Protokoll über die Beratung des Biedenkopf-Gutachtens durch den Arbeitskreis Mitbestimmung der Sozialausschüsse der CDA," February 27, 1970, ACDP/04–013/77/2; "DGB Bundesausschuss nimmt zum Biedenkopf-Gutachten Stellung," declaration of March 4, 1970, published in Karl Lauschke, ed., *Mehr Demokratie in der Wirtschaft. Die Entstehungsgeschichte des Mitbestimmungsgesetzes von 1976: Dokumente* (Düsseldorf, 2006), pp. 29–30; Vetter's speech of April 7, 1970, in Heinz Vetter, *Mitbestimmung –Idee, Wege, Ziel* (Cologne, 1979) pp. 36–58; Adolf Müller, "Mitbestimmung und Betriebsverfassung," manuscript of April 1971, published in the *Kolpingblatt* in June, ACDP/08–005/68/1; Karl Lauschke, *Mehr Demokratie in der Wirtschaft. Die Entstehungsgeschichte des Mitbestimmungsgesetzes von 1976* (Düsseldorf, 2006), pp. 54–55.

suffer from any polarizing debate over foreign policy.[46] Debates over foreign policy also took place within the Social Committees, but there a large majority agreed with Willy Brandt that old legal claims and "national rights" should be renounced to seek peaceful coexistence in today's Europe. Blüm predicted to a union congress in September 1970 that "the CDU too will be compelled to support this effort to build a bridge to the East, as long as it is built on the solid foundation of Western integration." Thus Jakob Kaiser's bridging metaphor from the year 1946 reentered political discourse, although Brandt differed from Kaiser in his willingness to improve ties with the German Democratic Republic, which Kaiser had always dismissed as a Soviet puppet.[47]

The CDU and CSU formed a joint panel in March 1970 to draft a co-determination bill in light of the Biedenkopf Report to reform both the elected factory councils and corporate supervisory boards. The small business lobbyist Thomas Ruf chaired the thirty-eight-member commission, and Norbert Blüm and Adolf Müller led the dozen representatives of the Social Committees. On April 20 Ruf proposed to publish a "statement of intent" to assist the CDU during the next state election campaigns, which promised to oppose any extension of parity co-determination beyond coal and steel. The labor representatives protested that only a party congress could issue such a pronouncement, and that it would cripple agitation among workers who were becoming disillusioned with the social-liberal government. Ruf's supporters replied that the FDP rejected parity co-determination emphatically, and the CDU must do likewise to avoid mass defections by businessmen.[48] Ruf held a weekend retreat in May 1970, where CSU colleagues demanded special representation outside the factory council for upper-level managers (leitende Angestellte). Current labor law classified the top-ranking managers as "employers" and everyone else as a blue- or white-collar "worker." The Social Committees and DGB opposed any recognition of

[46] CDU Bundesvorstand, April 23, 1970, Vorstandsprotokolle 1969–73, pp. 270–275; Werner Link, "Die CDU/CSU-Fraktion und die neue Ostpolitik in den Phasen der Regierungsverantwortung und der Opposition, 1966–1975," in Schwarz, Die Fraktion als Machtfaktor, pp. 116–139.

[47] "Bericht des ost- und deutschlandpolitischen Arbeitskreises ... zur CDA-Bundesvorstandssitzung am 17.1.1970," DGB-Archiv/5/DGCY000215; "Protokoll über die Sitzung des Geschäftsführenden Bundesvorstandes [der Sozialausschüsse]," February 16, 1970, and "Bundesvorstandssitzung der CDA," September 4, 1970, ACDP/04–013/15/2; Blüm's speech to the congress of IG Nahrung-Genuss, September 6, 1970, pp. 6–7 (enclosed in a circular by Zankl of October 26), ACDP/04–013/126.

[48] See the minutes of the joint meetings of the "Unterkommission Mitbestimmung der Programmkommission der CDU und der Arbeitsgruppe Mitbestimmung der CDU/CSU-Bundestagsfraktion" and the membership list of April 13, 1970, ACDP/08–005/68/2.

an intermediate group, because that would divide the labor force and weaken the factory council. The FDP had begun to court "upper-level managers," however, and the CSU resolved to compete for their support. When the Ruf Commission met again in June, the CSU representatives secured narrow majorities for their treatment of senior managers and the immediate publication of Ruf's "declaration of intent." The labor representatives publicly repudiated this declaration after Blüm reminded his colleagues that "for the Social Committees, parity belongs to our very essence."[49]

Katzer complained in a private meeting with Heinz Vetter in May 1970 that the passivity of the DGB crippled the efforts by the Social Committees to support co-determination. He was dismayed to hear Vetter explain that the DGB had decided to educate its own members about the issue, "because the mass of workers is not yet prepared to demonstrate for it." Only after a year or eighteen months would organized labor resume the campaign to influence public opinion. Vetter also noted that "the DGB cannot attack the SPD government sharply" without causing internal divisions.[50] Katzer complained repeatedly to the press thereafter that the DGB failed to defend its own program against the current government, and even some Social Democrats at DGB headquarters condemned Vetter's idea that they should refrain for eighteen months from efforts to mobilize public opinion. Katzer attracted enough publicity to goad Herbert Wehner into denouncing him as a "swindler" who had done nothing to help workers as labor minister but now made promises that he could not fulfill.[51]

After losing confidence in the Ruf Commission, the Social Committees sought new allies to influence the CDU program being drafted by a commission under Helmut Kohl. Their leaders conferred at length with Kurt Biedenkopf, leaders of the Young Union, the Ring of Christian Democratic Students, and Bavarian colleagues in the CSU Social Committees. They accepted Biedenkopf's advice to exclude government representatives from corporate supervisory boards (as proposed by

---

[49] "Kurzprotokoll über die Klausurtagung," May 1–4, 1970, "Kurzprotokoll über die Sitzung der kleinen Arbeitsgruppe 'Leitende Angestellte' der Mitbestimmungskommission," June 8, and "Kurzprotokoll über die Klausurtagung," June 22–25, 1970, ACDP/08–005/68/2; "Protokoll der Bundesvorstandssitzung [der Sozialausschüsse]," June 27, 1970, pp. 9–11 (source of Blüm quotation), ACDP/04–013/15/2; Adolf Müller, "Das neue Betriebsverfassungsgesetz," speech of December 5, 1971, pp. 2–3, ACDP/08–005/68/3.

[50] Heinz Bus, "Protokollentwurf, gemeinsame Sitzung der Bundesvorstände der Sozialausschüsse und des Deutschen Gewerkschaftsbundes" on May 21, 1970, ACDP/04–013/86 (quotations on p. 3).

[51] "Katzer/Wehner: Spielen und gaunern," Der Spiegel, XXIV/#48 (November 23, 1970), p. 42; "Notiz über die Sitzung des [DGB] Arbeitsausschusses zur Durchführung der Mitbestimmungskampagne," January 11, 1971, DGB-Archiv/5/DGCS000011.

Hermann Josef Wallraff), embracing instead a model developed by the Cologne industrialist Heinz Horn to elect an equal number of representatives of workers and shareholders, and then add three directors of the firm to break possible ties. The Horn Model broke with the German legal tradition of strict separation between management and oversight to propose a body resembling a British or American board of directors, with some top managers on the board, but with the addition of workers' representatives. The Social Committees hoped to attract business support for this model because of the likelihood that top managers would side with the shareholders. The CDU Business Council denounced the Horn Model as "worse than parity," however, because shareholders would only control a minority of seats.[52] When the CDU Program Commission met on September 30, 1970, the motion by the Social Committees was defeated by a vote of twenty-eight to twelve. Katzer warned, however, that the idea of parity co-determination would continue to be discussed no matter what it decided, so the commission agreed to present the Horn Model to the next party congress as a "minority report," while the majority endorsed the Biedenkopf Model. The Social Committees assumed thereafter that the mildly progressive Biedenkopf plan was the worst possible outcome if they continued to agitate for parity.[53]

Many business lobbyists argued that Kohl's majority and minority reports both went too far, and the conservative leader of the Hessian CDU, Alfred Dregger, championed that position. On December 21 Dregger persuaded the CDU Hessian state committee to endorse a motion for the party congress inspired by the Business Council of the CDU that simply granted the shareholders seven board seats and the workers five. The Frankfurt corporate lawyer Engelbert van de Loo orchestrated a campaign for this motion that included a direct appeal to Helmut Kohl by Bernhard Timm, the general director of the BASF plant in Ludwigshafen who had given Kohl his first job as a lobbyist for the chemical industry. Van de Loo informed Rainer Barzel

---

[52] "Protokoll der Bundesvorstandssitzung der Sozialausschüsse," April 25, 1970, and "Referat Prof. Dr. Biedenkopf und Diskussion," ACDP/04–013/124/2; Biedenkopf to Katzer, April 27, 1970, and reply of May 4, ACDP/01–684/1/2; Norbert Blüm, "Aktenvermerk" for Katzer, August 27, 1970, ACDP/04–013/86; minutes of the leadership conferences of the Social Committees on July 17, September 3, and September 4, 1970, ACDP/04–013/15/2; "Vorschlag des Bundesvorstandes der Sozialausschüsse zum Programmentwurf der CDU," September 4, 1970, and press release by the "Wirtschaftsrat der CDU" on September 8, ACDP/08–005/68/2; reports in *Der Spiegel*, XXIV/#37 (September 7, 1970), pp. 27–28, and XXIV/#38 (September 14, 1970), pp 30–31.
[53] "Informationen der Sozialausschüsse," September 30, 1970, ACDP/04–032/13/2; transcript of a television interview of Helmut Kohl and Heinrich Köppler, September 30, 1970, ACDP/08–005/68/2.

confidentially that Kohl promised not to "go to the trenches" to defend his own motion.[54] Dregger told the Düsseldorf CDU Party Congress in January 1971 that he belonged to no "party wing" or interest group but believed that the time had come for the "until now silent majority" of CDU members to bring the emotional debate over co-determination to a close. The Biedenkopf Model left the outcome of its procedures uncertain, while the parity demanded by the Social Committees would stifle economic growth, grant excessive power to the trade unions, and contradict the wishes of CDU voters. In reply Katzer, Blüm, and Adolf Müller cited the evidence from the Biedenkopf Report about the success of parity co-determination in coal and steel. Kohl's "majority report" was virtually ignored in this debate, and Josef Mick observed sarcastically that Dregger's silent majority obviously included the CDU leadership. The motion by the Social Committees suffered defeat by a vote of 111 to 411, a predictable result, but then something unexpected happened; the chair called next for a vote on Dregger's motion, which won narrowly, and Kohl's majority report never even came to a vote.[55]

The Social Committees felt betrayed, because Kohl himself and most other party leaders had voted for Dregger's motion in a public show of hands. Kohl insisted that he had simply blundered; returning to the congress hall from an interview with journalists, he saw Kiesinger and other party leaders raise their hands and assumed that they were voting on his motion. Norbert Blüm told reporters nevertheless that this congress gave the world the impression that the CDU had become a "businessman's party." Numerous letters of complaint after the congress by Catholic workers' clubs, Social Committees, and Christian Democratic factory cells expressed disillusionment with the CDU.[56] Katzer and

---

[54] Katzer's report in "Beschlussprotokoll der Bundesvorstandssitzung der Sozialausschüsse," December 12, 1970, ACDP/04–013/15/2; "CDU-Programm: Angst vor so was," *Der Spiegel*, XXIV/#50 (December 7, 1970), pp. 32–33; Christian Schwarz-Schilling to Otto Zink, January 11, 1971, ACDP/03–032/13/2; Otto Zink's circular to the Hessian Social Committees, January 5, 1971, ACDP/04–032/13/2; van de Loo to Rainer Barzel, November 23, 1970, and January 21, 1971, with attached photocopies of letters by Timm to Kohl on January 14, and H. Ley to Alfred Dregger on January 7, ACDP/08–005/119/2; Hans-Peter Schwarz, *Helmut Kohl. Eine politische Biographie* (Munich, 2012), pp. 90, 158.

[55] CDU, *18. Bundesparteitag der CDU. Düsseldorf, 25.– 27. Januar 1971* (Bonn, no date), pp. 249–275 (Dregger quotation on 257), 288–293, 298–300, 303–313.

[56] Interview with Blüm, *Der Spiegel*, XXV/#6 (February 1, 1971), p. 22 (source of quotation); CDA Rheinland, "Information," Nr. 4, February 11, 1971, ACDP/04–032/35/6; letters of complaint to Dregger from February 1971 in ACDP/04–032/35/6; Friedrich Högger to Bruno Heck, February 16, 1971, NL Blank/15; Sozialausschuss Ortsgruppe Bruchsal to CDU Bundesvorstand, February 9, 1971, ACDP/04–013/23; KAB Verbandsvorstand meetings of February 15 and March 18, 1971, with attached letters of complaint from member clubs, KAB Archiv/1/8; Schwarz, *Helmut Kohl*, pp. 158–159.

Blüm persuaded most activists in the Social Committees, however, to carry on the struggle for influence in their party. Katzer revealed in a closed meeting with colleagues that CDU leaders had experienced "strong pressure from business," exerted primarily through the CSU, which had "blackmailed" them with threats to dissolve their joint Bundestag delegation if the CDU endorsed parity. "This debate must be carried on," he concluded. Instead of retreating, the Social Committees must persuade their Bundestag delegation to present legislative proposals more attractive to organized labor than those of the social-liberal government.[57]

Willy Brandt's government declaration had ignored the issue of co-determination on corporate supervisory boards but did promise to strengthen the powers of the elected factory councils. The FDP flatly rejected, however, the labor ministry's proposals to update the Factory Councils Law of 1952. The coalition parties published a compromise bill in November 1970 disappointing to organized labor. The CDU's Ruf Commission then proposed a bill in January 1971 that was unfavorable to labor in some ways but did grant factory councils stronger powers to protect workers from dismissal and improved access to information about economic decisions by management.[58] The Social Committees protested against the anti-labor features in the CDU bill and deluged their Bundestag delegation with petitions. At the last minute, Rainer Barzel secured the inclusion of two of Katzer's demands in the final CDU bill submitted to the Bundestag on February 6: that there be no special representation in the factory for upper-level managers, and that workers retain the right to elect some union experts as their representatives on corporate supervisory boards.[59]

[57] "Protokoll der Bundesvorstandssitzung [der Sozialausschüsse]," February 27, 1971, three-page typescript, ACDP/04–013/15/2. See also Blüm's report to Katzer on conditions in the CSU, February 16, 1971, ACDP/04–013/149/4, and Blüm's circular of March 2, 1971, to the "CDA Arbeitskreis Mitbestimmung," ACDP/04–013/77/2.

[58] DGB Bundesvorstand, July 7, September 7, and December 1, 1970, Gewerkschaftsquellen, XVI: 300, 307–308, 344–345; "Notiz über die Sitzung der [DGB] Kommission zur Durchführung der Mitbestimmungskampagne," November 30, 1970, DGB-Archiv/5/DGCS000011; Ruf Commission minutes for December 1970-January 1971, ACDP/08–005/68/2; Adolf Müller, "Mitbestimmung und Betriebsverfassung," manuscript completed in March/April 1971 and published in the Kolpingblatt in June, ACDP/08–005/68/1.

[59] Katzer to Thomas Ruf, December 16 and December 22, 1970, ACDP/01–684/5/2; petitions to the CDU Bundestag delegation from the Social Committees and KAB, January/February 1971, ACDP/08–005/119/1; Thomas Ruf, "Was will die CDU in der Betriebsverfassung?" speech of December 22, 1970, and Katzer to Rainer Barzel, February 2, 1971, ACDP/08–005/68/2; CDU Bundestag delegation, February 1, 1971, pp. 3–4, and February 5, pp. 1–5, ACDP/08–001/1025/1; "Katzer: Arbeitnehmer wurden überstimmt," Kölner Stadt-Anzeiger, Nr. 31, February 6/7, 1971 (ACDP/08–005/119/2);

The DGB experts on labor law judged that both the government and CDU bills were unacceptable, but the union press only attacked the latter. Otto Brenner became especially harsh when he denounced the CDU bill for being "anti-worker," "anti-union," and "anti-democratic."[60] The Social Committees gained much publicity for their complaints that the DGB judged these bills with a double standard, and they achieved a breakthrough in March 1971 when DGB leaders extracted a pledge from Willy Brandt to "adopt the better passages from the CDU draft into the government bill." Heinz Vetter then addressed the national congress of the Social Committees in July to praise their record, and he met privately with their leaders to plan legislative strategy. Soon thereafter Adolf Müller secured large majorities on the Bundestag labor committee for a half dozen CDU amendments to the government bill, most notably to strengthen the factory council's power to protect workers from dismissal. Thomas Ruf declared nevertheless that "the CDU/CSU is not satisfied with the result . . ., after so many of its motions were rejected." The Social Committees and KAB replied that the CDU should claim credit for having greatly improved this popular bill and vote for it.[61]

CDA Rheinland, "Information," Nr. 4, February 11, 1971, ACDP/04–032/35/6; "Mitbestimmung: Schlucken oder machen," *Der Spiegel*, XXV/#7 (February 8, 1971), pp. 24–25.

[60] "Zum mündlichen Vortrag in der Bundesvorstandssitzung zum Thema Gesellschaftspolitik," briefing paper for Vetter by Friedhelm Farthmann, December 1, 1970, DGB-Archiv /5/DGAI000406; DGB Bundesvorstand, December 1, 1970, *Gewerkschaftsquellen*, XVI: 344–345; "Notiz über die Sitzung des Arbeitsausschusses zur Durchführung der Mitbestimmungskampagne," February 15, 1971, DGB-Archiv/5/DGCS000011; "CDA DOKUMENTATION: Parteipolitische Unabhängigkeit der Gewerkschaften," March 29, 1971 (quotation on pp. 4–5 from a letter sent by Brenner to Adolf Müller and other CDU workers' representatives), ACDP/04–013/149/4.

[61] "Begegnung des [DGB] geschäftsführenden Bundesvorstandes mit den CDU-Sozialausschüssen," March 25, 1971 (briefing paper for Vetter), DGB-Archiv/5/ DGCY000197; "Protokollentwurf über die gemeinsame Sitzung der Geschäftsführenden Bundesvorstände der Sozialausschüsse der CDA und des DGB," March 26, 1971 (quotation on p. 2 from the report by Gerd Muhr on what Willy Brandt had recently promised DGB leaders), ACDP/04–013/102; press clippings on the Social Committees' congress of July 2–4, 1971, in ACDP/04–032/14/1; "14. Bundestagung der Sozialausschüsse der CDA," report for DGB leaders in DGB-Archiv/5/DGAK000036; Norbert Blüm, "Aktenvermerk: Gespräch Vetter, Tacke, Otto, Katzer, Blüm," July 13, 1971, ACDP/04–013/149/4; Ruf's pamphlet published on July 26, 1971, "CDU/CSU-Entwurf eines Gesetzes über die Mitbestimmung der Arbeitnehmer . . . und Entwurf der Bundesregierung eines Betriebsverfassungsgesetzes. Eine Darstellung der wichtigsten Unterschiede," ACDP/08–005/68/1; letter by Thomas Ruf to all CDU/CSU Bundestag delegates, September 22, 1971 (Ruf quotation on p. 9), ACDP/ 08–005/119/2; petitions to the CDU Bundestag delegation from the KAB and Social Committees favoring the bill in ACDP/08–005/136/1.

Rainer Barzel appealed to his Bundestag delegation on October 19, 1971, for unified opposition to the government factory councils bill. He noted that the SPD insisted on unity even when its trade unionists were asked to vote for bills that contradicted the DGB program; the CDU must display similar discipline if it hoped to persuade the voters to entrust it with power.[62] Katzer soon persuaded Barzel, however, that a unanimous vote in the Bundestag could only be achieved through abstention, and that it would be better to allow the majority to vote No and twenty-one delegates from the CDU's left wing to vote Yes in the Bundestag on November 10. I G Metall then acknowledged that the final law was a great improvement over the government bill, and it published an honor roll of the CDU delegates who had advanced labor's cause. Adolf Müller felt that the courageous stand taken by this group "made such a powerful impression on the trade unions and in the factories that the 'No' by the large majority of the CDU/CSU delegation has receded into the background." He expressed regret, however, that only one-third of the nominal members of the CDU Workers' Group had taken this stand.[63] Some disillusionment with the social-liberal government became evident in the factory council elections of March/April 1972, and in the 349 large factories with a Christian Democratic factory cell, the proportion of "Christian social" council members rose from 10.5 to 16.5 percent. The Social Committees now had some evidence that their campaign to expose contradictions between the DGB program and cabinet policies was undermining Willy Brandt's popularity.[64]

The political strategy of the Social Committees was disrupted when the CDU provoked a fateful confrontation with the government over foreign policy. In February 1972 the Bundestag began to debate Willy Brandt's "Eastern Treaties" with the USSR and Poland, which renounced any attempt to alter European borders by force. Rainer Barzel had recently defeated Helmut Kohl in an election for the CDU chairmanship in October 1971, and then won approval by the CSU as the joint CDU/CSU chancellor candidate. To win the support of conservatives, Barzel argued passionately that the Eastern Treaties would have disastrous

---

[62] CDU Bundestag delegation, October 19, 1971, pp. 5–6, ACDP/08–001/1027/1.

[63] CDU Bundestag delegation, November 10, 1971, pp. 1–6, ACDP/08–001/1027/2; *Metall*, #24 (1971), p. 15 (NL Tacke/11/1); Adolf Müller, "Das neue Betriebsverfassungsgesetz," speech of December 5, 1971, pp. 7, 18–19, ACDP/08–005/68/3.

[64] Heinz Bus, "Vorläufige statistische Auswertung der Ergebnisse der Betriebsratswahl 1972," June 2, 1972, and "Abschlussbericht" of August 1972, pp. 21–22, 32–34, ACDP/04–013/127/2. These figures were not based on a scientific sample, of course, but the same technique of measurement had indicated stagnation or decline after the last three factory council elections.

consequences.[65] In April 1972 the government lost its Bundestag majority because of defections to the CDU by several FDP delegates opposed
to *Ostpolitik*. Opinion polls showed that over 75 percent of West German
voters supported the treaties, however, and Barzel's own discussions with
foreign leaders showed that the NATO allies regarded the opposition to
the treaties as a disturbing revival of old-fashioned German nationalism.
Barzel therefore arrived at the surprising conclusion that Willy Brandt
must be toppled, so that a government led by himself could ratify the
Eastern Treaties and preserve the NATO alliance. He never explained to
the public his conversion into a supporter of *Ostpolitik*, however, and most
observers assumed that he sought to prevent ratification. Hans Katzer
and Norbert Blüm implored CDU leaders to avoid any attempt to topple
Brandt. Blüm assured them that the SPD was losing support among
workers because of its ineffective economic policy; this erosion could only
be halted if a grab for power by the CDU allowed Social Democrats to
argue that chauvinists had toppled a great man of peace through shady
political deals. Barzel retorted that it would be more dangerous to allow
Willy Brandt and his allies in the DGB to abuse their powers of office
and defame their opponents until elections were required in 1973.
The CDU Bundestag delegation therefore moved on April 27 that
Barzel should replace Brandt as chancellor, but Barzel fell two votes
short of victory, because three members of his own delegation withheld
support. Spontaneous strikes in support of Brandt broke out in some
cities on the day of the vote, and as Blüm feared, most newspapers
reported that chauvinists had sought to topple a great man of peace
through shady political deals.[66]

In May Barzel persuaded Brandt to declare that the Eastern Treaties
were not intended to renounce the German people's right to self-
determination, and Barzel recommended that CDU Bundestag delegates
ratify them. Franz Josef Strauss insisted, however, that the CDU and
CSU both recommend abstention, with the condition that no Aye votes
would be tolerated, only Nays. On May 17 most Christian Democrats did

---

[65] See Barzel's inflammatory speech to the CDU Bundestag delegation, September 21,
1971, pp. 6–17, ACDP/08–001/1027/1; Geoffrey Pridham, *Christian Democracy in
Western Germany: The CDU/CSU in Government and Opposition, 1945–1976* (London,
1977), pp. 194–202; Hans-Otto Kleinmann, *Geschichte der CDU 1945–1982* (Stuttgart,
1993), pp. 322–333; and Manfred Uschner, *Die Ostpolitik der SPD* (Berlin, 1991),
pp. 57–100.

[66] CDU Bundesvorstand, April 24, 1972, *Vorstandsprotokolle 1969–73*, pp. 753–762,
774–783; CDU circular by Konrad Kraske, April 25, 1972, NL Lücke/144/1; Bracher,
Jäger, Link, *Republik im Wandel*, pp. 67–74; Baring, *Machtwechsel*, pp. 396–447; Peter
Koch, *Willy Brandt. Eine politische Biographie* (Frankfurt a.M., 1989), pp. 443–457;
Barzel, *Erinnerungen*, pp. 280–294.

abstain, assuring the treaties' passage, but several voted No. Katzer published a soothing declaration that the Eastern Treaties had been ratified "with the help of the Union," but the leader of the Young Christian Democratic Workers of the Rhineland wrote him that nobody in the factories could understand their party's maneuvers. Other reports confirmed that the CDU's attempt to topple Brandt alienated many workers and revived the sense of solidarity between trade unionists and the SPD.[67]

The debate over foreign policy also doomed the Social Committees' efforts to groom Adolf Müller for promotion within the DGB. At Katzer's urging, Bernhard Tacke notified Heinz Vetter in March 1972 that Müller was the candidate of the Christian Democratic minority to succeed him as DGB vice chair at the next union congress in June. Müller stumbled into controversy, however, after joining a unanimous vote by the DGB National Committee in February to urge ratification of the Eastern Treaties. Several newspapers reported that, for the first time, a CDU Bundestag delegate had committed himself to their support, but Müller responded that he had only cast a "proxy vote" for an absent superior and had not decided how to vote as a Bundestag delegate. That explanation was inaccurate – Müller was a full-fledged delegate at the conference, free to vote as he wished – and most union colleagues believed that he had switched positions because of pressure from the CDU.[68] The chairmen of the DGB-affiliated unions received many reports of growing opposition to Müller and agreed in May that they would not nominate him, because he could not win election. Katzer insisted, however, that the minority must be free to choose its own candidate, and that the DGB must elect Müller to demonstrate its independence from the SPD. Many Christian Democratic DGB functionaries concluded that Katzer's hard line jeopardized their few remaining power bastions, and

---

[67] CDU circular from Konrad Kraske, May 4, 1972, NL Lücke/144/1; CDU Bundesvorstand, May 15, 1972, *Vorstandsprotokolle 1969–73*, pp. 827–29; Katzer, "Ostverträge mit Hilfe der Union," *Soziale Ordnung*, XXVI/#5 (May 26, 1972), p. 2; Herbert Metzger to Katzer, May 26, 1972, NL Mick/9/4; Heinz Bus, "Abschlussbericht Betriebsratswahl 1972," August 1972, p. 33, ACDP/04–013/29/1; "Notiz über die Besprechung mit Vertretern der Sozialausschüsse der CDU am 24.5.72 im [DGB] Landesbezirk [Niedersachsen]," DGB-Archiv/5/DGAI001796; Bracher, Jäger, Link, *Republik im Wandel*, pp. 60–67; Werner Link, "Ostpolitik," in Schwarz, *Die Fraktion als Machtfaktor*, pp. 129–133; Kempter, *Eugen Loderer*, pp. 240–243.

[68] CDA "Dokumentation zur Nachfolge des stellvertretenden Bundesvorsitzenden des Deutschen Gewerkschaftsbundes," attached to the minutes of the "Geschäftsführende Bundesvorstand" of June 22, 1972, and Bernhard Tacke's rebuttal, "Zur Dokumentation: Einige grundsätzliche Ausführungen," ACDP/04–013/29/1; reports in *Der Spiegel*, XXVI/#7 (February 7, 1972), p. 24, and XXVI/#18 (April 24, 1972), pp. 50–52.

on June 16 Karl-Heinz Hoffmann persuaded nine of the thirteen leaders of their association to nominate Maria Weber as DGB vice chair, with Martin Heiss of the textile workers' union as their second candidate for the executive committee. Weber was very active in Catholic organizations but not the CDU and therefore did not face opposition.[69]

Katzer insisted that Adolf Müller could win election if his party colleagues remained united, and he secured a harsh condemnation by the Social Committees on June 22 of this "decision by a few Christian Democratic trade union colleagues at a private discussion" to withdraw support from Müller, an act which "caused the public to have doubts about the reliability of these colleagues." Müller's friends also denounced several long-time colleagues for betraying him out of shameful careerism. When Weber and Heiss were elected at the DGB congress nevertheless, *Social Order* termed the rejection of Müller an act of "collective stupidity."[70] This dispute gravely weakened the network of alliances between politicians and union functionaries that Katzer and Tacke had developed in the 1960s. Tacke became so angry over the resolution doubting his reliability that he compared his treatment by Katzer to what he had experienced in 1933. Maria Weber took charge of the Association of Christian Democratic DGB Trade Unionists soon thereafter and sent word to Katzer that many union colleagues were considering resignation from the CDU because of his imperious conduct.[71] Katzer's prestige among trade unionists sank so low that his Cologne local of the Public Service and Transport Workers' Union voted in October 1972 to expel him for "conduct harmful to the union." Katzer responded that he had fought for twenty-five years to preserve

---

[69] Eugen Stotz of IG Druck to Heinz Vetter, May 24, 1972, DGB-Archiv/5/DGAI001796; conflicting accounts in Adolf Müller's "Aktennotiz" of June 19, 1972, Horst Kowalak to Karl-Heinz Vorbrücken, June 22, and Hanshorst Viehof to Wilhelm Rieter, June 23, 1972, NL Breidbach/4; Adolf Müller's undated "Stellungnahme" in NL Breidbach/1; Stefan Remeke, *Anders links sein. Auf den Spuren von Maria Weber und Gerd Muhr* (Essen, 2012), pp. 285–333.

[70] "Protokoll der Sitzung des Geschäftsführenden Bundesvorstandes [der Sozialausschüsse]," with attached "Entschliessung" (source of quotation), June 22, 1972, ACDP/ 04–013/29/1; Bernhard Tacke's circular to the Social Committees, July 13, 1972, NL Tacke/12/3; Wilhelm Riether to Katzer, June 20, 1972, NL Breidbach/4; "Gewerkschaften: Erpressung verboten," and "Wie Benediktinerinnen," *Der Spiegel*, XXVI/#25 (June 12, 1972), pp. 75–76, and XXVI/#27 (June 26, 1972), p. 59; Lutz Esser, "Einheit ohne Realitätswert," *Soziale Ordnung*, XXVI/#7 (July 1972), pp. 8–9.

[71] Minutes of the conference of September 7, 1972, between the Social Committees and the "Arbeitsgemeinschaft Christlich-Demokratischer Gewerkschafter," ACDP/01–684/24; Heinz Bus, "Vermerk" for Katzer on January 2 and January 25, 1973, on his talks with DGB colleagues, ACDP/04–013/149/4; "Beschlussprotokoll über die Sitzung des Geschäftsführenden Ausschusses der DGB-Arbeitsgemeinschaft," January 31, 1973, DGB-Archiv/5/DGCS000098.

labor unity, and Karl-Heinz Hoffmann intervened to quash this expulsion verdict.[72]

Despite the failure of Barzel's motion of no confidence, Chancellor Brandt still lacked a Bundestag majority and soon arranged for new elections. The CDU/CSU voting share declined from 46.1 to 44.9 percent in November 1972, while the SPD overtook them for the first time with 45.8 percent, and the FDP rose to 8.4 percent. The CDU suffered its worst losses among Catholic workers. Its analyst Werner Kaltefleiter noted that they had experienced conflicting influences ever since the 1890s from the Catholic Church and their trade unions. In recent years, he concluded, "the Church has in general lost significance as a norm-defining institution, while the partisan political engagement of the trade unions on behalf of the SPD became stronger during the 1972 Bundestag election. Because of these trends, the magnetic attraction among Catholic workers shifted toward the SPD." Franz Varelmann, the leader of the Social Committees in Lower Saxony, rejected such fatalistic reflections about long-term trends, however, to focus attention on recent decisions by the CDU which created the impression that it rejected all progressive ideas.[73] Ferdi Breidbach conducted an energetic campaign in the blue-collar city of Duisburg and developed a powerful argument that the government's economic policy harmed workers, but the local SPD defeated the CDU by a demoralizing 43 percentage points. Breidbach and Adolf Müller returned to the Bundestag via their state nominations lists nevertheless, and Norbert Blüm won a seat for the Rhenish Palatinate. Breidbach was dismissed from his job at DGB headquarters shortly before the election, however, and he later recalled that a "genuine anxiety psychosis" regarding Franz Josef Strauss swept through the Ruhr during the campaign.[74]

Kaltefleiter was correct that the DGB supported the SPD with unprecedented fervor in this campaign. As in previous years, it sent a policy

[72] Press release by Heinz Soenius for the Cologne CDU, Katzer to Frau Liselotte-Maria Doebelt, October 28, 1972, and Katzer to the ÖTV Kreisverband Köln, October 31, 1972, ACDP/04–013/81/2; Tilman Mayer, "Gerechtigkeit schafft Frieden," p. 31.

[73] Bracher, Jäger, Link, *Republik im Wandel*, pp. 86–91; Werner Kaltefleiter, "Die Bundestagswahl 1972," January 1973, quotation from pp. 90–91, NL Lücke/145; Varelmann to Barzel, November 24, 1972, ACDP/01–684/14/3.

[74] Breidbach's stump speech, "Deutscher Gewerkschaftsbund, SPD, CDU/CSU," NL Breidbach/21; Rüdiger May, "Bundestagswahlkampf und Bundestagswahl 1972 [in Duisburg]: Eine Erste Bilanz," November 1972, NL Breidbach/1; "Gemeinsam werden wir ihn schaffen," *Der Spiegel*, XXVI/#49 (November 27, 1972), pp. 25–33; Breidbach to Barzel, December 1, 1972, ACDP/01–684/24; Breidbach, "Die politische Bewusstseinslage bei der Bevölkerung des Ruhrgebiets aus der Sicht der CDA," report to the Social Committees of the Rhineland, November 5, 1975, pp. 8–9, LANRW/CDA Rheinland/704.

questionnaire to every Bundestag candidate, and Rainer Barzel offered a carefully worded response for the CDU. Heinz Vetter departed from precedent, however, by publishing an emphatic refutation of each paragraph in Barzel's reply.[75] In early November the DGB county committee for Hannover issued leaflets on *Ostpolitik* and co-determination that linked Barzel with a scowling Franz Josef Strauss, and a smiling Willy Brandt with Heinz Vetter. On November 10 a DGB press release asserted that Barzel "sails in the wake of the right-wing nationalist Franz Strauss." These actions outraged Maria Weber, and two weeks before the election she persuaded her eight top-ranking CDU colleagues in the DGB to sign a protest letter to Vetter regarding the unions' loss of independence from the SPD. Vetter took great satisfaction in the SPD election victory, however, and felt no sense of urgency about addressing Weber's concerns; the conference she requested took over three years to arrange.[76]

6.3   The Co-Determination Law of 1976

From the perspective of the Social Committees, the one positive development during the election campaign of 1972 was the decision by the DGB to resume public agitation for parity co-determination. Heinz Vetter raised the issue in a private meeting with Willy Brandt the day after the election and informed his colleagues that "the DGB and trade unions will need to exert massive pressure in the co-determination issue." This demand enjoyed unprecedented support in the new Bundestag, where 48 percent of the delegates belonged to a DGB-affiliated union, and the SPD controlled 242 of 518 seats. The Social Committees would only need to deliver eighteen votes from the CDU to give the SPD an absolute majority. Willy Brandt's second government declaration also promised, unlike the first, to strengthen the organs of

---

[75] DGB "Wahlprüfsteine" sent by Vetter to Barzel on September 6, 1972, Barzel's reply of September 15, and "DGB-Wahlforderungen: Analyse des Antwortschreibens des CDU-Vorsitzenden Rainer Barzel," DGB-Archiv/5/DGAI001978; Vetter's open letter to Barzel of September 29, 1972, DGB-Archiv/5/DGCS000078.

[76] Norbert Blüm, "Totaler Wahlkampf," *Soziale Ordnung*, XXVI/#10 (October 31, 1972), p. 3; Heinz Bus to Vetter, November 8, 1972, with enclosed leaflets from Hannover, and reply by Dr. Bernd Otto on November 14, DGB-Archiv/5/DGCS000100; "Barzel versprach Fairness – er hält sie nicht," DGB press release of November 10, 1972, DGB-Archiv/5/DGCS00078; Maria Weber and colleagues, "An die Mitglieder des Bundesvorstandes des Deutschen Gewerkschaftsbundes. Betr.: Unabhängigkeit des DGB," November 2, 1972, and follow-up letter by Weber to her co-signers in mid-November, DGB-Archiv/5/DGCS000096; report by Vetter to the DGB Bundesausschuss, December 6, 1972, *Gewerkschaftsquellen*, XVI: 620–21; circular by Weber to CDU colleagues in the DGB, August 20, 1973, DGB-Archiv/5/DGCS000096.

co-determination based on the principle of equal rights for capital and labor.[77]

Helmut Kohl succeeded Barzel as CDU chair in June 1973, teamed with Kurt Biedenkopf as secretary general, and he sought to unify the party as it prepared for a congress in November to adopt a new program. The Social Committees gained pledges of support that summer for their Horn Model for parity co-determination from the KAB, the Young Union, the Ring of Christian Democratic Students, and the CDU state committees of the Rhineland, Westphalia, Saarland, and Oldenburg. As the newly elected chair of the Workers' Group in the CDU Bundestag delegation, Adolf Müller met twice with Kohl and Biedenkopf in September to explain that adoption of a party congress resolution intolerable for the Social Committees would cause great unrest; some activists in the Social Committees had even begun to discuss founding a new party. In October Katzer and Heinz Vetter issued a joint press release that the Social Committees and DGB agreed completely in support of parity co-determination. Katzer also arranged for Kohl to meet with Maria Weber and Martin Heiss of the DGB, who complained that the CDU never consulted them. Kohl promised to confer with the Association of Christian Democratic DGB Trade Unionists regularly in future, and he endorsed a plan to elect an equal number of representatives of capital and labor to corporate supervisory boards, provided that one "workers' representative" was an upper-level manager.[78]

Kohl's motion was certainly an improvement over the CDU's last co-determination resolution in January 1971, but Norbert Blüm told the press that it was really a plan for "parity with emergency exits," because the details guaranteed that the shareholders would have the final say. Blüm and Katzer led a fight at the Hamburg Party Congress for genuine parity. The press reported the outcome as a crushing defeat

---

[77] "Wir sind parteipolitisch unabhängig," interview with Vetter in *Der Spiegel*, XXVI/#45 (October 30, 1972), pp. 54–62; DGB Bundesvorstand, November 21, 1972, *Gewerkschaftsquellen*, XVI: 606–607 (source of quotation); Lauschke, *Mehr Demokratie*, pp. 61–66.

[78] "Denkmodelle zur Parteienkonstellation," memo by an aide to Ferdi Breidbach on the possibility of founding a new political party, sent by Breidbach to Hans Katzer on June 20, 1972, ACDP/01-684/24; Fritz Burgbacher to Katzer, May 14, 1973, and Kurt Biedenkopf to Katzer, May 15, ACDP/01-684/24; Adolf Müller, "Aktennotiz. Betr.: Gespräch Arbeitnehmergruppe der CDU/CSU-Bundestagsfraktion mit dem Generalsekretär der CDU Prof. Dr. Kurt Biedenkopf," written on October 23, 1973, ACDP/01-684/25/1; "CDA einig mit dem DGB," joint press release of October 16, 1973, and commentary by Lutz Esser, *Soziale Ordnung*, XXVII/#11 (November 12, 1973), p. 8; "Besprechung am 18.10.1973" of Kohl, Katzer, Maria Weber, and Martin Heiss, DGB-Archiv/5/DGCS000100; "Sieg der Parität. Auf zwei Parteitagen setzte sich der linke Flügel durch," *Die Zeit*, #46, November 9, 1973 (www.zeit.de).

for the Social Committees by a vote of 559 to 97, but that final vote only took place after their first proposed amendment received 200 Aye votes, and the second, 218. One-third of the delegates thus voiced a preference for genuine parity, meaning that the Social Committees had moved their party somewhat to the left since they first called for parity co-determination in the Offenburg Declaration of 1967. This development was doubtless related to the growth of CDU membership from 250,000 in 1962 to 450,000 in 1973 and 650,000 in 1976. With almost as many members as the SPD and stronger laws for public campaign financing, the CDU became far less dependent on business contributions.[79] After Maria Weber wrote him to protest against the Hamburg resolution, Kohl received his DGB colleagues again and denounced anti-worker prejudice in the CDU. "In future the party must," he declared, "make the concerns of the Social Committees its own concerns more than in the past. To do this it must liberate trade unionists and CDA people from the ghetto to which they have been confined within the party." Kohl then recruited trade unionists to serve on several CDU policy advisory committees.[80] He thus displayed sympathy for the workers' wing of his party without making any firm commitments.

Despite Vetter's call after the election for "massive pressure," the DGB remained passive when the government parties began serious negotiations over co-determination in September 1973. Vetter asked his National Committee on December 5 whether "the DGB should again organize a demonstration to underscore our demands or trust in the promises by our political friends [in the SPD] that a co-determination bill will be achieved that is acceptable for the DGB." He preferred the latter course and assured colleagues that the principle of genuine parity was not in jeopardy. Some Social Democratic union leaders criticized the idea that they should simply trust in "promises by our political friends," but they could not agree on a course of action.[81] Labor leaders were shocked when the SPD and FDP agreed on a bill in January 1974 that

---

[79] Interview with Blüm, *Der Spiegel*, XXVII/#42 (October 15, 1973), pp. 36–41 (quotation on 36); CDU, *22. Bundesparteitag der Christlich Demokratischen Union Deutschlands. Hamburg, 18. – 20. November 1973* (Bonn, 1973), pp. 279–326; "Niederlage für CDU-Sozialausschüsse," *Die Zeit*, #48, November 23, 1973 (www.zeit.de); Pridham, *CDU*, pp. 274–287; Kleinmann, *CDU*, pp. 352–366, 495; Schwarz, *Kohl*, pp. 166–180.

[80] Weber to Kohl, December 7, 1973, Adolf Müller, "Aktennotiz ... über das Gespräch [mit Kohl] am 24.1.1974," and "Bundesfachausschüsse der CDU und Arbeitsgemeinschaft christlich-demokratischer DGB-Gewerkschafter," November 1975, DGB-Archiv/5/DGCS000100.

[81] Minutes of a discussion with Willy Brandt on October 10, 1973, *Gewerkschaftsquellen*, XVI: 768–771; "6. Bundesausschuss-Sitzung, December 5, 1973, Punkt 2," DGB-Archiv/5/DGCS000011.

called for parity but gave senior managers the right to elect one "workers' representative" on the board, gave the annual shareholders' meeting the power to decide if a deadlock emerged, required no "labor director" in senior management, and gave the trade unions the right to nominate only one-third of the workers' representatives. Vetter wrote Willy Brandt that this bill violated core principles shared by the DGB and SPD for decades, and he told reporters that the DGB would employ "all means at its disposal" to prevent it from becoming law. Herbert Wehner told the SPD Bundestag delegation, however, that this bill was needed to preserve the coalition, and only one SPD delegate opposed it.[82]

The Social Committees sought to persuade the DGB to ally with them to achieve genuine parity. Katzer and Blüm assured DGB leaders in private meetings in October and December 1973 that parity enjoyed support from the "hard core" in the CDU Workers' Group, and *Social Order* proclaimed that the Bundestag delegates from the Social Committees would ignore party discipline "if it infringes on their responsibility for our social order and the rights of workers."[83] Most DGB leaders took alarm, however, when friends in the SPD warned that further agitation by the trade unions would topple the government and ruin the SPD's prospects in the next election. At DGB leadership conferences in February and March 1974, the representatives of IG Metall demanded genuine parity, but most colleagues agreed that they should avoid public demonstrations. In a published exchange with Blüm in April, Vetter insisted that "Social Democratic demands regarding co-determination are virtually identical with those of the trade unions," while the CDU and CSU distanced themselves more and more from labor's demands. Vetter concluded that "the SPD needs massive support from the trade unions to implement our common demands." Blüm replied that union leaders could not know how far the SPD might go to preserve its coalition with the FDP, and that "co-determination will only be achieved if the DGB launches a campaign for parity that transcends all political parties."[84]

---

[82] DGB leadership conference of January 29, 1974, Willy Brandt to Vetter, January 31, and reply of February 28, 1974, *Gewerkschaftsquellen*, XVI: 807–810, 835–839; "CDA Informationen," January 23 and January 30, 1974, DGB-Archiv/5/DGCS000012; "Kapitulation. Nur Farthmann gegen Koalitionsmodell," *Soziale Ordnung*, XXVIII/#1 (January 28, 1974), p. 1; Lauschke, *Mehr Demokratie*, pp. 58–60, 69–74.

[83] See the DGB press releases on these meetings on October 16, October 26, and December 12, 1973, DGB-Archiv/5/DGCS000012, and Lutz Esser's commentary in *Soziale Ordnung*, XXVII/#11 (November 1973), p. 8.

[84] Newspaper interview with Vetter of January 31, 1974, in Vetter, *Mitbestimmung*, pp. 106–110; DGB Bundesausschuss, February 16 and March 3, 1974, *Gewerkschafts-quellen*, XVI: 828–834, 852; Vetter, "DGB und politische Parteien," and Blüm, "Einheitsgewerkschaft und christlich-demokratische Arbeitnehmer," *Gewerkschaftliche*

In early May Vetter told an assembly of union functionaries in Essen that the leaders of all parties would insist that their Bundestag delegations vote as a united bloc regarding co-determination; he certainly described the position of Herbert Wehner correctly but ignored the fact that the CDU had a long history of split votes on social legislation. Blüm then invited the leaders of IG Metall, including its new chairman Eugen Loderer, to the Stegerwald House on May 11 to "serve notice officially that the leadership of the Social Committees has declared to the leadership of the DGB that it stands at your parliamentary disposal for parity. Whoever asserts that fluctuating majorities are impossible makes an assertion against their better knowledge, which obviously has no other purpose but to construct an excuse for Mr. Wehner."[85] Blüm and Adolf Müller were certainly prepared to risk their futures in the CDU with a vote for parity, and recent experience suggested that they could find at least twenty CDU Bundestag delegates willing to join them, enough to give the SPD an absolute majority.

DGB leaders chose not to put Blüm's offer to the test, in part because Willy Brandt's resignation in May 1974 following a spy scandal reinforced their desire to strengthen the SPD. At a congress of the teachers' union in June, Heinz Vetter heaped praise on the new chancellor, Helmut Schmidt, and pledged the support of organized labor for achieving his lofty goals. Vetter concluded that the "independence from political parties" guaranteed by union statutes simply meant that the unions were free to choose for themselves which party to support. "Unified trade unions must have the right to choose between the political possibilities . . . If they refrain from making a choice, they will lose all political and social influence." The Social Committees found this speech disturbing; in their view the founding principle of the unified trade unions was that union members remained free to choose which party to support, while union leaders must respect their choices.[86] Vetter's rhetoric encouraged mid-level DGB functionaries to ridicule the Social Committees as an impotent "social figleaf" for the CDU, or perhaps an active agent of big business, and leaders of the Social Committees responded by comparing Vetter unfavorably to his predecessors Hans Böckler, Willi Richter, and Ludwig Rosenberg.

Monatshefte, #4, April 1974, pp. 201–205, 238–242 (quotations on 205, 240); Lauschke, *Mehr Demokratie*, pp. 74–76.

[85] Transcript of Blüm's remarks on May 11, 1974, ACDP/04–013/149/1, quotation on pp. 5-6.

[86] Heinz Vetter, "Grusswort" to the GEW Bundeskongress in Mainz, June 5, 1974, quotation on p. 2, and Katzer to Vetter, June 10, 1974, DGB-Archiv/5/DGCS000104; "Vorlage für die Sitzung des Geschäftsführenden Bundesvorstandes der CDA" on June 7, 1974, DGB-Archiv/5/DGCS000100.

Social Democratic aides at DGB headquarters compiled all such hostile utterances for Vetter to study, and they presented a highly selective digest of the statutes and history of the Social Committees to argue that their whole mission was to conduct propaganda for the CDU, not serve the interests of workers.[87]

Big business launched a media campaign against the government's co-determination bill, and labor leaders were taken by surprise again in spring 1974 when the Free Democratic interior minister Hans Dietrich Genscher declared that it violated the Basic Law's guarantee of property rights. Genscher organized lengthy Bundestag hearings about constitutional law, and the Free Democrats demanded new concessions. Their arguments were implausible, because parity co-determination had existed in coal and steel since 1951 without serious court challenge. The FDP had good reason, however, to conclude that the DGB would accept any bill the government proposed, and that the SPD would pay almost any price to maintain the coalition. Indeed, SPD leaders themselves had deep reservations with regard to the DGB's demands and sometimes cited the FDP as an excuse to reject proposals that also offended increasingly powerful elements within the SPD, including the civil service lobby, small business, and the white-collar German Employees' Union, to which Willy Brandt himself belonged. For years the SPD had proclaimed its resolve to transform itself from a "class party" into a "people's party," and this strategy required a certain distance from the DGB.[88] Vetter had become fatalistic by autumn 1974, when he told DGB leaders that they must take account of the delicate balance of power in Bonn and "not conduct any public campaign against the planned regulation of co-determination." He argued that public opinion had become hostile to social reform, and that efforts to improve the government bill would

---

[87] Gerhard Orgass to Katzer, September 18, 1974, ACDP/01–684/11/3; "Christlich-demokratische Arbeitnehmerschaft und Deutscher Gewerkschaftsbund," dossier for Vetter completed on October 7, 1974, DGB-Archiv/5/DGCS000100. Already in December 1972 advisors adhering to a Marxist view of class struggle, Rolf Ebbighausen and Wilhelm Kaltenborn, had sent Vetter a memorandum to demonstrate the impotence of the Social Committees, "Arbeiterinteressen in der CDU?", which was later published; see the manuscript in DGB-Archiv/DGB Bundesvorstand/Abteilung Gesellschaftspolitik/24/1353 (alte Signatur), and the final version in Jürgen Dittberner and Rolf Ebbighausen, eds., *Parteiensystem in der Legitimationskrise* (Opladen, 1973), pp. 172–199.

[88] "Vermerk. Betr.: Verhältnis Gewerkschaften – SPD," by "Hen[sche]," May 2, 1974, DGB-Archiv/DGB Bundesvorstand/Abteilung Gesellschaftspolitik/24/1391 (alte Signatur); memorandum by Vetter, "Mitbestimmung und Grundgesetz," September 26, 1974, DGB-Archiv/5/DGCS000039; Lauschke, *Mehr Demokratie*, pp. 71–81; Peter Lösche and Franz Walter, *Die SPD. Klassenpartei – Volkspartei – Quotenpartei* (Darmstadt, 1992), pp. 81–100, 146–162.

doubtless fail; Vetter concluded that the DGB must accept whatever law the government proposed, and nobody disagreed.[89]

Hans Katzer meanwhile sought to persuade business leaders in the CDU that the Horn Model was a suitable basis to negotiate a compromise. They all replied firmly, however, that it was worse than parity, because only a minority on the supervisory board would be elected by the shareholders.[90] On only one point did they agree that the Social Committees proposed a superior alternative, the direct election by the workers of all their representatives on the supervisory board. The DGB had persuaded the cabinet to endorse elections by the factory council, which favored union influence. Opinion polls revealed that this was the bill's most unpopular feature, however, even among union members, and the Social Committees had long argued that direct elections were the most democratic approach. Katzer and Blüm therefore joined the chorus of those who argued that the DGB displayed oligarchic tendencies regarding election procedure.[91]

Katzer sought to drive a wedge between Heinz Vetter and Eugen Loderer of IG Metall by persuading Loderer that the CDU was more progressive than the FDP, and that workers would benefit from a revival of the Great Coalition. Loderer had applauded Katzer's performance as labor minister and came from a pious Catholic family, although he had broken with the Church as a young man. He believed that the struggle for full employment must be labor's top priority, however, and that Helmut Schmidt deserved support for his willingness to incur public debt to alleviate unemployment. The dominant forces in the CDU/CSU, Loderer concluded, had resolved to slash government outlay and reduce public debt. Any prospect for a challenge to Vetter's course within the DGB vanished in September 1975, when Loderer declared publicly that the trade unions must support the Schmidt government.[92] The DGB reiterated its old demands at one mass rally for co-determination

---

[89] DGB Bundesvorstand, September 30/October 1 and December 3, 1974, *Gewerkschaftsquellen*, XVI: 906–909, 932 (quotation on 907).

[90] See Hans Dichgans to Katzer, October 15, 1974, ACDP/01–684/7/5, and Philipp von Bismarck to Katzer, May 23, 1975, ACDP/01–684/8.

[91] CDU press release of January 28, 1974, DGB-Archiv/5/DGCS000012; "Die paritätische Mitbestimmung. Ergebnisse einer Umfrage unter Berufstätigen in der Privatwirtschaft," *Allensbacher Berichte*, 1974/Nr. 31 (November 1974), DGB-Archiv/5/DGCS000039; Norbert Blüm, "Der DGB und die Dinosaurier," *Der Spiegel*, XXIX/#22 (May 26, 1975), pp. 24–26.

[92] Note for Katzer of September 30, 1974, on a telephone call from Ferdi Koob, ACDP/01–684/10/2; "Eugen Loderer: Friderichs muss zwischen seinen beiden Rollen wählen," Metall Pressedienst, September 23, 1975, Katzer to Loderer, September 24, and Loderer's reply of October 23, 1975, ACDP/01–684/10/2; Kempter, *Eugen Loderer*, pp. 27–51, 230, 300–307.

in November, but Vetter also assured the SPD that organized labor would respect any law it enacted. The final version of the government bill, published on December 8, provided not only that one workers' representative on the supervisory board must be a senior manager, but also that the chairman of the board (who must represent the shareholders) enjoyed a second vote to resolve ties. The DGB responded meekly on December 11 that "after passage of this bill the trade unions will do everything they can to make optimum use of the possibilities it offers and will continue in future to seek the complete fulfillment of their demands." Contrary to Loderer's expectations, Helmut Schmidt also enacted a drastic plan to reduce government spending in December 1975 that went further than any austerity measures proposed by the CDU. His economic and fiscal policy had become quite similar to the FDP's, but he persuaded labor leaders that this action was unavoidable.[93] Katzer had a powerful argument that organized labor would benefit from a Great Coalition, but no Social Democrats in the DGB leadership were prepared to listen.

Big business still denounced the government bill for going too far, and the FDP might well have secured even more concessions if the CDU had opposed it. Hans Katzer persuaded Helmut Kohl and the CDU parliamentary leader Karl Carstens to endorse the government bill, however, and their Bundestag delegation agreed on December 12. Norbert Blüm responded with the following appeal for permission to introduce amendments calling for genuine parity:

I believe . . . that a socialist party and socialist government allied with the trade unions is difficult to topple. Scandinavian examples provide impressive evidence for this. As long as the CDU was in the government, the trade unions were compelled to cooperate with it, but not when the CDU is in opposition. If we do not succeed at loosening the bonds or emotional fixations linking Social Democrats, socialism, and the trade unions, then I believe that the Swedish model could become a European model, and that parties like ours would no longer be a genuine alternative.

Blüm appealed for an opportunity to give CDU colleagues in the DGB "arguments to defend themselves and the opportunity to force their Social Democratic colleagues to justify their position." Carstens and

---

[93] Vetter's speeches to the DGB rally on November 8, 1975, and SPD Party Congress on November 11, in Vetter, *Mitbestimmung*, pp. 194–205; Vetter's memorandum, "Betrifft: Koalitionsvereinbarungen über die Mitbestimmung," December 1, 1975, his remarks to the DGB Bundesausschuss on December 3, and DGB press release of December 11, 1975 (source of quotation), DGB-Archiv/5/DGCS000009; Lauschke, *Mehr Demokratie*, pp. 74–88; Markovits, *Trade Unions*, pp. 126–133.

Biedenkopf replied sternly, however, that the CDU could only persuade voters that it was capable of governing if it adopted a unified position.[94]

Blüm spoke on behalf of the Association of Christian Democratic DGB Trade Unionists, which had been galvanized into action when Social Democratic colleagues abandoned core union principles. Maria Weber assembled several dozen colleagues on December 12/13 to declare their steadfast support for parity co-determination. "The Association is dismayed," they told the press, "to learn that the government coalition has introduced a bill that lags far behind this demand ... This solution will steer developments in the wrong direction ... We expect a law that corresponds to the Co-Determination Law in coal and steel, which has worked so well for twenty years." The participants exhorted all DGB members in the Bundestag to introduce amendments to achieve full parity, and Adolf Müller and Blüm promised them to do so. Weber wrote Helmut Kohl afterward that all genuine supporters of the Catholic social movement had embraced parity co-determination ever since the Bochum Catholic Congress of 1949. "If this path is blocked under your chairmanship, and a solution is sought that lags behind that introduced by Konrad Adenauer for coal and steel, then many ties between workers and the CDU will rupture."[95]

Blüm, Adolf Müller, and their Hessian colleague Otto Zink resolved to press forward with amendments in the Bundestag labor committee. Blüm requested assistance from Eugen Loderer and DGB headquarters to draft co-determination amendments corresponding to the DGB program. The DGB only sent him an old pamphlet, however, and Loderer replied tersely after six weeks that there was no hope to achieve parity at this time. In February 1976 Blüm and his two friends nevertheless introduced two amendments in committee to implement in all large corporations parity co-determination as it existed in coal and steel, with a "neutral" eleventh board member to break ties, and a labor director hired by the workers' representatives. All committee members from the government parties rejected these motions, including three Social Democratic DGB functionaries. There were only two Free Democrats on this committee, so the motions would have passed if supported by the SPD. *Der Spiegel* reported that Vetter had erupted to aides: "I won't have that lout Blüm ruining our

---

[94] Declaration by Philipp von Bismarck on December 11, 1975, in Lauschke, ed., *Mehr Demokratie: Dokumente*, pp. 118–120; CDU Bundestag delegation, December 12, 1975, pp. 5–20 (quotations from 8–10), ACDP/08–001/1044/1.

[95] "Kompromissvorschlag der Entschliessung der Arbeitsgemeinschaft Christlich-Demokratischer DGB-Gewerkschafter in den Sozialausschüssen der CDA," December 13, 1975, and letters by Weber on December 19 to Helmut Kohl, Hans Katzer, and Adolf Müller, DGB-Archiv/5/DGCS000100.

[SPD] election campaign!" Vetter denied that report, but the official DGB response on February 23 certainly displayed hostility by alleging that "Blüm does not care about co-determination, only about party tactics."[96]

Vetter received so many complaints that he agreed at last to hold on March 9, 1976, the summit conference with Christian Democratic DGB colleagues that they had requested in November 1972. Weber was ill, so Martin Heiss and Adolf Müller led twelve Christian Democrats for a frank discussion with Vetter, Loderer, and other top union leaders. Vetter revealed distrust of the minority by declaring at the outset that "members of political parties are bound to party resolutions and statutes ... According to the statutes of the CDU and CDA, ... the members of the Social Committees are obliged to defend the resolutions of the CDU." Karl-Heinz Hoffmann replied that the Social Committees had always been more than just an organ of the CDU; they were also a component of the labor movement, dedicated to the emancipation of workers. He explained that "our three colleagues who introduced the motion for parity in the Bundestag Labor Committee certainly did not please their own party thereby. This initiative came not from the CDU but from our circle." Vetter confessed that he knew nothing about this background, and all DGB leaders agreed that they must avoid entanglement in the next election campaign and seek to hire more Christian Democratic functionaries. Vetter then issued a rare apology, telling the next DGB leadership conference that he had misconstrued Blüm's motives.[97] Despite this positive outcome, the Christian Democratic participants concluded that there was a growing chasm between their views and those of Social Democratic colleagues. Vetter described Christian social ideas as a vital "intellectual source" of the DGB program but not a living current today. Other union leaders stated explicitly that the DGB championed "democratic socialism," and they grossly underestimated the proportion of union members who voted CDU. Vetter's remarks about the obligations of party membership obviously reflected the

---

[96] "Blüms Solo für die Parität," *Der Spiegel*, XXX/#9 (February 23, 1976), p. 18; "Parität bleibt auf der Tagesordnung," *Soziale Ordnung*, XXX/#1 (February 5, 1976), p. 4; "Chance für die Parität vertan," *Soziale Ordnung*, XXX/#2 (March 10, 1976), pp. 4–5; Blüm to Loderer, December 15, 1975, reply of February 2, 1976, and DGB press release of February 23, 1976 (source of second quotation), in DGB-Archiv/5/DGCS000104.

[97] "Geschäftsführender Ausschuss der Arbeitsgemeinschaft christlich-demokratischer DGB-Gewerkschafter," February 24, 1976, DGB-Archiv/5/DGCS000098; "Notizen über das Gespräch zwischen dem Geschäftsführenden Ausschuss ... und dem Bundesvorstand des DGB," March 9, 1976, quotations on pp. 3–4, 10–12, and Vetter's remarks to the DGB Bundesausschuss on March 10, DGB-Archiv/5/DGCS000096.

traditions of the SPD; he had sacrificed his own scruples to party discipline so often, these Christian Democrats concluded, that he refused to
acknowledge the existence of colleagues who followed their conscience.[98]

After their amendments were rejected, Blüm and Adolf Müller
joined with Katzer to recommend approval of the government's
co-determination bill. All three men told their Bundestag delegation
that it was virtually identical to the CDU Hamburg Party Congress
resolution of November 1973; the CDU therefore had no plausible
reason to oppose it and would be branded as anti-worker if it did.
Katzer also took pride in the fact that the final bill incorporated the
Social Committees' proposal that workers' representatives on corporate
boards be elected directly by the entire work force. Kohl and Carstens
endorsed their reasoning, and on March 18 the Co-Determination Law
(*Mitbestimmungsgesetz*) sailed through to final passage against the votes
of just one Social Democrat who did not think it went far enough and
twenty-one pro-business delegates from the CDU/CSU who thought it
went too far. Blüm argued during the final Bundestag debate that the
SPD could have achieved genuine parity by voting with Christian
Democratic workers, but he provoked derisive laughter from the Left
and a cry, "You are so naive!" Labor Minister Walter Arendt reproached
Blüm for dishonesty, because he had introduced committee amendments designed "to lead every supporter of co-determination into temptation," despite knowing that his own Bundestag delegation would
never support them. Arendt ignored the fact that Blüm only needed to
deliver eighteen votes to enable the SPD to pass any bill it desired.[99]

The agitation for co-determination by the Social Committees raised
doubts about their party loyalty, and they encountered headwinds as
CDU county committees nominated Bundestag candidates in 1976.
The boldest champions of parity retained their seats nevertheless. After
the election, the new CDU Bundestag delegation included twenty-two
members of DGB-affiliated unions (versus 204 in the SPD), seven from
the white-collar German Employees' Union, and eleven from the Christian
trade unions, an improvement for the DGB presence.[100] Despite the

---

[98] See the "Tischvorlage," an analysis of the meeting sent by Albert Keil to Martin Heiss
on May 21, 1976, DGB-Archiv/5/DGCS000096.

[99] CDU Bundestag delegation, February 10, 1976, pp. 2–29, ACDP/08–001/1045/1,
and March 16, 1976, pp. 14–31, ACDP/08–001/1046/1; Bundestag debate in
Lauschke, *Mehr Demokratie: Dokumente*, pp. 121–130 (quotations on 123, 126);
Katzer's speech of March 13, 1976, in the "CDA Betriebsräte Brief," March-April
1976, pp. 5–6, DGB-Archiv/5/DGCS000104; Lauschke, *Mehr Demokratie*, pp. 88–90.

[100] "Gewerkschafter im VIII. Deutschen Bundestag," August 9, 1977, enclosed in
a circular by Albert Keil to Christian Democratic trade unionists on August 11, DGB-
Archiv/5/DGCS000096.

promises by DGB leaders to avoid entanglement in the election campaign, Eugen Loderer soon denounced the CDU slogan, "Freedom or Socialism," as "hostile to democracy." Kurt Biedenkopf escalated the conflict when he launched a whirlwind campaign in the Ruhr against the "corrupt entanglement" (*Verfilzung*) between the SPD and trade unions. In September he published two thick dossiers on the issue, but many of his allegations, provided mostly by business lobbyists, were trivial or inaccurate. These attacks offended most Ruhr workers and energized the SPD campaign, and in October the CDU voting share in the Ruhr declined from 38.5 percent in the last state election to 36.3 percent. Nationwide Helmut Kohl led the CDU/CSU to an impressive 48.6 percent, and some commentators suggested that Biedenkopf's failed campaign in the Ruhr had deprived Christian Democrats of an absolute majority.[101] The leading Christian Democratic DGB functionaries became angry with Biedenkopf for disrupting their sensitive negotiations with Vetter, and on September 21 they drafted a press release attacking Chancellor Schmidt and Biedenkopf alike for meddling in union affairs. Katzer refused to authorize publication during the campaign of a statement attacking the CDU secretary general, so Maria Weber and her colleagues published their declaration independently of the Social Committees, and their feud with Katzer resumed.[102]

In this election, 57.8 percent of all DGB members voted SPD, 28.4 percent CDU/CSU, and 8 percent FDP. This ratio of 2:1 between Social and Christian Democrats in the unions had remained largely unchanged since 1949. The CDU's popularity among workers rose thereafter, and an Allensbach Institute poll the following summer indicated that 34.6 percent of union members supported the CDU/CSU,

---

[101] "Eugen Loderer: Parole 'Freiheit statt Sozialismus' demokratiefeindlich," IG Metall press release of June 1, 1976, ACDP/01–684/18/2; Kurt Biedenkopf, "Dokumentation über den Missbrauch gewerkschaftlicher und politischer Macht durch SPD und Gewerkschafts-Funktionäre," September 3, 1976, "Richtigstellung des Hauptvorstandes der IG Bergbau und Energie zur angeblichen Dokumentation der CDU," and Biedenkopf's "Erweiterte Dokumentation" of September 22, DGB-Archiv/5/DGCS000086; "Wahrnehmbar schmutzig machen," and "Ruhrgebiet: Allet nich gehabt," *Der Spiegel*, XXX/#38 (September 13, 1976), pp. 36–38, and #42 (October 11, 1976), pp. 128–133; Schwarz, *Helmut Kohl*, pp. 206–214.

[102] Maria Weber and Adolf Müller to the DGB Bundesvorstand, September 3, 1976, DGB-Archiv/5/DGCS000096; "Ergebnisprotokoll der Sitzung des Geschäftsführenden Ausschusses der Arbeitsgemeinschaft christlich-demokratischer DGB-Gewerkschafter," September 21 and September 24, 1976, with attached "Anmerkung" of September 26, DGB-Archiv/5/DGCS000097; "CDA Informationen," October 9, 1976, DGB-Archiv/5/DGCS000086.

and 52 percent of non-unionized workers.[103] For the Social Committees the obvious conclusion from these polls was that the trade unions must respect the views of Christian Democratic workers to preserve unity and expand their appeal among unorganized workers. Heinz Vetter drew very different conclusions, however; he sent DGB leaders an analysis of the election results which argued that rational workers could not support the CDU, because it was aligned with big business.

> Rather, it appears that the attempts to foment anxiety and uncertainty in recent years have clouded people's judgment... To a disturbing extent, conservative and authoritarian explanations and solutions have gained resonance ... Under the influence of conservative propaganda, the uncertainty created by recent economic developments ... has fomented a false consciousness [eine illusionäre Bewusstseinsverfassung]. Clutching at their positive experiences in the past, people are inclined to hope and believe that the return to stability and the solution of economic and social problems can be achieved by those forces which support the market economy.

Vetter refused to consider the possibility that the Schmidt cabinet might have made some mistakes; unlike every previous DGB chair, he evidently regarded all Christian Democratic DGB colleagues as the dupes or agents of big business.[104]

The Social Committees had claimed 52,000 members in 1967, but that figure declined to 32,000 in 1976. The KAB had also begun to shrink, and it suffered a financial crisis in 1972 that led to the dismissal of one-third of the staff.[105] Internal conflict weakened the Social Committees further. Some activists grumbled in 1976 that all their leaders had become mere politicians who had lost touch with workers, and the Social Committees around Aachen threatened to found a new party if the CDU did not dramatically increase representation for workers in all party organs.[106] Norbert Blüm then spread the word that he would campaign for the chairmanship at the Social Committees' next congress. Helmut

---

[103] Horst Schmollinger, "Zur politisch-gesellschaftlichen Beteiligung von Gewerkschafts-mitgliedern: Gewerkschafter in Parteien, Kirchen und Vereinen," in Ulrich Borsdorf et al., eds., Gewerkschaftliche Politik: Reform aus Solidarität. Zum 60. Geburtstag von Heinz O. Vetter (Cologne, 1977), pp. 135–157 (esp. p. 137); "Sommer 1977: Berufstätige Arbeitnehmer," Allensbach Institute report sent by Helmut Kohl to Vetter on November 4, 1977, DGB-Archiv/5/DGCS000108.

[104] "Analyse der Bundestagswahl 1976," sent by Vetter to the DGB Bundesvorstand on October 28, 1976, quotation from pp. 15–17, DGB-Archiv/5/DGCS000086.

[105] Kleinmann, Geschichte der CDU, p. 468; minutes of the KAB Verbandsvorstand, June 12, 1972, KAB Archiv/1/8.

[106] "Sauer auf Hans Katzer," report on the annual assembly of the Social Committee of Euskirchen, Kölner Stadtanzeiger: Ausgabe Euskirchen, June 24, 1976 (ACDP/ 01–684/20/1); circular by Leo Frings, chair of the Social Committees, Bezirk Aachen, December 1976, ACDP/01–684/10/2.

Kohl favored him, and Katzer suffered a prolonged illness in spring 1977, during which he decided to withdraw his name from consideration. Katzer was healthy again by the time he announced this decision at the Social Committees' congress in June 1977, and he felt that Blüm did not appreciate his generous decision to step aside.[107]

Katzer remained chair of the Jakob Kaiser Foundation, the charitable institute for adult education that owned the Stegerwald House, published *Social Order*, and collected tax-deductible contributions for the Social Committees. Blüm was stunned when Katzer insisted on a strict financial separation between the foundation and the Social Committees and gained the support of all members of the foundation board, whom he had appointed. In November 1977 Blüm was compelled to agree that the Social Committees would pay rent for their own offices, and Katzer retained control of the Kaiser Foundation bank accounts. The leaders of the Association of Christian Democratic Trade Unionists observed with exasperation that the substantial union contributions to the Kaiser Foundation which they had arranged since 1961 had been given solely to assist the work of the Social Committees. Blüm soon founded a new charitable foundation, but Bernhard Tacke warned that most union leaders would refuse to contribute to either body in future. The Social Committees experienced financial crisis thereafter, while the Kaiser Foundation pursued its own course as a sponsor of adult education seminars, and Katzer served in the European Parliament. Katzer's feud with Blüm nurtured an impression among journalists that the Social Committees had become irrelevant.[108]

The Social Committees reached the nadir of their influence in July 1979, when the CDU and CSU agreed to nominate Franz Josef Strauss as their chancellor candidate. Several leading Christian Democratic DGB functionaries threatened to resign from the CDU if Strauss was chosen. They

[107] "CDU: Ende der Ein-Mann-Schau," *Der Spiegel*, XXXI/#20 (May 9, 1977), p. 36; "Geschäftsführender Ausschuss der Arbeitsgemeinschaft Christlich-Demokratischer DGB-Gewerkschafter," meeting with Blüm on April 20, 1977, DGB-Archiv/5/DGCS000097; Katzer to Erwin Ortmann, June 20, 1977, ACDP/01–684/23/1; Mayer, "Gerechtigkeit schafft Frieden," pp. 34–37.

[108] "Jakob-Kaiser-Stiftung für Fortsetzung der Zusammenarbeit mit den Sozialausschüssen," press release of September 7, 1977, DGB-Archiv/5/DGCS000096; "Geschäftsführender Ausschuss der Arbeitsgemeinschaft Christlich-Demokratischer DGB-Gewerkschafter," November 8, 1977, and February 22, 1978, DGB-Archiv/5/DGCS000097; Elfriede Kaiser-Nebgen, "Unser Haus in Königswinter," October 1, 1977, and Bernhard Tacke to Hans Katzer, March 3, 1978, NL Tacke/11/5; correspondence between Josef Mick and Elfriede Kaiser-Nebgen in October-November 1977, NL Katzer/306; *Der Spiegel*, XXXI/#35 (August 22, 1977), p. 24, XXXII/#10 (March 6, 1978), pp. 68–76, and XXXII/#15 (April 9, 1979), pp. 41–44; "Bonner Kulisse," *Die Zeit*, December 14, 1979, www.zeit.de; Kleinmann, *Geschichte der CDU*, pp. 468–470.

fought in alliance with the influential Helmut Kohl and many north German Protestants, but they could not prevent their Bundestag delegation from embracing the theory that the candidate best able to mobilize their base of conservative supporters had the best chance to win. This campaign strategy was influenced by the revival of anti-socialism among the Catholic bishops, who condemned the social-liberal government's decisions to legalize pornography and abortion. Ferdi Breidbach offered Strauss advice and support for his campaign rallies in the Ruhr but could not prevent a hostile reception, and Breidbach himself failed to win reelection. Nobody listened to "bridge builders" during this polarized campaign. Strauss suffered a humbling defeat in October 1980, however, when the CDU/CSU vote slumped from 48.6 percent to 44.5 percent. This result led to a comeback for Helmut Kohl as leader of the opposition and thereby revived the influence of the Social Committees to some extent.[109]

Norbert Blüm served for sixteen years as labor minister under Chancellor Kohl, by far the longest tenure for any labor minister in German history, and he became one of the most influential cabinet members. He achieved at least a few policy victories through sheer force of personality and media presence. Blüm helped to mend ties with the DGB by championing its thesis that the government should encourage a shorter work week and earlier retirement age to help maintain full employment.[110] Blüm sought as labor minister to go beyond the traditional issues of labor-management relations to address the problems of people with disabilities, senior citizens, and neglected or abused children. He took special pride in the *Erziehungsgeld* law of 1986; in addition to parental leave from the workplace, the government now offered modest compensation for up to three years to any parent who pledged to work fewer than thirty hours a week while raising a child. These benefits were claimed almost exclusively by mothers, and many observers concluded that Blüm's policies made life more difficult for women who wanted to combine motherhood with a career, because he did not seek government

---

[109] Protest telegrams to the CDU by DGB functionaries, June 21/22, 1979, Blüm's circular to the Social Committees on July 4, and related press releases in DGB-Archiv/5/DGCS000096; "CDU/CSU: Linke Liste," *Der Spiegel*, XXXIII/#31 (July 30, 1979), pp. 21–22; Ferdi Breidbach to Herrn Frühauf, September 17, 1980, and "Passagen zur Mitbestimmung für die Rede von Dr. Strauss am 24. September in Duisburg," NL Breidbach/37; "Das ist geistliche Nötigung," and "Helmut Schmidt ja, SPD na ja," *Der Spiegel*, XXXIV/#39 (September 22, 1980), pp. 17–29, and #41 (October 6, 1980), pp. 6–17; Remeke, *Anders links sein*, pp. 372–388; Schwarz, *Helmut Kohl*, pp. 239–256; Thomas Gauly, *Katholiken. Machtanspruch und Machtverlust* (Bonn, 1992), pp. 255–293.

[110] See the summary by Irmgard Blättel of Blüm's discussion with Heinz Vetter on July 15, 1977, DGB-Archiv/5/DGCS000106, and the report for DGB leaders, "Bericht über den 30. Bundesparteitag der CDU, 2.-5.11.81," pp. 6–7, DGB-Archiv/DGB Bundesvorstand/Abteilung Gesellschaftspolitik/24/5949 (alte Signatur).

funding for child day-care centers. The Social Committees' tendency to defend traditional family values limited their appeal to women and contributed to their decline.[111]

In 1996 Helmut Kohl acceded to demands by his FDP coalition partner to repeal the law for "continued payment of wages" to sick blue-collar workers enacted by Hans Katzer in 1969. Labor Minister Blüm capitulated in that debate and thus provoked anger among trade unionists. In 1997 Kohl also embraced tax cuts as the only hope to stimulate economic recovery, provoking serious disputes with Blüm, who sought to preserve social insurance programs with taxpayer subsidies. From the perspective of the Christian Democratic trade union functionary Helmut Wagner, Kohl went badly astray during his last years in office, and the repeal of "continued payment of wages" was the worst mistake he ever made. Kohl himself later judged that it played a major role in his election defeat in 1998.[112]

The Social Committees enlisted the support in the 1980s and '90s of several idealistic and talented party colleagues from middle-class backgrounds. Heiner Geissler, a former Jesuit novice, became a powerful ally as CDU secretary general, and the East German Evangelical pastor Rainer Eppelmann, who helped to topple the Communist dictatorship, rose to chair the Social Committees from 1994 to 2001. A similar figure was Ulf Fink, a university-educated economist who was drawn to the Social Committees as a young labor ministry official serving under Hans Katzer. He later served as social minister in the Berlin municipal government and was elected national chairman of the Social Committees in 1987. The Social Committees achieved an old dream when they persuaded the DGB to elect Fink as DGB vice chair in 1990. Fink had no trade union experience, however, and refused to give up any of his political offices when he joined the DGB leadership team; he was widely judged ineffective and lost his leadership roles in both the DGB and Social Committees by 1994. Fink and Eppelmann helped to call the attention of the Social Committees to new social problems involving the ill and the aging, immigrants, and the integration into German society of

---

[111] Kleinmann, *CDU*, pp. 468–470; speech by Blüm to the national congress of the Social Committees in 1987, in Schummer, *CDA 1945–1995*, pp. 133–145; Jan Ondrich, C. Katharina Spiess, and Qing Yang, "Barefoot and in a German Kitchen: Federal Parental Leave and Benefit Policy and the Return to Work after Childbirth in Germany," *Journal of Population Economics*, 9 (1996): 247–266; Petra Radke and Wiebke Störmann, "Erziehungsurlaub und Chancengleichheit am Arbeitsmarkt," *Jahrbuch für Wirtschaftswissenschaften*, 49 (1998): 180–197.

[112] Schwarz, *Helmut Kohl*, pp. 819–855; "'Wir gehen da ran.' Wie die Regierung bei den Kranken sparen will," *Der Spiegel*, L/#16 (April 15, 1996), pp. 34–36; Helmut Wagner, *Meine Lebensgeschichte. Zwischen schwarz und rot* (Hamburg, 2003), pp. 528–556.

those who grew up in Communist East Germany, but they failed to revive the connection with organized labor that was the original mission of the Social Committees.[113] In recent years the DGB has ignored the tradition that a vice chair should come from the CDU, and Chancellor Angela Merkel has ignored the tradition that a CDU-led cabinet should appoint a labor minister from the Social Committees.

The Social Committees and Catholic workers' clubs still exist, of course, and tens of thousands of activists in them continue to defend the interests of workers in the CDU, contribute a special perspective to debates in the trade unions, and develop creative proposals to deal with new social problems. The KAB has long since renounced the scramble to gain political offices as a distraction from its proper mission, however. CDU politicians retain a strong interest in winning the votes of workers but no longer nominate working-class candidates to accomplish this. The number of CDU Bundestag delegates who identify themselves as "blue-collar workers" (*Arbeiter*) sank from two in 1980 to zero by 2009, while the number of trade union functionaries sank from three to zero. Several delegates are still unionized white-collar workers, but the proportion of business lobbyists and those with university degrees has grown significantly. In 2015 the Social Committees only had five representatives in the Bundestag.[114] It seems fair to conclude that the co-determination debate of the 1970s was the last crucial issue in German politics upon which the Social Committees exerted vital influence.

---

[113] Thomas v. Winter, "Die Sozialausschüsse der CDU: Sammelbecken für christdemo-kratische Arbeitnehmerinteressen oder linker Flügel der Partei?" *Leviathan*, 18 (1990): 390–416; Yorck Dietrich's interview with Tacke on August 7, 1990, NL Tacke/15/5; "Spürbar entkrampft: Der CDU-Mann Ulf Fink, stellvertretender DGB-Vorsitzender, hat zu viele Posten gesammelt," *Der Spiegel*, XLV/#9 (February 25, 1991), p. 122; Ingrid Völker and Franz Dormann, eds., *Soziale Ordnungspolitik im 21. Jahrhundert. Festschrift für Ulf Fink zum 70. Geburtstag* (Stuttgart, 2012), with biographical introduction on pp. v–xi.

[114] Adalbert Hess, "Berufsstatistik der Mitglieder des 10. Deutschen Bundestages," *Zeitschrift für Parlamentsfragen*, 14 (1983): 486–489; Melanie Kintz, "Die Berufsstruktur der Abgeordneten des 17. Deutschen Bundestages," *Zeitschrift für Parlamentsfragen*, Heft 3/2010, pp. 491–503; c.v.'s for the leadership of the Social Committees available online at www.cda-bund.de/die-cda/bundesvorstand.html.

Conclusion: The Legacy of the Christian Labor Movement

German business lobbyists have always held that the CDU should not concern itself with the arguments of organized labor, and SPD leaders have long taught that no other party can serve the interests of workers. Both groups have always had powerful motives to deride Christian Democratic labor activists as bleeding heart Marxists or hopeless romantics, to exaggerate their failures and ignore their successes. This negative stereotype has influenced many journalists and even some scholars. To sort out the complex network of Christian social organizations with overlapping memberships, understand their occasional feuds with each other, and evaluate their cumulative impact requires considerable intellectual effort. To understand German politics as a contest between a "bourgeois" CDU and a laborite SPD is much easier. The SPD has never won much more than 50 percent of blue-collar votes in any German election, however, and the CDU always outpolled it among the working class, if that term is defined broadly to include lower-ranking white-collar workers and civil servants. The whole future of organized labor depends on the effort to define "working class" broadly.

Most top leaders of the trade unions and CDU understood after 1945 that their organizations benefitted greatly from the Christian social labor movement, and they did what they could to protect it. The CDU could not win elections without gaining a very large share of workers' votes, and labor leaders needed allies against the radical Left and the support of millions of workers who stood to the right of the SPD. Astute politicians such as Konrad Adenauer, Heinrich Krone, Rainer Barzel, and Helmut Kohl always sought to recruit credible workers' representatives as CDU candidates, allowed them to provoke debates within the party, and shielded them from reprisals. Astute labor leaders such as Hans Böckler, Walter Freitag, Willi Richter, and Ludwig Rosenberg made similar efforts to defend "minority rights" in the German Labor Federation. By doing so they preserved important channels of communication between the CDU and organized labor and helped to de-escalate many political confrontations. The most noteworthy exceptions to this rule, Ludwig Erhard, Kurt Georg Kiesinger, and Heinz Oskar Vetter, undermined their own effectiveness by permitting themselves to be influenced by the negative stereotypes of Christian Democratic workers.

The list of political victories for Christian Democratic workers is fairly impressive. The firm decision in 1945 by veterans of the Christian trade unions in favor of the CDU and unified labor unions shaped the political landscape of the Federal Republic. In 1948 the veterans of the old Christian trade unions tipped the balance at the Frankfurt Economic Council in favor of Ludwig Erhard's proposal to deregulate consumer prices. At the Parliamentary Council in 1948/1949, Josef Schrage prevented inclusion in the Basic Law of provisions that anyone was free NOT to join a trade union, and that strikes were permissible only if carried out for "economic" reasons. After Adenauer and Hans Böckler struck their historic bargain in 1951 to introduce parity co-determination in coal and steel, fierce opposition emerged within the CDU Bundestag delegation, but its Workers' Group secured parliamentary approval. As the CDU prime minister of North Rhine-Westphalia, Karl Arnold resisted Adenauer's tendency to demonize the SPD by supporting a Great Coalition during the most anxious phase of the Cold War. The influence of the CDU Workers' Group on social legislation peaked during Adenauer's second term as chancellor, and its greatest victory came with the "dynamic" pension reform of 1957. Theodor Blank and Jakob Kaiser also promoted consensus over rearmament and NATO membership when they insisted that Adenauer address the concerns of the SPD and trade unions. Kaiser placed reunification with the Saarland on the West German foreign policy agenda, and Blank imposed very strong parliamentary oversight on the new *Bundeswehr*. The Social Committees took the lead in agitating for a Great Coalition with the SPD in the 1960s and thereby overcame an era of social policy stagnation. Interior Minister Paul Lücke forged consensus in favor of "emergency powers" in 1967/1968. Labor Minister Hans Katzer greatly enhanced adult education programs for workers with the Jobs Promotion Act of 1969 and promoted equality between blue- and white-collar workers with the law for the "continued payment of wages" to sick workers.

The Social Committees sometimes advocated policies whose utility can be questioned, for example with regard to "co-ownership" of the means of production. They focused on a crucial issue for German workers, however, when they launched a campaign in 1967 to extend parity co-determination to all large-scale enterprise. Now they attacked directly the most vital interests of big business, and this task exceeded their strength. They argued with passion and skill nevertheless that co-determination laws were the most authentic expression of the Christian ideal of "social partnership," and they gained allies among the clergy, idealistic lay church activists, a handful of progressive businessmen, and youth groups. By the mid-1970s the Social Committees had moved the CDU far enough to the left to deny the FDP leverage as it sought to remove from the government co-determination bill all provisions that favored organized labor. The hard core among the CDU workers' delegates also provided a rare display of civic courage by volunteering to defy their own party and vote for genuine parity. They helped to achieve a Co-Determination Law in March 1976 that strengthened the influence of workers on management decisions, although it only applied to joint-stock corporations with 2,000 or more employees, i.e. about 650 firms. It left Germany with a four-tiered system after 1976: twenty-eight firms in coal and steel retained genuine parity co-determination, hundreds more still fell under the terms of the 1952 Factory Councils Law (amended in 1971) that only gave workers one-third of the seats on corporate supervisory boards, and "family firms" (including a few of Germany's largest) had no legally required organs of co-determination, only what was agreed upon in their collective labor contracts.[1]

Looking back after four decades, it appears that the year 1976 marked the last opportunity to extend parity co-determination, and that an alliance between Social Democrats and Christian Democratic workers offered the only viable strategy. All analysts agree that co-determination makes strikes far less likely and encourages cooperation among management, industrial unions, and elected factory councils in vocational training and other programs; this is often called the "German Model" for industrial relations. Scholars still debate the impact on economic performance when organs of co-determination are strengthened. The most detailed study of their functioning in the steel industry finds that they promoted management strategies far more beneficial to workers than in other German industries, but that they did not make German steel firms less capable of adjusting to structural crisis than those of other countries. The skeptical economist Kornelius Kraft found in 1993 that the firms which switched from the 1952 system to "near parity" in 1976 experienced "a productivity loss of 13–14 per cent of value added" and

---

[1] Heinz Vetter, "Die ersten Erfahrungen mit dem Mitbestimmungsgesetz 1976," speech of September 12, 1978, in Heinz Vetter, *Mitbestimmung – Idee, Wege, Ziel* (Cologne, 1979), pp. 291–303; Wolfgang Spieker, "Gewerkschaftliche Grundfragen der Mitbestimmung auf Unterenehmensebene," in Ulrich Borsdorf, Hans Hemmer, Gerhard Leminsky, and Heinz Markmann, eds., *Gewerkschaftliche Politik: Reform aus Solidarität* (Cologne, 1977), pp. 353–372; Andrei S. Markovits, *The Politics of the West German Trade Unions: Strategies of Class and Interest Representation in Growth and Crisis* (Cambridge, 1986), pp. 53–60.

a corresponding dip in profits, apparently because management became more reluctant to dismiss workers. In 2006, however, he concluded after reviewing far more data that "near parity" had increased the rate of return on investment in the firms affected, apparently by improving communication between management and labor. On balance, it seems clear that co-determination improved job security for German workers, promoted a collegial environment in the workplace, and contributed to a more egalitarian distribution of national income than that of the US or Great Britain, while German economic performance remains the envy of most European countries. The success of co-determination certainly depends on the quality of the educational opportunities available to workers who participate in factory councils and corporate supervisory boards, and the Social Committees and Catholic workers' clubs have always supported adult education alongside the trade unions. The Social Committees have good reason to celebrate their role in the passage and ongoing implementation of the co-determination laws of 1951, 1952, and 1976.[2]

It remains very difficult to analyze the extent to which Catholic social theory contributed to the emergence of the German Model. Papal encyclicals from *Rerum novarum* to *Quadragesimo Anno* nurtured sweeping claims by many Catholics that the Church possessed a comprehensive "social theory." These encyclicals did not inspire any useful proposal to alleviate mass unemployment during the Great Depression, however, and they hindered the search for political compromise by presenting a hostile caricature of democratic socialism. As the Second Vatican Council acknowledged, a variety of political programs are always compatible with any set of religious ethical norms. Catholic teaching did nevertheless encourage Christian Democratic workers with extensive experience of labor relations to identify somewhat more quickly than their Social Democratic colleagues specific issues where labor and management could cooperate to mutual advantage. Social Democratic trade unionists

---

[2] Karl Lauschke, *Die halbe Macht. Mitbestimmung in der Eisen- und Stahlindustrie, 1945 bis 1989* (Essen, 2007), pp. 231–334; Felix FitzRoy and Kornelius Kraft, "Economic Effects of Codetermination," *The Scandinavian Journal of Economics*, 95 (1993): 365–375 (quotation from 374); Kornelius Kraft and Marija Ugarković, "Gesetzliche Mitbestimmung und Kapitalrendite," *Jahrbücher für Nationalökonomie und Statistik*, 226 (2006): 588–604; Hyeong-ki Kwon, "The German Model Reconsidered," *German Politics and Society*, 20 (2002): 48–72; Heinz-Adolf Hörsken, "Noch eine Chance für mehr Mitbestimmung," and Regina Görner, "Die Gewerkschaften als Ordnungsfaktor der Sozialen Marktwirtschaft," in Uwe Schummer, ed., *CDA 1945 bis 1995* (Bergisch Gladbach, 1995), pp. 49–73. For the extraordinary decline of strike rates in the Federal Republic in comparison both with other countries and previous eras of German history, see Heinrich Volkmann, "Modernisierung des Arbeitskampfs? Zum Formwandel von Streik und Aussperrung in Deutschland 1864–1975," in Hartmut Kaelble, ed., *Probleme der Modernisierung in Deutschland* (Opladen, 1978), pp. 110–170.

have always sought, however, to weigh the costs and benefits of strike action with great care, basing their strategy on careful analysis of economic data. This attitude, shared by the old Free and Christian unions, made the most important contribution by organized labor to the emergence of the German Model. The Catholic principle of "subsidiarity" has proved helpful in the Federal Republic for designing social insurance programs that command broad public support, especially in the field of health insurance.

During Germany's economic slump of the 1990s, many analysts proclaimed that the German Model was not viable in a globalized economy. The SPD-led government of Gerhard Schröder therefore sought in 2003/ 2004 to promote flexibility on the labor market with the Hartz Reforms, which lowered jobless benefits and pressured the unemployed to accept part-time jobs or short-term employment contracts. These reforms left Germany's organs of co-determination intact but reduced the proportion of workers who participate in them. Economic performance improved significantly thereafter, and the German economy adjusted remarkably well to the global financial crisis of 2008. Most economists now agree that the German Model survives, although it is constantly evolving. The economic sociologist Wolfgang Streeck has identified powerful trends, however, that encourage German corporate management to maximize profits without restraint, including a steep decline in union organization rates, a decline in the proportion of workers covered by a collective labor contract, and a weakening of government power to regulate the economy, related to the massive increase in public debt. Streeck has provided a scholarly foundation for urgent warnings raised by Norbert Blüm in retirement, based on his personal experience as an automobile worker, labor activist, and long-time labor minister, about the consequences of "neo-liberalism" and "globalization". Nobody can predict how long Germany's consensual approach to labor relations will endure.[3]

[3] Harald Bathelt and Meric Gertler, "The German Variety of Capitalism: Forces and Dynamics of Evolutionary Change," *Economic Geography*, 81 (2005): 1–9; David P. Conradt and Eric Langenbacher, *The German Polity*, 10th edn. (Lanham, 2013), pp. 62–71, 249–250, 278–279, 363–365; Wendy Carlin and David Soskice, "German Economic Performance: Disentangling the Role of Supply-side Reforms, Macroeconomic Policy and Coordinated Economy Institutions," *Socio-Economic Review*, 7 (2009): 67–99; Steffen Mueller, "Works Councils and Establishment Productivity," *Industrial and Labor Relations Review*, 65 (2012): 880–898; Andreas Rödder, "'Modell Deutschland' 1950–2011. Konjunkturen einer bundesdeutschen Ordnungsvorstellung," in Tilman Mayer, Karl-Heinz Paqué, and Andreas Apelt, eds., *Modell Deutschland* (Berlin, 2013), pp. 39–51; Christian Dustmann, Bernd Fitzenberger, Uta Schönberg, and Alexandra Spitz-Oener, "From Sick Man of Europe to Economic Superstar: Germany's Resurgent Economy," *The Journal of Economic Perspectives*, 28 (2014): 167–188; Wolfgang Streeck, *Re-Forming Capitalism: Institutional Change in the German Political*

DGB leaders could probably have achieved significant gains for their members if they had embraced Norbert Blüm's proposal in 1974 for an alliance with the Social Committees to achieve parity co-determination. They refused to jeopardize the social-liberal coalition, because they believed that they enjoyed far more influence on it than on any previous government led by the CDU. Thereafter they endured several more political defeats under Chancellor Helmut Schmidt, however, and gained few victories. Schmidt displayed great skill at building personal relationships with individual union leaders, but from 1976 onward he pursued a policy of fiscal austerity and appealed repeatedly for wage restraint. One of Schmidt's first acts after winning reelection in 1976 was to dismiss the union leader Walter Arendt as labor minister and appoint an academic social policy expert, Herbert Ehrenberg. When Ehrenberg paid his first visit to DGB headquarters, Heinz Vetter observed that "the chancellor has appointed a labor minister without any consultation with the DGB. Even under Adenauer that has never happened before. If he had been asked, he would have suggested someone else."[4] It appears doubtful whether the DGB accomplished anything for its membership through alliance with Schmidt of a value comparable to the missed opportunity to achieve parity co-determination. What Blüm called the "emotional fixation" of union leaders on the SPD remained powerful until the 1990s but weakened under Chancellor Schröder. Anger over the Hartz Reforms drove many labor activists to join with former East German Communists in the new party that calls itself simply "The Left."[5]

It was difficult for DGB leaders to take Norbert Blüm's offer of alliance seriously, because the CDU now included few trade union activists. Before the attempt to revive separate Christian trade unions in 1955, Jakob Kaiser had counted 700 Christian social functionaries in the DGB; in 1962 there were apparently around 280, and Maria Weber could only identify 145 colleagues in 1975, many of whom ignored her letters. In 1973 Bernhard Tacke observed that this group had lost more positions in the last three years than in all previous years, not because of bias among

Economy (Oxford, 2009); Wolfgang Streeck, How Will Capitalism End? Essays on a Failing System (London, 2016); Norbert Blüm, Gerechtigkeit. Eine Kritik des Homo oeconomicus (Freiburg, 2006).

[4] DGB Geschäftsführender Bundesvorstand, December 20, 1976, Punkt 2, DGB-Archiv/5/DGCS000079 (source of quotation); Markovits, Trade Unions, pp. 131–157; Hans-Otto Hemmer and Kurt Thomas Schmitz, eds., Geschichte der Gewerkschaften in der Bundesrepublik Deutschland. Von den Anfängen bis heute (Cologne, 1990), pp. 361–374, 408–409.

[5] Jochem Langkau, Hans Matthöfer, and Michael Schneider, eds., SPD und Gewerkschaften, 2 vols. (Bonn, 1994); Conradt and Langenbacher, German Polity, pp.158–164, 170–172; Dan Hough, Michael Koss, and Jonathan Olsen, The Left Party in Contemporary German Politics (Basingstoke and New York, 2007).

union leaders, but because it could not identify plausible candidates for open positions. Tacke and Fritz Biggeleben (who retired in 1972 and 1973) were two of the last DGB functionaries trained by the old Christian trade unions of the Weimar Republic, and the poorly financed adult education seminars of the Social Committees had only inspired a few talented young colleagues to choose a career as labor organizer.[6] Germany's Catholic bishops acknowledged responsibility for this situation in November 1975, when they declared that many priests had displayed an attitude "unfriendly to trade unionism" since 1945, with the result "that it has mostly been not Catholic workers but others who have molded the unified trade unions." Helmut Kohl acknowledged in 1974 that Christian Democrats shared responsibility for this problem. "I sometimes observe still today," he declared to a rally of factory council members, "a remnant of the 19th-century bourgeois point of view in their emotional distance from Christian Democratic people who work full time within the DGB." Kohl insisted that it was an honorable vocation to become a labor organizer but acknowledged that many party colleagues disagreed. It had always been a difficult path for those who sought to combine activism in the CDU and trade unions; they had always been branded as "too red" by one set of colleagues and "too black" by the others. In the 1970s very few young people were motivated to shoulder this burden.[7]

The old idea of a "transmission belt," i.e. that the CDU needs a regional network of working-class activists to inform party leaders about the desires of workers and explain CDU policies to workers, appears quaint in an age when scientific polling and focus groups dominate politics. That transmission belt exerted a very positive influence on German social and political development from 1945 to 1976 nevertheless, and it surely remains important today that organized labor have some meaningful channel of communication with the government, based on personal relationships, regardless of whether the SPD is in power.

[6] "Niederschrift über die Aussprache mit der KAB am 27. Januar 1955," NL Katzer/618/ Aktionsausschuss; Heinrich Wittkamp to Lutz Esser, April 13, 1962, ACDP/ 04–013/141/1; "Geschäftsführender Ausschuss der Arbeitsgemeinschaft christlich-demokratischer DGB-Gewerkschafter," July 8, 1975, DGB-Archiv/5/DGCS000098; Bernhard Tacke, "Die Christlich-Sozialen in der Einheitsgewerkschaft in Vergangenheit und Zukunft," speech of May 12, 1973, NL Tacke/14/1; Rüdiger May, "Zur Strategie der CDA. Bemerkungen und Thesen zur Arbeit der Sozialausschüsse," September 1974, NL Breidbach/2.

[7] "Kirche und Arbeiterschaft: Ein Beschluss der Gemeinsamen Synode der Bistümer in der Bundesrepublik Deutschland," November 21, 1975, in KAB, *Texte zur katholischen Soziallehre. Band II: 2. Halbband* (Kevelaer, 1976), pp. 1469–1519 (quotation on 1482); "Rede Dr. Helmut Kohl," September 28, 1974, NL Zankl/1/3, quotation on p. 3; Helmut Wagner, *Meine Lebensgeschichte. Zwischen schwarz und rot* (Hamburg, 2003).

Perhaps the greatest achievement of the old Christian social labor movement was to promote respect for minority viewpoints and vigorous internal debate within the CDU and trade unions alike. Christian social activists helped both the CDU and DGB to integrate members with diverse outlooks and engage the attention of younger Germans. In the Bundestag elections of 1972 and 1976, the combined vote for the SPD and CDU/CSU exceeded 90 percent, and the voter participation rate also exceeded 90 percent. In 2013 their combined vote was around 60 percent, with a participation rate of 71.5 percent. Thus the proportion of voters who support the two large "people's parties" has plummeted from well over 80 percent to 43 percent. The membership of the DGB briefly surged to eleven million after national reunification in 1990 but has sunk again to six million, no more than it enrolled in a much smaller West Germany in 1953.[8] Political scientists and sociologists are investigating the causes of these trends, but it should be noted that with the decline of the Christian social labor movement, the CDU and DGB have both become more hierarchical organizations, and their congresses have become less interesting.

[8] Conradt and Langenbacher, *German Polity*, pp. 197–213; election returns at www.bundeswahlleiter.de/de/bundestagswahlen/; DGB membership figures at www.dgb.de.

Bibliography

Archival Sources

Archiv des Deutschen Gewerkschaftsbundes, Friedrich-Ebert-Stiftung, *Bonn (historical archive of the German Labor Federation)*

DGB-Archiv/5/DGAI [DGB Bundesvorstand/Abteilung Vorsitzender]: records of the DGB chair.

DGB-Archiv/5/DGCS [DGB Bundesvorstand, Sekretariat Martin Heiss]: records of the office of Martin Heiss.

DGB-Archiv/5/DGCY [DGB Bundesvorsstand, Sekretariat Bernhard Tacke]: records of the office of Bernhard Tacke.

DGB-Archiv/DGB Bundesvorstand/Abteilung Gesellschaftspolitik [alte Signatur]: records of the Department of Social Policy at DGB headquarters.

DGB-Archiv/NL Imbusch (partial collection of the papers of Heinrich Imbusch).

NL Dörpinghaus: personal papers of Karl Dörpinghaus.

NL Fahrenbrach: personal papers of Heinrich Fahrenbrach.

NL Föcher: personal papers of Matthias Föcher.

NL Hansen: personal papers of Werner Hansen.

Archiv für Christlich-Demokratische Politik, Konrad-Adenauer-Stiftung, *Sankt Augustin (historical archive of the Christian Democratic Union)*

ACDP/01–684: Hans Katzer's correspondence as a Bundestag delegate in the 1970s.

ACDP/03–002: records of the Westphalian Social Committees.

ACDP/04–013: *Christlich-Demokratische Arbeitnehmerschaft* (records of the national headquarters of the Social Committees).

ACDP/04–032: records of the Hessian Social Committees.

ACDP/06–021: *Stegerwald Bund* (records of the club of retired trade union functionaries from the Christian trade unions).

ACDP/07–004: *CDU Bundesgeschäftsstelle*, records of the office for trade union affairs at the CDU national party headquarters.

ACDP/08–001: records of the CDU/CSU Bundestag delegation.

ACDP/08–004: records of the Social Policy working group of the CDU/CSU Bundestag delegation (*Arbeitskreis IV*).

NL Albers [ACDP/01–079]: personal papers of Johannes Albers.

NL Andre [ACDP/01–208]: personal papers of Josef Andre.

NL Arndgen [ACDP/01–343]: personal papers of Josef Arndgen.

NL Arnold [ACDP/01–069]: fragmentary personal papers of Karl Arnold.

NL Blank [ACDP/01–098]: personal papers of Theodor Blank.

NL Braukmann [ACDP/01–193]: personal papers of Karl Braukmann.

NL Breidbach [ACDP/01–265]: personal papers of Ferdinand Breidbach.

NL Deus [ACDP/01–561]: personal papers of Franz Deus.

NL Ernst [ACDP/01–385]: personal papers of Johannes Ernst.

NL Even [ACDP/01–184]: personal papers of Johannes Even.

NL Lemmer [ACDP/01–280]: personal papers of Ernst Lemmer.

NL Lücke [ACDP/01–077]: personal papers of Paul Lücke.

NL Mick [ACDP/01–035]: personal papers of Josef Mick.

NL Rott [ACDP/01–101]: personal papers of Michael Rott.

NL Sabel [ACDP/01–275]: personal papers of Anton Sabel.

NL Stegerwald [ACDP/01–206]: personal papers of Adam Stegerwald.

NL Tacke [ACDP/01–455]: personal papers of Bernhard Tacke.

NL Winkelheide [ACDP/01–091]: personal papers of Bernhard Winkelheide.

NL Zankl [ACDP/01–329]: personal papers of Hans Zankl.

Bundesarchiv, *Berlin-Lichterfelde (German National Archive)*

NL Giesberts [N 2097]: personal papers of Johannes Giesberts.

Bundesarchiv, *Koblenz (German National Archive)*

NL Erkelenz [N 1072]: personal papers of Anton Erkelenz.

NL Kaiser [N 1018]: personal papers of Jakob Kaiser.

NL Katzer [N 1362]: voluminous personal papers of Hans Katzer (including many files of the Social Committees, Johannes Albers, and Elfriede Kaiser-Nebgen).

NL Otte [Kleine Erwerbung 461]: records of the League of Christian Trade Unions in the Weimar Republic, preserved by Bernhard Otte.

Haus der Geschichte des Ruhrgebiets: Bibliothek des Ruhrgebiets, *Bochum (affiliated with the Ruhr University of Bochum)*

NL Imbusch (Bochum): personal papers of Heinrich Imbusch.

Historisches Archiv des Erzbistums Köln *(archive of the Catholic Archdiocese of Cologne)*

HAEK/CR II [Cabinetts-Registratur II]: records of the archdiocese regarding bishops' conferences and the Catholic workers' clubs.

HAEK/NL Schmitt: fragmentary personal papers of Hermann-Josef Schmitt.

KAB Archiv, Ketteler-Haus, Cologne (records at the headquarters of the Catholic Workers' Movement).

Landesarchiv Nordrhein-Westfalen, Abteilung Rheinland, *Duisburg (state archive of North Rhine-Westphalia)*

CDA Rheinland [RW 277]: records of the Social Committees of the Rhineland.

NL Gockeln [RW 260]: personal papers of Josef Gockeln.

NL Gronowski [RWN 108]: personal papers of Johannes Gronowski.

NL Platte [RW 91]: personal papers of Johannes Platte.

NL Strunk [RWN 181]: personal papers of Heinrich Strunk.

Stadtarchiv Mönchengladbach (municipal archive of Mönchengladbach)

NL Elfes: personal papers of Wilhelm Elfes (SAMG/15/8).

Published Primary Sources

Akten der Reichskanzlei der Weimarer Republik. Die Kabinette Brüning I und II, 1930–32, ed. Tilman Koops, 3 vols. Boppoard am Rhein, 1982–90.

Barzel, Rainer. *Ein gewagtes Leben. Erinnerungen.* Stuttgart, 2001.

Blankenhorn, Herbert. *Verständnis und Verständigung. Blätter eines politischen Tagebuchs, 1949 bis 1979.* Frankfurt a.M., 1980.

Beier, Gerhard, ed. "Dokumentation: Zur Entstehung des Führerkreises der Vereinigten Gewerkschaften Ende April 1933." *Archiv für Sozialgeschichte,* 15 (1975): 365–392.

Borsdorf, Ulrich, Hans Hemmer, and Martin Martiny, eds. *Grundlagen der Einheitsgewerkschaft.* Cologne, 1977.

Brüning, Heinrich. *Briefe 1946–1960*, ed. Claire Nix. Stuttgart, 1974.

Briefe und Gespräche 1934–1945, ed. Claire Nix. Stuttgart, 1974.

Memoiren 1918–1934. Stuttgart, 1970.

Bundesarchiv, *Die Kabinettsprotokolle der Bundesregierung: Online Version, 1949–1969*, www.bundesarchiv.de/cocoon/barch/0000/index.html.

CDA Kongresse (congresses of the Social Committees of Christian Democratic Workers)

"Neues Wollen, neue Ordnung. Bericht über die Tagung der Sozialausschüsse der CDU Nordrhein-Westfalen," in Herne on November 8/9, 1946. No place or date.

"Erbe und Aufgabe. Bericht über die Tagung der Sozialausschüsse der CDU der britischen Zone in Herne in Westfalen am 21. und 22. Februar 1947," als Manuskript gedruckt, ed. Karl Zimmermann. Recklinghausen, no date.

"Erste Reichstagung der gesamtdeutschen Sozialausschüsse der CDU/CSU in Herne in Westfalen am 28., 29. und 30. November 1947," als Manuskript gedruckt, ed. Karl Zimmermann. Heidelberg, 1948.

Essener Kongress 1950 der christlich-demokratischen Arbeitnehmerschaft: Christlich, Deutsch, Demokratisch, Sozial, Europäisch. Bonn, no date.

Bundestagung der Sozialausschüsse der christlich-demokratischen Arbeitnehmerschaft. Köln, 28. Februar und 1. März 1953. Königswinter, no date.

CDU Fraktionsprotokolle (minutes of the CDU/CSU parliamentary delegation)

Die CDU/CSU im Frankfurter Wirtschaftsrat. Protokolle der Unionsfraktion 1947–1949, ed. Rainer Salzmann. Düsseldorf, 1988.

Die CDU/CSU im Parlamentarischen Rat. Sitzungsprotokolle der Unionsfraktion, ed. Rainer Salzmann. Stuttgart, 1981.

Die CDU/CSU-Fraktion im Deutschen Bundestag. Sitzungsprotokolle 1949–1953, ed. Helge Heidemeyer. Düsseldorf, 1998.

Die CDU/CSU-Fraktion im Deutschen Bundestag. Sitzungsprotokolle 1953–1957, ed. Helge Heidemeyer, 2 vols. Düsseldorf, 2003.

Die CDU/CSU-Fraktion im Deutschen Bundestag. Sitzungsprotokolle 1957–1961, ed. Reinhard Schiffers, 2 vols. Düsseldorf, 2004.

Die CDU/CSU-Fraktion im Deutschen Bundestag. Sitzungsprotokolle 1961–1966, ed. Corinna Franz, 3 vols. Düsseldorf, 2004.

Die CDU/CSU-Fraktion im Deutschen Bundestag. Sitzungsprotokolle 1966–1969, ed. Stefan Marx, 2 vols. Düsseldorf, 2011.

CDU Parteitage (minutes of the CDU party congresses)

Erster Parteitag der Christlich-Demokratischen Union Deutschlands. Goslar, 20.–22 Oktober 1950, Bonn, no date.

Zweiter Parteitag der Christlich-Demokratischen Union Deutschlands. Karlsruhe, 18. bis 21. Oktober 1951. Bonn, no date.

4. Bundesparteitag der CDU, 18.–22. April 1953. Hamburg and Bonn, no date.

5. Bundesparteitag der CDU. Köln, 28.–30. Mai 1954. Bonn, no date.

6. Bundesparteitag der CDU, 26.–29. April 1956 in Stuttgart. Hamburg, no date.

7. Bundesparteitag der CDU. Hamburg, 11.–15. Mai 1957. Hamburg, no date.

8. Bundesparteitag der CDU. Kiel, 18.–21. September 1958. Hamburg, no date.

9. Bundesparteitag der CDU. Karlsruhe, 26.–29. April 1960. Hamburg, no date.

11. Bundesparteitag der CDU. Dortmund, 2.–5. Juni 1962. Hamburg, no date.

12. Bundesparteitag der CDU. 14.–17. März 1964, Hannover. Hamburg, no date.

13. Bundesparteitag der CDU. der CDU. Düsseldorf, 28.–31. März 1965: Niederschrift. Oberhausen, no date.

15. *Bundestagung der CDU. Braunschweig, 22./23. Mai 1967.* Oberhausen and Düsseldorf, 1967.
16. *Bundesparteitag der Christlich Demokratischen Union Deutschlands. Berlin, 4. bis 7. November 1968.* Monschau in Eifel, 1968.
17. *Bundesparteitag der CDU. Mainz, 17./18. November 1969.* Bonn, 1969.
18. *Bundesparteitag der CDU. Düsseldorf, 25.–27. Januar 1971.* Bonn, no date.
22. *Bundesparteitag der Christlich Demokratischen Union Deutschlands. Hamburg, 18.–20. November 1973.* Bonn, 1973.

CDU Vorstandsprotokolle (minutes of the CDU leadership conferences)

Konrad Adenauer und die CDU der britischen Besatzungszone, 1946–1949. Dokumente zur Gründungsgeschichte der CDU Deutschlands, ed. Helmuth Pütz. Bonn, 1975.
Die Unionsparteien 1946–1950. Protokolle der Arbeitsgemeinschaft der CDU/CSU Deutschlands und der Konferenzen der Landesvorsitzenden, ed. Brigitte Kaff. Düsseldorf, 1991.
Adenauer: "Es mußte alles neu gemacht werden." Die Protokolle des CDU-Bundesvorstandes 1950–1953, ed. Günter Buchstab, 2nd edn,. Stuttgart, 1986.
Adenauer: "Wir haben wirklich etwas geschaffen." Die Protokolle des CDU-Bundesvorstands 1953–1957, ed. Günter Buchstab. Düsseldorf, 1990.
Adenauer: "… um den Frieden zu gewinnen." Die Protokolle des CDU-Bundesvorstands 1957–1961, ed. Günter Buchstab. Düsseldorf, 1994.
Adenauer: "Stetigkeit in der Politik." Die Protokolle des CDU-Bundesvorstands 1961–1965, ed. Günter Buchstab. Düsseldorf, 1998.
Kiesinger: "Wir leben in einer veränderten Welt:" Die Protokolle des CDU-Bundesvorstands 1965–1969, ed. Günter Buchstab. Düsseldorf, 2005.
Barzel: "Unsere Alternativen für die Zeit der Opposition." Die Protokolle des CDU-Bundesvorstands 1969–1973, ed. Günter Buchstab and Denise Lindsay. Düsseldorf, 2010.

Der Parlamentarische Rat, 1948–1949: Akten und Protokolle. Band 5: Ausschuss für Grundsatzfragen, ed. Eberhard Pikart and Wolfram Werner, 2 vols. Boppard am Rhein, 1993.
Der Parlamentarische Rat, 1948–1949: Akten und Protokolle. Band 14: Hauptausschuss, ed. Michael Feldkamp, 2 vols. Munich 2009.
Der Spiegel, 1947–2015, go to www.spiegel.de.

DGB KONGRESSE (proceedings of the congresses of the German Labor Federation)

Gewerkschaftliches Zonensekretariat, *Protokoll: Gewerkschafts-Konferenz der britischen Zone vom 21. bis 23. August 1946 in Bielefeld.* Bielefeld, no date.

DGB, *Protokoll: Ausserordentlicher Bundeskongress des Deutschen Gewerkschaftsbundes für die britische Zone, vom 16.-18. Juni 1948 in Recklinghausen.* Cologne, no date.

DGB, *Protokoll. Gründungskongress des Deutschen Gewerkschaftsbundes.* München, 12.-14. Oktober 1949. Cologne, 1950.

DGB, *Protokoll: Ausserordentlicher Bundeskongress des Deutschen Gewerkschaftsbundes, Essen, 22. und 23.* Juni 1951. Cologne, 1951.

DGB, *Protokoll. 2. Ordentlicher Bundeskongress, Berlin, 13.* bis 17. Oktober 1952. Düsseldorf, no date.

DGB, *Protokoll: 3. ordentlicher Bundeskongress, Frankfurt a.M., 4.* bis 9. Oktober 1954. Frankfurt a.M., no date.

DGB, *Protokoll: 4. ordentlicher Bundeskongress Hamburg, 1.* bis 6. Oktober 1956. Cologne, no date.

DGB, *Protokoll: 5. ordentlicher Bundeskongress. Stuttgart, 7.* bis 12. September 1959. Cologne, no date.

DGB, *Protokoll: 6. ordentlicher Bundeskongress. Hannover, 22.* bis 27. Oktober 1962. Cologne, no date.

Die Zeit, 1946–2015, go to www.zeit.de.

Elfes, Wilhelm. "Ich bitte ums Wort. Zur Diskussion mit meinen Freunden," als Manuskript gedruckt. Mönchen-Gladbach, 1945 (found in NL Elfes/2/ 133–57).

Erb, Dirk, ed. *Gleichgeschaltet. Der Nazi-Terror gegen Gewerkschaften und Berufsverbände 1930 bis 1933: Eine Dokumentation.* Göttingen, 2001.

Fait, Barbara, and Alf Mintzel, eds. *Die CSU 1945–1948. Protokolle und Materialien zur Frühgeschichte der Christlich Sozialen Union*, 3 vols. Munich, 1993.

Gesamtverband der christlichen Gewerkschaften Deutschlands

Niederschrift der Verhandlungen des 10. Kongresses der christlichen Gewerkschaften Deutschlands, 20–23 November 1920, Cologne, 1920.

Niederschrift der Verhandlungen des 13. Kongresses der christlichen Gewerkschaften Deutschlands, 18–20 September 1932, Berlin, 1932.

Die Essener Richtlinien 1933 der christlich-nationalen Gewerkschaften, Berlin, 1933.

Gradl, J.B. *Anfang unter dem Sowjetstern. Die CDU 1945–1948 in der sowjetischen Besatzungszone Deutschlands.* Cologne, 1981.

Heck, Bruno. "Adenauer und die Christlich-Demokratische Union Deutschlands," in Dieter Blumenwitz, Klaus Gotto, and Hans Maier, eds., *Konrad Adenauer und seine Zeit. Band I: Beiträge von Weg- und Zeitgenossen*, 2nd edn. Stuttgart, 1976, pp. 186–203.

Kaiser, Josef, ed. "'Wir können da keine Heimat finden, wo wir mit unseren Auffassungen immer wieder erdrückt werden.' Jakob Kaiser vor dem Bundesausschuss des Deutschen Gewerkschaftsbundes am 11. Dezember 1953." *Internationale wissenschaftliche Korrespondenz zur Geschichte der Arbeiterbewegung*, 34 (1998): 37–81.

Katholische Arbeitnehmer-Bewegung Deutschlands. *Texte zur katholischen Soziallehre: Die sozialen Rundschreiben der Päpste und andere kirchliche Dokumente*, 6th edn. 3 vols. Kevelaer, 1985.

Krebs, Albert. *The Infancy of Nazism: The Memoirs of Ex-Gauleiter Albert Krebs, 1923–1933*, ed. William S. Allen. New York, 1976.

Krone, Heinrich. *Tagebücher, 1945–1969*, ed. Hans-Otto Kleinmann, 2 vols. Düsseldorf, 1995–2003.

Lauschke, Karl, ed. *Mehr Demokratie in der Wirtschaft. Die Entstehungsgeschichte des Mitbestimmungsgesetzes von 1976: Dokumente.* Düsseldorf, 2006.

Lemmer, Ernst. *Manches war doch anders. Erinnerungen eines deutschen Demokraten.* Frankfurt am Main, 1968.

Lenz, Otto. *Im Zentrum der Macht. Das Tagebuch von Staatssekretär Lenz, 1951–1953*, ed. Klaus Gotto, Hans-Otto Kleinmann, and Reinhard Schreiner. Düsseldorf, 1988.

Lücke, Paul. *Ist Bonn doch Weimar? Der Kampf um das Mehrheitswahlrecht.* Frankfurt a.M., 1968.

Marx, Stefan, ed. *Der Kressbronner Kreis. Die Protokolle des Koalitionsausschusses der ersten Grossen Koalitiou aus CDU, CSU und SPD.* Düsseldorf, 2013.

Mayer, Tilman, ed. *Jakob Kaiser: Gewerkschafter und Patriot. Eine Werkauswahl.* Cologne, 1988.

Mensing, Peter, ed. *Adenauer – Heuss. Unter vier Augen: Gespräche aus den Gründerjahren 1949–1959*, 2nd edn. Berlin, 1999.

Morsey, Rudolf, ed. *Die Protokolle der Reichstagsfraktion und des Fraktionsvorstands der Deutschen Zentrumspartei 1926–1933.* Mainz, 1969.

Müller-List, Gabrielle, ed. *Montanmitbestimmung. Das Gesetz über die Mitbestimmung der Arbeitnehmer in den Aufsichtsräten und Vorständen der Unternehmen des Bergbaus und der Eisen und Stahl erzeugenden Industrie vom 21. Mai 1951.* Düsseldorft, 1984 (cited as *Quellen: Montanmitbestimmung*).

Pope Leo XIII, *Rerum novarum.* 1891. Go to w2.vatican.va.

Pope John XXIII, *Mater et Magistra.* 1961. Go to w2.vatican.va.

Pope John XXIII, *Pacem in Terris.* 1963. Go to w2.vatican.va.

Pope Pius XI, *Quadragesimo Anno.* 1931. Go to w2.vatican.va.

Quellen Zur Geschichte der Deutschen Gewerkschaftsbewegung im 20. Jahrhundert (cited as *Gewerkshaftsquellen*)

Band IV: Die Gewerkschaften in der Endphase der Republik, 1930–1933, ed. Peter Jahn. Cologne, 1988.

Band V: Die Gewerkschaften im Widerstand und in der Emigration 1933–1945, ed. Siegfried Mielke and Matthias Frese. Frankfurt a.M., 1999.

Band VI: Organisatorischer Aufbau der Gewerkschaften 1945–1949, ed. Siegfried Mielke. Cologne, 1987.

Band VII: Gewerkschaften in Politik, Wirtschaft und Gesellschaft 1945–1949, ed. Siegried Mielke and Peter Rütters. Cologne, 1991.

Band IX: Die Industriegewerkschaft Metall in den Jahren 1956 bis 1963, ed. Felicitas Merkel. Frankfurt a.M., 1999.

Band X: Die Industriegewerkschaft Metall in der frühen Bundesrepublik, 1950–1956, ed. Walter Dörrich and Klaus Schönhoven. Cologne, 1991.

Band XI: Der Deutsche Gewerkschaftsbund, 1949 bis 1956, ed. Josef Kaiser. Cologne, 1996.

Band XII: Der Deutsche Gewerkschaftsbund, 1956–1963, ed. Jens Hildebrandt. Bonn, 2005.

Band XIII: Der Deutsche Gewerkschaftsbund, 1964–1969, ed. Wolther von Kieseritzky. Bonn, 2006.

Band XVI: Der Deutsche Gewerkschaftsbund, 1969–1975, ed. Klaus Mertsching. Bonn, 2013.

Ruhl, Klaus-Jörg, ed. *Neubeginn und Restauration. Dokumente zur Vorgeschichte der Bundesrepublik Deutschland 1945–1949*, 3rd edn. Munich, 1989.

Schroeder, Wolfgang, ed. *Gewerkschaftspolitik zwischen DGB, Katholizismus und CDU, 1945 bis 1960. Katholische Arbeiterführer als Zeitzeugen in Interviews*. Cologne, 1990.

Schwering, Leo. *Frühgeschichte der Christlich-Demokratischen Union*. Recklinghausen, 1963.

Siemer, Laurentius. *Aufzeichnungen und Briefe*. Frankfurt am Main, 1957.

Soziale Ordnung, 1947–1976 (the monthly journal of the Social Committees of Christian Democratic Workers).

Storch, Anton. "Lebenserinnerungen," in Deutscher Bundestag, *Abgeordnete des Deutschen Bundestages. Aufzeichnungen und Erinnerungen*, vol. 2, Boppard am Rhein, 1983, pp. 319–344.

Vetter, Heinz Oskar. *Mitbestimmung –Idee, Wege, Ziel*. Cologne, 1979 (collected speeches).

Wagner, Helmut. *Meine Lebensgeschichte: Zwischen schwarz und rot. 50 Jahre in der CDU, 50 Jahre in der Gewerkschaft*. Hamburg, 2003.

Welty, Eberhard. *Die Entscheidung in die Zukunft. Grundsätze und Hinweise zur Neuordnung im deutschen Lebensraum*. Heidelberg, 1946.

Udo Wengst, ed. *Auftakt zur Ära Adenauer. Koalitionsverhandlungen und Regierungsbildung*. Düsseldorf, 1985 (cited as *Quellen: Koalitionsverhandlungen*).

Secondary Sources

Angster, Julia. *Konsenskapitalismus und Sozialdemokratie. Die Westernisierung von SPD und DGB*. Munich, 2003.

Aretz, Jürgen. *Katholische Arbeiterbewegung und Nationalsozialismus. Der Verband katholischer Arbeiter- und Knappenvereine Westdeutschlands, 1924–1945*. Mainz, 1978.

Aretz, Jürgen, Rudolf Morsey, and Anton Rauscher, eds. *Zeitgeschichte in Lebensbildern. Aus dem deutschen Katholizismus des 20. Jahrhunderts*. 12 vols., Münster, 1973–2007.

Balderston, Theo. *Economics and Politics in the Weimar Republic*. Cambridge, 2002.

The Origins and Course of the German Economic Crisis, November 1923 to May 1932. Berlin, 1993.

Baring, Arnulf. *Machtwechsel. Die Ära Brandt-Scheel*, 3rd edn. Stuttgart, 1982.

Baus, Ralf Thomas. *Die Christlich-Demokratische Union Deutschlands in der sowjetisch besetzten Zone, 1945 bis 1948*. Düsseldorf, 2001.

Beier, Gerhard. *Der Demonstrations- und Generalstreik vom 12. November 1948*. Frankfurt a.M., 1975.

Die illegale Reichsleitung der Gewerkschaften 1933–1945. Cologne, 1981.

"Einheitsgewerkschaft. Zur Geschichte eines organisatorischen Prinzips der deutschen Arbeiterbewegung." *Archiv für Sozialgeschichte*, 13 (1973): 207–242.

Willi Richter. Ein Leben für die soziale Neuordnung. Cologne, 1978.

Benz, Wolfgang. *Von der Besatzungsherrschaft zur Bundesrepublik. Stationen einer Staatsgründung 1946–1949*. Frankfurt a.M., 1984.

Besier, Gerhard, with Francesca Piombo. *The Holy See and Hitler's Germany*. Trans. W.R. Ward, New York, 2007 (first published as *Der Heilige Stuhl und Hitler-Deutschland*, Munich, 2004).

Blüm, Norbert. *Gerechtigkeit. Eine Kritik des Homo oeconomicus*. Freiburg, 2006.

Borsdorf, Ulrich, and Hans Hemmer, eds. *Vom Sozialistengesetz zur Mitbestimmung. Zum 100. Geburtstag von Hans Böckler*. Cologne, 1975.

Borsdorf, Ulrich, Hans Hemmer, Gerhard Leminsky, and Heinz Markmann, eds. *Gewerkschaftliche Politik: Reform aus Solidarität. Zum 60. Geburtstag von Heinz O. Vetter*. Cologne, 1977.

Bösch, Frank. *Die Adenauer-CDU. Gründung, Aufstieg und Krise einer Erfolgspartei 1945–1969*. Stuttgart and Munich, 2001.

Bracher, Karl Dietrich, Wolfgang Jäger, and Werner Link, *Republik im Wandel, 1969–1974. Geschichte der Bundesrepublik Deutschland: Band 5/1*. Stuttgart, 1986.

Brady, Steven. *Eisenhower and Adenauer: Alliance Maintenance under Pressure, 1953–1960*. Lanham, 2010.

Braunthal, Gerard. *The West German Social Democrats, 1969–1982: Profile of a Party in Power*. Boulder, 1983.

Brose, Eric Dorn. *Christian Labor and the Politics of Frustration in Imperial Germany*. Washington, DC, 1985.

Brunner, Detlev. *Bürokratie und Politik des Allgemeinen Deutschen Gewerkschaftsbundes 1918/19 bis 1933*. Cologne, 1992.

Buchstab, Günter, Brigitte Kaff, and Hans-Otto Kleinmann, eds. *Christliche Demokraten gegen Hitler. Aus Verfolgung und Widerstand zur Union*. Freiburg, 2004.

Buchstab, Günter, Brigitte Kaff, and Hans-Otto Kleinmann, eds. *Verfolgung und Widerstand 1933–1945. Christliche Demokraten gegen Hitler*. Düsseldorf, 1986.

Buchstab, Günter, Philipp Gassert, and Peter Thaddäus, eds. *Kurt Georg Kiesinger, 1904–1988. Von Ebingen ins Kanzleramt*. Freiburg, 2005.

Bücker, Vera. "Bernhard Letterhaus (1894–1944)," in Karl-Joseph Hummel and Christoph Strohm, eds., *Zeugen einer besseren Welt. Christliche Märtyrer des 20. Jahrhunderts*. Leipzig, 2000, pp. 276–296.

Nikolaus Gross. Politischer Journalist und Katholik im Widerstand des Kölner Kreises. Münster, 2003.

Buschak, Willy. "*Arbeit im kleinsten Zirkel.*" *Gewerkschaften im Widerstand gegen den Nationalsozialismus*. Hamburg, 1993.

Carlin, Wendy, and David Soskice. "German Economic Performance: Disentangling the Role of Supply-side Reforms, Macroeconomic Policy and Coordinated Economy Institutions." *Socio-Economic Review*, 7 (2009): 67–99.

Cary, Noel. *The Path to Christian Democracy: German Catholics and the Party System from Windhorst to Adenauer.* Cambridge, MA, 1996.

Ciampani, Andrea, and Massimiliano Valente. "The Social and Political Dynamics of the Christian Workers in Unified Trade Union Movements: The Experiences of Italy and West Germany after World War II," in Lex Heerma van Voss, Patrick Pasture, and Jan de Maeyer, eds., *Between Cross and Class: Comparative Histories of Christian Labour in Europe, 1840–2000.* Bern, 2005, pp. 203–223.

Conradt, David, and Eric Langenbacher. *The German Polity,* 10th edn. Lanham, MD, 2013.

Conze, Werner. *Jakob Kaiser: Politiker zwischen Ost und West, 1945–1949.* Stuttgart, 1969.

Creuzberger, Stefan. *Kampf für die Einheit. Das gesamtdeutsche Ministerium und die politische Kultur ds Kalten Krieges, 1949–1969.* Düsseldorf, 2008.

Crew, David. *Germans on Welfare: From Weimar to Hitler.* Oxford, 1998.

Dahrendorf, Ralf. *Society and Democracy in Germany.* New York, 1969 (first published as *Gesellschaft und Demokratie in Deutschland,* Munich, 1965).

Dietrich, Yorck. *Eigentum für jeden. Die vermögenspolitischen Initiativen der CDU und die Gesetzgebung, 1950–1961.* Düsseldorf, 1996.

Drummond, Gordon D. *The Social Democrats in Opposition, 1949–1960: The Case Against Rearmament.* Norman, OK, 1982.

Edinger, Lewis. *Kurt Schumacher: A Study in Personality and Political Behavior.* Stanford, 1965.

Eisenberg, Carolyn. *Drawing the Line: The American Decision to Divide Germany, 1944–1949.* Cambridge, 1996.

Engel, Helmut, ed. *Ludwig Erhard.* Berlin, 2010.

Esser, Albert. *Wilhelm Elfes, 1884–1969. Arbeiterführer und Politiker.* Mainz, 1990.

Feldman, Gerald. *The Great Disorder: Politics, Economics, and Society in the German Inflation, 1914–1924.* Oxford, 1997.

Feldman, Gerald, and Irmgard Steinisch. *Industrie und Gewerkschaften 1918–1924. Die überforderte Zentralarbeitsgemeinschaft.* Stuttgart, 1985.

Fichter, Michael. *Besatzungsmacht und Gewerkschaften. Zur Entwicklung und Anwendung der US-Gewerkschaftspolitik in Deutschland, 1944–1948.* Opladen, 1982.

Fink, Ulf, ed. *Hans Katzer. Partnerschaft statt Klassenkampf.* Cologne, 1989.

Focke, Franz. *Sozialismus aus christlicher Verantwortung. Die Idee eines christlichen Sozialismus in der katholisch-sozialen Bewegung und in der CDU.* Wuppertal, 1978.

Forster, Bernhard. *Adam Stegerwald (1874–1945). Christlich-nationaler Gewerkschafter, Zentrumspolitiker, Mitbegründer der Unionsparteien.* Düsseldorf, 2003.

Friedrich, Norbert. *"Die christlich-soziale Fahne empor!" Reinhard Mumm und die christlich-soziale Bewegung.* Stuttgart, 1997.

Führer, Christian. *Arbeitslosigkeit und die Entstehung der Arbeitslosenversicherung in Deutschland 1902–1927*. Berlin, 1990.

Fürtwangler, Franz Josef. *ÖTV. Die Geschichte einer Gewerkschaft*. Stuttgart, 1955.

Gauly, Thomas. *Katholiken. Machtanspruch und Machtverlust*. Bonn, 1992.

Gimbel, John. *The American Occupation of Germany: Politics and the Military, 1945–1949*. Stanford, 1968.

Granieri, Ronald. *The Ambivalent Alliance: Konrad Adenauer, the CDU/CSU, and the West, 1949–1966*. New York and Oxford, 2003.

Gray, William Glenn. *Germany's Cold War: The Global Campaign to Isolate East Germany, 1949–1969*. Chapel Hill, 2003.

Grebing, Helga, ed. *Geschichte der sozialen Ideen in Deutschland: Sozialismus, Katholische Soziallehre, Protestantische Sozialethik*. Essen, 2000.

Grossmann, Thomas. *Zwischen Kirche und Gesellschaft. Das Zentralkomitee der deutschen Katholiken 1945–1970*. Mainz, 1991.

Gruber, Ludger. *Die CDU-Landtagsfraktion in Nordrhein-Westfalen, 1946–1980*. Düsseldorf, 1998.

Gundelach, Herlind. "Die Sozialausschüsse zwischen CDU und DGB. Selbstverständnis und Rolle 1949–1966," phil. diss. Bonn, 1983.

Hamel, Iris. *Völkischer Verband und nationale Gewerkschaft. Der Deutschnationale Handlungsgehilfen-Verband 1893–1933*. Frankfurt am Main, 1967.

Hamerow, Theodore. *On the Road to the Wolf's Lair: German Resistance to Hitler*. Cambridge, MA, 1997.

Harsch, Donna. *German Social Democracy and the Rise of Nazism*. Chapel Hill, 1993.

Heitzer, Horstwalter. *Der Volksverein für das katholische Deutschland im Kaiserreich 1890–1918*. Mainz, 1979.

Die CDU in der britischen Zone 1945–1949. Gründung, Organisation, Programm und Politik. Düsseldorf, 1988.

Hemmer, Hans-Otto, and Kurt Thomas Schmitz, eds. *Geschichte der Gewerkschaften in der Bundesrepublik Deutschland. Von den Anfängen bis heute*. Cologne, 1990.

Hentschel, Volker. *Ludwig Erhard. Ein Politikerleben*. Bremen, 1998.

Herbers, Winfried. *Der Verlust der Hegemonie. Die Kölner CDU, 1945/46–1964*. Düsseldorf, 2003.

Herbert, Ulrich. "Arbeiterschaft im 'Dritten Reich': Zwischenbilanz und offene Fragen." *Geschichte und Gesellschaft*, 15 (1989): 320–360.

Hiepel, Claudia. *Arbeiterkatholizismus an der Ruhr. August Brust und der Gewerkverein christlicher Bergarbeiter*. Stuttgart, 1999.

Hildebrand, Klaus. *Von Erhard zur Grossen Koalition, 1963–1969. Geschichte der Bundesrepublik Deutschland: Band 4*. Stuttgart, 1984.

Hirsch-Weber, Wolfgang. *Gewerkschaften in der Politik. Von der Massenstreikdebatte zum Kampf um das Mitbestimmungsrecht*. Cologne, 1959.

Hockerts, Hans Günter. *Der deutsche Sozialstaat. Entfaltung und Gefährdung seit 1945*. Göttingen, 2011.

Sozialpolitische Entscheidungen im Nachkriegsdeutschland. Alliierte und deutsche Sozialversicherungspolitik 1945 bis 1957. Stuttgart, 1980.

Hoffmann, Peter. *The History of the German Resistance, 1933–1945.* Cambridge, MA, 1977.

Hong, Young-Sun. *Welfare, Modernity, and the Weimar State, 1919–1933.* Princeton, 1998.

Hough, Dan, Michael Koss, and Jonathan Olsen. *The Left Party in Contemporary German Politics.* Basingstoke, Hampshire, and New York, 2007.

Hüwel, Detlev. *Karl Arnold. Eine politische Biographie.* Wuppertal, 1980.

Jacoby, Wade. *Imitation and Politics: Redesigning Modern Germany.* Ithaca, 2000.

Jäger, Wolfgang. *Bergarbeitermilieus and Parteien im Ruhrgebiet. Zum Wahlverhalten des katholischen Bergarbeitermilieus bis 1933.* Munich, 1996.

James, Harold. *The German Slump: Politics and Economics 1924–1936.* Oxford, 1986.

Jones, Larry Eugene. "Between the Fronts: The German National Union of Commercial Employees, 1928 to 1933." *Journal of Modern History,* 48 (1976): 462–482.

German Liberalism and the Dissolution of the Weimar Party System, 1918–1933. Chapel Hill, 1988.

Jones, Larry Eugene, ed. *The German Right in the Weimar Republic: Studies in the History of German Conservatism, Nationalism, and Antisemitism.* New York and Oxford, 2014.

Kempter, Klaus. *Eugen Loderer und die IG Metall. Biografie eines Gewerkschafters.* Filderstadt, 2003.

Kent, Peter. *The Lonely Cold War of Pope Pius XII: The Roman Catholic Church and the Division of Europe, 1943–1950.* Montreal, 2002.

Kettenacker, Lothar. *Germany since 1945.* Oxford, 1997.

Kitzinger, U.W. *German Electoral Politics: A Study of the 1957 Campaign.* Oxford, 1960.

Klein, Gotthard. *Der Volksverein für das katholische Deutschland 1890–1933.* Paderborn, 1996.

Klein-Reesink, Andreas. *Textilarbeiter und Nationalsozialismus im Westmünsterland. Eine regionale Untersuchung zur Auseinandersetzung katholischer Arbeiter mit dem Faschismus.* Münster, 1981.

Kleinmann, Hans-Otto. *Geschichte der CDU 1945–1982.* Stuttgart, 1993.

"Theodor Blank," in Jürgen Aretz, ed., *Zeitgeschichte in Lebensbildern,* VI: 171–188.

Klemperer, Klemens von, Enrico Syring, and Rainer Zitelmann, eds. *"Für Deutschland." Die Männer des 20. Juli.* Frankfurt a.M., 1993.

Klessmann, Christoph, "Betriebsgruppen und Einheitsgewerkschaft. Zur betrieblichen Arbeit der politischen Parteien in der Frühphase der westdeutschen Arbeiterbewegung, 1945–1952." *Vierteljahrshefte für Zeitgeschichte,* 31 (1983): 272–307.

Klessmann, Christoph, and Peter Friedemann. *Streiks und Hungermärsche im Ruhrgebiet 1946–1948.* Frankfurt a.M., 1977.

Klotzbach, Kurt. *Der Weg zur Staatspartei. Programmatik, praktische Politik und Organisation der deutschen Sozialdemokratie 1945 bis 1965.* Bonn, 1982.

Koch, Bernhard. *100 Jahre Christliche Gewerkschaften.* Würzburg, 1999.

Koch, Peter. *Willy Brandt. Eine politische Biographie.* Frankfurt a.M., 1989.

Koerfer, Daniel. *Kampf ums Kanzleramt. Erhard und Adenauer.* Darmstadt, 1987.

Kosthorst, Erich. *Jakob Kaiser: Der Arbeiterführer.* Stuttgart, 1967.

Jakob Kaiser: Bundesminister für gesamtdeutsche Fragen, 1949–1957. Stuttgart, 1972.

Krenn, Dorit-Maria. *Die Christliche Arbeiterbewegung in Bayern vom Ersten Weltkrieg bis 1933.* Mainz, 1991.

Krüger, Dieter. *Das Amt Blank. Die schwierige Gründung des Bundesministeriums für Verteidigung.* Freiburg, 1993.

Lange, Erhard. "Landrat Josef Schrage (1881–1953). 'Dem heimatgebundenen Wirken am nächsten …'." *Olpe in Geschichte und Gegenwart. Jahrbuch des Heimatvereins für Olpe und Umgebung,* 10 (2002): 105–142.

Large, David Clay. *Germans to the Front: West German Rearmament in the Adenauer Era.* Chapel Hill, 1996.

Lauschke, Karl. *Die halbe Macht. Mitbestimmung in der Eisen- und Stahlindustrie, 1945 bis 1989.* Essen, 2007.

Hans Böckler. Band 2: Gewerkschaftlicher Neubeginn, 1945 bis 1951. Frankfurt a. M., 2005.

Mehr Demokratie in der Wirtschaft. Die Entstehungsgeschichte des Mitbestimmungsgesetzes von 1976. Düsseldorf, 2006.

Leithäuser, Joachim. *Wilhelm Leuschner: Ein Leben für die Republik.* Cologne, 1962.

Lösche, Peter, and Franz Walter. *Die SPD: Klassenpartei – Volkspartei – Quotenpartei. Zur Entwicklung der Sozialdemokratie von Weimar bis zur deutschen Vereinigung.* Darmstadt, 1992.

Maier, Charles. *Recasting Bourgeois Europe: Stabilization in France, Germany, and Italy in the Decade after World War I.* Princeton, 1975.

Mallmann, Klaus-Michael, and Horst Steffens. *Lohn der Mühen. Geschichte der Bergarbeiter an der Saar.* Munich, 1989.

Markovits, Andrei S. *The Politics of the West German Trade Unions: Strategies of Class and Interest Representation in Growth and Crisis.* Cambridge, 1986.

Mason, Tim. *Social Policy in the Third Reich: The Working Class and the "National Community,"* trans. John Broadwin. Oxford and Providence, 1993.

Matthias, Erich, and Rudolf Morsey, eds. *Das Ende der Parteien 1933. Darstellungen und Dokumente.* Düsseldorf, 1960.

Matthias, Erich, and Klaus Schönhoven, eds. *Solidarität und Menschenwürde. Etappen der deutschen Gewerkschaftsgeschichte von den Anfängen bis zur Gegenwart.* Bonn, 1984.

Mayer, Tilman. "'Gerechtigkeit schafft Frieden.' Die Gesellschaftspolitik Hans Katzers," in Ulf Fink, ed., *Hans Katzer. Partnerschaft statt Klassenkampf,* Cologne, 1989, pp. 11–37.

Mayer, Tilman, Karl-Heinz Paqué, and Andreas Apelt, eds. *Modell Deutschland.* Berlin, 2013.

Mergel, Thomas. "Das Scheitern des deutschen Tory-Konservatismus. Die Umformung der DNVP zu einer rechtsradikalen Partei 1928–1932." *Historische Zeitschrift,* 276 (2003): 323–368.

Parlamentarische Kultur in der Weimarer Republik. Politische Kommunikation, symbolische Politik und Öffentlichkeit im Reichstag. Düsseldorf, 2002.

Merkl, Peter. *The Origin of the West German Republic*. Westport, Conn., 1982.

Mielke, Siegfried, and Günter Morsch, eds. *"Seid wachsam, dass über Deutschland nie wieder die Nacht hereinbricht."* *Gewerkschafter in Konzentrationslagern 1933–1945*. Berlin, 2011.

Mierzejewski, Alfred. *Ludwig Erhard: A Biography*. Chapel Hill, 2004.

Militärgeschichtliches Forschungsamt, ed. *Anfänge westdeutscher Sicherheitspolitik 1945–1956*, 4 vols. Munich, 1982–1997.

Misner, Paul. *Social Catholicism in Europe: From the Onset of Industrialization to the First World War*. New York, 1991.

Catholic Labor Movements in Europe: Social Thought and Action, 1914–1965. Washington, DC, 2015.

Mitchell, Maria. "Materialism and Secularism: CDU Politicians and National Socialism, 1945–1949." *Journal of Modern History*, 67 (1995): 278–308.

The Origins of Christian Democracy: Politics and Confession in Modern Germany. Ann Arbor, 2012.

Mockenhaupt, Hubert. *Weg und Wirken des geistlichen Sozialpolitikers Heinrich Brauns*. Paderborn, 1977.

Moeller, Robert. *Protecting Motherhood: Women and the Family in the Politics of Postwar West Germany*. Berkeley, 1993.

Möller, Martin. *Evangelische Kirche und Sozialdemokratische Partei in den Jahren 1945–1950. Grundlagen der Verständigung und Beginn des Dialoges*. Göttingen, 1984.

Mommsen, Hans. *Alternative zu Hitler. Studien zur Geschichte des deutschen Widerstandes*. Munich, 2000.

Mommsen, Hans, and Ulrich Borsdorf, eds. *Glück auf, Kameraden! Die Bergarbeiter und ihre Organisationen in Deutschland*. Cologne, 1979.

Morsey, Rudolf. *Der Untergang des politischen Katholizismus. Die Zentrumspartei zwischen christlichem Selbstverständnis und "Nationaler Erhebung" 1932/33*. Stuttgart, 1977.

Mueller, Steffen. "Works Councils and Establishment Productivity." *Industrial and Labor Relations Review*, 65 (2012): 880–898.

Mühlen, Patrik von zur. *"Schlagt Hitler an der Saar!" Abstimmungskampf, Emigration und Widerstand im Saargebiet, 1933–1935*. Bonn, 1979.

Müller, Dirk. *Arbeiter, Katholizismus, Staat. Der Volksverein für das katholische Deutschland und die katholischen Arbeiterorganisationen in der Weimarer Republik*. Bonn, 1996.

Nebgen, Elfriede. *Jakob Kaiser: Der Widerstandskämpfer*, 2nd edn. Stuttgart, 1970.

Nell-Breuning, Oswald von. *Wie sozial ist die Kirche? Leistung und Versagen der katholischen Soziallehre*. Düsseldorf, 1972.

Nicholls, A.J. *Freedom with Responsibility: The Social Market Economy in Germany, 1918–1963*. Oxford, 1994.

Niethammer, Lutz, ed. *"Die Jahre weiss man nicht, wo man die heute hinsetzen soll." Faschismuserfahrungen im Ruhrgebiet*. Bonn, 1983.

Nonn, Christoph. *Die Ruhrbergbaukrise. Entindustrialisierung und Politik, 1958–1969*. Göttingen, 2001.

O'Malley, John W. *What Happened at Vatican II*. Cambridge, MA, 2008.

Opitz, Günter. *Der Christlich-soziale Volksdienst. Versuch einer protestantischen Partei in der Weimarer Republik.* Düsseldorf, 1969.

Pasture, Patrick. *Histoire du syndicalisme chrétien international. La difficile recherche d'une troisième voie.* Paris and Montreal, 1999.

Patch, William L. *Christian Trade Unions in the Weimar Republic, 1918–1933: The Failure of "Corporate Pluralism."* New Haven, 1985.

"Fascism, Catholic Corporatism, and the Christian Trade Unions of Germany, Austria, and France," in Lex Heerma van Voss, Patrick Pasture, and Jan De Maeyer, eds., *Between Cross and Class: Comparative Histories of Christian Labour in Europe 1840–2000*, Bern, 2005, pp. 173–201.

Heinrich Brüning and the Dissolution of the Weimar Republic. Cambridge, 1998.

"The Catholic Church, the Third Reich, and the Origins of the Cold War: On the Utility and Limitations of Historical Evidence." *Journal of Modern HIstory*, 82 (2010): 396–433.

"The Legend of Compulsory Unification: The Catholic Clergy and the Revival of Trade Unionism in West Germany after the Second World War." *Journal of Modern History*, 79 (2007): 848–880.

Pirker, Theo. *Die blinde Macht. Die Gewerkschaftsbewegung in der Bundesrepublik*, 2 vols. Berlin, 1979.

Plener, Ulla. *Theodor Leipart (1867–1947). Persönlichkeit, Handlungsmotive, Wirken, Bilanz – Ein Lebensbild in Dokumenten*, 2 vols. Berlin, 2000–2001.

Potthoff, Erich. *Der Kampf um die Montanmitbestimmung.* Cologne, 1957.

Potthoff, Heinrich. *Freie Gewerkschaften 1918–1933. Der Allgemeine Deutsche Gewerkschaftsbund in der Weimarer Republik.* Düsseldorf, 1987.

Preller, Ludwig. *Sozialpolitik in der Weimarer Republik*, reprint. Düsseldorf, 1978.

Pridham, Geoffrey. *Christian Democracy in Western Germany: The CDU/CSU in Government and Opposition, 1945–1976.* London, 1977.

Pyta, Wolfram. *Hindenburg. Herrschaft zwischen Hohenzollern und Hitler.* Munich, 2007.

Remeke, Stefan. *Anders links sein. Auf den Spuren von Maria Weber und Gerd Muhr.* Essen, 2012.

Reucher, Ursula. *Reformen und Reformversuche in der gesetzlichen Krankenversicherung (1956–1965). Ein Beitrag zur Geschichte bundesdeutscher Sozialpolitik.* Düsseldorf, 1999.

Reulecke, Jürgen, ed. *Arbeiterbewegung an Rhein und Ruhr. Beiträge zur Geschichte der Arbeiterbewegung in Rheinland-Westfalen.* Wuppertal, 1974.

Richter, Ludwig. *Die Deutsche Volkspartei 1918–1933.* Düsseldorf, 2002.

Ritter, Gerhard. *Carl Goerdeler und die deutsche Widerstandsbewegung.* Stuttgart, 1954.

Ritter, Gerhard A. *Social Welfare in Germany and Britain: Origins and Development.* Leamington Spa and New York, 1983.

Ritter, Gerhard A., and Klaus Tenfelde, *Arbeiter im Deutschen Kaiserreich 1871 bis 1914.* Bonn, 1992.

Rohe, Karl. "Political Alignments and Re-alignments in the Ruhr, 1867–1987: Continuity and Change of Political Traditions in an Industrial Region," in Karl Rohe, *Elections, Parties, and Political Traditions: Social Foundations of German Parties and Party Systems, 1867–1987*, New York, 1990, pp. 107–144.

Rueckert, George, and Wilder Crane. "CDU Deviancy in the German Bundestag." *Journal of Politics*, 24 (1962): 477–488.

Schäfer, Michael. *Heinrich Imbusch. Christlicher Gewerkschaftsführer und Widerstandskämpfer.* Munich, 1990.

Schmädeke, Jürgen, and Peter Steinbach, eds. *Der Widerstand gegen den Nationalsozialismus. Die deutsche Gesellschaft und der Widerstand gegen Hitler.* Munich, 1985.

Schmidt, Eberhard. *Die verhinderte Neuordnung 1945–1952. Zur Auseinandersetzung um die Demokratisierung der Wirtschaft in den westlichen Besatzungszonen und in der Bundesrepublik Deutschland*, 7th edn. Frankfurt a.M., 1977.

Schmidt, Ute. *Zentrum oder CDU. Politischer Katholizismus zwischen Tradition und Anpassung.* Opladen, 1987.

Schneider, Michael. *Arbeiter und Arbeiterbewegung 1933 bis 1939. Unterm Hakenkreuz.* Bonn, 1999.

Arbeiter und Arbeiterbewegung 1939 bis 1945. In der Kriegsgesellschaft. Bonn, 2014.

Demokratie in Gefahr? Der Konflikt um die Notstandsgesetze: Sozialdemokratie, Gewerkschaften und intellektueller Protest (1958–1968). Bonn, 1986.

Die christlichen Gewerkschaften 1894–1933. Bonn, 1982.

"Jakob Kaiser und das Ende der Christlichen Gewerkschaften 1932/33," in Tilman Mayer, ed., *"Macht das Tor auf." Jakob-Kaiser-Studien*, Berlin, 1996, pp. 11–42.

Schroeder, Wolfgang. "Christliche Sozialpolitik oder Sozialismus. Oswald von Nell-Breuning, Viktor Agartz und der Frankfurter DGB-Kongress 1954." *Vierteljahrshefte für Zeitgeschichte*, 39 (1991): 179–220.

"Die gewerkschaftspolitische Diskussion in der evangelischen Kirche zwischen 1945 und 1955," in Frank von Auer and Franz Segbers, eds., *Sozialer Protestantismus und Gewerkschaftsbewegung. Kaiserreich – Weimarer Republik – Bundesrepublik Deutschland*, Cologne, 1994, pp. 221–241.

Katholizismus und Einheitsgewerkschaft. Der Streit um den DGB und der Niedergang des Sozialkatholizismus in der Bundesrepublik bis 1960. Bonn, 1992.

Schulz, Günther. *Wiederaufbau in Deutschland. Die Wohnungsbaupolitik in den Westzonen und der Bundesrepublik von 1945 bis 1957.* Düsseldorf, 1994.

Schulz, Günther, ed. *Geschichte der Sozialpolitik in Deutschland seit 1945. Band 3: Bundesrepublik Deutschland, 1949–1957.* Baden-Baden, 2005.

Schummer, Uwe, ed. *CDA 1945 bis 1995.* Bergisch-Gladbach, 1995.

Schwarte, Johannes. *Gustav Gundlach S.J. (1892–1963). Massgeblicher Repräsentant der katholischen Soziallehre während der Pontifikate Pius' XI. und Pius' XII.* Munich, 1975.

Schwarz, Hans-Peter. *Adenauer*, 2 vols. Stuttgart, 1986–1991.

Die Ära Adenauer, 1949–1957. Geschichte der Bundesrepublik Deutschland: Band 2. Stuttgart, 1981.

Helmut Kohl. Eine politische Biographie, Munich, 2012.

Schwarz, Hans-Peter, ed. *Die Fraktion als Machtfaktor. CDU/CSU im Deutschen Bundestag, 1949 bis heute.* Munich, 2009.

Steenson, Gary. *"Not One Man! Not One Penny!" German Social Democracy, 1863–1914*. Pittsburgh, 1981.

Steininger, Rolf. "England und die Gewerkschaftsbewegung 1945/46." *Archiv für Sozialgeschichte*, 18 (1978): 41–116.

Streeck, Wolfgang. *How Will Capitalism End? Essays on a Failing System*. London and New York, 2016.

Re-Forming Capitalism. Institutional Change in the German Political Economy. Oxford, 2009.

Stürmer, Michael. *Koalition und Opposition in der Weimarer Republik 1924–1928*. Düsseldorf, 1967.

Thiesen, Helene. "Christlich-soziale Arbeitnehmerschaft und Gewerkschaftsfrage 1945–1953," phil. diss. Bonn, 1988.

Thompson, Wayne. *The Political Odyssey of Herbert Wehner*. Boulder, 1993.

Thum, Horst. *Mitbestimmung in der Montanindustrie. Der Mythos vom Sieg der Gewerkschaften*. Stuttgart, 1982.

Trippen, Norbert. *Josef Kardinal Frings (1887–1978)*, 2 vols. Paderborn, 2003–2005.

Turner, Henry A. *German Big Business and the Rise of Hitler*. Oxford, 1985.

Hitler's Thirty Days to Power: January 1933. Reading, MA, 1996.

Uertz, Rudolf. *Christentum und Sozialismus in der frühen CDU. Grundlagen und Wirkungen der christlich-sozialen Ideen in der Union 1945–1949*. Stuttgart, 1981.

Uschner, Manfred. *Die Ostpolitik der SPD*. Berlin, 1991.

Vogelsang, Thilo. *Das geteilte Deutschland*, 9th edn. Munich, 1978.

Volkmann, Heinrich. "Modernisierung des Arbeitskampfs? Zum Formwandel von Streik und Aussperrung in Deutschland 1864–1975," in Harmut Kaelble, ed. *Probleme der Modernisierung in Deutschland*, Opladen, 1978, pp. 110–170.

Warner, Isabel. *Steel and Sovereignty: The Deconcentration of the West German Steel Industry, 1949–54*. Mainz, 1996.

Weinacht, Paul-Ludwig, ed. *Die CDU in Baden-Württemberg und ihre Geschichte*. Stuttgart, 1978.

Wengst, Udo. "Unternehmerverbände und Gewerkschaften in Deutschland im Jahre 1930." *Vierteljahrshefte für Zeitgeschichte*, 25 (1977): 99–119.

Wiesen, Jonathan. *West German Industry and the Challenge of the Nazi Past, 1945–1955*. Chapel Hill, 2001.

Winkler, Heinrich August. *Arbeiter und Arbeiterbewegung in der Weimarer Republik. Von der Revolution zur Stabilisierung 1918 bis 1924*. Berlin and Bonn, 1984.

Arbeiter und Arbeiterbewegung in der Weimarer Republik. Der Schein der Normalität 1924 bis 1930, 2nd edn. Berlin and Bonn, 1988.

Arbeiter und Arbeiterbewegung in der Weimarer Republik. Der Weg in die Katastrophe 1930 bis 1933. Berlin and Bonn, 1987.

Wirz, Ulrich. *Karl Theodor von und zu Guttenberg und das Zustandekommen der Grossen Koalition*. Grub am Forst, 1997.

Zündorf, Benno. *Die Ostverträge*. Munich, 1979.

Index